Critical Criminological Perspectives

Series Editors
Reece Walters, Faculty of Law, Deakin University,
Burwood, VIC, Australia
Deborah H. Drake, Department of Social Policy &
Criminology, The Open University, Milton Keynes, UK

The Palgrave Critical Criminological Perspectives book series aims to showcase the importance of critical criminological thinking when examining problems of crime, social harm and criminal and social justice. Critical perspectives have been instrumental in creating new research agendas and areas of criminological interest. By challenging state defined concepts of crime and rejecting positive analyses of criminality, critical criminological approaches continually push the boundaries and scope of criminology, creating new areas of focus and developing new ways of thinking about, and responding to, issues of social concern at local, national and global levels. Recent years have witnessed a flourishing of critical criminological narratives and this series seeks to capture the original and innovative ways that these discourses are engaging with contemporary issues of crime and justice. For further information on the series and to submit a proposal for consideration, please get in touch with the Editor: Josephine Taylor, Josephine.Taylor@palgrave.com.

David Gordon Scott · Joe Sim
Editors

Demystifying Power, Crime and Social Harm

The Work and Legacy of Steven Box

Editors
David Gordon Scott
Social Policy & Criminology
The Open University
Milton Keynes, UK

Joe Sim
School of Justice Studies
Liverpool John Moores University
Liverpool, UK

ISSN 2731-0604　　　　　ISSN 2731-0612　(electronic)
Critical Criminological Perspectives
ISBN 978-3-031-46212-2　　ISBN 978-3-031-46213-9　(eBook)
https://doi.org/10.1007/978-3-031-46213-9

© The Editor(s) (if applicable) and The Author(s), under exclusive license to Springer Nature Switzerland AG 2023

This work is subject to copyright. All rights are solely and exclusively licensed by the Publisher, whether the whole or part of the material is concerned, specifically the rights of translation, reprinting, reuse of illustrations, recitation, broadcasting, reproduction on microfilms or in any other physical way, and transmission or information storage and retrieval, electronic adaptation, computer software, or by similar or dissimilar methodology now known or hereafter developed.
The use of general descriptive names, registered names, trademarks, service marks, etc. in this publication does not imply, even in the absence of a specific statement, that such names are exempt from the relevant protective laws and regulations and therefore free for general use.
The publisher, the authors, and the editors are safe to assume that the advice and information in this book are believed to be true and accurate at the date of publication. Neither the publisher nor the authors or the editors give a warranty, expressed or implied, with respect to the material contained herein or for any errors or omissions that may have been made. The publisher remains neutral with regard to jurisdictional claims in published maps and institutional affiliations.

This Palgrave Macmillan imprint is published by the registered company Springer Nature Switzerland AG
The registered company address is: Gewerbestrasse 11, 6330 Cham, Switzerland

Paper in this product is recyclable.

*You got criminals in high places,
And law-breakers making the rules.*

(Bob Dylan, cited in Box, 1983: 58).

For Steven Box

Preface

In the first of his great trilogy of books, *Deviance, Reality and Society*, published in 1971, Steven Box spent half of the first page of the Preface pointing out that when a reader has contact with a new book their initial thoughts are to turn to the Preface to find out about the author in order to build a picture in the reader's mind: their friends, family, students they taught, grants obtained and so on. Box decided not to perform this 'magician's trick', as he put it. Instead, he opted to spend the rest of the Preface—two and a half pages—discussing the book, its contents and why he wrote it. There were no 'identity blocks', as he called them, from which the reader could build an impression of him. And apart from some, small extra details provided in Jock Young's obituary in the *British Journal of Criminology* after Steven died, that has remained the case.

Looking back from the present moment—an age of celebrity culture—this invisibility might seem strange. However, as with Foucault's arguments about the need for masked, anonymised philosophising, the lack of detailed, biographical knowledge means that the words and concepts Box used, and the critical analysis he developed, provided the lens through which we read his work. Many might say, especially in the context of the developments in social media over the last four decades, that biography and content cannot and should not be separated, they are inseparable. That might be a valid, though debatable point but it was not the path Box chose, nor indeed Foucault. Instead, as Buddhists would argue, Box followed the mantra about 'the dissolution of the [academic] self'. The age of selfie criminology would have been anathema to him, and rightly so.

As for the reader, the great, feminist science fiction writer Ursula K. Le Guin noted 'we read books to find out who we are'. Her insight applies equally to the world of critical criminology as it does to the science fiction genre in which she wrote. In reading and recognising the originality and impact of *Power, Crime and Mystification*, with which this volume is concerned, we can find out who we are not only as academics, activist scholars and activists but also who we are as human beings. How should we respond emotionally, spiritually and politically to the areas he discussed forty years ago? Four decades on, in a world stalked and dismembered by the malevolent, malignant barbarism of neoliberalism which Box saw emerging when the book was published, how do, and should we respond now? That is the essence of this collection.

It was devised and written against a tumultuous social and political background which impacted on billions of sentient beings as well as on us as editors and contributors: the state-generated, socially murderous rampage of COVID-19; the impact of the steel claw of state and social authoritarianism; the unfolding climate catastrophe; and the desolation and devastation generated by atavistic, neoliberal social and economic policies pursued by a sociopathic, national and international ruling class.

In universities, where many though not all of the contributors work, there has been righteous industrial action pursued by academics as they demanded a reckoning with an increasingly deranged university managerial class who, in Harry Braverman's brilliant phrase, took the 'degradation of work' within higher education to a new, parasitic level. Their philistine antics have attempted to turn learning for its own sake into a soul-chilling, utilitarian study of hard facts, in effect training students to accept the iniquities and inequities of the capitalist labour market while ensuring a good salary for themselves and a healthy profit for their institutions.

Preface

As Leonard Cohen said, in language which Steven would have appreciated, 'there is a crack in everything. That's how the light gets in'. Together, with the contributors, we believe we have produced a volume which continues to ensure that the light is still getting in and shining on the remorseless carnage of contemporary, capitalist barbarism. Hopefully, if he had still been with us, he would have raised a glass of his favourite Grand Cru Chablis to toast this volume. As the chapters here illustrate, the light he shone still burns as brightly as ever.

Given the events described above, we want to say thank you to all the contributors for your enthusiasm for the original idea and for your patience. In a Boxian spirit, we do not intend to summarise each chapter in this collection. The words, concepts, insights and critical analyses developed in the chapters themselves provide a much better articulation of your ideas. We could not do justice to them in a brief outline here.

We also remember the contributors who did not make it into the final volume for personal reasons. We thank them for their initial input.

Thanks to Naveen Dass, Bhanya Rattan, Gopalakrishan Lakshminarasimha and Josic Taylor at Palgrave. Thanks also to Corina Rogerson for helping us edit the chapters end references and all others at Palgrave involved in the production process.

Ramsbottom, UK David Gordon Scott
Liverpool, UK Joe Sim
September 2023

Contents

Part I Introduction

1 Steven Box: A 'Realist of a Larger Reality' 3
   David Gordon Scott and Joe Sim

Part II Corporate Crime

2 Corporate Crime, Regulation and the State 57
   Steve Tombs

3 From Corporate Corruption to Rentiership: Extending Box's Power, Crime and Mystification 81
   Steven Bittle and Jon Frauley

4 Power, Crime and Deadly Deception 103
   David Whyte

5 '90 Seconds to Midnight': Climate Change, Planetary Collapse and the 'Mystification' of Environmental Crime 123
   Reece Walters

6 Fighting for 'Justice for All' in an Era of Deepening
   Exploitation and Ecological Crisis   147
   Elizabeth Bradshaw and Paul Leighton

Part III Power, State Crime and Social Harm

7 The Neoliberal State: Then and Now   181
   Samantha Fletcher and William McGowan

8 The Austerity State, 'Social Junk'
   and the Mystification of Violence   203
   Chris Grover

9 Steven Box and Police Crime: Understanding
   and Challenging Police Violence and Corruption   223
   Will Jackson

10 The Mystification of Police Institutional Violence   247
   Lisa White and Patrick Williams

11 Immigration Control, Mystification and the Carceral
   Continuum   273
   Jon Burnett

12 Criminal Law Categories as Ideological Constructs:
   The Case of Human Trafficking   299
   Shahrzad Fouladvand and Tony Ward

Part IV Power, Gender and Sexual Violence

13 Power, Sexual Violence and Mystification   327
   Kym Atkinson and Helen Monk

14 'Rape Kills the Soul': The Use of Sexual Violence
   by State and non-State Actors in War and Conflict   351
   Brenda Fitzpatrick

15 Gender, Power and Criminalisation   379
   Kathryn Chadwick and Becky Clarke

| 16 | Mystification, Violence and Women's Homelessness
Vickie Cooper and Daniel McCulloch | 407 |

Part V Demystifying Social Harm

17	Standing on the Shoulders of a Criminological Giant: Steven Box and the Question of Counter-Colonial Criminology *Biko Agozino*	433
18	The Policing of Youthful 'Social Dynamite' and Neo-liberal Capitalism: Continuities, Discontinuities and Alternatives *Jodie Hodgson*	455
19	Demystifying Injustice: Joint Enterprise Law and Miscarriages of Justice *Janet Cunliffe and Gloria Morrison*	481
20	Punishment in 'This Hard Land': Conceptualising the Prison in Power, Crime and Mystification *Joe Sim*	507
21	Demystifying Murder: Open University Pedagogy, Social Murder and the Legacy of Steven Box *Deborah H. Drake and David Gordon Scott*	531

Index   557

Notes on Contributors

Biko Agozino is Professor of Sociology and Africana Studies, Virginia Tech, Blacksburg, VA. He is ranked as one of the top Criminologists in the world today by AcademicInfluence.com and has published the following books: *Community Policing in Nigeria* (co-authored, 2021); *Routledge Handbook on Africana Criminologists* (co-edited, 2020); *Critical, Creative and Centered Scholar-Activism* (2016, FDP); *ADAM: Africana Drug-Free Alternative Medicine*, (2006); *Counter-Colonial Criminology*, (2003); *Pan African Issues in Crime and Justice* (co-edited, 2004); and *Black Women and the Criminal Justice System*, (1997, republished by Routledge, 2018). Also, he is the Director-Producer of *'Shouters and the Control Freak Empire'*, Winner of the Best International Short Documentary, Columbia Gorge Film Festival, USA, 2011; Director-Producer of *'IE: Inclusive Excellence'*, Premiered on Blue Ridge PBS ECHO Channel, September 2021; and Selected for the Open Vision Film Festival, September 2021. He was appointed Professor Extreaordinasrius 2021–2024 by the Faculty of Law, University of South Africa.

Kym Atkinson is a lecturer in Criminology and Human Rights at Sheffield Hallam University. Her doctoral research explored women students' experiences of sexual violence at university and institutional responses to this violence. Her research interests broadly relate to violence against women, gendered experiences of the criminal justice system and state regulation, feminist theory and methodologies. She is a co-editor of *Feminist Responses to injustices of the State and its Institutions: Politics, Intervention, Resistance*, published in 2023 by Policy Press.

Steven Bittle is Associate Professor of Criminology at the University of Ottawa. He has published widely on issues of corporate crime and crimes of the powerful, with a particular focus on corporate killing and the political economy of law reform. His publications can be found in *The Journal of White Collar and Corporate Crime*; *Capital and Class*; *The Howard Journal of Crime and Justice*; *Critical Criminology*; *Justice, Power and Resistance,* among others. He co-edited (with Laureen Snider and Dean Curran) the December 2018 special issue of *Critical Criminology* on 'Crimes of the Powerful: The Canadian Context', and is co-editor (with Laureen Snider, Steve Tombs and David Whyte) of *Revisiting Crimes of the Powerful: Marxism, crime and deviance* (Routledge, 2018).

Elizabeth Bradshaw is Professor of Sociology in the School of Politics, Society, Justice, and Public Service at Central Michigan University. Her research focuses on the environmental harms resulting from state-corporate criminality and social movements as a form of resistance to crimes of the powerful. Dr. Bradshaw's work has been published in multiple edited books and peer-reviewed journals including *Theoretical Criminology*, *Critical Criminology*, and *State Crime Journal*.

Jon Burnett is a lecturer in Criminology at Swansea University. He has written widely on issues relating to asylum and immigration control, criminalisation and power, and has published work in a range of academic and non-academic fora. He is on the council of the management of the *Institute of Race Relations* (IRR).

Kathryn Chadwick is a principal lecturer in the Sociology Department at Manchester Metropolitan University. Her main areas of research and publication focus on gendered processes of marginalisation, criminalisation and punishment, challenging state injustice, penology and the theoretical imperatives of critical criminology. Current work focuses on the gendered policing and prosecution narratives in Joint Enterprise women's cases.

Becky Clarke is a senior lecturer in the Sociology Department at Manchester Metropolitan University. Her interests centre around the gendered and racialised experiences of criminalisation and punishment; processes of Othering in research, policy and media; and the relationship between research and intervention or activism to challenge injustice. Her current work focuses on the criminalisation of women and girls, through a critical examination of legal and welfare intervention in their lives.

Vickie Cooper is a senior lecturer in Criminology and Social Policy at The Open University. Vickie's research background is in evictions, homelessness and the criminalisation and incarceration of homeless people. Vickie was co-editor (with David Whyte) of *The Violence of Austerity* (Pluto Press, 2017) and has published in the area of evictions, homelessness and criminal justice.

Janet Cunliffe is co-founder of the grassroots organisation *Joint Enterprise Not Guilty by Association*. JENGbA raises awareness about the thousands of wrongful convictions of defendants sentenced under the draconian doctrine of joint enterprise which allows for more than one person to be convicted of the most serious offence. She recently gave evidence to the UN who, in January 2023, published its report on systemic racism in the UK's criminal justice system. and, with the advocacy of Liberty, has successfully litigated the Crown Prosecution Service because they do not collate data on joint enterprise. JENGbA supports over 1500 prisoners, all serving mandatory Life sentences, and the campaign group is currently raising a Private Members Bill in the UK's House of Commons to ensure the appeal system is fit for purpose.

Deborah H. Drake is Senior Lecturer in Criminology at The Open University. She is the author of *Prisons, Punishment and the Pursuit of Security* (Palgrave, 2012) and co-editor of the *Palgrave Handbook of Prison Ethnography* (Palgrave, 2015). She has also carried out research and published in the areas of community development, movements of dissent and resistance in Higher Education.

Brenda Fitzpatrick has a Ph.D. in Global Politics and has had experience in refugee camps and conflict zones. Her reports were circulated to/by United Nations, governments and NGOs demanding recognition that deliberate, tactical rape in war breaches international law, violates human rights and constitutes war crimes or crimes against humanity, genocide and ethnic cleansing. Her book, *Tactical Rape in War and Conflict* was judged ground-breaking. She respects the voices of victims and survivors and her novel, *Gwennie's Girl* presented women in war to a wider audience. She volunteers with remote desert Indigenous communities and with 'Care for Africa', which works in Tanzania.

Samantha Fletcher is Senior Lecturer in Criminology at Manchester Metropolitan University. Samantha's main research and teaching interests are focused on matters of 'crime', harm, global justice and state power. Samantha is particularly interested in social movements that seek to challenge global inequalities and injustice. Central to all Samantha's research concerns is a commitment to active scholarship that can contribute to discourses and activities seeking to redress inequalities and harms, caused by powerful persons, in the pursuit of capitalist accumulation of wealth.

Shahrzad Fouladvand is Senior Lecturer of International Criminal Law at the University of Sussex. Her research focuses on two forms of Transnational Crime: Human Trafficking and Corruption. Particularly, she is interested in the ways in which these two wrongdoings are interrelated. She is a member of the Editorial Board of the *Journal of Economic Criminology* and a member of the UK Research and Innovation (UKRI) Talent Peer Review College.

Jon Frauley is Associate Professor of Criminology at the University of Ottawa, Canada, where he teaches social and criminological theory, epistemology and methodology, and creative analytics. He has published numerous book chapters and articles in journals such as *The British Journal of Criminology*, *Social & Legal Studies*, *Critical Criminology*, and the *International Journal of Law, Crime & Justice*. He is the author of *Criminology, Deviance, and the Silver Screen* (Palgrave, 2010) and is the editor of and contributor to *The Routledge Intl. Handbook of C. Wright Mills Studies* (Routledge, 2021), *C. Wright Mills and the Criminological Imagination* (Ashgate, 2015), and (with Frank Pearce), *Critical Realism and the Social Sciences* (Univ. of Toronto Press, 2007).

Chris Grover works in the Department of Sociology at Lancaster University. His main research interest is in the political economy of social security policy. In the past, he has written about relationships between social security, and crime and criminal justice. More recently, he has focused on violence and 'austerity' in Britain's social security system (Violent proletarianisation: Social murder, the reserve army of labour and social security 'austerity' in Britain, *Critical Social Policy*).

Jodie Hodgson is a lecturer in Criminology at Manchester Metropolitan University and is based in the Manchester Centre for Youth Studies. Jodie has previously worked as a lecturer at Leeds Beckett University and The University of Liverpool. Jodie is the author of *Gender, Power and Restorative Justice: A feminist critique* (Palgrave, 2022). Her research interests are situated within the areas of youth justice, feminism and critical criminology.

Will Jackson is a lecturer in Criminology at the Centre for the Study of Crime, Criminalisation and Social Exclusion at Liverpool John Moores University. His research is focused on policing and state responses to political activism. He is co-editor of *Destroy Build Secure: Readings on Pacification* (Red Quill Books, 2017) and his recent work has been published in *Policing and Society*, *Social Justice*, *Feminist Review* and *Critical Social Policy*.

Paul Leighton is a professor in the Department of Sociology, Anthropology and Criminology at Eastern Michigan University. He is the co-author of *Punishment for Sale; Class, Race, Gender and Crime*; and *The Rich Get Richer and the Poor Get Prison*. Dr. Leighton is also a co-editor of the *Palgrave Handbook of Social Harm* (2021). He has been president of the board of his local domestic violence shelter and is currently head of the advisory board of his university's food pantry.

Daniel McCulloch is a lecturer in Social Policy and Criminology at The Open University. His research interests are in constructions of homelessness, experiences of d/Deaf people in prison and understandings of 'voice' in participatory visual methods.

William McGowan is a senior lecturer in Criminology and Co-Director of the Centre for the Study of Crime, Criminalisation and Social Exclusion at Liverpool John Moores University. His recent research has explored the lived experiences of political violence survivors in the contemporary war on terror, the involvement of the state in the UK funeral industry, funerals as commodities, ordinary yet marginalised mortalities, and methodological practice within the social sciences.

Helen Monk is a lecturer in Criminology at Liverpool John Moores University where she is also Co-Director of the Centre for the Study of Crime, Criminalisation and Social Exclusion. Her research interests include violence against women, gendered understandings of policing and social control, and intersectional and feminist theory. She is a co-editor of *Feminist Responses to injustices of the State and its Institutions: Politics, Intervention, Resistance*, published in 2023 by Policy Press.

Gloria Morrison is co-founder of the grassroots organisation *Joint Enterprise Not Guilty by Association*. JENGbA raises awareness about the thousands of wrongful convictions of defendants sentenced under the draconian doctrine of joint enterprise which allows for more than one person to be convicted of the most serious offence. She recently gave evidence to the UN who, in January 2023, published its report on systemic racism in the UK's criminal justice system. and, with the advocacy of Liberty, has successfully litigated the Crown Prosecution Service because they do not collate data on joint enterprise. JENGbA supports over 1500 prisoners, all serving mandatory Life sentences, and the campaign group is currently raising a Private Members Bill in the UK's House of Commons to ensure the appeal system is fit for purpose.

David Gordon Scott works at The Open University. His books include *Controversial Issues in Prisons* (Open University Press, 2010, with Helen Codd), *Why Prison?* (Cambridge University Press, 2013), *Against Imprisonment* (Waterside Press, 2018), *For Abolition* (Waterside Press, 2020) and the *International Handbook of Penal Abolition* (Routledge, 2023, co-edited with Michael Coyle). David is the co-founding editor (with Emma Bell) of the international journal *Justice, Power and Resistance*. A former coordinator of the *European Group for the Study of Deviance and Social Control* (2009–2012), he is chair of the *Weavers Uprising Bicentennial Committee.*

Joe Sim is Emeritus Professor of Criminology at Liverpool John Moores University. He has published a number of books including *Medical Power in Prisons* (Open University Press), *Punishment and Prisons* (Sage), *British Prisons* (Basil Blackwell, with Mike Fitzgerald) and *Prisons Under Protest* (Open University Press, with Phil Scraton and Paula Skidmore). He has also published a range of academic articles and blogs about prisons and law and order more generally. Finally, he is a Trustee of the charity *INQUEST*, which supports the families of those who die in the custody of the state and the families of the bereaved at Grenfell.

Steve Tombs is Emeritus Professor at The Open University. He has a long-standing interest in the incidence, nature and regulation of corporate and state crime and harm. His most recent books are *The Emerald Handbook of Activist Criminology* (edited with Victoria Canning and Greg Martin, 2023); *From Social Harm to Zemiology* (with Victoria Canning, 2021); *Revisiting Crimes of the Powerful* (edited with Steven Bittle, Laureen Snider and David Whyte, 2018); *Social Protection After the Crisis* (2016); and *The Corporate Criminal* (with David Whyte, 2015). He has long collaborated with the Hazards movement and The Institute of Employment Rights and is a Trustee and Deputy Chair of *INQUEST*.

Reece Walters is Professor of Criminology in the Faculty of Arts and Education at Deakin University, Melbourne, Australia. He was formerly Head of the Social Policy and Criminology Department at the Open University, Associate Dean of Law at QUT; and Director of the Institute of Criminology, Victoria University of Wellington. He is the recipient of Radzinowicz Prize in Criminology and has published extensively on crimes of the powerful, the sociology of criminological knowledge and green criminology. His books include *Deviant Knowledge* (2003), *Criminology and Genetically Modified Food* (2010), *Emerging Issues in Green Criminology* (2013), *Southern Criminology* (2018) and *Water Crime in the 21st Century* (2019). He is particularly interested in the ways in which corporations and governments exploit and compromise the 'essentials of life', namely air, food and water for power and profit.

Tony Ward is Professor of Law and Convener of the Centre for Evidence and Criminal Justice Studies at Northumbria University, Newcastle upon Tyne. He is the Co-Director of the International State Crime Initiative and one of the Editors-in-Chief of its journal, *State Crime*. With Penny Green, he is co-author of *State Crime: Governments, Violence and Corruption* (Pluto, 2004) and *State Crime and Civil Activism: On the Dialectics of Repression and Resistance* (Routledge, 2019). With Gerry Johnstone, he also co-authored *Law and Crime* (Sage, 2010), a critical introduction to law for criminology students. He and Shahrzad Fouladvand have co-authored several articles on human trafficking and the law.

Lisa White is a senior lecturer in Criminology at Liverpool John Moores University. Her current research is concerned with deaths in detention and custody, while previous work has explored the motivation, significance and consequences of narrating state torture in relation to N. Ireland. She is particularly interested in the lived impact of official discourse around state violence and how this is experienced by the most marginalised.

David Whyte is Professor of Climate Justice at Queen Mary University of London. He is the author of a number of texts including *Ecocide: Kill the Corporation Before it Kills Us; The Violence of Austerity* (edited with Vickie Cooper); *The Corporate Criminal* (with Steve Tombs); and the edited collection *How Corrupt is Britain?*

Patrick Williams is a senior lecturer in Criminology at Manchester Metropolitan University. He undertakes critical social research and publishes in the area of 'race' and ethnicity, with a particular focus on racial disparity, disproportionality and differential treatment within the Criminal Justice System. His most recent work foregrounds the experiences of those impacted by the 'Gangs Matrix' and the use of 'Joint Enterprise'.

Part I

Introduction

1

Steven Box: A 'Realist of a Larger Reality'

David Gordon Scott and Joe Sim

Introduction

James Baldwin, the great American writer and political activist, once noted that '[t]he world changes according to the way people see it, and if you alter, even by a millimeter, the way a person looks or people look at reality, then you can change it' (cited in Romano 1979). Baldwin's typically poetic words perfectly encapsulate Steven Box's work, in general, and his acclaimed classic *Power, Crime and Mystification [PCM]*, in particular.

Le Guin (2014).

D. Gordon Scott
Social Policy and Criminology, The Open University, Milton Keynes, UK
e-mail: david.scott@open.ac.uk

J. Sim (✉)
School of Justice Studies, Liverpool John Moores University, Liverpool, UK
e-mail: J.Sim@ljmu.ac.uk

The book was published on 24 November 1983, four years before his untimely death aged 50 on 22 September 1987. Box's critical theoretical, methodological, political *and* moral trajectory was clear from the first page: demystifying crime as a concept; recognizing and evidencing the devastating impact of avoidable harms, injury, suffering and deaths generated by the systemic criminality of the powerful; detailing the institutionalized indifference of state agents to pain and suffering; highlighting the deeply embedded culture of immunity and impunity which protected them, and the powerful more generally, from being held to account; critiquing the cynical criminalization of the actions of the powerless, and its hypocritical obverse, the non-criminalization of the actions of the powerful; and demanding a radical shift away from institutionalized criminal injustice to a system built on democratic accountability and 'justice for all' (Box 1983: 219). He explored these themes through four case studies—corporate crime, police crime, sexual violence and female crime—and situated them within the wider, lacerating context of deeply entrenched, capitalist, social divisions that destroyed lives, obliterated psyches and grievously stunted human growth. In criminological terms, it was a book based on 'visionary dissent' (Harding 2017).[1]

The chapters in this volume reflect Box's 'visionary dissent' and are linked by two considerations. They revisit his original arguments and the theoretical, political, moral and activist doors he opened in *PCM*. Additionally, they demonstrate the continued relevance of his thinking four decades on, decades which have been dominated by a ferocious intensification in the exercise, *and* non-exercise, of state power. However, it has also been a period of fearless contestation and resistance by critical criminologists, activists and grassroots organizations often working together, whose interventions have denied the state the capacity to impose a hegemonic 'truth' around crime and punishment, a point we return to below.

This Introduction is divided into six parts. First, it outlines the personal and academic context in which the book was written. Second,

---

[1] This phrase was used by Luke Harding in an obituary for the poet Heathcote Williams so while Harding was not talking about Box specifically the phrase seemed appropriate to what he was attempting in *PCM* (Harding 2017).

it considers the contribution of Box's key concept of ideological mystification. Third, it discusses the political background at the time of its publication. Fourth, it explores the reception the book received in the mid-1980s. Fifth, it reflects on some issues the book could have developed further when it was originally published. Finally, it considers the relevance of *PCM* to the 'Iron Times' of the twenty-first century (Hall 1988: vii).

Genesis and Influences

In the Preface to *PCM*, Box linked its genesis to a drink-fuelled interaction in London:

> The germ of this book infected me on Trent Park underground station nearly five years ago. I asked Jock Young if he had any explanation for corporate crime. He gave me the wide-eyed, glazed stare of a man suddenly possessed by the light of truth (or finally overcome by the magical influence of too much *grand cru* Chablis – two bottles of Les Preuses 1970). After a moment he yelled "greed!", and silenced the noise of the incoming train. (Box 1983: ix)

The last few lines in the first of his great trilogy of books, *Deviance, Reality and Society* (1971/1981) provided a less dramatic insight into its origins. Here he challenged the common-sense claim that a society gets the criminals it deserves, a recurring theme in *PCM*. In fact, the opposite was the case:

> In the end, we don't get the criminals we deserve, but the criminals who nicely mask the extent of serious crime being committed by those who seek, or who strongly support those who seek, to control the criminals we get. In this way the vast bulk of the population is mystified as to the extent of crime, the persons committing it, and those being victimised. Perhaps this mystification is something *which should occupy a high place on the agenda of critical criminology during the 1980s*. (Box 1971/1981: 240, emphasis added)

In the context of a world being turned upside down by the scorching, radical convulsions which erupted in the 1960s and 1970s, the self-reinforcing doom loop of traditional criminology and the politics of acquiescence—a criminology of grovelling[2]—which dominated the rarified cloisters of its academic practitioners, was also turned upside down. Despite, or perhaps because of, being pompously patronized as 'naughty schoolboys' by Sir Leon Radzinowicz, the Director of Cambridge University's Institute of Criminology (cited in Plummer 2013), their scholarship, politics *and* policies for radical change presented an emancipatory alternative to the reductive, suffocating straightjacket of individual and sociological positivism and the 'self-neutering empiricism' (Nairn 1988: 235) within which traditional criminology was constrained and trapped, *and within which its practitioners allowed themselves to be constrained and trapped.* The new generation confronted the intellectual and political stagnation of traditional criminologists, their stifling conformity and the moral compromises they made to conduct research whose outcomes, more often than not, reinforced existing power structures by accepting the state's 'truth' about crime and punishment which meant, in reality, working-class criminality.

Essentially, they had unconditional access to state institutions to conduct research resulting in policy recommendations which again, more often than not, legitimated what state agents *thought* they already knew, and the policies they wanted to implement. To paraphrase Alvin Gouldner, they were 'technicians of the [crime control] state',[3] offering, in Ralph Miliband's terms, 'straightforward apologetics' for the operational power of its institutions (Miliband cited in Panitch 2009: xix). The fact that the Home Office, a 'strategic sponsor' of research at the time, was also the 'patron of the Cambridge Institute of Criminology and the Oxford Centre for Criminological Research' indicated the intertwined nature of the crime control state as funders of research and the practice of criminology. It was a link that Paul Rock also patronizingly described as

---

[2] We have paraphrased Tom Nairn here who talked about the 'sociology of grovelling' regarding the response of some sociologists to the Coronation of Elizabeth II in 1953 (Nairn 1988: 115–120).

[3] Gouldner had used the term 'technicians of the welfare state' (Hall and Scraton 1981: 464).

being 'much criticized by younger and rather more belligerent members of the fortunate generation...' (Rock 1988: 64).

As with any social phenomenon, there were contradictions in this process. Critical criminologists were not entirely excluded from applying for, and obtaining, research grants. In the year *PCM* was published, Pat Carlen wrote *Women's Imprisonment: A Study in Social Control* which was also to become a classic text within critical criminology. The funding came from the state through the Scottish Home and Health Department while Carlen was given access to conduct interviews with women in Cornton Vale prison which formed the basis for her pioneering study (Carlen 1983). Previously in 1975, Rebecca and Russell Dobash had been funded by the Social Science Research Council (later the Economic and Social Research Council) to study violence against women in Scotland, which formed the basis of another classic study *Violence Against Wives: A Case Against the Patriarchy* (Dobash and Dobash 1979).

In general, however, the regressive trajectory of criminological research left the power of the punitive state undiminished and the academic status quo intact, as traditional criminologists shared a regressive echo chamber that reverberated with the endless mantra that more empirical research, *not* research on structures of power and powerlessness, was needed if the problem of working-class crime was to be solved. This empirical orientation, and the lack of structural analysis, was a form of 'psychic bondage' which, historically, has bedevilled criminology and other academic disciplines (Nairn 1988: 93). The fact that the new criminologists also wanted to, and did, make alliances with different 'deviant' groups, and provided an academic space for them to articulate their righteous anger about their often-violent, humiliating and terrifying torment generated by the state's interventions, or the torment of being ignored by its institutions, as in the case of survivors of domestic violence, was enough to condemn them as 'unscientific', academic reprobates, accusations, which, as we indicate below, also befell Box.

Attempting to shift the criminological tectonic plates, and refusing to be frozen in time, condemned critical criminologists to the seventh ring of criminological hell as punishment for two other sins: not being proportionate and not being objective. They had rejected so-called academic neutrality for active, political engagement supported by a relentless demand for radical social change. In contrast, a sense of proportionality was central to the world view of state agents and politicians who uncritically utilized and disseminated the research conducted by traditional 'scientific' methods. As Howard Zinn noted, this had profound implications: '[A] learned sense of moral proportion, coming from the apparent objectivity of the scholar, is accepted more easily than when it comes from politicians at press conferences. *It is therefore more deadly*' (Zinn 2015: 9, emphasis added). The fetish for insisting on academic objectivity had also been critiqued by Stuart Hall as far back as 1966:

> ....the social inquiry approach has a strong tendency to make people the objects rather than the agents of change. By demoting the role of human agency, it robs the situation of its historical dimensions and of its potential for change....for all the refinement of measurement involved, the descriptions of our society accumulated in this way lack agency, historical perspective, existential meaning or a proper subjectivity. Instead what seems to reign as a dominant mood in the whole intellectual climate just at present is a spurious search for "objectivity", a bogus pseudo-scientism. Such an intellectual climate - especially when mediated to an even wider public by the press and the journals – is one covertly hostile to politics. (Hall 1966/2017: 87–88)

The 'seminal texts' published in the 1960s and 1970s which preceded *PCM*, while 'advocating a diverse range of theoretical perspectives and methodological positions' (Monk and Sim 2017: 2)[4] were, nonetheless, clearly different from the theoretically reductive and snake oil,

---

[4] Along with Carol Smart's *Women, Crime and Criminology*, these texts included: Jock Young's *The Drugtakers*; Steven Box's *Deviance, Reality and Society*; Stan Cohen's *Images of Deviance*; Stan Cohen's *Folk Devils and Moral Panics*; Stan Cohen and Laurie Taylor's *Psychological Survival*; Ian Taylor and Laurie Taylor's *Politics and Deviance*; Ian Taylor, Paul Walton and Jock Young's *The New Criminology*; Thomas Mathiesen's *The Politics of Abolition*; Ian Taylor, Paul Walton and Jock Young's *Critical Criminology*; Michel Foucault's *Discipline and Punish*; Douglas Hay, Peter Linebaugh, John Rule, E.P. Thompson and Carl Rule's *Albion's Fatal Tree*; Geoff Pearson's *The Deviant Imagination;* Susan Brownmiller's *Against Our Will*; Pat Carlen's *Magistrates' Justice*; Frank Pearce's *Crimes of the Powerful*; Mike Fitzgerald's *Prisoners in Revolt*; Steve Chibnall's *Law and Order News*; Carol Smart and Barry Smart's *Women, Sexuality and Social Control*; Mick Ryan's *The Acceptable Pressure Group*; Michael Ignatieff's *A Just Measure of Pain*; Mike Fitzgerald and Joe Sim's *British Prisons*; the National Deviancy Conference's *Capitalism and the Rule of Law* and Rebecca and Russell Dobash's *Violence Against Wives* (cited in Monk and Sim 2017: 1).

quantitative, 'scientific' research uncritically pursued by traditional criminologists. The searching question posed by William Chambliss and Milton Mankoff seven years before *PCM* was published—*Whose Law? What Order?* (Chambliss and Mankoff 1976)—captured the political and moral essence, and electrical charge, of the new criminologists' perspective. They rejected the idea of value-free knowledge, and allegedly neutral research, in favour of a 'criminology from below' based on the voices and experiences of those on the razor's edge of a criminal injustice system built on the state's threat, and use of, violence and the systemic indifference of its institutions to the social harms experienced overwhelmingly by the powerless (Sim et al. 1987: 7). The answer was *not* liberal, piecemeal reform which, as Foucault (1979) recognized, had been an abject failure for two centuries, but a radical transformation in state institutions, including their democratization and eventual abolition. Abolishing the searing, wider social divisions that stunted human growth and generated avoidable harms and death for the powerless was the logical political *and* moral conclusion to realizing these demands (Scott 2018, 2020).

By the time *PCM* was published, the theoretical, political and moral concerns of this new, insurgent criminology had coalesced around a number of themes: challenging the 'truth' articulated by the state/media/criminological complex about the nature and extent of conventional crime; disputing the vacuous claim that state agents were neutral in how they exercised their capricious, discretionary power; analysing the structural violence of state institutions which transcended the 'bad apple' theory of individual state agents; pinpointing the institutionalized misogyny, racism and homophobia which directed the interventions and non-interventions these agents made, or failed to make, on the ground; documenting the culture of immunity and impunity underpinning the systemic non-response to crimes committed by the powerful; illustrating the long history of criminal justice coercion and repression dating back centuries; and critically analysing the role of parasitic, state institutions in defending, legitimating and reinforcing a deeply unequal, and morally reprehensible, decaying social order brutally divided along the jagged fault-lines of social class, gender, 'race', sexuality and ability/disability which eviscerated the human side of human beings. Central to this work was deconstructing the ideological mystification surrounding crime, social harm and the state which Box had developed and applied, often brilliantly, in *PCM*. It is to a consideration of this concept that we now turn.

'Nothing but Mystification'[5]

PCM is replete with descriptions of the avoidable harms committed by the powerful, which stole lives, killed and maimed individuals and defrauded and destroyed communities while leaving their families bereft and traumatized. An explicit aim of the book was to address a deficit of intellectual consideration and political action in response to such avoidable harms. For Box (1983: x–xi):

> People in powerful positions will do, and have done some pretty dreadful things. Unfortunately, this is all lost to those who concentrate entirely on crimes committed by the powerless. I hope that this book, in a modest way, redresses the balance. Crimes of the powerful can only be ignored at the risk of enormously increasing our chances of being victimised by them.

These 'pretty dreadful things' were largely not part of the remit, culture and focus of the criminal law which was systemically indifferent towards them. Furthermore, those laws which did exist, which, theoretically, were supposed to respond to those avoidable harms of power that had been criminalized, were often themselves ideological camouflage and were either ignored, dismissed or not appropriately enforced. The endemic wrongdoing and associated social harms generated by the powerful were hidden, which produced 'public ignorance' (ibid.: 17) and, in the case of corporate crime, 'very little social scandal' (ibid.: 53), resulting in a lack of awareness about the 'social consequences of the most serious, avoidable harms in the wider society' (ibid.: 31).

---

[5] Box (1983: 12).

The ocean-deep callousness and dangerousness of the powerful, and the carnage and terror their behaviour generated, were not the state's concern in the majority of cases. Turning away was the first course of action of its agents. At the same time, the state's laser focus on the powerless, and their punishment, was integral to its institutional praxis. The dominant discourse that the law offered protection to the powerless would have been laughable had it not been for the sheer sense of dread felt by the millions to whom it offered no protection from violence, terror, harm and death in the home, in institutions, on the streets and in workplaces.

As many of the chapters in this collection illustrate, the key concept of ideological mystification was central to Box's analysis, a concept which was not without its limitations (Fletcher and McGowan, this volume). Significantly, for Box, mystification arose even before the application and enforcement of the law began. Criminal laws were ideological constructions that reflected the vested interests of the powerful rather than being objective moral and legal categories that focused on the avoidable harms which caused the greatest hurt, injury and suffering (Fouladvand and Ward, this volume). The law was partially blind. Whereas it could perfectly well see the deviance and criminality of the powerless, legal institutions were either unable or unwilling, or both, to see criminal behaviour when perpetrated by those with power, prestige, privilege and wealth.

However, there were contradictions in the operationalization of the law. To claim that it was an unmitigated evil working only for the powerful and doing nothing to benefit or protect the powerless (sometimes dismissed as 'bourgeois law'), would clearly be false. It was also equally false and implausible to claim that the enforcement of the law was neutral, impartial and fair. Elaborating on the analytical insights of Stephen Spitzer, Box captured this contradiction, if grudgingly, when discussing the process of criminalization:

> [The argument] does not maintain that all criminal laws directly express the interests of one particular group, such as the ruling class. Clearly some legislation reflects temporary victories of one interest or allied interest groups over others, and none of these may necessarily be identical or

> coincide with the interests of the ruling class. Yet the above argument does not demand or predict that every criminal law directly represents the interests of the ruling class. It recognises that some laws are passed purely as symbolic victories which the dominant class grants to inferior interest groups, basically to keep them quiet; once passed they need never be efficiently or systematically enforced. It also recognises that occasionally the ruling class is forced into a tactical retreat by organised subordinate groups, and the resulting shifts in criminal law enshrine a broader spectrum of interests. But these victories are short lived. Powerful groups have ways and means of clawing back the spoils of tactical defeats. In the last instance, definitions of crime reflect the interests of these groups who comprise the ruling class. This is not to assume that these interests are homogenous and without serious contradictions…..Indeed, it is just the space between these contradictions that subordinate groups fill with their demands for legal change. (Box 1983: 8)

It was in these spaces that the application and non-application of the law was fiercely contested and resisted and where the state's ideological mystification was challenged as an alternative truth was constructed. Critical criminologists, in alliance with activists and grassroots organizations, spoke not just truth *to* power but demanded truth *from* power (Sim 2023). This was apparent in their support for, and involvement with, community-based, independent inquiries into the police killing of Blair Peach at an anti-fascist demonstration in April 1979, the material context of the disturbances in Handsworth in Birmingham and Tottenham in London in 1985 and in exposing the violence generated by state agents in the year-long miners strike in 1984/5 (Sim et al. 1987).

In supporting these struggles, critical criminologists navigated a theoretical and political tightrope to avoid either being obsequiously assimilated and 'defined-in' by the state through using its language and definition of reality, or being 'defined-out', through wrongly, and often offensively, being caricatured as idealistic, ivory tower utopians, divorced from the grim, everyday reality of crime and its impact on victims (Mathiesen 1980). In fact, the reverse was the case. It was the perfidious network of state agents, politicians, and an increasingly unhinged and uncontrollable mass media, that ignored the crimes and the social harms generated by the rampant criminality of the powerful. This network's systemic indifference to violence against women and girls, and racist, homophobic and transphobic violence, illustrated the cynical depth of their hypocrisy surrounding crime victims. The state and mass media *did* support victims but only those victims, or their relatives, who demanded vengeance and retribution. Victims who articulated empathic compassion, even when terrible crimes had been committed against them or against a family member, were systematically ignored, and dismissed (Sim 2023). Critical criminologists, and activist groups, not only critiqued the hypocritical use and crass mobilization of loaded terms such as crime and victims but also demanded that *social justice* rather than *criminal injustice* should be the basis for responding to crime and social harms (Sim et al. 1987). And *PCM* both reflected, and was reflected in, these demands.

PCM in an 'Age of Mixed Tyrannies'[6]

The Conservative Party's General Election victory in May 1979 was a profound, conjunctural moment in consolidating 'the great moving right show', and the 'authoritarian populism' that sustained it (Hall 1988). This moment was represented in the apocalyptic dyad 'free economy/ strong state' (Gamble 1988). The Party's victory ushered in a 'regression to a stone-age morality', based on:

> ….a blind spasm of control; the feeling that the *only* remedy for a society which is declared to be "ungovernable" is the imposition of order, through a disciplinary use of the Law by the State. (Hall 1980a: 3, original emphasis)

This 'blind spasm of control' was legitimated by linking the importation of specific forms of criminality with the unwelcome presence of black people who were socially constructed as being pathologically disconnected from the traditional values of British culture. As Paul Gilroy noted in 1982:

---

[6] Bedford cited in Lynskey (2019: 257).

> The imagery of alien violence and criminality personified in the "mugger" and the "illegal" immigrant has become an important card in the hands of politicians and police officers whose political authority is undermined by the political fluctuations of the crisis. For them, as for many working class Britons, the irresolvable difference between themselves and the undesired immigrants is clearly expressed in the latter's culture of criminality and inbred inability to cope with that highest achievement of civilization – the rule of law. (Gilroy 1982: 48)

In October 1983, a month before *PCM* was published, the Conservative Party held its annual conference. This was four months after the Party's second, successive General Election victory. By then, law and order—at least law and order for the powerless—was deeply embedded in the collective psyche of the 'delegates' who unequivocally supported, Margaret Thatcher's 'ultra-capitalist tyranny' (Nairn 1988: 242). In her Prime Ministerial address, Thatcher told the enraptured audience that:

> We were elected to strengthen the forces of law and order. Thanks to Willie Whitelaw there are now more policemen, better paid, better equipped, than ever before, and more of them back on the beat. But as you heard from Leon Brittan, this Government is reinforcing its efforts. But it is not just a case of more of them back on the beat. But it is not just the case of "leave it to Leon". Law and order is not just his problem - it involves every citizen in the land. None of us can opt out. (Thatcher 1983)[7]

Thatcher had ruthlessly culled her first Cabinet to ensure that each Minister was 'One of Us' (Young 1989). She had capitulated to the demands of the Tory press, and many in her party, to replace William Whitelaw as Home Secretary, who was caricatured as a 'weak and ineffectual procrastinator in the fight against crime' (Sim 2009: 32). Yet in reality, Whitelaw had been proactive in pushing forward the law and order agenda. Most notably, in 1983, he initiated and signed off a secret

---

[7] Ironically, given what has since transpired with Brexit, Thatcher said of the European Union: 'We are in, and we are in to stay' (Thatcher 1983).

police manual for the repressive control of protest and industrial action (Foot and Livingstone 2022).

For Thatcher, Leon Brittan, Whitelaw's successor, 'would have no time for the false sentimentality which surrounds the causes of crime' (Thatcher, cited in Sim 2009: 33). In his conference speech, Brittan turned the law and order screw even tighter by introducing a range of new policies, which, as ever, were overwhelmingly targeted downwards towards those on the lowest rung of the corrosive ladder of social inequality. The policies included: funding the biggest prison-building programme of the twentieth century; increasing the sentencing powers of the courts; and restricting parole for certain categories of offenders (Ryan and Sim 1984).

However, despite the hard-line social and criminal justice policies relentlessly articulated by Thatcher's Ministers, their callous and compassionless fixation on delivering punishment for the powerless did little, if anything, to stabilize a deeply fractured society. Nor did their speeches and actions generate legitimacy for the government's policies, and for the neoliberal social order more generally, which remained deeply divided. Inner city disturbances in 1981, the police's ongoing, racist use of stop and search powers, disturbances in both long-term and short-term prisons culminating in the biggest prison demonstration in UK history in April 1990, deaths in custody, male, racist and homophobic violence which generated abject responses from state agents and a series of miscarriages of justice, many linked to the war in Northern Ireland (White and Williams, this volume), graphically illustrated that the 'politics of Thatcherism' (Hall and Jacques 1983) had failed to achieve hegemony.

After *PCM's* publication, there were other, tumultuous, political events including the bombing of the Conservative Party conference by the IRA in 1984; the miners strike in 1984/5; and the inner city disturbances in 1985. The government responded by passing the draconian *Public Order Act* in 1986. This Act reflected the brutal authoritarianism of the Conservative Party's law and order agenda. And like governments before and after, Thatcher's government focused on re-establishing and maintaining order in the world of the public. Order in the private sphere which was often maintained through the threat, and use, of male violence towards women and girls, was, as ever, systematically ignored (Edwards 1989).

Dialectically linked to this authoritarian, interventionist strategy was an anti-statist strategy, defined by Stuart Hall as:

> ...not one which refuses to operate thought the state; it is one which conceives a more limited state role, and which advances through the attempt, ideologically, to *represent itself* as anti-statist, for the purposes of popular mobilisation. (Hall 1988: 152, original emphasis)

In practice, this meant that the policing of the powerless, including their morals as well as their behaviour, intensified while the policing and regulation of the powerful, which was already abject, became even more circumspect and withdrawn in areas such as health and safety at work, factory inspections, with the avoidable deaths that followed and the non-prosecution of companies for illegally underpaying workers (Sim 2009: 43–44).

Thatcher's third government was elected in June 1987. In August, the last of Box's great trilogy, *Recession, Crime and Punishment* was published (Box 1987). He died a month later on September 22nd. By this point, for the powerless, the unrelenting drive towards, and iron consolidation of, the authoritarian state was becoming desperately clear (Scraton 1987). For the powerful, it was 'business as usual' (Tombs 2016a: 51). As ever, the pliers of punishment cut only one way.

PCM: Reception and Reviews[8]

Like Carol Smart's *Women, Crime and Criminology* (Smart 1976), *PCM* can be considered a 'classic....that has never finished saying what it has to say' (Calvino, cited in Monk and Sim 2017: 10). And, as with another seminal text at the time, *Policing the Crisis*, the book was 'an intervention in the battleground of [criminological] ideas' (Hall et al. 1978: x). Given this, how was *PCM* received at the time of its publication?

---

[8] This method is based on one suggested and developed by Helen Monk and utilized in Monk and Sim (2017).

Looking back at a number of reviews published between 1983 and 1987, it is clear that the book's importance was recognized relatively quickly. Reviewers noted that it was a: 'highly competent pithy text' (Ditton 1983: 497); was '[w]ritten as though ideas really count and rational thought will make a difference' (Quicker 1987: 58); and was 'impassioned, witty, and, on the whole, convincing' (Waddington 1985: 73). It was also described as 'provocative', 'innovative' and 'illuminating' which pointed criminology 'in an important direction' (Brown 1986: 840–841). For Quicker (1987: 58), 'Box presents an insightful examination' whereas Jones (1985: 341) noted that '[a]nyone with the slightest interest in social justice should find this a welcome and necessary book'. What is also interesting is the way in which the reviewers interpreted its key themes and ideas (Ditton 1983; Jones 1985; Brown 1986; Quicker 1987; see also Grover, this volume).

First, both Brown (1986: 840) and Jones (1985: 340) drew attention to how avoidable harm and suffering, which may or may not be defined by the state as a crime, were made visible. In other words, the reviewers recognized the central role of demystification in Box's analysis. Second, Ditton (1983: 497), highlighted the significance of the interrelationship between the exercise of power and the generation of social harms, and how many of these harms, such as corporate criminality, were simply 'exaggerated forms of normal behaviour'. Third, Quicker (1987) argued that following Box, criminologists should look beyond the issue of intention and focus their attention on the indifference of the wealthy, privileged and powerful—in other words to the actions and inactions of the state. Fourth, both Jones (1985: 341) and Brown (1986: 841) emphasized how Box raised concerns about the limits of jurisprudence. This was clear not only in the processes through which only certain harms were criminalized but also when the powerful were caught and prosecuted, 'they will be treated with kid gloves' (Jones 1985: 341). Finally, Fielding (1985: 494) identified the book's pedagogical significance.[9]

---

[9] For further discussion on critical pedagogy and Box see Drake and Scott, this volume.

Box's core argument that crime and criminalization are social control strategies may be familiar but, as he notes, the indignation with which this prospect is generally met reveals the resilience of mystification, and the need to bring each generation of students over this ground.

For defenders of the criminological status quo like Waddington (1985: 74), it was 'particularly important that [Box's] arguments should not go without some critical scrutiny and become thereby a new conventional wisdom'. In the attempt to prevent the critical arguments from becoming 'conventional wisdom', *PCM* was criticized for being polemical and empirically flawed. Brown (1986: 840) argued that it made 'unsubstantiated assertions' and Box's attempt to 'draw inferences from data too scanty' was its key weakness (ibid.: 841). Waddington also argued that Box was 'like all "law and order" polemicists' (Waddington 1985: 74), in that he had produced what 'amounte[d] to a party manifesto for democratic socialism' (ibid.: 73) which resulted in too much 'speculation and assertion substituted for fact'. While Box raised some important questions, Waddington had doubts 'about how well his polemic will translate into criminological analysis' (ibid.).

However, despite the alleged deficiencies in Box's data—which rarely stop non-critical criminologists from almost universally pointing to the dark figure of street-level crime without demanding firm empirical data sets for these invisible crimes—as Jock Young noted, *PCM* was teeming with empirical data and other forms of evidence to support its arguments:

> The key characteristics of Box's work are an extraordinarily wide range of empirical data coupled with a striving for comprehensive theory.......His remorseless exposure of the hypocrisy of the powerful and of the crimes of the corporations and the wealthy was well documented and never stooped to simple conspiracy. Nor was he slow to develop in terms of criticism. In his later work he took on board much of the feminist critique of criminology, developing well-thought-out analyses of rape, of the female criminal and of women, crime and the labour market. (Young 1988: 95)

Box marshalled extensive evidence throughout the book to develop a sophisticated analysis of the social harms and depredations of the powerful. It is disingenuous to argue otherwise. His points were, in the main, meticulously researched and argued. Claiming that the book was not sufficiently empirically substantiated in the context of the available data was misplaced. Fielding (1985: 493) puts this point well:

> The art of the argument is such that Box denies the unsympathetic the chance to dismiss this analysis as being akin to a catchy but superficial slogan; a determined use of official sources and sophisticated marshalling of criminological research provides a solid base to support the heckling.

The book was also criticized for its style, specifically for swimming against academic convention. Ditton (1983: 497) pointed to its 'irritating juvenility' and how the discussions of the Beatles, Bob Dylan and Woody Guthrie were placed, by a 'hapless indexer [who] pops [them] into the index' as if they were 'learned criminologists'. In a more subtle assertion of this critique, Brown (1986: 840) noted how Box 'deviates from his generally "scientific" approach, with a liberal sprinkling of quotes from literary works and song lyrics'. This concern, on the face of it, seems like an abject example of academic elitism and intellectual snobbery, implying that academics should only read books and 'scientifically' observe the social world from the privileged, armchair isolation of their ivory towers. However, Quicker (1987: 57) offered a different interpretation of Box's writing: '[b]eing fearful of neither humour nor prose, the author's style is steeped in the Millsian ethos of *The Sociological Imagination*'.

As well as some clearly ideological objections—Waddington's review (1985) was polite but fundamentally hostile noting that those in positions of power could give adequate responses to Box's claims but decided not to provide any in his response—the reviews identified some other important tensions in the book. According to Jones (1985), in discussing the relationship between women's liberation and the nature and extent of women's crimes, Box ignored the fact that 'the debate itself is another mystification' (ibid.: 341). This debate is now a historical artefact, yet in fairness to Box at the time, and indeed at least until the mid-1990s, it was still on the curriculum in critical criminology programmes in the UK. These debates have moved on, mainly due to feminist-inspired research. Clearly, there are more analytical ways to conceive the relationship between women, power and social harm in terms of critically analysing how the behaviour of 'deviant' women and girls' is criminalized and punished as well as the state's systemic indifference and non-response to sexual violence against women and girls more generally (Chadwick and Clarke this volume; Hodgson, this volume; Atkinson and Monk, this volume).

Another area of contention raised by Brown, Quicker and Waddington concerned Box's conceptualization of 'avoidable harm'. For Quicker (1987: 60), Box struggled to maintain a 'consistent analytical quality' to his application of 'avoidable harms' throughout *PCM's* different case studies, whereas Brown (1986: 840) noted that Box's arguments about the nature and extent of avoidable harms, for example, the increasing prevalence of police brutality were, like other data on crime, 'artifacts of a reporting process' and the categories deployed in the recording of such harm by the state. Certainly, the categorization of harm, and its measurement, is still a point of significant tension for studies of social harm today.

Waddington (1985) raised similar points but did so in a more controversial way. His comments are worth considering at length as, in themselves, they revealed another level of mystification related to the social harms of the powerful:

> However, the danger of using a criterion of "avoidable harm" lies in its inclusiveness. Few would disagree with the view that most of the cases cited are callously reckless, or worse. However, to take a deliberately contentious example, would there be similar agreement about the non-criminal, avoidable harm that follows a decision by a trade union to take industrial action? Or, again, the decision of some developed nations to export unemployment to the Third World by adopting protectionist measures for their own industries? Sometimes, perhaps often, the choice is not between causing or not causing harm but involves balancing harm to some against benefits to others. The problem is that it is much easier to identify harm that is done, as opposed to that which was avoided. A trade union, for example, may well act in the correct belief that the defence of certain rights avoids more harm in the long term than is immediately caused through industrial action. Likewise, an employer or

a government may also correctly judge that to pursue a policy which involves risk for some may entail more than compensating benefits for others. (Waddington 1985: 74)

While Waddington did partly temper his critique of the harms of 'trade unions', his arguments seem to be a clear attempt to further mystify the avoidable harms of corporations and states which Box so strongly identified. In muddying the waters here, Waddington completely negated the political context around contestation and resistance to power, oppression and exploitation, which is absolutely crucial when distinguishing between, for example, trade unions taking industrial action and the decisions of a company to maximize profits.

Finally, reviewers were concerned about the difficulties in both conceptualizing the immorality of corporate harms (i.e. the problem of resolving the tension between identifying individual and institutional immorality as highlighted by Fielding [1985]) and how best to respond to such harms. We return to this question below.

PCM: A Critical Review

Cliché ridden though it might be, but hindsight, including criminological hindsight, is a wonderful thing when discussing any book. Often such hindsight disassociates the book from the personal, academic and political context in which it was written. At the same time, like any book, academic or otherwise, critical or not, critiques can be made of its arguments without losing sight of their relevance, power and impact (Whyte, this volume; Tombs, this volume; Chadwick and Clarke, this volume). With respect to *PCM*, the points below are raised in that spirit.

First, there is the question of the state. While Box brilliantly used labelling theory in *Deviance, Reality and Society* (Box 1971/1981), *PCM* does not get beyond labelling theory's reluctance to engage with the issue of the state, and the exercise of its power, to criminalize and punish. In places, he tends to conflate the government with the state. More broadly, there is no real engagement with the rich literature on the state that had appeared in the late 1970s and early 1980s (Fletcher and McGowan, this volume; Tombs this volume). This literature—(Hall et al. 1978; Hall 1979/2017; Jessop 1982; Poulantzas 1978)—is missing. Theorizing the state remains tantalizingly just out of reach. It is there but not there, a schematic presence rather than being critically considered as a network of institutions, and formal and informal connections, orientated towards punishing the powerless.

He does though provide some important insights into state institutions including identifying the link between the state and '…its control agencies, criminologists, and the media who [not only] conceptualise a particular and partial ideological version of serious crime and who commits it, but it does so by concealing and hence mystifying its own propensity for violence and serious crimes on a much larger scale' (Box 1983: 14). He also provides an important but still neglected insight into the power of the police to demand 'autonomy from gross political interference; they got this in the shape of organizational and operational control with only the hint of public accountability being anything more than a smokescreen to comfort the faint libertarian heart' (ibid.: 116; see also Jackson, this volume).

Second, there is a tension in *PCM*, as there is in much of the brilliant, critical criminological work done in the 1970s and 1980s, concerning the conceptual time-line underpinning Box's analysis. Implicitly and explicitly, it is built on the assumption that a shift had taken place from a social democratic, consensual state to a coercive, authoritarian state form during those decades. It could be argued, however, that statist authoritarianism and violence *and* anti-statist, non- interventions have a much longer history dating back, at least, to the emergence of the capitalist state in the eighteenth century. And as Alberto Toscano has noted, while 'social war' against internal enemies is central to how neoliberalism, or 'neoliberal lawfare' governs, '[w]e may also wonder whether social war is not in fact the norm rather than the exception in capitalist social formations before neoliberalism…'. Toscano cites Engels who pointed out in *The Condition of the Working Class in England* that '[s]ince capital, the direct or indirect control of the means of subsistence and production, is the weapon with which this social warfare is carried on, it is clear that all the disadvantages of such a state must fall upon the poor' (Toscano 2023: 190).

Therefore, what transpired in the 1970s and 1980s marked the *normalization and intensification* of these processes, rather than a shift (Gilroy and Sim 1987). The long history of the exercise of brutal, racist colonial and imperial power illustrates the first dimension in this dialectic (Hillyard 1987; Elkins 2022), while the equally long history of the non-policing and non-regulation of sexual violence against women and girls illustrates the second dimension (Clarke 1987).

Third, there is the question of how power and powerlessness is conceptualized. There had been a number of analytical discussions on the exercise of power prior to *PCM*, Foucault's work being the most obvious example (Elden 2017). However, the Foucauldian analysis of power and governmentality is not considered. At one level, this is not surprising given the well-documented tension between Foucault's decentering of the macro exercise of power via the state in favour of a focus on the 'micro physics of power' (Smart 1985: 79). Nonetheless, *PCM* does not engage with the interrelationship between power and knowledge, in particular, the social construction of dominant discourses, and their devastating impact, formulated by expert 'judges of normality' working in the human sciences like criminology (Foucault 1979: 304). Additionally, the application and understanding of powerlessness could have been explored further through analysing how powerlessness, in itself, is accumulative. When power is exercised, its impact can be corrosive: individuals give up, lose hope, disengage and internalize blame (Scott 2006). Indeed, creating feelings of powerlessness, and generating political inaction, are crucial for the maintenance of social order. There is also the question of how powerlessness and gender are conceptualized in the book in relation to women and girls with respect to the power structures involved in the generation of their criminality (Chadwick and Clarke, this volume).

Fourth, while Box rightly demanded 'justice for all' (Box 1983: 219), he tended to present an homogenized vision of justice. Academics and grassroots organizations, then and now, have conceptualized justice in ways which are specific to the concrete concerns of the different groups they have campaigned for such as the struggles of women and girls for a gendered form of justice based on feminist praxis (Atkinson and Monk, this volume); the demands for climate justice by the new social movements which have emerged in the last four decades (Bradshaw and

Leighton, this volume); and the justice demanded for those sentenced to life imprisonment without having committed a crime (Cunliffe and Morrison, this volume). When reflecting on the different calls for justice today, it is important to be vigilant about their contingent nature, pay close attention to the diversity and plurality of any such calls and recognize that they will be situated in different subject positions, standpoints or worldviews.

Finally, Box refers to the issue of how critical criminologists should respond to the deadly harms generated by the powerful but, again, he does not develop his arguments in any great depth. In terms of corporate crime, he maintained that '[n]o piecemeal reform will make one iota of difference. Only when the means of production and distribution are *socialized* will the incidence of corporate crime diminish' (Box 1983: 63, original emphasis). He also raised the question of punishment and its relationship to the delivery of justice:

> If there is no way of implementing justice for the largest and worst offending corporations then it is surely unjust to pursue with such ruthless and cruel tenacity the majority of those eventually condemned to prison. By all means punish those committing violence against us, but when we fail to punish those practicing minor acts of genocide, let us be merciful on those committing comparatively minor acts of violence. (ibid.: 79)

It is important to recognize that Box was prepared at least to engage with this issue which had existed on the margins of critical criminology and, not unexpectedly, had been ignored by traditional criminologists. We return to this key philosophical and political question below.

PCM Forty Years On: Continuities and Discontinuities

A key theme in this collection is a critical consideration not only of Box's original analysis but also the relevance of this analysis forty years on in a world where the 'modern power-seeker [seeks to assemble] whatever combination of coercion, seduction and distraction [which proves] most effective' (Bedford cited in Lynskey 2019: 257). There are six issues we consider here.

Authoritarian State Power

Writing in 2009, Stuart Hall pointed out how the exercise of state power had changed since the late 1970s and early 1980s. Following Gramsci, he noted, that a 'dual perspective' around the use of force, and the social construction of consent, was still key to analysing the exercise of state power within the political economy of neoliberalism:

> „„„the force/consent dialectic marks the distinction between two kinds of power – between a reliance on coercive dimensions, and a form of "hegemonic power" which, of course, always has its coercive aspects. The latter has real effects, and the state is massively involved in it: for example in restructuring institutions around the market forces principle, giving capital access to every aspect of public and social life, saturating society from end to end with a "free market" common sense which is visible today in every department of society, and educating society to meet the needs of that "new type of civilization and citizen" [sic] required by capitalist globalization. (Hall 2009: xvii)

Hall also recognized that neoliberalism had mutated since Thatcher's conjunctural moment (and the moment of *PCM*):

> Under Thatcherism, the emphasis was on economic liberalization and privatization of public assets and the dismantling of the mixed economy; with the more coercive side deployed to undermine and break the collective defences and constraints on market forces (for example the criminalization of opposition in the miner's strike). Its leading edge was "privatization". In broad principle, New Labour…have been converted to and loyally followed through this economic liberalization approach. But it focused its attention on the *management of society* – a more regulatory social regime altogether. This has included the "entrepreneurialization" of public life, the public sector, public services, government and social institutions and expanding the regulation of civil society and of social

and individual behavior. It has replaced "privatization" with the broader process of "marketization"...... involve[ing] the obligation of all social institutions to comply with the obligation to re-model themselves on the private market, adapt market disciplines and ways of calculating value. (ibid.: xviii, original emphasis)

The impact of the privatization/marketization dyad, Hall identified above, has impacted in a number of ways. Through mobilizing the discourses of responsibilization and managerialism, new layers of mystification have been added to what the state does in practice (Hodgson, this volume). And contrary to liberal and governmental readings of how and why state power is exercised, these layers, often including charities and voluntary sector organizations, have augmented rather than diminished the exercise of this power (Davies 2011). In that sense:

> ….the public-private assemblage governing the poor, spectacularly illustrated in England by privatized probation and prisons and by the treatment of migrants and asylum seekers, points to the growth of an "authoritarian periphery" of the coercive management of the poor, harking back to the nineteenth century and the view of the poor not as citizens but as the "dangerous classes". (Fitzgibbon and Lea 2020: 166)

The violent degradation and humiliation of detainees in immigration detention centres brutally illustrate Fitzgibbon and Lea's point (Burnett, this volume).

Outside state institutions, this dyad has had a devastating impact. The attempted rape and murder of Zara Aleena by Jordan McSweeney in June 2022 was connected to the drive for profit arising from the probation service being split so that private community rehabilitation companies were left to supervise low to medium-risk cases while the National Probation Service (NPS) supervised high-risk cases. In this profit-driven environment:

> McSweeney was the responsibility of the profit-driven London Community Rehabilitation Company. Despite McSweeney's known risk being present in custody, such as his possession of weapons and threatening behaviour, as well as subsequent information received about the serious

risk he posed to women, the company assessed him to be medium-risk. With inaccurate risk assessment a key feature of the case....... The funding arrangements for the private, profit-oriented companies provided a monetary incentive for employees not to assess cases as high-risk, as this would result in them being passed on to the state-owned NPS, and a loss of income. Consequently, risk was routinely downgraded. If anyone has "blood on their hands", it is the neoliberal ideologues in this government who, ignoring warnings issued in 2015 and 2016 by the inspectorate that resettlement arrangements were not fit for purpose, pursued this flawed and ultimately doomed experiment to its predictable tragic end. (Hobbs 2023)

In the searing and mutating context of the political economy of neoliberalism, and the emergence of a 'new moving right show' (Knott 2020: 111), the exercise and non-exercise of state power described by Hall above, remains a key issue that unites the historical themes explored in *PCM* with contemporary developments. Despite internal contradictions and contingencies, the 'toxic trinity of state, capital and media' (Calderbank 2011: 3) is integral to maintaining a grossly unequal national and international social order, whatever the cost to sentient beings (Walters, this volume; Bradshaw and Leighton, this volume).

And while the 'techniques of neutralisation' mobilized by the state to mystify and deny the culpability of its agents in the criminal activities of the powerful remains undiminished (Sykes and Matza cited in Box 1983: 153; see also Whyte, this volume), the consolidation in the surveillance capabilities of, and data sharing between, state institutions, nationally and internationally has added another dimension to this process (Statewatch 2022; Zuboff 2019). This 'technological/security complex' (Gilroy 2019) has both 'strengthened the neo liberal ethos' and generated an international social order where 'paranoia is entangled with reality' while 'simultaneously weaken[ing] many social protections and pay[ing] less attention to the ways the social order produces bad choices and collective problems' (Marx 2005: 42).

In Karl Marx's terms, the ratcheting up of the coercive and surveillance capabilities of state institutions, increasingly ensures that 'the force of argument' is being replaced by the 'argument of force'.[10] In the UK, this has included: building more prisons, extending police powers, increasing sentencing powers for the courts, introducing greater restrictions on the right of trade unions to take strike action and instituting draconian measures on the streets and in the courts to punish direct action by climate change activists, and other protesters, as well as arresting journalists reporting on this action. In March 2022, 13 protestors were sentenced to over 55 years in prison for their part in demonstrations against the *Police, Crime, Sentencing and Courts Act 2022* (Anderson 2022). The direct action undertaken by *Just Stop Oil* and *Insulate Britain* to prevent the 'earth [from dying] screaming'[11] intensified the state's thirst for punishment. The 2022 Act, for example, 'made the offences of public nuisance and obstruction of the highway more serious and more likely to result in prison sentences' (Walter 2023). In April 2023, the Act became law. On May 2nd, the *Public Order Act* received Royal Assent from Charles Windsor, four days before he was crowned King. On the day itself, the Acts were used to arrest dozens of people, not only Republicans demonstrating peacefully against the coronation and the reputed cost of the event—between £50 and £100 million pounds (Elston 2023)—when more people than ever in Britain were using food banks (Bryant and Ungoed-Thomas 2023), but also other groups including volunteers accredited to the police to stop the sexual harassment of women and girls on the day. The police claimed that their rape alarms might be used to frighten the parading horses. They were arrested and detained for 14 hours and then released on bail (Monbiot 2023). As Monbiot notes:

> The *Police [Crime, Sentencing and Courts] Act* 2022 was bad enough, redefining "serious disruption" so widely that it could be applied to almost any situation, greatly increasing the penalties for acts of peaceful protest and creating a new and remarkably vague offence of "intentionally or recklessly causing public nuisance", with a penalty of up to 10 years in prison. Half the people arrested at or around the coronation were

---

[10] This is a quote from Marx used by Stuart Hall in an ITV documentary, *Karl Marx and Marxism*, first broadcast on 15 October 1983 (Hall 1983).
[11] From the song *The Earth Dies Screaming* by UB40.

detained on this charge. But the *Public Order Act* 2023 is much worse. The new offences it creates have been designed to allow the police to shut down every form of effective protest. If you chain yourself to the railings or attach yourself to anything or anyone else you could be jailed for 51 weeks. If you carry equipment that the police claim could be used for such a purpose, you could also be breaking the law: at the coronation, protesters were arrested for the possession of string and luggage straps. The act imposes blanket bans on protests against new roads, fracking or any other oil and gas works. If......you dig a tunnel – or even enter one – you can be imprisoned for three years. The act greatly expands the police power of suspicion-less stop and search, which has been used to such discriminatory effect against black people. Anyone can now be searched if a police inspector or any other senior officer "reasonably believes" protests might happen somewhere in the area, or that someone somewhere might be carrying a "prohibited object". If you resist a search, you can be imprisoned for 51 weeks. (ibid.)

Mobilizing a compassionless strategy of 'authoritarian austerity' has further reinforced the state's coercive interventions. This austerity is based on:

> .... a one-sided class war, conducted in numbers and defended by economists' jargon. And when that fails to do the trick, dissenters can be silenced. Already, you can see the forces of law and order mustering. Theresa May's former right-hand man, Nick Timothy, rails in the *Telegraph* against the weak policing at our borders and at protests while the deputy prime minister, Dominic Raab, wants our human rights laws to be ripped up entirely. A clampdown on public finances, a crackdown on public disorder: the two went together in the 80s, in the 2010s – and they are what lie ahead now. (Chakrabortty 2022)

The impact of this 'enduring austerity state' (Jessop 2016: 233) has been disastrous for the socially vulnerable (Grover, this volume). The decimation of the already brittle support for criminal and civil justice cases has led inevitably to miscarriages of justice (Cohen-Ennis 2021). Since 2010, the brutal cuts imposed on public services have 'contributed to 335,000 excess deaths – twice as many as previously thought, ... More people in Britain died due to austerity in the five years before the pandemic, than died from COVID-19 in the first three years of the pandemic. The effects of austerity continued after the pandemic hit, but initially became harder to discern' (Dorling 2022).

And, as noted above, while Box used Spitzer's (1975) initial insights concerning the policing and punishment of those pejoratively labelled as 'social dynamite' and 'social junk', forty years on this binary has 'morphed into a broader mass that encompasses both elements but who face the same state response: systemic indifference, lacerating punishment and structural violence' (Sim 2021: 127). At the same time, the human debris targeted as 'social junk' has expanded nationally and internationally due to the 'bulimic over- criminalization' of the behaviour of contemporary paupers forced onto the unforgiving ratchet of '*punitive welfare*' (Vegh Weis 2017: 226, emphasis in the original). For those caught in the pliers of an increasingly calibrated, demonstrably punitive, criminal injustice and state welfare system, the deeply damaging impact has been, and remains, profound (Grover, this volume).

At the same time, the drive towards greater authoritarianism, and the uninhibited state violence that often follows, continues to be ideologically mystified and legitimated through the mobilization of the nefarious discourse of the 'victimised state' (Sim 2004; Burnett, this volume). The allegedly disproportionate victimization of state agents at the heads, hands and feet of a deranged and dangerous criminal underclass, has been immensely powerful in cementing the drive towards more law and order. In Box's terms, this discourse has played a key role in ideologically mystifying the deaths, destruction, harm and pain caused by these same agents through '*exaggerati[ng]*……the numbers [of state agents] who are assaulted and murdered and *overdramtis[ing]* the seriousness of the violence against them' (Sim 2004: 126, emphasis in the original; see also Scott and Sim 2018; Scott 2020; Sim and Tombs 2021). This is not just a UK phenomenon. In America, during the demonstrations in Minneapolis after the state-sanctioned murder of George Floyd, no police officers were 'known to have been wounded [while] many protestors were severely hurt by the police'. Eighty-nine people aged between 15 and 77 were hospitalized for injuries including 'skull fractures and traumatic brain injuries. Others, including a reporter were partially blinded. One man lost an eye' (Mogelson 2022: 68).

Anti-statism

The anti-statist strategy, described above, has continued to be ruthlessly pursued over the past four decades. Contemporaneously, the policing and regulation of the powerful generally remains abject. At the same time, like the mutation and intensification in state authoritarianism since the early 1980s, so too has the anti-statist strategy mutated. Writing in 2009, Coleman et al. (2009: 5, emphasis in the original) pointed to '*how* the state form over the last three decades has further reinforced and intensified [the] process of differential law and its enforcement...'. For Tombs and Whyte, since Thatcher's (and Box's) time, the rhetoric of deregulation contained within the anti-statist discourse has had less to do with the 'punitive enforcement' of the law with respect to regulating corporations and, by extension, their depredations. Successive UK governments have been 'much more interested in changing the terms of the enforcement, towards greater compliance-type techniques which imply less actual impact on business' (cited in ibid.).

Within this brutal, unforgiving context, mercy, care and empathy towards the poor, nationally and internationally, do not tug at the neoliberal heartstrings. Since the financial crash of 2008, the protection offered to the poor by the post-war settlement—contingent and contradictory though that often was—has been increasingly eroded as the social state has been 'dismembered', resulting in further desolation and devastation (Toynbee and Walker 2017). The avoidable fire at Grenfell Tower in 2017 where 72, mainly minority ethnic and disabled people died, with hundreds injured and thousands traumatized, provides a profound and poignant example of the shattering harms generated by this dismembering process (Tombs 2020; Drake and Scott, this volume).

Furthermore, the use of critical concepts—social murder (Grover, this volume; Drake and Scott, this volume), femicide (Atkinson and Monk, this volume), climate catastrophe (Walters, this volume; Bradshaw and Leighton, this volume), genocide (Agozino, this volume; Fitzpatrick, this volume), organized neglect and mystification (Cooper and McCulloch, this volume), zemiology (Hillyard et al. 2004), social harm (Canning and Tombs 2021), social death (Price 2015; Scott 2020), preventable deaths and corporate manslaughter (Tombs 2017) and racialized criminalization and state violence (Williams and Clarke 2018)—have immeasurably widened the scope for analysing the social harms perpetrated by states, corporations, institutions and organizations, as well as powerful individuals. This work has also highlighted the deeply embedded culture of immunity and impunity which has legitimated and protected them from being held accountable for their collective policies and individual actions and the resulting deaths of millions of sentient beings globally (Bradshaw and Leighton, this volume). Furthermore, the social construction of transnational, criminal law categories such as 'human trafficking' and 'modern slavery' in practice mystify, in a Boxian sense, injustice, exploitation and state crime while legitimating repressive policies pursued by states domestically and internationally (Fouladvand and Ward, this volume).

The pandemic also demonstrated how the theory, methodology and methods of critical criminology have generated a deeper, more analytical understanding of the state-induced carnage that has occurred since March 2020: the lack of value placed on human life, particularly for those existing on the bottom rung of the brutal ladder of social inequality; the millions of avoidable deaths that have occurred; the lies and deceit perpetrated by different states and media outlets; the silencing of discussion about infection and death rates and the creation of a 'curated ignorance'[12] around them; the systemic, institutionalized corruption around the buying and selling of Personal Protective Equipment (PPE) and the systemic, unconscionable indifference to the differential impact of the virus on the lives and deaths of the poor, minority ethnic groups and those with disabilities (Sim and Tombs 2022). As Box noted, such indifference to 'who suffers - it could literally be anybody - ...does display disdain for humanity in general' (Box 1983: 21).

---

[12] Paul Gilroy used this phrase in his brilliant 2019 Holberg Lecture: 'Never Again: Refusing Race and Salvaging the Human'. While he was not talking about the virus it seemed to us to sum up what has been happening in terms of understanding its origins and impact (Gilroy 2019).

Resistance, Democratic Accountability and Delivering Justice

PCM was one of the few texts in critical criminology published in the early 1980s that discussed the democratic accountability of state institutions. Central to this concern was the capricious discretion used by state agents on the streets and in institutions which delivered injustice on a daily basis. Throughout the book, Box wrestles with these issues. In the chapter on police crime, he excoriates the police complaints procedure and its dismal failure not only to make the police publicly accountable: it was also a system which 'enabled[d] them to discredit the complainants and protect their own "deviants"' (Box 1983: 111; see also Jackson, this volume).

His analysis illustrated that critical criminologists *were* concerned about intervening to develop policy responses that would make a radical difference. They were not the out-of-touch idealists caricatured by the state, media, liberal academics *and* traditional political parties like the Labour Party. Nor did it prevent them, and the grassroots organizations they worked with, from being labelled as subversives by the security services.[13]

Importantly, Box's demand for a reckoning with the state through democratizing its institutions, and the institutions of the wider society, curtailing discretion and delivering social justice, was *not* a liberal concession to the powerful. It was, in fact, quite the opposite. It reflected Marx's demand a century earlier for the democratization of the state as a fundamental prerequisite for the democratization of the wider society which itself was a fundamental prerequisite for abolishing the capitalist

---

[13] At the time of writing, July 2023, the ongoing Undercover Policing Inquiry (https://www.ucpi.org.uk/) released state documents showing how grassroots organizations regarded as 'subversive' were kept under surveillance and infiltrated by Special Branch agents including the campaign to achieve justice for Stephen Lawrence murdered in a racist attack in 1993. Those working for democratically elected organizations such as the Greater London Council were also kept under surveillance See Special Branch report entitled *Political Extremism and the Campaign for Police Accountability within the Metropolitan Police District*—Undercover Policing Inquiry ucpi.org.uk. There were further revelations in June 2023 into the failings of the police investigation into the murder of Stephen Lawrence, this time with regard to the identification of the 'sixth suspect' and the failure of the police to pursue clear lines of inquiry.

shards that splintered human lives (Sim, this volume). In the twenty-first century, the demand for democracy has not disappeared. Although writing about democracy in Latin America, Hugo Chavez raises an important question about how democracy should be defined:

> It is not the same thing to talk about a democratic revolution and a revolutionary democracy. The first concept has a bridle, like a horse: revolutionary, but democratic. It is a conservative bridle. The other concept is liberating, it is like a discharge…like a horse without a bridle: revolutionary democracy, democracy for the revolution. (cited in Therborn 2022)

Since Box's time, this demand for revolutionary democracy has been propelled forward by critical criminologists, activists, grassroots, organizations, charities and the voices and experiences of bereaved families working together to generate 'truth, justice and accountability'[14] across old and new sites of contestation (Jackson, this volume; Bradshaw and Leighton, this volume; Cunliffe and Morrison, this volume; Chadwick and Clarke, this volume). They have attempted to transgress what Stuart Hall called the 'difficult business of making alliances' (Hall 1988: 280) and exploit the crisis of legitimacy inside the state as well as the contradictions and contingencies within and between its institutions. Generating a politics of dissent and resistance, developing alternative truths, seeking justice and demanding radical policy alternatives stand in marked contrast to the sterile, reformist 'realism' of state agents, liberal academics, media personnel and the regressive forces of traditional social democracy where a change of policy is defined as realistic 'to the extent that it approaches what already exists' (Unger, cited in Williams 2013).

The Gramscian emphasis on articulating a 'war of position' and turning 'common sense' into 'good sense' has been central to these alliances, particularly in a political context where 'the left as a whole, in its one-sided rationalism, has utterly failed to comprehend the necessity to educate the common sense of the common people, in order to constitute a popular bloc, a practical, material force, against traditional

---

[14] This is the campaigning slogan used by the charity INQUEST which, in many ways, sums up the goals of these different campaigns. See inquest.org.uk.

ideas' (Hall 1980b: 178). Hall's point about the wretched failure of the forces of social democracy remains entirely relevant, perhaps even more so forty years on. Two examples below illustrate how this 'war of position' has unfolded over the last four decades.

INQUEST's work has shifted the terrain in terms of how deaths inside and outside of state institutions have been perceived as well as the state's role in these deaths. In February 2023, the charity published *I can't breathe: Race, death & British policing* (INQUEST 2023). Combining academic research and family testimonies the report showed that black men were seven times more likely to die at the hands of the police. This report illustrated how the state continued to use the racist discourse of 'big, black and dangerous' to legitimate the violence perpetrated by its agents against black men. Additionally, the spiteful treatment of the families at inquests, and their often self-imposed silence around discussing racism due to the fear of being accused of 'playing the race card', and thereby being dismissed, provided a grim reminder, and as the chapters here show, that justice, for many, remains a distant star which has yet to be reached (see White and Williams, this volume).

The gruelling, decades-long campaign for justice for the 97 football fans who died at Hillsborough in 1989, as well as justice for their families and survivors, provides the second example. This campaign was central to uncovering the truth about how the deaths were preventable, the role of the police in the deaths and the scurrilous, unconscionable role of the media in blaming the deceased for their own deaths (Scraton 2016). The work of the *Hillsborough Independent Panel* illustrated how the contradictions within the state could be mobilized by critical academics not only to challenge and defeat the lies and deceit of the Thatcher government and the media and articulate an alternative, critical analysis but also to develop an alternative critical method for excavating the truth:

> The Hillsborough panel heralded a departure from the unfettered operational autonomy of previous non-government-funded panels. While funded by the state and supported by state officials its full independence in setting research priorities and examining the accessed material and publishing its findings was secured. This underpinned the confidence and

support of those whose interests were paramount – the bereaved families, survivors and wider public. (Scraton 2020: 133)

Responding to the Social Harms of the Powerful

As we noted above, Box raised questions about how the abysmal depredations of the powerful should be regulated and controlled. However, there was a tension in how he conceptualized this issue, particularly around the nature of regulation within capitalist societies and its relationship to the state (Tombs, this volume). Forty years on, questions concerning the regulation, control and punishment of the powerful remains a pivotal, if still problematic, issue for critical criminologists. For Anne Alvesalo and Steve Tombs:

> Accepting the premise that for a long time society will criminalize activities by the marginalized and relatively powerless, then the crimes of the powerful – which on any criterion are more serious in terms of level of economic, physical, and social harm – also should be subject to such processes. This means both resisting some efforts to criminalize conventional crimes, while promoting some efforts to criminalize economic crimes. (2002: 37)

Tombs (2016b: 193) has also discussed the obstacles involved in attempting to hold the 'harmful corporation' to account:

> ….in the realm of criminal law, we can still identify reforms which have the potential to be transformative – that is, which maintain the potential for more radical reform, rather than ultimately bolstering the power of capital through a limited instrumentalism, a mere symbolism, or indeed both. Key contemporary examples of legal reforms which might radically undermine the legal protections which corporations currently enjoy are those which seek to pierce the corporate veil – that ideological and material, legal construction through which the corporate form exists as if independent of those who own and control it, guaranteeing a compartmentalisation of legal (and moral) liability. (ibid.: 205)

Using the 'tortuous passage of the [*Corporate Manslaughter and Corporate Homicide Act* 2007] CMCH Act' through the UK Parliament as an example, he noted that:

> .....an early Home Office consultation document on the law proposed that, alongside a corporation being convicted for manslaughter, company directors should be able to be disqualified if it is found that their conduct has 'contributed' to the company committing the offence, while the Government also stated that it 'would welcome comments' on whether company directors should be able to be prosecuted for such conduct.... Ultimately, organised lobbying from employers organisations, and notably the Institute of Directors, saw the potential criminalisation of Directors removed from the law. Yet, this debate represented a sustained period in which there was a genuine possibility to pierce the corporate veil. Similar proposals continue to circulate in the context of legal liability for workplace killings that precisely establish a clear legal relationship between such deaths, the corporate form, and the senior officers and shareholders of that corporation. These are potentially radical, and are on various political agendas....... (ibid.: 205–206)[15]

Indeed, the actual implementation of the *Corporate Manslaughter and Corporate Homicide* [CMCH] *Act 2007* provides a recent illustration of what Box (1983: 8) referred to as a 'symbolic victory', where the state concedes ground and introduces criminal legislation, only then to systematically fail to enforce the legislation in any systematic, coherent or principled way. The profound limitations of the criminal law in response to the deadly harms of the corporation have led Tombs and Whyte (2015) to call for its abolition. For Tombs and Whyte (2015), it is necessary to challenge the legal basis of the corporation; remove the principle of limited liability for shareholders; and put an end to the idea of the 'corporate personhood' (ibid: 82) as having the same legal rights as people. Abolishing the corporation offers a radical agenda outside of the remit of the criminal law which presents a full frontal attack on the unbridled accumulation of profits, and indeed the very foundations

---

[15] Thanks to Steve Tombs for the references and for discussing the complexities involved in this issue with us.

of capitalism. The call by Tombs and Whyte (2015) for such a radical dilution of corporate power is very much in line with the arguments of Box (1983: 202) forty years ago, who also noted that it is only through dispersing of power as 'thinly' as possible that we can hope to avoid the harms of the powerful in the future.

In campaigning against prisons, feminist abolitionists have also captured the tensions in mobilizing conventional criminal justice responses to the systemic, brutal, social harms generated by male violence against women and girls. For Ardath Whynacht, safeguarding and protecting women from domestic homicide is crucial given that 'there are some incarcerated people who are tremendously dangerous to our individual and collective safety' (Whynacht 2021: 29). Crucially, however, a 'system that never addresses the *why* behind a harm never actually contains the harm itself' (Kaba cited in ibid.: 118, original emphasis). Responding to male violence through incarcerating violent men is therefore problematic:

> ……we can banish those who commit harm without asking questions about why they harmed in the first place… [A] refusal to acknowledge the causes of violence allows us to scapegoat individuals for forms of violence that are taught and maintained in everyday life. (Whynacht 2021: 118)

A hardened commitment to punishment and criminalization will never generate the conditions required for 'answerability' (Scott 2020). In the last 40 years, debates among critical criminologists regarding which interventions should be advocated in response to the harms of the powerful have ebbed and flowed, but it is clear that the dilemmas Box (1983) grappled with in *PCM*, and the need to think through, formulate, promote and then implement responses which reflect the ethico-political principles of socialism remains as pertinent today as it has ever been.

Box and Contemporary Criminology

What would Box have made of contemporary criminology? At one level, the criminological landscape he discussed 40 years ago has changed.

The binary between critical criminology and traditional and administrative criminology is arguably less clear cut now as evidenced by the number of critical papers presented at the British Society of Criminology's annual conference, the book prizes awarded to critical scholars from the Society and the debate about what public-facing criminology should look like (Hughes 2005; Loader and Sparks 2010; Christie et al. 2011). All of these developments, while not leading to a rapprochement between the different criminological strands, have ensured a more nuanced, 'complex and contested' arena compared with 40 years ago (Hughes 2005: 158). The fragmentation of critical criminology in Box's lifetime between left realism and left idealism also contributed to this shifting landscape and today it is important to acknowledge the overlaps between different criminological strands as well as the critical thought of abolitionists, zemiologists and other radicals promoting emancipatory knowledge who do not sit within the intellectual boundaries of the discipline of criminology.

And yet, having said this, the key critical criminological concerns which Box raised, and which have been identified over the last four decades still remain marginal at best, and neglected at worst, within mainstream criminology: the dominance of empiricism and reformist ethnographies; the lack of a structural analysis of state violence and corporate crime; the abject processes for funding research and its ties to career progression; the reductive definition of impact and the overly rigid criteria of the research excellence framework which can stifle rather than foster critical thinking; the role of 'pseudo-scentific procedure[s]' in 'disciplining critics of the status quo' (Carlen 2005: 87); the continuation of research agendas 'that ignore…crimes committed by the most powerful and wealthy in society, while endorsing policies that aim to regulate the already over-regulated in society' (Walters 2009: 209); the dismissive, academic snobbery towards radical, grassroots and activist organizations; the marginalisation of key concepts such as structural violence; the failure to demand the democratic accountability of state agents and corporate executives for the social harms they generate; and the reluctance to countenance the emancipatory politics and praxis of social justice and, by implication, the radical transformation, dissolution and abolition of parasitic state institutions and the deeply embedded social divisions of neoliberal capitalism which they defend. In short, although written in 2002, Kerry Carrington and Russell Hogg's, succinct point remains entirely relevant in 2023: there remains a 'kind of criminology that takes so much of the status quo for granted' (Carrington and Hogg 2002: 2).[16]

At the same time, he might well have been surprised by the hegemonic and policy impact of critical criminology due, in large part, to the radical seeds he, and his contemporaries, planted between the 1960s and the early 1980s. In William Blake's terms, they broke free from the 'mind-forg'd manacles' (cited in Higgs 2021: 99)[17] which constricted criminological thinking. As academics and activists, '*how* we see is as important as *what* we see' (ibid.: 338), a point that traditional criminology had ignored in its distorted emphasis on human beings as criminals rather than criminals as human beings and in its distorted, collective failure to see the social harms generated by corporations and the state.

Despite the regressive detour into the theoretical and political cul-de-sac of left realism pursued by some critical criminologists referred to above (Sim et al. 1987), and the moral and political hypocrisy of successive New Labour governments around law and order for the poor while simultaneously ignoring the crimes of the powerful (Sim 2000), overall, the impact of critical criminology can be seen in the sheer number of undergraduate and postgraduate courses and modules available; the books, journals, journal articles and contributions to grassroots newsletters; the links with national and international grassroots organizations; the media interventions and in the radical research that is still being conducted, despite the obstacles generated by the suffocating, governance culture dominating the research agenda in universities (Squires 2013).

The influence of *PCM* might have surprised him given the book's huge impact on critical criminology, a point to which this collection testifies. The global forums for critical criminology which have emerged in the last four decades in Europe, Australasia and North America, and

---

[16] Thanks to Steve Tombs for discussing this point with us.
[17] Coincidently, this phrase was also used by the late Eric Allison in a *Guardian* article written in 2007 which we rediscovered after writing this section (Allison 2007).

more recently in the Global South, with their emphasis on critical analysis and activist interventions, at the very least, share the core ideas and values expressed in *PCM*. The *European Group for the Study of Deviance and Social Control*, is a good example of this point (Gilmore et al. 2013). In addition, the diversity and scope of the following chapters, which include considering the impact of post-colonial criminology and post-structural feminism (Agozino, this volume; Atkinson and Monk, this volume), both of which have evolved since *PCM* was published, demonstrate the durability of the book's key ideas, themes and concepts. That the chapters continue to grapple with many of the same intellectual, ethical and political dilemmas as Box did in 1983, also demonstrate that 40 years on the *spirit* of the book remains powerfully relevant and intact.

Without engaging in a full audit of the critical criminological curriculum, or a search of the indexes of criminology textbooks, it is impossible to give a definitive answer to the extent to which *PCM* remains a key text for criminology students today. However, one contemporary example of Box's influence can be found in an Open University module, DD105 *Introduction to Criminology*. Along with C. Wright Mill's *The Sociological Imagination*, *PCM* was a key inspiration for this module, which is the largest criminology module in the UK, and one of the largest in Europe. It has quite literally introduced the ideas of Box to tens of thousands of students since it was launched in October 2019 (Drake and Scott, this volume).

Finally, like many of us, Box would have been astonished by universities, nationally and internationally, acting as training grounds for state agents through 'disciplines' such as Police Studies (Jackson, this volume). The sheer number of undergraduate and postgraduate degrees, operating 'neutrally' within a state/higher education complex, has not only generated huge income streams, buttressed by the rush to obtain research grants, *at whatever cost, from whatever source*, but also has allowed university managers to ideologically legitimate the police by validating and teaching academic degrees *and* allowed the police to legitimate universities through the vacuous and offensive claims made by these managers that they, and their students, are in touch with 'real life' issues. And what could be more 'real life' than crime and punishment? These degrees, much like Psychology and its forensic variants, are supported both by managerial structures, pathologically obsessed with not jeopardizing research income by asking 'awkward' questions and 'a rampant epidemic of censorious mission creep by criminal justice agencies (metaphorically pulling up the drawbridges and circling the wagons via their new research protocols)' (Squires 2013).

In operating as 'disimagination machine[s]' (Giroux 2013: 257), the yearly production of thousands of '[criminal justice] judges of normality' (Foucault 1979: 304) remains, as in Box's time, driven by a laser focus on working-class crime. The 'correspondence of interests' (Hall and Scraton 1981: 474) universities share with state institutions, allows these degree courses to systematically disregard critical concepts like social harm, social murder, social death and structural violence and effectively ignore, indeed are contemptuous of, radical social policies designed to prevent social harm and embed a revolutionary praxis of democratic accountability to hold to account those responsible for the egregious harms they inflict on the wider society. For university managers, studying malfunctions of the mind is more market-friendly, and ideologically acceptable, than studying Marx, studying forensics is more acceptable than studying feminism and studying allegedly disorganized families is more acceptable than studying disorganized capitalism.[18] As Box might have said, in the modern, university, 'money doesn't talk, it swears'.[19]

A Boxian Morality

The final point we want to make about Box's work is that it is a profoundly *moral* as well as a political enterprise. This was recognized by Pat Carlen, the year after his death. In 1988, she made a key observation about radically transforming the response to social harms and wrongdoing by developing a more complex, critical understanding of what responsibility, culpability and accountability mean. Like Box, she

---

[18] It would be interesting to add up, and audit, *all* of the research funds and grants that traditional criminology has had poured into it since Box wrote *PCM*, never mind beforehand to arrive at a global sum. And then the question becomes: who has benefitted from such largesse given the abject state of criminal justice systems around the world?
[19] From the song *It's All Right Ma (I'm Only Bleeding)* by Bob Dylan.

rejected deterministic visions of how individuals behave in favour of recognizing the complex links between agency, action and meaning and their dialectical relationship to wider structures of social and economic power (Carlen 1988). She illustrated how Box stripped away the hypocritical obfuscation around how social harms, wrongdoing and crime *should* be understood in relation to the poor, in this case, poor women caught up in the pliers of a compassionless, criminal injustice system:

> ... although people choose to act, sometimes criminally, they do not do so under conditions of their own choosing. Their choice makes them responsible, but the conditions make the choice comprehensible. These conditions, social and economic, contribute to crime because they constrain, limit or narrow the choices available. Many of us, in similar circumstances, might choose the same course of action. (Box, cited in ibid. 1988: 162)

This fundamental questioning of the scope and meaning of criminal responsibility and culpability, and, by extension, the ability to competently assess and judge the choices and conduct made by others in a deeply divided, socially unjust and brutal world, leaves the basic claims of the criminal justice system—that it is fair, equal, transparent and accountable—in tatters. Forty years on, this is perhaps the most important lesson of all that we can learn from Box's work.

Conclusion

In November 2014, the feminist writer Ursula K. Le Guin was honoured for her huge contribution to science fiction. Although working in a different discipline, her acceptance speech captured the emancipatory spirit that Box reached for, and embraced, in *PCM*:

> Hard times are coming, when we'll be wanting the voices of writers who can see alternatives to how we live now, can see through our fear-stricken society and its obsessive technologies to other ways of being, and even imagine real grounds for hope. We'll need writers who can remember

freedom – poets, visionaries – realists of a larger reality…We live in capitalism, its power seems inescapable – but then, so did the divine right of kings. Any human power can be resisted and changed by human beings. Resistance and change often begin in art. Very often in our art, the art of words… We who live by writing and publishing want and should demand our fair share of the proceeds; but the name of our beautiful reward isn't profit. Its name is freedom. (Le Guin 2014)

In Le Guin's terms, Box *was* a 'realist of a larger reality'. As this collection shows, his analysis was prescient and remains entirely relevant to understanding and responding to the devastating social harms generated by the systemic wrongdoing of the powerful in the twenty-first century. He compels us not just to whisper in hushed tones about these harms and wrongdoings, then and now, but to shout about them and demand a reckoning with the perpetrators if they are not to be normalized and endlessly repeated. Box also compels us to shout about the systemic indifference of state agents to social harm, and the culture of immunity and impunity that protects them and the governments they serve nationally and internationally, in the twenty-first century. As Steve McQueen has pointed out, justice and truth 'need[s] to be shouted from the highest rooftops' (cited in Booth 2023).

For many on the left, these issues are still invisible as their political and Parliamentary representatives—aptly and pointedly described by Stuart Hall as 'the great moving nowhere show' (Hall 1998/2007: 283)—remain ideologically welded to doing something—*anything*—about the crimes of the powerless, through imposing draconian punishments on the allegedly malevolent individuals, problem families and disorganized communities from whom these 'real' criminals are supposedly drawn.[20] *PCM*'s insurgent analysis illustrated the reductive, hypocritical limitations of this perspective and the abject policy responses to it. In a

---

[20] At the time of writing, the resurgence of a 'tough on crime, tough on the causes of crime' rhetoric in the Labour Party gives us little hope that we will see 'clear red water' (Sim 2000) between the current Sunak administration and any future government led by Keir Starmer. Rather than looking for responses to the social harms of the Conservative government, or searching for inspiration in socialist ethics and politics, the Labour Party is peddling a disciplinarian crackdown on a society that it portrays as a 'criminal dystopia where people are unable to go out at night and youths huddle ominously in parks and public areas getting high and menacing the public' (Malik 2023).

'fear-haunted world' (H.G. Wells cited in Lynskey 2019: 73), they have offered, and continue to offer, nothing by way of achieving the inclusive and emancipatory 'justice for all' which Box so eloquently, poignantly and compellingly demanded. Forty years on, the yearning to fulfil this demand burns as brightly as ever.

Acknowledgements Thanks to Steve Tombs for reading an earlier draft of this chapter and for his encouragement and his usual insightful comments and to Sam Fletcher and Will McGowan for the excellent discussions about the nature of contemporary state power. Also thank you to Raj Harrison, Learning and Teaching Librarian at the Open University, for his help in compiling the reviews of *PCM* discussed above in the section *PCM: Reception and Reviews*.

References

Allison, E. 2007. Breaking the Mind-Forged Manacles. *The Guardian*, November 23. https://www.theguardian.com/commentisfree/2007/nov/23/breakingconceptualshackles. Accessed 1 Dec 2022.

Alvesalo, A., and S. Tombs. 2002. Working for Criminalization of Economic Offending: Contradictions for Critical Criminology? *Critical Criminology* 11: 21–40.

Anderson, T. 2022. A Bristol Riot Defendant Explains How She Was Traumatised after Police Kneed Her to the Ground. *The Canary*, March 4. https://www.thecanary.co/exclusive/2022/03/04/a-bristol-riot-defendant-explains-how-she-was-traumatised-after-police-kneed-her-to-the-ground/. Accessed 8 Mar 2022.

Booth, R. 2023. "People Will Be Disturbed": Steve McQueen on Airing His Grenfell Film. *The Guardian*, March 27. https://www.theguardian.com/uk-news/2023/mar/27/steve-mcqueen-grenfell-tower-film-serpentine-gallery. Accessed 27 Mar 2023.

Box, S. 1971/1981. *Deviance, Reality and Society*, 2nd ed. Eastbourne: Holt, Rinehart and Winston.

Box, S. 1983. *Power, Crime and Mystification*. London: Tavistock.

Box, S. 1987. *Recession, Crime and Punishment*. Basingstoke: Macmillan Education.

Brown, S. 1986. Power, Crime and Mystification. *Social Forces* 64 (3, March): 840–841.

Bryant, M., and J. Ungoed-Thomas. 2023. Revealed: Record Number of Households in UK Depending on Food Banks. *The Guardian*, February 19. https://www.theguardian.com/society/2023/feb/19/record-number-of-uk-households-depending-on-food-banks. Accessed 31 May 2023.

Calderbank, M. 2011. Editorial: Explanation Not Excuses. *Red Pepper* 180 (October/November): 3.

Canning, V., and S. Tombs. 2021. *From Social Harm to Zemiology: A Critical Introduction*. London: Routledge.

Carlen, P. 1983. *Women's Imprisonment: A Study in Social Control*. London: Routledge and Kegan Paul.

Carlen, P. 1988. *Women, Crime and Poverty*. Milton Keynes: Open University Press.

Carlen, P. 2005. In Praise of Critical Criminology. *Outlines* 2: 83–90.

Carrington, K., and R. Hogg. 2002. Critical Criminologies: An Introduction. In *Critical Criminology: Issues, Debates, Challenges*, ed. K. Carrington and R. Hogg, 1–12. Cullompton: Willan.

Chakrabortty, A. 2022. Discipline the Poor, Protect the Rich—It's the Same Old Tories, Same Old Class War. *The Guardian*, November 10. https://www.theguardian.com/commentisfree/2022/nov/10/poor-rich-tories-brexit-austerity-cameron-osborne-sunak. Accessed 6 Dec 2022.

Chambliss, W., and M. Mankoff, eds. 1976. *Whose Law? What Order?* New York: Wiley.

Christie, N., E. Currie, H. Kennedy, G. Laycock, R. Morgan, J. Sim, J. Tombs, and R. Walters. 2011. A Symposium of Reviews of *Public Criminology?*: By Ian Loader and Richard Sparks (Oxford: Key Ideas in Criminology, Routledge, 2010, 196pp.) with contributions from Nils Christie, Elliott Currie, Helena Kennedy, Gloria Laycock, Rod Morgan, Joe Sim, Jacqueline Tombs and Reece Walters'. *The British Journal of Criminology* 51 (4, July): 707–738.

Clarke, A. 1987. *Women's Silence, Men's Violence: Sexual Assault in England and Wales 1770–1845*. London: Pandora.

Cohen-Ennis, C. 2021. Claims Cuts to Legal Aid Has Led to "Broken" Criminal Justice System. *ITV News Wales*, March 11. https://www.itv.com/news/wales/2021-03-11/claims-cuts-to-legal-aid-has-led-to-broken-criminal-justice-system. Accessed 13 Feb 2023.

Coleman, R., J. Sim, S. Tombs, and D. Whyte. 2009. Introduction. In *State Power Crime*, ed. R. Coleman, J. Sim, S. Tombs, and D. Whyte, 1–19. London: Sage.

Davies, J.S. 2011. *Challenging Governance Theory: From Networks to Hegemony*. Cambridge: Polity.
Ditton, J. 1983. Power Play. *New Society*, December, 22/29: 497.
Dobash, R.E., and R.P. Dobash. 1979. *Violence Against Wives: A Case Against the Patriarchy*. New York: Free Press.
Dorling, D. 2022. Austerity Led to Twice as Many Excess UK Deaths as Previously Thought—Here's What That Means for Future Cuts. *The Conversation*, October 6. https://theconversation.com/austerity-led-to-twice-as-many-excess-uk-deaths-as-previously-thought-heres-what-that-means-for-future-cuts-192033. Accessed 28 Dec 2022.
Edwards, S. 1989. *Policing 'Domestic' Violence: Women, Law and the State*. London: Sage.
Elden, S. 2017. *Foucault: The Birth of Power*. Cambridge: Polity.
Elkins, C. 2022. *Legacy of Violence: A History of the British Empire*. London: The Bodley Head.
Elston, L. 2023. Multimillion-Pound Coronation "A Slap in the Face". *The Independent*, May 9. https://www.independent.co.uk/life-style/royal-family/how-much-coronation-cost-2023-b2335324.html. Accessed 31 May 2023.
Fielding, N. 1985. Power, Crime and Mystification by Steven Box Review. *The British Journal of Sociology* 36 (3): 493–494.
Fitzgibbon, W., and J. Lea. 2020. *Privatising Justice: The Security Industry, War and Crime Control*. London: Pluto.
Foot, P., and M. Livingstone. 2022. *Charged*. London: Verso.
Foucault, M. 1979. *Discipline and Punish: The Birth of the Prison*. Harmondsworth: Peregrine.
Gamble, A. 1988. *The Free Economy and the Strong State*. Basingstoke: Palgrave Macmillan.
Gilmore, J., J.M. Moore, and D. Scott, eds. 2013. *Critique and Dissent*. Ottawa: Red Quill Books.
Gilroy, P. 1982. The Myth of Black Criminality. In *The Socialist Register 1982*, ed. M. Eve and D. Musson, 47–56. London: The Merlin Press.
Gilroy, P. 2019. Never Again: Refusing Race and Salvaging the Human. The 2019 Holberg Lecture. The University Aula, Bergen, Norway. https://www.youtube.com/watch?v=Ta6UkmlXtVo. Accessed 12 Jan 2023.
Gilroy, P., and J. Sim. 1987. Law, Order and the State of the Left. In *Law, Order and the Authoritarian State*, ed. P. Scraton, 71–106. Milton Keynes: Open University.
Giroux, H.A. 2013. The Disimagination Machine and the Pathologies of Power. *Symploke* 21 (1–2): 257–269.

Hall, S. 1966/2017. Political Commitment. In *Stuart Hall: Selected Political Writings: The Great Moving Right Show and Other Essays*, ed. S. Davison, D. Featherstone, M. Rustin, and B. Schwartz, 85–106. Chadwell Heath: Lawrence and Wishart.

Hall, S. 1979/2017. The Great Moving Right Show. In *Stuart Hall: Selected Political Writings: The Great Moving Right Show and Other Essays*, ed. S. Davison, D. Featherstone, M. Rustin, and B. Schwartz, 172–186. Chadwell Heath: Lawrence and Wishart.

Hall, S. 1980a. *Drifting into a Law and Order Society*. London: The Cobden Trust.

Hall, S. 1980b. Popular Democratic vs Authoritarian Populism: Two Ways of "Taking Democracy Seriously." In *Marxism and Democracy*, ed. A. Hunt, 157–185. London: Lawrence and Wishart.

Hall, S. 1983. *Karl Marx and Marxism*. Television Documentary, Thames TV, broadcast 15 October, 1983. https://archive.org/details/karl-marx-and-marxism. Accessed 10 Feb 2023.

Hall, S. 1988. *The Hard Road to Renewal*. London: Verso.

Hall, S. 1998/2017. The Great Moving Nowhere Show. In *Stuart Hall: Selected Political Writings: The Great Moving Right Show and Other Essays*, eds. S. Davison, D. Featherstone, M. Rustin, and B. Schwartz, 283–300. Chadwell Heath: Lawrence and Wishart.

Hall, S. 2009. Preface. In *State Power* Crime, eds. R. Coleman, J. Sim, S. Tombs, and D. Whyte, xii–xviii. London: Sage.

Hall, S., C. Critcher, T. Jefferson, J. Clarke, and B. Roberts. 1978. *Policing the Crisis: Mugging, the State and Law and Order*. London: Macmillan.

Hall, S., and M. Jacques, eds. 1983. *The Politics of Thatcherism*. Lawrence and Wishart.

Hall, S., and P. Scraton. 1981. Law, Class and Control. In *Crime and Society: Readings in History and Theory*, compilers. M. Fitzgerald, G. McLennan, and J. Pawson, 460–497. London: Routledge and Kegan Paul.

Harding, L. 2017. Heathcote Williams, Radical Poet, Playwright and Actor, Dies Aged 75. *The Guardian*, July 2. https://www.theguardian.com/books/2017/jul/02/heathcote-williams-radical-poet-playwright-actor-dies-aged-75. Accessed 6 July 2017.

Higgs, J. 2021. *William Blake vs The World*. London: Weidenfeld and Nicolson.

Hillyard, P. 1987. The Normalisation of Special Powers: From Northern Ireland to Britain. In *Law, Order and the Authoritarian State*, ed. P. Scraton, 279–312. Milton Keynes: Open University Press.

Hillyard, P., C. Pantazis, S. Tombs, and D. Gordon, eds. 2004. *Beyond Criminology: Taking Harm Seriously*. London: Pluto Press.

Hobbs, S. 2023 Letter, *The Guardian*, January 26. https://www.theguardian.com/uk-news/2023/jan/26/zara-aleena-was-failed-by-a-privatised-probation-service. Accessed 27 Jan 2023.

Hughes, G. 2005. Book Review: Beyond Criminology: Taking Harm Seriously. *Social and Legal Studies* 15 (1): 157–159.

INQUEST. 2023. *I Can't Breathe: Race, death & British policing* London: INQUEST.

Jessop, B. 1982. *The Capitalist State: Marxist Theory and Methods*. Oxford: Martin Robertson.

Jessop, B. 2016. *The State: Past Present Future*. Cambridge: Polity.

Jones, A. 1985. Power, Crime, and Mystification by Steven Box Review. *Political Science Quarterly* 100 (2, Summer): 340–341.

Knott, A. 2020. The New Moving Right Show. *Soundings* 75 (Summer): 111–123.

Le Guin, U. K. 2014. Ursula K Le Guin's Speech at National Book Awards: "Books Aren't Just Commodities". *The Guardian*, November 20. https://www.theguardian.com/books/2014/nov/20/ursula-k-le-guin-national-book-awards-speech. Accessed 6 June 2022.

Loader, I., and R. Sparks. 2010. *Public Criminology?* Oxford: Routledge.

Lynskey, D. 2019. *The Ministry of Truth: A Biography of George Orwell's 1984*. London: Picador.

Malik, N. 2023. Why Labour's "Law and Order" Tribute Act Feels Hollow and Overblown. *The Guardian*, April 10. https://www.theguardian.com/commentisfree/2023/apr/10/labour-law-and-order-england-wales-justice-system-crime. Accessed 14 Apr 2023.

Marx, G.T. 2005. Soft Surveillance: Mandatory Voluntarism and the Collection of Personal Data. *Dissent* 52 (4): 36–43.

Mathiesen, T. 1980. *Law, Society and Political Action*. London: Academic Press.

Mogelson, L. 2022. *The Storm Is Here: America on the Brink*. London: Riverrun.

Monbiot, G. 2023. The Coronation Arrests Are Just the Start. Police Can Do What They Want to Us Now. *The Guardian*, May 12. https://www.theguardian.com/commentisfree/2023/may/12/coronation-protest-arrests-police. Accessed 31 May 2023.

Monk, H., and J. Sim. 2017. Introduction. In *Women, Crime and Criminology: A Celebration*, ed. H. Monk and J. Sim, 1–15. Liverpool: Centre for the Study of Crime, Criminalization and Social Exclusion/European Group for the Study of Deviance and Social Control.

Nairn, T. 1988. *The Enchanted Glass: Britain and Its Monarchy*. London: Radius.
Panitch, L. 2009. Foreword: Reading the State in Capitalist Society. In *The State in Capitalist Society*, R. Miliband, x–xvii. Merlin Press/Fenwood Publishing.
Pearce, F. 1976. *Crimes of the Powerful*. London: Pluto.
Plummer, K. 2013. Inspirations: The National Deviancy Conference. https://kenplummer.com/2013/02/08/inspirations-the-national-deviancy-conference/. Accessed 27 June 2021.
Poulantzas, N. 1978. *State Power Socialism*. London: Verso.
Price, J. 2015. *Prison and Social Death*. New Brunswick: Rutgers University Press.
Quicker, J.C. 1987. Power, Crime and Mystification Book Review. *Journal of Contemporary Criminal Justice* 1 (February): 58–60.
Rock, P. 1988. The Present State of Criminology in Britain. In *A History of British Criminology*, ed. P. Rock, 58–69. Oxford: Oxford University Press.
Romano, J. 1979. James Baldwin Writing and Talking. *The New York Times*, September 23. https://www.nytimes.com/1979/09/23/archives/james-baldwin-writing-and-talking-baldwin-baldwin-authors-query.html. Accessed 10 May 2023.
Ryan, M., and J. Sim. 1984. Decoding Leon Brittan. *The Abolitionist* 16: 3–7.
Scott, D. 2006. *Ghosts Beyond Our Realm: A Neo-abolitionist Analysis of Prisoner Human Rights and Prison Officer Occupational Culture*. Unpublished PhD Thesis, University of Central Lancashire.
Scott, D. 2018. *Against Imprisonment*. Hook: Waterside Press.
Scott, D. 2020. *For Abolition: Essays on Prisons and Socialist Ethics*. Hook: Waterside Press.
Scott, D., and J. Sim. 2018. *Prisons: Dangerous for Whom?* https://ccseljmu.wordpress.com/2018/09/20/prisons-dangerous-for-whom/. Accessed 10 May 2023.
Scraton, P., ed. 1987. *Law, Order and the Authoritarian State*. Milton Keynes: Open University Press.
Scraton, P. 2016. *Hillsborough: The Truth*. Edinburgh: Mainstream.
Scraton, P. 2020. The Hillsborough Independent Panel and the UK State: An Alternative Route to "Truth", "Apology" and "Justice." In *Justice Alternatives*, ed. P. Carlen and L.A. Franca, 121–134. London: Routledge.
Sim, J. 2000. "One Thousand Days of Degradation": New Labour and Old Compromises at the Turn of the Century. *Social Justice* 27 (2): 168–192.

Sim, J. 2004. The Victimised State and the Mystification of Social Harm. In *Beyond Criminology: Taking Harm Seriously*, ed. P. Hillyard, C. Pantazis, S. Tombs, and D. Gordon, 113–132. London: Pluto.

Sim, J. 2009. *Punishment and Prisons: Power and the Carceral State*. London: Sage.

Sim, J. 2021. "Help Me Please": Death and Self-Harm in Male Prisons in England and Wales. In *The Routledge International Handbook of Penal Abolition*, ed. M. Coyle and D. Scott, 119–130. London: Routledge.

Sim, J. 2023. Confronting State Power: Dissenting Voices and the Demand for Penal Abolition. In *The Oxford Handbook of Criminology*, ed. A. Liebling, S. Maruna, and L. McCara, 7th ed., 884–908. Oxford: Oxford University Press.

Sim, J., P. Scraton, and P. Gordon. 1987. Introduction. In *Law, Order and the Authoritarian State*, ed. P. Scraton, 1–70. Milton Keynes: Open University Press.

Sim, J., and S. Tombs. 2021. *Policing, Violence and State 'Truths'*. https://ccseljmu.wordpress.com/2021/04/21/policing-violence-and-state-truths/.

Sim, J., and S. Tombs. 2022. Narrating the Coronavirus Crisis: State Talk and State Silence in the UK. *Justice, Power and Resistance* 5 (1–2, May): 67–90.

Smart, B. 1985. *Michel Foucault*. London: Tavistock.

Smart, C. 1976. *Women, Crime and Criminology*. London: Routledge.

Spitzer, S. 1975. Toward a Marxian Theory of Deviance. *Social Problems* 22 (5): 638–651.

Squires, P. 2013. Research Prevention and the Zombie University. *Criminal Justice Matters* 91 (1): 4–5. https://www.tandfonline.com/doi/full/10.1080/09627251.2013.778740?scroll=top&needAccess=true. Accessed 9 Nov 2022.

Statewatch. 2022. *Building the Biometric State: Police Powers and Discrimination*. London: Statewatch.

Thatcher, M. 1983. *Speech to Conservative Party Conference*. Washington: Thatcher Foundation. https://www.margaretthatcher.org/document/105454. Accessed 2 June 2022.

Therborn, G. 2022. The World and the Left. *New Left Review*. No. 137, September/October. https://newleftreview.org/issues/ii137/articles/goran-therborn-the-world-and-the-left?pc=1478. Accessed 11 November 2022.

Tombs, S. 2016a. *Social Protection After the Crisis: Regulation Without Enforcement*. Bristol: Policy Press.

Tombs, S. 2016b. What to Do with the Harmful Corporation? The Case for a non-penal Real Utopia. *Justice, Power and Resistance Foundation Issue.* 1 (September): 193–216.

Tombs, S. 2017. The UK's Corporate Killing Law: Un/Fit for Purpose? *Criminology and Criminal Justice* 18 (4): 488–507.

Tombs, S. 2020. Home as a Site of State-Corporate Violence: Grenfell Tower, Aetiologies and Aftermaths. *Howard Journal of Crime and Justice* 59 (2): 120–142.

Tombs, S., and D. Whyte. 2015. *The Corporate Criminal: Why Corporations Must Be Abolished.* Abingdon: Routledge.

Toscano, A. 2023. Review of Le Choix de la Guerre Civile. In *Une Autre Histoire Neoliberalisme*, ed. P. Dardot, H. Gueguen, C. Laval, and P. Sauvetre. *New Left Review.* No. 140/141, May/June. 181–190.

Toynbee, P., and D. Walker. 2017. *Dismembered: How the Attack on the State Harms Us All.* London: Faber and Faber.

Vegh Weis, V. 2017. *Marxism and Criminology: A History of Criminal Selectivity.* Chicago: Haymarket Books.

Waddington, P.A.J. 1985. Power, Crime and Mystification by S. Box. *British Journal of Criminology* 23 (1, January): 73–75.

Walter, N. 2023. "They've Taken Away My Freedom": The Truth About the UK State's Crackdown on Protesters. *The Guardian*, February 5. https://www.theguardian.com/world/2023/feb/05/protest-laws-state-police-crackdown-uk-activists-prison. Accessed 5 Feb 2023.

Walters, R. 2009. The State, Knowledge Production and Criminology. In *State Power Crime*, ed. R. Coleman, J. Sim, S. Tombs, and D. Whyte, 200–213. London: Sage.

Whynacht, A. 2021. *Insurgent Love: Abolition and Domestic Homicide.* Halifax: Fernwood Publishing.

Williams, P., and B. Clarke. 2018. Contesting the Single Story: Collective Punishment, Myth-Making and Racialised Criminalisation. In *Media, Crime and Racism*, ed. M. Bhatia, S. Poynting, and W. Tufail, 317–336. Basingstoke: Palgrave Macmillan.

Williams, Z. 2013. Why Does Wonga Even Exist? It's a Question No One on the Left Asks. *The Guardian*, December 17. https://www.theguardian.com/commentisfree/2013/dec/17/why-wonga-exist-no-one-on-left-asks. Accessed 19 Nov 2018.

Young, H. 1989. *One of Us: A Biography of Mrs Thatcher.* London: Macmillan.

Young, J. 1988. Note: Steven Box (1937–1987). *The British Journal of Criminology* 28 (1, Winter): 95–96.

Zinn, H. 2015. *A People's History of the United States*, 6th ed. New York: HarperCollins.

Zuboff, S. 2019. *The Age of Surveillance Capitalism*. London: Profile Books.

Part II
Corporate Crime

2

Corporate Crime, Regulation and the State

Steve Tombs

Introduction

Quite incredibly for a wide-ranging text—a key contribution to critical criminology at the time, I would say, but with significant enduring legacies, as this edited volume admirably demonstrates—well over one quarter of *Power, Crime and Mystification* consists of an extended chapter on 'Corporate Crime'. To this point, neither mainstream nor the burgeoning critical criminology in the UK had focused on this form of offending—a fact noted by Box (1983: ix–x) in his 'Preface', where he also recognised the two 'notable exceptions' (ibid.: x) to this observation, namely Frank Pearce and Kit Carson. What is more, for a 'non-specialist' text on the topic, Box's treatment of the scale and dimensions, the nature and aetiologies and the relative merits of state and societal responses to corporate crime remains one of the most sophisticated ever written.

S. Tombs (✉)
The Open University, Milton Keynes, UK
e-mail: steve.tombs@open.ac.uk

This chapter begins, first, by acknowledging some of these remarkable achievements, and specifically those around the complex aetiology and the organisational production of corporate crime. Second, I consider what I refer to as key presences in the chapter, namely Box's discussion around how to respond to corporate crime via his considerations of 'Control, regulation and justice' (ibid.: 63–79). Such considerations stand the test of time and are certainly not without merit—quite the opposite—but I argue that they betray some theoretical naivety, not least through their assumptions about the potential role of 'the state and its criminal justice system' (ibid.: 66). Third, I go on to discuss absences in the chapter—namely Box's twin failure here to address theoretically the nature of the state and what, therefore, is meant by 'regulation', and both the essence and limits of this latter term. Crucially, he fails to consider the role of regulation in *producing* corporate crime, examining regulation simply through the prism of *control*. Thus. the problematic aspects of both the presences and absences are, I claim, intimately related to each other. I argue that thinking through regulation and its relationship to both the state and the corporation allows us subsequently to focus more sharply on the limits of reforms under a system of production that is dominated by corporate capital.

The Achievements of 'Corporate Crime'

What follows is not intended to be a summary of Steven Box's chapter on Corporate Crime. Rather it is to highlight what I believe to be some of the key achievements of this chapter. This implies at least two features of what is to follow. First, there are some weaknesses in Box's work that are not discussed here—for example the poorly evidenced (and I think misleading) claim that there was at the time 'a growing awareness of corporate crime' (ibid.: 18–19). Second, it does not drill into the detail of all of the enduring contributions made to subsequent corporate crime scholarship—for example, his turning to 'anomie' to understand motivation for individuals' involvement in corporate crime, an analysis crucially strengthened by his reference to Durkheim's discussion of this concept in *Suicide* (1898/1951) rather than Merton's subsequent (1938/1957) popularisation of this in his claims regarding social structure, strain and crime.

The key, outstanding contribution made here by Box is to set out a sophisticated framework for understanding the organisational production of corporate crime, which spans the heart of the chapter (1983: 34–63). This analysis itself is predicated on a definitional contribution to knowledge. Indeed, Box's definition of corporate crime is one that myself and colleagues[1] have adopted and adapted in various writings and which has become a central reference point in the literature—cutting through what had been intense definitional controversy since Sutherland coined the term 'white-collar crime' to define this area, thus highlighting individuals, but in fact going on to research and publish around corporate crime, that is crimes of organisations.

Thus, drawing very heavily on Box's discussion of Schrager and Short's earlier (1977) definition, we have defined corporate crime as:

> illegal acts or omissions of an individual or a group of individuals in a legitimate formal organisation, in accordance with the operative goals of the organisation, which are punishable by the State under administrative, civil or criminal law, as the result of deliberate decision making or culpable negligence within a legitimate formal organization and which have serious physical or economic impact on employees, consumers, the general public, and other organisations. (Pearce and Tombs 1998, 108–109, following Box 1983; Schrager and Short 1977)

Lest they are not immediately obvious, there are several key elements of this definition, which mostly draw upon Box's seminal contribution in this chapter. I set out each of these elements here, following Box (1983: 20–34):

- 'illegal acts or omissions' marks the fact that corporate crimes—as some conventional crimes—are likely to involve failures to meet legal requirements as opposed to any organisation 'doing' anything to violate law;

---

[1] Notably Frank Pearce, David Whyte and Gary Slapper.

- 'an individual or a group of individuals' highlights that while corporate crimes are organisational crimes, they always implicate one or generally some individual men and women, even if the production of crime may escape the intention and sometimes even knowledge of any of these individuals—that is, notwithstanding the legal fiction of the corporate person, organisations per se cannot do anything;
- 'legitimate formal organisation' marks off corporate crime from organized crime, even if the two phenomena share some key characteristics;
- 'in accordance with the operative goals of the organisation' marks off those illegalities which do, or were intended to, benefit the organisation as opposed to those committed within the organisation where the organisation itself is the victim;
- 'punishable by the State' raises the issue of the under- or non-enforcement of law against organisations in general and corporations in particular, so that we are dealing here with illegalities which are clearly violations of law but are never formally processed as such—punish*able* but not punish*ed* whether through, for example, a lack of political will, lack of enforcement resources, or the social or financial resources at the disposal of potential defendants;
- 'administrative, civil or criminal law' incorporates Sutherland's earlier insight that the distinctions between different forms of illegalities—that is, whether these are classed as criminal, civil, administrative—are contingent and to a great extent reflect the ability of the powerful, including corporations, to have activities in which they may be implicated classified out with criminal law, and thus as less serious;
- 'as the result of deliberate decision making or culpable negligence within a legitimate formal organization' crucially, and following Reiman (1979), emphasises that crime is not solely a consequence of intent—the *mens rea* which in criminal law generally denotes seriousness and invokes moral and legal opprobrium - but also of various degrees of legally-defined negligence;
- 'which have serious physical or economic impact on employees, consumers, the general public, and other organisations' indicates the range of impacts that such crimes can and do have—while Box himself sets out in powerful empirical detail how, and the extent to which,

corporate crime kills and injures alongside a host of other deleterious economic and social costs. (Box 1983: 23–34)

But to be clear, Box's discussion here is much more than providing a robust *definition* of the phenomenon at issue—it is both the basis, and at the heart, of a sophisticated framework for understanding the *organisational production* of corporate crime within the context of corporate capitalism. He demonstrates to us how any full-blown theory of corporate crime would both encompass a range of elements and levels and seeks to represent the articulation of these elements and levels (Slapper and Tombs 1999; Tombs and Whyte 2007, 2015). These are set out originally and brilliantly in Box's chapter, and represented diagrammatically in Fig. 2.1, here.

A detailed discussion of the explanatory framework summarised in this Figure is neither appropriate nor necessary—Box sets this out far better than any commentator upon it could. But here I wish to draw attention to some of its key elements, before engaging in a critique of some of the less developed aspects.

Reading from the top left of the Figure, Box's starting point is with the goals of any organisation—corporation—which essentially entail maximising profit through growth, or market share and control, or both. While these are common to all forms of private corporations—and some public ones in terms of growth or market share and control—the extent to which these are realised (or not) relies upon the men and women who work within the organisation, and particularly corporate executives who take key decisions and set the values of the organisation.

In the context of the goals of the organisation, Box sets out a series of sources of 'environmental uncertainties' (1983: 37)—competitors, the state, employees, consumers and the general public—each or all of whom may impinge detrimentally upon achieving corporate goals of profit, growth and control. It is in this relationship—the contradictions between the goals of the corporation and the claims, power and interests of other stakeholders within and around the corporation—that a motive for the corporate crime is produced which can lead to a range of violations of law. In this ingenious schema, then, Box accounts for the role of individuals in the organisational production of corporate crime without a

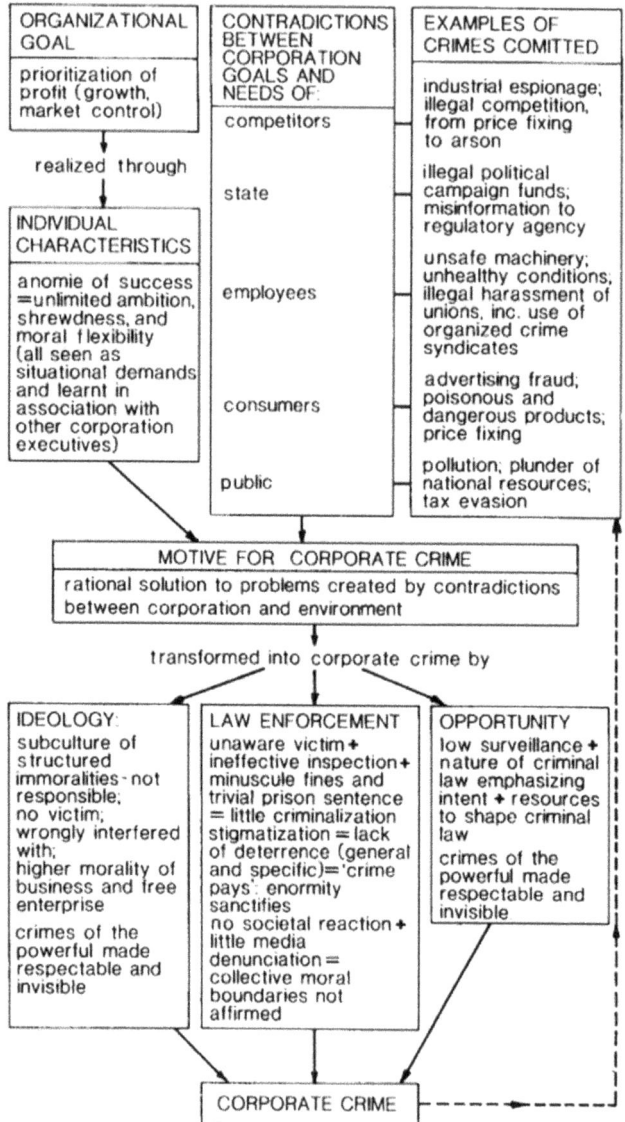

Fig. 2.1 Understanding corporate crime (Reproduced from Box 1983: 64)

reductionist interpretation of this involvement as an effect of proclivities of the men and women implicated therein.

Simultaneously, these points concerning the organisational nature of corporate crime are not made to absolve individuals of any responsibility:

> the pursuit of organisational goals is deeply implicated in the cause(s) of corporate crime. But it is important to realise that these goals are not the manifestation of personal motives cast adrift from organisational moorings, neither are they disembodied acts committed in some metaphysical sense by corporations. Rather, organisational goals are what they are perceived to be by officials who have been socialised into the organisational "way of life" and who strive in a highly co-ordinate fashion to bring about collectively their realisation. (Box 1983: 21)

This is, then, a recognition that organisations are the sites of complex relationships, invested with power and authority, between individuals and wider groups; between these groups themselves; between these groups and something called the 'organisation'; and between the organisation and its various operating environments—key actors within the latter being other organisations.

The significance of the need to understand corporate crimes in terms of their *organisational production* cannot be overstated. These are extra-individual phenomena: it has been argued that 'most corporate crimes cannot be explained by the perverse personalities of their perpetrators' (Braithwaite 1984: 2), and this claim calls into question the tendency within individualistic liberal or bourgeois cultures to locate the source of evil deeds in evil people (ibid.). Corporate crime is produced through the interaction of men and women through an organisation's structure, its culture, its unquestioned assumptions, its very *modus operandi*, the markets and geographical contexts in which it operates, as well as a range of external pressures upon it.

Crucial among these external pressures is the nature and level of law enforcement, that is, regulation, to which organisations are subject—Box spends some time here discussing the failures of general and specific deterrence through law enforcement as if these could actually 'work', and as if the deterrence of corporate crime is an unproblematic goal of regulation, on which, more below. In effect, however, what Box highlights in the bottom half of Fig. 2.1, and upon which he elaborates in his chapter, is that the relative lack of criminalisation is in part an effect of and in part cultivates the general ideological constructs around corporate crime as not *real* crime—something which many scholars since have taken as central within media, political and indeed criminological understandings of it as a phenomenon (see, for example, Davies, Francis and Wyatt 2014). Where corporate crime is under-policed, rarely prosecuted and hardly ever punished with severe sanctions, the very focus, structure, and functioning of the criminal justice system itself also contributes to the facilitation of corporate crime as an option for achieving business goals. These characteristics—a social, political, ideological and legal tolerance of what is relatively obscured albeit systematic offending creates the perfect opportunity structure within which corporate crimes can proliferate. Thus corporate crime is organisational and socially produced—to greater or lesser extents depending upon different organisational and societal contexts.

Brilliantly, then, Box reveals organisational crime production as being understood via a series of factors ranging from the individual through to the structural, each of which is complexly related to the other, and which can in brief, be identified as follows.

At the individual level, we need to take account of personality and other characteristics, not least the kinds of personalities that are valued within companies, as well as 'individual' factors that are socially constructed as relevant, such as position within the hierarchy, age, gender, and ethnicity. For example, it is relevant to enquire whether an organisation is one where being female diminishes one's social power, or in which time served adds authority.

At the level of the immediate work-group or sub-unit within the organisation, we must take account of inter-personal dynamics, the culture of the work-group (and the extent to which this coheres or clashes with the culture of the wider organisation) and its location within the overall organisation, both structurally and geographically—that is, is it relatively autonomous or highly supervised, part of one large organisational complex, an autonomous cost-centre, or geographically isolated?

There are also key sets of issues relating to the organisation itself. We need to understand its structure, its internal lines of decision-making and accountability, its geographical scope of operations and the nature, volume and complexity of internal transactions. Issues of organisational culture must also be addressed: is the organisation risk-taking or risk-averse; gendered; authoritarian; dominated by a blame culture? The products or services that are the focus of the organisation are also relevant: are these opaque or transparent, are they sold to consumers or other organisations, is their production labour or capital intensive? Further, we also need to know something of levels of profitability, how that is calculated, and how that relates to rewards systems.

Lastly, there are key questions regarding the wider economic, political and social environments within which the organisation operates. Among these are: the nature of the market structure; the size and scope of the market; the nature and level of regulation; the general nature of state-business relationships; and the dominant form of political economy, and concomitant societal values, including the nature and degree of pro- or anti-business sentiment. Again, the overall economic 'health' of the economies in which the corporation operates is of relevance.

This is only a brief summary of an extensive and complex inter-related set of factors. Following Box, there have been numerous attempts to develop this outline schema—whether consciously or not—into a full-blown integrated explanatory framework of corporate crime production. This much was subsequently urged by some commentators on corporate crime (Coleman 1987; Vaughan 1996; Punch 2000). And if theoretical development here remains at an early stage, there are now a number of book-length studies that attempt to use some of this range of factors set out so schematically by Box. These include studies of safety crimes generally (Tombs and Whyte 2007) and specifically in the offshore oil industry (Woolfson et al. 1996); corporate crime in the asbestos (Tweedale 2000), chemicals (Pearce and Tombs 1998) and pharmaceutical industries (Braithwaite 1984); a national-case study in the control of 'economic' crime (Alvesalo 2003); the production of corporate manslaughter (Slapper 2000); and varieties of symbiotic corporate and state illegalities associated with the fateful launch of the Challenger space shuttle (Vaughan 1996); urbanisation in parts of the Global South (Lasslett 2018); and even the very survival/death of the planet (Whyte 2020).

Regulation: Presences and Absences?

While contributing to our understanding of the aetiology of corporate crime, Box's chapter also attempts to consider the ways in which this might best be controlled and regulated. His discussion here begins with the recognition that such crimes are endemic within capitalism, so that the answer to 'what is to be done' is, tersely:

> **** all. According to a more polite version of this argument, these crimes are embedded and endemic within the capitalist system. The prioritisation of profit under conditions of environmental uncertainties inevitably leads to persistent and chronic levels of corporation crime. No piecemeal liberal reform will make one iota of difference. Only when the means of production and distribution are socialised will the incidence of corporate crime diminish. (Box 1983: 63, asterisks in original)

This 'may or may not be true' states Box, as the preface to a discussion of various such reforms that might better mitigate or respond to corporate crimes—based on awareness-raising for key stakeholders and victims alongside shaming 'the state and legal institutions' into action (ibid.: 67). This reveals a tension in his view of what regulation can achieve and indeed more generally of the extent to which demystification can be achieved under capitalism—which in turn reveals a failure to attend to sufficiently, theoretically, the source of regulation, namely the state. On the latter, more below, but on what is *in* rather than missing from Box's discussion here is that, curiously, his subsequent consideration of better 'justice' for corporate crime is based entirely around sanctions, not regulation. Here it should be emphasised that his discussion around 'Enterprising ideas for sanctioning deviant enterprises' is imaginative, thoughtful and, with rare notable exceptions (see, for example, Braithwaite and Geis 1982; Coffee 1977), entirely original; moreover, the issues he raises and grapples with therein still pose challenges for criminologists of corporate punishment four decades later (Tombs 2016b). These points made, a weakness of the discussion about punishment is that it is almost entirely divorced from his earlier discussion of how the level of regulation adds to the opportunity structure for corporate crime (Box 1983: 58–63) and completely devoid of any insights from the then emerging descriptive, normative and conceptual literatures on regulation. In short, regulation is present here, but only partially and thus problematically: while Box describes in fragments how some forms of regulation proceed—notably in its inability to produce any forms of deterrence—he fails to address conceptually nor to think theoretically about regulation, its essence, what it can and is intended to 'achieve'. It is to these questions—and therefore a sympathetic critique of Box's chapter—that this chapter now turns.

Some Presences …

In the forty years since Box's contribution, there has emerged a substantial body of work, within criminology and indeed across socio-legal studies, political science and organisational and management studies, which has focused on regulation. To preface the argument here, this is of interest not simply because it allows us to reflect upon Box's claims about 'Control, regulation, and justice' (ibid.: 63), but because if regulation is the manifest empirical link between apparently distinct and separate state and corporate sectors, then theorising regulation requires an understanding of the state–corporate relationship and, indeed, of the nature of the state itself—each of which is absent from Box's chapter here.

While academic work on regulation in the forty years since *Power, Crime and Mystification* is enormous and, in many ways, diverse, it can, for some, be categorised into three dominant theoretical approaches (Whyte 2004): a 'compliance' school, the neo-liberal perspective, and capture theories. In each of these quite different bodies of literature, the state either does not appear at all or is treated as a 'black box', a reference point rarely described, analysed or theorised—and, I would suggest, a feature in many respects shared with Box's contribution on corporate crime and, indeed, more generally across *Power, Crime and Mystification* (see Fletcher and McGowan, this volume) None of this work places a critical analysis of 'the state' at its core, albeit that each is based upon an implicit theory of state institutions and regulatory capacities and tendencies.

The compliance perspective is derived from the 'fact' that compliance-oriented enforcement techniques (enforcement styles that seek to bargain with, and persuade, corporations to comply with law) dominate in most advanced economies. It is the acceptance of this fact that leads much of the research on regulation towards a normative endorsement of compliance-oriented approaches or versions of it (see Pearce and Tombs 1998: 223–246), a normative position that is usually based upon a recognition and acceptance of the constraints upon state resources required to regulate corporations more punitively; a recognition of the power of business vis-à-vis regulators; and thus a concern not to provoke counter-productive tendencies through punitive enforcement.

Second, neo-liberal theorists, most closely associated with Friedman's Chicago School of Economics, argue that, in general, states have an interventionist tendency that obstructs efficient economic activity. A key element of the neo-liberal ideology that took hold of political systems in the late 1970s and 1980s was the institutionalisation of 'deregulation' as a centrepiece of economic policy, perhaps best summed up by the UK Conservative government's anti 'red-tape' and 'burdens on business' campaigns that were then enthusiastically adapted by the subsequent Blair and Brown governments (Tombs 2016a). Here, then, the somewhat misleading mantra is that a smaller state and a freer economy is always the preferred regulatory outcome.

Third, there are theories which characterise state regulatory agencies as vulnerable to 'capture' by big business. Capture is achieved by a mixture of intense corporate lobbying, the consolidation of elite interests in public and private sectors, and a 'revolving door' of personnel between regulator and regulated. The implication of capture theory is therefore that regulation is counter-productive, since it has an inherent tendency to institutionalise corporate influence. Originally developed by Bernstein (1955), capture theory was somewhat revived at the turn of the century, often adopted by left analysis and by the critics of globalisation (Monbiot 2000) in order to demonstrate the increasing and overwhelming power of capital in the global market.

These three bodies of literature take very different positions on the question of the extent to which corporate crime is a significant crime problem and, therefore, of the necessities for and tasks of regulation. But aside from this question of the need for regulation, each of these different perspectives reaches a very similar conclusion as to the likelihood of the efficacy of regulation—that is, albeit by very different paths, each reaches the conclusion that corporate crime evades effective control as crime. In short, each ends up largely agreeing with Box as to what can be done—that is, '**** all' (Box 1983: 63).

This is not the only common consideration that extends across these very different views of regulation. A further, common view across these three apparently very different perspectives is that regulation involves a process of an autonomous (state) agency intervening against an autonomous (capitalist) organisation. For compliance theorists, regulatory activities aim to forge consensus across a plurality of competing claims on the part of potentially—but not fundamentally—antagonistic parties ('business', 'workers', 'consumers', other 'interests'), all of whom, ultimately, are viewed as having a mutual interest in an effective business sector. For neo-liberals, the optimal role of the state is to withdraw from economic and social life and to perform any arbitration role as a last resort when market mechanisms have manifestly failed. For capture theorists, the state is there to be seized and dominated by powerful, organised, *external* interests and their ways of understanding the world.

Despite what are, on the surface, significant differences between compliance, neo-liberal and capture theories of the state and regulation, a common, key *presence* within each of these is a view of the relationship between the state and corporations or 'business' as one of *opposition* and *externality*—that is, the state stands as an institution or ensemble of institutions which is ontologically separate and distinct from economy and civil society. This is, too, precisely the view expressed by Box in his discussion of the extent to which state control can generate justice in respect of corporate crime. It is highly a-theoretical, a view devoid of any extended consideration of state—corporate relationships and, indeed and relatedly, of the state per se. The major distortion that this leads to is that regulatory agencies are mostly viewed in one-dimensional terms, from a limited understanding of the state that Gramsci termed the 'state as policeman' (Coleman et al. 2009). Gramsci used the term to suggest that we could only ever have a selective, uni-dimensional view of the state if we limited our understanding to the negative, repressive, law-centred role of the state. If the state is always the negative enforcer, then the relationship between state institutions and corporations is always going to be antagonistic—one facing the other in a battle of opposing wills, one seeking to secure compliance with the law, the other seeking to avoid this, and so on.

The relation of externality—the positioning of the state in direct opposition to capital—that we find in the three dominant perspectives in the regulation literature and also in Box's work here oversimplifies the role that the state plays in mediating and re-constituting class conflict. And there is a significant irony here in the context of a discussion of Box's text. For the very idea of externality reinforces the mystificatory social and legal order upon which Box (and others, not least Reiman 1979; Pearce 1976) is centrally focused because it presents a way of thinking about states as acting in the public interest. Thus, if the relationship between the state and capital is one of externality, *and* the regulatory agency expresses the basic dynamic of the 'state as policeman', then state and capital can be portrayed in antagonistic terms. This logic allows the regulatory relationship to be represented as a heroic effort on the part of the state to control the excesses of capital. Of course, this idea is not mere ideology, since control efforts are part of this relationship, so there often *is* a struggle between state and capital; indeed, this is why we might expect at particular times to see tough regulatory responses against the interests of individual businesses. An element of this may also be symbolic—albeit not to be read as *merely* symbolic. Thus, at times, the harmful practices generated by some business or businesses may be so egregious that there needs to be a formal, state recognition of this. Such recognition, for example by way of some form of inquiry, a new law, or even a new regulatory body if the scale of harm and public and political outrage that follows is significant enough (see below), need not be, and generally is not, 'effective' in the terms it has been proposed—but the very fact of there *being* some formal recognition helps to restore legitimacy to what is an unchanged or slightly reformed area of business practice.

However, while we can see struggle, contradictions, contingencies and so on, ultimately the role of the capitalist state is to reproduce unequal relations of power inherent within capitalism, a key issue to which we return, below. Box simultaneously recognises and ignores this key aspect of power and mystification in relation to corporate crime. That is, while he does not advance a theory of regulation nor any theory of the state—each is notable for its absence—he still in fact offers key fragments to understanding both and their inter-relationship.

... and Absences

A body of research produced by critical and neo-Marxist scholars emphasises the importance of *conflict* in the formation and implementation of regulatory regimes (Bernat and Whyte 2017; Bittle and Hebert 2019; Tombs and Whyte 2015; Whyte 2014). This literature notes that regulatory controls have often been established only after long and bitter struggles by organised groups of workers and other social movements (Kramer 1989; Snider 1991). At the same time, historically, businesses and their representatives have fought bitterly in opposition to regulation when it is not in their clear interest. They obfuscate, lie, cheat and make threats to disinvest, often fighting fierce public relations campaigns and behind-the-scenes political manoeuvres to avoid or to influence regulatory reform (Palast 2003). Critical scholars and neo-Marxist commentators therefore argue that conflicts between pro- and anti-regulatory forces from outside the state are crucial to understanding the emergence or otherwise of regulation, and its subsequent level of enforcement (for example, Carson 1979; Pearce and Tombs 1998)—even if such conflicts around the definition and enforcement of the law are not always visible (Grigg-Spall and Ireland 1992).

On this view, regulatory agencies emerge as a compromise borne out of social conflict, so that the nature of the regulatory body and its formal mission reflect the balances of forces between *and within* states, capital and populations (Snider 1991)—an observation with which Box seems to concur (Box 1983: 60–63). Regulatory agencies, then, are not simply 'policemen'—that is, their relation to capital is not merely one of opposition and externality, but rather they play a much more general role in reproducing the social conditions necessary to sustain a capitalist social order. In other words, they do not only have a command-and-control function—this function is part of a much broader role in dissipating conflict, providing an outlet for social conflict and so on. The visible aspects of regulatory agencies (how they persuade corporations to comply with the law, enforcement and prosecution and so on) is therefore merely part of their general function in maintaining a stable social order.

Thus regulatory agencies can be said to be formed by states in order to absorb and dissipate struggles between conflicting social groups and do this by claiming to represent the interests of pro-regulatory groups alongside, and at the same time as protecting, the interests of other stake-holding groups, and thus some wider general or national interest. This leads Mahon to observe that regulatory agencies are not neutral or balanced in the way that they deal with corporate crime; rather they are 'unequal structures of representation' (Mahon 1979: 154). According to this claim, regulatory bodies subordinate the interests of non-hegemonic groups to the interests of business, but since their purpose is a stabilising one for capitalist social orders, they may at specific times subordinate the immediate interests of particular businesses to the long-term interests of capital as a whole. This latter observation was beautifully demonstrated by Marx in *Capital Volume 1* as he accounted in empirical and theoretical detail for the emergence of the early Factory Acts in England (Tombs 2021).

This discussion of regulatory agencies demonstrates clearly how corporations exist with some degree of autonomy from states, but also that this autonomy can never be complete, since the state—through regulation—plays a crucial role in reproducing the social conditions necessary for them to survive and thrive. This analysis therefore warns us against adopting an over-simplified idea, inherent within neo-liberal and pluralist literatures, of the 'roll back' of the state (see Coleman et al. 2009). This obscures the fact that the power of capital depends not merely or even largely upon the rolling *back* of the state, or the diminution of state power thereby implied, but also on the simultaneous roll-*out* of the state to secure successful mediation and dissipation of particularly contentious issues, or issues that threaten a stable social order. In this sense we can see very clearly how states intervene in ways that are essential to the long-term interests of capital. Here, the roll-out and roll-back of the state are complementary rather than antagonistic characteristics and functions of any existing state form.

In a much more profound sense, states are essential to the survival of profit-making corporations within capitalist social orders. Indeed, it is not an exaggeration to say that corporations are given life by states: corporations are institutions that are created for the mobilisation, utilisation and protection of capital within recent socio-historical state formations. As such, they are wholly artificial entities whose very existence is provided for, and maintained, through the state via legal institutions and instruments, which in turn are based upon material and ideological supports. They can only invest, extract surplus value, and make profits because of the existence of a complex set of rules that formally permit then structure their activities. Institutions of government and law establish the basis of their incorporation as organisations with particular juridical and administrative characteristics. Corporations are thus given form by the rules that govern labour and commodity markets, and by regulatory laws that establish the social and economic obligations of corporations, shareholders and so on. In capitalist societies, then, we cannot view the state as standing in binary opposition to markets *or* to corporations. The way that those juridical/administrative conditions position the corporation in relation to the state provides further evidence to show how capital's autonomy from the state can never be complete but is always in a relationship of *relative autonomy*.[2] Corporations always exist simultaneously 'inside' and 'outside' of state rules

---

[2] This point can be understood as the mirror image of the Miliband/Poulantzas debate (Hay 2006) about the degree to which we can say that the state (superstructures) possess autonomy from the economic base (structure).

and institutions. On this view, state–corporate relationships are best understood as *symbiotic* (Tombs 2012).

Thus the markets within which corporations act are themselves created and maintained by state activity—not least the re-emerged, so-called 'free' market. This observation reveals state complicity in the production of corporate crime: for *just as states create and sustain markets, so too can and do they create and sustain criminogenic markets, that is, markets that are conducive to, or facilitate, the production of harms and crimes.* Indeed, when it comes to the production of corporate crime, Kramer and Michalowski (2006) show very clearly how corporate crime is often either *initiated* or *facilitated* by states. This understanding of the relationship between states and corporations suggests the need to reject a notion of the state as a passive (external) bystander to the production of corporate crime; rather, it locates the relationship between states and corporations as complexly imbricated and at times consciously collusive. Corporate crime is thus a product of this complex relationship between states and corporations within which regulation is a key process—and in this sense, regulation produces rather than simply 'controls' corporate crime.

Conclusion

Throughout Box's chapter, his analysis of corporate crime contains a tension—a tension, indeed, present throughout the book as a whole. As I have argued, he analyses corporate crime production with significant original insight, and in this context he therefore at times recognises, or at least states explicitly, that only the socialisation of production or the transcendence of capitalism can really eradicate it, seeing corporate crime as inevitable within and endemic to capitalism. But at the same time, both in the chapter and in the book's concluding chapter, 'Crime, power and justice', he makes an appeal to a 'truly democratic society' (1983: 223)—not, he insists, a utopian demand (ibid.)—which may allow for the greater control of corporate crime, albeit he seems slightly unconvinced by this. Forty years after Box made this appeal, decades of 'regressive modernisation' (Hall 1988: 2) have edged the UK and other societies further from any democratic ideal, so that it is even more important, I would argue, to have such demands placed on social and political agendas. But Box implicitly engages in an attempt to determine potentially effective reforms that inevitably fail to do that which they are intended—that is, significantly mitigate corporate crime. This ambiguity, tension or contradiction is hardly unique to him— see, for example, Alvesalo and Tombs (2002), Tombs (2016b)—but perhaps better that this tension is explicitly recognised and explored (Tombs and Whyte 2015) rather than left somewhat unsaid. This leaving unsaid is, in my view, based upon a failure to theorise what regulation *is*—which in turn requires a treatment of 'the state' which is absent from this book.

Regulation, then, as Box glimpses but ultimately obscures, is about much more than simply 'controlling' corporate harms. Regulation in capitalist societies is as much about social order maintenance as it is about control efforts per se. Regulation maintains the steady rate and function of the machinery of industry and commerce. And for this reason, regulation per se can never be a solution to corporate harm or crime.

The consequence of looking at regulation from this perspective is that we have to accept that the regulation of corporate activity by the state may seek to ameliorate the harms of corporations, but that this is by no means its primary purpose. And it is by pursuing its *primary* purpose, that is, to maintain the current state of affairs, that regulation produces and reproduces corporate harm and, in a variety of ways, prevents such harms from being identified, processed *or formally recognised as crimes*, rendering such crimes invisible. I would argue that reading Box's brilliant text in the context of this observation produces another level of understanding of the relationships between power, corporate crime and mystification in a capitalist social order.

In this respect, corporate crime is nothing more or less than a power relationship that is guaranteed, under-written and indeed often partly also enjoined by states. Thus the intensification and concentration of corporate power—recognised by Box, not least with the emerging to dominance of transnational corporations (Box 1983: 78)—is a manifestation of the infrastructural power of states; and a major aspect of this form of state–corporate power-mongering is the production of corporate crime. As Box's explanatory framework reveals—albeit inadequately pursued through his subsequent discussion of regulation and control—through a variety of political, legal and ideological processes, processes always ongoing, requiring a great deal of state work, corporations have been and are more or less empowered *within states* in ways that allow them to cause large scale social harms with relative impunity. It is this empowerment by states that remains the key source of corporate power. It is for this reason that capitalist states can never provide a lasting solution to corporate power, crime and harm, but will always in the long term enable corporate profit-seeking to prevail over human needs and social protection. Box's seminal contribution to understanding corporate crime both recognised yet simultaneously mystified this basic observation. This is not to deny of course that the struggle for democratic accountability raised by Box—in the spirit of Marx (1871/1977: 285–297), for example, on the Paris Commune—is insignificant. Even as democratic accountability appears beyond reach under capitalism, the struggle for some element of this is now more rather than less significant in societies where the most liberal norms of political accountability have been systematically dismantled since the publication of *Power, Crime and Mystification*.

Acknowledgements Many of the ideas expressed here have been developed over many years through a long, enjoyable collaboration with David Whyte, while the focus on Box specifically as well as other issues raised here have benefited from extended conversations with Joe Sim over more years than I care to remember. My thanks also go to the editors of this volume, David Scott and Joe Sim, for their enduring collegiality and in particular for their encouragement of and patience with my efforts here.

References

Alvesalo, A. 2003. *The Dynamics of Economic Crime Control.* Espoo, Finland: Poliisiammattikorkeakoulun tutkimuksia.

Alvesalo, A., and S. Tombs. 2002. Working for Criminalisation of Economic Offending: Contradictions for Critical Criminology? *Critical Criminology* 11 (1): 21–40.

Bernat, I., and D. Whyte. 2017. State-Corporate Crime and the Process of Capital Accumulation: Mapping a Global Regime of Permission from Galicia to Morecambe Bay. *Critical Criminology* 25 (1): 71–86.

Bernstein, B.H. 1955. *Regulating Business by Independent Commission*. Princeton, NJ: Princeton University Press.

Bittle, S., and J. Hebert. 2019. Controlling Corporate Crimes in Times of De-regulation and Re-regulation. In *The Handbook of White-Collar Crime*, ed. M. Rorie, 484–501. New York: Wiley.

Box, S. 1983. *Power, Crime and Mystification*. London: Tavistock.

Braithwaite, J. 1984. *Corporate Crime in the Pharmaceutical Industry*. London: Routledge and Kegan Paul.

Braithwaite, J., and G. Geis. 1982. On Theory and Action for Corporate Crime Control. *Crime and Delinquency* 28 (2): 292–314.

Carson, W. 1979. The Conventionalisation of Early Factory Crime. *International Journal of the Sociology of Law* 7 (1): 37–60.

Coffee, J.C. 1977. Beyond the Shut-Eyed Sentry: Toward a Theoretical View of Corporate Misconduct and an Effective Legal Response. *Virginia Law Review* 63 (November): 1099–1278.

Coleman, J.W. 1987. Toward an Integrated Theory of White-Collar Crime. *American Journal of Sociology* 93 (2): 406–493.

Coleman, R., J. Sim, S. Tombs, and D. Whyte. 2009. Introduction: State, Power, Crime. In *State, Power, Crime*, ed. R. Coleman, J. Sim, S. Tombs, and D. Whyte, 1–19. London: Sage.

Davies, P., P. Francis, and T. Wyatt, eds. 2014. *Invisible Crimes and Social Harms*. London: Palgrave Macmillan.

Durkheim, E. 1898/1951. *Suicide*. New York: Free Press.

Grigg-Spall, I., and P. Ireland, eds. 1992. *The Critical Lawyers' Handbook*. London: Pluto.

Hall, S. 1988. *The Hard Road to Renewal: Thatcherism and the Crisis of the Left*. London: Verso.

Hay, C. 2006. (What's Marxist about) Marxist State Theory? In *The State: Theories and Issues*, ed. C. Hay, M. Lister, and D. Marsh, 59–78. Basingstoke: Palgrave Macmillan.

Kramer, R.C. 1989. Criminologists and the Social Movement Against Corporate Crime. *Social Justice* 16 (2): 145–164.

Kramer, R.C., and R.J. Michalowski. 2006. The Original Formulation. In *State-Corporate crime*, ed. R.J. Michalowski and R.C. Kramer, 18–26. New Jersey: Rutgers University Press.

Lasslett, K. 2018. *Uncovering the Crimes of Urbanisation: Researching Corruption, Violence and Urban Conflict*. London: Routledge.

Mahon, R. 1979. Regulatory Agencies: Captive Agents or Hegemonic Apparatuses? *Studies in Political Economy* 1 (1): 154–168.

Marx, K. 1871/1977. The Civil War in France. *Marx-Engels Selected Works in One Volume*, 248–309. London: Lawrence and Wishart.

Merton, R. 1938. Social Structure and Anomie. *American Sociological Review* 3 (5): 672–682.

Monbiot, G. 2000. *Captive State: The Corporate Takeover of Britain*. London: MacMillan.

Palast, G. 2003. *The Best Democracy Money Can Buy*. London: Robinson.

Pearce, F. 1976. *Crimes of the Powerful. Marxism, Crime and Deviance*. London: Pluto.

Pearce, F., and S. Tombs. 1998. *Toxic Capitalism: Corporate Crime and the Chemical Industry*. Aldershot: Ashgate.

Punch, M. 2000. Suite Violence: Why Managers Murder and Corporations Kill. *Crime, Law and Social Change* 33: 243–280.

Reiman, J.H. 1979. *The Rich Get Richer and the Poor Get Prison. Ideology, Class, and Criminal Justice*. New York: Wiley.

Schrager, L.S., and J.F. Short. 1977. Towards a Sociology of Organisational Crime. *Social Problems* 25 (4): 407–419.

Slapper, G. 2000. *Blood in the Bank. Social and Legal Aspects of Death at Work*. Aldershot: Ashgate.

Slapper, G., and S. Tombs. 1999. *Corporate Crime*. London: Addison Wesley Longman.

Snider, L. 1991. The Regulatory Dance: Understanding Reform Processes in Corporate Crime. *International Journal of the Sociology of Law* 19 (2): 209–236.

Tombs, S. 2021. Social Justice and the Limits of Regulation: The Enduring Insights of Marx's Capital. In *Leading Works in Law and Social Justice*, ed. F. Gordon and D. Newman, 141–161. London: Routledge.

Tombs, S. 2016a. *Social Protection After the Crisis: Regulation Without Enforcement*. Bristol: Policy Press.

Tombs, S. 2016b. What to Do with the Harmful Corporation? *Justice, Power and Resistance* 1 (1): 193–216.

Tombs, S. 2012. State-Corporate Symbiosis in the Production of Crime and Harm. *State Crime* 1 (2, October): 170–195.

Tombs, S., and D. Whyte. 2015. *The Corporate Criminal. Why Corporations Must Be Abolished*. London: Routledge.

Tombs, S., and Whyte, D. 2007. *Safety Crimes*. Cullompton: Willan.

Tweedale, G. 2000. *Magic Mineral to Killer Dust. Turner and Newall and the Asbestos Hazard*. Oxford: Oxford University Press.

Vaughan, D. 1996. *The Challenger Launch Decision. Risky Technology, Culture, and Deviance at NASA*. Chicago: Chicago University Press.

Whyte, D. 2004. Regulation and Corporate Crime. In *Student Handbook of Criminal Justice*, ed. J. Muncie and D. Wilson, 134–148. London: Cavendish.

Whyte, D. 2014. Regimes of Permission and State-Corporate Crime. *State Crime* 3 (2): 237–246.

Whyte, D. 2020. *Ecocide. Kill the Corporation Before It Kills Us*. Manchester: Manchester University Press.

Woolfson, C., J. Foster, and M. Beck. 1996. *Paying for the Piper? Capital and Labour in the Offshore Oil Industry*. Aldershot: Mansell.

3

From Corporate Corruption to Rentiership: Extending Box's Power, Crime and Mystification

Steven Bittle and Jon Frauley

Introduction

Whether we are consumers or citizens, we stand more chance of being robbed by persons who roam corporate suites than we do by those who roam public streets. Furthermore, in the aggregate we stand to be robbed of far more by these fine gentlemen acting in the good name of their corporation [or state] than by the common rogues apparently acting from some morally worthless motive. (Box 1983: 31)

The 'suite' crimes of 'fine gentlemen' referred to by Steven Box, above, diverge markedly from the stereotypical 'street crimes' that are the focus of criminal justice administration and most criminologists.

S. Bittle (✉) · J. Frauley
University of Ottawa, Ottawa, ON, Canada
e-mail: steven.bittle@uottawa.ca

J. Frauley
e-mail: jonathan.frauley@uottawa.ca

The astoundingly widespread invisibility of and ignorance about 'crimes of the powerful' is largely due to a political-legal definition of 'crime' that operates as a mystifier: the concept distorts and misdirects public attention away from economically and politically powerful actors who routinely and with callous indifference engage in wrongdoing, producing in Box's (1983: 30–31) view, 'avoidable' harms.

Box makes clear that crime is first and foremost a concept and as such must be constructed and then reproduced. This process, Box notes, is monopolised by a political-legal machinery populated by the privileged and wealthy. Additionally, as with any concept attempting to capture something about social life, exclusions are necessary. These exclusions are of central interest to Box because their practical manifestations in law making, enforcement, and adjudication display a bias against the poor and disenfranchised. As Box (1983: 8–9) argues, '[I]n the criminal law, definitions of murder, rape, robbery, assault, theft, and other serious crimes are so constructed as to exclude many similar, and in important respects, identical acts, and these are just the acts likely to be committed more frequently by powerful individuals'. These harmful acts of privilege are not simply designed out of the criminal law, they are excluded from the very conception of what is and whom might be credibly viewed as criminal.

In this chapter we extend and refine some of Box's seminal ideas through an analysis of one particularly prolific activity engaged in by powerful actors: corruption. In so doing, we follow Box's notion of power crime and define corruption as *an act of avoidable harm to persons and/or democratic processes and institutions, produced by indifferent politically or economically powerful actors and rooted in and supported by collective ignorance.* Our goal is to make sense of corruption as an outcome of the criminogenic structure of political and economic power within capitalism. In culturally dominant terms, we are encouraged to view corruption in a very narrow and stereotypical way, as victimless acts taking the form of bribes paid to public officials, political interference, collusion between corporate actors and public officials, or as abuses of public office for private gain. Much like the political-legal conception of crime, the stereotypical notion of corruption is mystifying as it distorts our understanding not only of what corruption is but of who are its victims. Like other crimes of the powerful, corruption remains 'undiscussed, unrecognized and uncontrolled' (ibid.: 221).

We begin the chapter by addressing what we take as Box's most prominent explanatory concepts: mystification, collective ignorance, and indifference. Following this, we extend and update Box's ideas by noting an affinity with Pierre Bourdieu's theory of social action. Because Box's concerns are less theoretical and more empirical, he does not fully elaborate on his most important concepts or how they are related to one another. We seek to explicate, extend, and connect these to outline what amounts to Box's implicit theory of action. In using Bourdieu's ideas to more fully elaborate Box's work, we provide a theoretical grounding for understanding and explaining corruption as a crime of the powerful and, importantly, avoid naïve and untenable explanations based on self-interest and rational choice theory. We then use insights from Box and Bourdieu to critique the corruption literature, demonstrating how mainstream definitions of corruption are mystifying of both the harms caused by corruption and the underlying social, political, and economic forces that generate them. Finally, we build from this analytical framing to argue that rentierism—the *raison d'être* of contemporary capitalism wherein the overriding goal is to control and commercialise assets to help gain a distinct market advantage 'under conditions of limited or no competition' (Christophers 2020: xxiv)—is a particular type of power crime neglected by the corruption literature. We conclude that as rentierism produces avoidable harm to persons and democratic processes—harm produced by indifferent politically and economically powerful actors supported by collective ignorance—it should be treated as a type of corruption.

Mystic Reality and the Failure of Corporate Corruption Literature

Box's work was part of a small body of critical literature at the time that attended to the ideological nature of crime, cogently arguing that crime was not a product of powerlessness but of power. In fact, for

Box, the concentration of wealth and power helped explain why corporations routinely committed crimes with impunity (1983). Power, from his perspective, was both 'dangerous' and 'criminogenic' (1983: 202), therein challenging much criminological thinking that took political-legal definitions of crime at face value and, in the process, ignored crimes of the powerful—a situation we argue still stands today.

A selective and narrow political-legal conception of crime, the amplification of street crime by mass media and popular culture, and the ignoring of power crime by the majority of criminology combine to produce what we will call a 'mystic reality'.[1] Box attempted to capture this through his use of the term mystification. This essentially refers to the production and reproduction of distorted pictures of social reality that obfuscate or render opaque the activities that produce widespread avoidable harms engaged in by those with economic and political power. As Box (1983: 14) argues, 'for too long too many people have been socialized to see crime and criminals through the eyes of the state. There is nothing left, as [David] Matza points out, but mystification' We want to explore this mystification process in more detail and tie it to two other of Box's important concepts: collective ignorance and indifference.

Ideological constructs that become doxic tend to be understood less as dominant ideas and more as facts. According to Box (1983: 16), one very important but misunderstood outcome of ideological distortion is 'collective ignorance' about the existence and extent of the damage caused by what many simply regard as routine business practices or political activities. Here Box approaches a mass society thesis with respect to criminal justice. There is a mystified reality that most, including those who should know better, are ignorant about. This ignorance facilitates the complicity of criminologists and others in the reproduction of an Illusory or mystic reality wherein the criminogenic structure of economic and political power within capitalist democracies is rendered invisible.

A key feature of Box's argument is that there is a mass of potential and actual victims of avoidable harms produced through the indifference of those who wield high levels of political and economic power, and

---

[1] This is inspired by Harold Lasswell's (1941) account of 'mystic democracy'. This mystic reality is framed by 'doxic' assumptions that comprise naturalised and universalised precepts that are the outcome of struggle and competition between actors.

that these potential and actual victims are ignorant of their victimisation (ibid.: 13). What is more, collective ignorance as a structural situation impacts not only victims of avoidable harms but also perpetrators. 'Thus corporate officials are both mystified as to their own crime, and misdirected as to the distribution of crime in general. Both mystification and misdirection preserve the *appearance* of corporate respectability and help keep invisible, to themselves and others, the underlying ugly reality of corporate crime'(ibid.: 57, emphasis added). Here collective ignorance is linked to the indifference displayed by powerful actors.[2] According to Box (1983: 21), the goals of organisations such as corporations induce ignorantly indifferent action that can lead to avoidable harms.

Indifference, then, is not merely a characteristic of the rational choices of individuals but rather is systemic in that it reflects an organisational culture and, in particular, the collective ignorance that is embedded within this culture. Personal motives become aligned with the organisational field as the organisation's goals are enacted through the employee (through what Bourdieu, below, terms one's habitus). Box defines corporate crime in a way that recognises the range of harms caused by corporate offending, acknowledges that these offences often lack intention as conventionally defined, and stresses that the 'pursuit of organizational goals is deeply implicated in the cause(s) of corporate crime' (ibid.: 20–21).

It is important to realise, Box (1983: 21—emphasis original) argues:

> … that these goals are not the manifestation of *personal* motives cast adrift from organizational moorings, neither are they disembodied acts committed in some metaphysical sense by corporations. Rather, organizational goals are what they are perceived to be by officials who have been socialized into the organizational "way of life" and who strive in a highly co-ordinate fashion to bring about collectively their realisation. … These confront new employees at all bureaucratic levels as "solid facts" to

---

[2] More recent work raises similar points regarding the social production of ignorance and indifference. Barton and Davis (2018) argue the powerful actively work to obscure, deny, and avoid accountability for their many harms and crimes, while McGoey (2014) suggests ignorance is a resource used by the powerful to obscure and conceal truths.

be learnt and practised rather than queried and altered. … they feel the corporation acting through them as mere passive intermediaries.

This is a particularly important passage for it is where Box outlines why he thinks intention alone is an insufficient condition to recognise criminality. More than this, Box's account of crimes of the powerful relies on an unarticulated theory of action displayed here, or what can be viewed as the productive aspects of mystification—that it not only obscures but produces and makes possible other forms of oppression and abuses of power. Overall, then, embedded in Box's text is a theory of action which we argue can be explicated and further developed through Bourdieu's concepts of field, habitus, and doxa.

What Bourdieu terms the 'habitus' animates the actions of the subject. The habitus is a 'structuring structure' (Bourdieu 1994: 13), the cognitive structure of social actors that is formed within structured organisational fields of knowledge and practice. 'Fields' are more or less hierarchically organised spaces structured by the distribution of actors (according to the amount and type of know-how they possess) as well as by the distribution of the various forms of economic, social, or cultural/informational capital that actors will struggle over and compete for in order to gain dominance within a field (1986, 1987, 1994, 1998). In part, habitus refers to embodied capital, acquired practical know-how, frames of reference, and the 'right' family-social connections. What are desirable forms of educational capital or practical know-how, for example, will be field specific and will carry a higher exchange rate for economic capital within the labour market than other forms (see Frauley 2012). As habitus is instilled within the context of a structured and organised field of struggle it becomes aligned with the demands and needs of that field. Thus, actors' personal motives are never merely personal or subjective.

For Bourdieu, habitus does not refer to the subjective quality of social subjects. He is clear that habitus in part refers to the doxic assumptions that transcend any one field of practice. Different organisational fields, Bourdieu (1973: 66) argues, will produce different '…classes of habitus … by instilling different definitions of what is impossible, possible, probable and certain…'.

The political-legal sphere and commercial-economic are highly co-ordinated, dynamic, and stratified spaces of action or fields in which actors compete and struggle for dominance over various forms of capital. If one is to be successful, one must *intuitively* understand not only the goal to be advanced but how best to advance this goal or meet an organisational objective. Thus, the organisation's objectives and interests become that of the organisational subject as they are aligned one to the other for practical purposes. In this way one tacitly agrees to and internalises the objectives and intuitive understanding of a field of practice. In this way certain agreed upon precepts and principles escape cognition and scrutiny.

One basic need of any field is for it to be reproduced. This in turn requires reproduction of the doxic or unthought rationalities and precepts that have been naturalised within the field as foundational and which are consequently not subjected to scrutiny, taken to be facts and immutable. Habitus is central to this reproductive process, and it is through this that the process of misrecognition operates. Doxa is distinguished by Bourdieu (1977: 164) from the 'orthodox or heterodox belief [which imply] awareness and recognition of the possibility of different or antagonistic beliefs'. Doxa is referred to elsewhere as a 'feel for the game', an embodied practical knowledge that enables one to compete successfully for dominance within one's field. Importantly, as Bourdieu explains, this doxic relation to the social world is enacted through the subject's recognition of legitimacy (ibid.: 168) as doxa is that which is naturalised, existing below and beyond the level of opinion, argument, or debate. Although the habitus enables us to formulate (ideological) orthodox or heterodox points of view or opinion, and this can lead to transformative action, it also equips us with a practical and doxic understanding that exists below the level of critical scrutiny and which is reproduced through these struggles (ibid.: 164). The domain of doxa is 'beyond question and to which each agent tacitly accords by the mere fact of acting in accord with social convention' (ibid.: 169). What is doxic, what 'goes without saying', runs deeper than merely belief. The habitus as 'embodied structures' (Bourdieu 1994: 14) enables an actor to formulate beliefs and opinions but habitus as such does not refer to 'forms of consciousness but *dispositions of the body*' (Bourdieu 1994: 14—emphasis original). Bourdieu theorises an ideological consciousness as stemming from habitus, (as embodied capital) but also the more deeply embedded doxa that transcends any one field of action. Thus, habitus is best understood as a mechanism through which various forms of embodied capital (including field specific ideologies) and doxa come together in practice.

Although actors do formulate decisions and do have intentions, an intention is not sufficient in and of itself to explain an outcome. Decision making is less about 'subjective intention' and more about the doxic precepts that are embedded in the habitus of actors, and which reflect the organisational structure of any given field of action. *Thus, we can view mystification as being secured by the production and reproduction of the habitus*, which occurs in structured and historically specific contexts. Although it might be thought that actors simply make decisions that are oriented toward generating profits and/or market share for the corporation, or self-interest, more fundamentally their actions serve to enact deeply embedded doxic precepts and serve to reproduce their professional field of practice to which their habitus is aligned.

We contend that Bourdieu's work is useful for extending Box's notion of indifference. As with collective ignorance, indifference is structural and systemic, and not subjective. We can see in Box's work at least three uses of indifference and collective ignorance. First, it suggests *a lack of empathy and concern* for others by those in positions of power and authority. Box (1983: 13) defines a power crime as an act of indifference to others that produces avoidable harms. He thus rejects a political-legal notion of crime that revolves solely around intention, and which is premised upon rational choice theory, and emphasises what was done and the outcome. This is the most visible sense of indifference advanced by Box. This indifference is a characteristic of the culture of an elite stratum—or 'culture of delinquency' to follow David Matza whom Box (1983: 54) cites approvingly.[3] The second sense is of an indifference by the public (including criminologists) to these avoidable harms, as in an *unawareness of the prevalence and scope* of these abuses of political and

---

[3] Here Box also cites C. Wright Mills' (1956) *The Power Elite* as inspiration for his formulation.

economic power. Here there is a direct linkage to Box's idea of collective ignorance. Third, there is indifference as in *fatalism or apathy*, where one might understand the criminogenic nature of unchecked political and economic power but lack the capacity to change the situation and so therefore must begrudgingly accept it. This might be the result of exclusion from democratic processes.

The structure of the corporation—its organisational goals and culture, and alignment of habitus to field—render it 'inherently criminogenic' (ibid.: 35). This process produces a routine indifference to the outcome of 'action or inaction' (ibid.: 25). What is more, the fact that powerful corporations significantly influence processes of law-making factors into their ability to avoid legal scrutiny (and enjoy relative impunity) for their harms and crimes by helping to set the parameters within law of what ought to be considered normal and even necessary with respect to its own activity, thus contributing to the doxa of crime and harm. For Box, the mystification of the criminogenic structure of the corporation as well as the effects of this—the routine production of avoidable harms—contributes to its ability to avoid being subjected to '*criminal sanctions in the first place*' (ibid.: 59—emphasis original), which in turn helps facilitate corporate offending.

It goes without saying that the personal characteristics of actors are important, but we should not understand the production of avoidable harms only in relation to personal characteristics for 'the relatively unaccountable and unconstrained power of being at or near the top of a large national, but especially transnational corporation' enables the enhancement of already existing 'competitive ambition, shrewdness, and moral flexibility' and provides for their unhindered realisation (ibid.: 41). These characteristics are needed within the fields in which these actors struggle over capital—i.e., competition for economic, social, or cultural power—from the business school to the boardroom. Where 'corporate officials are frequently placed in a position where they are required to choose between impairing their career chances or being a loyal organizational person' they seem to overwhelmingly choose the latter. This suggests 'successful methods of persuading them that their interests and the corporation's interests happily coincide' (ibid.: 42). It is the alignment or elision of actor's and institutional goals through habitus that is important. It is this process of the acquiring of a habitus and the enactment of this habitus in action that we think complements Box's views on the role of mystification in capitalist democracies.

Mystifying Corruption

We can see this process of the production of habitus and of mystification in the corruption literature. Box was not only critical of criminology's failure to penetrate the mystification process but argued it facilitated this process (ibid.: 4–12). This critique continues to be relevant, particularly as it concerns scholarship on corruption. Wedel (2015) suggests that a driving force behind the corruption scholarship is the anti-corruption industry that first emerged in the late 1990s in response to growing concerns internationally with the bribery of public officials by private sector actors competing for lucrative government infrastructure projects. These anti-corruption initiatives, lead primarily by the business sector and focused largely on bribery in so-called underdeveloped countries, have worked to entrench what is known as the 'anti-corruption consensus' (Bukovansky 2006: 182). Supported by the academic knowledge claims of primarily orthodox economists, the focus became 'principal-agent theory' in which a government agent takes a bribe from a third party, thus acting in their own interests as opposed to those of the principal, or government. From this perspective, the challenge became how to incentivise the agent to work in the 'best interests' of the 'principal' (Wedel 2015: 7). For Wedel, Bratsis (2014), Hindess (2005, 2008), and others, the motivations for these anti-corruption efforts were corporations looking to secure access to burgeoning global markets—premised on the idea that good anti-corruption policies are good for business—and embraced by states of the Global North interested in distracting from their own corruption problems by pointing to 'less developed' countries with illiberal markets and weak governance. Corruption thus became synonymous with bribery (Wedel 2015: 14) and anti-corruption with the need for transparency and 'more' democracy.

An entire industry of anti-corruption scholars and entrepreneurs sprang-up to root-out and prevent these corrupt practices, but as many critics have argued, anti-corruption discourse rings hollow not least because corruption is very narrowly defined and understood, neglecting the activities of politically and economically powerful actors in favour of attention to the administrative/bureaucratic/enforcement realm (Bratsis 2014; Warren 2015). Corruption as a crime of the powerful cannot be understood merely as bribery of public officials or as a lack of transparency at the bureaucratic level. Political corruption involves the very making and formation of laws and policies at a level that is 'necessarily very removed from the lives of common citizens' while bureaucratic corruption is far more visible, as it concerns 'the junction where the institutions of the state mostly directly come into contact with citizens' (Bratsis 2014: 110).

A narrow administrative understanding of corruption fundamentally obscures the callous indifference of a political and economically powerful stratum at the highest levels of law and policy making which produces avoidable harms suffered by everyday people and democratic institutions (see Bratsis 2014; Mills 1956; Nyberg 2021). 'Political corruption', argues Warren (2006: 804), 'attacks democracy by excluding people from decisions that affect them. The very logic of corruption involves exclusion: the corrupt use their control over resources to achieve gains at the expense of those excluded from collective decision making, or organization of collective actions'. Here Warren (2006: 804) is clear to enter the caveat that not every form of exclusion is an act of corruption, but any 'corrosion of public norms by those who profess them' which 'harms those who are excluded' (ibid.) is corruption. This 'duplicitous exclusion' (ibid.) concerns the highest levels of government rather than simply the work of bureaucrats in relatively public facing roles who are charged with enforcing law and policies and who are the routine object of anti-corruption laws and rhetoric.

The great irony of the anti-corruption movement is that the campaigns, many of which are supported by transnational corporations, hold out 'transparency' as the remedy to corruption, but political corruption is left opaque as most anti-corruption campaigners instead focus on the activities of the public service. 'The focus on bureaucratic corruption', maintains Bratsis (2014: 110),

> displaces any serious effort to address the question of political corruption as a matter of private interests within the policy-making process. … Unsurprisingly, Transparency International, Exxon, Shell, and the IMF do not seem particularly concerned about the role of private interests, especially their own, within the policy-making process and certainly are not out to challenge the influence of the economically powerful within politics.

As with many crimes of the powerful, law operates according to the principal of duplicitous exclusion where democratic institutions and agencies are reduced to 'instruments of private benefit' (Warren 2006: 803).

There are three conclusions we make about the orthodox corruption literature that cohere with Box's framework. First, it is dominated by neglect of political corruption and instead focuses predominantly on corruption involving public officials (Barutciski and Bandali 2015). The source of the corruption can either be the supply side—a private sector actor looking for a 'competitive advantage through bribes' (Carr and Outhwaite 2011)—or demand side of the equation—a public official abusing their position to solicit bribes for their 'private economic advantage' (Cooley and Sharman 2015: 11). However, in either case corruption is considered a legal problem concerning the administrative/bureaucratic level of enforcement of policies, regulations, and laws. A corporate agent bribing a foreign government official (Mijares 2015) to secure a lucrative government contract or favourable regulatory environment (David-Barrett 2017), contrary to jurisdictional criminal codes (Gottschalk 2020) or the OECD's Convention on Combating Bribery of Foreign Public Officials in International Business Transactions (Barutciski and Bandali 2015: 233), is a predominant example within the literature.

Second, the literature commonly treats corruption as the product of weak governance (Allum et al. 2019). In essence, corruption results from some collusion between parties within a weak legal and policy context that favours certain (corrupt) interests. Here too the focus is on the middling level of the bureaucrat with transparency and 'more' democracy as remedies. The corruption as weak governance approach emphasises the problems of so-called 'developing states' while emphasising that it is largely a public sector problem, with private sector companies having to navigate these difficult political environments when operating abroad (Hindess 2012).

Third, there is an overwhelming concern with developing effective anti-corruption measures. Corruption in this instance is seen as undermining the economic development of a country, signalling the need to intervene through law and policy (Loughman and Sibery 2011). Unsurprisingly, within a neoliberal context, Corporate Social Responsibility (CSR) is touted as a strategy to ensure companies act ethically and legally when operating abroad (Mijares 2015). Corruption from this perspective is the result of 'degenerate' leadership (i.e., corporate leaders who undertake illegal or unethical activities and set the corporate culture accordingly) or individuals in a company who act for personal gain (Arbogast 2017: 27–28). The overall suggestion is that corruption is solvable through new laws or robust CSR measures.

From Box's perspective, legalistic approaches: exclude most forms of corporate or systemic corruption; obscure the construction of laws and what gets excluded from these; gloss over the fact that laws vary from country to country, and give the erroneous perception that laws are neutral and objective (Sissener 2001: 4–5). There is also a tendency to individualise corruption—that it is a problem of bad apples, either bad individuals, bad organisations, or bad political cultures. This, of course, obscures the criminogenic nature of the political and economic structure of capitalist democracies, in particular corporations, something that Box cogently illustrates. Debates about the problems and measures needed to address corruption are therefore highly individualised in that they focus on something that has changed in the character of individuals, who have become greedier or morally corrupt—their moral compass has gone awry (Wiegratz 2015: 50). There is also a tendency to define deviance down by putting the onus for corruption on so-called developing countries—corruption is not about us, but them (the 'others'). Corporations are thus positioned as victims of weak governance structures, lack of transparency, or rogue individuals who are only out for their own best interests!

Rentierism [or Parasitism] as Crime of the Powerful

The preceding demonstrates how Box's account of mystification as generating collective ignorance and indifference speaks to structural characteristics within capitalist democracies that facilitate the production of the avoidable harms characteristic of an economically powerful stratum. It moves us away from considering crimes of the powerful as simply the result of 'bad apples' or 'bad actors'. The structure of power as criminogenic suggests that crimes of the powerful cannot be reduced to the choices and actions of only individuals. Rather, the structure of political and economic power within capitalist democracies is perverting or corrupting of democracy (Box 1983: 223, passim). This account supports our efforts to extend Box's implicit theory of action via Bourdieu's notions of field and habitus to explore the doxic practices that fuel corporate power and exploitation on a global scale, which inform anti-corruption scholarship, and, ultimately, produce corruption in its various guises. It is in this respect, we argue, that corruption needs to be understood as avoidable harm stemming from the callous indifference of an economically powerful stratum within the context of contemporary capitalism.

We believe that scholarly focus should move away from political-legal definitions of corruption—what we referred to earlier as the anti-corruption consensus—to interrogate the ways in which a central mechanism of wealth extraction, baked into the very system of modern capitalism, is itself a form of corruption. It is here that the literature on the 'moral economy' can help us (Sayer 2007: 268). Sayer (2015) argues that wealth extraction today has been mystified as wealth production. There is little distinction between, for example, earned and unearned income. Those who work to produce income might produce useful goods and services, but others might extract wealth without producing anything useful in return. One form of work is socially useful and beneficial while one is destructive, or productive of avoidable harms through callous indifference to any outcome beyond wealth extraction. Sayer (2000: 80) uses the term 'moral economy' in reference to the 'moral-political norms and sentiments' that are infused with economic forces in ways that serve 'entrenched power relations'. From this perspective, 'the immorality of capitalism lies substantially in the fact that once our means of existence is dependent on market forces, the latter tend to trump considerations of the good' (ibid.: 89). In recent decades the moral and class context of the powerful has been dominated by a pernicious form of capitalism referred to in political-economic terms as rentiership. Rentierism should be treated as a type of corruption as it owes to the practices of an indifferent politically and economically powerful stratum of actors who routinely produce avoidable harm to persons and democratic processes.

Christophers conceptualises rentierism broadly and flexibly to include the control and commercialisation of an asset which provides the rentier with a distinct market advantage. As Christophers (2020: xxiv) argues, rentierism is 'income derived from the ownership, possession or control of scarce assets under conditions of limited or no competition'. Once a peripheral part of the economic system, rentierism is now a central practice and mode of conceptualising contemporary capitalism and a main driver of profound and growing inequalities around the world.

Neoliberalism provided a 'convenient rationale for rentier capitalism' (Standing 2016: 12) via the liberalisation of markets, along with the 'commodification and privatisation of everything that could be commodified and privatised and the systemic dismantling of all institutions of social solidarity that protected people from "market forces"'. In essence, rentiership is the byproduct of efforts to shrink social democracy in order to financially exploit every inch of the globe. It is what Christophers (2020: xvii) refers to as 'balance-sheet capitalism' in which the main goal is maximal profits based on what is controlled, not what is done, meaning the predominant concern is with what assets a company holds and how these can be utilised to produce (unearned) income.

As powerful individuals and corporations virtually tripped over each other to take advantage of the privatisation bonanza, there were myriad bribes and insider deals to ensure access to an increasingly exclusive global oligarchy (Standing 2016: 42–45). As crony capitalism spread its tentacles into the political realm, politicians were effectively tethered to the rich and powerful who funded 'politicians and political parties' (ibid.: 46). As Sayer (2016: 26) argues:

> Economic power is also political power. The very control of assets like land and money is a political issue. Those who control what used to be called 'the commanding heights of the economy' – and increasingly that means the financial sector – can pressure governments, including democratically elected ones, to do their bidding. They can threaten to take their money elsewhere, refuse to lend to governments except at crippling rates of interest, demand minimal financial regulation, hide their money in tax havens and demand tax breaks in return for political funding.

Crony capitalism allowed for the proliferation of rentiership. As Standing (2016: 46) argues, widespread privatisation not only transferred 'public assets to private interests' but also provided the foundation for 'selected individuals or firms' to receive 'considerable rental income'. Rent, or the money received from providing access to something owned or controlled by someone, therein reinforcing the exclusion of capitalist property relations, has always been a staple of capitalism (the landlord renting property to someone is the quintessential example). Since the advent of neoliberalism, economic and political conditions have cohered to increase the scope of rent-seeking to include a whole host of money-making activities geared primarily to wealth extraction without social benefit (Christophers 2020; Standing 2016; Sayer 2016).

The focus on corruption in legal terms or as a problem that is treatable through the right mix of anti-corruption measures obscures how the economy works. It is tantamount to tinkering at the edges while the truly corrupt nature of the structure of political and economic power goes under-examined and uncontested. When a corporate agent bribes a government official to secure a contract, it is not simply about two people acting greedily, nor is it just about the betterment of one or both agents involved. While it is these things, it is fundamentally about the dynamics or common sense associated with sustaining economic relations which prioritise wealth extraction at the expense of almost everything that happens along the way. In addition, driving these relations are the wealthy and powerful rentiers who derive 'unearned income from ownership of existing assets or resources' (Sayer 2016: 50). Indeed, many of these are privately held resources, but some are publicly owned but controlled by private interests. These are the people who get richer and more powerful without having to do anything or produce anything, yet their needs must be met and are met through others' labour. As capital scours the earth looking for ways to make money, new sources of profit have been fabricated which:

> include the income lenders gain from debt interest; income from ownership of "intellectual property" (such as patents, copyright, brands and trademarks); capital gains on investments; "above normal" company profits (when a firm has a dominant market position that allows it to charge high prices or dictate terms); income from government subsidies; and income of financial and other intermediaries derived from third-party transactions. (Standing 2016: 3)

Thinking of corruption through a rentier lens is needed because of the profound problems of social and income inequality on a global scale—all linked to the 'rise of the rentier' (Standing 2016: 2). We therefore need to look beyond narrow notions of corruption that dwell on the level of bureaucratic or 'office' corruption and that emphasise visible expressions of these narrow notions (Bratsis 2014; Heywood 2018; Warren 2015), to consider 'circumstances that allow' (Sayer 2016: 9) the rich to get richer and more powerful and act in ways that economically and physically harm others and de-democratise democratic processes and institutions with impunity. Corruption is rampant in part because the political structures within capitalist democracies are specifically designed to facilitate the concentration of economic power. Box draws attention to the anti-democratic nature of this concentration of power, witnessed by the transfer of authority from elected parliamentarians to unelected bodies like the European economic community and the IMF (Box 1983: 203). Likewise, the call to protect the 'Nation' at a time of economic need (something that still resonates today) serves to ensure the burden of these challenges falls to those at the lower end of the socio-economic hierarchy, leaving the powerful unburdened in their quest for even more wealth and power (ibid.: 210).

Overall, Box's arguments surrounding the concentration of power as undemocratic and criminogenic, of how corporate organisation and objectives become embedded in subjectivity and action, that what is accepted as natural and factual is a mystic reality, is relevant for understanding why corruption is commonly understood narrowly as a distinctly legal phenomenon and for why it is that rentier capitalism is reinforced on a global scale. We argue rentierism, as part of efforts to (re)secure unearned income through wealth extraction, ought to be considered as a crime of the powerful.

Conclusion

What we find particularly doxic in the contemporary era is that parasitism is considered beneficial although its unearned spoils are not merited. From Box's perspective, the lens is cast downward toward the powerless, with 'solutions' to social problems such as workfare and residualism having the goal of increasing dependency on the market where one necessarily becomes dependent on private corporations as providers of goods and services, and with this subjected to dire working conditions to make use of the market mechanism for provision of needs. If the same lens was cast upward, however, financialisation and rentierism—as forms of wealth extraction with no tangible benefit to our society—would appear as destructive to both democracy and capitalism.

Endemic globally is a parasitical transnational capitalist class that reproduces itself through extracting wealth from property ownership and control of assets without producing anything that is socially useful. The rentier's 'subsidized' existence 'goes unnoticed' states Sayer (2015: 48), and the costs of subsidising the rich 'diverts resources away from the productive economy' (ibid.: 52). This unjust and unethical parasitism is 'authorized by the legal system and supported by a common-sense moral code, which presents [rent as wealth extraction] as a reasonable payment to a provider of a service' (ibid.: 48). The harms produced include those to exploited populations of workers who in manufacturing and industry often face unsafe working conditions as a means of boosting productivity; those from resource extraction and environmental despoliation, income inequality, and economic harms to those preyed upon by saving and loans schemes, and high interest rates that amount to usury. This is carried out through what is a privatised economy that is mainly beneficial to those with a property stake in it.

National and international economies that are owned by private commercial interests that present debt (i.e., credit) as freedom rather than as dependency on private enterprise, offer a form of indenture to those whom Box referred to as the collectively ignorant. Indeed, Sayer (2015: 51) attributes the common elision of wealth extraction with wealth-generating practices to ignorance. 'Mere ownership, whether it is of land, buildings, money or technology produces nothing, but can be used for extracting value from others' (ibid.: 47). Given the prominence within neoliberal economics of a corporatised culture and the need to be an enterprising self, one's habitus is largely attuned to the commercial interests of private industry; personal interests, aspirations, and practices become aligned with and support the needs of the subsidised existence of the wealth extraction class as people 'freely' engage in their daily lives and are constituted as potential victims of the avoidable harms of rentierism. As rentierism produces avoidable harm to persons and democratic processes and that it emanates from and is supported by collective ignorance and produced by indifferent politically and economically powerful actors, it should be treated as a type of corruption.

References

Allum, F., S. Gilmour, and C. Hemmings, eds. 2019. *Handbook of Organised Crime and Politics*. London: Edward Elgar.
Arbogast, S.V. 2017. *Resisting Corporate Corruption: Cases in Practical Ethics Through the Financial Crisis*, 3rd ed. Beverly: Scrivener Publishing.

Barton, A., and H. Davis, eds. 2018. *Ignorance, Power and Harm*. London: Palgrave Macmillan.
Barutciski, M., and S. Bandali. 2015. Corruption at the Intersection of Business and Government: The OECD Convention, Supply-Side Corruption, and Canada's Anti-corruption Efforts to Date. *Osgoode Hall Law Journal* 53 (1): 231–267.
Bourdieu, P. 1973. The Three Forms of Theoretical Knowledge. *Social Science Information* 12 (1): 53–80.
Bourdieu, P. 1977. *Outline of a Theory of Practice*. New York: Cambridge University Press.
Bourdieu, P. 1986. Forms of capital. In *Handbook of Theory and Research for the Sociology of Education*, ed. J. Richardson, 241–258. Westport: Greenwood Press.
Bourdieu, P. 1987. The Force of Law: Toward a Sociology of the Juridical Field. *Hastings Law Journal* 38: 814–853.
Bourdieu, P. 1994. Rethinking the State: Genesis and Structure of the Bureaucratic Field. *Sociological Theory* 12 (1): 1–18.
Bourdieu, P. 1998. *Practical Reason: On the Theory of Action*. Stanford: Stanford University Press.
Box, S. 1983. *Power, Crime and Mystification*. London: Tavistock.
Bratsis, P. 2014. Political Corruption in the Age of Transnational Capitalism. *Historical Materialism* 22 (1): 105–128.
Bukovansky, M. 2006. The Hollowness of Anti-corruption Discourse. *Review of International Political Economy* 13 (2): 181–209.
Carr, I., and O. Outhwaite. 2011. Controlling Corruption Through Corporate Social Responsibility and Corporate Governance: Theory and Practice. *Journal of Corporate Law Studies* 11 (2): 299–341.
Christophers, B. 2020. *Rentier Capitalism: Who owns the economy and who pays for it*. London: Verso.
Cooley, A., and J.C. Sharman. 2015. Blurring the Line Between Licit and Illicit: Transnational Corruption Networks in Central Asia and Beyond. *Central Asian Survey* 34 (1): 11–28.
David-Barrett, E. 2017. Business Unusual: Collective Action Against Bribery in International Business. *Crime, Law and Social Change* 71: 151–170.
Frauley, J. 2012. Post-social Politics, Employability, and the Security Effects of Higher Education: Foucault, Bourdieu Governance. *Journal of Pedagogy* 3 (2): 219–241.

Gottschalk, P. 2020. Convenience in White-Collar Crime: A Case Study of Corruption Among Friends in Norway. *Criminal Justice Studies* 33 (4): 413–424.

Heywood, P. 2018. Combatting Corruption in the Twenty-First Century: New Approaches. *Daedalus* 147 (3): 83–97.

Hindess, B. 2005. Investigating International Anti-corruption. *Third World Quarterly* 26 (8): 1389–1398.

Hindess, B. 2008. International Anti-corruption as a Programme of Normalization. In *Governments, NGOs and Anti-corruption: The New Integrity Warriors*, ed. L. de Sousa, B. Hindess, and P. Lamour, 19–32. New York: Routledge.

Hindess, B. 2012. Introduction: How Should we Think About Corruption? In *Corruption*, ed. M. Barcham, B. Hindess, and P. Lamour, 1–24. Canberra: ANU Press.

Lasswell, H.D. 1941. The Garrison State. *American Journal of Sociology* 46 (4): 455–468.

Loughman, B., and R. Sibery. 2011. *Bribery and Corruption: Navigating the Global Risks*. New York: John Wiley and Sons Inc.

McGoey, L., ed. 2014. *An Introduction to the Sociology of Ignorance: Essays on the Limits of Knowledge*. London: Routledge.

Mijares, S.C. 2015. The Global Fight against Foreign Bribery: Is Canada a Leader or Laggard? *Western Journal of Legal Studies* 5 (4): 1–24.

Mills, C.W. 1956. *The Power Elite*. Oxford: Oxford University Press.

Nyberg, D. 2021. Corporations, Politics, and Democracy: Corporate Political Activities as Political Corruption. *Organization Theory* 2: 1–24.

Sayer, A. 2000. Moral Economy and Political Economy. *Studies in Political Economy* 61 (1): 79–103.

Sayer, A. 2007. Moral Economy as Critique. *New Political Economy* 12 (2): 261–270.

Sayer, A. 2015. Moral Economy, Unearned Income, and Legalized Corruption. In *Neoliberalism and the Moral Economy of Fraud*, ed. D. Whyte and J. Wiegratz, 44–56. New York: Routledge.

Sayer, A. 2016. *Why We Can't Afford the Rich*. Chicago: Policy Press.

Sissener, T.K. 2001. *Anthropological Perspectives on Corruption*. London: CMI Working Papers.

Standing, G. 2016. *The Corruption of Capitalism: Why Rentiers Thrive and Work Does Not Pay*. London: Biteback Publishing.

Warren, M.E. 2006. Political Corruption as Duplicitous Exclusion. *Political Science and Politics* 39 (4): 803–807.

Warren, M.E. 2015. The Meaning of Corruption in Democracies. In *The Routledge Handbook of Political Corruption*, ed. P. Heywood, 42–55. Oxford: Routledge.

Wedel, J.R. 2015. High Priests and the Gospel of Anti-corruption. *Challenge* 58 (1): 4–22.

Wiegratz, J. 2015. The New Normal: Moral Economies in the 'Age of Fraud.' In *How Corrupt Is Britain?*, ed. D. Whyte, 47–58. London: Pluto Press.

4

Power, Crime and Deadly Deception

David Whyte

Introduction

This chapter highlights one aspect of the contribution made by Steven Box's *Power, Crime and Mystification* (*PCM*) to the study of corporate and white-collar crime: his use of deviance theory to illuminate the criminal subculture of corporate executives. It does so for two reasons. First, to recognise, and pay some attention to, the influence that this work has had on critical criminology, and particularly on those who have studied and written about corporate crime since the publication of *PCM*. And second, to offer a constructive critique which revisits Box's perspective and suggest a modification of his approach. This modification argues for a materialisation of the ways that elite subcultures—their belief systems and patterns of behaviour—are sustained and reproduced. In doing so, the chapter will argue that techniques of neutralisation (ToN) do not stem from power that is derived from within the subculture, but from

---

D. Whyte (✉)
Queen Mary University of London, London, England
e-mail: david.whyte@qmul.ac.uk

the material social relationships that exist beyond the subculture. The chapter begins by outlining Box's arguments on corporate subcultures. It then explores how a selection of some of the most deadly processes and substances to emerge in the industrial era have been 'neutralised', before offering some reflective comments on the concrete ways in which corporate impunity is guaranteed by a set of power relations that underpins a regime of permission to commit extreme forms of physical harm and 'slow violence' (Nixon 2011).

Box on Elite Subcultures

For Box (1983), to start from the perspective of the subculture itself allows us to view *formal* criminal legal definition as less persuasive guides to conduct, in comparison to the social mores and moral codes followed by powerful groups. In this sense he is part of a long tradition of critical criminology that seeks to marginalise, ridicule or disable dominant discourses of crime and criminality. Box was of course interested in *ideological* constructions of crime and criminality. In a highly influential passage in *PCM* (pp. 54–57) he mobilised Sykes and Matza's (1957) ToN to show how the moral bind of crime is substantially weakened or rendered irrelevant by elite subcultures. Thus:

> each subculture softens criminal acts so that they assume the appearance of 'not really' being against the law, or it transforms them into acts required by a morality higher than that enshrined in a parochial criminal law. (ibid: 54)

It is in this respect that sub-cultural theory has much in common with the 'harm' or 'zemiology' perspective that has evolved since Box's contributions in the 1980s. The former perspective similarly asserts that crime is a *parochial* political and social construction. For Box, the construction of 'harm' and 'crime' is part of the praxis of the state and criminal justice apparatuses. At the same time, he argues that the subculture has the capacity to *neutralise* how it internalises this praxis. For Box, particularly when it comes to elite subcultures, 'crime' can be made significantly less relevant as a morally binding force to the immediate social group of perpetrators. Equally it can be argued that 'harm' is rendered less significant here. Just as the subculture has the capacity to justify any crime done by particular forms of conduct, in the same breath, *harm* is justified. Indeed, from a sub-cultural perspective, there is little difference between 'crime' and 'harm': both are the effects of elite conduct that can be neutralised by more dominant moral assertions of the social group.

Box's approach to sub-cultural theory is of the variety espoused by more radical scholars, rather than the liberal formulae developed by the likes of Becker and Cohen. As such, Box is interested in the agency of actors and the ways in which actors shape the world around them within a broader structure of power. Thus, Box's insights on elite subcultures were explicitly influenced by C Wright Mills.

In *PCM* he makes reference to concepts that were developed in the conclusion to Wright Mills' *The Power Elite,* and in particular, his reflections on the 'higher immorality' of the ruling class. Wright Mills had railed against the morality that serves the interests of the ruling class, rather than any general social or public interest:

> Within the corporate worlds of business, war-making and politics, the private conscience is attenuated—and the higher immorality is institutionalized. (Wright Mills, 2000: 343)

Just like youth subcultures, corporate officials follow the rules of their subculture, not the law of the land. The originality of Box's approach to sub-cultural theory springs into life when he refuses to accept that those different commitments to conventional 'law and order' practices directly translate into different levels of commitment to observing the law. For Box, it is precisely the higher [im]morality of elites that informs their perspective and helps create a culture of being 'above the law'. It is therefore a mistake to assume that the difference in the threat posed by the criminal justice system to elites—compared say, with young working class people—corresponds to a difference in how each social group respects the law. In fact, Box argues, corporate executives use precisely the same 'techniques' to do precisely the same thing: to rationalise and therefore neutralise their own offending behaviour, both to themselves and to external audiences:

> By the use of these techniques of neutralization, which are themselves embedded in the 'structural immorality' of corporations, executives are able to violate the law without feeling guilt or denting their respectable self-image. (Box 1983: 57)

Ultimately, for Box, there are major differences between upper class and lower class subcultures. Not least of those is the differential threat they face from law enforcers. The latter are generally locked into ongoing confrontation with the criminal legal system and the former confront a system that is generally on their side. This implies a contradiction. Since corporate officials generally have more invested in the system and the social order, this intensifies the importance of their own ToN:

> they have an even greater need to neutralize the moral bind of the law and thus protect their respectability and self-identity from the signs of discreditability implicit in corporate crimes. (ibid: 54)

This means, for Box, that there is even more of an urgent necessity for corporate officials to rely on more sophisticated and more expansive (but essentially the same) ToN that deviance theorists Sykes and Matza had set out. And this is the simple beauty of Box's conclusion: Sykes and Matza's ToN may indeed be a more convincing framework for explaining the subcultures of elite groups than it is for youth subcultures. He illustrates this claim across 5 key dimensions. First, officials can deny responsibility (they plead 'ignorance', 'accident', 'acting under orders' or 'for the good of the company'). Second, they deny the victim (they blame workers, consumers, state bodies like tax authorities other corporations) in order to deflect or displace blame and responsibility. As part of this process, the injury experienced by victims is denied. Third, they condemn the condemners (they can deny the legitimacy of the law that they transgress, the political authority that introduced it or the regulatory authority trying to enforce it). Fourth, they appeal to higher loyalty (they are loyal to the corporation, they are protecting public interests by generating wealth and jobs, or they obey the rules of the market, of free enterprise and of economic progress). Fifth, a central part of the 'Identity cosmetic' (ibid: 57) that executives are able to present is the plausible claim that what they do is not 'real' crime; that crime is essentially a lower class phenomenon. Thus:

> …[c]orporate officials are both mystified as to their own crime, and misdirected as to the distribution of crime in general. Both mystification and misdirection preserve the appearance of corporate respectability and help keep invisible, to themselves and others, the underlying ugly reality of corporate crime. (ibid: 57)

Box's analysis of how elites use ToN inspired a significant sub-genre of work, fronted by Benson (1985) and Coleman (1987) in the 1980s. The influence of this work has endured and this literature continued to develop more than 3 decades later (Piquero et al. 2005; Heath 2008; Vieraitis et al. 2012; Fooks et al. 2013; Whyte 2016). This literature used Box's work as a point of departure to add a number of other ToN used by corporate executives. I summarise three of the most prominent of those below.

First, because of the structural power that corporate officials draw upon and because of their sphere of influence, they can justify their deviance with an appeal to 'harm avoidance'. This is an explicitly utilitarian rationale that claims that a particular behaviour is justified by the avoidance of a 'greater' harm. This rationale is essentially the flipside—a reversal of precisely the same logic—of the denial of harm or of the injury (denial of victim) discussed above. This rationale assumes that harm or injury would have occurred if the corporate officer had not done what he or she is being censured for. As Coleman (1987) notes, when a particular offence is committed, a logic of survival is very commonly invoked, either to ensure that an employee keeps her job, or to ensure that the business stays competitive and therefore is able to survive in a tough market place (see also Health 2008; Minor 1981 in Fooks et al. 2013). This justification is often linked to a series of moral spin-offs: that jobs and livelihoods will be preserved; that the business's contribution to the community will be preserved and so on. In other words, not committing an offence in those circumstances might have exposed a corporate officer to moral censure.

Second, the social power of executives allows them to claim that *they are* the culture norm. Thus, an 'everybody's doing it' rationale in which corporate officers point to the culture of the industry, can have a powerful force, particularly in criminogenic industries. Coleman (1987) recalls one respondent in Cressey's study of embezzlers: 'We did a little juggling and moving around, but everyone in the real estate business has to do that. We didn't do anything that they all don't do' (Cressey 1953: 137, cited in ibid: 413). This type of rationale begins to locate the event or process or behaviour in a 'normal' structure of business. It is powerful because of its invoking of what is normal cultural practice and therefore cannot be deviant. Third, a further ToN occurs as corporate officials portray their behaviour as out of character or an aberration for an individual who, because of their social position, can claim an exemplary record in previous behaviour. This is sometimes called the 'ledger technique' (Moore and McMullan 2009; Fooks et al. 2013) and is illustrated well by Benson's (1985) tax evaders, who portrayed their crimes as an uncharacteristic flaw in their otherwise unblemished record.

Ultimately, for Box, as noted above, there are major differences between upper class and lower class subcultures. Not least of those is their relationship with the law. The structural power of the latter means that they can draw upon both their social prestige and material resources to construct their ToN from a dominant and privileged position. It is for this reason that corporate offenders are likely to be able to exist in a paradoxical relationship to law and legality. After all, as Benson (1985: 599) notes, for the labelling of white-collar criminals to be successful, the criminal event or practice must be shown to be out of the ordinary, or 'revealed as obviously and unquestionably profane' *and* at the same time must be 'indicative of a pattern of behavior that is the opposite of that expected of the normal citizen' (ibid).

Elsewhere I have used Box's work on ToN as a point of departure for understanding how car manufacturers are empowered by their structurally dominant position to conceal basic facts about the safety of their products, the true costs of production and so on (Whyte 2016). The routine deception that we can observe in this industry is simply part and parcel of a never-ending struggle between manufacturers for market share. As a long history of work on corporate crime and corporate fraud shows, corporations across all sectors engage in exactly the same pattern of routine deception.

Precisely the same process of corporate denial and distortion surrounding the fatal nature of their products can be found in food production and sales, in pharmaceuticals, in agricultural products, in textile and clothing production, in electronics production and on and on and on (Stauber and Rampton 1995; Lubbers 2012; Pellow 2007; Michaels 2008;). This is a pattern that seems to pervade all industries that are hazardous to the environment. In the following sections we explore some examples of environmental violence in order to deepen our analysis of the ways in which ToN are used by corporate executives for competitive advantage.

Denial of the Victim

In the early 1970s, the industrial use of chlorofluorocarbons (CFCs), a group of chemicals used in the manufacture of a range of products, including aerosols, fridges and air conditioning units rang some alarm bells about global warming. The main brand was a coolant that General Motors made in partnership with the chemical company DuPont as 'Freon'. In 1974, two significant scientific studies demonstrated that a build-up of CFCs was responsible for depleting the ozone layer, thus depleting one of the earth's essential mechanisms for absorbing the sun's ultraviolet radiation and cooling down the earth. The GM-DuPont coolant, once released into the environment, was quickly heating the atmosphere. It is highly unlikely that GM, DuPont or other chemical companies manufacturing CFCs knew, or could have known, their irreversible environmental effects before the findings of those studies were published.

However, when they *were* published, the US Chemical Manufacturers Association, led by DuPont, initiated a research programme by academic investigators. The research programme was part of a search for a safe alternative chemical. Coupled to this programme was a concerted effort in the industry to lobby against and organise political resistance to a regulatory ban on CFCs (Maxwell and Briscoe 1997). In 1980, as it became more likely that a global ban would be implemented, DuPont withdrew all research funding for its safe alternative (Weisskopf 1988). And it was not until 1986 (when British scientists had discovered a gaping hole in the ozone layer over Antarctica) that DuPont re-committed to finding an alternative; later the company was to support a phase out of CFCs by 2000. James Lovelock, the British scientist who had discovered the problem of CFC build-up in 1971, noted with regret almost 50 years later:

> Manufacturers were determined to deny they had any effects on the global environment, notably the depletion of the ozone layer in the atmosphere. (Lovelock 2019)

The story of the chemical industry's attempt to prevent or at least slow down the CFC ban reveals a pattern of corporate denial and deliberate cover-up that seems to prevail, even in the face of scientific evidence. This is a pattern of slow violence that has typified the production of our most persistent and deadly products (Nixon 2011).

The tobacco story is perhaps best known. Medical research evidence linking smoking to lung cancer began to appear in the 1920s. In the early 1950s, as it became apparent that the mounting evidence could threaten its interests, the tobacco companies organised a major campaign to disrupt scientific research, and to lie about and distort health evidence (Bero 2005; Montague 2018). The industry used front organisations such as the Council for Tobacco Research (founded by United States [US] tobacco companies in 1954) and the Center for Indoor Air Research (founded by Philip Morris, R.J. Reynolds and Lorillard in 1988) in the US to attack and discredit public health advocates. In the United Kingdom (UK), the key right wing think tanks, including Centre for Policy Studies and the Institute of Economic Affairs were funded by British tobacco firms from 1963 onwards to do the same job (Monbiot 2017).

4 Power, Crime and Deadly Deception

The very brief details of those stories tell us something different, but related, about the power that corporate executives have to deceive us. This power to deceive adds a further dimension to the discussion set out above. Commissioning research to create doubt about the science and to distort what we know about the harmful effects of substances can clearly be understood as ToN. Of all the Box and 'post-Box' categories of ToN set out above, perhaps 'denial of the victim' and its associated rationalisations around denial of injury fits best here. After all, the publication of research that downplays the harms of a substance or an industrial process does precisely this: it downplays the extent and the seriousness of the harms, and therefore the effects suffered by victims and their families and communities.

We are, of course, talking about a very specific group of victims here: consumers. And it is their status as consumers that enables a particular type of victimisation: their victimisation through their consumption of deadly products. And this is where denial of victim takes on a special characteristic in the case of corporate harms. In capitalist ideologies, the consumer always has a choice. And it is in the acting out of this 'choice' that victimhood can be neutralised. Tobacco consumers have the choice to either purchase or not purchase the harmful substance that they use; consumers had the choice to buy products using CFCs or not. Of course, in the case of CFCs, it was impossible to buy a fridge, or any aerosol product in early the 1980s that did not contain CFCs. So much for consumer choice.

But there is another important dimension to the figure of the consumer as victim. This figure is used to argue against regulation. In both cases, the manufacturers of their products argued that state intervention in the form of legal regulation could not be allowed to compromise *consumers'* interests. In the case of CFCs, the argument was that a slower phase out of the chemicals would prevent consumers from absorbing the costs of developing alternatives. In the case of tobacco, rather contradictory messaging from the major manufacturers has pursued a dual line of argument: first that the health effects are overstated, and that in any case consumers are aware of the effects and can make their own choice (and in the background of course the companies suppressed any medical evidence of adverse health effects; Bero 2005).

In the case of tobacco, the idea of consumer choice can be challenged when the highly addictive nature of the product is considered; consumer choice is influenced by addiction. Nonetheless, it is clear that 'consumer choice' is used to justify the marketing of harmful products by corporate officials. How do we interpret this in relation to Box's techniques of neutralisation? First, we can read it as a kind of *weak* blaming of the victim. Second, it fits as an 'appeal to higher loyalties'; loyalty to the free market principle of consumer choice is a form of 'higher loyalty' that corporate executives would be expected to adhere to.

No Choice

If, in the examples set out above, it is actually quite difficult to deny victimhood. It is a stretch to imagine that consumers are in some way responsible for harming themselves and the environment, because they make a 'choice' to do so, this particular form of neutralisation narrative cannot, even at a stretch, be applied to other deadly substances. Indeed, there are endless examples of deadly substances that have been manufactured and distributed to consumers, where no 'choice' has been cultivated, because those consumers have simply not been told about the risks.

For example, nobody *chose* to have lead added to the petrol they use in their cars, and yet it was done for most of the twentieth century. Indeed, it is not clear at all *who* demanded the addition of lead into petroleum. The potentially deadly effects of adding lead compounds to petrol were discovered by scientists 100 years ago, in the 1920s. Despite this knowledge, a trio of major corporations: General Motors, DuPont (the same partnership that developed CFCs) and Standard Oil of New Jersey (now the largest oil company in the world under the name of ExxonMobil) aggressively marketed and promoted the addition of tetraethyllead to petrol. They were supported by the US Surgeon General who ensured that the US government gave the green light to the export of this deadly additive (Gardiner 2019). Those major—and deadly—public health effects of adding lead to petrol were well known; and the benefits were marginal. Although in the early days, the additives made engines slightly more efficient, the main effect was to reduce engine 'knock', a problem that had no major effect on the mechanics of the car, but was largely cosmetic. Yet the industry did all it could to hide and distort our knowledge, and ensure leaded petrol was standard in most countries for at least 60 years. Indeed, as recently as 2017, Greenpeace reported that British company Innospec was still producing lead additive and exporting it to Libya, despite acknowledging the deadly health risks and pledging to stop exporting the chemical to African countries by the end of 2012 (Sandler Clarke 2017).

The story of PVC or vinyl chloride is one of many other groups of chemical substances that essentially has the same plotline. The US Environmental Protection Agency now classifies vinyl chloride as a Group A human carcinogen. Studies have identified a causal link with brain cancer, lung cancer, lymphoma, leukemia, oral cancer and liver cancer in particular, as well as a number of other series illnesses. Indeed, academic research commissioned by one of the chemical's largest producers Union Carbide and published in 1930 showed exposure to the vinyl chloride polymers caused serious liver damage (Patty et al. 1930). A Dow Chemical memo in 1959 acknowledged that exposure to vinyl chloride produces 'appreciable injury when inhaled seven hours a day, 5 days a week' (Robin 2014: 195). The internal memo went on '[a]s you can appreciate this opinion is not ready for dissemination and I would appreciate it if you would hold it in confidence'. In 1973, an internal Ethyl Corporation memo noted lab results showing a 'positive carcinogenic effect' (ibid). And yet, in 1998, a full 25 years after the Ethyl Corporation research, and almost 70 years after the first scientific research showed that vinyl chloride was killing people, it was discovered by investigative journalists that US chemical companies had conspired to manipulate the results of scientific studies to avoid liability for worker exposure and had deliberately failed to warn local communities of extensive and severe chemical spills of vinyl chloride (Morris 1998). The motivation for using PVC in industrial processes is commercial: as a chemical in the manufacture of synthetic materials, it provided a much wider range of malleable products at a relatively cheap price.

There are countless more chemicals that we could tell a very similar story about, including Bisphenol A (BPA); Polychlorinated biphenyl (PCB); Polyvinyl chloride (PVC) and organophosphates (Whyte 2020).

There is certainly a process of victim denial going on here. The impacts of tetraethyllead and vinyl chloride on their victims are denied. But unlike the cases of CFCs and tobacco, there is no attempt here to introduce the figure of the 'free' consumer. At the same time, there seems to be something more going on in those cases that is not captured very well by the ToN approach.

In those cases, we do not merely see a passive or dismissive denial here: it is not only a denial based upon a shared set of beliefs. Rather, a great deal of effort has gone into building a concrete, often new, base of evidence that has been actively commissioned and disseminated for this purpose. The ability to deny and neutralise those harms is derived from the capacity to commission research, to publish it and then to get media outlets and politicians to promote this evidence. The ability to neutralise the psychological impact of those harms, both *within* and *beyond* the subculture, is derived directly from the significant infrastructural power that profit making corporations enjoy. Having access to networks of researchers, as well as having the capital to pay for research, having access to national media, and to politicians; all of those things are derived from a power that reaches well beyond the narrow confines of a 'subculture'.

Regimes of Permission and the State

To put the argument set out in the previous section more succinctly, it is their social power that enables corporate executives to produce deadly substances with impunity. And it is their social power that enables them to justify and neutralise what they do when they market and distribute deadly substances. Yet there is another, crucial source of this social power: the power that is organised in the state. This is the source of power that Box is explicitly referring to in *PCM* where he carefully details how corporations and their executives draw upon to shape legal outcomes and to neutralise the enforcement of the law against them:

In comparison with "conventional" offenders, corporate executives find themselves in an enviable position. Not only do they have a greater opportunity to commit their favoured types of crimes, but they have the capacity to influence which of their behaviours will be regarded as corporate crimes in the first place. (Box 1983: 63)

This is not simply because they hold 'power' in an abstract sense. Corporations are able to influence the law, because they occupy a central role in the economy, in the social fabric and in the culture of capitalist societies. Corporations are the key market actors, who must be protected as market actors, because that is precisely the role of state in capitalist social orders. The role of the state is to make sure that regulation does not interfere too much with their right to accumulate value and make commercial products. In this social order, even the negligent and avoidable killing of consumers, even the ultimate human catastrophe—global warming—is seen as a mere annoyance, an obstacle in the uninterrupted right of corporations to accumulate value.

This is the case in all of the substances discussed in this chapter: at every turn, state regulators initially accepted the evidence presented to them by corporations, and allowed those products to be sold with very little restriction. In the case of lead added to petrol and CFCs, worldwide bans came eventually. But in the case of tobacco and of deadly chemicals that are industrially produced, they are regulated in ways that tend to place the commercial goals of their commercial producers ahead of the interests of consumers, workers and communities. Often this is part of a complex balance that sometimes restricts their use. But generally, as a rule, most of the harmful substances that are in our air and water and food are under government licence.

For the purposes of this chapter, what this means is that the process of denying victims, on which corporate executives rely, are always in some way related to the degree to which regulators and public bodies are prepared to disrupt those ToN. In other words, corporate executives' freedom to deceive is always underpinned by the state.

Let's turn briefly to another example to illustrate this point in further detail.

The Volkswagen 'dieselgate' case which broke in 2015 involved the use of 'defeat device' software to fraudulently understate deadly NOx emissions from 11 million cars. The real level of NOx emissions in Volkswagen, Audi and Porsche cars was up to 40 times more than the test results showed, and research subsequently showed that this pollution led to around 1200 premature deaths (Chossière et al. 2017). As well as the Volkswagen brands, we know now that 'defeat' devices were used by Fiat Chrysler, Nissan, Renault, Mercedes-Benz, General Motors and Mitsubishi, amongst others (Whyte 2016). The lack of any systematic inquiry into those brands is evidence that the right to deceive is always carefully protected by governments.

It is difficult to imagine that the dieselgate case could have proceeded in this way had the industry itself not been granted a formative role in shaping the standards that regulate the industry, and if the system of regulation declined to make adequate checks for legal compliance. Regulatory systems across North America and Europe permitted the car manufacturers full autonomy over the conditions of their compliance with emissions rules. This principle of full autonomy was made very clear in the negotiations around the Transatlantic Trade and Investment Partnership between the US and the European Union before the defeat device scandals emerged. According to a series of documents obtained by Corporate Europe Observatory, Commission representatives concluded after meetings with car lobbyists in 2012 that 'any action proposed should be demand driven, based on input from industry'. In a position paper published in May 2014, the same month that the Volkswagen crisis began to emerge, the European Commission stated:

> Pending a more detailed, data-driven analysis, the lists of matching regulations submitted by the industry in their joint contributions already provide a valuable indication of industry's expectations for this negotiation. Regulators would conduct such an equivalence assessment based on data provided by the industry as well as other available data.[1]

---

[1] See the Corporate Europe Observatory report online at: https://corporateeurope.org/en/international-trade/2015/10/vw-tested-once-approved-everywhere. Accessed 3 Aug 2023.

This remains the position of the European Commission: any future system of automobile industry regulation is to be driven by data produced by auto manufacturers!

And this is the principle that generally shapes the regulation of *all* substances that are harmful to us and to our environment: states define and implement regulatory standards in close co-operation with those that have the greatest incentive to minimise regulatory controls. The basic approach to regulating the car industry is precisely the same approach taken to the regulation of other hazardous industries.

In each of the cases noted above, corporations were involved in a process of 'denial' (Cohen 2000); they used extensive access to financial and social resources to mobilise networks and state structures outside the subculture to ensure the production and sale of highly deadly substances could proceed uninterrupted. The executives that willfully ignored and actively sought to bury the evidence of the devastating effects of their products on human health and the eco-system did so with a regulatory stamp of approval. And yet those mass killings, organised and planned by corporate executives, are barely recognised as crimes, either by the subculture, or by those outside the subculture. They are crimes that barely require neutralising. Corporate executives derive their ability to deny from the hard-wired infrastructural power of the state.

Crucially, the *right* to deceive is formally underpinned by the state: by government departments, by regulatory authorities, by expert committees of inquiry and so on. The examples discussed so far involve a process of recognition by state and public authorities that has not only failed to challenge the manipulation of scientific evidence, but has ultimately licensed those products, and therefore encouraged their use. States establish *regimes of permission* for the slow violence perpetrated by corporations (Whyte 2014). Corporate denial is therefore never simply a matter for the subcultures that control the corporation; it is also a matter of *state*.

Conclusion

In a great many cases of harmful and deadly products, corporate executives have known at an early stage in their production about the extent that of the damage that they are doing to human, non-human animals and the environment. In a very broad sense, we can say that in the cases discussed here, corporate executives had full knowledge of what they were doing and of the consequences of their actions. And yet they have gone to great lengths to hide information that would certainly have saved countless lives. It is part of the habitus of the corporate executive that they actively prevent us knowing about harmful products in ways that prevents us being able to do anything about them.

Box's analysis of corporate crime in *PCM* always comes back to the *contradictions* in capitalist law. I suspect that this is really why he wants to apply Sykes and Matza (1957) to elites: to expose the hypocritical bias within criminal justice systems that proclaims universal application, but in the end punishes poor, racialised, working class 'deviants'. And this takes him in some unexpected directions. Box is not an abolitionist; his overall perspective is one that seeks to *remedy* the system, not to rip it up and start again. As he seeks less punishment as a remedy for class and gender inequalities, he seeks more punishment for elite offending, not less. This much is clear in his proposals that are set out in the closing sections of Chapter 2 of *PCM*. But his answer to the undercriminalisation of the elite is not merely that the criminal justice system could put 'some old ideas…into effective operation' (Box 1983: 67).

After all, Box's project is not really about seeking legal solutions to the problems that law has created. He is a sociologist who is interested in social change, and knows that the answers do not lie in demands for more law. Yet one of the paradoxes that he raises is a rare one that was never really taken up by scholars of corporate crime. The implication is that a focus on corporate criminals, and a demand for more punishment, may heighten sympathy for the groups that *are* criminalised. Whereas, he argues, in the vast majority of cases, the usual suspects in state 'law and order' campaigns do not correspond to democratic pressures from below, the demand for the punishment of serious crimes committed by of elites is fundamentally a democratic one. This raises the possibility, implied, and not developed by Box, that democratic demands to act on corporate crime will plausibly weaken the public demand for punitive responses against the usual suspects.

And ultimately, Box is not optimistic about the effectiveness of exposing the contradictions inherent in criminal law. Indeed, his response to the question, 'What can be done to reduce significantly the volume of killing, maiming, and economic deprivation caused by corporate crime?' is a resounding: 'Fuck all!' (ibid: 63). Whilst a constant rally against the contradictions of law is a hallmark of Box's work, at the same time, he is very well aware of the limits of this approach:

> Pushing the state and its legal institutions to act consistently with their own principles at least brings out the contradictions between what they say they are doing and what they are actually doing. Publicizing this may undermine their legitimacy, an outcome they would want to avoid. In response, they may close the gap, if only slightly, between principles and practices. (ibid: 67)

What would Box say about the specific examples discussed in this chapter? Perhaps he would go back to the legal category of 'pre-meditated crime'. In most jurisdictions, if a crime is planned or designed in any way, then this is taken to be something that aggravates or makes it worse. In the US, for example, the most serious category of murder is first degree murder. The premeditated nature of a killing is something that would render it serious enough to be considered first degree murder, or indeed, first degree manslaughter. From a criminal lawyer's perspective, the prior knowledge that corporate executives had about the deadly effects of the substances they sold, and how they then positively acted to cover up the effects, makes the examples discussed in this chapter more serious in strictly doctrinal legal terms. But it is a stretch to suggest that by merely naming something, by 'labelling' or 'hailing' something, that this will be enough to precipitate social transformation.

Box did not write a book about social transformation, but it is clear in Chapter 2 of PCM that his analysis leads us inevitably to conclude that law reform cannot reset power. Transformation depends upon the balance of social forces. Talking about and writing about and shouting about corporate crime is only useful if:

> employees, consumers, and other corporate victims had their awareness sharpened and supported by trade unionism, consumerism, and environmentalism, and if the state and legal institutions could be shamed into closing the gap between lofty principles and tawdry practices. (ibid: 67)

We can find another way out of the seemingly endless cycle of corporate crime. It is buried just a little deeper in *PCM*. This is a way out that is not about criminal justice, or law, but about the structure of social power. At two places in the text, Box argues that the very best the law can do is reveal contradictions that lead to popular demands for the *public ownership* of corporations. And this is precisely where he ends Chapter 2 of *PCM*. There is no better message to end this chapter on:

> If the price of achieving justice for offending corporations is a more socialized mode of production, that may be a price worth paying if our lives, limbs, and property are protected from predatory transnational corporations. (ibid: 79)

References

Benson, M. 1985. Denying the Guilty Mind: Accounting for Involvement in a White-Collar Crime. *Criminology* 23: 583–607.

Bero, L. 2005. Tobacco Industry Manipulation of Research. *Public Health Reports* 120: 9.

Box, S. 1983. *Power, Crime and Mystification*. London: Sage.

Chossière, G.P., R. Malina, A. Ashok, I.C. Dedoussi, S.D. Eastham, R.L. Speth, and R.H. Barrett. 2017. Public Health Impacts of Excess NOx Emissions from Volkswagen Diesel Passenger Vehicles in Germany. *Environmental Research Letters* 12: 3.

Cohen, S. 2000. *States of Denial: Knowing About Atrocities and Suffering*. London: Polity.

Coleman, J. 1987. Toward an Integrated Theory of White-Collar Crime. *American Journal of Sociology* 93 (2): 406–439.
Cressey, D. (1953). *Other people's money: A study of the social psychology of embezzlement.* The Free Press.
Fooks, G., A. Gilmore, J. Collin, C. Holden, and K. Lee. 2013. The Limits of Corporate Social Responsibility: Techniques of Neutralization, Stakeholder Management and Political CSR. *Journal of Business Ethics* 112: 283–299.
Gardiner, B. 2019. *Choked: The Age of Air Pollution and the Fight for a Cleaner Future.* London: Granta.
Heath, J. 2008. Business Ethics and Moral Motivation: A Criminological Perspective. *Journal of Business Ethics* 83: 595–614.
Lubbers, E. 2012. *Secret Manoeuvres in the Dark: Corporate and Police Spying on Activists.* London: Pluto Press.
Lovelock, J. 2019. *Novascene: The Coming Age of Hyperintelligence.* London: Allen Lane.
Maxwell, J., and F. Briscoe. 1997. There's Money in the Air: The CFC Ban and DuPont's Regulatory Strategy. *Business Strategy and the Environment* 6 (5): 276–286.
Michaels, D. 2008. *Doubt is Their Product.* Oxford: Oxford University Press.
Minor, W. W. (1981). Techniques of neutralization: A reconceptualization and empirical examination. *Journal of Research in Crime and Delinquency, 18*(2), 295–318.
Monbiot, G. 2017. *Out of the Wreckage: A New Politics for an Age of Crisis.* London: Verso.
Montague, B. 2018. How the Neoliberal Dream Became the Reality of Thatcherism. *The Ecologist*, August 9. https://theecologist.org/2018/aug/09/how-neoliberal-dream-became-reality-thatcherism. Accessed 3 Aug 2023.
Moore, R., and E. McMullan. 2009. Neutralizations and Rationalizations of Digital Piracy: A Qualitative Analysis of University Students. *International Journal of Cyber Criminology* 3 (1): 441–451.
Morris, J. 1998. In Strictest Confidence. The Chemical Industry's Secrets. *Houston Chronicle*. Part One: Toxic Secrecy. June 28, 1A, 24A–27A; Part Two: High-Level Crime, June 29, 1A, 8A, 9A; and Part Three: Bane on the Bayou, July 26, 1A, 16A.
Nixon, R. 2011. *Slow Violence and the Environmentalism of the Poor.* Cambridge Mass.: Harvard University Press.
Patty, F., W. Yant, and C. Waite. 1930. Acute Response of Guinea Pigs to Vapors of Some New Commercial Organic Compounds: V. Vinyl Chloride. *Public Health Reports* (1896–1970) 45 (34): 1963.

Pellow, D. 2007. *Resisting Global Toxins*. Cambridge: MIT Press.

Piquero, N., S. Tibbetts, and M. Blankenship. 2005. Examining the Role of Differential Association and Techniques of Neutralization in Explaining Corporate Crime. *Deviant Behavior* 26 (2): 159–188.

Robin, M. 2014. *Our Daily Poison: From Pesticides to Packaging, How Chemicals Have Contaminated the Food Chain and Are Making us Sick*. New York: The New Press.

Sandler Clarke, J. 2017. British Company Still Exporting Dangerous Lead Petrol, Years After Saying It Would Stop. *Unearthed*, August 22. https://unearthed.greenpeace.org/2017/08/22/innospec-uk-lead-petrol-exports/. Accessed 3 Aug 2023.

Stauber, J., and S. Rampton. 1995. *Toxic Sludge is Good for You*. New York: Common Courage.

Sykes, G., and D. Matza. 1957. Techniques of Neutralization: A Theory of Delinquency. *American Sociological Review* 22: 664–670.

Vieraitis, M., N. Piquero, A. Piquero, S. Tibbetts, and M. Blankenship. 2012. Do Women and Men Differ in Their Neutralizations of Corporate Crime? *Criminal Justice Review* 37 (4): 478–493.

Weisskopf, M. 1988. CFCs Rise and Fall of Chemical 'Miracle'. *The Washington Post*, April 10. https://www.washingtonpost.com/archive/politics/1988/04/10/cfcs-rise-and-fall-of-chemical-miracle/9dc7f67b-8ba9-4e11-b247-a36337d5a87b/. Accessed 3 Aug 2023.

Whyte, D. 2014. Regimes of Permission and State-Corporate Crime. *State Crime* 3 (2): 237–246.

Whyte, D. 2016. It's Common Sense, Stupid! Corporate Crime and Techniques of Neutralization in the Automobile Industry. *Crime, Law and Social Change* 66 (2): 165–181.

Whyte, D. 2020. *Ecocide*. Manchester: Manchester University Press.

Wright Mills, C. 2000. *The Power Elite*. Oxford: Oxford University Press.

5

'90 Seconds to Midnight': Climate Change, Planetary Collapse and the 'Mystification' of Environmental Crime

Reece Walters

Introduction

As the introduction to this book attests (Scott and Sim, this volume), Steven Box's confronting scholarship laid bare the hypocrisy and corruption of state and corporate power; radically challenged and championed the sociology of deviance through his critical analyses of the criminalisation process with an astute inculcation of discourses in science, law and political economy (Box 1981, 1983, 1987). He was an avid activist, standing toe-to-toe with campaigners for nuclear disarmament, condemning social inequality and thus shaping the lives of critical criminology's most esteemed pioneers (cf Young 1988)—an inspiration for modern academics working in a world dominated by neoliberal political ideologies that suppress dissent, ferment mediocrity, and endorse the status quo of state conformity and employee obsequiousness. There is

---

Bulletin of the Atomic Scientists (2023).

R. Walters (✉)
Deakin University, Melbourne, VIC, Australia
e-mail: reece.walters@deakin.edu.au

© The Author(s), under exclusive license to Springer Nature Switzerland AG 2023
D. G. Scott and J. Sim (eds.), *Demystifying Power, Crime and Social Harm*, Critical Criminological Perspectives, https://doi.org/10.1007/978-3-031-46213-9_5

no shortage of academic scholarship per se, and criminological research specifically; that has been silenced, dismissed and marginalised for its expertise that has shattered contemporary thinking and rocked the foundation of government predisposition (Hope and Walters 2008; Drake and Walters 2015; Butler 2022). I am not for a moment suggesting that all academic endeavour should be integral to political and public debate, most of it is not. Nor, however, should it be actively cherry-picked or ruthlessly debunked by those in power for political and profitable means. Yet, knowledge of all sorts should be permitted to 'breathe', to be disseminated openly and widely, for all people to make up their own minds without fear or favour. As Box (1983: 223) so forthrightly and eloquently observed; …

> in a truly democratic society, citizens should have the right to criticize effectively those in power to arrest, prosecute and imprison. The criminal justice system personnel should be accountable not only for *who* they criminalize, but *why*, and in *whose* interests.

However, herein lies a dilemma. Not all knowledge is openly available nor is it disseminated widely; it is controlled and manipulated by those in power to advance specific political and corporate agendas; most often without public input and oversight.

As an illustration of this manipulation and mystification of knowledge, this chapter focuses on the perils of human-induced climate change through escalating greenhouse gas emissions that continue to pose devasting challenges for future environmental security and preservation. The compelling knowledge of climate catastrophe has been deliberately obscured from the public for decades through 'climate denial but the comprehensive and most recently released reports of the Intergovernmental Panel on Climate Change [IPCC] emphasises the stark and dire consequences of unmitigated CO_2 outputs and increased global warming' (Intergovernmental Panel on Climate Change [IPCC] 2022, 2023). The United Nations Secretary-General, António Guterres, has made an urgent warning to all nations stating: 'This report is a clarion call to massively fast-track climate efforts by every country and every sector and on every timeframe. Our world needs climate action on all fronts: everything, everywhere, all at once' (cited in Harvey 2023: 1). The climate change debate and its links to global insecurity, financial and environmental loss perpetuate exacerbated victimisation on the world's most marginal and impoverished (White 2019). Moreover, the global increases in environmental crime are a devastating and significant factor deleteriously impacting on climate change (United Nations Office on Drugs and Crime [UNODC] 2022).

This chapter, in honour of Steven Box, emphasises the avarice of the powerful, within normalised discourses of fiscal prosperity and market regulation and examines the contexts for environmental crime and despoliation to flourish. It seeks to demystify the global harms associated with environmental crime, and in doing so, critique how constructed legal apparatuses continue to reflect and perpetuate the interests and actions of the powerful that result in 'avoidable killing' (Box 1983: 9), dislocation and widespread harm of the world's most powerless.

The Mystification of Climate Change and Environmental Crime

Who are the real villains; those most dangerous offenders of harm and suffering in society? Steven Box challenges us to critique public and political discourses and the official statistics and narratives routinely and repeatedly portrayed by criminal justice agencies. As he cogently argues:

> Who are these 'villains' driving us into a state of national agoraphobia? We are told a fairly accurate and terrifying glimpse can be obtained of 'our' Public Enemies by examining the convicted imprisoned populations… Thus the typical people criminally victimizing and forcing us to fear each other and fracture our sense of 'community' are young uneducated males, who are often unemployed, living in a working-class impoverished neighbourhood, and frequently belong to an ethnic minority. (Box 1983: 2)

It is essential that we grasp Box's challenge and seek to identify villains and topics of villainy often absent from justice, yet responsible for immense global environmental harm.

The Intergovernmental Panel on Climate Change (IPCC) continues to highlight the hazardous consequences of ongoing greenhouse gas emissions inertia, and the urgent need to transition to renewable energies (IPCC 2022, 2023). A position endorsed at the November 2022 COP27 in Egypt by the United Nations Secretary-General, António Guterres. In his opening address reiterating the urgency and emergency of the impending climate disaster stating:

> …We are in the fight of our lives and we are losing … And our planet is fast approaching tipping points that will make climate chaos irreversible …. We are on a highway to climate hell with our foot on the accelerator. (cited in Harvey and Carrington 2022: 2)

This is a powerful statement, it is a call to arms, and it is a challenge to world leaders to do more in the fight for ongoing human existence against those who deny climate change and perpetuate planetary demise. Yet, twelve months on from this urgent global warning from a respected world leader and the situation has worsened. The IPCC (2023: 3) report asserts a more dire and condemning global position; arguing that the planetary position has deteriorated stating:

> …in 2018, IPCC highlighted the unprecedented scale of the challenge required to keep warming to 1.5°C. Five years later, that challenge has become even greater due to a continued increase in greenhouse gas emissions. The pace and scale of what has been done so far, and current plans, are insufficient to tackle climate change.

The perils of humanity and non-human species are globally monitored by various international institutions. The most influential and reputable is the Doomsday Clock, established in 1947 by atomic scientists who had worked on the Manhattan Project.[1] Its intention was to provide

---

[1] The Manhattan Project was a nuclear weapons research and development initiative undertaken by the United States, United Kingdom and Canadian Governments between 1942 and 1946.

5 '90 Seconds to Midnight': Climate Change, Planetary ...

a symbolic representation, based on the evidence of available destructive technologies, contemporary conflicts and geopolitical instability, of the likelihood of humanity annihilating itself. Throughout the past six decades, the Clock has become a symbol or warning to humanity of the likelihood of human extinction. When the Clock is set at midnight, then a panel of world nuclear, physical and climate scientists, who meet twice a year, will have decided that based on available scientific facts, humanity is facing imminent extinction. The Clock's latest setting was positioned at 90 seconds to midnight, its most alarming positioning in six decades (Bulletin of the Atomic Scientists 2023).

The perils identified by the Doomsday Clock are for Steven Box alluded to in his analyses of crimes and injuries of the powerful that are normalised within the capitalist system. Box challenges us all with his stern and sharp assertion:

> What can be done to reduce significantly the volume of killing, maiming and economic deprivation caused by corporate crime? One brief terse answer is **** all!'. According to a more polite version of this argument, these crimes are embedded and endemic within the capitalist system. The prioritization of profit under conditions of environmental uncertainty inevitably leads to persistent and chronic levels of corporate crime. No piecemeal liberal reform will make one iota of difference. Only when the means of production and distribution are socialized will the incidence of corporate crime diminish…But there is no hope of that occurring in the foreseeable future…there is no reason to believe that we will see the lights going down on capitalism in our lifetime. (Box 1983: 63)

This quote from Box sets the scene for the mystification examined throughout this chapter. Human-induced climate change is the most pressing and significant problem facing humanity's ongoing safety and security (UN Human Rights 2023). The threats posed by nuclear weapons, military and rogue dictatorships, and political corruption are deemed less dramatic than the realities presented by global warming and

---

The project's laboratory was based in Las Alamos in New Mexico USA, and was responsible for developing the deadly atomic bombs that were dropped on the Japanese cities of Hiroshima and Nagasaki in August 1945 (see Reed 2019).

its impacts on human and non-human species alike. The French philosopher and anthropologist Bruno Latour, who sadly passed away in 2022, challenged world leaders and the international community to urgently address what many are calling an 'extinction crisis'. As Latour (2017: 80) asks:

> If there is no planet, no earth, no soil, no territory to house the Globe of globalization to which all countries claimed to be heading, what should we do? Either we deny the existence of the problem, or else we seek to come down to earth. For each of us, the question now becomes: 'Are you going to keep nursing dreams of escape, or are you going to search for a land in which you and your children might live?' This is what now divides people, much more than knowing whether you are politically on the right or the left. The United States had two solutions. By finally realising the extent of the change in circumstances, and the hugeness of their responsibility, they could finally become realistic, leading the free world out of the abyss; or they could sink into denial.

The abyss Latour identifies is the midnight hour on the Doomsday Clock, the moment at which humanity's extinction is looming (cf South and Walters 2020). Yet despite these warnings, air pollution and toxic emissions are accelerating, and environmental crime is emerging as a key threat to global security and 'the survival of all living things' (Europol 2022). Air pollution kills an estimated seven million people each year (World Health Organisation 2023). These 'avoidable killings' or 'deaths', to quote Box (1983: 10), are caused by greenhouse gas emissions and linked to fossil fuel combustion, deforestation, and the industrial activities of the world's most economically wealthy and powerful nations (Evans 2021). Moreover, the post-Covid period of mounting capital production and global trade has witnessed a substantial rise in international air pollution and a dramatic reduction in air quality (United Nations Climate Change 2022). This acceleration of greenhouse emissions continues to have devastating consequences for the world's lowest producing emission countries (Walters 2020). Indeed, what Steven Box (1983: 78) referred to as 'the internationalization of capital and the concentration of power' or the 'political economy of speed', has arguably resulted in the escalating release of methane, one of the deadliest and most damaging greenhouse gas emissions, to an all-time high (World Meteorological Organisation 2022). Moreover, it is the low-lying South Pacific nations with insignificant carbon footprints such as Tuvalu, Vanuatu and Maldives that experience the worst impacts of climate change; something such nations have highlighted and lamented for years (Natano 2022). The perils faced by such nations is the creation of environmental refugees in what some argue is a form of 'climate apartheid' (Brisman et al. 2018: 303).

In 2022, a total of 18 nations, led by Vanuatu, pursued their case for climate justice in the United Nations General Assembly seeking the intervention of international courts (Amnesty International 2022). The resolution championed by Vanuatu was unilaterally adopted and was supported by more than 100 nations, however, the world's biggest polluters notably the USA and China, strenuously objected. In early 2023, the United Nations General Assembly accepted the resolution and submission of the eighteen nations and has referred the matter to the International Court of Justice (ICJ) for a decision (United Nations High Commissioner for Refugees 2023). The (ICJ) will now assess the legal obligations of states to protect current and future generations from climate change after countries backed the UN resolution (Hodgson 2023). The decision of the ICJ could increase the risk of future litigation for countries failing to adhere to existing international laws, while providing legal guidance to governments about what they must do to defend human rights and the environment from climate polluting harm (Lakhani 2023). This legal development has significant repercussions for international criminal law (discussed below) and the responsibilities of nation states to uphold the human right to a safe, clean and healthy environment for present and future generations.

As Steven Box (1983: 12) argued four decades ago, criminal laws should reflect assaults 'whose injuries become apparent years later, such as those resulting from working in a polluted factory where the health and risk was known to the employer but concealed from the employee'. The contemporary and influential political theorist, Steve Vanderheiden, agrees with Box and has called for 'atmospheric justice'. He suggests an international pollution and climate change regulatory regime based on equity, harm and compensation. In essence, he advocates for the 'polluter pay principle' within a framework of 'fault-based liability' that includes responsibility and accountability for historical emissions. However, such measures suggested in the draft stages of the Kyoto Protocol were successfully defeated by the United States and other major polluting countries. As Vanderheiden (2008: 231) argues:

> Rather than holding the bigger historical polluters responsible for their greater contributions to the problem by assessing them greater remedial burdens, the protocol in effect rewarded them by grandfathering their historical pollution rates, allowing those nations that had done the least to minimise pollution in the past to continue polluting at significantly higher levels than those nations that lower historical emissions.

To remedy this, he foresaw the importance of internationally agreed upon air pollution targets with a system for compensating low emitting nations for the environmental and human impacts of atmospheric injustices not of their doing. Unlike Kyoto and the carbon credit system, he asserts that a new international independent climate change committee, with representatives from various nations, collects and analyses air quality data and policies from individual countries. The recent resolution of the UN General Assembly to potentially hold polluting nations to account for their impact on low-carbon-footprint countries is a poignant reminder of the international community seeking to redress, albeit slowly, the injustice experienced by victims of rapacious capitalist accumulation. Again, the insightful forethought of Steven Box must be revered for his insistence on being in the 'polemicists camp' (cf, Taylor 1972: 14).

For other commentators, the deliberate violations of air pollution targets combined with climate denial is a form of intentional killing (Hertsgaard 2017), and for others, it constitutes an act of ecocide (Higgins 2015). For the now-departed highly acclaimed and internationally renowned environmental lawyer, Polly Higgins, the term 'ecocide' (discussed below) is 'the extensive damage, destruction to or loss of ecosystems of a given territory, whether by human agency of by other causes, such an extent that peaceful enjoyment by the inhabitants of that territory has been severely diminished' (cf Higgins 2010: 12). If humans are responsible for this ecological loss, then Higgins argues that ecocide should be included into the Statute of Rome where perpetrators of mass environmental destruction can be convicted in similar ways to offenders processed for crimes against humanity (Higgins 2015). As such, the remit and definition of 'environmental crime' must be expanded beyond existing national and transnational protocols, directives and laws that seek to protect ecosystems and biodiversity; to include those powerful elected personnel and legitimate commercial entities that authorise, or fail to redress, actions that decimate natural habitats or create and perpetuate conditions that compromise and erode human health and well-being (South and Walters 2020; Walters 2017, 2019).

However, David Whyte in his powerful critique of the evolving processes of the criminalisation of ecocide provides a stark warning of how corporations are not only expertly astute at avoiding responsibility for their actions through existing mechanisms of global justice but may utilise such legal developments as those proposed in the amendments to the Statue of Rome to their commercial and legal advantage (Whyte 2020—discussed further later).

Green Criminology and Climate Criminality

Green criminology continues to evolve as a dynamic multidisciplinary approach to addressing behaviours and actions that compromise and threaten the integrity of the planet. Discourses in green criminology have for some time unearthed, exposed, examined and critiqued harmful actions, notably of powerful elites within frameworks of environmental crime (Beirne and South 2007; Brisman and South 2020). As a criminological enterprise it is:

> a collection of new and innovative voices within the criminological lexicon, and its engagement with diverse narratives seeks to identify, theorise and respond to environmental issues of both global and local concern. The expansion of green criminological perspectives serves to harness and mobilise academic, activist, and governmental interests to preserve, protect and develop environmental issues. (Walters 2013: 4)

It is an enterprise consistent with Boxian endeavour, notably that green criminology, in its 'pursuit of social justice and human rights', can identify and expose 'environmental problems' and converting them to 'historical facts' (South and Brisman 2013: 99). Such an agenda inevitably involves an examination of the intersection of the concepts of harm, power and justice and also of the ways in which power is mobilised to justify a market model of capitalism with unjust and harmful consequences for the environment and the world's most vulnerable peoples. Therefore, green criminologies extend critical rethinking of the parameters and horizons of the criminological landscape. Such a rethinking requires a reflection on how humans relate to the environment and what constitutes acceptable and unacceptable exploitations of flora, fauna and natural resources. While legal interventions seek to protect the environment, the imperatives of market economies and free trade perpetuated by powerful institutions and governments provide the impetus for the continuance of environmental crimes. Moreover, environmental harms caused by nations and corporations that continue to exceed pollution targets, have acerbated climate change dramatically and worsened global air quality. Again, Box when referring to the silence of state crime over the bombing of innocent civilians at the hands of the US Government, reminds us:

> …that the criminal law…condemns the importation of murderous terrorist acts…but goes all quiet when governments export or support avoidable acts of killing usually against the underdeveloped countries' poor. (Box 1983: 9–10)

As such, those states and corporations that deliberatively, intentionally and repeatedly exceed pollution targets must be viewed as the pariahs of global security and as the environmental criminals of future generations. To further support this point, the World Meteorological Organization identifies that increasing hot and dry conditions have produced unprecedented wildfires that have resulted in rapidly declining air quality that will destroy ecosystems, human livelihoods and health (United Nations Climate Change Learning Partnership 2022). Such wild or bushfires have been identified as a major cause of biodiversity mortality, rises in carbon emissions and the death and illness of the world's most vulnerable people. The increase in greenhouse gas emissions acerbates global warming including sea temperatures that act as fire accelerates, with devastating impacts on global fauna and flora (Walters 2022).

A new term emerging alongside environmental criminal is 'climate criminal', a label applied to climate deniers and perpetrators responsible for global ecological catastrophes. It is also a label attributed to powerful political and corporate leaders who execute their authority in ways that decimate the natural environment (South and Walters 2020). The interface of green criminological scholarship with discourses of climate emergency remainsq environmentally and politically salient (White 2021). As such, green criminological narratives have for several years continued to assert and promote 'ecocide' (discussed below) as an international crime to hold powerful elites to account for actions that substantially destroy the natural environment (White and Kramer 2015; Lynch et al. 2021).

The Center for Biological Diversity (2018: 1) argues that … 'Unlike past mass extinctions, caused by events like asteroid strikes, volcanic eruptions, and natural climate shifts, the current crisis is almost entirely caused by *us* — humans'. This insightful and factful position has shaped the terminological development and inculcation of 'climate criminality' within the criminological landscape and seeks to capture those in positions of state and corporate power whose action result in climate change and devastating planetary demise.

Planetary Protection—'Boxian' Forays and Forecasts

Having demystified the harmful actions of climate criminals, it is pertinent to draw inspiration from Steven Box in asserting planetary protection. Hence, Box's argument for an ideological turn, combined with grassroots activism provides the platform for a criminological scholarship seeking environmental justice. The first leaf from the Steven Box book of not only speaking truth to power but confronting power head-on; is to deconstruct existing legal landscapes that promotes an alternative that captures and prosecutes the worst environmental offenders.

The legal and criminological momentum for holding corporate and political leaders accountable for their environmental destructive decision-making is taking hold. What may once have been seen radical and futuristic within the earliest discussions of corporate crime, is no longer the case, when the preservation of the planet is now a global imperative and compromising environmental integrity is increasingly being framed within discourses of criminalisation and emerging ecocide debates (Walters 2022). As the Head of the Law Unit at the Division of the United Nations Environment Programme has recently stated; 'The right to a safe, clean, healthy and sustainable environment is legally recognised in 155 countries' (Raine, cited in United Nations Environment Programme [UNEP] 2021). Emerging ecocide laws, therefore, seek to ensure that not only is the global environment protected and preserved, and that deleterious impacts of climate change are averted, but also that all human rights are comprehensively realised. As such, the global increase in climate litigation has witnessed more than a thousand cases brought in the past six years from school children to senior citizens against governments and corporations across dozens of countries (Setzer and Higham 2021).

The issue of ecocide and its concomitant connection with climate criminality is in its infancy within socio-legal and criminological debates (White 2021). The bourgeoning ecocidal laws and emerging environmental international treaties, conventions and protocols provide legal pathways to hold governing and corporate leaders to account for the despoliation of the environment continues to gather momentum where green criminological discourses seek to push new horizons (Gacek and Jochelson 2022). In doing so, such scholarship ensures that the discipline of criminology remains not only relevant, but at the forefront of human security and planetary protection (White and Hasler 2019).

As such, proposals are before the UN seeking to include ecocide as the 5th international crime against within the Rome Statute, alongside genocide, crime against humanity, war crimes and crimes of aggression (Hesketh 2021). The Stop Ecocide Foundation, a global NGO and a consortium of international legal experts drafted a formal submission to make ecocide a recognised and triable crime within the International Criminal Court where it means 'unlawful or wanton acts committed with knowledge that there is a substantial likelihood of severe and either widespread or long-term damage to the environment being caused by those acts' (Stop Ecocide International 2021: 5).

To date, ten countries, influenced by global legal debates, have inculcated 'ecocide law' within their domestic legal arrangements to hold individuals, corporations and governments to account for various acts of environmental destruction. The defining and framing of the ecocide debate remains fluid and contested. If ecocide is to be implemented within the International Criminal Court as a crime, similar to genocide, war crimes, crimes against humanity and crimes of aggression it must be substantiated as having identifiable devastating impacts, and potentially proven with evidence of intention, maleficence and or negligence by powerful and political actors (Alberro, and Daniele 2021). As a criminological concept, ecocide is evolving within an unprecedented and uncharted political and legal terrain. If it is to be adopted by the necessary seventy-five per cent of signatory countries to the ICC to formally enact it as a new State of Rome criminal offence, it must be defined, framed and prosecuted within the lived trauma, loss and long-term ecological impacts of victims (human and non-human) that are most affected. As a current judge of the International Criminal Court, His Honour Sir Howard Morrison has recently stated:

> I've always said, and I maintain it, that if an environmental offence is egregious enough to affect a large number of people, then why not prosecute it as a crime against humanity, which is already on the statute book of the ICC? I don't see why an inventive prosecutor could not make out a perfectly proper case, if enough people are egregiously affected. (cited in Turok-Squire 2022: 2)

The framing of the ecocide debate should be influenced by criminological discourses of harm, environmental injustice and political deviance. In doing so, such framing of ecocide must move beyond the limitations of existing national and international criminal law (Whyte 2020). Moreover, as South (2014: viii) has argued, it is imperative that criminology and criminologists unearth, examine and highlight harms and crimes omitted by state scrutiny and subsequent judicial processes. In doing so, the discipline of criminology must continue in 'making visible the invisible', or as Brisman (2014: 63) incisively argues, the importance of 'visual acuity', where the intellectually grasping of ideas such as climate change, for example, are embedded in experiences where the 'see' and 'feel' of environmental devastation become realised within a broader public conscience beyond those immediately effected (cf Walters 2022).

The second leaf from the Boxian book is the path of activism and direct action (see Cunliffe and Morrison, this volume). The *modus operandi* of this trajectory of scholarship and frontline intervention is best surmised by the powerful words of Elie Wiesel, Nobel Laurette and holocaust survivor. He stated:

> We must always take sides. Neutrality helps the oppressor, never the victim. Silence encourages the tormentor, never the tormented. Sometimes we must interfere. When human lives are endangered, when human dignity is in jeopardy, national borders and sensitivities become irrelevant. Wherever men or women are persecuted because of their race, religion, or political views, that place must—at that moment—become the center of the universe. (Wiesel 1986:1. cf Wiesel 1987)

This quote is a powerful reminder of Steven Box's 'radical reflexiveness'—as mentioned, a call 'to get up early', and seek out the real harms in society often overlooked by the established infrastructure of criminal law and criminal justice. Such an approach requires academic criminologists to be bold, assertive, confrontational and always at the front lines of agitation and contestation. An activist criminology promotes 'dissent', revolution', 'active engagement', 'grassroot social movement' and 'protest' in pursuit of justice. It is, quite simply, 'one of criminologists engaging in social and/or legal justice at individual, organizational, and/or policy levels' (Belnap 2015: 7). The activist enterprise within critical criminology is premised on progressive, left-leaning ambitions seeking peace, social equality and justice (DeKeersedy and Dragiewicz 2018). It is a knowledge of resistance that speaks truth to power, advocates for the voices of injustice and champions social, economic and environmental inequality—it is a deviant knowledge (Walters 2003)

Such Boxian voices of dissent have never before been more needed than in the area of environmental crime and climate criminality. The deniers of climate change comprise a powerful global lobby (Frumhoff and Oreskes 2015). Indeed, the link between climate change denial and politically conservative think tanks has been well-established, where non-peer-reviewed books and articles are disseminated as powerful 'science' in a persuasive attempt to control, censure and neutralise the overwhelming caucus of reputable science identifying the undeniable existence of global warming and its devastating effects (Walters 2018).

Furthermore, in recent years, we have witnessed emerging discourses in knowledge politics and information technology. The German cultural studies expert Nico Stehr has written extensively on the ways that science and technology have coalesced around market forces to dominate the agendas of politics and innovation (Stehr 2005). In this hierarchy of knowledge, it is science and, notably, its market branding in 'innovation' that triumph and assert a dominant position in political priorities. For many commentators, this science-driven era of knowledge politics is viewed as the 'scientification of public policy', where the values and needs of people are secondary to the aspirations and discoveries of science (Frickel 2013: 6). It is here that the climate deniers, exacerbated by populist and Trumpian politics, have systemically eroded the democratisation of knowledge and, in its place, is emerging a knowledge politics (grown out of ignorance, self-interest and the desire to maintain power and profit that were forewarned by Box in *Power, Crime and Mystification*), that emphasise specific scientific developments that the public may embrace, yet serve to enhance economic innovation at the expense of social and environmental innovation. Of course, the corporate tentacles of climate denial are embedded in the fossil fuel industry and in those technological innovations all receiving political support through tax cuts and key government advisory and policy-making appointments (Walters 2018; Mazzoni 2017). The need to robustly action a greening of the criminological landscape with global networks of collective environmental concern is paramount to future human and ecological security.

Climate 'Justice For All'

Steven Box's unorthodoxy and his willingness to stand alone and agitate is a key message that this chapter has advanced—notably his fore-running force, leadership and advocacy for an activist criminology coupled with his desire to tear down the edifice of a safe, pretentious and sycophantic state-discipline, into a people's criminology of social justice for a more equitable world. Nowadays, there exists an 'academic fear', an unwillingness to speak out, to stand up and to disagree; all in favour of a career-advancing compliance and a neoliberal university ethos of financial avarice. In the spirit of Box, it is important to stand up for the fight first. To strategically advance the career in line with the managerial and safe politics of an academic institution—will probably result in promotion but may cost you your soul. I am reminded of Oscar Wilde's powerful 1891 (Wilde 2004) critique of capitalism and its desolation of the human soul in his 'The Soul of Man Under Socialism'. Influenced by the socialist and anarchist historian Peter Kropotkin, the famous poet and playwright provides an expose of his political views and the deteriorating state of British society governed by principles of private property and capital accumulation. For Wilde, the compliance of nineteenth-century English society, notably those educated and status individuals that should stand against injustice and the plight of the impoverished but did not—were akin to slave owners who perceived their treatment of slaves as kind and just. For Wilde, the human spirit was not only crushed but corrupted by the shackles of the capitalist enterprise.

Hence, within contemporary criminological scholarship, those who choose to make money from states and corporations seeking policy or product endorsement, become complicit in perpetuating injustice. To stand outside the increasingly lucrative financial domain of commercial funding, is to take a risk; it is to be an advocate of deviant knowledge (Walters 2003). Failure to do so, may result in you losing that piece of yourself that matters most. However, as Steven Box has taught us, it is important to look inside ourselves and ask these fundamental and life-changing questions: what do I stand for? And what do I stand up for? Two simple questions that define and differentiate the true critical scholar. Someone willing to put aside the perceived benefits of conformity and neutrality, to pursue the path of tackling social injustices. As the influential and inspirational scholar Joy James has argued, 'show up' and represent your cause without fear and with a willingness to revolutionise ideas, whatever the cost—in doing so, there is no better peace of conscience or pride in one's ambition and, for example, the *European Group for the Study of Deviance and Social Control* is a beacon of such values (James 2022: 4; cf Gilmore et al. 2013).

The discipline of criminology must continue to pick up the mantle of Box and engage with national and global injustices, topics he referred to as 'mystified', issues concealed by the real 'villains', (discussed throughout this collection); notably those powerful and privileged that shape the social and political order and in doing so create a new ideology of crime and criminal justice—one that omits, protects and mystifies actions of immense and actual harm (cf Quicker 1987).

Conclusion

Steven Box did not mince words—he vociferously advocated for, unearthed and advanced, the plight and struggle of society's most marginalised and discriminated against peoples. He also charted a clear passage for pursuing the great injustices laid bare before all to see—the unashamed actions of political and corporate elites who prioritise profit and personal interest, and in doing so, disregard and undermine the needs of the most hurting and vulnerable. I never had the privilege of meeting Steven Box, but his written words are immortalised in the pen for all to admire. His words ooze social justice and express a passion to end the pain of an ideologically misguided political and criminal justice system that overwhelmingly targets and condemns the poor and needy, while strategically and conveniently ignoring the most harmful actors in society—the powerful, who exert privilege to maintain a status quo that perpetuates self-interest and an enduring inequity for maximum political and fiscal gain.

Steven Box is an inspiration for the critical criminological scholar; he pioneered and charted unknown or unfavourable horizons. And did so at personal and professional risk, with an unwavering commitment to expose the unseen; to shine light on the shadows and to bring unspoken and unspeakable harms into the spotlight of social and intellectual scrutiny.

The Doomsday's Clock current setting of 90 seconds to midnight can only be redressed with global political will and grand-scale community action. It is incumbent upon academic and criminological scholars to ensure that such transnational momentum is harnessed, mobilised and operationalised in ways that expose, apprehend and hold to account those individuals and corporations that compromise and destroy the essentials of human and non-human life.

Steven Box was not a person of half measures. He detested academic neutrality and cowardice and taught us to seek out injustice—and to unreservedly stand up and speak out against the gravest harms in society. Like all species on this planet, humanity is vulnerable to extinction; we require fundamental and basic needs for survival—the free-market ideologies of rampant capitalism are extinguishing the breath of all living things. It is time to act; to put aside immaterial things, to demystify, expose and challenge the narratives, ideological and prejudices of the powerful and prevent planetary extinction. As Steven Box (1983: 14) poignantly and powerfully advises:

> For too long too many people have been socialized to see crime and criminal through the eyes of the state. There is nothing left, as Matza points out, but mystification. This is clearly revealed in the brick wall of indignation which flattens any suggestion that the crime problem defined by the state is not the only crime problem, or that criminals are not only those processed by the state. There is more to crime and criminals than the state reveals. But most people cannot see it.

As Boxian scholars and adherents to his message, it is now our charge to ensure that people 'do see it', to question the status quo, to challenge official discourse and in doing so, to seek out harm and injustice not defined nor investigated and processed by agents of the State. But to shine light on, to 'unearth' and 'excavate' society's most deviant actors and most deleterious actions in an ongoing exercise of 'radical reflexiveness'. Arguably, an uncomfortable and often risky process that requires relentlessness perseverance, 'to get up early' as Box suggested, and shake the ideological foundations of established criminological thinking—but a worthwhile and enduring endeavour that speaks truth to power in the pursuit of justice for a better world.

Acknowledgements I would like to acknowledge Nigel South for his insightful input into this chapter. Moreover, my immense thanks to editors, David Scott and Joe Sim, for discerning and knowledgeable feedback that vastly improved this chapter.

References

Alberro, H., and L. Daniele. 2021. Ecocide: Why Establishing a New International Crime Would Be a Step Towards Interspecies Justice. *The Conversation*, June 29.
Amnesty International. 2022. Climate Crisis: International Court Should Play Key Role in Delivering Climate Justice. https://www.amnesty.org/en/latest/news/2022/12/climate-crisis-international-court-should-play-key-role-in-delivering-climate-justice/. Accessed 3 Apr 2023.
Beirne, P., and N. South (eds.). 2007. *Issues in Green Criminology*. Collumpton: Willan.
Belnap, J. 2015. Activist Criminology: Criminologists' Responsibility to Advocate for Social and Legal Justice. *Criminology*. https://doi.org/10.1111/1745-9125.12063.
Box, S. 1981. *Deviance, Reality and Society*, 2nd ed. London: Holt, Rinehart and Winston.
Box, S. 1983. *Power, Crime and Mystification*. London: Tavistock.
Box, S. 1987. *Recession, Crime and Punishment*. London: Bloomsbury.
Brisman, A. 2014. The Visual Acuity of Climate Change. In *Invisible Crimes and Social Harms*, eds. P. Davies, P. Francie, and Y. Wyatt, 61–80. London: Palgrave.
Brisman, A., N. South, and R. Walters. 2018. Climate Apartheid and Environmental Refugees. In *The Palgrave Handbook of Criminology and the Global*

South, eds. K. Carrington, R. Hogg, J. Scott, and M. Sozzo, 301–323. London: Palgrave.

Brisman, A., and N. South (eds.). 2020. *Routledge International Handbook of Green Criminology*, 2nd ed. London: Routledge.

Bulletin of Atomic Scientists. 2023. Timeline: It is 90 Seconds to Midnight. https://thebulletin.org/doomsday-clock/2021-doomsday-clock-statement/. Accessed 1 Apr 2023.

Butler, J. 2022. Endangered Scholarship, Academic freedom, and the Life of Critique. *Critical times* 5 (2): 399–425.

Center for Biological Diversity. 2018. The Extinction Crisis. https://www.biologicaldiversity.org/programs/biodiversity/elements_of_biodiversity/extinction_crisis/. Accessed 12 Feb 2023.

DeKeseredy, W., and M. Dragiewicz (eds.). 2018. *Routledge Handbook of Critical Criminology*, 2nd ed. London: Routledge.

Drake, D., and R. Walters. 2015. Crossing the Line. Criminological Expertise, Policy Advice and the "Quarrelling Society". *Critical Social Policy* 35 (3): 414–433.

Europol. 2022. *Environmental Crime in the Age of Climate Change: 2022 Threat Assessment*. https://www.europol.europa.eu/publications-events/publications/environmental-crime-in-age-of-climate-change-2022-threat-assessment. Accessed 7 Jan 2023.

Evans. 2021. *Analysis: Which Countries Are Historically Responsible for Climate Change?* https://www.carbonbrief.org/analysis-which-countries-are-historically-responsible-for-climate-change/. Accessed 9 Feb 2023.

Frickel, S. 2013. Knowledge Politics. *Mobilizing Ideas.* https://mobilizingideas.wordpress.com/2013/04/01/knowledge-politics/. Accessed 12 Mar 2023.

Frumhoff, P., and O. Oreskes. 2015. *Fossil Fuel Firms Are Still Bankrolling Climate Denial Lobby Groups.* https://www.theguardian.com/environment/2015/mar/25/fossil-fuel-firms-are-still-bankrolling-climate-denial-lobby-groups. Accessed 4 Jan 2023.

Gacek, J., and R. Jochelson (eds.). 2022. *Green Criminology and the Law.* London: Palgrave.

Gilmore, J., D. Scott, and J. Moore (eds.). 2013. *Critique and Dissent: An Anthology to Mark 40 Years of the European Group for the Study of Deviance and Social Control.* Ottawa: Red Quill Books.

Harvey, F. 2023. Scientists Deliver 'Final Warning' on Climate Crisis: Act Now or It's Too Late. https://www.theguardian.com/environment/2023/mar/20/ipcc-climate-crisis-report-delivers-final-warning-on-15c. Accessed 21 Mar 2023.

Harvey, F., and D. Carrington. 2022. The World is on a "Highway to Climate Hell", UN Chief Warns at COP27 Summit. https://www.theguardian.com/environment/2022/nov/07/cop27-climate-summit-un-secretary-general-António-guterres. Accessed 10 May 2023.

Hesketh, R. 2021. How Ecocide Could Become an International Crime. https://www.bloomberg.com/news/articles/2021-06-25/how-ecocide-could-become-an-international-crime-quicktake. Accessed 18 Feb 2023.

Hertsgaard, M. 2017. Climate Denialism is Literally Killing Us'. *The Nation.* https://www.thenation.com/article/climate-denialism-is-literally-killing-us/. Accessed 4 Feb 2023.

Higgins, P. 2010. *Eradicating Ecocide: Laws and Governance to Prevent the Destruction of Our Planet.* London: Shepheard-Walwyn.

Higgins, P. 2015. *Eradicating Ecocide: Exposing Corporate and Political Practices Destroying the Planet*, 2nd ed. London: Shepheard-Walwyn.

Hodgson, C. 2023. Top UN Court to Assess Countries' Climate Obligations After Resolution Passes. https://www.ft.com/content/16bda3ea-a09c-4b31-b42d-0bf8d946841f. Accessed 4 Apr 2023.

Hope, T., and R. Walters. 2008. *Critical Thinking About the Uses of Research.* London: Centre for Crime and Justice Studies.

Intergovernmental Panel on Climate Change. 2022. *Climate Change 2022: Impacts, Adaptation and Vulnerability.* https://www.ipcc.ch/report/ar6/wg2/. Accessed 3 Feb 2023.

Intergovernmental Panel on Climate Change. 2023. Sixth Assessment Report. https://www.ipcc.ch/assessment-report/ar6/. Accessed 1 Apr 2023.

James, J. 2022. *In Pursuit of Revolutionary Love.* London: Divided Publishing.

Lakhani, N. 2023. United Nations Adopts Landmark Resolution on Climate Justice. https://www.theguardian.com/environment/2023/mar/29/united-nations-resolution-climate-emergency-vanuatu. Accessed 4 Apr 2023.

Latour, B. 2017. Europe as Refuge. In *The Great Regression*, ed. H. Geaselberger, 78–87. Cambridge: Polity.

Lynch, M., A. Fegadel, and M. Long. 2021. Green Criminology and State-Corporate Crime: The Ecocide-Genocide Nexus with Examples from Nigeria. *Journal of Genocide Research* 23 (2): 236–256.

Mazzoni, M. 2017. Top 10 Climate Deniers in Trump Administration. *Eco Watch.* https://www.ecowatch.com/climate-deniers-in-trump-administration-2518894384.html. Accessed 19 Jan 2023.

Natano, K. 2022. The Climate Crisis Is Making the Pacific Islands Uninhabitable. Who Will Help Preserve Our Nations? *Time Magazine.* https://time.com/6217104/climate-crisis-pacific-islands-uninhabitable/. Accessed 2 Apr

2023.

Quicker, J. 1987. Book Review: Power, Crime and Mystification. Steven Box. *Journal of Contemporary Criminal Justice* 3 (1). https://doi.org/10.1177/104 398628700300107. Accessed 14 Jan 2023.

Reed, B. 2019. *The History and Science of the Manhattan Project*. New York: Springer.

Setzer, J., and C. Higham. 2021. *Global Trends in Climate Change Litigation. 2021 snapshot.* https://www.lse.ac.uk/granthaminstitute/wp-content/uploads/2021/07/Global-trends-in-climate-change-litigation_2021-snapshot.pdf. Accessed 19 Nov 2022.

Stehr, N. 2005. *Knowledge Politics: Governing the Consequences of Science and Technology*. Abingdon: Routledge.

South, N. 2014. Foreword. Seeing the Invisible. In *Invisible Crimes and Social Harms,* eds. P. Davies, P. Francies, and T. Wyatt, 3–9. London: Palgrave.

South, N., and A. Brisman. 2013. Critical Green Criminology. Environmental Rights and Crimes of Exploitation. In *New Directions in Crime and Deviance*, eds. S. Winlow, and R. Atkinson, 99–111. London: Routledge.

South, N., and R. Walters. 2020. Power, Harm and the Threat of Global Ecocide. In *Crime, Harm and the State*, ed. L. Copson, E. Dimou, and S. Tombs, 139–178. Walton Hall: The Open University Press.

Stop Ecocide International. 2021. Legal Definition of Ecocide. https://www.stopecocide.earth/legal-definition. Accessed 20 May 2023.

Taylor, I. 1972. Book Review—S. Box. Deviance, Reality and Society. *The British Journal of Criminology* 12 (2): 201–203. https://academic.oup.com/bjc/article-abstract/12/2/201/345731?redirectedFrom=fulltext. Accessed 21 May 2023.

Turok-Squire, R. 2022. Inside the Mind of an International Criminal Court Judge. Sir Howard Morrison QC. https://lacuna.org.uk/justice/international-criminal-court-icc-judge-sir-howard-morrison-qc/. Accessed 4 Feb 2023.

United Nations Climate Change Learning Partnership. 2022. Air Quality Sinks as Climate Change Accelerates. https://unfccc.int/news/air-quality-sinks-as-climate-change-accelerates. Accessed 8 Feb 2023.

United Nations Environment Programme. 2021. How New Laws Could Help Combat the Planetary Crisis. https://www.unep.org/news-and-stories/story/how-new-laws-could-help-combat-planetary-crisis. Accessed 14 Nov 2022.

United Nations Human Rights. 2023. Comment by Human Rights Chief on Request for Climate Change Opinion from International Court of Justice. https://www.ohchr.org/en/taxonomy/term/790. Accessed 5 Apr 2023.

United Nations Refugees Agency. 2023. Global Appeal. https://reporting.unhcr.org/globalappeal.
United Nations Office on Drugs and Crime (UNODC). 2022. *Crimes that Affect the Environment*. https://www.unodc.org/res/environment-climate/resources_html/Crimes_that_Affect_the_Environment_and_Climate_Change.pdf. Accessed 12 Mar 2023.
Vanderheiden, S. 2008. *Atmospheric Justice. A Political Theory of Climate Change*. Oxford: Oxford University Press.
Walters, R. 2003. *Deviant Knowledge: Criminology, Politics and Policy*. Cullompton: Willan.
Walters, R. 2013. Ecomafia and Environmental Crime. In *Crime, Justice and Social Democracy*, ed. K. Carrington, M. Ball, E. O'Brien, and J. Tauri, 281–294. London: Palgrave.
Walters, R. 2017. Green Criminologies. In *Alternative Criminologies*, eds. P. Carlen, and F. Leandro Ayres, 165–181. London: Taylor and Francis.
Walters, R. 2018. Climate Change Denial: Making Ignorance Great Again. In *Ignorance, Power and Harm: Agnotology and the Criminological Imagination*, ed. A. Barton and H. Davis, 163–187. London: Palgrave.
Walters, R. 2019. Green Justice. In *Justice Alternatives*, eds. P. Carlen, and F. Leandro Ayres, 110–131. London: Routledge.
Walters, R. 2020. Air Pollution, Climate Change and International (in) Action. In *Emerald Handbook of Crime, Justice and Sustainable Development*, ed. J. Blaustein, K. Fitzgibbon, N. Pino, and R. White, 533–550. London: Emerald Publishing.
Walters, R. 2022. Ecocide, "Climate Criminals" and the Politics of Bushfires. *The British Journal of Criminology*. https://doi.org/10.1093/bjc/azac018/6574885.
White, R. 2019. Resisting Ecocide: Engaging in the Politics of the Future. In *Progressive Justice in an Age of Repression: Strategies for Challenging the Rise of the Right*, eds. W. DeKeseredy, and E. Currie. New York: Routledge.
White, R. 2021. *Theorising Green Criminology. Selected Essays*. London: Routledge.
White, R., and O. Hasler. 2019. Ecocide. In *The Routledge International Handbook of Violence Studies*, ed. W. DeKeseredy, C. Rennison, and A. Hall-Sanchez, 102–106. London: Routlege.
White, R., and R. Kramer. 2015. Critical Criminology and the Struggle Against Climate Change Ecocide. *Critical Criminology* 23 (4): 383–399.
Whyte, D. 2020. *Ecocide: Kill the Corporation Before it Kills Us*. Manchester: Manchester University Press.

Wiesel, E. 1986. The Nobel Prize. Acceptance Speech. Elie Wiesel. https://www.nobelprize.org/prizes/peace/1986/wiesel/acceptance-speech/. Accessed 24 May 2023.

Wiesel, E. 1987. *The Night Trilogy: Night, Dawn, The Accident*. London: Hill and Wang.

Wilde, O. 1891/2004. *The Soul of Man under Socialism*. London: Kessinger Publishing.

World Health Organisation. 2023. Air Pollution. https://www.who.int/health-topics/air-pollution#tab=tab_1. Accessed 4 Apr 2023.

World Meteorological Organization. 2022. More Bad News for the Planet: Greenhouse Gas Levels Hit New Highs. https://public.wmo.int/en/media/press-release/more-bad-news-planet-greenhouse-gas-levels-hit-new-highs. Accessed 6 Apr 2023.

Young, J. 1988. Note. Steven Box. 1937–1987. *The British Journal of Criminology*. https://academic.oup.com/bjc/article/28/1/95/363553. Accessed 9 Sep 2022.

6

Fighting for 'Justice for All' in an Era of Deepening Exploitation and Ecological Crisis

Elizabeth Bradshaw and Paul Leighton

Introduction

Reading Box's *Power, Crime and Mystification* (1983) today evokes a sense of familiarity. The general problems he raised have festered in Western democracies; variations of his critique are still being written—and largely ignored by traditional criminology. Decades of passionate critical criminologists have taken to heart the ideas of Box (and similar thinkers):

> The possible clue to our understanding most serious crimes can be located in power, not weakness, privilege, not disadvantage, wealth, not poverty. This is not an idea that has found much elbow room within traditional criminology. (Box 1983: 202)

E. Bradshaw
Central Michigan University, Mount Pleasant, MI, USA
e-mail: brads2ea@cmich.edu

P. Leighton (✉)
Eastern Michigan University, Ypsilanti, MI, USA
e-mail: pleighton@emich.edu

© The Author(s), under exclusive license to Springer Nature
Switzerland AG 2023
D. G. Scott and J. Sim (eds.), *Demystifying Power, Crime and Social Harm*, Critical Criminological Perspectives, https://doi.org/10.1007/978-3-031-46213-9_6

However, few who share this perspective would necessarily weave together the same strands of analysis, or do so in Box's direct and colorful language:

> (i) the growing concentration of economic power in national and transnational corporations is sometimes utilized to victimize large numbers of employers, consumers, and the general public; (ii) the enhanced legal powers of apprehension and investigation coupled with improved technological capacity of the police is sometimes used by officers to victimize criminally citizens and business, and; (iii) men who are powerful economically, politically, and physically occasionally impose themselves sexually on relatively powerless and vulnerable women. As opposed to all this unpleasantness, it was argued that women, a relatively powerless group, commit hardly any serious crimes in comparison with the endless spread-eagled trail of lifeless, injured, and robbed victims left in the path of predatory powerful men. (1983: 201)

In the 40 years since then, all three dynamics have intensified for the worse despite ongoing activism and social movements. Corporations are larger, have lobbied to make more harmful conduct legal, made regulatory and enforcement agencies defective by design, and bought mass media to spread messages that this is a just society (Reiman and Leighton 2023). Poor and minority adolescents face a school to prison pipeline or nexus (Goldman and Rodriguez 2022), and the wayward affluent end up in the for-profit Troubled Teen Industry (Mooney and Leighton 2019). While the #MeToo movement led to increases in reporting of sex crimes and arrests for sexual assault, there was a lesser effect on the number of cases solved by police (Levy and Mattsson 2022). An increasingly militarized police force does harm by responding to problems often caused by the malign neglect of public policy. They also harass residents over trivial infractions, often to raise revenue for the city through fines and fees, and too frequently do so with deadly violence against minorities. Decades of wars on crime and drugs have privileged increasingly harsh sentences and expanded police powers over crime prevention, drug treatment, and harm reduction in the face of a credible body of knowledge that 'get tough' policies would be ineffective in reducing crime (Reiman and Leighton 2023). Understanding why is a question with enormous significance for the next 40 years.

Further, Box's (1983: 202) call for a more robust democracy to contain the problem of corrupt power is still highly relevant. But it seems almost quaint to believe that governments can work against concentrated power and patriarchy, and for a wider public good that includes the most vulnerable. For example, a survey of 10,000 people aged 16–25 years, 1000 from each of ten countries, found young people felt a strong sense of betrayal. More than 60 percent said the government was dismissing people's distress, not doing enough to avoid a climate catastrophe, cannot be trusted, and were 'lying about the effectiveness of the actions they are taking'(Hickman et al. 2021: e869). They are not wrong. And in many ways, these struggles could frame a contemporary analysis if Box were to (re)write *Power, Crime and Mystification (PCM)*—as would his conclusion that 'the growth of a generation of young people in the decaying inner-cities, vast numbers of them with little or no experience of work and employment, is…not simply a set of social problems and deprivations, it is also a crisis for the political process' (Box 1983: 216). But if a crisis continues for 40 years, is it a crisis? If there isn't a crisis, what does it take to create enough of one to get meaningful change?

In honoring Box's legacy and advocacy for 'justice for all,' our chapter aims to connect Box to the young people growing up amid increasing exploitation, environmental destruction, and governments more intent on criminalizing youth than helping them. We reaffirm the reality of the crisis facing youth and the importance of nurturing rebellions by youth. Specifically, in the first section, we examine why, 40 years after Box, the dynamics of power, crime, and criminal justice have changed so little. We build on Box's discussion by integrating ideas from *The Rich Get Richer and the Poor Get Prison (RGR)* (Reiman and Leighton 2023) to offer a fuller but compatible theoretical explanation for the continuing injustice. Second, we critically examine the mystifications around the climate crisis by discussing the reality of climate crimes and carbon criminals (Kramer 2020). While traditional criminology has largely neglected the violence to our environment and the capitalist dynamics behind it, the fields of green criminology and state-corporate crime have maintained a focus on crimes of the powerful in a manner that Box would have appreciated. In the third section, consistent with Box's wider aspiration to challenge and diffuse existing power relations, we explore the ways in which power is being challenged in a variety of ways by people engaged in democratic protest against state and corporate elites set on criminalizing their dissent. In conclusion, we discuss how the challenge for the next 40 years is what we do about these injustices, so that a future retrospective can celebrate some progress. To this end, we examine several recent books about militant protest and the need for a more coherent politics and praxis to connect protest to the abolition of the criminal justice system and fossil fuel use.

'The Carnival Mirror': Concealing the Crimes of Power, Exaggerating the Crimes of the Poor

Box saw the real harms of street crimes but critiqued the disproportionate enforcement against them compared to the equally real and often more harmful crimes of the powerful. He further noted the 'very strong desire to move wayward adolescents from the "caring" hands of social workers and probation officers to the calloused hands of prison officers' (1983: 220). This process neutralizes potentially dangerous youth as well as controlling the poor, who are seen as the 'dangerous class.' At the same time, Box (1983: 6) recognizes the ideological functions of these patterns:

> The outcome of these processes is that the official portrait of crime and criminals is highly selective, serving to conceal crimes of the powerful and hence shore up their interests, particularly the need to be legitimated through maintaining the appearance of respectability. At the same time, crimes of the powerless are revealed and exaggerated, and this serves the interests of the powerful because it legitimizes their control agencies, such as the police and prison service, being strengthened materially, technologically, and legally, so that their ability to survey, harass, deter, both specifically and generally, actual and potential resisters to political authority is enhanced.

Perhaps 40 years later the situation is worse because crimes of the powerful have been hidden, including by mainstream criminology. Perhaps, too, the exaggeration of the crimes of the poor continues enough to drive further expansion of the system. Although *PCM* explores failures of the criminal justice system in different ways, *RGR* (Reiman and Leighton 2023) expands on Box by arguing that criminal justice policy continues to embrace three failures that serve to maintain the status quo through ideology.

The first failure is to fight crime in effective ways. Nations have pursued 'get tough' laws in the face of substantial evidence that such policies would be ineffective at best and criminogenic at worst. Further, ineffective strategies focused on police and mass incarceration have been pursued while ignoring crime prevention, drug treatment, and the social causes of crime. These concerns open up a new line of analysis, taking seriously the idea that it is almost like nations are trying to have a high crime rate. After all, Durkheim argued that crime and deviance are functional for promoting social solidarity. But if a society benefitted from deviance, was society 'organized in such a way as to promote this resource' with forces that 'recruit offenders and to commit them to long periods of service in the deviant ranks?' (cited in Reiman and Leighton 2023: 49).

While neither Durkheim nor Erikson critically interrogated how power, including state power, played into the drawing of in- and out-groups, it is not coincidental that the failure of criminal justice policy sets up the poor as criminals to be feared and hated instead of those who engage in financial predation, mass pollution, or hasten environmental catastrophe. Thus, while the system in the U.S. does repress millions of poor and marginalized people, the failures of criminal and social justice policies ensure that crimes by the poor will be at a level to be of ongoing public concern—and is an important way the poor remain identified with 'criminal' and 'dangerous.'

The second failure is to criminalize the harms of the powerful. The criminal justice system—from law making to sentencing—is like a carnival mirror that throws back a distorted image of the harms that threaten people (Reiman and Leighton 2023). It magnifies the real threats from street crime while mystifying the real (and often more significant) harms of the powerful. The process of enforcing the law, Box similarly observed, 'operates in such a way as to *conceal* crimes of the powerful against the powerless but to *reveal* and *exaggerate* crimes of the powerless against "everyone"' (1983: 6).

The third failure is to acknowledge and reduce class bias (while other social divisions based on gender, race, age, sexuality, and ability apply here too, we will be focusing specifically on class bias). The rich are less likely to be investigated, arrested, charged, convicted, and sentenced to prison when they commit the same crime (say, drug dealing) as the poor. The same applies when they commit versions of theft and fraud that are only available to the rich (wage theft, financial frauds).

Departing from *PCM*, *RGR* notes that none of these failures creates effective demand for change among those with the power to change the system. For example, the rich live in gated communities so they are less victimized by street crime; they benefit from the lack of criminalization of harms of the powerful (it is easier to run a profitable business) and class bias. These failures also confer *ideological benefits* for corporations and the affluent. While Box saw these as legitimating crime control targeted against the poor, the *RGR* adds that the identification of the poor with crime deflects the fear of the middle classes from the rich—who are harming and exploiting them—onto the poor. The corporate- and billionaire-owned media, as well as mainstream criminology, tell people that the threat is from the poor below them, not from the rich above. As the rich are not associated with criminality, solutions to the 'crime problem' do not advocate for increased business regulation, inspection, and sanction.

Further, justice systems focus on individual guilt in a way that 'diverts our attention from the possible evils in our institutions, and thus puts forth half the problem of justice as if it were the whole problem' (Reiman and Leighton 2023: 187). For example, the law against theft is 'a law against stealing what individuals presently own,' thereby legitimating current inequality. The criminal justice process also does not allow 'social adversity' defenses, so it implicitly reaffirms the reasonableness of that inequality. Such defenses, which have been proposed for decades, would allow courts to hear arguments about whether selling sex or drugs or committing property crimes was common in a neighborhood 'because that is the least worst—or only—way they can obtain enough money to survive' (Tonry 2020: 2). Without such defenses, inequality is obscured, and so too are the many criminogenic features of capitalism.

Because of the criminal justice system and broader ideological messages, both crime and poverty are seen as individual problems. Thus, inequality, capitalism, and neoliberalism are not scrutinized or targeted for change. When crime is seen as 'pathological' (Box 1983: 4), resulting from personality and bad choices, there are no social causes of crime and crime prevention programs seem less relevant. Although Americans, and others elsewhere, know we have the highest incarceration rate and police do violence to minorities, more cops and more prisons—with maybe a bit of reform—seems like the only answer.

Importantly, Box (1983: 214) did not want macro-level arguments to sound like conspiracies, and the *RGR* also avoids this (Reiman and Leighton 2023: 180). Despite examples of widespread and long-term elite wrongdoing, a conspiracy does not make the most sense of decades worth of public policy, both about street crime and business regulation, that has been the subject of public hearings and votes. The *RGR* suggests that 'historical inertia' (ibid: 181) best describes how the failures of justice generate no effective demand for change among those with the power to enact change.

Mystifications of State-Corporate Crime

In *PCM*, Box uses the concept of mystification to understand the ways in which the criminal justice system distorts the realities of crime. Questioning the disproportionate focus on street crimes at the expense of crimes by state officials and corporate elites, Box (1983: 3) posits:

> Maybe what is stuffed into our consciousness as *the* crime problem is in fact an illusion, a trick to deflect our attention away from other, even more serious crimes and victimizing behaviours, which objectively cause the vast bulk of avoidable death, injury, and deprivation.

Casting doubt on the view that the real crime problem stems from the pathologies of the poor, Box (1983: 4) draws attention toward those above us in the social hierarchy to observe 'serious crimes being committed by the people who are respectable, well-educated, wealthy, and socially privileged.' By concealing the crimes of the powerful against the powerless while exaggerating crimes committed by the powerless, the criminal legal system functions to paint a distorted image of crime. The real crime problem, Box (1983: 4) contends, comes from political leaders responsible 'for being or for protecting the "real" culprits.'

Although Box did not address the issue of climate catastrophe, it is a good example of his analysis and builds off his recognition of harm to the public because of air pollution and the failure of criminology to account for such harms (1983: 29). While Green Criminology has emerged to study pollution and climate change, mainstream criminology remains fixated on street crime and neglects to account for climate chaos that undermines the earth's ability to sustain life (Whyte 2020). Box keenly understood the criminogenic nature of the oil industry and seemingly anticipated the formal articulation of state-corporate crime (Michalowski and Kramer 2006), which examines social harm stemming from the facilitation of corporate misdeeds by the government. This section, then, discusses climate crimes and explores them as an example of state-corporate crime. Box's other examples of corporate wrongdoing could similarly be analyzed through the framework of state-corporate crime, which is seen in many large-scale social harms—whether technically illegal or not—that need to be highlighted, understood, and resisted.

Box explored how oil companies resolve 'contradictory demands' for productivity and safety by pressuring employees to take unnecessary risks and violating company protocol, all with tacit support from successive British governments (1983: 29). In another major case of corporate law-breaking, Box describes how the company believed that 'their actions, although technically illegal, were informally condoned by governmental officials' (ibid: 46).

While such problems still regularly occur, the larger concerns with the fossil fuel industry are the release of greenhouse gasses that are causing human deaths, increased illness and injury, and damage to ecosystems that sustain life (Intergovernmental Panel on Climate Change (IPCC)

2022; see also Walters, this volume). Governments and corporations alike have known this but pursued—and continue to pursue—a course of conduct usually described as 'catastrophic' and 'apocalyptic' (Atwoli et al. 2021; *Juliana v U.S.* 2020). Without intervention, unbridled corporate power and the pursuit of profit will continue to perpetuate climate catastrophe and ecocide (Whyte 2020).

In the short to medium term, the climate emergency will bring about more heat waves, drought, war, sea-level rise, pandemics, ocean acidification, and severe storms and flooding (Masters 2022). Still understudied are how problems of food shortages, infrastructure destruction, disease, and climate refugees interact, amplify each other, and/or create cascading harmful impacts (Kemp et al. 2022). Such disasters harm the most vulnerable, and research about the effects of natural disasters describe 'mental stress, substance abuse, economic hardship, food insecurity and poor social infrastructure' (Rodrigues 2022). Further, the 'weather events were linked to various forms of gender-based violence, from physical and sexual assault to forced marriage, trafficking and psychological abuse' (ibid). The punitive neoliberal cuts in social support and funding increases for criminal justice and 'security' agencies ensure that:

> social control mechanisms that already predominantly punish the powerless and those at the margins of society will be aggravated. In the growing climate emergency, more punitive societies will have even less tolerance for minor criminal behavior caused by desperation. (Twyman-Ghoshal et al. 2022: 807)

The high level of knowledge about the harmfulness of greenhouse gasses and the affirmative actions taken to further their use by both the government and the fossil fuel industry make their actions morally blameworthy—and criminal. Moral blameworthiness arises from acts that threaten physical security (or failure to act when obligated to do so), are both voluntary and intentional (including those done knowingly, recklessly, and negligently), and are not considered justifiable or excusable (for example, by duress or necessity) (Agnew 2011: 37). While some morally blameworthy serious harm is criminalized, Agnew (2011) suggests that the category of 'unrecognized blameworthy harms' encompasses crimes of the powerful broadly and can be applied to the concept of climate crimes specifically (Kramer 2020). The failure to criminalize blameworthy harms stems from the impact of the mystification strategies used to conceal the climate emergency.

In *Juliana v U.S.* (2015), a suit where young people sued the U.S. government to slow climate chaos, a federal Court of Appeals concluded: 'A substantial evidentiary record documents that the federal government has long promoted fossil fuel use despite knowing that it can cause catastrophic climate change, and that failure to change existing policy may hasten an environmental apocalypse' (*Juliana v U.S.* 2020: 11). The record 'conclusively establishes that the federal government has long understood the risks of fossil fuel use' with a warning as early as 1965 'that fossil fuel emissions threatened significant changes to climate, global temperatures, sea levels' (ibid: 15). The court noted the government 'affirmatively promotes fossil fuel use in a host of ways, including beneficial tax provisions, permits for imports and exports, subsidies for domestic and overseas projects, and leases for fuel extraction on federal land' (ibid: 15–6). Further, 'the government by and large has not disputed the factual premises of the plaintiffs' claims' (2020: 16), although the government spent years delaying, obstructing, and seeking to have the suit dismissed. Morally blameworthy government action and inaction have obscured the harms of climate chaos and facilitated conditions conducive to social murder.

The larger fossil fuel industry is also morally blameworthy because as early as 1954 leaders of the American Petroleum Institute (API) shared with its members research linking greenhouse gasses with potentially dangerous consequences (Franta 2018). The energy industry monitored academic research starting in the 1950s, then developed their own research teams, and by the 1970s 'Exxon strove to be on the cutting edge of inquiry' (Kramer 2020: 69). However, as oil companies acquired knowledge that their business model would wreak havoc with the planet, 'they used this knowledge to plan for future explorations of oil' as the Arctic warmed. They also 'climate-proof[ed] their facilities, all the while doing nothing to reduce the resulting carbon pollution and climate disruption' (ibid: 59). While the research was originally intended to help companies like Exxon participate meaningfully in discussions about greenhouse gas regulation, they later 'engaged in a concerted effort to deny that global warming was occurring at all' (ibid: 59). The industry funded politicians, think tanks, and organizations that denied the climate emergency and created doubt about the severity of climate crisis, which they knew would strategically delay reforms that would hurt their profitability (Oreskes and Conway 2012). They also 'lobbied effectively to prevent government regulation of carbon emissions and to block the development of renewable energy' (Kramer 2020: 59–60; see also Lynch et al. 2010).

Building on this background, Kramer's *Carbon Criminals, Climate Crimes* uses a 'persuasive definition' (2020: 25) of crime to identify four specific forms of state-corporate climate crimes: (1) crimes of continued fossil fuel extraction and rising emissions, (2) crimes of political omission, (3) crimes of socially organized denial, and (4) climate crimes of empire (including wars for oil, emissions from military operations, and militaristic adaptations to climate chaos). As this analysis demonstrates, corporations in the fossil fuel industry, energy trade associations, conservative think tanks and foundations, the U.S. government, and the international political community have all engaged in forms of climate crimes, and as such, can be defined as carbon criminals. The combination of private and government entities working together to advance the fossil fuel industry is a state-corporate crime (Kramer 2013, 2014, 2020; Kramer and Michalowski 2012; Kramer and Bradshaw 2020), even if the parties are in conflict over some specifics (Lynch et al. 2010; White 2011, 2012, 2018).

Governments facilitate corporations engaging in corrupt, harmful, and illegal practices when the government's dual mandate of oversight and promotion of business interests is resolved in favor of industry (Tombs and Whyte 2015). State-facilitated corporate crime occurs when government regulatory agencies fail to control deviant corporate behavior or neglect to adopt regulations and inspections to protect the public, workers, consumers, and the environment. This often results from normalized but problematic practices such as revolving doors of personnel between government and industry (Pons-Hernández 2022) that create regulatory capture. Lobbying and congressional bribery through political contributions enable social harm (Peoples and Sutton 2015; Hogan et al. 2006, 2010; Long et al. 2007) and 'criminogenic industry structures' (Bradshaw 2015).

State-corporate crime is thus responsible for widespread social murder (Engels 1845, 2009) (see also Scott and Sim, this volume; Drake and Scott this volume; Grover, this volume; Tombs, this volume), which involves how living and working conditions contribute to premature and avoidable death, similar to the concerns Box explored. Social murder involves capitalist exploitation and failed public policy resulting from racism, patriarchy, and masculinity, rape, and poverty (Medvedyuk et al. 2021), including damaging cuts to social security policy in Britain (Grover 2019). And, 'by calling social murder what it is – the premeditated causing of death — writers can mobilize the public to resist the powerful economic and political interests that control the media, academia, and indeed, our own lives' (Medvedyuk 2022).

Fear of Revolt: Youth Activism, Power, and the Climate Emergency

A third theme explored by Box in this chapter is power. Recognizing the criminogenic effects of power, Box (1983: 202) advocated for its broad diffusion as a means of curtailing its most harmful effects: 'by spreading power thinly, just as a good farmer would spread manure over a field, instead of concentrating it in one place, the stink of rotten absolute power can be avoided.' Moreover, by establishing institutionalized democratic checks and balances to hold elected representatives accountable can also reduce the criminogenic effects of power and limit 'the chances of people in powerful positions inflicting too much avoidable and technically illegal damage on citizens lives, limbs, and property' (ibid). Providing a case study of Box's call to challenge those perpetuating crime and harm, youth activists are taking direct action to prevent climate catastrophe by trying to find ways to hold state and corporate officials accountable for climate crimes.

White (2011: 36) argues that 'from the vantage point of future generations, present action and lack of action around climate change will most likely constitute the gravest of transnational crimes… Failure to act, now, is criminal.' Research on resistance to state-corporate climate crimes has highlighted the power of social movements to challenge and disrupt fossil fuel infrastructure projects (Bradshaw 2015, 2018). Indeed, Kramer (2020: 193–4) suggests:

> These organizational actors (and some specific individuals who occupy powerful positions within organizational structures), enmeshed in a larger global capitalist political economy, must be the intended targets for social, political and legal actions if the human species is to have any hope of avoiding extreme climate catastrophe and achieving some form of climate justice.

The prevention and amelioration of the climate emergency depend on social movements, and 'youth provide a powerful referent for a discussion about the long-term consequences of neoliberal policies, while also gesturing towards the need for putting into place those economic, political, and cultural institutions that make a democratic future possible' (Giroux 2012: 7). Further, the well of emotions that climate catastrophe taps into both hinders and facilitates youth 'speaking of a deep longing for a future they thought they had but that is disappearing' because 'adults fail to act on the reality that we are in an emergency' (Klein 2020: 7). In the survey of 10,000 youth (mentioned in the introduction), at least half of the young people said they felt helpless, afraid, angry, and powerless—and 75% of young people said that they think the future is frightening (Hickman et al. 2021: e863). Put together with the feelings of betrayal (noted in the introduction), meant that 'more than 45% of respondents said their feelings about climate change negatively affected their daily life and functioning' (ibid: e866).

However, growing numbers of concerned youth also view climate activism as a means of addressing the problem. In comparison to older generations, Millennial or younger adults are more likely to view global warming as personally important and/or to express a readiness to engage in climate activism. Even across party lines, young people are more likely to support or identify with climate activists, and to support non-violent civil disobedience against corporations or governments such as sit-ins and blockades (Ballew et al. 2020).

Representing complementary and mutually reinforcing avenues for youth to express opposition, O'Brien et al. (2018) draw attention to dutiful dissent, disruptive dissent, and dangerous dissent. 'Dutiful dissent' describes cases in which young people's concerns about unjust practices are expressed within existing political and economic institutions. While challenging the status quo, this form of youth resistance ultimately reinforces the dominant institutions and includes membership in mainstream environmental organizations and seeking solutions through existing political, economic, and religious traditions. Explicitly challenging political authority and power relations rather than working within them, 'disruptive dissent' is a type of activism that seeks to change political and economic institutions through petition campaigns, boycotts, disrupting official climate meetings, protesting through marches or rallies, and other forms of direct action. Referring to the degree of threat that alternatives pose to established power elites, 'dangerous dissent' involves political activism that moves beyond existing paradigms to initiate and sustain new social, political, and economic transformation in the long term.

> The 'danger' also lies in the way that youth are claiming, taking back, or generating their own power and strengthening their personal and political agency, or simply questioning what to others appears to be inevitable, such as a fossil fuel–based economy, hyperconsumption, and increasing social inequality. (O'Brien et al. 2018: 7)

As more explosive forms of 'social dynamite' (Spitzer 1975; Box 1983) that threaten the existing social order and necessitate more repressive social control, the school strikes of Fridays for Future, direct action protests of Extinction Rebellion, disruptive tactics of Just Stop Oil and other groups, and the Indigenous youth resistance to fossil fuel infrastructure, all provide varying degrees of disruptive and dangerous dissent. While each example embraces different tools, tactics, and techniques, they remain collectively committed to spurring government action on the climate crisis.

Fridays for Future

Representing a form of disruptive dissent, Fridays for Future (FFF) originated in 2018 when Greta Thunberg, then 15 years old, began a school strike by sitting outside of the Swedish Parliament every school day to demand that legislators take action on the climate crisis. Soon, other young people around the country and the world joined the strike by skipping school to protest. FFF makes three demands of government: (1) keep the global temperature rise below 1.5 degrees Celsius compared to pre-industrial levels, (2) ensure climate justice and equity, and (3) listen to the best science currently available (Fridays for Future 2023). The hashtag #FridaysForFuture was created to encourage others to protest outside their local governments for urgent action on the climate crisis. In addition to weekly protests, the group has also organized Global Climate Strikes on seven separate Fridays as well as two week-long events. Organized by FFF with an explicit call for adults to join, the third week-long Global Climate Strike in September 2019 mobilized 7.6 million participants across 6000 protest events in 185 countries. Participants in this protest were disproportionately (60 percent) young women, with youth aged 19 and under representing almost one third of all demonstrators and many were engaging in activism for the first time (Wahlstrom et al. 2019; de Moor et al. 2020).

Extinction Rebellion

Extinction Rebellion (XR) provides an example of dimensions of both disruptive dissent through their use of arrestable disruption tactics, as well as dangerous dissent, reflected in the group's transformative goal of cultivating greater democratic power. Increasingly developing an international youth presence (XR Youth 2023), Extinction Rebellion is a decentralized, international social movement that uses non-violent direct action and civil disobedience to encourage government action on the climate emergency. Founded in 2018 in response to inaction by the U.K. government, the organization quickly spread to more than 30 countries.

Although XR has no formalized organizational structure, those identifying with the group adhere to three demands: that governments 'tell the truth' about the climate emergency, 'act now' to stop the loss of biodiversity and reduce greenhouse gas emissions to net zero by 2025, and 'go beyond politics' to create citizens' assemblies to give greater political power to citizens on climate justice (Extinction Rebellion 2023a).

XR has used civil disobedience like marches, demonstrations, blocking roads, and gluing themselves to corporate and government buildings, to cause economic disruption. Many XR activists are willing to risk going to jail. However, critics suggest that XR's techniques risk alienating supporters by using such high-profile public disruptions (Shenker 2023; Berglund and Schmidt 2021), especially when they prevent the poor and minorities from getting to their jobs (Malm 2021). In 2022, Extinction Rebellion released a public statement stating, 'We Quit' and announcing that it would instead focus its efforts on inclusive bridge-building that prioritizes 'attendance over arrest and relationships over roadblocks' (Extinction Rebellion 2022). An indication of the strategy changes of XR, in April 2023 the group organized a four-day action nicknamed 'The Big One,' which relied on more conventional forms of protest that were 'family friendly,' 'accessible and welcoming,' 'creative,' and 'engaging' (Extinction Rebellion 2023b).

Just Stop Oil and Other Disruptive Groups

Even as XR shirks away from its emphasis on arrestable disruption, other coalitions continue to rely on disruptive dissent to draw public attention to inaction on the climate emergency and invoke critical questions about the ideological assumptions underlying everyday life amidst a world on fire. However, the extent to which they can be classified as examples of dangerous dissent differs depending on their degree of commitment to larger sustained social transformation. Embracing more militant tactics such as strikes, boycotts, mass protests, and other forms of arrestable disruption, Just Stop Oil (2023) is a coalition of groups dedicated to using non-violent civil resistance to ensure that the U.K. government immediately ends support for all new fossil fuel exploration, development, and production. In 2022 activists with the group threw soup on Van Gogh's famed Sunflowers painting at the National Gallery and then glued themselves to the wall, asking the questions 'what is worth more, art or life?' and 'are you concerned more about the protection of a painting or the protection of our planet?' (Gayle 2022a). In similar subsequent protests at the Royal Academy of Arts, where activists glued themselves to the frame of Leonardo da Vinci's The Last Supper, activists were convicted of criminal damage (Quinn 2023).

And Just Stop Oil is not alone. Under this umbrella, other groups are embracing direct action and sabotage in the fight to stop climate chaos. Using similar tactics, members of the Scottish climate activist group This is Rigged smashed and spray painted a glass case housing the sword of knight William Wallace (Chen 2023). The organization Insulate Britain (2023) utilizes arrestable disruption to pressure the U.K. government to insulate all social housing by 2025 and to advocate for a nationally funded plan to retrofit housing as part of a just transition to full decarbonization. To draw attention to the carbon emissions of large gas guzzling vehicles, the Tyre Extinguishers movement releases the air from the tires of SUVs under the anonymity of darkness and has reported that the response from the public was 'more welcoming than expected' (Gayle 2022b). Casting doubt onto the frequently cited assumption that radical tactics have a negative impact on the overall environmental movement, Ozden and Ostarek (2022) found a 'positive radical flank effect,' whereby high-profile public disruption campaigns by Just Stop Oil resulted in increased public support for and identification with more moderate environmental organization Friends of the Earth.

Indigenous Youth Activists

Indigenous youth resistance to the extractive industries driving climate chaos has helped sway public debate on fossil fuels and Indigenous rights through the use of non-violent direct action, political lobbying, multimedia campaigns, divestment, and more. Over the last decade, Indigenous resistance has stopped or delayed pipeline projects emitting greenhouse gas pollution roughly equivalent to at least one-quarter of the annual U.S. and Canadian emissions (Indigenous Environmental Network and Oil Change International 2021). Climate activism by Indigenous youth seeks to reform both the climate justice movement itself as well as fundamentally alter the political-economic power structures that facilitate dependence on fossil fuel. The movement's focus on transforming the status quo through decolonization provides an apt example of dangerous dissent. Pushing the movement itself to decolonize, Indigenous youth are at the forefront of climate activism (Ritchie 2020). Yet, despite their leadership, in formal decision-making policy structures such as UN climate negotiations and in activist spaces, Indigenous youth experience intersectional exclusion (Crenshaw 1989) whereby people with multiple marginalized identities are excluded from decision-making policy structures (Grosse and Mark 2020). But the voices of Indigenous youth in climate change policy are necessary to counter 'colonial ecological violence' (ibid: 4). Indeed, 'moving toward decolonization and realizing climate justice require meaningful involvement of and leadership by Indigenous peoples, youth, the queer community, people from the Global South, and women' (ibid: 24). The dangerousness of this form of dissent stems from its goal of ending the cycle of colonial ecological violence by seeking alternatives to capitalist extractive industries while simultaneously changing the social relationships perpetuating colonialism and marginalization.

Justice for All: Fighting for Survival in an Era of Extinction

In the call for 'Justice for All,' Box (1983) stressed the need for a radical democratization and diffusion of power, including direct action by ordinary people, if there is any hope of confronting the crimes of the powerful. While the non-violent direct action that characterizes disruptive and dangerous forms of dissent may violate civil and sometimes criminal laws, activists justify their behavior as necessary for the higher moral purpose of forcing government action on catastrophic climate change (Malm 2021; Berglund and Schmidt 2021). Furthermore, their social protest and peaceful demonstrations in defense of the environment and humankind are frequently criminalized by authorities, and activists are subjected to arbitrary detention, unwarranted and excessive legal charges, inadequate due process guarantees, and public stigmatization by officials (Birss 2017). Non-violent civil disobedience by activists has successfully transformed the debate on the climate catastrophe, and in response, criminalizing climate protests is now a growing fossil fuel industry strategy (Taylor 2021). Additional actions targeting protestors include surveillance against protestors because of labels of extremism, and retaliatory lawsuits against climate protesters and supporting organizations (Nosek 2020).

Take, for example, the U.K.'s controversial *Police, Crime, Sentencing and Courts Act* of 2022 that expands the power of state and criminal justice institutions including specific restrictions on 'unacceptable' protests to target the disruptive tactics of climate activists like XR and Just Stop Oil. The impetus for the controversial anti-protest law came from a report by Policy Exchange, a secretive right-wing think tank funded by ExxonMobil with close ties to government officials, which urged for stronger police powers over planned protests to control mass law-breaking tactics more effectively. Repeating claims made by Policy Exchange that XR should be considered an extremist group, Tory MPs and ministers refer to climate protesters as 'criminals' and XR as an 'attack on capitalism' (Bychawski 2022). Obscuring the harm caused by powerful carbon criminals, from this perspective, it is not profit from continuing fossil fuel extraction and emissions amidst a burning planet which poses the greatest threats to humanity, but instead non-violent activists fighting against extinction that requires criminalization.

As Box (1983: 222) asserted, those in power 'should be accountable not only for *who* they criminalize, but *why*, and in *whose* interests.' Criminalizing climate activists and their non-violent disruptive tactics conceal the structural violence and state-corporate crimes perpetuated by carbon criminals. Not only do economic benefits continue to accrue for corporations as repression intensifies, but suppressing protests also provides important ideological benefits to the state through the maintenance of law and order. Responding to 'their own fears of growing social indiscipline,' the criminalization of climate protests functions to not only 'demoralize and fracture potential resistance to domination' but also legitimates the 'portrait of crime and criminals so artfully and cynically constructed by legislators' (ibid: 222).

To fully pursue Box's (1983) call for 'justice for all,' it is necessary to expose the crimes of the powerful and establish institutional democratic procedures for citizens to express their grievances to political leaders in an effective manner. But this transformation will require the continued development of 'social dynamite' that is backed by an ethical analysis of social injustices—and tactics that effectively drive society toward their visions of a better future.

Dismantling the Theatres of Control

Building on Spitzer (1975), Box (1983: 209) notes that able-bodied unemployed youth, are 'social dynamite' who have to be '*controlled*' and not just managed because they constitute a threat 'real or imagined' to the ideological hegemony of law and order under capitalism. This population was expanding, throwing into 'question the ability of the capitalist mode of production to generate enough work and wealth' to avoid a legitimacy crisis (ibid). But 40 years on, the system has expanded further as economic inequality and exploitation became worse, and as governments cut social supports. In response, the U.S. 'has become an open-air theater of punishment and control' (Shanahan and Kurti 2022: 70). The criminal justice system has expanded even though it obviously does not result in greater public safety, because 'police and prisons have proven cheaper for the ruling class than guaranteeing free health care, housing, and education, and other minimum demands for a comfortable life' (ibid: 165). While there have been continuities and discontinuities (Sim 2009) in crime and the state response, the enlarging and empowering criminal justice system of the 1960s and 1970 has gone beyond a 'stopgap response to the crisis of that era. This solution has today entered a crisis of its own' (Shanahan and Kurti 2022: 58).

Since nations have been managing 'crises' for at least the last 40 years—with some reforms mixed with policies to promote inequality and exploitation—to what extent is our current situation a 'crisis'? While there is more social dynamite and people see themselves as having little to lose, the crises of neoliberalism tap into a deep well of emotion that drives activism as well as debilitating mental health impacts. In this environment, youth are increasingly subjected to a predatory and punishing youth crime-control complex in the forms of 'soft' and 'hard' wars. Referring to the changing conditions of a global consumer society that devalues and exploits youth by treating them as markets or commodities, the low-intensity soft war commercializes every aspect of young peoples' lives and thrives on the technological advancements of social media. The hard war, on the other hand, draws attention to the 'the harshest elements, values, and dictates of a growing youth crime-control complex that increasingly governs poor minority youth through a logic of punishment, surveillance, and control' (Giroux 2012: 5). Rooted in fear of youth revolution, these forces culminate to subject young people to a perpetual environment of control, containment, and criminalization. As Box astutely noted, the 'real or imagined, fancied or fabricated' anxieties of state and corporate elites motivating the decades-long 'law and order' campaign 'is fed by fear of youthful rebellion, riot or resistance' (1983: 220).

In this exploitative and repressive environment, where inaction on climate change is 'a species-wide death wish' (Malm 2021: 118), two significant topics stand out if another retrospective on Box 40 years from now is to report some successes. The first is the study of ideology, which secures allegiance to the current destructive and oppressive status quo. The second is the development of long-range praxis and politics of protest, meaning 'a set of coherent practices guided by a commonly held political vision and an understanding of how actions in the here and now relate to a liberated future' (Shanahan and Kurti 2022: 66).

In addition to the material conditions and forces of control is an ideological onslaught that also disengages youth and others from activism. While many try to equate ideology with a belief system or worldview, the *Rich Get Richer* notes that: 'When ideas, however unintentionally, distort reality in a way that justifies the prevailing distribution of power and wealth, hides society's injustices, and thus secures uncritical allegiance to the existing social order, we have what Marx called ideology' (Reiman and Leighton 2023: 200). Ideological messages often admit the need for some limited reforms, but the messages broadcast by the corporate- and billionaire-owned media do not allow for questions about the legitimacy of fossil fuel capitalism and criminal justice under it.

Although the study of ideology has moved beyond the thinking of Box and his contemporaries, they wrestled with some important questions about political consciousness that are still relevant. Discussions centered on the status of crime across a 'range from unconscious reactions to exploitation, to conscious acts of survival, to politically conscious acts of rebellion' (Quinney 1977: 93). Currie (in Quinney 1977: 90–1) goes the next step in moving from crime to suggesting that:

> the main task of Marxian theory of deviance is to uncover the conditions in which "deviance" becomes politically progressive and those in which it doesn't; the conditions in which deviance represents the beginnings of conscious political action, and those in which it is simply the action of people ground down by a system they neither understand nor challenge.

Perhaps we should return to these general questions, but not be focused on crimes or deviance by those living in the system. Instead, the question is about how to transform crime victims—those harmed by corporate domination, economic exploitation, and climate catastrophe—into more conscious political actors opposing the causes of their victimization and protesting for their survival.

Further, the question of praxis and politics arises because even when youth—and others—protest, rebel, and riot, there are legitimate questions about the effectiveness of their actions for social change. The rebellion in response to the police killing of George Floyd in the U.S. was met with huge repressive force. But even while the ongoing Black Lives Matter protests against police violence show great courage and tactical ingenuity when confronting police, 'there was no coherent politics' (Shanahan and Kurti 2022: 65) to burning down a police station and damaging hundreds of police cars in cities across the U.S. This made it easier for the crowd's militancy to dissipate and accept the same type of non-reformist reform that has happened over decades but does not change anything.

With protests of fossil fuels too, the question about politics is whether protesters have fetishized strategic pacifism and why tactics do not include property damage (see also Gelderloos 2007). In *How to Blow Up a Pipeline*, Malm (2021) discusses not so much 'how' but 'why': In the face of increasing concentrations of greenhouse gasses that are, with a high degree of scientific certainty, warming the planet, when do tactics escalate? Malm argues that the history of social movements and campaigns has obscured the positive radical flank effect. More to the point, 'devices emitting CO_2 have been physically disrupted for two centuries by subaltern groups indignant at powers they have animated – automation, apartheid, occupation – but not yet as destructive forces *in and of themselves*' (ibid: 78, emphasis original). Even within criminology, sabotage and other forms of direct action have been explored as 'powerful methods of resistance that expose, define and challenge state/corporate crimes' and impose a sense of consequence on powerful actors who are alienated from the harms they produce (Lasslett et al. 2015: 530).

Following this analysis, protests against fossil fuels and the carceral state both need to sharpen the long-range praxis to fulfill their own goals and Box's rousing plea for justice for all. For fossil fuel protests, Greta Thunberg has stated, 'If the emissions have to stop, then we must stop the emissions' (in Malm 2021: 19). Taking this seriously so the planet can stay below 1.5 degrees of warming, means, *in part*, the movement must:

> Announce and enforce the prohibition. Damage and destroy new CO_2-emitting devices. Put them out of commission, pick them apart, demolish them, burn them, blow them up. Let the capitalists who keep on investing in the fire know that their properties will be trashed. (Malm 2021: 67)

He notes that if that seems radical now, it will be less so in the future as the planet heats up more, making people appreciate the violence that is being done to life-sustaining ecosystems and less concerned with 'violence' to property that is fueling an existential crisis.

Conclusion: Putting Up a Fight for Justice

With the carceral state, all the reforms enacted in the face of previous crises have legitimated a coercive system of social control that 'has been deployed, not as a response to crime but to manage daily life, tightly regulating how they [poor and minorities] are allowed to congregate, support themselves when consigned to informal economies, shop, and even drive their cars' (Shanahan and Kurti 2022: 74). What is needed is abolition, 'the proactive rejection of an entire way of life defined by the state's reliance on police, courts and prisons to administer America's racialized capitalist order' (ibid: 69). Following Gramsci, this work of turning 'penal common sense' into nonpenal 'good sense' (Sim 2009; Scott 2020) involves simultaneously divesting from the carceral state and investing in communities in ways that build fulfilling lives and community safety.

It is impossible for us to say how militant Box would have been if he bore witness to the politics and problems that have unfolded in spite of his sharp analysis. We appreciate that his emphasis on the importance of power for understanding crime and justice inspired others and helped create a vibrant critical criminology that continues to expose new manifestations of the same problem as criminal justice is continually 'reformed' and legitimated. Paying tribute to Box today involves working on the wide range of possibilities articulated by Shanahan and Kurti (2022: 66) when they write: 'The politics that will save the world can only emerge from rigorous theoretical engagement with how people are struggling, capable of theorizing and implementing the bridge from the struggles of today to the post-capitalist society of tomorrow.' Then, as eloquently captured by a protest sign, 'Put up a FUCKING fight for what you LOVE' (Malm 2021: 132, emphasis original).

References

Agnew, R. 2011. *Toward a Unified Criminology*. New York: New York University Press.
Atwoli, L., A.H. Baqui, T. Benfield, R. Bosurgi, F. Godlee, S. Hancocks, R. Horton, L. Laybourn-Langton, C.A. Monteiro, I. Norman, K. Patrick, N. Praities, M.G.M. Olde Rikkert, E.J. Rubin, S. Peushi, R. Smith, N. Talley, S. Turale, and D. Vasquez. 2021. Call for Emergency Action to Limit Global Temperature Increases, Restore Biodiversity, and Protect Health. *New England Journal of Medicine* 385: 1134–1137.
Ballew, M., J. Marlon, J. Kotcher, E. Maibach, S. Rosenthal, P. Bergquist, A. Gustafson, M. Goldberg, and A. Leiserowitz. 2020. *Young Adults, Across Party Lines, Are More Willing to Take Climate Action*. Yale University and George Mason University. New Haven, CT: Yale Program on Climate Change Communication. https://climatecommunication.yale.edu/publicati ons/young-adults-climate-activism/. Accessed 22 Feb 2023.
Berglund, O., and D. Schmidt. 2021. *Extinction Rebellion and Climate Change Activism: Breaking the Law to Change the World*. London: Palgrave.
Birss, M. 2017. Criminalizing Environmental Activism. *NACLA Report on the Americas* 49 (3): 315–322.
Box, S. 1983. *Power, Crime, and Mystification*. London: Routledge.
Bradshaw, E. 2015. Blockadia Rising: Rowdy Greens, Direct Action and the Keystone xl Pipeline. *Critical Criminology* 23 (4): 433–448.
Bradshaw, E. 2018. Pipelines, Presidents and People Power: Resisting State-Corporate Environmental Crime. In *Revisiting Crimes of the Powerful*, ed. S. Bittle, L. Snider, S. Tombs, and D. Whyte, 157–173. London: Routledge.
Bychawski, A. 2022. Revealed: Policing Bill was Dreamed Up by Secretive Oil-Funded Think Tank. *openDemocracy*. June 15. https://www.opende mocracy.net/en/dark-money-investigations/policing-bill-policy-exchange-exxonmobil-lobbying/. Accessed 1 Mar 2023.
Chen, M. 2023. A Pair of Climate Activists in Scotland Smashed and Spray-Painted a Glass Case Housing Knight William Wallace's Sword. *Artnet*. March 6 from https://news.artnet.com/art-world/climate-activists-this-is-rig ged-william-wallace-sword-2265843. Accessed 7 Mar 2023.
Crenshaw, K. 1989. *Demarginalizing the Intersection of Race and Sex: A Black Feminist Critique of Antidiscrimination Doctrine, Feminist Theory and*

Antiracist Politics, vol. 139, 139–167. The University of Chicago Legal Forum.

de Moor, J., K. Uba, M. Wahlstrom, M. Wennerhag, and M. De Vydt. 2020. *Protest for a Future II: Composition, Mobilization and Motives of the Participants in Fridays for Future Climate Protests on 20–27 September 2019, in 19 Cities Around the World*. The Institute for Protest. https://osf.io/3hcxs/download. Accessed 1 Aug 2022.

Engels, F. 1845/2009. *The Conditions of the Working Class in England*. London: Penguin Classics.

Extinction Rebellion. 2022. *We Quit*. https://extinctionrebellion.uk/2022/12/31/we-quit/. Accessed 1 Mar 2023.

Extinction Rebellion. 2023a. *About Us*. https://rebellion.global/about-us/. Accessed 1 Mar 2023.

Extinction Rebellion. 2023b. *The Big One*. https://extinctionrebellion.uk/the-big-one/#. Accessed 5 May 2023.

Franta, B. 2018. Early Oil Industry Knowledge of CO_2 and Global Warming. *Nature Climate Change* 8 (12): 1024–1025.

Fridays for Future (FFF). 2023. *What We Do: Our Demands*. https://fridaysforfuture.org/what-we-do/our-demands/. Accessed 1 Mar 2023.

Gayle, D. 2022a. Just Stop Oil Activists Throw Soup at Van Gogh's Sunflowers. *The Guardian*, October 14. https://www.theguardian.com/environment/2022/oct/14/just-stop-oil-activists-throw-soup-at-van-goghs-sunflowers. Accessed 1 Mar 2023.

Gayle, D. 2022b. Tyre Extinguishers-Deflating SUV Tyres as a Form of Climate Action. *The Guardian*, March 18. https://www.theguardian.com/environment/2022/mar/18/tyre-extinguishers-deflating-suv-tyres-as-a-form-of-climate-action. Accessed 1 Mar 2023.

Gelderloos, P. 2007. *How Nonviolence Protects the State*. New York: South End Press.

Giroux, H. 2012. *Disposable Youth: Racialized Memories and the Culture of Cruelty*. London: Routledge.

Goldman, M., and N. Rodriguez. 2022. Juvenile Court in the School-Prison Nexus: Youth Punishment, Schooling and Structures of Inequality. *Journal of Crime and Justice* 45 (3): 270–284.

Grosse, C., and B. Mark. 2020. A Colonized COP: Indigenous Exclusion and Youth Climate Justice Activism at the United Nations Climate Change Negotiations. *Journal of Human Rights and the Environment* 11 (3): 146–170. https://digitalcommons.csbsju.edu/cgi/viewcontent.cgi?article=1008&context=environmental_studies_pubs. Accessed 1 Aug 2022.

Grover, C. 2019. Violent Proletarianisation: Social Murder, the Reserve Army of Labour and Social Security in Britain. *Critical Social Policy* 39 (3): 335–355.

Hickman, C., E. Marks, P. Pihkala, S. Clayton, R.E. Lewandoski, E.E. Mayall, B. Wray, C. Mellor, and L. van Susteren. 2021. Climate Anxiety in Children and Young People and Their Beliefs About Government Responses to Climate Change: A Global Survey. *The Lancet Planetary Health* 5 (12): e863–e873.

Hogan, M., M. Long, and P. Stretesky. 2006. Campaign Contributions, Post-War Reconstruction Contracts and State Crime. *Deviant Behavior* 27 (3): 269–297.

Hogan, M., M. Long, and P. Stretesky. 2010. Campaign Contributions, Lobbying and Post-Katrina Contracts. *Disasters* 34 (3): 593–607.

Indigenous Environmental Network and Oil Change International. 2021. *Indigenous Resistance Against Carbon.* https://www.ienearth.org/wp-content/uploads/2021/09/Indigenous-Resistance-Against-Carbon-2021.pdf. Accessed 1 Aug 2022.

Insulate Britain. 2023. https://insulatebritain.com/. Accessed 3 Mar 2023.

Intergovernmental Panel on Climate Change (IPCC). 2022. *Climate Change 2022: Impacts, Adaptation and Vulnerability.* Working Group II Contribution to the Sixth Assessment Report of the Intergovernmental Panel on Climate Change. https://www.ipcc.ch/report/ar6/wg2/. Accessed 1 Aug 2022.

Just Stop Oil. 2023. https://juststopoil.org/. Accessed 1 Mar 2023.

Kemp, L., C. Xu, L. Depledge, and T. M. Lenton. 2022. Climate Endgame. *Proceedings of the National Academy of Sciences* 119. 34: e2108146119. https://doi.org/10.1073/pnas.2108146119. Accessed 1 Aug 2022.

Klein, N. 2020. *On Fire: The Burning Case for a Green New Deal*. New York: Penguin Press.

Kramer, R. 2013. Carbon in the Atmosphere and Power in America: Climate Change as State-Corporate Crime. *Journal of Crime and Justice* 36 (2): 153–170.

Kramer, R. 2014. Climate Change: A state-Corporate Crime Perspective. In *Environmental Crime and Its Victims: Perspectives Within Green Criminology*, ed. T. Spapnes, T.R. White, and M. Kluin, 22–39. New York: Routledge.

Kramer, R. 2020. *Carbon Criminals, Climate Crimes*. New Brunswick: Rutgers University Press.

Kramer, R. and E. Bradshaw. 2020. Climate Crimes: The Case of ExxonMobil. In *Routledge International Handbook of Green Criminology* ed. A. Brisman and N. South, 2nd ed., 167–186. New York: Routledge.

Kramer, R., and R. Michalowski. 2012. Is Global Warming a State-Corporate Crime? In *Climate Change from a Criminological Perspective*, ed. R. White, 71–88. New York: Springer.

Lasslett, K., P. Green, and D. Stańczak. 2015. The Barbarism of Indifference: Sabotage, Resistance and State-Corporate Crime. *Theoretical Criminology* 19 (4): 514–533.

Levy, R., and M. Mattsson. 2022. The Effects of Social Movements: Evidence from #MeToo. *Social Science Research Network*. https://ssrn.com/abstract=3496903. Accessed 1 Aug 2022.

Long, M., M. Hogan, P. Stretesky, and M. Lynch. 2007. The Relationship between Postwar Reconstruction Contracts and Political Donations: The Case of Afghanistan and Iraq. *Sociological Spectrum* 27: 453–472.

Lynch, M., R. Burns, and P. Stretesky. 2010. Global Warming and State-Corporate Crime: The Politicization of Global Warming Under the Bush Administration. *Crime, Law and Social Change* 54 (3–4): 213–239.

Malm, A. 2021. *How to Blow Up a Pipeline*. London: Verso.

Masters, J. 2022. *The Future of Global Catastrophic Risk Events from Climate Change*. Yale Climate Connections, July 28. https://yaleclimateconnections.org/2022/07/the-future-of-global-catastrophic-risk-events-from-climate-change. Accessed 1 Sept 2022.

Medvedyuk, S. 2022. Why a 19th Century Concept of 'Social Murder' is Very Much Relevant Today. *Marxist Sociology Blog*. https://marxistsociology.org/2022/09/why-a-19th-century-concept-of-social-murder-is-very-much-relevant-today/. Accessed 22 Feb 2023.

Medvedyuk, S., P. Govender, and D. Raphael. 2021. The Reemergence of Engels' Concept of Social Murder in Response to Growing Social and Health Inequalities. *Social Science and Medicine* 289: 114377.

Michalowski, R., and R. Kramer. 2006. *State-Corporate Crime: Wrongdoing at the Intersection of Business and Government*. New Brunswick: Rutgers University Press.

Mooney, H., and P. Leighton. 2019. Troubled Affluent Youth's Experiences in a Therapeutic Boarding School. The Elite Arm of the Youth Control Complex and Its Implications for Youth Justice. *Critical Criminology* 27 (4): 611–626. https://doi.org/10.1007/s10612-019-09466-4.

Nosek, G. 2020. The Fossil Fuel Industry's Push to Target Climate Protestors in the U.S. *Pace Environmental Law Review* 38 (1): 53–108.

O'Brien, K., E. Selboe, and B. Hayward. 2018. Exploring Youth Activism on Climate Change Dutiful, Disruptive, and Dangerous. *Ecology and Society* 23 (3): 42. https://doi.org/10.5751/ES-10287-230342.

Oreskes, N., and E. Conway. 2012. *Merchants of Doubt: How a Handful of Scientists Obscured the Truth on Issues from Tobacco Smoke to Global Warming*. London: Bloomsbury Publishing PLC.

Ozden, J., and M. Ostarek. 2022. *The Radical Flank Effect of Just Stop Oil*. Social Change Lab. https://www.socialchangelab.org/_files/ugd/503ba4_a18 4ae5bbce24c228d07eda25566dc13.pdf. Accessed 1 Mar 2023.

Peoples, C., and J. Sutton. 2015. Congressional Bribery as State-Corporate Crime: A Social Network Analysis. *Crime, Law, and Social Change* 64 (1): 103–125.

Pons-Hernández, M. 2022. Power(ful) Connections: Exploring the Revolving Doors Phenomenon as a Form of State-Corporate Crime. *Critical Criminology* 30 (2): 305–320.

Quinn, B. 2023. Leonardo Would Have Backed Gallery Protest, Say Just Stop Oil Activists. *The Guardian*, February 8. https://www.theguardian.com/environment/2023/feb/08/leonardo-da-vinci-gallery-protest-just-stop-oil-activists. Accessed 1 Mar 2023.

Quinney, R. 1977. *Class, State and Crime*. New York: David McKay Co.

Reiman, J., and P. Leighton. 2023. *The Rich Get Richer and the Poor Get Prison*, 13th ed. New York: Routledge.

Ritchie, J. 2020. Movement from the Margins to Global Recognition: Climate Change Activism by Young People and in Particular Indigenous Youth. *International Studies in Sociology of Education* 30 (1–2): 53–72.

Rodrigues, M. 2022. How Climate Change Could Drive an Increase in Gender-Based Violence. *Nature*, July 13. https://www.nature.com/articles/d41586-022-01903-9. Accessed 1 Aug 2022.

Scott, D. 2020. *For Abolition*. Hook: Waterside Press.

Shanahan, J., and Z. Kurti. 2022. *States of Incarceration: Rebellion, Reform and America's Punishment System*. London: Reaktion Books.

Shenker, J. 2023. The Existential Question for Climate Activists: Have Disruption Tactics Stopped Working? *The Guardian*, March 6. https://www.theguardian.com/commentisfree/2023/mar/06/british-eco-activists-disruption-extinction-rebellion. Accessed 8 Mar 2023.

Sim, J. 2009. *Punishment and Prisons: Power and the Carceral State*. London: Sage.

Spitzer, S. 1975. Towards a Marxian Theory of Deviance. *Social Problems* 22 (5): 638–651.

Taylor, M. 2021. Environment Protest Being Criminalised Around World, Say Experts. *The Guardian*, April 19. https://www.theguardian.com/environment/2021/apr/19/environment-protest-being-criminalised-around-world-say-experts. Accessed 1 Mar 2023.

Tombs, S., and D. Whyte. 2015. *The Corporate Criminal: Why Corporations Must Be Abolished*. New York: Routledge.

Tonry, M. 2020. *Doing Justice, Preventing Crime*. New York: Oxford University Press.

Twyman-Ghoshal, A., E. Patten, and E. Ciaramella. 2022. Exploring Media Representations of the Nexus Between Climate Change and Crime in the United States. *Critical Criminology* 30: 799–820. https://doi.org/10.1007/s10612-022-09608-1.

Wahlstrom, M., P. Kocyba, M. De Vydt, and J. de Moor (eds.). 2019. *Protest for a Future: Composition, Mobilization and Motives of the Participants in Friday For Future Climate Protests on 15 March 2019 in 13 European Cities*. The Institute for Protest. https://protestinstitut.eu/wp-content/uploads/2019/07/20190709_Protest-for-a-future_GCS-Descriptive-Report.pdf. Accessed 1 Aug 2022.

White, R. 2011. *Transnational Environmental Crime: Towards an Eco-Global Criminology*. New York: Routledge.

White, R., ed. 2012. *Climate Change from a Criminological Perspective*. New York: Springer.

White, R. 2018. *Climate Change Criminology*. Bristol: Bristol University Press.

Whyte, D. 2020. *Ecocide: Kill the Corporation Before It Kills Us*. Manchester: Manchester University Press.

XR Youth. 2023. https://xryouthus.org/. Accessed 1 Mar 2023.

Legal Cases Cited

Juliana v. United States. 2020. United States Court of Appeals for the Ninth Circuit Court. https://cdn.ca9.uscourts.gov/datastore/opinions/2020/01/17/18-36082.pdf. Accessed 1 Nov 2022.

———. 2015. First Amended Complaint. https://www.ourchildrenstrust.org/court-orders-and-pleadings. Accessed 29 Jul 2023.

Part III

Power, State Crime and Social Harm

7

The Neoliberal State: Then and Now

Samantha Fletcher and William McGowan

Introduction

We meet in the aftermath of a General Election...We were elected to strengthen the forces of law and order...Of course, our opponents could never begin to match our record, once again trying to pin on us all the adjectives in the dictionary of denigration - harsh, uncaring, uncompassionate and the rest...The election showed that something remarkable has happened in this country - and our opponents were just as aware of it as those millions of people who supported us...And by giving voice to these convictions in 1979, by holding fast to them for four years, by having them reaffirmed in 1983, I believe we have altered the whole course of British politics for at least a generation. We have created the

S. Fletcher (✉)
Manchester Metropolitan University, Manchester, UK
e-mail: samantha.fletcher@mmu.ac.uk

W. McGowan
Liverpool John Moores University, Liverpool, UK
e-mail: w.j.mcgowan@ljmu.ac.uk

new common ground, and that is why our opponents have been forced to shift their ground. Both the policy and direction of State Socialism on which they have been fighting for years have been utterly rejected by our people...We are told the Social Democrats now see the virtues of capitalism, competition, and the customer. We have entered a new era...We have set a true course - a course that is right for the character of Britain, right for the people of Britain and right for the future of Britain. To that course we shall hold fast. We shall see it through - to success. (Thatcher 1983)

In June 1983, the Conservative Party in the UK won their second consecutive general election under the leadership of Margaret Thatcher. The win was monumental not only because of the number of seats won in Parliament—by far the Party's most decisive general election victory since Labour's in 1945—but because of what it signified in terms of concretising a new course for the British state and, by definition, domestic and international publics. As indicated in Margaret Thatcher's leadership address at the Conservative Party Conference in Blackpool four months later, this election win for the Conservatives was the firming up of a new era. This era was neoliberalism, or what we refer to here as the neoliberal conjuncture. Understandably, the Party's 1979 general election win is often cited as the birth of neoliberalism in Britain, consolidated internationally by Ronald Reagan's US Presidential Election victory in November 1980, but this whole period of political foment provides an important contextual backdrop against which to read *Power, Crime, and Mystification* published in the November of 1983.

The augmentation of the neoliberal project through the Conservative Party election win of 1983 was significant for myriad reasons. For one, it represented an intensification of state authoritarianism under the guise of 'rolling back' the state's direct interference in people's private, civic, and social lives. As a political project, neoliberalism was initially concerned with dismantling what had come before, namely, the social democratic state (for more nuanced discussions than we can provide here, especially pertaining to the so-called crime problem, see Hall et al. 1978; Hall 1979/2017; Scraton 1987). The support the neoliberal project had garnered since its first election win in 1979 had shown no signs of abating, quite the contrary. The elicitation of support had many aspects to it, but one of the major cornerstones for its public success hinged on the promise of a delivery of effective law and order in tackling the so-called 'crime problem'. The crime problem, as articulated by the new architects of the neoliberal project, was one of rising street crime, a loose term for criminal offences perceived to be committed typically by individuals from the working classes in public view. The official record of state-recorded crime added theft, burglary, murder, and robbery to this picture. Neoliberal champions for more effectual law and order offered a convincing and 'strident moral rhetoric' (Box 1983: 2) for more robust and punitive responses *to their depictions* of the crime problem.

In November of 1983, Steven Box published *Power, Crime, and Mystification*. At its core was an alternative, radical message: that the crime problem presented to us by the advocates of neoliberalism was instead 'only *a* crime problem and not *the* crime problem' (Box 1983: 3 original emphasis). Box begins with an astute acknowledgement that a denial of the victimisation experienced through the conventional crimes contained within the neoliberal depiction of 'the crime problem' would likely result in rejection from the public. In addition, with a deft persuasiveness of his own, he (1983: 3) sets out to demonstrate the limitations of the crime problem defined by the neoliberal project, as being in no way capable of depicting those 'even more serious crimes and victimizing behaviours, which objectively cause the vast bulk of avoidable death, injury, and deprivation'. Integral to the neoliberal project's law and order mandate was to maintain its vision of the crime problem thus, in turn, mystifying the full set of 'actors, instruments, situations, and motives' (Box 1983: 9) involved in the fully exhaustive list of social harms in existence. Crucially, the power of the neoliberal state to mystify the true extent of the crime problem, including the nefarious actions of the state itself, was a central tenet of *Power, Crime, and Mystification*. The book ultimately encouraged a 'radical reflexiveness' (Box 1983: 6), supporting the recognition 'that the crime problem defined by the state is not the only crime problem, [and] that criminals are not only those processed by the state' (ibid.: 15). Drawing on both the advantages of intellectual hindsight, and the disadvantages of having lived through neoliberalism's heyday to date, how are we to assess the legacy of Steven Box's contribution? More specifically, how are we to assess the legacy of *Power, Crime, and Mystification* for making sense of the neoliberal state today, a conceptualisation of governance in its relative infancy when Box's book was first published?

In attempting to answer these questions, this chapter first provides an 'orthodox' account of the neoliberal state. We do this in the knowledge that what constitutes neoliberalism and whether neoliberalism's days are numbered, or even over altogether, are live and contested debates. These debates are bracketed off from this section for the practical purposes of simply setting some initial parameters around what we mean by 'the state', in this case 'the neoliberal state', something Box did not do explicitly. In the three sections that follow this, we explore the book's eponymous subject matter—power, crime, and mystification—as each relates to the neoliberal state. Ultimately, we argue that assessing the book's contribution to our understanding of how the neoliberal state works can, and should, be treated as discrete questions, dependent on our disciplinary vantage point and cognisant of the pedagogical work that *Power, Crime, and Mystification* has enabled so many of us to do.

The Neoliberal State: A Working Definition?

The neoliberal conjuncture refers to a period with a distinct set of economic, social, and political arrangements. Although neoliberalism is a disputed term, we are broadly referring to the dominant economic, political, and ideological arrangements emerging out of the late 1970s and early 1980s onwards (Thorsen 2010). The first experiment in neoliberal state formation took place in Chile following Augusto Pinochet's coup in 1973; since then, a recurring feature of neoliberal state formation has been the West's aggressive implementation of neoliberal trade rules in strategically occupied countries whose domestic assets and services have been channelled into global chains of value extraction (Harvey 2005: 6–7). Neoliberalism comprises several elements. These include the unyielding drift towards mass privatisation and commodification of all aspects of public life, public space and, in turn, the selling of as many major public (that is, publicly funded) services as possible to corporate entities to elicit profit for shareholders. This has resulted in the unremitting accumulation of wealth by the most powerful and dominant classes and, in turn, the acute dispossession of the less powerful. Enshrined within the social, economic, and political arrangements of neoliberalism is the mantra of the free market and, whilst the economically and politically powerful reap the benefits of free market conditions, the people are met with increasingly aggressive fiscal and civil discipline (Harvey 2005).

Like neoliberalism, 'the state' is a contested concept. Mair (2021) suggests that the social and political sciences have focused primarily on either the state's constitutional make up, or on empirical critiques of constitutional theorists' accounts, in what might broadly be termed 'constructionist' approaches. Without space to do justice to Mair's contribution, which advocates for a radical freeing from both such approaches, the latter group of state theorists (the 'constructionists', including the likes of Nicos Poulantzas, Michel Foucault, Bob Jessop, among others) conceive of the state as a social relation. The state conceived of as a social relation sits in contrast to instrumental conceptions of the state. An instrumentalist conception of the state supposes that the state is an object capable of manipulation or being seized. Conceptualising the state in this way infers one group at any given time has ownership and control of the state, whilst another group, or groups, lie in wait until such a time that they might take control of the state themselves.

An instrumental conception of the state reveals itself to be unsatisfactory in several ways. Although at any given time the state presents itself as having distinct capacities and tendencies, this does not equate to a state that is a 'pure power' or a 'monolithic block without cracks of any kind' (Poulantzas 2014 [1978]: 337). We know this to be the case through any number of examples where the state acts in ways that are contradictory to its everyday typical inclinations. In recognition of this, instead, we argue that the state is better understood as a social relation. That relation is, to paraphrase Poulantzas (2014 [1978]), the condensation of the relationship of class forces. The capacities and tendencies of the state, within a particular conjuncture, are therefore the material representation of the condensation of the relationship of class forces at that time. As it is neatly put by Poulantzas (2014 [1978]: 342–343):

power is not a quantifiable substance held by the State that must be taken out of its hands, but rather a series of relations among the various social classes. In its ideal form, power is concentrated in the State, which is thus itself the condensation of a particular class relationship of forces. The State is neither a thing-instrument that may be taken away, nor a fortress that may be penetrated by means of a wooden horse, nor yet a safe that may be cracked by burglary: it is the heart of the exercise of political power.

Therefore, the neoliberal state is not the state as wholly and successfully commandeered by the neoliberal project, as it would be in an instrumentalist conception. Instead, the neoliberal state is the material condensation of the relationship of class forces within a particular conjuncture, representing the outcome of complex and considerable struggle. Within this condensation-based outcome, the state presents itself as exhibiting both the capacity and tendency to act in favour of the continuation and advancement of the neoliberal project.

Notably, within *Power, Crime, and Mystification* itself, Box makes no direct reference to either neoliberalism or to the neoliberal state. However, despite the literal absence of this specific terminology, the text clearly makes a series of significant contributions to our understanding of these phenomena—not least, of course, in relation to the eponymous subject matter of power, crime, and mystification. How each of these subjects and concepts in turn relate to, and illuminate, the activities of the neoliberal state forms the basis of the following three sections of the chapter.

Power and the Neoliberal State

To talk about the neoliberal state is to talk about state power in the neoliberal conjuncture. Much like the various key terminology under discussion here, power too is a term subjected to frequent deliberation. At the end of the second edition of *Power: A Radical Critique*, Lukes (2005) provides an excellent guide to further reading on theories of power, including the classic contributions of authors such as Hobbes,

Spinoza, Kant, Wollstonecraft, Marx, Mill and Nietzsche, among others, and also to the debates contemporaneous to Box (1983), such as the famous Poulantzas/Miliband debate in the 1960s and 1970s (see for example Poulantzas 1969; Miliband 1973). Gramscian notions of hegemony and their critiques, feminist contributions from the likes of Raewyn Connell, Nancy Fraser, and Nancy Hartsock, Pierre Bourdieu's sociological framing of power, and, of course, Foucault's body of work. Furthermore, we might also refer to the work of Stuart Hall in *The Great Moving Right Show* (1979/2017) and the edited collection *The Politics of Thatcherism* put together by Stuart Hall and Martin Jacques (1983). Far from a simple concept, in either theory or practice, power, broadly speaking, refers to the presence of the capacity or ability to influence and shape actions and events, either directly or indirectly, in one's own life or the lives of others. The exercise of power, therefore, takes shape in multiple and diverse formats. To consider power in the neoliberal state means to be concerned with political power in the neoliberal conjuncture. Political power refers precisely to the ability and capacity to influence and shape the course of events in public life. This includes examining its various manifestations and the various actors and institutions of power involved.

Despite the book's title, *Power, Crime, and Mystification* makes very few explicit references to the concept of power. When it does its concern lies with the shape that political power takes, at that precise point in time, through an emphasis on the role of the corporation on the global stage. To illuminate our understanding of political power within the neoliberal conjuncture, Box (1983) focuses his attention on the role of the transnational corporation.[1] His observations are broadly threefold; firstly, he notes the increasing concentration of power into fewer transnational corporate hands; secondly, Box highlights the ability of the corporation to intervene in the construction of criminal law; and, thirdly, the subsequent lack of political accountability achieved through the former two points.

---

[1] We should be clear that Box also concerns himself with an examination of power within other contexts including an examination of sexual violence and female criminality, however here we are drawn to focus on this particular aspect of his analysis.

In the neoliberal conjuncture, capitalism takes the express form of monopoly finance capitalism. For Poulantzas (1979 [1974]), writing less than a decade before Box (1983), monopoly finance capitalism denotes the development of capitalism over a prolonged period. After earlier historical periods of intense competition, capitalism is established as the dominant mode of production. The monopoly finance capitalist stage marks out the period thereafter and can be understood as 'the product of a process of a "merger" chiefly between industrial and banking capital' (Poulantzas 1979 [1974]: 107). There is a lots to be said about capitalism during this period but in the context of the promotion of the neoliberal project, the salient feature that defines this epoch is the emergence of monopoly capital. Monopoly capital is the concentration of corporate power into fewer corporate hands with a huge international reach. The transnational corporate entities of monopoly capital exhibit an intensive exploitation of labour, taking advantage of the differences in the internationalisation of capitalist relations for obtaining 'super profits', most notably via the exploitation of 'cheap labour' (Poulantzas 1979 [1974]: 112 and 156). Most importantly, monopoly capital is the hegemonic fraction that plays the dominant role in the economy and enjoys political hegemony within this conjuncture (Poulantzas 1979 [1974]).

It was these emerging patterns of corporate power that Box (1983: 41) was beginning to identify for his reader. He was rightly concerned with the impact such patterns of 'unrestrained power' would have on the already opaque accountability of corporations. He was particularly concerned with the impact that such increasingly concentrated corporate power would have on the possibilities of corporations being able to evade accountability for the 'crimes' and social harms they committed. He saw this as occurring in two ways. Firstly, through the ability of corporations to exploit their transnational nature in order to export their day-to-day harmful activities to places where sanction was far less likely (see also Pearce and Tombs 1998). As Box (1983: 78) notes:

> With the internationalization of capital and the concentration of power in the hands of fewer and fewer transnational corporations, national law violation may well become old fashioned. These giant corporations may simply opt for law evasion. That is, they may choose to export, say,

plants emitting too much (illegal) pollution, or manufacturing processes where the labour costs are legally maintained at a 'high' level, or products banned for safety reasons, to other countries where pollution laws, legal wage levels, and product safety regulations are all less stringent.

Failing this, Box (1983: 58) argues that corporations could successfully evade accountability for their actions by way of 'the power of corporations to intervene in the process by which corporate behaviour becomes incorporated into criminal behaviour [or not]'.

These initial ideas have, of course, seen even further refinement. This is with specific reference to explicating in greater detail the relationship between the state and corporation. Given the intensification of monopoly capital, intellectual thought from some scholarly quarters has deduced that an increase in corporate power signifies a reduction in state power. However, more astute arguments have expressed that such presumptions about the impact of intensified corporate power overlook the reality of the symbiotic relationship between states and corporations (Michalowski and Kramer 2006; Tombs and Whyte 2003). Rather than seeing corporate power replacing state power, Tombs and Whyte (2003) argue that the corporation augments the power of the state. For example, when the forces of neoliberalism successfully see public institutions and activities sold and delivered by private entities for profit, all and any errors, failures, and harms happening within these spaces are used to justify massive economic restructuring. Blame is often attributed to the vestiges of the social democratic state, rather than private corporations, making the continued sell-off of public assets and general failure of state regulation easier to accomplish and seem positively commonsensical in the face of public sector crises.

Scholars of the state have long continued to argue about the nature of state power in action. The debate typically tends to question if state power is expressed through explicit apparatuses such as the law or the judicial system, or through more subtle forms of internalised repression (see Poulantzas 2014 [1978]: 111–112). This suggests that the two are mutually exclusive. In the neoliberal state, what emerges is state power of a variegated nature, and it is precisely this dynamic nature of power, that secures the continued propagation of the system. The full and comprehensive details of power within the neoliberal state are not depicted within *Power, Crime, and Mystification*. However, what Box (1983) does achieve is to give his readers an indicative set of guiding landmarks about some of the typical arrangements of power found within this conjuncture. His astute and prescient warning concerning the intensification of corporate power, then, is one key contribution he makes to the study of the neoliberal state at a time when that project was in its infancy. It is to his commentary on 'the crime problem' more broadly, and the ways the neoliberal state crafts its response to this through processes of mystification, that we now turn.

Crime and the Neoliberal State

The power to define both 'crime' and the 'crime problem' is a strategically important feature of the neoliberal state. Crime, as those reading this are likely already aware, has no objective ontological reality (Hulsman 1986; Tombs and Hillyard 2008). Crime is not a concrete object but rather an act to which the marker of 'crime' has been successfully applied. Yet its subjective construction is not one of serendipitous relativism. What is, and what is not, defined into, or out of, 'crime' and the 'crime problem', rather than mere happenstance, is a central tenet of the exercise of political power in the neoliberal state. The power of 'crime' and the 'crime problem' lies within its moralising discourse. The construction of 'crime' and the crime problem shapes our social and public understanding of right, wrong, good, and bad. That which is ascribed as 'crime' or criminal by the state and the various other overseers of neoliberalism becomes the benchmark for immoral behaviour. That which does not fall under the remit of 'crime' and the 'crime problem' as defined by the neoliberal state fails to be taken as seriously, even where objectively more harm has been caused.

According to Box (1983: 4), there are two potential routes for analysts to take when it comes to 'crime' and the 'crime problem'. The first is the liberal 'scientific' approach. For liberal scientism the role of the researcher is that of an excavator—detecting, digging, and unearthing all the 'underreported, under recorded and non-prosecuted crimes' (ibid.). To the liberal scientific mind, the trouble with the 'crime problem' is a practical one, where resolution lies within the remit of greater administrative care, higher rates of efficiency, and reform. Whilst there is clear value in successfully recovering some of the less documented official crimes, and bringing them back into the crime picture, liberal scientism is in no way sufficient to uncover the whole truth of the crime problem. Liberal scientism, no matter its apparent successes, 'will still be denied an adequate view of those whose crimes and victimizing behaviours cause us most harm, injury and deprivation' (Box 1983: 6). The reason for this is that all its 'excavation work occurs so late in the process of constructing 'crime' and 'criminals' that it never gets to the foundations' (ibid.). Box (1983: 6) continues:

> those committed to self-report and victimization surveys do not start off asking the most important question of all: "what is serious crime?" Instead, they take serious crime as a pre- and state- defined phenomenon. But by the time crime categories or definitions have been established, the most important foundation stone of "our crime problem" has been well and truly buried in cement, beyond the reach of any liberal "scientific' shovel".

In contrast, Box (1983) then describes a 'radical reflexive' approach to the question of 'crime' and the 'crime problem'. This considers how, within a particular period of history, it comes to be that out of all the vast swathes of harmful behaviours and activities in existence, only some come to be included in state definitions of 'crime'. The answer is simple but frequently estranged from us.

As detailed by Box (1983: 7), 'criminal law categories are ideological reflections of the interests of particular powerful groups'. In the case of the neoliberal conjuncture specifically, this translates to criminal law categories and constructions of the 'crime problem' through those laws, being in the specific interests of the proliferation of the neoliberal project. The power to define 'crime' and the 'crime problem' through state law affords the neoliberal state enormous amounts of power. As

Box (1983: 7) writes, 'criminal law categories are resources, tools, instruments, designed and then used to criminalize, demoralize, incapacitate, fracture and sometimes eliminate those problem populations perceived by the powerful to be potentially or actually threatening the existing distribution of power, wealth, and privilege'. He continues, 'they [criminal laws] constitute one, and only one way by which social control over subordinate, but 'resisting', populations is exercised. For once behaviour more typically engaged in by subordinate populations has been incorporated into criminal law, then legally sanctioned punishments can be 'justifiably' imposed. In a society such as ours, populations [are] more likely to be controlled in part through criminalization' (ibid.).

Under these conditions, neoliberalism not only persists but thrives. The enormous transfers of public wealth, natural resources, and political power from domestic economies, local environments, and civil societies into the hands of multinational corporations, whose behavioural incentives revolve around profit generation and returns for shareholders at the expense of exploited classes, demand that such adjustments to our shared sense of morality take place. Just as magicians work to ensure their audience is looking precisely where they want them to, enabling even a relatively clumsy sleight of hand to go unnoticed, the state depicted by Box (1983) is shaped by a set of powerful actors working expediently to signpost our senses. In practical terms we can also argue that the limited regulation and policing of the powerful also plays an important role (see Hall et al. 1978). How this is achieved is taken up in the next section.

Mystification and the Neoliberal State

Whilst we know that processes associated with the neoliberal state have significantly skewed the public view of 'crime' and the crime problem in both the specific ways depicted by Box (1983), but also as part of broader efforts to promote and subsequently capitalise on crises for opening up new markets (Klein 2007), it often seems puzzling how such situations endure. If radically reflexive accounts of 'crime' and the 'crime problem' are available, then how do their revelations fail to breach the projected falsehoods of the neoliberal project's 'crime problem' discourse? Mystification is the idea Box (1983) finds utility in for explaining its endurance. He writes:

> for too long too many people have been socialized to see crime and criminals through the eyes of the state. There is nothing left, as Matza points out, but mystification. This is clearly revealed in the brick wall of indignation which flattens any suggestion that the crime problem defined by the state is not the only crime problem, or that criminals are not only those processed by the state. There is more to crime and criminals than the state reveals. But most people cannot see it. (ibid.: 15)

In short, when the magician whips the sheet off the cage, all we are left with is an audience aghast at where the doves, and indeed the cage itself, have gone. Our inability to see the workings of the trick rarely occupy our minds for long, for we are so overawed by the artifice and skill of the trick itself. Box's (1983) work on the concept of mystification has two aspects to it. Firstly, he seeks to readily identify key actors who play a defining role in the mystification within the neoliberal epoch. In this sense, he identifies both the police and the corporation as key actors in this process (see Chapters 2 and 3 of *Power, Crime, and Mystification*). However, the real triumph within *Power, Crime, and Mystification* lies in its illumination of the concept of mystification via its ability to explicate some of the finer important details about the state's role in misdirection and deceit on this scale. As previously depicted, most state law is designed to work in the interests of the powerful. The key term here is *most*. Whilst most laws within this conjuncture serve the interests of ruling class fractions, there crucially remain some laws that do not directly represent the interests of the ruling classes. Instead, there are several laws that seem to serve the interests of the people—those not implicated in the mass scale corruption and dishonesty of neoliberalism. The reason for their existence is twofold. Firstly, they reflect the struggles of the less powerful whose tenacity can have the capacity to elicit tangible change. These changes, or 'pertinent effects' (see Poulantzas 1982 [1968]), however, remain fragile whilst the overall balance of class forces continues to condensate into the neoliberal state overall. Secondly, it is often the case that the existence of these laws is no careless mistake on the part of the superintendents of the neoliberal project. In fact, it is quite deliberate. These laws that seem at odds with, or not in the direct interest of, the dominant discourses of the conjuncture serve a clear purpose in the process of mystification. These laws typically represent either a short-lived tactical retreat, born out of a successful pocket of resistance and/or, most importantly, a misdirection in the search for truth. What we mean by this is that it is precisely the existence of such laws within the neoliberal state that provide adequate fodder for the effective obfuscation of the truth about 'crime' and social harm (see also Pearce 1976). Laws that seem to, or do in fact, serve the interests of the people are mostly symbolic and rarely adequately or systematically enforced (Box 1983: 8). Instead, their existence is exploited by the power of the neoliberal state to project the falsehood that criminal law acts in the interests of the people. Examples are lauded as 'justice delivered as standard', rather than as isolated concessions. Whilst most laws continue to serve the interests of neoliberalism and its beneficiaries, the neoliberal state is highly proficient in taking the exception and making it the rule. This is done through 'structuring' the sparse cases of law that are not expressly in the interests of the powerful (see Hall et al. 1978: 35, 41, 55 and 66), as the 'truth' of criminal law. This depiction of criminal law is then 'amplified' (ibid.) as the 'truth' of criminal law writ large above all other alternatives, and far more accurate, portrayals.

Mystification by typical dictionary-styled definition infers the quality, or state, of being mystified; of being utterly confused and bewildered. Mystification within the neoliberal state leans far more towards a definition of mystification steeped in deception and falsehood. The dexterity of the neoliberal state results in an ability to mystify in a way that, for many, delivers satisfaction by way of the 'crime problem' and criminal law as it is presented to them in the current conjuncture. In fact, for those that partake in the neoliberal project's common-sense constructions of 'crime' and the 'crime problem', their confusion leads to their surprise when the persistent, repeated, and increasingly punitive measures of the neoliberal state's law and order mandate fails to address their concerns. By such a time, our gaze has quickly been moved onto the magician's next trick.

The Neoliberal State Then and Now: *Mystification* Pure and Simple?

Despite the attractiveness of 'mystification' as an explanatory concept, and its undeniable utility for Box in framing his selected examples, it invites several further questions which are arguably never really resolved within *Power, Crime, and Mystification*. This is because Box couples it with an underdeveloped conceptualisation of power. We must be careful not to misread him here, nor to judge his contribution unfairly, but a couple of points deserve some attention. The second part of his key claim, that '[t]here is more to crime and criminals than the state reveals. But *most people cannot see it*' (Box 1983: 15; emphasis added), seems perhaps less convincing today than it may have been four decades ago. This becomes particularly apparent if we use the book to try and reflect on contemporary statecraft and the Covid-19 pandemic (Sim and Tombs 2022), or the perennial issue of state-corporate greenwashing (Nurse 2022). Clearly, millions of people truly were *mystified* when the UK government continued to promote success stories of a vaccine rollout, all whilst the same government awarded Party donors PPE contracts with no competition, and key figures in government acted with reckless disdain for a country in lockdown. Indeed, the almost inexplicable resilience of the UK Conservative Party since 2010 at the time of writing would suggest so. Yet there are similarly millions of people who vote for and benefit from the kind of status quo critiqued by Box. There are also millions more who know full well that there is more to crime than the state reveals, but who feel relatively powerless to change things. Box (1983: 223) is well aware of this and acknowledges as much on the final page of the book: 'The autonomy of the criminal justice system, constitutionally congealed as "separation of power"', is left untampered with by those with the power, but not the will, to redirect it. Those with the will, but not the power are unable to alter the situation without much more organized and solidaristic action'.

So, whether people in 1983 were as genuinely mystified about state-corporate corruption, political nepotism, and related systemic harms as Box is suggesting they were throughout much of the book remains a moot point. Even fairly mainstream or 'status quo' accounts of 1960s counterculture, 1970s trade union activism, or the 1980s AIDS and heroin epidemics paint a cynical picture of the state's moral legitimacy. How power practically circulates among the demons (see Brown 2015) what its local and specific effects are, and what non-mystified people successfully and unsuccessfully do to resist remain unanswered questions. To be clear, we are not suggesting that Box's analyses concerning financial and legal inequalities are wrong. His longest chapter on corporate crime, for instance, is especially good at concretising the very real ways in which people, communities, and indeed entire societies, are dispossessed of their power by the financial might of the corporation due to its immense influence over markets, health and safety standards, precedents set in the criminal courts, and other key sites of decision-making and moral regulation. But Box's somewhat inconsistent clarifications on power leave him open to the critique that *Power, Crime, and Mystification*'s everyday actors are cultural or psychological 'dopes' following preestablished grounds for action (Garfinkel 1967: 68). As Lukes (2005: 150, emphasis in original) argues, 'It would be simplistic to suppose that "willing" and "unwilling" compliance to domination are mutually exclusive: one can *consent* to power and *resent* the mode of its exercise'. Box (1983) evidence that the deconstruction of 'crime' is his most compelling contribution; his accounts of power, mystification, and indeed the neoliberal state all leave readers seeking deeper explanations.

Box Forty Years On

At the start of this chapter, we provided a brief and familiar sketch of what the neoliberal state is often taken to be. We set Box's (1983) landmark work in the context of neoliberalism's ascendency in the UK. It is obviously one among many sketches. Notwithstanding the above critiques of Box, what might the relationship between neoliberalism and mystification be today? To echo a somewhat vacuous truism of all generations, we have lived through strange times. The period of austerity beginning in 2010 could be described as a major turning point in the shifting dynamics of mystification. The mask which adorns the front cover of Box's (1983) book had mostly slipped for an entire generation, only to be ripped clean off with the Brexit referendum of 2016 and empty promises of money for the NHS and endless economic prosperity for the UK. The election of Donald Trump as US President and his explicit emboldening of the American right, the Johnson government's handling of, and behaviour during, the Covid-19 pandemic, and institutional corruption, and the culture of immunity and impunity that still protects those involved, at the highest levels of government throughout this period furnish no end of interesting examples to consider the utility of 'mystification'. The pageantry of Trump, the buffoonery of Johnson, and the immense levels of real harm and corruption undergirding these superficial exterior plays have been met with mass resistance, mockery, and, worryingly, support. In the UK, when political satire actually parodied the news, the likes of *Spitting Image* or *Not The Nine O'clock News* felt like a reminder that the public could channel their anger into laughter, belittling political authority, if mostly symbolically, but occasionally materially quite powerful ways. Today, political satire which uses state mystification as its primary source material fails to trigger quite the same response. It does not just feel too close to the truth, it often *is* the truth.

Today's cost of living crisis, with further recessions on the horizon, mass stagnation of wages, crippling house prices, dangerously unaffordable energy prices, the list goes on. Within a decade, a generation of new voters has been schooled in both austerity economics ('there's no money left in the UK bank account'), emergency economics ('there's as much money as we want in the UK bank account, we must keep greasing the wheels of commerce'), and now back to those familiar artificial grimaces from our leaders waxing lyrical about 'knowing how hard it is', a sure fire cue for Austerity 2.0 (see also Flohr and Harrison 2016). If this is still mystification in action, then the novelty of Box's original tricksters has worn off somewhat since 'The Iron Lady' took aim at her familiar folk devils. Furthermore, as we have argued, voters occupying certain class positions may embrace mystifying discourses, often without believing a word of it.

Then there is the recurrent question of whether evermore frequent crises, such as the 2008 crash, Covid-19, or the war in Ukraine and its impact on fuel and food supplies have hastened the end of neoliberalism (see for example Kılıç 2021) or just its next iteration. However, whilst early neoliberals liked the classic metaphor furnished through Adam Smith's 'invisible hand' to describe the market, there was nothing invisible about the handshakes between the public state and the private market. Deregulation meant endorsing less safe production practices, but it never really meant 'free market competition'. The market may have appeared more or less free, or more or less competitive, at points between 1983 and today, but the neoliberal state has always played an active role in maintaining 'those military, defence, police, and legal structures and functions required to secure private property rights and to guarantee, by force if need be, the proper functioning of markets' (Harvey 2005: 2). It is also the case that the neoliberal state has intensified its authoritarian powers even further through changes to Trade Union Laws and the *Police, Crime, Sentencing and Court Act* 2022 (Webber 2021) reminiscent of the authoritarian state populism identified by Stuart Hall in the 1970s, 1980s, and beyond (Hall 1979/2017; 2009).

On the question of ideological epochs, Garland (2001: 168, emphasis in original) is instructive here when he writes: 'History is not the replacement of the old by the new, but the more or less extensive modification of one by the other. The *intertwining* of the established and the emergent is what structures the present, and our analysis should reflect that fact'. To understand the materiality of mystification then and now, we would need to compare general living standards, corporation tax, wages, house prices, education, healthcare, and geopolitical stability. After decades of deteriorating public transport systems, strained national healthcare, massive inequalities in education, and ongoing housing crises, we have seen time and again successive governments forced to spend big, but in ways purposefully designed to extract maximum wealth from the public and funnel it up the class structure. Arguably, mystification only works if the working classes truly believe that migrants are stealing their jobs, or that we really cannot afford to close down prisons and invest in social care and community restoration, or that street crime is something to fear more than men in suits brokering shareholder deals. Whilst social media provides the working classes with unbridled access to counter-narratives today, does it productively combat the kind of mystification concerning Box, or simply breed endemic cynicism?

Conclusion: The Importance of Holding Radical Ground

Having given Box a fair reading, we suggest his thesis leaves unanswered questions concerning the relationship between power and mystification. We have considered where his work 'sits' in relation to today's neoliberal state, furnished as we are with such examples of contemporary statecraft as Brexit and Covid-19, alongside social media as a political communication network. To say that Box's (1983) contribution to our conceptual understanding of the state in *Power, Crime, and Mystification* is modest should not be read as barbed criticism. In comparison to other intellectual works produced both prior to and during the neoliberal conjuncture, found within the humanities and social sciences, the text lacks a comprehensive conceptualisation of the neoliberal state. Yet it does do something quite extraordinary at the time, in rendering some of the capacities of the state intelligible as criminological research objects. For intellectuals concerned with the power of the state and its ability to construct a 'crime problem' that obscures a wider, and often more potent, set of harms within society, *Power, Crime, and Mystification* (and other notable texts from this period) performed a crucial role. That role was to resist the neoliberal deluge of the 1970s onwards by holding radical ground at a time when intellectual acquiescence to the project of neoliberalism was rife. *Power, Crime, and Mystification* becomes a seminal text in this context. The book's commitment to keeping alive a radical agenda for those for whom the politics of 'crime', deviance, and social harm were major concepts within their scholarly concerns was of vital importance. Without *Power, Crime, and Mystification*, and other works like it, the hegemonic project of capitalist imperialism in its neoliberal form would surely have secured the relevant disciplines entirely for its own ends. Instead, there is an endurance of a radical project within the study of 'crime' and deviance. Although this project remains a path less travelled in comparison to the Goliath of mainstream criminology, the radical pluck of Box (1983) and others is a major driving force in the dogged persistence of their contemporary successors. As the mystifying powers of the neoliberal state persist, the task for radical scholars is to not only reveal the true scope of 'crime' and harm but to summon the necessary dedication and commitment to subjecting the neoliberal state to continued rigorous scrutiny.

A commitment to revealing the composite nature of state power within the neoliberal conjuncture today is as important as it ever was. Never has this been more the case than with reference to the increased abilities of the state, and its concomitant corporate entities, to structure and amplify (Hall et al. 1978) the 'crime problem', having exponentially increased its capacity for obscuring the truth through the commodification and use of surveillance technology (Zuboff 2018). The task ahead remains a long and arduous one, but when it comes to the possibility of subjecting the neoliberal state to continued scrutiny on matters of 'crime', deviance, and social harm, to Steven Box and his fellow radically reflexive scholars, we can, and should be, truly thankful.

Acknowledgements With thanks to Becky Clarke whose articulation of the construction of 'crime' and the 'crime problem' within our shared endeavours is a constant source of intellectual nourishment.

References

Box, S. 1983. *Power, Crime, and Mystification*. London: Routledge.
Brown, W. 2015. *Undoing the Demos: Neoliberalism's Stealth Revolution*. Massachusetts: The MIT Press.
Flohr, M., and Y. Harrison. 2016. Reading the Conjuncture: State, Austerity, and Social Movements, an Interview with Bob Jessop. *Rethinking Marxism* 28 (2): 306–321.
Garfinkel, H. 1967. *Studies in Ethnomethodology*. Cambridge: Polity Press.
Garland, D. 2001. *The Culture of Control*. Oxford: Oxford University Press.
Hall, S., C. Critcher, T. Jefferson, B. Roberts, and J. Clarke. 1978. *Policing the Crisis: Mugging, the State and Law and Order*. London: Bloomsbury Publishing.

Hall, S. 1979/2017. The Great Moving Right Show. In *Selected Political Writings: The Great Moving Right Show and Other Essays Stuart Hall*, ed. S. Davison, D. Featherstone, M. Rustin, and B. Schwarz, 172–185. Chadwell Heath: Lawrence and Wishart.

Hall, S., and M. Jacques, eds. 1983. *The Politics of Thatcherism*. London: Lawrence and Wishart.

Hall, S. 2009. Preface. In *State Power Crime*, ed. R. Coleman, J. Sim, S. Tombs, and D. Whyte, xii–xviii. London: Sage.

Harvey, D. 2005. *A Brief History of Neoliberalism*. Oxford: Oxford University Press.

Hulsman, L.H. 1986. Critical Criminology and the Concept of Crime. *Contemporary Crises* 10: 63–80.

Kılıç, S. 2021. Does COVID-19 as a Long Wave Turning Point Mean the End of Neoliberalism? *Critical Sociology* 47 (4–5): 609–623.

Klein, N. 2007. *The Shock Doctrine*. London: Penguin Books.

Lukes, S. 2005. *Power: A Radical View*, 2nd ed. Basingstoke: Palgrave Macmillan.

Mair, M. 2021. *The Problem of the State*. Oxon: Routledge.

Michalowski, R.J., and R.C. Kramer, eds. 2006. *State-Corporate Crime: Wrongdoing at the Intersection of Business and Government*. Michigan: Rutgers University Press.

Miliband, R. 1973. Poulantzas and the Capitalist State. *New Left Review* 82: 83–92. https://newleftreview.org/issues/i82/articles/ralph-miliband-poulantzas-and-the-capitalist-state. Accessed 31 Mar 2023.

Nurse, A. 2022. *Cleaning Up Greenwash: Corporate Environmental Crime and the Crisis of Capitalism*. Rowman and Littlefield.

Pearce, F. 1976. *Crimes of the Powerful: Marxism, Crime, and Deviance*. London: Pluto Press.

Pearce, F., and S. Tombs. 1998. *Toxic Capitalism: Corporate Crime and the Chemical Industry*. Oxon: Routledge.

Poulantzas, N. 1969. The Problem of the Capitalist State. *New Left Review* 58: 67–78. https://newleftreview.org/issues/i58/articles/nicos-poulantzas-the-problem-of-the-capitalist-state. Accessed 31 Mar 2023.

Poulantzas, N. 1979 [1974]. *Classes in Contemporary Capitalism*. London: Verso.

Poulantzas, N. 1982 [1968]. *Political Power and Social Classes*. London: Verso.

Poulantzas, N. 2014 [1978]. *State, Power, Socialism*. London: Verso.

Scraton, P., ed. 1987. *Law, Order and the Authoritarian State*. Milton Keynes: Open University Press.

Sim, J., and S. Tombs. 2022. Narrating the Coronavirus Crisis: State Talk and State Silence in the UK. *Justice, Power and Resistance* 5 (1–2): 67–90.

Thatcher, M. 1983. Speech to Conservative Party Conference. Washington: Thatcher Foundation. https://www.margaretthatcher.org/document/105454. Accessed 2 June 2022.

Thorsen, D.E. 2010. The Neoliberal Challenge: What Is Neoliberalism? *Contemporary Readings in Law and Social Justice* 2: 188–213.

Tombs, S., and P. Hillyard. 2008. Beyond Criminology? In *Criminal Obsessions: Why Harm Matters More Than Crime*, ed. D. Dorling, D. Gordon, P. Hillyard, C. Pantazis, S. Pemberton, and S. Tombs, 2nd ed., 6–23. https://www.crimeandjustice.org.uk/publications/criminal-obsessions-why-harm-matters-more-crime-2nd-edition. Accessed 28 Oct 2022.

Tombs, S., and D. Whyte. 2003. Unmasking the Crimes of the Powerful: Establishing Some Rules of Engagement. In *Unmasking the Crimes of the Powerful: Scrutinizing States and Corporations*, ed. S. Tombs and D. Whyte, 261–272. Oxford: Peter Lang.

Webber, F. 2021. Britain's Authoritarian Turn. *Race and Class* 62 (4): 106–120.

Zuboff, S. 2018. *The Age of Surveillance Capitalism: The Fight for a Human Future at the New Frontier of Power*. London: Profile Books Ltd.

8

The Austerity State, 'Social Junk' and the Mystification of Violence

Chris Grover

Introduction

This chapter focuses upon austerity in Britain and the social harms it is inflicting upon working-class people there. In particular, the chapter examines cuts to social security provision during the 'age of austerity' (2010 to 2019), the consequences of which endure through its cumulative impact that will be felt for many years to come and which, for example, have left those in the most economically perilous positions, notably working class, disabled and BAME[1] people, and women, especially exposed during the current cost of living crisis. The chapter draws upon and extends arguments from Box's (1983) *Power, Crime and Mystification* that the most harmful acts are committed by institutions

---

[1] The BAME category was questioned in a report by David Lammy in 2017, although there is still some debate as the best alternative language to be adopted in its place.

C. Grover (✉)
Department of Sociology, Lancaster University, Lancaster, UK
e-mail: c.grover@lancaster.ac.uk

© The Author(s), under exclusive license to Springer Nature
Switzerland AG 2023
D. G. Scott and J. Sim (eds.), *Demystifying Power, Crime and Social Harm*, Critical
Criminological Perspectives, https://doi.org/10.1007/978-3-031-46213-9_8

(including the state), but such acts are rendered invisible through the criminalisation of the least powerful people; that criminal justice operates within and reproduces capitalism's inequities, which, and closely linked, creates a need to control and manage people deemed outside of capitalist social and economic relations.

Bringing these foci together the chapter examines ways enduring austerity and its role in deepening and extending poverty and destitution can be understood as a form of violence because of the detrimental impacts it has upon what Spitzer (1975: 638 and 645) describes as 'problem populations', most notably the 'social junk'. These are people who Vegh Weis (2017) argues are over-criminalised for their exclusion from capitalist production and as an economic burden. The impacts of poverty and destitution upon the life chances (e.g. poorer education, increased likelihood of unemployment and 'scarred' working lives) are well known and, therefore, are avoidable and alterable. Nevertheless, enduring austerity has exacerbated such conditions through punitive welfarism, whose intention, rather than relieving needs, is, on the constant threat of sanction and censure, to surveil and demand conformity (Sim 2014). In doing so, the chapter argues, the British state has acted to harm (injure and kill) the poorest people through austerity-driven developments to impoverish them and systemic indifference to the consequences of that impoverishment. Consequently, the chapter goes on to argue that the impacts of austerity, rooted in long-standing capitalist concerns with (re)commodifying labour power, are contradictory, degrading labour power, and for many reducing the possibility that it will be (re-)commodified.

Power, Crime and Mystification

While it was not unique, the strength of Box's (1983, 13) *Power, Crime and Mystification* lies in its argument that definitions of crime are ideological and have little to do with 'those behaviours which objectively and avoidably cause… most harm, injury, and suffering'. Notably, he argued that crime and criminalisation can be understood as social control strategies that, among other things:

...render invisible the vast amount of avoidable harm, injury, and deprivation imposed upon the ordinary population by the state, transnational and other corporations, and thereby remove the effects of these "crimes" from the causal nexus for explaining "conventional crimes" committed by ordinary people. (ibid.: 14)

At the time, this dimension of Box's work was criticised by more orthodox criminologists. Waddington (1985), for instance, argued it was too inclusive of 'non-criminal' acts concerned with the harms caused by corporations and the police. This, he argued, was a reflection of liberal criminological sentiments, and, in a utilitarian kind of way, Waddington (1985: 76) suggested that 'often, the choice is not between causing or not causing harm but involves balancing harm to some against benefits to others'. Such critiques, however, were embedded in traditional criminological concerns with acts defined as being criminal by the state and made little effort to acknowledge or explain why the harms of which Box (1983) wrote were endured by the least powerful in society—working-class people who were income poor and socially and culturally excluded through the stigma attached to their poverty and their over-criminalised statuses. And, of course, Box's critics could not have foreseen later intellectual developments, in part informed by his work, but also by zeimiology.[2] This extended the argument that criminology was too narrowly focused upon those acts and behaviours defined as being criminal by the state.

Arguably, however, Box (1983) was too limited in his focus. While Waddington (1985) bemoans his inclusivity, the argument in this chapter is that *Power, Crime and Mystification* was not expansive enough. Reference in the above quote to 'deprivation imposed… upon the ordinary population by the state' (Box 1983: 14) is helpful but needs extending from Box's (1983) focus upon the systems and agencies of law and order. The 'avoidable harm' of the state, for instance, in *Power, Crime and Mystification* is restricted to various issues related to policing and a lack of law enforcement in relation to particular types of crime

---

[2] In a narrow sense zeimiology is the study of social harms. In a broader sense, Kotzé (2018) argues that, in addition to social harms, zeimiology can also be understood as being concerned with the traditional focus of criminology, punishment and (in)justice.

(e.g. corporate crime and sexual offences). Important though they are, this chapter broadens Box's (1983) concerns to focus upon relationships between material deprivation imposed by the state and social harm. The substantive focus is upon austerity in social security policy for working-age people.

This argument for extending Box's (1983) analysis is consistent with his concern, drawing upon Spitzer (1975) with the ways criminal justice is embedded in the economic foundations and social relations of capitalism in which the processes of capital accumulation create the conditions where some groups are constructed as needing to be controlled (the 'social dynamite') and others (the 'social junk') are in need of being managed. The 'social dynamite', Spitzer (1975) argues, tends to be younger, more disaffected and politically volatile than 'social junk', and, therefore, tends to be dealt with via the criminal justice system. In contrast, the 'social junk', although not exclusively, tends to be dealt with via the services and interventions of the welfare state. Spitzer (1975) is careful to argue that the two problem populations are not necessarily discreet and that there is fluidity in their categorisation, which was embedded, among other things, in the economic, ideological and political dimensions of deviance production.

Nevertheless, the focus in this chapter is upon the ways in which enduring austerity has impacted upon the 'social junk', expanded by Vegh Weis (2017) to include all those people who survive upon social assistance and precarious forms of wage-labour and self-employment. Following Vegh Weis (2017), the 'social dynamite' in their refusal to be incorporated into such activity as wage-labour often do not apply or qualify for social assistance because they are unable or unwilling to meet its demands for labour power commodification. While the 'social junk' presents little political threat, Vegh Weis (2017) argues it is over-criminalised as a consequence of its minimally harmful survival strategies and an embedding of social assistance in a crime-informed logic via punitive social welfare provision. This can be seen in Britain, for example, in changes since Spitzer's (1975) and Box's (1983) work in the ways in which lone mothers, sick and disabled people and (low-paid) part-time workers have all come to be viewed in policy terms as uncommodified or under-commodified labour power. And they are subject to increasingly parsimonious and conditional social security provision, which is embedded in crime-informed discourses that criminalise working-age benefit receipt and recipients (Grover 2012).

This chapter brings together these concerns to argue that in Britain austerity cuts to working-age social security policy is ingrained in longer-term concerns with the (re-)commodification of under- and unemployed labour power[3] in ways that were meant to be, and which were experienced, as being socially violent.

Britain's Austerity State and Social Security

Blyth (2013: 2) notes that austerity 'is a form of voluntary deflation in which the economy adjusts through the reduction of wages, prices and public spending to restore competitiveness, which is (supposedly) best achieved by cutting the state's budget, debts and deficits'. This describes austerity in a techno-economic way. Jessop (2015), however, argues that austerity is better understood as having various forms with different chronologies and aims. What he describes as '*conjunctural austerity policies*' (Jessop 2015: 97, emphasis in the original) are short-term responses to immediate difficulties, with the aim of safeguarding existing economic and political arrangements. In contrast, what Jessop (ibid.) calls the '*enduring politics of austerity*' is longer term and has transformative potential to increase the power of capital. In this form, austerity can be understood as a concerted attack upon social democracy and the welfare state (Farnsworth and Irving 2016) and, as Jessop (2015) argues, can be a response to a real crisis or one manufactured for political purposes.[4]

---

[3] The offer of working people's ability to do wage-labour as a commodity, something to be sold to those employers willing to pay for it. While labour power is not a true commodity because it is not produced in a profit-orientated process, it is nevertheless treated as a commodity in capitalist societies, as something that can be bought and sold in labour markets. Forcing benefit recipients to turn their labour power into such a commodity is central to social security provision for working-age people in Britain and many other welfare capitalist countries.

[4] In this chapter, it is argued that while the 'real' origins of austerity in Britain were primarily in the 2008–09 North Atlantic Financial Crisis, social security austerity was 'manufactured' via ideologically informed discourses through which the alleged detrimental impacts of extant

Following Seymour (2014), the transformative potential of austerity, includes such things as the promotion of precarity, the redistribution of income from workers to capital and a shift from welfarism to workfarism. In this version, austerity can be understood as being an offensive strategy to the benefit of capitalism, to which, and through a range of economic and social policies, the state is central in institutionalising enduring austerity (c.f. Jessop 2016), which is embedded in 'coercion, [and] casual sadism' (Jessop 2015: 98).

Since the inception of collectively organised support for working-age people a central principle has been that it should not economically or socially undermine the idea that individuals should support themselves (and, if they have one, their families) through wage-labour. This is demonstrated in such ideas as 'less eligibility' in the eighteenth and nineteenth centuries, 'work incentives'; 'the why work syndrome'; the 'unemployment trap' and 'replacement ratios' in the twentieth century. And policies, such as the nineteenth century workhouse and labour tests, the genuinely seeking work test of the period between WWI and WWII; labour and instruction centres (what Hannington (1937) described as 'slave' and 'concentration' camps) of the 1930s; the operation of the wage-stop between the 1930s and 1970s; cuts to the real value of out-of-work benefits and their scope in the 1980s; the introduction of Jobseeker's Allowance in the 1990s; the conditionality turn of 1997–2010 Labour governments; and the extension of supplementing low wages with social security benefits since the 1970s. These ideas and policy developments demonstrate a continuous policy elite concern with the foundations of capitalism, most notably that the actions of the state (at whatever scale) should not undermine the need of working people to do wage-labour, otherwise its source of profit and wealth accumulation (the commodified labour power of working people) would be threatened.

Given those observations of the fundamentalism of labour power commodification to poor relief and social security policy, it is possible to argue that a 'crisis of commodification' which frames contemporary enduring social security austerity was manufactured by the state. So, for

---

provision on the behaviour and morality of poor people, and on capital accumulation were constructed.

example, the then British Prime Minister, David Cameron (2012, npn), argued that existing working-age social security 'encourages the worst in people – that [it] incites laziness, ...excuses bad behaviour, ...erodes self-discipline, ...discourages hard work' and ...'has sent out some incredibly damaging signals. That it pays not to work. ...It gave us millions of working-age people sitting at home on benefits... It created a culture of entitlement'. Cameron's words were part of a broader discursive attempt of governments of all political hues in the 2010s to construct unemployment and poverty as a consequence of social security policy acting to decommodify labour power. As noted above, there was little new about this. Edmiston (2017), however, suggests that both the scale of cuts and the enhanced role of sanctions and benefit withdrawal, denoted social security policy in the 2010s as being different to previous times.

The cuts to social security were eye-watering. In 2010 savings of £18 billion a year were announced followed by a further £3.7 billion and £12 billion per annum announced in 2012 and 2015 respectively. It is estimated that by 2023 'welfare spending' would be £40 billion a year lower than it would have been had the cuts not occurred (Garnham 2020). These cuts, however, were not evenly spread across claimant groups, but focused upon working-age 'social junk'. Taylor-Gooby (2017) estimates that the 2010s' austerity announcements amounted to about a third of the social security budget for such people. They had a disproportionate impact upon women, racialised and disabled people, and families with children.

The cuts were made through over 50 changes that have slashed the real and nominal value of benefits, made them more difficult to claim, extended the breadth and depth of conditionality and extended means-testing (Garnham 2020). Despite claims to the contrary during the crisis of commodification, even before the cuts Britain's benefit system condemned recipients to living below measures of subsistence and poverty (Grover 2019). The immediate impact, therefore, of austerity was to impoverish further already poor people. Unsurprisingly, data suggests that the number of people in Britain living in poverty and destitution has increased in the twenty-first century. It is estimated, for instance, that the number of children living in relative poverty increased by 700,000 between 2011/12 and 2017/19[5] and that in 2019 a million households (2.4 million people) experienced destitution (a lack of access to essentials, such as clothing, food, heating and shelter and extremely low or no income). Such observations were before the Covid pandemic and the more recent 'cost of living crisis', both of which saw temporary, and often selective and exclusionary measures (Wiggan and Grover 2022; Adam et al. 2022), which did nothing to address the impact of the preceding decade of austerity on benefit incomes. The casual sadism of austerity continues.

Violence and Austerity

We have seen that Box (1983: 7) alluded to a need for the criminological gaze to be extended to also focus upon what he described as 'avoidable harm'. Most notably for this chapter, Box (1983) pointed to the fact that the criminal law focused only upon some forms of avoidable killings as murder. Deaths, for instance, resulting from negligence (such as unsafe working conditions); a lack of safety standards; a lack of regulatory oversight/enforcement and the manufacture of unsafe products were excluded from definitions of murder. Equally, Box (1983) could have noted those people not killed, but maimed and disabled by such activities and which were (and are) excluded from understandings of other forms of violence against the person. In many senses, Box's (1983) observations can be understood as being (partly) the intellectual roots of more contemporary concerns with social harm, the ways in which over the life-course people are economically, physically, and psychologically and emotionally damaged by the policy decisions and developments of the state.

In these instances, death and injury are a consequence of institutional action and inaction, and the operation of systems and structures. Such violence has been described as 'structural' or 'indirect' by Galtung (1969), who argues it can be understood as violence because of the impact they have upon the mental and physical 'realisations' of people, in particular, causing differences between the potential (what could have

---

[5] https://ifs.org.uk/publications/15512. Accessed 6 April 2022.

been) and the actual (what is). It is the detrimental impacts upon people and the fact they are a consequence of alterable social conditions and relations that make austerity a form of violence. There is obvious resonance here with Box's (1983) concerns with avoidable harm and that less powerful people are 'physically and psychologically damaged through the greed, apathy, negligence, indifference and the unaccountability of the relatively more powerful' (Box 1983: 11).

The harmful effects of poverty upon working-class people have been acknowledged since the mid-nineteenth century when both orthodox (e.g. French surgeon René Villermé and English utilitarian Edwin Chadwick) and heterodox (for example, Friedrich Engels, 1993, originally 1845) analyses highlighted what is now described as the social gradient of health (Birn 2009). The orthodox analyses found the causes of the poorer health and earlier death of working-class people, not to be related to the conditions in which working-class people were forced to labour and live, but in a need for more moral education and laissez-faire industrialism, or action that addressed such things as sanitation, but left unaddressed poor wages and labour conditions. In contrast, Engels' (1993) analysis pointed to the impact of the conditions of wage-labour upon the physical health of working-class people. He argued poor working conditions and wages, and consequential poor diets and housing, injured and killed working people.

For Engels (1993: 106), the condemnation of large numbers of working people to lives that killed them at ages younger than otherwise would have been the case and that meant they often lived with capitalist-induced poor health, could be understood as social murder. In recent years the idea of social murder has seen an intellectual and popular revival, with it, for example, being used to examine a concern with the destruction of regulations designed to mitigate some of the harmful effects of capitalism (Tombs 2017); a critique of conservative economics (Chernomas and Hudson 2007); and specific events, such as the Grenfell Fire that in its immediacy killed at least 72 people in tower block accommodation in London (Tombs 2019; see also Drake and Scott, this volume) and responses to the Covid-19 pandemic in the United Kingdom and other countries (Abassi 2021; McGibbon 2021). Notably, I have argued elsewhere (Grover 2019) that social security austerity in the 2010s can be understood as a form of social murder because of the ways in which it has undoubtedly led to early death via destitution and, drawing upon Mills (2018) 'austerity suicide' and, in the longer term, will detrimentally impact upon the lives and life chances of poor people by worsening, for instance, their health, their educational achievement and further embedding their material and cultural exclusion. In a material sense, enduring social security austerity has starved people of the economic resources needed for such necessities as food, heat and shelter and via the affective economy it has acted to stigmatise benefit receipt and recipients, and to increase anxiety through the fetishising of being productive and economically independent.

While criminologically the idea of social murder is difficult because of the importance of intent (mens rea) to criminal law, studies of social violence point to the fact that social harms, including social murder, can be the consequence of both intent and indifference. Indeed, Box (1983: 21) argues that while the criminal law is concerned with acts of intent, 'indifference rather than intent may well be the greater cause of avoidable human suffering'. Social security austerity is embedded in such indifference, an indifference that Pemberton (2004) highlights is embedded in wage-labour-related capitalist hegemony.

Capitalism, Violence and the Austerity State

The dominant discourse constructing enduring social security austerity for working-age 'social junk' in Britain was a need to control public spending in the context of the North Atlantic Financial Crisis. However, as was seen above, central to that discourse was a manufactured crisis of commodification; that extant social security provision acted to decommodify labour power. Such discourse produced the idea that, not only was social security unaffordable in its pre-austerity forms, but that it disincentivised the 'social junk' from fulfilling their socio-economic responsibilities.

In this sense, cuts to benefits were part of a strategy to force workless people to (re)commodify their labour power with the aim of swelling the size and the closeness of the reserve army of labour to labour markets to increase the number of people in wage-labour without igniting wage inflation. From a British government's point of view, it has been a successful strategy. It, for example, pointed to the record number of people in wage-labour (32.78 million in Summer 2019) (Leaker 2019) and a falling proportion of children living in households where there was no adult in wage-labour (9.3 per cent of children in 2019, compared to 19.7 per cent in 1996) (Watson 2019). Rightly, however, critics note concerns with the quality of many jobs, for instance, the number of zero-hour contracts; the incidence of part-time and low paid wage-labour and the fact that the majority of children living in poverty live in households where at least one person is in wage-labour (Child Poverty Action Group 2019).

Such observations, however, provide a weak critique of the (re)commodifying aims of social security austerity. First, they imply it would have been acceptable had 'good' wage-labour been its consequences, and, second, the focus upon outcomes ignores the violence upon which the commodification of labour power was (and is) premised. To make 'social junk' compete for and take wage-labour, they were in a contemporary version of 'less eligibility' to be further impoverished through severe and enduring austerity in social security provision. Hence, it is possible to argue that the mechanisms of commodification were socially violent, for they created harms that were avoidable and alterable, and had a detrimental impact on, in Galtung's (1969: 168) words, 'what could have been' for many people and families. Given the centrality of the (re-)commodification of labour power to ensuring the supply of labour, it is possible to argue that the exploitative basis of capitalist societies is embedded in social violence. The enforcing of labour power commodification via coerced destitution means social security austerity by its very nature is socially violent, further harming the 'social junk'.

Similar to Engels' (1993) observations of the mid-nineteenth century, contemporary austerity-driven poverty and destitution detrimentally impact upon the health of working-class people. Infant mortality, for example, has recently increased in England, particularly in the poorest local authorities, the most likely causes of which are increasing poverty and austerity-related cuts to preventative services (Taylor-Robinson et al. 2019). Research comparing the situation in Glasgow, Liverpool and

Manchester (Schofield et al. 2021) highlights the impact of austerity in stalling improvements to mortality rates in each city. To help reverse this Schofield et al. (2021: 67) argue that policies 'to protect, and restore, the income of the poorest in society are... urgently needed'.

'Austerity deaths' are recorded in hardcopy (We are Spartacus 2015) and electronically (for instance, Calum's List[6] and Remember the Dead),[7] and poor material circumstances brought about by austerity have been recorded by coroners as being linked to deaths (O'Hara 2017). British newspapers are replete with examples of people who have died following problematic interactions with the Department for Work and Pensions (DWP), and which had detrimental impacts upon their mental and physical health.[8] The recording of malnutrition on death certificates, increased by nearly a fifth (18 per cent, from 399 to 471) in England and Wales between 2010 and 2017,[9] although it is estimated that poor diets, which are most likely to be endured by the poorest people, contribute to 64,000 deaths per year in England (Dimbleby 2021).

Meanwhile, Mills' (2018: 317) conceptualisation of 'austerity suicide' provides a counter to orthodox explanations of self-killing that are embedded in individualised and medicalised explanations to highlight that 'people are killing themselves because austerity is killing them'. Evidence, for example, suggests that Employment and Support Allowance (ESA)[10] recipients are much more likely to have considered killing themselves in comparison to the general population (66.4 per cent, compared to 21.7) and had tried to do so (43.2 per cent, compared to 6.7 per cent) (McManus et al. 2016: 3). This demonstrates

---

[6] http://calumslist.org/. Accessed 7 May 2023.

[7] https://www.facebook.com/ribbonsforwelfare/. Accessed 7 May 2023.

[8] The British Broadcasting Corporation, for instance, has compiled a database of press reports of 82 people who have died after DWP activity, such as the termination of benefit claims (Homer, A. [2021], *Deaths of people on benefits prompt inquiry call*, www.bbc.co.uk/news/uk-56819727. Accessed 7 May 2023).

[9] Office for National Statistics (2018) *Deaths where malnutrition was the underlying cause of death or was mentioned anywhere on the death certificate, persons, England and Wales, 2001 to 2017*, https://www.ons.gov.uk/peoplepopulationandcommunity/birthsdeathsandmarriages/deaths/adhocs/009065deathswheremalnutritionwastheunderlyingcauseofdeathorwasmentionedanywhereonthedeathcertificatepersonsenglandandwales2001to2017. Accessed 7 May 2023.

[10] ESA is a benefit in Britain for people adjudged through a medicalised assessment to be unable to work.

the psycho-social effects of what is described as a fear of the brown envelope arriving to call disabled people for disability-related assessments to establish or confirm benefit receipt (Soldatic and Morgan 2017). Quantitative research points to the impacts of this. It is estimated, for example, that for every 10,000 Work Capability Assessments[11] there are an additional six suicides, 2,700 reported cases of 'mental health problems' and 7,020 antidepressant items prescribed (Barr et al. 2015).

Austerity, however, does not just have such immediate impacts. As Cooper and Whyte (2017: 24) note, the 'slow violence' of austerity – that which has 'the most damaging effects… will take years to be fully realised'. An increasing number of people in Britain, for instance, are reliant upon charitable provision (food banks) to feed themselves and their families, and parents (primarily mothers) are regularly missing meals (Garthwaite 2016). Evidence paints a bleak austerity-related picture of hunger in Britain's poorest families caused by falling incomes, administrative delays and the imposition of sanctions (Loopstra 2018; Loopstra et al. 2018). In a survey of foodbank users Loopstra and Lalor (2017, cited in Loopstra 2018: 57) found that the majority (78 per cent) of households could, according to the United States Department of Agriculture Adult Food Security Module, be classed as 'severely food insecure' as they 'had skipped meals, gone without eating, lost weight or gone whole days without eating, due to a lack of money for food' (ibid.). The evidence points to social security provision in Britain for working-age people being 'not sufficient for low-income households to meet their basic food needs' (ibid.).

While the Marmot Review (Marmot 2010) on health inequalities was problematic in its wage-labour-related orthodoxy (it was embedded in a discourse of not reducing incentives for people to (re-)commodify their labour power), it recommended that to help address inequalities in England a healthy standard of living for all was required. At the time, England's social security benefits were set at levels below what was then described as a minimum income for a healthy living (MIHL) and a

---

[11] The medical assessment that determines whether an applicant is sick or disabled enough to receive ESA.

Minimum Income Standard (MIS) (Marmot 2010). Since then the situation has worsened. By 2019 social security benefits for couples and lone mothers with two dependent children were less than 60 per cent of the MIS (56.2 per cent and 58.3 per cent respectively) and less than a third (31.5 per cent) for a single working-age person (Hirsch 2019: Table 4). This worsening position was acknowledged in Marmot et al.'s (2021) update a decade later after his original review was published.

Although, not couched in the language of social violence, nevertheless, Marmot et al.'s (2021: 5) report reinforced the point that austerity would have long-term effects—that it would, for example, 'cut a long shadow over the lives of the children born and growing up under its effects'. And while this undoubtedly relates to the health impacts of austerity, it equally relates to the harms that poverty wrecks upon the broader potential of people enduring austerity to flourish. In Britain, for example, children from the poorest households are much less likely to gain 'good' educational qualifications (Exley 2016). While governments choose to focus upon an alleged lack of aspiration and a lack of engagement with opportunity among poorer pupils and households (Spohrer et al. 2018), poverty undoubtedly impacts upon the education of income poor children. Evidence suggests that poorer children often have difficult educational experiences (for example, being unable to partake in school trips and activities that have to be paid for; poorer relationships with teachers; and have to cope with feelings of anxiety and uncertainty linked to concerns with inclusion) (Exley 2016). Social security austerity has exacerbated such issues.

What these various observations suggest is that while the aim of social security austerity was to commodify labour power, its violence means for many people it is having the opposite effect. In the short and longer term it reduces potential labour power by both restricting its possible supply and increasing its distance from labour markets through, for instance, its impacts upon the mental and physical health of working-class people and the ability of their children to thrive in education. This points to the problematic nature of (re)commodifying labour power through poverty and destitution; that it ignores the economic basis of the various factors that are required to reproduce labour power. This should not be surprising, for it is embedded in a 'work first' approach where the focus upon immediate, entry-level employment means qualification and longevity in wage-labour are less important than the supply of labour. In other words, as Peck and Theodore (2000: 123) note, the concern is with reproducing a 'secure labour supply for insecure work'.

Conclusion

This chapter has focused upon the harms that enduring austerity has created in Britain. It draws upon and extends Steven Box's (1983) arguments in *Power, Crime and Mystification* that harms enacted by the state are rarely seen as being criminal, even though they are greater in scope and effect than many acts criminalised by the law. The chapter, however, has argued that *Power, Crime and Mystification* was too narrowly focused upon the acts of the criminal justice-related institutions. By conjoining this argument with Box's (1983) concern with the broader context in which criminal justice operates, notably the regulation and management of 'social junk', and embedding it in a manufactured crisis of commodification, the chapter has examined enduring austerity for 'social junk' in Britain. Its aim has been to transform social security in ways that have created a forced labour supply for precarious forms of employment. The poorest people are being coerced through destitution into competing for such wage-labour through cuts to social security provision and the ratcheting up of restrictions to it.

In doing so, the chapter has demonstrated the ways in which 'social junk' are criminalised because their receipt of social assistance is taken as an indication of behavioural and moral deficiencies, rather than economic need. It has also shown how this involves the mystification of the violence of state-enacted social security austerity, through which structural and systemic problems and their impacts are constructed as being the responsibility of poor people, rather than being embedded in the social relations and economic practices of capitalism and the state's role within them. This has involved the state taking a socially violent approach through punitive social welfare policies and is linked to an ideological anti-statism, the aim of which is withdrawing of state responsibility for supporting poor people.

The chapter, however, has also demonstrated that while the aim may have been the (re)commodification of labour power austerity can be understood as having effects that are inconsistent with this. In many senses, this reflects the contradictory position of 'social junk' embedded in the hegemony of capitalist economic and social relations. On the one hand, it is required to maintain downward pressure on wages as part of the reserve army of labour. On the other hand, it is seen as an economic drain upon the fundamental capitalist aim of ever-greater levels of capital accumulation. There can, however, be no doubt that enduring austerity is socially violent, harming working-class people by detrimentally impacting upon those dimensions of their lives—their health, education and so forth—in which their ability to labour is embedded. Such impacts have been known about for many years and, therefore, they are avoidable and alterable, but since 2010 governments have, beyond short-term and often exclusionary measures in relation to specific events (e.g. Covid support), refused to change course. It is then, as Box (1983) argued, the systemic indifference of the political and policy elite to the impacts of social security austerity that is particularly damaging to that group of people constructed as the 'social junk', the least powerful working-class people.

References

Abassi, K. 2021. Covid-19: Social Murder, They Wrote—Elected, Unaccountable, and Unrepentant. *British Medical Journal* 372: n314.

Adam, S., C. Emmerson, H. Karjalainen, P. Johnson, and R. Joyce. 2022. *IFS Response to Government Cost of Living Support Package, Institute for Fiscal Studies*. https://ifs.org.uk/publications/16066.

Barr, B., D. Taylor-Robinson, D. Stuckler, R. Loopstra, A. Reeves, and M. Whitehead. 2015. First, Do No Harm: Are Disability Assessments Associated with Adverse Trends in Mental Health? A Longitudinal Ecological Study. *Journal of Epidemiology Community Health* 70 (4): 339–345.

Birn, A.-E. 2009. Making It Politic(al): Closing the Gap in a Generation: Health Equity Through Action on the Social Determinants of Health. *Social Medicine* 4 (3): 166–182.

Blyth, M. 2013. *Austerity: The History of a Dangerous Idea*. Oxford: Oxford University Press.

Box, S. 1983. *Power, Crime and Mystification*. London: Tavistock.

Cameron, D. 2012. *Speech by the Prime Minister David Cameron on welfare*, June 25. www.gov.uk/government/speeches/welfare-speech.

Chernomas, R., and I. Hudson. 2007. *Social Murder and Other Shortcomings of Conservative Economics*. Winnipeg: Arbeiter Ring Publishing.

Child Poverty Action Group. 2019. *Child Poverty in Working Families on the Rise*. Downloaded at: https://cpag.org.uk/news-blogs/news-listings/child-poverty-working-families-rise. Accessed 6 Nov 2019.

Cooper, V., and D. Whyte. 2017. Introduction: The Violence of Austerity. In *The Violence of Austerity*, ed. V. Cooper and D. Whyte, 1–31. London: Pluto Press.

Dimbleby, H. 2021. *National Food Strategy: Independent Review. The Plan*. https://www.nationalfoodstrategy.org/the-report/.

Edmiston, D. 2017. Review Article: Welfare, Austerity and Social Citizenship in the UK. *Social Policy and Society* 16 (2): 261–270.

Engels, F. 1845/1993. *The Condition of the Working Class in England*. Oxford: Oxford University Press.

Exley, S. 2016. Inside and Outside the School Gates: Impacts of Poverty on Children's Education. In *Improving Children's Life Chances*, ed. J. Tucker, 38–48. London: Child Poverty Action Group.

Farnsworth, K., and Z. Irving. 2016. Austerity: More Than the Sum of Its Parts. In *Social Policy in Time of Austerity: Global Economic Crisis and the New Politics of Welfare*, ed. K. Farnsworth and Z. Irving, 9–41. Bristol: Policy Press.

Galtung, J. 1969. Violence, Peace and Peace Research. *Journal of Peace Research* 6 (3): 167–191.

Garnham, A. 2020. Secure Futures: After the Pandemic. *Poverty* 166: 7–10.

Garthwaite, K. 2016. *Hunger Pains. Life Inside Foodbank Britain*. Bristol: Policy Press.

Grover, C. 2012. 'Personalised Conditionality': Observations on Active Proletarianisation in Late Modern Britain. *Capital and Class* 36 (2): 283–301.

Grover, C. 2019. Violent Proletarianisation: Social Murder, the Reserve Army of Labour and 'Austerity' in Britain. *Critical Social Policy* 39 (3): 335–355.

Hannington, W. 1937. *The Problem of Distressed Areas*. London: Victor Gollancz Ltd.

Hirsch, D. 2019. *A Minimum Income Standard for the United Kingdom in 2019*. York: Joseph Rowntree Foundation.

Homer, A. 2021. *Deaths of People on Benefits Prompt Inquiry Call*. www.bbc.co.uk/news/uk-56819727. Accessed 7 May 2023.

Jessop, B. 2015. Neoliberalism, Finance-Dominated Accumulation and Enduring Austerity: A Cultural Political Economy Perspective. In *Social Policy in Time of Austerity: Global Economic Crisis and the New Politics of Welfare*, ed. K. Farnsworth and Z. M. Irving, 87–111. Bristol: Policy Press.

Jessop, B. 2016. The Heartlands of Neoliberalism and the Rise of the Austerity State. In *Handbook of Neoliberalism*, ed. S. Springer, K. Birch, and J. McLeavy, 410–421. London: Routledge.

Kotzé, J. 2018. Criminology or Zemiology? Yes, Please! On the Refusal of Choice Between False Alternatives. In *Zemiology: Reconnecting Crime and Social Harm*, ed. A. Boukli and J. Kotzé, 85–106. London: Palgrave Macmillan.

Leaker, D. 2019. *Labour Market Overview, UK: September 2019*. https://www.ons.gov.uk/employmentandlabourmarket/peopleinwork/employmentandemployeetypes/bulletins/uklabourmarket/september2019.

Loopstra, R. 2018. Rising Food Bank Use in the UK: Sign of a New Public Health Emergency? *Nutrition Bulletin* 43: 53–60.

Loopstra, R., J. Fledderjohann, A. Reeves, and D. Stuckler. 2018. Impact of Welfare Benefit Sanctioning on Food Insecurity: A Dynamic Cross-Area Study of Food Bank Usage in the UK. *Journal of Social Policy* 47 (3): 437–457.

Marmot, M. 2010. *Fair Society, Healthy Lives. The Marmot Review*. London: The Marmot Review.

Marmot, M., J. Allen, T. Boyce, P. Goldblatt, and J. Morrison. 2021. *Health Inequality in England: The Marmot Review 10 Years On*. www.instituteofhealthequity.org/the-marmot-review-10-years-on.

McGibbon, E. 2021. The COVID-19 Pandemic: On the Everyday Mechanisms of Social Murder. *Critical Studies: An International and Interdisciplinary Journal* 16 (1): 35–42.

McManus, S., P. Bebbington, R. Jenkins, and T. Brugha (eds.). 2016. *Mental Health and Wellbeing in England: Adult Psychiatric Morbidity Survey 2014*. Leeds: NHS Digital.

Mills, C. 2018. 'Dead People Don't Claim': A Psychosocial Autopsy of UK Austerity Suicides. *Critical Social Policy* 38 (2): 302–322.

Office for National Statistics. 2018. *Deaths Where Malnutrition Was the Underlying Cause of Death or Was Mentioned Anywhere on the Death Certificate, Persons, England and Wales, 2001 to 2017*. https://www.ons.gov.uk/peoplepopulationandcommunity/birthsdeathsandmarriages/deaths/adhocs/009065deathswheremalnutritionwastheunderlyingcauseofdeathorwasmentionedanywhereonthedeathcertificatepersonsenglandandwales2001to2017. Accessed 7 May 2023.

O'Hara, M. 2017. Mental Health and Suicide. In *The Violence of Austerity*, ed. V. Cooper and D. Whyte, 35–43. London: Pluto Press.

Peck, J., and N. Theodore. 2000. 'Work First': Workfare and the Regulation of Contingent Labour Markets. *Cambridge Journal of Economics* 24: 119–138.

Pemberton, S. 2004. A Theory of Moral Indifference: Understanding the Production of Harm by Capitalist Society. In *Beyond Criminology: Taking Crime Seriously*, ed. P. Hillyard, C. Pantazis, S. Tombs, and D. Gordon, 67–83. London: Pluto Press.

Schofield, L., D. Walsh, N. Bendel, and R. Piroddi. 2021. Excess Mortality in Glasgow: Further Evidence of 'Political Effects' on Population Health. *Public Health* 201: 61–68.

Seymour, R. 2014. *Against Austerity: How We Can Fix the Crisis They Made*. London: Pluto.

Sim, J. 2014. 'Welcome to the Machine': Poverty and Punishment in Austere Times. *Prison Service Journal* 213: 17–23.

Soldatic, K., and H. Morgan. 2017. 'The Way You Make Me Feel': Shame and the Neoliberal Governance of Disability Welfare Subjectivities in Australia and the UK. In *Edges of Identity: The Production of Neoliberal Subjectivities*, ed. J. Louth and M. Potter, 106–133. Chester: University of Chester Press.

Spitzer, S. 1975. Toward a Marxian Theory of Deviance. *Social Problems* 22 (5): 638–651.

Spohrer, K., G. Stahl, and T. Bowers-Brown. 2018. Constituting Neoliberal Subjects? 'Aspiration' as Technology of Government in UK Policy Discourse. *Journal of Education Policy* 33 (3): 327–342.

Taylor-Gooby, P. 2017. Re-Doubling the Crises of the Welfare State: The Impact of Brexit on Welfare Politics. *Journal of Social Policy* 46 (4): 815–835.

Taylor-Robinson, D., E. Lai, S. Wickham, T. Rose, P. Norman, C. Bambra, M. Whitehead, and B. Barr. 2019. Assessing the Impact of Rising Child Poverty on the Unprecedented Rise in Infant Mortality in England, 2000–2017: Time Trend Analysis. *British Medical Journal*. https://doi.org/10.1136/bmjopen-2019-029424.

Tombs, S. 2017. Undoing Social Protection. In *The Violence of Austerity*, ed. V. Cooper and D. Whyte, 133–140. London: Pluto Press.

Tombs, S. 2019. Grenfell: The Unfolding Dimensions of Social Harm. *Justice, Power and Resistance* 3 (1): 61–88.

Vegh Weis, V. 2017. *Marxism and Criminology: A History of Criminal Selectivity.* Leiden: Brill.

Waddington, P. 1985. Power, Crime, and Mystification by S. Box Review. *The British Journal of Criminology* 25 (1): 73–75.

Watson, B. 2019. *Working and Workless Households in the UK: April to June 2019.* https://www.ons.gov.uk/employmentandlabourmarket/peopleinwork/employmentandemployeetypes/bulletins/workingandworklesshouseholds/apriltojune2019.

We Are Spartacus. 2015. *Work Capability Assessment: Deaths and Suicide.* https://www.centreforwelfarereform.org/uploads/attachment/456/work-capability-assessment-deaths-and-suicides.pdf.

Wiggan, J., and C. Grover. 2022. The Politics of Job Retention Schemes in Britain: The Coronavirus Job Retention Scheme and the Temporary Short Time Working Compensation Scheme. *Critical Social Policy.* https://doi.org/10.1177/02610183221086515.

9

Steven Box and Police Crime: Understanding and Challenging Police Violence and Corruption

Will Jackson

Introduction

How do we talk about police today? In *Power, Crime, and Mystification* (PCM), Box suggested that the law-and-order climate of the 1980s made it very difficult to even mention police violence and corruption without being accused of adopting a 'hysterical and anti-police stance' (1983: 82). His attempt to highlight the nature and extent of what he refers to as 'police crime', and his efforts to situate this within a transformative criminological analysis of crimes of the powerful, would have been more than enough for him to be dismissed by the institution, its supporters, and the mass media. Forty years on, for those scholars and activists seeking to demystify the exercise of police power, very little has changed in the responses to the way that we talk and write about the police. The political climate in Britain in the third decade of the

W. Jackson (✉)
Liverpool John Moores University, Liverpool, UK
e-mail: W.H.Jackson@ljmu.ac.uk

twenty-first century continues to make it very difficult to advance a critical analysis of policing that foregrounds the violence and abuse of power perpetrated by police without this being dismissed as hysterics.

This chapter begins by considering the contribution of Box's work on police crime to the contemporary development of a critical empirical, and theoretical analysis of the institution and the wider exercise of police power. The chapter then considers the value of the concept of police crime for both scholarly and activist work on policing today. To do this, the chapter examines how Box approached police as a *state* institution, distinguishing his analysis from the liberal work being done at the time, and considers how he situated his critique of police violence and corruption in relation to his understanding of crime, law, and social order. Recognising that we can learn much from Box's attempt to develop our understanding of the general function of police under capitalism, the chapter suggests that we also need to think carefully about the concept of 'police crime' as the best way to understand the social harms caused by police and the role of violence in the exercise of police power.

The chapter assesses the relevance of Box's analysis by considering the state of policing in Britain today and the current political and academic climate within which policing is discussed and debated. The chapter suggests that the tendency to dismiss critical work on policing as hysterical and 'anti-police' has been heightened due to the expansion of police studies and the growing interrelationship of the police institution and the discipline of criminology. Understanding the role of academic work in the mystification of police power, the chapter advocates an alternative analysis of police that draws on, and develops, Box's work. The chapter reflects on what we can learn from Box today, considering the role and value of critical research in an era in which police powers are being increased despite its problems. Reflecting on current debates about the future of policing, the chapter concludes by considering Box's view on the potential for the reform and control of police in its current form.

Police Crime as a Systemic Issue

Critical criminology, as both an intellectual and activist project, needs a critical theory of police power and PCM makes an important contribution to this through a series of interventions. Firstly, by focussing on the everyday nature of police violence and corruption, Box challenges the mystification of the institution of police and the practice of policing. Secondly, by framing police crimes as crimes of the powerful, he positions a critical analysis of policing at the centre of a radical criminology. Finally, Box's approach to policing and his reorientation of criminology demands a radical rethinking of the question of justice and challenges dominant ideas on who, or what, is the answer to the 'crime problem'.

For Box, a critical understanding of policing must begin from a recognition that it is Janus-faced. There are two sides of police work, and most people remain ignorant of the 'ugly face', seeing only a 'media-projected image of the police which is both partial and idealized' (1983: 80). The two faces reflect the two major functions of policing, only one of which—the *service* function (1983: 111)—is emphasised by most politicians, media representations, and academic research. The service function provides us with the acceptable face of police emphasised in dominant depictions of policing (including by the police themselves), while the *control* function is underplayed, and mystified, generally only experienced, and thus recognised, by a minority of predominantly powerless people. For Box, the emphasis on the service function obscures the reality of policing and mystifies the extent and nature of police crime perpetrated against particular segments of the public.

Crucially, for Box, the existence of 'police crime'—'law violations by police in their capacity as police officers' (1983: 81)—is not always denied in the dominant representation of police, but instead the meaning of police violence, corruption, and rule-breaking is transformed. Framing misconduct as 'bending the rules' in popular representations of policing is viewed as 'good and necessary police work' (ibid.) because it effectively achieves justice and protects the community. Box noted that where explicit forms of violence and corruption cannot be transformed, they are denied or blamed on 'bad apples' in such a way as to sustain the image of the institution. The dominant representation of policing means that police crime is 'never presented as something endemic and inherent in the nature of police work' (ibid.). Box was acutely aware that any attempt to expose the nature and extent of police crime would be dismissed as a 'gross exaggeration' (ibid.: 82) and would lead to accusations of being anti-police.

Box details the extent of the problem in subsections on police brutality and police corruption highlighting issues like deaths in police custody that had been, up to that point, effectively ignored in criminological scholarship. From this starting point, Box sets out the necessary components of a fully social theory of police crime:

> A full social theory of police crime requires relating the micro factors of opportunities, career socialization, determinants of career advancement, occupational subculture, and (lack of) deterrence to the macro processes of social control in an unequal society where the problems of legitimacy has not been resolved successfully. (1983: 93)

Box's approach here moves us beyond the dominant explanations of police misconduct (then and now) by linking police crime to the broader role of policing. Violations of the law by police in their capacity as police officers cannot be explained away by isolating individual deviants—the 'bad apples' in the otherwise good barrel. We have to understand the micro factors within the police station, the police force, or the institution more generally, but we must relate these to the broader function of policing within a specific social, political, and historical context.

The macro dimension of Box's framing of police crime is critical to explain not just 'why they do it' but also 'why they are allowed to do it' (1983: 93). The answer to the latter question firstly comes from the 'magical cloak of immunity' (1983: 99) enjoyed by police due to the inadequacy of accountability mechanisms. Understanding precisely why the police complaint and oversight systems are ineffective requires us to understand the power dynamics that define the relationship between police and those groups who are the focus of police power. In earlier work (Box and Russell 1975) Box argued that the police complaints procedure served to discredit complainants, and he developed this critique in PCM with reference to Becker's (1967) work on social inequality and the moral hierarchy of society. Box explains that those who most often have cause to complain about police sit low on what Becker (1967 cited in Box 1983: 103) referred to as the 'dominant hierarchy of credibility'. Put simply, the police version of events is almost always taken as read, leaving those who seek to challenge the police version of these events lacking credibility.

The lack of police accountability is heightened by the fact that those who sit at the intersections of the social attributes that mark groups out as what Lee (1981) referred to as 'police property' are most likely to experience the effects of police crime. For Box, some groups are 'virtually "open territory"' (1983: 104) for police crime and this is reflected in the experiences of women as well as working class, minoritized, and LGBTQ+ communities. This stems from the status these groups are afforded in the current social order but also reflects the general role of policing under capitalism (Neocleous, 2021a; Jackson 2021). The 'licence' afforded to the officer and the institution to behave outside the law is intrinsically tied to the police function. For Box, situating the police in historical context requires us to understand the police as 'an agency for, and deriving benefit from, supporting, and reproducing forms of domination, and suppressing, fracturing, and demoralizing forms of resistance' (1983: 93). Here the police function is primarily *repressive* focussed on managing the 'usual suspects', preserving power relations, and maintaining social order.

Theorising police crime in this way challenges the dominant framings of the problem and brings into question the potential of those solutions so often muted for dealing with police misconduct. If police crime is endemic, and is tied to the general function of police, then reforms to policy and procedure are likely to have limited impact no matter how 'sweeping' they are said to be. In this sense, Box's analysis provides us with an explanation for *why* police crime remains as significant a problem today. He makes a direct comparison between deviant police and corporate criminals as both are a product of their 'occupational experiences and socialization' (1983: 94) and in doing so, he reinforces the view that a liberal reformism is doomed to failure. His analysis in Chapter 2 of PCM concludes that the very nature and status of the corporation gives rise to corporate offending and his analysis of police crime leads us to the same conclusion. To suggest that reform to policy and practice is sufficient to tackle the criminality inherent in the corporation or the police is at best naïve and at worst serves to further mystify the harms perpetrated by the state and the corporation.

Crime, Law, and Order

Box's focus on 'police crime' was key to the aims of PCM. It played a central role in the challenge posed to mainstream criminology, disturbing the dominant understanding of the crime problem and the failures of the justice system. Reconceptualising police as part of—rather than the response to—the crime problem was vital in this endeavour and was a truly radical move. The continued relevance and importance of Box's analysis to critical criminology reflects how transgressive his work was. Challenging how we talk about police remains essential to both critical scholarship and activism today, but we need also to think about what the emphasis on police crime specifically provides us in our attempt to develop a critical theory of police power.

Focusing our critique of police power on the perpetration of illegal acts infers that the proper relationship between policing and the law should, and could, be different. In the same way, a focus on police corruption infers a deviation from a previous state of police in which violence, brutality, and illegality were not inherent in the exercise of police power. As Gilroy and Sim (1985) noted of critiques of Thatcherism, there is a tendency on the left to highlight issues with policing as though they are new and reflective of a departure from a previous, if not 'golden', then at least less problematic, age. The focus on crimes perpetrated by police in critical accounts is inevitable (and necessary) given the seemingly inseparable relationship between police, crime, and law. Police remain intelligible in the popular imagination through the correlation with crime-fighting and thus we position police and crime in opposition. This is why Box's emphasis on police crime was, and still is, a radical move in relation to the hegemonic view of police. However, the opposition between police and crime is predicated on the reproduction of a fundamental liberal opposition between law and violence. The construction of law as a neutral force—central to depiction of the 'rule of law' as an 'unqualified human good' (Thompson in Gilroy and Sim 1985: 35)—positions police as the defenders of the law. We need to rethink the place of crime and law in a critical theory of police power, and this involves a development of Box's work.

It is arguably the status of police as defenders of 'law and order' that offers more to our attempt to develop a critical understanding of policing. As Box recognised, a critical understanding of the history of policing is key to making sense of the police function. In this regard, a critical history of police illustrates that from the original police scientists in the eighteenth century to the contemporary advocates of 'quality of life' policing, the central concern has always been, above all else, about 'good order' (Correia and Wall 2018; Neocleous 2021a). The usual suspects in the eyes of police are not those who pose the greatest threat to life and property (as an analysis of corporate crime makes clear) but those who pose a threat to social order understood in classed, raced, gendered and heterosexualised terms. The primary concern with disorderly conduct rather than crime is clear throughout the history of police and the concern with (dis)order is reflective of the fact that the central function of police is the reproduction of social order. This *productive* dimension of police power is underplayed in Box's emphasis on the repressive dynamic of the control function. A critical history of police reveals the central place of police power in the *fabrication* of bourgeois social order and its enduring role in the subsequent reproduction of this order (Neocleous 2021a). Understanding the centrality of police power to the (re)production of capitalist order helps us to make sense of why police power has been, and continues to be, ranged against the powerless.

If we recognise that the concern with order has always, and will always, be prioritised over a concern with law, the violence and illegality inherent in the exercise of police power make more sense. This violence is not exceptional, but a *normal* dynamic of police power deployed legitimately in the pursuit of order. Police illegality thus needs to be understood in the context of this pursuit of order. Some examples of police crime clearly expose individual and/or collective attitudes towards specific communities and a desire to exploit the dynamics inherent in the policing of powerless groups, but the endemic nature of police violence and corruption should not be understood as a departure from the regular exercise of police power. As Mark Neocleous has argued, 'police violence is policing; policing is violence' (2021b: 28), and those populations marked as police property know this all too well. The pursuit of order has always justified the police acting outside of the law even if the official presentation of policing is at pains to deny this.

A commitment to the law and principles of democracy are important to the mystification of policing in the Boxian sense but are not reflected in the way the institution functions today or has at any point in its history. The institution's enduring culture of denial, obfuscation, and secrecy and its continued defence of all but the most egregious offenders in its ranks, makes clear how the police view illegality when perpetrated by their own, but we perhaps understand more about the relationship between police and law if we consider the power of *discretion*. The power of discretion, central to modern policing from its inception, makes clear that the enforcement of the law need not be consistent and is, by design, unaccountable to the law; discretionary power allows for the exercise of power 'with the law standing at arms-length' (Neocleous 2021a: 200). The extra-legal dynamic of discretionary power is central to the (re)production of order. As Neocleous explains: 'for police, it matters little if the police action is legal so long as it is regarded as an *efficient technique for achieving order*' (2021a: 31 original emphasis). Despite this, it would be wrong to suggest that police violence, discrimination and misdeeds occur exclusively outside the law. A critical reading of the power of discretion demonstrates that its discriminatory nature 'has its foundation in the *permissive* structure of the law' (Neocleous 2021a: 197 emphasis added). The result of this foundation is that 'the effect of law on police practice at street level is permissive rather than restrictive' (Gilroy and Sim 1985: 36).

Such an analysis of the nature and function of discretionary power suggests that police are better understood as a form of *administration* as opposed to law enforcement (Neocleous 2021a; Wall and Linnemann 2021). For Neocleous (2021a: 199) this distinction becomes clearer if we understand that discretion is 'exercised in accordance with the key principle of administrative law that discretion be exercised reasonably'. Discretionary powers—of arrest and stop and search—are regulated by the standard of 'reasonable grounds' but "reasonableness" is assessed according to the standards applicable to executive officers and measured by basic principles of administrative law' (ibid.). Therefore, rather than the notion of reasonableness constraining what the police can do, it enables 'vast discretionary power' (ibid.: 200) that is very difficult to challenge. This is not a flaw in the design, or regulation, of police powers. It is reflective of both the way they were designed from the outset of modern policing and the way that they have been sustained to facilitate, and legitimate, the police in fulfilling their central role in managing disorderly populations. As Gilroy and Sim (1985: 36) explain, 'legal powers which were framed with the control of street populations in mind, become a unified resource with which officers are able to legitimate any course of action they engage in' (ibid.).

Calls for legal regulation and control of police have to be (re)evaluated in light of this reframing of police power. We have to recognise that police violence is *routine* and also acknowledge that the law actually facilitates rather than restricts much of what we identify as problems in policing. In this sense, the impunity police enjoy is not a reflection of the failure of specific regulations or particular accountability mechanisms. Instead, what Box refers to as 'police crime' is inherent to policing and is a product of the impotence of legal regulation. This suggests that while the concept of police crime may be useful to shift popular conceptions of policing, it is of limited value to a critical theory of police power. This is not to say that scholars and activists stop monitoring and exposing police violence and abuse of power, or abandon calls for reform and accountability regarding specific problems in policing. However, we have to recognise that while such calls may have the potential to expose and restrain police violence in limited circumstances, we cannot build a transformative politics on the basis of an imagined return to a previous, idealised form of policing in which violence and corruption were absent.

The State of Contemporary Policing

The need for a critical analysis of policing today is clear from even a limited review of the state of the institution. Such a review begins from a recognition that policing in Britain is in crisis. While this does not mean that the place of the institution is necessarily under threat, British policing is experiencing a real crisis of legitimacy for several reasons. Firstly, the uncovering of a 'litany' of 'systemic failings' in the response to crime and in the service of victims (Dodd 2022) has led the police inspectorate to place a record six police forces, including the two biggest, the Metropolitan Police and Greater Manchester Police, into special measures. Secondly, a series of inquiries, reports, and public scandals in recent years have exposed long hidden or ignored aspects of policing to the public and have challenged the dominant view of police defined by commitments to impartiality and upholding the law. In conjunction with these cases, campaigns such as Black Lives Matter, Campaign Opposing Police Surveillance, Police Spies Out of Lives, United Friends and Families, along with organizations like The Network for Police Monitoring and INQUEST, have opened the police institution to public criticism in a way not seen before.

In March 2023, Baroness Casey published her report (Casey 2023) into the standards of behaviour and internal culture of the Metropolitan Police Service. This landmark review, commissioned in the wake of the 2021 murder of Sarah Everard by a serving Metropolitan Police officer, found 'institutional racism, sexism and homophobia' (2023: 7) in the largest police force in the UK. Casey did recognise that she was not the first to highlight these problems. The existence of institutional racism in the Metropolitan Police was confirmed 24 years earlier in the landmark Macpherson inquiry into the racist murder of Stephen Lawrence. While its publication was a watershed moment in the history of British policing the promises of action on the part of politicians and police leaders have not resulted in any substantive change in the policing of minoritised communities in the intervening decades. Data on issues such as racial discrimination, particularly in the use of stop and search powers (Home Affairs Committee 2021), the use of force (Grierson 2020), and deaths in police custody (INQUEST 2022), expose the nature and scale of the over-policing of minoritized communities today. Black communities have long been constructed as synonymous with crime and disorder (Gilroy 1987) and this continues to be reproduced through the endurance of racialised gang narratives that seek to legitimise the continued intrusion of police power into these communities (Williams 2015).

Women's experiences of policing have also received significant attention in recent years coming to the fore in a most profound way following the murder of Sarah Everard in March 2021. The murder, and the police response to the vigil held in Sarah's memory (Graham-Harrison 2021), reignited long-standing debates about women's experiences of men's violence, highlighting the role of police as both perpetrators of that violence and as ineffective, indeed uninterested, protectors. The Everard case was not alone in provoking a charge of institutionalised misogyny. The case of Bibaa Henry and Nicole Smallman, two black sisters murdered in June 2020, was marked by initial failures in the police response and then by the actions of two police officers who took photographs of themselves with the women's bodies and shared them on social media (Dodd 2021). The intersection of racism and misogyny evident in the dehumanising police response to this case was again reflected in the 2022 case of Child Q, a fifteen-year-old black girl strip searched by police officers while at school (Davies 2022). These cases have heightened criticisms of the police response to women, children, and minoritised communities but have also occurred against the backdrop of wider problems with police responses to systemic violence against women and girls.

The problem of domestic violence perpetrated by police has been referred to as an 'epidemic' in the force (Stephenson 2021) and the institution appears unwilling to tackle the problem effectively (Grierson 2022). In 2023, this was brought to the public's attention in a very high-profile way by the case of David Carrick, a serving Metropolitan police officer who was convicted of 85 serious offences including 48 rapes against 12 women over a 17-year 'campaign of terror and attacks' (Dodd and Sinmaz 2023). The problem of police as perpetrators of violence against women is also laid bare by the wider problem of 'abuse of position for sexual purpose', which appears to be on the increase (Ambrose 2021). The failure to respond effectively to tackle men's violence is indicative of a 'systemic failure' to protect women as a 'highly vulnerable section' of the population from multiple forms of men's violence (Oppenheim 2019). These failures are made most explicit by Karen

Ingala Smith's 'Counting Dead Women' project (2022) and the annual Femicide Census (2022).

The problem of institutionalised discrimination has also been highlighted in relation to the policing of LGBTQ+ communities in particular in response to the murders of Anthony Walgate, Gabriel Kovari, Daniel Whitworth, and Jack Taylor by Stephen Port between 2014 and 2015. The apparent failures of police to respond effectively to the death of these young men, and previous murders of LGBTQ+ people, have led to further allegations of institutionalised homophobia (Tatchell 2021). In 2022, the Independent Office for Police Conduct [IOPC] (2022) found evidence of a culture of sexism, racism, bullying, and homophobia following its Operation Hotton investigation into misconduct in the Metropolitan Police. The IOPC concluded that this culture could not be dismissed as the behaviour of a few 'bad apples' as allegations of misconduct in policing so often are.

A review of systemic problems in British policing must also include the recent allegation of 'institutional corruption'. In 2021, the Metropolitan police was described as 'institutionally corrupt' by an independent panel set up to inquire into the police handling of the murder of private detective Daniel Morgan in 1987 (Dodd and Sabbagh 2021). The findings related to historic corruption that shielded his killers from arrest but also highlighted an enduring approach that concealed or denied failings, for the sake of the force's public image. But this was not the first time in recent years that evidence of systemic misconduct and the prioritisation of reputation by police has been exposed. Revelations about the undercover policing of political activists—including environmental campaigners, trade unionists, and justice activists—demonstrated that the use of undercover police in the response to political activism is a central component of national policing in Britain, beginning in its current form in the late 1960s (Evans and Lewis 2013). The additional disclosure of the role police and security services played in colluding with major construction firms in the UK to produce and administer a blacklist of trade union activists (Smith and Chamberlain 2015) laid bare the fallacy of the police as an apolitical, independent institution whose sole concern is upholding the law.

The revelation of these issues in contemporary policing has come as a surprise to many members of the public whose perception of the police is defined only by its acceptable face. The fact that the police are now regarded as institutionally racist, misogynistic, homophobic, and corrupt by many observers comes as less of a surprise to those communities long marked out as police property. Those with lived experience of the violence and corruption in policing that Box sought to expose have always been aware of its 'ugly face'. As Box noted, it is 'part of their everyday harsh reality' (1983: 90) and yet the state continues to reproduce a sanitised image of British policing portrayed as the best in the world. Box's aim to develop an alternative, critical account of police power, and to take a risk as a researcher and scholar, is arguably even more important today in an era in which most of the scholarship on policing is informed by partnership working with the institution. It is to this issue to which the chapter now turns.

The Mystifying Role of Academic Research

It is unlikely that Box would have been surprised about the nature and extent of problems with British policing given what he documented in PCM and what he argued about the general role of policing. What might have shocked him is the extent to which the interrelationship of criminology (including its subdiscipline of police studies) and the institution of police has intensified in the intervening decades. At the heart of Box's project was a challenge to mainstream criminology and its emphasis on the crimes of the powerless. His vision of a radical criminology was a direct challenge to the ideological alignment of criminology and the state, and he recognised that because of this link the state was able to 'muster a galaxy of skilled Machiavellian orators to defend its definitions' (1983: 9). While such orators may also be drawn from a wealth of places in government, the media, and think tanks, the role of the academic is significant.

Criminology, the disciplinary home of police studies in the contemporary university, has continued to grow at a phenomenal rate in the twenty-first century as it has kept pace with expanding criminal justice systems around the world, providing them with both a vital source of legitimacy and a steady supply of labour. In the last twenty years, we have seen 'a dizzying expansion in the number of institutes, posts, publications, conferences, courses and academic and quasi-academic journals devoted to research and teaching in policing' (Loader 2011: 449). In Britain, universities have consolidated their position as centres for police training and this has been turbocharged since 2020 by the requirement for all police recruits in England and Wales to have a degree. A search of the UK Universities and Colleges Admissions Service [UCAS] in early 2023 finds 250 course matches for 'police studies' from 79 different higher education providers. The closeness of the discipline and its object of study mean that the distinction is blurred; exchanges of personnel make this most explicit, with the academic-cop and the cop-academic now a growing presence in the corridors of both the university and the police station and the position of professor of police studies a common post for retired Chief Constables. The legitimating function of this relationship cuts both ways: the collaboration with academic institutions and research is important to the professionalisation agenda in policing; and the collaboration with police enables universities to bolster their 'impact' agenda and promotion of 'real world' research.

Even if contemporary police studies is, in reality, just another branch of administrative criminology, its establishment as a specific discipline—marked by its own courses, departments, journals, etc.—illustrates the further intensification of the 'university-sponsored imposition of bourgeois "disciplinarity"' (Neocleous 2006: 19). This was already reflected in twentieth-century criminology, as it sought to isolate the study of the policing from the examination of other exercises of power, but contemporary police studies push this separation to its end point. Here the police institution exists in glorious isolation, detached from any wider concept of policing or recognition of the exercise of state power. The nature and scale of its expansion in recent years reveals much about the enduring importance of liberal police science to the state.

Much of the work in police studies is 'mirror work' (Manning 2005, p. 39) that reflects the priorities of government, and 'mimics rather than challenges police-centred visions of order' (Loader 2011: 451). This is better understood *not* as a failure of scholarship, but as a reflection of the essential function of the discipline, illustrating why its expansion has been so vociferously supported by the state. Police studies supplies police with the 'useable knowledge' (Bradley and Nixon 2009: 427) they require, and an institutional framework has been constructed within and between British universities as well as at a national level (notably through the College of Policing, the professional body for police in England and Wales established in 2013) to help academics be more useful.

Research *with* rather than *on* police (Goode and Lumsden 2018: 76) is prioritised and this has intensified the development of what Peter Manning (2005) referred to as a sociology *for*, rather than *of*, the police. Despite calls for piecemeal reform, the scholars of modern police studies are, like the original police scientists, firmly '*on the side* of police powers' (Neocleous 2006: 21 original emphasis) defending the institution in scholarly and public debate. Positioning police as 'co-producers' of research has produced a discipline which is 'embarrassingly eager to study any currently fashionable question without theorizing it' (Manning in Loader 2011: 450).

Theorising police is not attempted in any substantive way because this is ultimately unnecessary and unhelpful to the discipline. As Foucault (1980) noted of criminology, the value of police studies to the functioning of the system relieves it of any need to seek a theoretical justification. The utility of academic research is measured by its ability to produce evidence of 'what works' in policing; a commitment to 'evidence-based practice' (Sherman 1998)—within which research produces evidence that subsequently guides policy and practice—has made the relationship between researchers and the institution even more important in the last twenty years. 'Scientific' research begets 'scientific' policing, and the positivism of police science and administrative criminology provides a vital source of legitimacy in this context. Such research seeks, through incremental reforms, to enhance efficiency in police practice, and academic inquiry plays a key role in maintaining a facade of openness, responsiveness, and accountability.

Critical examination is neither desired nor attempted; in reality, it is not possible. Just as criminology cannot deconstruct crime (Smart in Hillyard et al. 2004: 374), police studies cannot deconstruct police. The priorities of police studies as a discipline (as well as its blind spots) reflect the demands of the institution. The function of police studies is thus to reinforce the liberal concept of police and, as a result, to mystify policing. As Box knew so well, mystification serves to limit what can be said, and in turn what can be done, in response to the exercise of police power.

The Mystification of Contemporary Policing

The most important insight we can draw from Box's analysis is the need to focus a critical lens on the strategies of mystification that obscure both the nature and extent of police violence and corruption and the general role of police. To continue Box's work, we need to consider what has changed since the publication of PCM. While the fundamental features of policing and the general function of the institution remain constant, there have been fundamental changes to the way that policing is presented and thus the way it is mystified. Box's example of Sir Robert Mark, former Commissioner of the Metropolitan Police, nostalgically recalling examples of police officers administering 'rough justice' appears very dated in an era of 'professional policing'. This is not to say that nostalgic ruminations about a golden age of police are a thing of the past. A yearning for a past in which policing was 'free' of the limitations imposed by human rights and 'political correctness' is a recurring feature in political discourse (for example, Davies 2017) and in popular representations of police, but the official image of policing has been redefined through a process of *professionalisation* (Martin 2021). The drive to professionalise the police is as old as the modern police (Correia and Wall 2018), but in the last decade it has become the primary vehicle through which police reform is presented and is thus central to appeals for police legitimacy and pivotal to sustaining the mystification that surrounds the exercise of police power.

There are several dynamics to the contemporary drive for professionalisation in the UK which include 'the creation of a professional body, developing a framework of accredited qualifications across the organisation, adopting a code of ethics, and developing a knowledge base dictated by scientific evidence' (Martin 2021: 5). The establishment of the College of Policing and the move to graduate entry have been key to this agenda as has the adoption of a code of ethics, a theoretical commitment to democratic accountability, and an increasing emphasis on evidence-based policing (NPCC 2016). The move to graduate entry and the emphasis on the link between scientific research and scientific policing has increased the proximity and importance of the university to the police institution in the pursuit of this apparent transformation. As noted above, the rapid expansion of police studies and the proliferation of police-academic partnerships are key to the reform and subsequent legitimation of policing. Police studies have advanced the model of 'criminology as industry' (Hillyard et al. 2004: 384) within which academic labour is openly employed in the service of the state, helping to both 'professionalise' the institution and produce the next generation of disciplined workers.

However, the brief review of problems in British policing provided above demonstrates that the drive for professionalisation has not had a significant impact on the nature and extent of police crime. Even taken on its own terms, the focus on public service and making communities safer is failing. In its Police Vision 2025 report (2016), the National Police Chiefs' Council (NPCC) set out its vision for a professional police that will 'embed consistent, professional practice that is ethically based and informed by a shared understanding of what works to deliver public value' (ibid.: 4). For the NPCC, professionalisation included a commitment to equality and a 'role in helping to create a fair, just and peaceful society and helping citizens to live confident, safe and fulfilling lives' (ibid.). To be kind, professionalisation could be viewed as an aspiration not yet achieved, but more likely, its primary function is to mystify the behaviour of police officers, the priorities of police forces, and the function of the institution.

For Correia and Wall (2018: 25), professionalisation is a 'reformist fairy tale'. It is first and foremost a strategy of legitimation that 'masquerades as self-critique while at the same time rescuing the police as a flawed but fundamentally well-intentioned and necessary institution for the public good' (ibid.: 125). The place of police-academic partnership working in the professionalisation agenda is reflective of the rescue-work that police studies does; that this relationship has not led to a transformation in transparency and accountability is unsurprising as it is not the aim. The aim of police studies is to shore up the pretence of critique and in turn to reinforce the liberal concept of policing. In doing so, this work seeks to emphasise the acceptable face of police and limit both what can be said about policing today and what can be imagined about the future of policing.

Conclusion

By centralising the processes of mystification, Box provides a guide for critical criminology today and a review of his work should focus our efforts on providing a challenge to the depoliticising effects of police studies. Such a challenge requires a critical theory of police power from which to build our alternative analysis. We need to develop the terminology through which a critical theory of police power is advanced. The concept of 'police crime' does important work in challenging the dominant understanding of the relationship between police and crime/violence/corruption. However, to be counter-hegemonic, our work requires a challenge to the way that we think about the relationship between police, law, and order and, in this regard, framing problems with policing through the concept of 'police crime' may well obscure the cause(s).

Recognising this should inform the way that we speak about police as well as what we focus on in our critical research and what we demand in response. To call for further legal regulation is in reality to ask for more of the same and we should be mindful of this as politicians, police leaders, and their academic allies seek to respond to the current crisis of legitimacy. As the current crisis of police misconduct is addressed, there may well be an increase in convictions of police officers found guilty of criminal offences. Recent data that suggests that roughly 1 in 100 police officers in England and Wales (in excess of 1400 officers) faced criminal charges in 2022 (Kersley and Townsend 2023) demonstrates the size of the task. While we can be sceptical as to the effectiveness of these changes, they should not be dismissed outright. Stopping the likes of Couzens or Carrick when their criminality is first identified to police could save lives and prevent untold harm. However, the current response by police and government remains focussed on the existence of 'bad apples' in a redeemable barrel, motivated as it is with regaining legitimacy in the eyes of the public. The Casey report reinforced the view that the occupational culture that defines policing from the leadership down to the rank and file is a barrier to effective reform. Calls for tighter regulation, better training, and enhanced vetting, among other solutions, do not get at the violence of everyday policing and they do not challenge the institutionalised discrimination enabled by the discretionary exercise of police power.

Critical research on policing has an important role to play in exposing police violence and to enable this we must keep open a space for research *on* rather than *with* police (Jackson 2020). But from this point, what is to be done? Greater accountability is understandably the demand made by many, but we have to think about what demands for public, community, or democratic accountability in this field involve and what they could achieve. Critical scholars and activists must determine if there is an effective model of democratic accountability beyond the model of Police and Crime Commissioners heralded by government that serves only to legitimate policing by annexing accountability mechanisms to the electoral system. In contrast, the appeal for a system in which state servants could be controlled and responsibilised for their actions has been made in other sectors of the criminal justice system and making demands on state institutions in the name of democratic control could be a radical intervention on the road to abolition.

The Black Lives Matter movement in the US has prompted a (re)turn to debates about the defunding and abolition of police in the UK (Duff 2021; Elliott-Cooper 2020; Fleetwood and Lea 2022, 2023; McElhone et al. 2023). The call for defunding brings together a range of perspectives that aim varyingly for a reduction, redirection, or abolition of police, and share a view that not only is effective reform of policing in its current state impossible but, as Fleetwood and Lea (2022: 168) argue, 'reforms shore up a failing institution'. In a key contribution, US scholar and proponent of defunding, Alex Vitale (2017: 221), has argued that the failure of reform is tied to the central role of police: 'as long as the basic mission of police remains unchanged, none of these reforms will be achievable'. In response, the debate about the defunding of police in the

UK has focussed on the potential for transformations in the size, role, and very existence of the police, as well as the potential for democratic control now and as we seek to move away from the status quo.

Box's work makes an important contribution to a critical criminology of policing and should inform the way that we engage in these debates. It is fitting though to conclude this discussion with reference to his work and his view of the potential for reform. Crucially for Box, the state maintains conditions under which the police are able to fulfil their role. In his words, the state reassures the police that it will make sure that mechanisms of accountability 'can never be effective' (1983: 116). To maintain the façade of accountability, a handful of officers must be periodically offered up as 'patsies in order to keep up the good appearances of having an honest police force' (ibid.). On current evidence, it would seem that the role of the police remains too vital to the reproduction of social order for the state to allow its work to be hindered. As we consider the potential for democratic alternatives, we should be wary of the offer of nothing more than 'patsies' as the police appears to seek to get its house in order today.

References

Ambrose, T. 2021. Cases of Police Abusing Role for Sexual Gain Have Risen Sharply, Says Watchdog. *The Guardian*, October 26. https://www.theguardian.com/uk-news/2021/oct/26/cases-of-police-abusing-role-for-sexual-gain-have-risen-sharply-says-watchdog. Accessed 24 Apr 2023.

Box, S. 1983. *Power, Crime, and Mystification*. London: Tavistock Publications.

Box, S., and K. Russell. 1975. The Politics of Discreditability: Disarming Complaints Against the Police. *The Sociological Review* 23 (2): 315–346.

Bradley, D., and C. Nixon. 2009. Ending the 'Dialogue of the Deaf': Evidence and Policing Policies and Practices: An Australian Case Study. *Police Practice and Research: An International Journal* 10 (5): 423–435.

Casey, L. 2023. *Baroness Casey Review: Final Report—An Independent Review into the Standards of Behaviour and Internal Culture of the Metropolitan Police Service*. https://www.met.police.uk/SysSiteAssets/media/downloads/met/about-us/baroness-casey-review/update-march-2023/baroness-casey-review-march-2023a.pdf. Accessed 24 Apr 2023.

Correia, D., and T. Wall. 2018. *Police: A Field Guide*. London: Verso.
Davies, C. 2022. Child Q: Four Met Police Officers Facing Investigation Over Strip-Search. *The Guardian*, June 15. https://www.theguardian.com/uk-news/2022/jun/15/child-q-four-met-police-officers-facing-investigation-over-strip-search. Accessed 26 July 2022.
Davies, P. 2017. Why Political Correctness Is Killing Our Police Force. *Yorkshire Post*, October 26. https://www.yorkshirepost.co.uk/news/why-political-correctness-killing-our-police-force-1767620. Accessed 26 July 2022.
Dodd, V. 2021. Two Met Police Officers Jailed Over Photos of Murdered Sisters. *The Guardian*, December 6. https://www.theguardian.com/uk-news/2021/dec/06/two-met-police-officers-jailed-photos-murdered-sisters-deniz-jaffer-jamie-lewis-nicole-smallman-bibaa-henry. Accessed 26 July 2022.
Dodd, V. 2022. Met Police Placed in Special Measures Due to Litany of New 'Systemic' Failings. *The Guardian*, June 28. https://www.theguardian.com/uk-news/2022/jun/28/met-police-placed-special-measures-series-scandals. Accessed 27 July 2022.
Dodd, V., and D. Sabbagh. 2021. Daniel Morgan Murder: Inquiry Brands Met Police 'Institutionally Corrupt'. *The Guardian*, June 15. https://www.theguardian.com/uk-news/2021/jun/15/daniel-morgan-met-chief-censured-for-hampering-corruption-inquiry. Accessed 26 July 2022.
Dodd, V., and W. Sinmaz. 2023. David Carrick Jailed for Life Over Series of Rapes While Met Police Officer. *The Guardian*, February 7. https://www.theguardian.com/society/2023/feb/07/david-carrick-jailed-life-rapes-met-police-officer.
Duff, K., ed. 2021. *Abolishing the Police*. London: Dog Section Press.
Elliott-Cooper, A. 2020. 'Defund the Police' Is Not Nonsense: Here's What It Really Means. *The Guardian*, July 2. https://www.theguardian.com/commentisfree/2020/jul/02/britain-defund-the-police-black-lives-matter. Accessed 24 April 2023.
Evans, R., and P. Lewis. 2013. *Undercover: The True Story of Britain's Secret Police*. London: Faber & Faber.
Femicide Census. 2022. *Femicide Report 2020*. https://www.femicidecensus.org/wp-content/uploads/2022/02/010998-2020-Femicide-Report_V2.pdf.
Fleetwood, J., and J. Lea. 2022. Defunding the Police in the UK: Critical Questions and Practical Suggestions. *The Howard Journal of Crime and Justice* 61 (2): 167–184.
Fleetwood, J., and J. Lea. 2023. Not If —But How—To Defund the Police: Response to Our Critics. *The Howard Journal of Crime and Justice*.

Foucault, M. 1980. Prison Talk. In *Power/Knowledge: Selected Interviews & Other Writings 1972–1977*, ed. C. Gordon, 37–54. New York: Pantheon Books.

Gilroy, P. 1987. The Myth of Black Criminality. In *Law, Order and the Authoritarian State*, ed. P. Scraton, 107–120. Milton Keynes: Open University Press.

Gilroy, P., and J. Sim. 1985. Law, Order and the State of the Left. *Capital and Class* 9 (1): 15–55.

Goode, J., and K. Lumsden. 2018. The McDonaldization of Police-Academic Partnerships: Organisational and Cultural Barriers. Encountered in Moving from Research on Police to Research with Police. *Policing & Society* 28 (1): 75–89.

Graham-Harrison, E. 2021. Police Clash with Mourners at Sarah Everard Vigil in London. *The Guardian*, March 13. https://www.theguardian.com/uk-news/2021/mar/13/as-the-sun-set-they-came-in-solidarity-and-to-pay-tribute-to-sarah-everard. Accessed 26 July 2022.

Grierson, J. 2020. Black People Five Times More Likely to Have Force Used on Them by Police. *The Guardian*, December 17. https://www.theguardian.com/uk-news/2020/dec/17/black-people-five-times-more-likely-to-be-subjected-to-police-force. Accessed 24 Aug 2022.

Grierson, J. 2022. Watchdogs Condemn Police Response to Domestic Abuse Claims Against Officers. *The Guardian*, July 30. https://www.theguardian.com/uk-news/2022/jun/30/watchdogs-condemn-police-response-domestic-abuse-claims-against-officers. Accessed 26 July 2022.

Hillyard, P., J. Sim, S. Tombs, and D. Whyte. 2004. Leaving a 'Stain Upon the Silence': Contemporary Criminology and the Politics of Dissent. *The British Journal of Criminology* 44 (3): 369–390.

Home Affairs Committee. 2021. The Macpherson Report: Twenty-Two Years On—Third Report of Session 2021–22. https://committees.parliament.uk/publications/7012/documents/89144/default/. Accessed 26 July 2022.

Ingala Smith, K. 2022. Counting Dead Women. https://kareningalasmith.com/category/counting-dead-women/

INQUEST. 2022. BAME Deaths in Police Custody. https://www.inquest.org.uk/bame-deaths-in-police-custody. Accessed 26 July 2022.

Independent Office for Police Misconduct (IOPC). 2022. *Operation Hotton: Learning Report*. https://www.policeconduct.gov.uk/sites/default/files/Operation%20Hotton%20Learning%20report%20-%20January%202022.pdf. Accessed 26 July 2022.

Jackson, W. 2020. Researching the Policed: Critical Ethnography and the Study of Protest Policing. *Policing and Society* 30 (2): 169–185.

Jackson, W. 2021. Police Power and Disorder: Understanding Policing in the 21st Century. *Social Justice* 47 (3–4): 95–114.

Kersley, A., and M. Townsend. 2023. Revealed: One in 100 Police Officers in England and Wales Faced a Criminal Charge Last Year. *The Guardian*, February 25. https://www.theguardian.com/uk-news/2023/feb/25/revealed-one-in-100-uk-police-officers-faced-a-criminal-charge-last-year.

Lee, J.A. 1981. Some Structural Aspects of Police Deviance in Relations with Minority Groups. In *Organizational Police Deviance*, ed. C. Shearing. Toronto: Butterworth.

Loader, I. 2011. Where Is Policing Studies? *The British Journal of Criminology* 51 (2): 449–458.

Manning, P. 2005. The Study of Policing. *Police Quarterly* 8 (1): 23–43.

Martin, D. 2021. Understanding the Reconstruction of Police Professionalism in the UK. *Policing and Society* 32 (7): 931–946. https://doi.org/10.1080/10439463.2021.1999447.

McElhone, M., K. Kemp, S. Lamble, and J.M. Moore. 2023. Defund—Not Defend—The Police: A Response to Fleetwood and Lea. *The Howard Journal of Crime and Justice* 8.

Neocleous, M. 2006. Theoretical Foundations of the "New Police Science". In *The New Police Science: The Police Power in Domestic and International Governance*, ed. M. Dubber and M. Valverde, 17–41. Stanford: Stanford University Press.

Neocleous, M. 2021a. *A Critical Theory of Police Power*. London: Verso.

Neocleous, M. 2021b. 'Original, Absolute, Indefeasible': Or, What We Talk About When We Talks About Police Power. *Social Justice* 47 (3–4): 9–32.

National Police Chiefs' Council (NPCC). 2016. *Policing Vision 2025*. https://www.npcc.police.uk/documents/Policing%20Vision.pdf. Accessed 26 July 2022.

Oppenheim, M. 2019. 'Bad Apple' Police Officers Must Be Fired, Mother of Murdered Sisters Tells 'Racist' Met Police. *The Guardian*, June 6. https://www.independent.co.uk/news/uk/home-news/bibaa-henry-nicole-smallman-mother-met-police-b2094841.html. Accessed 26 July 2022.

Sherman, L.W. 1998. *Evidence-Based Policing: Ideas in American Policing*. Washington, DC: Police Foundation.

Smith, D., and P. Chamberlain. 2015. *Blacklisted: The Secret War Between Big Business and Union Activists*. Oxford: New Internationalist Publications.

Stephenson, M. 2021. More Than 100 Women Accuse Police Officers of Domestic Abuse, Alleging "Boys Club" Culture. *Channel 4 News*, May 18. https://www.channel4.com/news/more-than-100-women-accuse-police-officers-of-domestic-abuse-alleging-boys-club-culture. Accessed 26 July 2022.

Tatchell, P. 2021. Why Should We Have Uniformed Police at Pride Marches When the Met Is so Homophobic? *The Guardian*, December 14. https://www.theguardian.com/commentisfree/2021/dec/14/met-homophobic-police-investigation-stephen-port-gay-men. Accessed 26 July 2022.

Vitale, A. 2017. For a Critical Criminology. https://www.versobooks.com/blogs/3434-for-a-critical-criminology. Accessed 21 Sept 2022.

Wall, T., and T. Linnemann. 2021. No Chance: The Secret of Police, or the Violence of Discretion. *Social Justice* 47 (3–4): 33–54.

Williams, P. 2015. Criminalising the Other: Challenging the Race–Gang Nexus. *Race & Class* 56 (3): 18–35.

10

The Mystification of Police Institutional Violence

Lisa White and Patrick Williams

Introduction

Today, across England and Wales, policing is in a state of crisis. Following a catalogue of high-profile police crimes driven by what Casey (2023) determined as the institutionalisation of 'racism, sexism and misogyny', the 'thin blue line' has momentarily blurred, revealing to the public, what racially, socially and economically marginalised groups and communities have long known. According to Kersley and Townsend (2023) the number of police officers facing criminal charges across England and Wales has risen by 590%, with one in every 100 police officers reportedly now facing criminal charges, including for sexual offences. We have also witnessed police crimes characterised by *inaction*, a dereliction

---

L. White (✉)
Liverpool John Moores University, Liverpool, UK
e-mail: l.m.white@ljmu.ac.uk

P. Williams
Manchester Metropolitan University, Manchester, UK
e-mail: p.williams@mmu.ac.uk

of duty to the interpersonal violence experienced by women and girls within their homes; a sometimes fatal lack of compassion in policing responses to people who experience mental health crises; and a *laissez-faire* strategy to the violence experienced and endured by LGBTQI groups and communities.

Yet paradoxically, our politicians boast of the recruitment of 20,000 new police officers employed to discharge a raft of controversial new policing powers submerged within the *Police, Crime Sentencing and Courts Act* (2022); the *Nationality and Borders Act* (2022); and the *Public Order Act* (2023). For Box (1983) within the 'fog' is mystification—state-enacted processes through which the public's attention is necessarily turned away from the violence of the police and onto the 'usual suspects' of racially, socially, and economically marginalised groups and communities. Further, there is 'nothing but mystification' marked by the political construction and (re)production of evermore 'objects to be policed' and manufactured 'crime' problems to be solved (Williams, 2015; Williams and Clarke, 2018). Mystification is therefore enacted by the police to 'create the illusion' that 'crimes' as defined and determined by the powerful are the preserve of pathological groups who are (deliberately) marginalised within supposedly criminogenic communities who threaten the normative boundaries of society. To enhance our understanding of contemporary policing our knowledge can be framed through 'historically informed macro analysis' (Box, 1983: 119). Building on this, the decade in which *Power, Crime and Mystification* was published was marked by the consolidation of free market economics, the spread of neoliberalism and shifts towards increasing authoritarian populism (Hall, 1979). The Thatcher-led Conservative government elected in 1979 sought to employ 'a strong interventionist law and order state on the one hand [and] a rolled-back non-interventionist state form on the other' (Coleman et al., 2009: 4). The former was buttressed by the expansion of police powers and the 'ideological communication … of tough sentencing, more deterrence, more punishment, more police efficiency, and more social defence against "the enemy within…"' (Box, 1983: 25).

Today, austerity-scarred, brexited communities are now contending with an energy and cost-of-living crisis popularly mediated as being caused by a war in Ukraine. To police these crises, there is a need for 'illusion'. This chapter honours Box's legacy, by tracing a history of police abuses since the publication of Box's work. It shows how processes of mystification distort public understandings of 'crime', obfuscate the violent reality of policing and continue shaping (and concealing) how the role, function and purpose of the police institution is framed and understood in the present day.

Enemies Within

In the years surrounding *Power, Crime and Mystification*, purported 'enemies within' were subjected to discrimination, control and criminalisation, perceived as a threat to security, stability and prosperity, and deemed 'open territory… for police crimes' (Box 1983: 104). These 'enemies' included the poor, the unemployed, LGBT communities, political dissidents, striking workers, traveller groups, racially minoritised communities and the Irish (Scraton 1985, 1987), whilst those existing at certain intersections (e.g. Black unemployed young men) were viewed as particularly risky 'social dynamite' (Box 1983: 207–219). The racially discriminatory use of 'sus' powers (Section 4 of *The Vagrancy Act* 1824, though officially repealed in 1981) contributed to uprisings across the UK during the early-mid 1980s (Fryer 1984) and so-called 'community policing' targeted economically depressed inner-city communities predominantly populated by racially, socially and economically marginalised people (Gordon 1984). Police violence against striking miners at Orgreave in 1984 was symbolic of wider patterns of institutional abuses against the working class (Bunyan 1985; Gilmore 2019) whilst 'New' travellers intending to set up a free festival were subjected to mass arrests, violence and aggression at the 'Battle of the Beanfield' in 1985.

For Box, police oppression was (and is) not limited to these visible acts of so-called 'public order' policing, but also occurs within the often-hidden world of police surveillance and interrogation, operating as a further form of social disciplining (Choongh 1988). The Irish community in Britain remained subject to suspicion, with draconian counter-terror legislation continuing throughout the 1980s (Hillyard

1993, 1994; Pantazis and Pemberton 2009). As *the* 'suspect community' (Hillyard 1993) police actions against Irish women and men would continue a trend of miscarriages of justice seen throughout the 1970s (such as in the 'Birmingham Six', 'Guildford Four' and 'Maguire Seven' cases).

Police corruption and abuse against Black men e.g. the Tottenham Three also occurred despite the Royal Commission on Criminal Procedure (1981) and the resultant *Police and Criminal Evidence Act* (1984)—a supposedly professionalising reform following the policing 'scandals' of the 1970s. Corruption was present in the deaths of 97 Liverpool supporters at Hillsborough, Yorkshire in 1989—each a preventable death caused by a dangerous and negligent policing approach guided more by stereotypes and prejudices rather than public safety. These 97 institutional killings were 'covered up' in a process clearly reminiscent of the mystification observed by Box (1983). Police statements were changed to absolve police of responsibility and redirect blame onto Liverpool football supporters, whilst false media coverage slandered survivors as thieves, sexual predators and drunken 'hooligans', who had stolen from, assaulted and urinated upon the dead and injured (Scraton 2016). The impact of these deaths and dehumanisation further contributed to the growth of resistance within Liverpool's communities—communities which had already experienced economic underinvestment, high unemployment and rising inequality and were secretly considered suitable for a policy of 'managed decline' within the upper echelons of Thatcher's government (BBC 2011; Parker 2019).

Reproducing and Regulating the Enemy Within

The murder of Black teenager Stephen Lawrence in London in 1993 illustrates the ongoing racialised nature of policing and the differential treatment of minoritised communities perceived to be a 'threat' to an imagined white social order. Stephen was murdered by a group of white men, who subjected him and his friend Duwayne Brooks to racist abuse prior to killing Stephen. The police response was characterised by repeated failings and allegations of corruption, and by what the MacPherson Inquiry (1999) called 'institutional racism'. The police response demonstrated how little of substance had changed since the 1980s evidencing how racially minoritised communities were (and are) still viewed with suspicion. Stephen's killing was marred by police inaction, evidencing the material effects of police racism, where the police first responders to the murder scene had initially thought that Stephen's fatal injuries were caused by his Black friend Duwayne Brooks. The institutional inability for the police to *see* Stephen as an innocent victim of racist violence manifested as police inaction which hindered the critical stages of the investigation.

By the 2000s, Middle Eastern and South Asian communities (or those perceived to be) were increasingly targeted for policing, now under the guise of so-called 'counter-terrorism' following the September 11th 2001 attacks in the United States of America (USA) and the London bombings on July 7th 2005. Whilst the 'PREVENT' strategy contributed to the heightened surveillance and 'othering' of Muslim communities across a range of settings (Cohen and Tufail 2017; Lavalette 2013; Pantazis and Pemberton 2009; Younis 2021; Younis and Jadhav 2020) counter-terrorist policing led to the police killing of Brazilian Jean Charles De Menezes on a Stockwell tube in 2005 and the wounding of Mohammed Abdul Kahar in Forest Gate, shot by police during a counter-terrorist operation involving hundreds of officers (Mythen et al. 2013). Racism against South Asian and Muslim communities continues today, mostly tied to an Islamophobic construction of 'the terrorist threat' (Sabir 2022), yet Muslim and South Asian communities had been viewed as the 'enemy within' before this period, as a cursory reading of racism in Britain illustrates the state-sanctioned political narratives that persistently presented South Asian and Muslim communities as unassimilable and incompatible with so-called British values (Kapoor 2013; Poynting and Mason 2007). The racist murders of Gurdip Singh Chaggar, Altab Ali and Ishaque Ali in the 1970s—alongside police failures to protect minoritised communities from the actions of the Far Right, such as in Southall in 1979 (Bunyan 1985)—evidence this history.

The political reproduction of 'enemies within' continued during the Coalition Government (2010–2015). Whilst police technologies took new forms, the construction of threats remained (and remains) broadly familiar. Racially minoritised communities across the UK lack protection from far-right violence[1] and remain subjected to over-policing, partly illustrated by Stop and Search disproportionality (Keeling 2017; Long 2018). Police and state justifications for the over-policing of racially minoritised people converge around the attribution of criminality, including to an increasing array of non-criminal popular youth products. For example, the creation and consumption of popular culture such as Grime and Drill music is today presented by police as risky, dangerous signifiers for violent crime, 'gang' involvement and drug distribution (Fatsis 2019) with police officers phishing social media spaces in order to compile databases of drill music videos in what Clarke and Williams (2020) describe as 'guilt-producing' practices. Whilst the 'gang' in and of itself remains a racialised construction lacking in any ontological value, significant numbers of Black children and young peoples' details are now recorded onto 'gang databases' including the 'Gangs Matrix' operated by the Metropolitan Police (Amnesty International 2018). Such databases reify the unreliable and racist construct of the 'gang' and increase 'conviction maximising' opportunities through the hyper-criminalisation and punishment of Black and Brown people (Waller 2022).

LGBT+ Queer communities have also found themselves subjected to the harms of policing in the years surrounding the publication of *Power, Crime and Mystification*. As in previous decades, homophobia continued to operate within policing throughout the 2010s with concerns around the investigation of the murder of four young men—Anthony Walgate, Gabriel Kovari, Daniel Whitworth and Jack Taylor—in separate incidents, carried out by Stephen Port in 2014–2015. Police failed to carry

---

[1] In Rotherham in 2015, a peaceful anti-fascist vigil called after the racist murder of Mushin Ahmed was subjected to police 'kettling' before being diverted past a pub frequented by supporters of Britain First, a far-right group. In the legal case which followed, the Prosecution argued that although the supporters of the vigil came under attack first, the response of twelve Asian men had not been justified as self-defence. All twelve men would later be acquitted (Institute of Race Relations 2016).

out basic checks, send evidence for forensic testing or exercise professional curiosity throughout the 16 months between Port's first and last known murders (Davies 2021). This lack of care shown towards LGBT+ Queer communities follows similar patterns seen in previous decades. In 1989, sixteen men were arrested and charged with offences (including actual bodily harm) in the so-called 'Spanner case' following the discovery of a videotape showing consensual same-sex sadomasochist expression (White 2006). The institutional heteronormativity of the police helped to build and re-enforce the construction of Queer communities as a source of threat, assisted by the chilling effect of policies such as the *Local Government Act*'s (1988) Section 28, which prohibited the 'promotion of homosexuality' (Waites 2003) and by wider moral panics around HIV and AIDS.

Furthermore, a growing awareness of 'undercover policing' has highlighted how enmeshed and interwoven constructions of 'social order', 'deviance' and 'threats' are within policing, as bereaved families, activist groups, community organisers and politicians are now known to have been subjected to police surveillance via the 'Special Demonstration Squad' (Gilmore 2019; Lubbers 2012; Schlembach 2018). Police also worked with the privately owned Consulting Association, sharing 'intelligence' about worker activism and union organising (Evans 2020; Lubbers 2012; Smith and Chamberlain 2016). The close relationship between police and capital was also been laid bare by the harassment and sexualised violence inflicted against peaceful environmental protesters in 2015 when oppressive public order policing approaches were employed to ensure that I-Gas Energy had access to a potential hydraulic fracturing site in Barton Moss (Jackson et al. 2019).

The decision to employ a policing response to the Covid-19 pandemic has provided police with enhanced powers to surveil, stop, search and summarily punish the public (Harris et al. 2021, 2022). Again, racially minoritised groups remain demarcated as sites of dangerousness and have been disproportionately subjected to fines under these police powers (Gidda and Busby 2020). The period also highlighted ongoing police misogyny and cultures of violence against women, reflecting previous systemic and institutionalised failures to take violence against women seriously. At least 53 offences (including 27 rapes) by officer David

Carrick occurred despite frequent reports against him for sexual violence, whilst the murder of Sarah Everard by officer Wayne Couzens in March 2021 took place despite serious allegations surrounding the officer's previous behaviour, including repeated allegations of 'indecent exposure' (Grierson 2021). At a public vigil following Sarah's killing police engaged in violence against mourners and trampled upon tributes. Developments in technology during this time have also uncovered further examples of abuse, as violent, misogynist, homophobic and racist texts between officers were revealed (Atkinson et al. 2023). Officers have also taken and shared 'selfie' images of the dead bodies of Bibaa Henry and Nicole Smallman—two young women from racially minoritised backgrounds who were murdered in 2020 (Akram 2022).

This (inevitably incomplete) list highlights the systematic and systemic nature of police violence, repression and abuse. In line with Box (1983), rather than view police abuses as emerging from the toxic synthesis between underlying ideologies and the violent possibilities of police powers/practices and consequently as a problem *intrinsic to policing*, processes of mystification are still employed today so that events are recast as the actions of individual officers or occasionally as rogue elements of the culture of a single police force. Within the disciplinary architecture of the British state, these events do not lead to a critical and meaningful questioning of the position or presence of the police *as an institution in society*, nor to a careful analysis of the legitimacy of their powers.

Transforming the Meaning of 'Police Crimes'

The following sections explore how these mystificatory processes work in reference to police institutional killings. These killings highlight the absolute control over life and death which lies at the heart of state power made manifest through policing. At the time of writing (May 2023), there have been 1,851 deaths in police custody or otherwise following police contact in England and Wales since 1990 (INQUEST Casework and Monitoring 2023). Black people are seven times more likely than white people to die following police restraint (ibid: 38). The official

10 The Mystification of Police Institutional Violence

discourse which surrounds these deaths represents the continuation of racialised processes of mystification which aim to dismiss, dehumanise and deny the experiences of the policed. As succinctly put by one of the families affected by police killings, the 'first narrative that is put out' is too often a police narrative formulated around racialised tropes of drugs, 'gangsterism' and 'dangerousness', designed to mystify police actions and invisibilise or re-cast police violence as something other than how it appears (Williams et al. 2023).

As Williams et al. (2023) have shown, the storied recollections of bereaved families show the regularity of police harassment for Black communities deemed 'objects to be policed' (Williams and Clarke 2018: 234). For Box (1983: 90) 'experiences of domination are…everyday harsh reality' for those deemed a threat by the police and those in positions of power. The mere presence of Blackness i.e. to simply exist, marks Black families out as suspicious thereby necessitating and 'deserving' of surveillance, punishment and control (Puwar 2004).

Fatal encounters between the police and members of racially marginalised communities are not random or unfortunate moments, but manifestations of the racist violence and othering at the core of policing. The 'protective shield…around police-caused homicides' noted by Box (1983: 86) remains in place whilst racialised regimes of truth construct Black people as a dangerous source of threat (Elliot-Cooper 2021; Williams and Clarke 2018; White 2017). Stop and search encounters between the police and Black men are precipitated and characterised by police organisational instructions of risk and riskiness that work to escalate interactions between the police and Black people (Harris et al. 2021) towards arrest, criminalisation, use of painful restraint techniques and ultimately death (INQUEST 2023).

> Any trouble around where we lived [the police] came to our house… and that was my life for that amount of time [living] at my parents [house], all negative connotations with the police … That's one of the things that hit me right in my mind when they said Junior died … I thought they've [police] managed to kill one of us now (Relative of Junior in Williams et al. 2023: 255).

The object of the 'Black mugger' critiqued in Hall et al.'s (1978) *Policing the Crisis* has become subsumed into the 'gangsta' tropes of today and the mystification of police violence is writ large through the institutional killing of Mark Duggan in 2011.[2] Mark was killed by a firearms officer following a so-called 'Hard Stop' in Tottenham, London. Attempts at obfuscation contained within state talk followed his death, as the Independent Police Complaints Commission (IPCC) initially reported that shots had been fired at police (Elliott-Cooper 2011) only to acknowledge eight days later the injuries sustained by an officer had been caused by police bullets (Barkas 2014). Despite the lack of forensic evidence, the fact that no officers could recall seeing a weapon being thrown and the jury's own disbelief that Mark had been holding a gun when shot, the inquest jury reached a lawful killing conclusion. This conclusion followed extensive media coverage which operationalised imagery around dangerousness:

> The same photo appeared, of Duggan the hard man, staring defiantly into the camera as if no one and nothing could touch him. Hidden by the head and shoulders frame, cropped from a larger photo, was the floral heart plaque he was holding in his hands, as he attended the grave of his still-born daughter. Not defiance, but grief. (Erfani-Ghettani 2015: 110).

Yet as Box (1983) suggests, to simply focus on police shootings would present a misleading picture of police institutional violence and killing:

> Police can kill citizens in many ways…Any brutal assault, executed with truncheon or other blunt instruments, or involving boots, knees, heads or fists, can and sometimes does result in a citizen being killed or severely injured (ibid: 87).

Dogs, CS/PAVA irritant sprays and 'TASER' electro-shock weaponry further extend police violence, with use of the latter increasing by 500% between 2009/2010 and 2018/2019 (Resistance Lab 2020). The former professional footballer Dalian Atkinson was 'TASERED' for six times longer than recommended and, in echoes of the state talk which

---

[2] See also the killing of Chris Kaba at the time of writing (May, 2023).

10 The Mystification of Police Institutional Violence

described a previous victim of police violence—5'10 Shiji Lapite—as 'the biggest, strongest, most violent Black man [the officer had ever seen]' (cited in Pemberton 2008: 249), Dalian was imagined as 'quite simply huge... towering above me, absolutely towering...literally fill[ing] the frame of the door' (BBC 2011) by the heavier, taller, white police officer who—in a rare instance—would later be convicted of Dalian's manslaughter (Logan 2022). Within police 'regimes of truth' (Foucault 1980) stereotypes of superhuman strength necessitate extreme police force to contain, and thus the meaning of police violence is transformed (Long 2018: 87; Long and Joseph-Salisbury 2018). It is 'rendered as "good and necessary police work" because it effectively administers and achieves justice (albeit it rough) and thereby protects us from those criminals who pose a real threat to the community' (Box 1983: 81). To borrow from Sykes and Matza (1957) responsibility, victimhood and the injury are denied and an appeal is made to higher loyalties around safety, security and order, which has the effect of emphasising and exaggerating the dangerousness of police work (Sim 2010) and encourages the public to evaluate police killings in 'stark "him (sic) or me" terms' (Linnemann et al. 2014: 521).

In 1998, Christopher Alder was dragged face down along the floor of a custody suite in Hull, by officers who stood around watching him struggle to breath for over eleven minutes (Alder 2015; Angiolini 2017; INQUEST 2000). Sean Rigg died in 2008 after police responded to his mental health crisis with a dangerous form of restraint (Angiolini 2017; Baker 2016a; Bruce-Jones 2021). In both cases, police chose not to recognise the seriousness of each man's loss of consciousness and in Sean's case had responded to a mental health crisis with prolonged use of restraints, just as they would later do to Olaseni (Seni) Lewis in 2010, Leon Briggs in 2013 and Kevin Clarke in 2018. A similar lack of concern for the health of those under police 'care' can be observed in the death of Leroy 'Junior' Medford, whose preventable death occurred in 2017 following a heroin overdose, taken whilst supposedly under observation in a police cell. Officers had failed to suitably monitor Junior, had not adhered to Standard Operating Procedures regarding detention and had delayed getting medical assistance despite suspicions that Junior might have swallowed drugs (INQUEST 2019). These and other police institutional killings which result from the violence of neglect, non-intervention and inaction (both coupled with and separated from the use of restraint) evidence significant failures in the duty of care shown to Black men encountering police.

Perhaps the clearest example of racist forms of mystification is observable in comments from Dr Margaret Branthwaite, former Assistant Deputy Coroner (Inner South London), who described the police suffocation of Joy Gardner in the following terms:

> Mrs Joy Gardiner (sic), a lady of Caribbean extraction … was large, powerful and vociferous. Irked by her noise, the police taped her mouth, with disastrous consequences but it is quite characteristic of the black community that they are unable to breathe adequately – or perhaps at all – through the nose (Braithwaite 2001:114, *our emphasis*)

Something about the person killed is therefore 'disordered'—with all the reductionism and dehumanisation that implies—and it is that disordering which is responsible for the death, *not* the actions of the police. It imbibes the deaths with a sense of inevitability and is, as Cohen (2001) might describe, an 'interpretive denial' as what looks like a death caused by police action is now re-interpreted into an inevitable and unpreventable sudden death, where the police were simply unfortunate to be present. Braithwaite's account fails to mention that Joy Gardner died after being sat on by four officers, her wrists handcuffed to a body belt, her ankles and thighs bound with belts whilst her nose and mouth were gagged with 12 feet of adhesive bandage (Athwal 2015; Erfani-Ghettani 2015). When Rashan Charles was killed as a result of police action in July 2017, the initial Independent Police Complaints Commission (later the Independent Office for Police Conduct) statement similarly referred to Rashan as 'taking ill' but said nothing about an officer violently throwing him to the floor by his neck, locking him into a neck hold and forcibly trying to prise open his mouth, whilst another person[3] knelt on the back of his legs and helped apply 'rear stack' handcuffs.

Occasionally mystificatory state talk responsibilises the body of the person killed in other ways, as Pemberton (2008) has shown. Inquests reference 'Excited Delirium' and 'Acute Behavioural Disturbance' despite a lack of medical agreement about their scientific validity (Baker 2017; Angiolini 2017). Here the emphasis is placed upon something 'disorderly' about the person's psychological and physical health rather than police (in)action individually and/or institutionally. Thus, the validity of Box's (1983) arguments about police violence is evident throughout the forty years since the publication of *Power, Crime and Mystification*.

Mystification and Technological Change

In 1983, Box could not have envisaged the pace of technological change and its relationship to processes of mystification. Internet access, social media and phone camera technologies now permeate much of British society, leading to new forms of police visibility (Goldsmith 2010, 2013; Goldsmith and McLaughlin 2021). The shared CCTV footage of the institutional killing of Rashan Charles challenges the narrative which stated he 'took ill' and begins to fracture the imagery around his 'uncaused' death. Recordings have also been published showing the premature deaths of Christopher Alder, Sean Rigg and Kevin Clarke. Publicised videos of police institutional killings serve a powerful purpose, raising awareness of the visceral and brutal reality of policing that may become a catalyst for social movements (Linnemann et al. 2014) and as part of the public record of abuses, shared footage grants particular police institutional killings a hypervisibility which might not otherwise occur when such things are not recorded or the recordings are not made publicly available.

---

[3] The official version of events has stated that this man (known as Witness 1) is not a police officer, yet the CCTV evidence suggests some familiarity with use of restraint techniques and cuffing, and some confidence in communicating with the officer present.

Whilst on the surface, camera phone sousveillance of the police from below (i.e. by individuals, 'cop watch' organisations and civil society groups) can provide some public scrutiny, the history of recorded cases suggests caution when it comes to *criminal accountability* for police institutional killing. The surveillance state remains potent and typically casts its gaze towards the policed—further creating objects to *be* policed—and whilst sousveillance might create the occasional crack in official narratives of police violence and neglect, they have limited power in *isolation* to deconstruct the entire architecture which grants institutional legitimacy to policing and police powers. As Glasbeek et al. (2020) have argued, the expansion of visual technologies may also mean that the police (and the institutions which support them) become more experienced and more skilled at mystification. Police *centred* video technologies have also become commonplace alongside the growth of mobile phone cameras, particularly in relation to Body Worn Cameras (BWC).[4] Police discretion regarding the operation of BWC alongside their physical location on the body of officers privileges a particular perspective, and the footage is not immune from the wider social cultural framing around dangerousness and disorder (Brucato 2015; McKay and Lee 2019; Bailey et al. 2021) which may underpin the encounter in the first place. Images of Black victims of police institutional killings do not exist within a vacuum, for as Beutin (2017) has argued in relation to the USA:

> …racism and racialized ways of seeing mediate the effectiveness of visual evidence in cases of police brutality. It also limits the potential usefulness of anti-police brutality tactics by individualizing the problem to specific police officers rather than 'indicting' an entire system (Beutin 2017: 8).[5]

Videos of police violence can thus be seen and shared but are 'read' as something else. Through the 'racist episteme', the victim's presence becomes read as the source of danger and as a risk necessitating violent

---

[4] The use of Facial Recognition Technology by the police is also worthy of further exploration.
[5] In January 2023, Memphis Police Department (USA) released footage showing 5 officers beating to death Tyre Nichols, a 29-year-old Black man. That the video featuring 5 Black officers was quickly released by the police is perhaps not without significance, adding further complexity to the arguments seen in Beutin (2017) and Butler (1993).

10 The Mystification of Police Institutional Violence

restraint, even when the footage suggests differently (Butler 1993: 16). Videos of police institutional killings exist in a wider social context where the 'visual evidence that requires society to be able to see black humanity will be persistently limited by the structures that have created racialized ways of seeing' (Beutin 2017: 10). Similar ways of seeing exist in England and Wales, tied to dominant narratives of 'Black criminality'. Thus, despite footage clearly showing police brutality, criminal prosecutions remain rare and none of the footage cases referred to here have so far resulted in successful criminal prosecutions for murder or manslaughter in England and Wales. The videos are therefore a way of both seeing and not seeing (Glasbeek et al. 2020), rendering the racialised victims of police institutional killing both visible as a site of supposed dangerousness and criminality, and invisible as victims (White 2017). This is not to suggest that videos showing police institutional killing and violence against non-Black victims are unproblematic. Rather, the argument is that footage of police violence against white victims (such as Ian Tomlinson)[6] is not (re)interpreted through the same racialised lens of risk and dangerousness. The relationship between footage of police institutional killings and criminal forms of accountability thus contains an intrinsic complexity which goes beyond equally challenging questions about the commodification, sharing and consumption of images of suffering (White 2017).

---

[6] Ian died following an assault by PC Simon Harwood, as the former was walking past the police in London in 2009. Footage of the attack recorded by journalists and members of the public was published in the media, challenging the police's initial statement. The Crown Prosecution Service refused to charge PC Harwood, though would later seek manslaughter charges following an inquest conclusion of unlawful killing. In 2012, a jury found the officer not guilty of manslaughter.

Accountability, Mystification and Police Crimes

Coroner's inquests which aim to establish who the victim was, where, when and how they died occur after deaths involving the police (and other state actors). These should be compliant with Article 2 of the *European Convention on Human Rights and Fundamental Freedoms* (1950) as enacted by the *Human Rights Act* (1998), meaning that the circumstances leading up to the death should also be explored. Criticisms of this system include its limited powers, over-reliance on IOPC/IPCC reports, discretion, regional differences and limited oversight, whilst underfunding has also impacted upon inquests, both for Coroners themselves and for the families who engage with them (Angiolini 2017; Bruce-Jones 2021).[7]

Processes of mystification emerge throughout inquests, yet on occasions, Coroners *have* issued findings which have been critical of police actions and inactions surrounding the deaths of racially minoritised victims. Kingsley Burrell was fatally restrained in 2011 and his 2015 inquest found that the actions of the police had 'more than minimally' contributed to this death (Rawlinson 2018). In some cases, they have reached unlawful killing conclusions—for example in the deaths of Christopher Alder, Azelle Rodney and Leon Patterson. Some suggest that Coroners inquests might provide a more thorough examination of deaths compared to IOPC/IPCC linked investigations (Casale et al. 2013; Baker 2016b; Angiolini 2017). Yet this is a low bar. As we have argued elsewhere (Williams et al. 2023), the IOPC's alleged independence from police and police cultures remains subjected to considerable and sustained critique (see e.g., Coles and Shaw 2012; Savage 2013a, 2013b; Smith 2013; Baker 2017; Mohdin 2022). *The Independent Review of Deaths and Serious Incidents in Police Custody* (Angiolini 2017: 8) noted families' concerns regarding the 'influence and culture' of former officers now working for the then IPCC, whilst also acknowledging the potential impact this had on trust and perceptions of legitimacy (see also Casale

---

[7] Work led by families and campaigners is beginning to bring some changes, such as the removal of means testing in exceptional case funding for inquests (see INQUEST 2021).

et al. 2013). In recent years, the IOPC has re-opened some of its own investigations into the deaths of racially minoritised men (Kevin Clarke and Darren Cumberbatch) whilst others have been followed by supplementary addendum years later (Anthony Grainger) and/or subjected to external review (Sean Rigg).

Yet the existence of supposedly 'independent' investigations, repeated talk of reform and the occasional unlawful killing conclusions strengthens rather than refutes the nuanced argument of Box (1983). He problematises simplistic readings of the police as automatonic instruments serving the state, suggesting instead that police are wooed through a promise of 'autonomy from gross political interference... [and gains in] organisational and operational control with only the hint of public accountability being anything more than a smokescreen' (Box 1983: 116). He argues:

> The exchange between the state and the police effectively granted the latter a licence to misbehave within tolerable limits. From the state's point of view, it is implied that if you carry out your control function, we in turn will not insist that your men [sic] keep strictly within the law, providing of course you keep your deviants relatively invisible and confine the more violent and brutal outbursts to those classes and sections of the community you are controlling for us...There will of course be machinery for processing complaints and for holding you publicly accountable, but do not lose any sleep over these, for we will make certain they can never be effective (ibid.).

Unlawful killings and critical narratives form part of this smokescreen, giving the *appearance* of accountability, but without actual democratic accountability. If and when these mystificatory processes are put under strain by families, activist and advocacy groups, these processes might partially break down, some awareness is raised and 'the haunting spectre of police murdering or illegally killing civilians' might emerge (ibid: 82). Yet in terms of criminal accountability, this haunting spectre is quickly exorcised—the Crown Prosecution Service remains reluctant to proceed with cases of police institutional killing and on the rare occasions when these cases do progress, juries have failed to convict. Instead, police actions are reduced to the errant behaviour of 'bad apples' who are subjected to disciplinary hearings and occasionally sacked, for as Box argues:

> We do not want to be seen condoning police brutality and corruption when the public become aware of them, so if they are seen occasionally as getting out of hand we will need a few wayward junior officers as patsies in order to keep up the good appearance of having an honest police force (ibid.: 116).

Individual officers can be disciplined, regional forces (such as the Metropolitan Police) can be criticised, but the dominant narrative avoids asking the challenging questions about the *institutional arrangements* that legitimise the police and their role in society. That only one case has thus far resulted in an officer being criminally convicted for murder or manslaughter[8] since 1986 suggests that Box's (1983: 52) claim that 'an occasional court appearance can become enshrined as mere ritual ceremony totally encapsulating a particular moment of time which can be easily forgotten' is most pertinent to our understanding of police crime today.

Conclusion

This outline of policing since the publication of *Power, Crime and Mystification* has illustrated the relevance of Box's (1983) analysis today, against a background characterised by the continuity of austerity policies and the cost-of-living crisis, the effects of Brexit, a European war playing out in Ukraine and the material effects of what has been described as an 'energy crisis'. It is within such moments that the state resolves to assuage crisis through the (re)production of enemies within and the enactment

---

[8] PC Benjamin Monk was cleared of murder and convicted of the manslaughter of Dalian Atkinson. During a mental health crisis, Dalian had been repeatedly Tasered for 33 seconds, beaten with a baton and kicked twice in the head whilst on the floor, including with enough force to leave imprints of the officer's bootlaces on his face. That Monk's trial took place in the immediate aftermath of the public sharing of videos showing the murder of George Floyd by officer Derek Chauvin in the USA, and that Dalian was a well-known Black footballer is perhaps not without significance.

of evermore intrusive forms of law enforcement, as alarmingly evidenced by the *Police, Crime, Sentencing and Courts Act* (2022)—a contemporary attempt to 'police the crisis' (Hall et al. 1978). It would be easy to conclude from this study of policing that the police are simply failing to protect, but in reality, they protect very well a system which mystifies the harmful actions and inactions of powerful actors and institutions, including the police themselves. The police are a key disciplinary instrument in the maintenance of inequality, the role of violence in society, the continuation of cultures of misogyny, racism, homo/bi/transphobia, and the coercive pacification of those deemed disorderly. Potential action against 'their own' appears *possible*, but typically only as an ever-receding horizon. On the rare occasions where attempts to hold police perpetrators to account progress—usually through the tenacious indefatigability of families, social movements and advocacy groups—legal processes represent perpetrators as pathologised individuals drained of any of the wider occupational and structural contexts common to policing.

Whilst we may understand victims of police institutional killings as being 'sacrificed to uphold the "greater good" of communal order' (Loader 2020: 405–406) actions against individual officers (or occasionally regional forces) can also be seen as a form of sacrifice. The scapegoat can be isolated and safely cast out, as once the sacrifice is made something *has been done*, and business as usual can then continue. Ritual offerings might follow in the form of paper recommendations and pacifying plans to 'learn lessons'. The harms are cleansed and things can continue as before. To acknowledge police killings as *institutional killing* thus directly challenges foundational concepts like policing by consent, force and legitimacy. It is thus not surprising that the full range of mystification processes are employed, as the alternative—full and meaningful accountability for police institutional killing *as institutional killing*—is so shattering, as it brings into question the very nature of the state and the social, political, economic and cultural place that the structural violence of policing occupies within so-called liberal democracies.

References

Akram, S. 2022. Police ça Change? Cressida Dick, Institutional Racism and the Metropolitan Police. *Political Quarterly* 93 (3): 383–391.
Alder, J. 2015. What's the Worst that Could Happen? The Death of Christopher Alder. *Criminal Justice Matters* 101 (1): 4–5.
Amnesty International. 2018. *Trapped in the Matrix: Secrecy, Stigma, and Bias in the Met's Gangs Database*. London: Amnesty International.
Angiolini, E. 2017. *Report of the Independent Review of Deaths and Serious Incidents in Police Custody*. ISBN: 978-1-78655-575-5.
Athwal, H. 2015. 'I Don't Have a Life to Live': Deaths and UK Detention. *Race and Class* 56 (3): 50–68.
Atkinson, K., U. Barr, H. Monk, and K. Tucker, eds. 2023. *Feminist Responses to Injustices of the State and its Institutions*. Bristol: Bristol University Press.
Bailey, R.L., G.L. Read, Y.H. Yan, J. Liu, D.A. Makin, and D. Willits. 2021. Camera Point-of-View Exacerbates Racial Bias in Viewers of Police Use of Force Videos. *Journal of Communication* 71 (2): 246–275.
Baker, D. 2016a. *Deaths After Police Contact*. London: Palgrave Macmillan.
Baker, D. 2016b. Deaths after Police Contact in England and Wales: The Effects of Article 2 of the European Convention on Human Rights on Coronial Practice. *International Journal of Law in Context* 12 (2): 162–177.
Baker, D. 2017. Making Sense of 'Excited Delirium' in Cases of Death after Police Contact. *Policing: A Journal of Policy and Practice* 12 (4): 361–371.
Barkas, B. 2014. The Framing of Mark Duggan. *Race and Class* [online] April 17, 2015. https://irr.org.uk/article/framing-the-death-of-mark-duggan/.
BBC. 2011. Thatcher Urged 'Let Liverpool Decline' after 1981 Riots. *BBC News*, 30 December. https://www.bbc.co.uk/news/uk-16361170. Accessed 19 Dec 2022.
Box, S. 1983. *Power, Crime and Mystification*. London: Routledge.
Branthwaite, M. 2001. Deaths in Custody—Causes and Legal Consequences. *Medico-Legal Journal* 69 (3): 107–116.
Brucato, B. 2015. Policing Made Visible: Mobile Technologies and the Importance of Point of View. *Surveillance and Society* 13 (3/4): 455–473.
Bruce-Jones, E. 2021. Mental Health and Death in Custody: The Angiolini Review. *Race and Class* 62 (3): 7–17.
Bunyan, T. 1985. From Saltley to Orgreave via Brixton. *Journal of Law and Society* 12 (2): 293–304.

Beutin, L.P. 2017. Racialization as a Way of Seeing: The Limits of Counter-Surveillance and Police Reform. *Surveillance and Society* 15: 1.

Butler, J. 1993 Endangered/Endangering: Schematic Racism and White Paranoia. In Gooding-Williams, R. (Eds.), *Reading Rodney King/Reading Urban Uprising*. New York: Routledge.

Casale, S., J. Lewis, and M.J. Corfee. 2013. *Report of the Independent External Review of the IPCC Investigation into the Death of Sean Rigg*. London: Independent Office for Police Conduct.

Review, Casey. 2023. *An Independent Review into the Standards of Behaviour and Internal Culture of the Metropolitan Police Service*. London: Metropolitan Police Service.

Choongh, S. 1988. Policing the Dross: A Social Disciplinary Model of Policing. *The British Journal of Criminology* 38 (4): 623–634.

Clarke, B., and P. Williams. 2020. (Re)producing Guilt in Suspect Communities: The Centrality of Racialisation in Joint Enterprise Prosecutions. *International Journal for Crime, Justice and Social Democracy* 9 (3): 116–129.

Cohen, B., and W. Tufail. 2017. *Prevent and the Normalization of Islamophobia*. London: Runnymede Trust.

Cohen, S. 2001. *States of Denial: Knowing about Atrocities and Suffering*. Cambridge: Polity Press.

Coleman, R., J. Sim, S. Tombs, and D. Whyte. 2009. *State, Power, Crime*. London: Sage.

Coles, D., and H. Shaw. 2012. *Learning from Death in Custody Inquests: A New Framework for Action and Accountability*. London: INQUEST.

Davies, C. 2021. Met Failings Probably a Factor in Deaths of Stephen Port Victims, says Inquest. *The Guardian* 10 December. https://www.theguardian.com/uk-news/2021/dec/10/mets-failings-contributed-to-deaths-of-stephen-ports-victims-inquest-finds. Accessed 21 Dec 2022.

Elliott-Cooper, A. 2021. *Black Resistance to British Policing*. Manchester: Manchester University Press.

Elliott-Cooper, A. 2011. The Second Death of Mark Duggan. *Ceasefire Magazine* 27 November. https://ceasefiremagazine.co.uk/anti-imperialist-14-mark-duggan/. Accessed 19 Dec 2022.

Erfani-Ghettani, R. 2015. The Defamation of Joy Gardner: Press, Police and Black Deaths in Custody. *Race and Class* 56 (3): 102–112.

Evans, R. 2020. Police Chief Who Spied on Activists Went on to Work for Union Blacklist, Inquiry Told. *The Guardian*, 17 November. https://www.theguardian.com/uk-news/2020/nov/17/police-chief-who-spied-on-activists-went-on-to-work-for-union-blacklist-inquiry-told. Accessed 21 Dec 2022.

Fatsis, L. 2019. Policing the Beats: The Criminalisation of UK Drill and Grime Music by the London Metropolitan Police. *Sociological Review* 67 (6): 1300–1316.

Fryer, P. 1984. *Staying Power: The History of Black People in Britain*. London: Pluto Press.

Foucault, M. 1980. *Power/Knowledge: Selected Interviews and Other Writings, 1972–1977*. Random House.

Gidda, M., and Busby, M. 2020. BAME People Disproportionately Targeted By Coronavirus Fines. *Liberty Investigates*. https://libertyinvestigates.org.uk/articles/bame-people-disproportionately-targeted-by-coronavirus-fines/. Accessed 21 Dec 2022.

Gilmore, J. 2019. Lessons from Orgreave: Police Power and the Criminalization of Protest. *Journal of Law and Society* 46 (4): 612–639.

Glasbeek, A., M. Alam, and K. Roots. 2020. Seeing and Not-seeing: Race and Body-worn Cameras in Canada. *Surveillance and Society* 18: 3.

Goldsmith, A. 2013. Disgracebook Policing: Social Media and the Rise of Police Indiscretion. *Policing and Society* 25 (3): 249–267.

Goldsmith, A., and E. McLaughlin. 2021. Policing's New Vulnerability Re-Envisioning Local Accountability in an Era of Global Outrage. *British Journal of Criminology* 62 (3): 716–733.

Goldsmith, A. 2010. Policing's New Visibility. *British Journal of Criminology* 50 (5): 914–934.

Gordon, P. 1984. Community Policing: Towards the Local Police State? *Critical Social Policy* 4 (10): 39–58. https://doi.org/10.1177/026101838400401003.

Grierson, W. 2021. Wayne Couzens Case Raises Questions Over How Police Officers Are Sanctioned. *The Guardian* 4 October. https://www.theguardian.com/uk-news/2021/oct/04/wayne-couzens-case-how-do-you-lose-your-job-in-the-police. Accessed 21 Dec 2022.

Hall, S. 1979. The Great Moving Right Show. *Marxism Today*, January 14–20.

Hall, S., C. Critcher, T. Jefferson, J. Clarke, and B. Roberts. 1978. *Policing the Crisis: Mugging, the State and Law and Order*. London: Springer Nature Limited.

Harris, S., R. Joseph-Salisbury, P. Williams, and L. White. 2022. Notes on Policing, Racism and the Covid-19 Pandemic in the UK. *Race and Class* 63 (3): 92–102.

Harris, S., R. Joseph-Salisbury, P. Williams, and L. White. 2021. *A Threat to Public Safety—Policing, Racism and the Covid-19 Pandemic*. London: Institute for Race Relations.

Hillyard, P. 1993. *Suspect Community : People's Experience of the Prevention of Terrorism Acts in Britain.* London: Pluto.

Hillyard, P. 1994. Irish People and the British Criminal Justice System. *Journal of Law and Society* 21 (1): 39.

INQUEST. 2023. Casework and Monitoring: Deaths in Police Custody. https://www.inquest.org.uk/deaths-in-police-custody. Accessed 13 Feb 23.

INQUEST. 2021. Casework and Monitoring. https://www.inquest.org.uk/pages/category/statistics-and-monitoring. Accessed 22 Feb 2022.

INQUEST. 2000. *Jury Concludes Unlawful Killing in Death of Christopher Alder* https://www.inquest.org.uk/christopher-alder-inquest-concludes. Accessed 31 Oct 2022.

INQUEST. 2019. *Critical conclusion at inquest of Leroy Junior Medford* https://www.inquest.org.uk/leroy-junior-medford-conclusion. Accessed 31 Oct 2022.

Institute of Race Relations (IRR). 2016. *Rotherham 12: The Jury Finds Defendants not Guilty.* Institute of Race Relations. 17 November https://irr.org.uk/article/rotherham-12-the-jury-finds-defendants-not-guilty/. Accessed 21 Dec 2022.

Jackson, W., J. Gilmore, and H. Monk. 2019. Policing Unacceptable Protest in England and Wales: A Case Study of the Policing of Anti-fracking Protests. *Critical Social Policy* 39 (1): 23–43.

Kapoor, N. 2013. The Advancement of Racial Neoliberalism in Britain. *Ethnic and Racial Studies* 36 (6): 1028–1046.

Keeling, P. 2017. *No Respect: Young BAME Men, the Police and Stop and Search.* London: Criminal Justice Alliance.

Kersley, A., and Townsend, M. 2023. Revealed: One in 100 Police Officers in England and Wales Faced a Criminal Charge Last Year. *The Guardian.* 25 May. https://www.theguardian.com/uk-news/2023/feb/25/revealed-one-in-100-uk-police-officers-faced-a-criminal-charge-last-year. Accessed 26 May 2023.

Lavalette, M. 2013. Institutionalised Islamophobia and the 'Prevent' Agenda: 'Winning Hearts and Minds' or Welfare as Surveillance and Control? In *Race, Racism and Social Work*, ed. M. Lavalette and L. Penketh, 167–190. Bristol: Policy Press.

Linnemann, T., T. Wall, and E. Green. 2014. The Walking Dead and Killing State: Zombification and the Normalization of Police Violence. *Theoretical Criminology* 18 (4): 506–527.

Loader, I. 2020. A Question of Sacrifice: The Deep Structure of Deaths in Police Custody. *Social and Legal Studies* 29 (3): 401–420.

Logan, L. 2022. We Can Stop the Police Brutality that Killed Dalian Atkinson, But Let's First Admit There is a Problem. *The Guardian*. 29 September. https://www.theguardian.com/commentisfree/2022/sep/29/police-dalian-atkinson. Accessed 22 Dec 2022.

Long, L. 2018. *Perpetual Suspects, A Critical Race Theory of Black and Mixed-Race Experiences of Policing*. London: Palgrave Macmillan.

Long, L., and R. Joseph-Salisbury. 2018. Black Mixed-Race Men's Perceptions and Experiences of the Police. *Ethnic and Racial Studies* 42 (2): 1–18.

Lubbers, E. 2012. *Secret Manoeuvres in the Dark: Corporate and Police Spying on Activists*. London: Pluto.

Macpherson, W. 1999. The Stephen Lawrence Inquiry. Report CM 4262-1. London: HMSO.

McKay, C., and M. Lee. 2019. Body-Worn Images: Point-of-View and the New Aesthetics of Policing. *Crime Media Culture: An International Journal* 16 (3): 431–450.

Mohdin, A. 2022. Family of Man Who Died After Release from Custody Demand Police CCTV, *The Guardian* [ONLINE], January 9. https://www.theguardian.com/uk-news/2022/jan/09/family-of-man-who-died-after-release-from-custody-demand-police-cctv. Accessed 22 Feb 2022.

Mythen, G., S. Walklate, and F. Khan. 2013. Why Should We Have to Prove We're Alright? Counter-Terrorism Risk and Partial Securities. *Sociology* 47 (2): 383–398.

Pantazis, C., and S. Pemberton. 2009. From the 'Old' to the 'New' Suspect Community Examining the Impacts of Recent UK Counter-Terrorist Legislation. *British Journal of Criminology* 49 (5): 646–666.

Parker, S. 2019. The Leaving of Liverpool: Managed Decline and the Enduring Legacy of Thatcherism's Urban Policy. British Politics and Policy at LSE. *LSE Politics Blog*. https://blogs.lse.ac.uk/politicsandpolicy/the-leaving-of-liverpool/. Accessed 19 Dec 2022.

Pemberton, S. 2008. Demystifying Deaths in Police Custody: Challenging State Talk. *Social & Legal Studies* 17 (2): 237–262. https://doi.org/10.1177/0964663908089614.

Poynting, S., and V. Mason. 2007. The Resistible Rise of Islamophobia: Anti-Muslim Racism in the UK and Australia before 11 September 2001. *Journal of Sociology* 43 (1): 61–86.

Puwar, N. 2004. *Space Invaders—Race, Gender and Bodies Out of Place*. London: Bloomsbury Academic.

Rawlinson, K. 2018. Kingsley Burrell Family Call for Inquiry after Sacking of Police Officer. *The Guardian.* 18 December. https://www.theguardian.com/uk-news/2018/dec/18/kingsley-burrell-family-call-for-inquiry-after-sacking-of-police-officer. Accessed 19 Dec 2022.

Resistance Lab. 2020. *A Growing Threat to Life: Taser Usage by Greater Manchester Police.* Manchester: Resistance Lab. https://resistancelab.network/our-work/taser-report/index.html

Sabir, R. 2022. *The Suspect: Counterterrorism, Islam and the Security State.* London: Pluto Press.

Savage, S.P. 2013a. Thinking Independence: Calling the Police to Account through the Independent Investigation of Police Complaints. *The British Journal of Criminology* 53 (1): 94–112.

Savage, S.P. 2013b. 'Seeking 'Civilianness': Police Complaints and the Civilian Control Model of Oversight. *The British Journal of Criminology* 53 (5): 886–904.

Schlembach, R. 2018. Undercover Policing and the Spectre of 'Domestic Extremism': The Covert Surveillance of Environmental Activism in Britain. *Social Movement Studies* 17 (5): 491–506.

Scraton, P. 1985. *The State of the Police.* London: Pluto.

Scraton, P. 1987. *Law, Order, and the Authoritarian State.* Milton Keynes: Open University Press.

Scraton, P. 2016 *Hillsborough: The Truth.* Mainstream Publishing.

Sim, J. 2010. Thinking about State Violence. *Criminal Justice Matters* 82 (1): 6–7. https://doi.org/10.1080/09627251.2010.525909.

Smith, D., and P. Chamberlain. 2016. *Blacklisted: The Secret War Between Big Business and Union Activists*, 2nd ed. London: New Internationalist.

Smith, G. 2013. Oversight of the Police and Residual Complaints Dilemmas: Independence, Effectiveness and Accountability Deficits in the United Kingdom. *Police Practice and Research*, 14 (2): 92–103.

Sykes, G.M., and D. Matza. 1957. Techniques of Neutralization: A Theory of Delinquency. *American Sociological Review*, 22 (6): 664–670.

Waites, M. 2003. Equality at Last? Homosexuality, Heterosexuality and the Age of Consent in the United Kingdom. *Sociology* 37 (4): 637–655.

Waller, N. 2022. *Gang Narratives and Broken Law: Why 'Joint Enterprise' Still Needs Fixing.* London: Centre for Crime and Justice Studies.

White, L. 2017 Sites of Dangerousness: The Visibility and Invisibility of Black Victims of Police Violence. European Group for the Study of Deviance and Social Control Conference, Lesvos.

White, C. 2006. The Spanner Trials and the Changing Law on Sadomasochism in the UK. *Journal of Homosexuality* 50 (2–3): 167–187.

Williams, P. 2015. Criminalising the Other: Challenging the Race-Gang Nexus. *Race & Class* 56 (3): 18–35.

Williams, P., and B. Clarke. 2018. The Black Criminal Other as an Object of Social Control. *Social Sciences* 7 (234): 1–14.

Williams, P., L. White, R. Joseph-Salisbury, and S. Harris. 2023. Omission, Erasure and Obfuscation in the Police Institutional Killing of Black Men. *Mortality* 28 (2): 250–268.

Younis, T. 2021. The Psychologisation of Counter-Extremism: Unpacking PREVENT. *Race and Class* 62 (3): 37–60.

Younis, T., and S. Jadhav. 2020. Islamophobia in the National Health Service: An Ethnography of Institutional Racism in PREVENT's Counter-Radicalisation Policy. *Sociology of Health and Illness* 42 (3): 610–626.

11

Immigration Control, Mystification and the Carceral Continuum

Jon Burnett

Introduction

Writing in the opening chapter of *Power, Crime and Mystification*, Steven Box (1983: 13) memorably and powerfully described constructions of crime and the parameters of criminalisation in Britain as 'social control strategies'. Elaborating further, he demonstrated how the criminal justice system's intense focus on the actions of marginalised populations was linked to its indifference to the crimes and harms of elites, corporations and the state. In turn, this reproduced an 'illusion' of an identifiable dangerous class at the same time as making invisible the crimes and harms of the powerful, he argued; simultaneously articulating the criminal justice system as a benevolent, apolitical 'service' (ibid.: 13–14). Against the backdrop of the deepening economic crisis throughout the 1970s and into the early 1980s, and a reworking (and in many respects intensification) of particular forms of criminalisation and state power,

J. Burnett (✉)
University of Hull, Hull, UK
e-mail: Jon.Burnett@hull.ac.uk

his analysis was a formidable example of neo-Marxist theorising: demonstrating how people became more reliant on particular state institutions at the same time as they victimised them. It showed how the criminal justice system's 'elastic ability to expand into areas not previously part of its jurisdiction' made it '*one* of the first lines of defences available to the powerful' in suppressing or eliminating those constituted as a threat, in order to shore up 'ideological and social hegemony' (ibid.: 209, see also Cunliffe and Morrison, this volume). So, a core task of radical analysis, he made clear, was to understand how particular state apparatuses both reinforce and reproduce unequal and unjust forms of social order, while moving beyond 'the imagery and logic of conspiracy theory' (ibid.: 213).

This chapter focuses on a further, diametrically related, area of state activity depicted by the powerful as a 'first line of defence' in securing ideological and social hegemony, but which was largely absent from Box's account: immigration control. Where immigration control did feature in *Power, Crime and Mystification* this was almost tangentially. Yet despite this gap, some four decades after its publication its analytical framework nonetheless both did, and does have plenty to say about immigration control's contours, its harms, functions and inequities. Immigration control operates as a central component of a carceral state in Britain which, while having long roots, has developed with intensity since the late twentieth Century. And what follows here consequently proceeds in two parts. First, it draws on Foucault's (1977) notion of a carceral continuum to set out how carceral logics are materialised and reproduced through immigration control. Second, building on Box's analysis, it explores how forms of mystification are central to these processes. 'Not only does the state with the help and reinforcement of its control agencies, criminologists, and the media conceptualize a particular and partial ideological version of serious crime and who commits it', Box (1983: 14) argued, 'but it does so by concealing and hence mystifying its own propensity for violence and serious crime on a much larger scale'. These insights, as we shall see, are prescient for British immigration control in the twenty-first Century which simultaneously criminalises, manages, subordinates and victimises. For, to paraphrase Box, there is more to immigration control than the state reveals, but only if we see it.

Braverman's Dreams

In December 2022, the High Court in England appeared to realise Home Secretary Suella Braverman's dreams by ruling that the mass deportation of asylum seekers to Rwanda was lawful. Three months earlier, soon after being appointed Home Secretary, she had told party members at the Conservative Party's annual conference about her passionate, heartfelt desire to deport people seeking asylum to central Africa. And referring to the government's already-existing 'Rwanda Asylum Plan', announced officially by the then Prime Minister Boris Johnson earlier that year, she expressed her disappointment that this had at that point been prevented by a legal challenge: telling her audience that 'unfortunately, we've got to let that play out … we've got to come out of the legal dispute we are currently embroiled in' (Braverman 2022). However, while previous attempts to put the plan into practice had been 'thwarted by our laws' (ibid.), she continued, she was nonetheless optimistic that it would be made possible in the future. For the 'time for words' was now 'over', she made clear; now was the 'time for action'. To a backdrop of cheers and rapturous applause, she continued to tell her audience how she would 'love to have a front page of *The Telegraph* with a plane taking off to Rwanda'. That's 'my dream', she explained. 'It's my obsession' (ibid.).[1]

As Braverman was very much aware, then, this 'obsession' drew on existing legal and policy measures: part of the 'foundations', as she described them, already been laid by Johnson and her predecessor Priti Patel. Indeed, it is in this context that she pledged to both build on a range of existing practices put in place or previously attempted, in her first major speech on immigration at this Party Conference and expand on them. This included a promise to 'cut' migration by tens of thousands of people, loosely echoing the 2010 to 2015 Conservative-Liberal Democrat coalition government's ultimately abandoned migration 'cap'.

---

[1] On 29 June 2023 the UK government lost a case in the Court of Appeal on the Rwanda deportations. The court ruled that this policy was 'unlawful'. However, Prime Minister Rishi Sunak immediately stated that the government planned to seek leave to appeal this decision. In the weeks that followed there were renewed calls within the Conservative Party to abolish the *Human Rights Act* (1998).

It included a pledge to target international students, reminiscent of the deportation of thousands of international students for alleged exam deception which an immigration tribunal later stated was based on 'hearsay' (Menon 2016). With pledges ranging from tackling those 'asylum seekers who are abusing the system' (Braverman 2022) to cracking down on the 'vocal minorities who attempt to undermine our common sense instincts' (ibid.), her vision for the future not only reproduced and reworked narratives about the asylum and immigration system utilised by her predecessors, it pledged to rework and build on policy frameworks established over decades. And although her dreams were seemingly interrupted when she resigned from her position shortly after this conference speech, as a result of a data breach, almost immediately after being reappointed under the leadership of new Prime Minister Rishi Sunak she returned to the same themes. Those attempting to enter the UK through the English Channel, she claimed, equated to 'an invasion of our southern coast' (cited in Clarke 2022). Within a few months, the government was pursuing plans targeting them with such ferocity that they were described by observers as an 'assault': putting lives 'at risk of extreme harm' and allowing 'the Government to abuse rights with impunity' (Liberty 2023).[2]

It is against this backdrop—feeding off and feeding into what has elsewhere been depicted as a 'war' on asylum and irregular migration (Bhatia and Burnett 2019)—that Braverman's ideological narratives and their proposed material realisations spoke to the expansion of a form of carceral continuum within Britain, which in turn operate as a core feature of a developing carceral state. Foucault (1977: 297) described the carceral continuum as the blurring of the frontiers between 'confinement, judicial punishment and institutions of discipline', and highlighted the diffusion of 'penitentiary techniques' (ibid.) into an array of policy domains, institutions and agencies. As he made clear, carcerality is not just reproduced within specific coercive institutions and forms of confinement, but embedded within and reproduced through a 'subtle, graduated carceral net' (ibid.). As such, Ruby Tapia (2019) has argued:

---

[2] This is the context to the tragic and high profile deaths of six Afghan me in their 30 on the 12 August 2023, when the small boat carrying them across the English Channel sunk.

> [T]he carceral state encompasses the formal institutions and operations and economies of the criminal justice system proper, but it also encompasses logics, ideologies, practices, and structures, that invest in tangible and sometimes intangible ways in punitive orientations to difference, to poverty, to struggles for social justice and to the crossers of constructed borders of all kinds.

Put another way, the 'concept of carcerality captures the many ways in which the carceral state shapes and organizes society and culture through policies and logics of control, surveillance, criminalisation, and unfreedom' (University of Michigan Carceral State Project 2019). What follows in the next section sets out some of the interlinked parameters of a carceral continuum reproducing such structures within a British context, particularly as they relate to immigration control, and how these have developed, expanded and intensified since Box's (1983) analysis in *Power, Crime and Mystification*.

Immigration Control and the Carceral Continuum

A central component of this carceral continuum is the immense detention and incarceration system that has been established as a core component of immigration enforcement and immigration control. In 1975, 188 people were detained for immigration purposes in the UK, while in 2015, some 32,447 people were incarcerated in immigration detention—an increase of over 17,000 per cent (Burnett 2022). Since that point, the number of people detained for immigration purposes per year have varied, decreasing slightly to 24,004 in the year to July 2022. However, this does not include the rapid outgrowth of satellite forms of incarceration over this same period. For example, over the last few years disused military barracks in England and Wales have been utilised to detain several hundreds of asylum seekers at any point, making barb-wired migrant 'camps' at some points a feature of the immigration landscape. While simultaneously, in January 2022 the Manston 'processing centre' opened on an out-of-use military airfield in the South of England and, despite having capacity to cage 1600 people, was holding around 4000 people within a few months (see Maggs 2022; as discussed below, by November 2022 this had been temporarily emptied of people). Such camps, operating alongside dedicated immigration removal centres (IRCs), euphemistically named short-term holding facilities (STHFs) and forms of pre-departure accommodation, have existed as an expansive carceral machinery through which entry into the UK, case-processing and removals can be administered. But, as is well established, they dovetail with the prison system itself. In 2022, there were 9671 foreign nationals held in prisons in England and Wales, making up some 12 per cent of its prison population (Ministry of Justice 2022).

This substantial increase in confinement is linked, in part, to political will. Against the backdrop of a moral panic in the mid-2000s over the release of foreign nationals from prison after serving a prison sentence (Griffiths 2017), policy and legislation have persistently lowered the bar towards a presumption for the automatic deportation of foreign nationals convicted of criminal offences. While, simultaneously, initiatives such as Operation Nexus in 2012 (involving closer collaboration between criminal justice and immigration agencies) have served as a carceral dragnet drawing in more foreign nationals and widening the scope of criminal offences and forms of police contact potentially precipitating immigration enforcement itself (Parmar 2020). At the same time, such measures have been buttressed by shifts in citizenship legislation rendering increasing numbers of people vulnerable to immigration enforcement (such as those with dual-citizenship; see de Noronha 2020). And in conjunction, the late 1990s and early twenty-first Century in particular saw a concerted, unprecedented increase in the number of immigration offences, with New Labour, for example, introducing more immigration offences in its thirteen years in power than in the 113 years previously (Aliverti 2016). Indeed, while Box developed a formidable analysis of the functions of criminalisation, and its reproduction of a particular form of capitalist order, he would not have been aware of the sheer extent to which immigration and criminal law and policy would grow closer over the next four decades, to the point that 'crimmigration' control now exists as a core feature of state policy. Crimmigration refers to the overlap and mutually reinforcing interrelations between criminal and immigration law, as well as the expansive mechanisms through which immigration is managed through crime control processes, the plethora of civil sanctions and exclusions, and the development of institutions, agencies and bodies tasked with enforcing its remit (Stumpf 2006). It is among the factors (but certainly not the only factor) directly underpinning substantial increases in immigration raids and attempted deportations and removals in the early twenty-first Century (Fekete 2009), alongside this expansive framework of sites of confinement.

However, while detention, prison and camps are key sites of the carceral continuum, carcerality further expands well beyond their walls. Following their 'release' from the Manston Processing Centre in 2022, for example—after (as will be discussed below) revelations about unsafe conditions and outbreaks of diphtheria—many of the same occupants were transferred to hotels across the UK, utilised as temporary 'contingency accommodation'. Some 37,000 asylum seekers were funnelled to hotel rooms in 2022, with many (but not all) sent to them after arriving in the UK via the waters of the English Channel (between southern England and France). Over 38,000 people were forced to enter the UK through such dangerous routes that same year (Home Office 2022), risking (again, as shall be discussed below) serious harm and in some cases death. And despite claims made by a range of political figures and media sources that such forms of accommodation are a 'luxury' (Cole et al. 2022), many have experienced restrictions on movement and association amounting to a 'form of incarceration', according to the charity Bail for Immigration Detainees: having been prevented from leaving by security officers and surviving on the barest financial support (cited in Walawalker and Bulman 2022). Nonetheless, this was not austere enough for the government, and after exploring plans to use buildings such as unused holiday sites or defunct student halls of residence (ideal as they are 'never luxurious'), according to one official (Hymas 2022), in 2023 it stated that it would begin corralling around 500 people into the cheaper and more 'basic' conditions of a giant barge. Other vessels too were being explored, it made clear, as well as looking for further disused army barracks (Walker 2023).

Indeed, this has both mirrored in some ways, and in others sought to make more punitive the conditions in the asylum housing market, with more than 40,000 asylum seekers dispersed around the UK in 2021, generally to towns and cities with available stocks of cheap (often dilapidated) housing (Berg and Dickson 2022). As Jonathan Darling (2022) has suggested, these outsourced networks of 'no-choice' accommodation can already be described as 'systems of suffering': their residents denied the ability to work and left languishing in state-sanctioned poverty and psychological limbo. Moreover, these systems simultaneously double-up as mechanisms of control, with asylum seekers unable to reside elsewhere, and who, in many cases, are required to 'report' regularly at immigration reporting centres to verify their presence and whereabouts. That this has generated intense fear is understandable, with impoverished people not only made to travel sometimes lengthy distances but also facing the very real threat of being detained when reporting; and it is only because of the actions of activists that in 2022 the Home Office announced that telephone reporting would at some point become the standard method of reporting. But as activists themselves have made clear, this is nonetheless only a 'first step towards eradicating the surveillance of migrants' embedded more broadly within the fabric of immigration control (Abolish Reporting 2022).

Surveillance is a core component of immigration control and the carceral continuum that is reproduced through its contours. For example, Monish Bhatia (2021) has documented how the expansive use of electronic monitoring technologies upon those released from detention on immigration bail not only operates as a form of permanent surveillance, but carries the very real threat of triggering a return to confinement through non-compliance, and in many ways reproduces the harms of detention itself. Meanwhile, for those whose immigration status has been irregularised, the essence of the hostile environment policy framework is to transform society itself into a web of immigration control with—as has been well documented—landlords, universities, employers, schools, airlines, transport companies, banks, the Driver and Vehicle Licensing Agency and the NHS among the sectors which have at various points been absorbed (not, in some cases without resistance) into the immigration enforcement apparatus (Goodfellow 2020). This is not exhaustive.

But again, it expands upon Box's (1983: 7) conceptualisations of social control, and indicates one arena within which the subordination, incapacitation, demoralisation and 'fracture' (to use his terminology) of particular populations has become part of the fabric of everyday life, and how carceral logics have enveloped a range of social arenas and areas that were not envisaged in *Power, Crime and Mystification*. Moreover, as we shall discuss below, such frameworks operate alongside and as part of forms of crimmigration and criminalisation, blurring the boundaries of 'care' and control, and 'support' and enforcement, and operate as central features of a British carceral state.

Power and Mystification

Late in 2015, London's Westminster council ran a joint operation with the Home Office called Operation Adoze. Described as a way of addressing homelessness, the initiative was underpinned by a change in policy defining rough sleeping by European Economic Area (EEA) nationals as an abuse of free movement. Doing so rendered those who found themselves unhoused—perhaps as a result of workplace exploitation, or eviction from London's extortionate rental housing markets—vulnerable to removal from the UK. The way to combat rough sleeping, in other words, was to get rid of rough sleepers (see Cooper and McCulloch, this volume).

Such cruelty—effectively rendering poverty an immigration offence—is not in and of itself anything new. Indeed, cruelty is one of British immigration and asylum policy's defining features (Kundnani 2007). However, by utilising and harnessing segments of the homelessness sector as a front for immigration control, Operation Adoze also embodied a broader trajectory inculcating its logics into a whole range of agencies, bodies and sectors. Those coming into contact with charities such as Thames Reach or St. Mungos, who may well have thought they were about to be supported, in at least some cases, instead found their details shared with Home Office Immigration Compliance and Enforcement (ICE) teams. Even prior to this operation, the charities had entered into contractual relationships with the Home Office involving collaborative working and operations to effect immigration enforcement (Corporate Watch 2017). Under the guise of providing support, this was part of the charity sector working as an appendage of state power.

In Box's (1983: 14) terms, such processes are indicative of ideological mystification: a grammar and vocabulary which is necessary to understand them not as isolated processes, but as manifestations of the ways power is concealed and actualised. 'For too long', he argued, 'too many people have been socialized to see crime and criminals through the eyes of the state' (ibid.), and in this regard he explored mystification not only by way of obfuscating the material roles and functions of criminal justice strategies and policies, but also how it is central to their reproduction. Conceptually, his analysis of mystification provided tools vital for exploring social relations as they exist, rather than as presented: the 'real' as opposed to the 'imaginary' social order, as Frank Pearce (1976: 80–81) put it. As such, what follows explores some of the forms of mystification embedded within immigration control, and how these reproduce a carceral state. Indeed, while carceral logics have enveloped a range of social arenas and areas that were not envisaged in *Power, Crime and Mystification*, these following sections will explore how its conceptual frameworks are nonetheless vital for understanding and resisting them.

Enforcement as 'Support'; 'Support' as Enforcement

Central to this is Box's (1983: 112–113) insights on the functions of police power, and the (apparent) dual functions of 'service' and 'control'. As he articulated, while the 'service' functions of policing have historically been (and continue to be) periodically foregrounded in state discourses (especially at points where police legitimacy has been challenged), these have never been separate from policing's core 'control' functions in practice. That is, while *at times* rationalised in different ways, these functions ultimately work to the same objectives of maintaining and (re)producing particular forms of social order, and within immigration (or crimmigration) control, such dynamics are manifested and have expanded in particular ways.

Sam Hanks (2021: 95), for instance, has documented extensively how discourses of safeguarding and vulnerability embedded within the immigration policing of migrant sex workers, promoted by the National Police Chief's Council (NPCC), provide an 'alibi for the exercising of power' by way of surveillance and monitoring. While simultaneously, as Emily Kenway (2021) demonstrates, mechanisms to 'rescue' victims of 'modern slavery' can all too often lead to their detention, destitution or deportation. Indeed, in 2022 it was revealed that police forces in England and Wales were reporting hundreds of victims of crimes per month—including those who had experienced domestic violence, abuse and sexual exploitation—to immigration authorities (Shehadi 2022). What is more, around a quarter of those experiencing domestic abuse referred to immigration agencies were subject to enforcement procedures (for example, attempted removal). Or put another way, forms of state of intervention instigated under the rubric of *protecting* people served in real terms to *punish* them: operating as pre-texts for forms of data sharing and immigration enforcement, and working to legitimise, mystify, and also to sustain repressive functions in practice.

At the same time, immigration enforcement policies themselves are frequently rationalised through languages of benevolence and care, with immigration raids precipitating evictions carried out under the pretext of protecting residents from 'rogue landlords', and raids targeting undocumented workers rationalised in part by claims to be tackling unscrupulous and hyper-exploitative forms of employment (Bhatia and Burnett 2022). However, at a point where the regulatory mechanisms designed to protect victims of labour exploitation have been systemically attacked by governments (Tombs 2015), the 'regulation' of irregular or undocumented working through immigration enforcement not only leaves the broader dynamics (such as the demands for 'flexible' labour forces) underlying exploitation intact, this can push working conditions down further (Burnett and Whyte 2010).

Of course, this should not detract from the ways that immigration enforcement is driven and rationalised *as enforcement*. However, where packaged under the garb of support this is by no means restricted to these domains. The prospect (and realisation) of the children's charity

Barnardo's helping to run supposedly 'child friendly' forms of immigration detention in 2011, for example, prompted sustained discussion in the charity sector, with some voices suggesting this mediated the harms of detention and others that it provided 'chintz curtains for a system of institutionalised disbelief, indifference and inhumanity' (Webber 2014). While in turn, this is not dissimilar to ongoing practices where undocumented migrants in need of medical care can have—and in many cases do have—their details shared with the Home Office. If government discourses of humanitarianism are integral to the actualisation of immigration control, as Côté-Boucher et al. (2022) have argued, their genealogy is 'inextricably linked with … restrictive enforcement strategies in border spaces'.

The State as Victim

In part, this is bound up with the Janus-faced construction of immigration and asylum in political discourse: as something to be controlled and managed, as something to which obligations are owed in certain regards, and as latent threat. It is such binaries which underpin artificial demarcations of 'good' vs 'bad' immigrants, a politically constructed dichotomy which says more about states themselves than about those subject to immigration control. But it resides on a further form of mystification: of a benevolent state which is perennially at risk of victimisation. As Sim (2001: 26) has suggested, the idea of the 'victimised state' has very real consequences: distracting attention from state violence, enabling state narratives to monopolise debate *about* violence, positing those who challenge such narratives as naïve or unthinking (or both) and binding together 'the mass media, government and opposition spokespersons, liberals and broader public opinion, cementing them into a moral and political force which uncritically accepts the criminal justice reality articulated by powerful interest groups'. Drawing on Box's work, he makes clear that such notions themselves operate as a form of 'ideological mystification': working dialectically to reproduce a particular form of 'state talk' and discourse (Sim 2004: 126). And his analysis resonates explicitly with immigration control. For this is one of the contexts where narratives of violence *against* the state or state servants mystify violence *by* the state.

Witness former Home Secretary Priti Patel's condemnation of those detained in the Napier Army Barracks after a fire broke out in 2021, for example, stating that 'This this type of action will not be tolerated and the Home Office will support the police to take robust action against those vandalising property, threatening staff and putting lives at risk' (Patel 2021). But there was no mention of the Crown Premises Fire Safety Inspectorate's (CPFSI) warnings several months earlier that there was 'no effective fire safety measure' in place (Bulman 2021).—warnings that were seemingly ignored, and which left people detained at the barracks seriously exposed to harm. Nor was there any mention of the detainees' well-established anguish, which just a month after the fire would be laid bare in an unpublished Prison Inspectorate report outlining seven suicide attempts, seven incidents of self-harm and over a third of the occupants disclosing suicidal thoughts (ibid.). Indeed, Box's (1983: 20–21) recognition that state violence and harm must be understood both in terms of intention and also indifference, abandonment and 'disdain for humanity' speaks directly to the conditions in the barracks that were later described by a barrister as 'squalid, ill-equipped, lacking in personal privacy and unsafe', with as many as 28 people sleeping in single rooms. Yet, this did not stop immigration minister Chris Philip appearing to blame the people residing there for a Covid-19 outbreak, stating that they were 'either refusing to self-isolate or follow social distancing rules' (Trilling 2021). In doing so, he became the latest in a long line of political figures reproducing racialised tropes associating migration with illness and disease; and not only are such tropes factually incorrect (UCL-Lancet Commission on Migration and Public Health 2018), they mystify the role of immigration policies and practices in putting people at serious, life-threatening risk. One of the reasons that the Manston processing centre was rapidly emptied in 2022, for example (before later being utilised again as a processing centre), was because outbreaks of diphtheria may have been related to a man's death, with conditions in the centre so appalling that the Council of Europe's Prevention of Torture and Inhuman or Degrading Treatment or Punishment Committee carried out an inspection in November 2022 (Taylor 2022).

However, as disturbing as the conditions in this and many other detention facilities were, and are, it is also the *condition* of detention itself which precipitates immense harm and fundamentally damages physical and mental health. Some 17 immigration detainees in prison, and 39 in immigration detention, died between 2000 and 2022, according to the charity INQUEST (2022), with more than half of these deaths overall 'as self-inflicted'. Such is the harm precipitated that around one-third of all of those detained in Brook House IRC (in London) between July to December 2020 were on constant suicide watch, according to the Independent Monitoring Board (IMB), with over 30 people removed from the UK while waiting to see doctors or being monitored with regard to concerns about self-inflicted death. This included a person bleeding and only partially clothed, and a person removed from netting after a suicide attempt (Taylor 2021).

Meanwhile, within such sites of incarceration, reports, investigations and exposés of violence against incarcerated people, their poor treatment, experiences of racist abuse and institutional indifference to their plights have been so frequent that they suggest something endemic, rather than exceptional (Cowen 2021), with the government's own review into immigration detention, published in 2016 (Shaw 2016) acknowledging that detention inflicts trauma lasting years after release/removal and that these impacts are gendered. Such pains, violence and damage can be understood as forms of social harm, according to those working within the field of zemiology: manifested through the structures of state activity themselves (Canning and Tombs 2021). Yet in many cases government responses to such scrutiny have been to try and shut it down. In 2014, UN special rapporteur Rashida Manjoo said that she had been blocked from entering Yarl's Wood IRC by the Home Office, which she had intended to visit as part of a wider investigation into violence against women (Sherwood 2014). While in 2023, with the government discussing expanding the use of detention and increasing the number of people subject to it, the Home Secretary discontinued a standing commission monitoring the impact of detention on adults 'at risk' (Neal and Shaw 2023). As the state claims to be victim, it victimises with impunity.

'Safe Routes' and Bogus Debates

The harms underpinned by immigration policy are continually, systemically obfuscated. When 39 Vietnamese people trying to enter the UK were found dead, suffocated while crammed into the trailer of a lorry in Essex in 2019, the then Prime Minister Boris Johnson condemned the 'callousness of those people responsible for this crime' (cited in Mills 2019), referring to those who had profited from facilitating their entry (two of whom were later given prison sentences for manslaughter. Similarly, when 31 people drowned in November 2021 as they tried to cross the channel by dinghy, his immediate response was to state he would 'leave no stone unturned' (cited in Therrien, 2021) in the effort to tackle 'human trafficking gangs' (cited ibid.). Yet, as has been pointed out elsewhere, there was no and never is any acknowledgement of the role of immigration policies themselves which make travelling in such dangerous ways—where human beings are frequently exploited and put at considerable risk—among the only viable options available (Rahman 2019). In 2020, for example, activists documented the deaths of nearly 300 people trying to enter the UK in and around the English Channel since 1999, many of whom drowned (Institute of Race Relations, the Permanent People's Tribunal and the Groupe d'Information et de Soutien des immigré 2020). However, not only has the government intensified efforts to restrict and control routes, increasing demand for those who can facilitate entry through dangerous routes in the process, it pressed forward with attempts to artificially construct and in very real terms demarcate 'desirable' or 'undesirable' migrants potentially claiming asylum, based in part on the routes utilised to try and enter or where they have travelled from (Webber 2022).

While 'paused' in 2023, as has been pointed out elsewhere (Laidman 2022), this was a two-tier system, with selective and limited resettlement schemes for some (even if in real terms often tokenistic in practice) operating alongside moves to punish and criminalise others (such as those crossing the Channel). It differentiated those seeking asylum "according to their mode of arrival, penalising those not coming directly from the country of persecution, who may be declared inadmissible, and liable to be 'offshored'" (either for 'processing' or permanently) (Webber 2022). And in this regard, it was Kafkaesque in its cruelty: closing down ways to claim asylum while punishing those who are then forced to enter the UK by other means (Mehrez 2022). However, what is at stake here is not just the inconsistencies in a two-tier system as it exists in practice, but its *existence in the first place* (Webber 2022). Refusing to acknowledge its own role in creating the conditions for travelling via particular means, the government criminalises those who do so. Refusing to acknowledge the deep structural forces which underline the need for people to flee or move, it responds by erecting systems which seek to eject, expunge and control those moving (Patel 2021). 'We are here because you were there', Sivanandan (2008) emphasised decades ago, referring to the global North's historical and ongoing role in creating the conditions from which people leave or flee from the Global South. But as the 'war' on irregular migration intensifies, it is those who flee who are depicted (and treated) as an 'invasion'.

Indeed, what is ultimately being mystified here is the manner in which carceral logics themselves are central components of an expansive system of racialised global inequality, segregation and subordination to the point where some describe this as a form of global apartheid. Drawing on Spitzer's (1975) work, Box demonstrated in substantial detail how states' control strategies at that point frequently split those 'unrequired' and rendered surplus to capitalist productive processes into two broad categories: with those not adapted to the vagaries of capitalist development, demonised and depicted as 'social junk', to be 'managed' by a range of institutions and frequently punitive practices; and with those potentially challenging and throwing up the direct contradictions of capitalist development depicted as 'social dynamite' to be controlled, suppressed or eliminated. And such analytical frameworks are prescient at a point where immigration control has moved to the forefront of strategies to manage a global surplus in the pursuit of upholding a vastly unequal and violent form of social order. For some of the primary contours of contemporary capitalist orders, as Haiven (2020: 11) makes clear, can be seen 'in the monstrous ways surplussed populations become the targets of both direct and systemic violence: made killable, left to drown, warehoused in prisons, chained by extortionate debt, or made to compete for the scraps'. What is more, as Kundnani (2021) has added, the underlying rationale of such violence, degradations, control and expulsions, is not just to target those who are immediately the focus of immigration control, but to reproduce the disposability and effect control of those who may at some point be.

Referring to the 'loosely integrated effort by countries in the global north to protect themselves against the mobility of the global south', global apartheid encompasses the measures and apparatuses utilised to facilitate the 'hierarchal integration' of those deemed desirable or temporarily exploitable, as well as the mechanisms used to prevent people from moving and from arriving, the technological mechanisms to monitor, track, repel and deport, and the legislative and policy measures which create new forms of criminalisation and criminality (Besteman 2019: S33). As a form of global order, it 'recasts the terms of sovereignty, citizenship, community, belonging, justice, refuge, and civil rights' and 'draws on and remakes historically sedimented racial formations that are highly localized but articulated with global imaginaries of race and racial difference' (ibid.: S26–S27). Not only does global apartheid 'rely on the fortification and policing of sovereign territory and on the delegation of this work regionally to third countries', as Lloyd (2015: 2) has argued; 'it also relies on domestic policing and crime policies and their infrastructure of detention facilities, jails, prisons, and the methods for moving people within this network or removing them through deportation'. Indeed, such is its breadth that a militarised security industry encompassing things like monitoring, biometrics, the construction of walls and fences, and deportation as well as audit and consultancy services has exploded since the late twentieth Century, with market predictions expecting growth of between 7.2 and 8.6 per cent to a value of $65–68 billion by 2025 (Akkerman 2021).

In the UK alone, a multi-billion-pound industry profits from and feeds into immigration control, including the technologies utilised for data sharing, data analytics, border surveillance and biometric scanning (see Privacy International 2021). These, in turn, are situated alongside the £4 billion (in 2019) contracts to accommodate asylum seekers (Home Office 2019). Meanwhile, in 2023, firms holding asylum seekers in hotels reported trebling their profits, while simultaneously some £70 million was announced to facilitate the running of centres described by migrants' rights charities as 'warehouses' blurring the line 'between detention and accommodation' (Taylor 2023). At the same time, the contracts for immigration detention routinely run into the hundreds of millions, as do those for 'escorting immigration detainees' as parts of removals or deportations (McGuirk and Pine 2020; Norris 2021). And as the unlawful killing of Jimmy Mubenga by privately contracted immigration escorts in 2010 testifies, such arrangements can compound, and have compounded risks of harm and ultimately death. 46-year-old Jimmy Mubenga's death in an attempt to deport him to Angola, with escorts 'using unreasonable force and acting in an unlawful manner', was 'the inevitable consequence of a privatised removals service that was out of control and where the duty of care and the wellbeing of deportees were undermined in the pursuit of profit', according to INQUEST's Deborah Coles (INQUEST 2013). However, such is the mystification of Britain's immigration and asylum systems that it is those subject to immigration control who are frequently accused of profiting from it.

Conclusion

On 14 December 2022, four people became the latest (at the time of writing) to die trying to enter the UK by sea as their small dinghy, carrying over 30 people, capsized in the icy waters between Britain and France. Speaking after the incident, while migrants' rights organisations depicted the seas as a 'graveyard', the Home Secretary insisted that the deaths highlighted the necessity and urgency of plans to ban those who contravened immigration legislation from remaining in the country, as doing so would 'act as a deterrent [to those trying to reach the UK], and it will save lives' (*BBC News* 2022). Presumably, this was part of the same logic behind the government's latest (at that point) new plan for immigration—announced in Parliament by Prime Minister Rishi Sunak just a day before these deaths—pledging to rework and mobilise immense state power by including promises (among other things) to: combine the military, civilians and the National Crime Agency (NCA) in a 'small boat command'; expand internal immigration controls by increasing workplace immigration raids by 50 per cent; increase the scale and breadth of data sharing and mass surveillance of those subject to immigration control between agencies; reduce appeal rights (further); instigate weekly flights to deport Albanian nationals while designating Albania itself as a 'safe' country; and introduce legislation facilitating the increased detention and removal of those whose claim for asylum is 'refused' (Grünewald 2022).

Presumably, too, was it part of the same logic underpinning the Government's Illegal Migration Bill, announced in 2023, marking an intention to eradicate some forms of legal challenge to detention, prevent some forms of family reunification, increase deportation and powers, solidify outsourced (outside of the UK) detention and effectively act as a 'ban' for some asylum claims (Gower et al. 2023). And so too was it presumably part of the same logic as Deputy Prime Minister Dominic Raab's pledge, in early 2023, to hold several hundred people seeking asylum in huge, austere barges: necessary, he would later claim, to stop the asylum system itself acting as a 'pull factor' (Lawton 2023). Such claims have been rebutted repeatedly—with substantial evidence (including that published by the Home Office) having long demonstrated that such 'pull factors' do not exist in the way that is commonly portrayed (Robinson and Segrott 2022)—appeared to matter little when such plans were announced. The reason is that these logics are driven by a notion that cruelty to some operates to discipline others.

It is the contention of this chapter that Box's *Power, Crime and Mystification*, some four decades after its publication, provides a mode of analysis which can contribute to the process of demystifying such logics, and ultimately dismantling them and the violent apparatus they reproduce. Certainly, this requires comprehending how the *forms* and *contours* of state power and mystification have developed since its initial publication, and in ways the text did not at that point comprehend. And as this chapter has made clear, immigration control is one arena in which such developments can be traced: through operating as a vehicle for immense data sharing and surveillance, for example, or through ensuring social control is administered through an increasing array of sites, bodies and agencies. Indeed, immigration control is one site through which carceral logics have been and continue to be reworked and reproduced. However, it is the *conceptual tools* that Box provided which render its analyses vital in challenging such frameworks. For, while his work was not focused on immigration control per se, they contribute to uncovering rationalisations of expansive carceral state power and their functions in reproducing—and mystifying—repressive forms of social order. Just as it was at the time it was published, the task is imperative, carrying with it an urgency that must be met. *Power, Crime and Mystification* contribute to the insurgent analysis necessary to meet this.

References

Abolish Reporting. 2022. Telephone Reporting—A Campaign Victory, but the Struggle Continues. *These Walls Must Fall*, 8 July. https://wallsmustfall.org/telephone-reporting-a-campaign-victory-but-the-struggle-continues/. Accessed 12 Oct 2022.

Akkerman, M. 2021. *Financing Borders Waters: The Border Industry, Its Financiers and Human Rights*. Amsterdam: Transnational Institute and Stop Wapenhandel.

Aliverti, A. 2016. *Immigration Offences: Trends in Legislation and Criminal and Civil Enforcement*. Oxford: Oxford University Press.

BBC News. 2022. Channel Migrant Asylum Ban Will Save Lives, says Braverman. *BBC News*, 15 December. https://www.bbc.co.uk/news/uk-politics-63975279. Accessed 13 Nov 2022.

Berg, E., and M. Dickson. 2022. *Asylum Housing in Yorkshire: A Case Study of Two Dispersal Areas*. London: University College London.

Besteman, C. 2019. Militarized Global Apartheid. *Current Anthropology* 60 (19): S26-38.

Bhatia, M. 2021. Racial Surveillance and the Mental Health Impacts of Electronic Monitoring on Migrants. *Race & Class* 62 (3): 18–36.

Bhatia, M., and Burnett, J. 2019. Torture and the UK's 'War on Asylum': Medical Power and the Culture of Disbelief. In *Tortura e migrazioni,* ed. F. Perocco, 161–179. Venice: Ca' Foscari Editions.

Bhatia, M., and J. Burnett. 2022. Immigration Raids and Racist State Violence. *State Crime Journal* 11 (1): 33–51.
Box, S. 1983. *Power, Crime and Mystification*. London: Routledge.
Braverman, S. 2022. Speech to the Conservative Party Conference, 4 October. https://www.ukpol.co.uk/suella-braverman-2022-speech-to-conservative-party-conference/. Accessed 19 Nov 2022
Bulman, M. 2021. Home Office Placed Hundreds of Asylum Seekers at "Serious Risk" of Fire in Napier Barracks, Document Reveals. *The Independent*, 14 April. Bulman. Accessed 19 Nov 2022.
Burnett, J. 2022. *Work and the Carceral State*. London: Pluto Press.
Burnett, J., and D. Whyte. 2010. *The Wages of Fear: Risk, Safety and Undocumented Work*. Leeds and Liverpool: PAFRAS and the University of Liverpool.
Canning, V., and S. Tombs. 2021. *From Social Harm to Zemiology: A Critical Introduction*. London: Routledge.
Clarke, N. 2022. Coast Crisis: Suella Braverman Warns UK Faces "Invasion of Southern Coast" as Migrants in Overcrowded Centre Each Get £6K Comp. *The Sun*, 1 November. https://www.thesun.co.uk/news/20281500/suella-braverman-invasion-coast-illegal-migrants/. Accessed 19 Nov 2022.
Cole, H., Pattinson, R., Clark, N., and Sabey, R. 2022. Five-Star Migrants: Thousands of Migrants Living in Luxury Hotels with Brits Forking Out £6.8m a Day to House Them. *The Sun*, 2 November. https://www.thesun.co.uk/news/20305829/migrants-five-star-hotels-housing/. Accessed 22 Nov 2022.
Corporate Watch. 2017. Court Victory against St Mungos and Thames Reach Rough Sleeper Raids: What Next? *Corporate Watch*, 16 December. https://corporatewatch.org/court-victory-against-st-mungos-and-thames-reach-rough-sleeper-raids-what-next/. Accessed 13 Nov 2022.
Côté-Boucher, K., L. Vives, and L.-P. Jannard. 2022. Chronicle of a "Crisis" Foretold: Asylum Seekers and the Case of Roxham Road on the Canada-US Border. *Environment and Planning C: Politics and Space* 41 (2): 408–426.
Cowen, L. 2021. *Border Nation: A Story of Migration*. London: Pluto Press.
Darling, J. 2022. *Systems of Suffering: Dispersal and the Denial of Asylum*. London: Pluto Press.
de Noronha, L. 2020. *Deporting Black Britons: Portraits of Deportation to Jamaica*. Manchester: Manchester University Press.
Fekete, L. 2009. *A Suitable Enemy: Racism, Migration and Islamophobia in Europe*. London: Pluto Press.

Foucault, M. 1977. *Discipline and Punish: The Birth of the Prison*. London: Penguin.

Goodfellow, M. 2020. *Hostile Environment: How Immigrants Became Scapegoats*. London: Verso.

Gower, M., McKinney, C., Dwawson, J., Foster, D., and Sturge, G. 2023. *Illegal Migration Bill 2022–23*. CBP-9747. London: House of Commons Library.

Griffiths, M. 2017. Foreign, Criminal: A Doubly Damned Modern British Folk Devil. *Citizenship Studies* 21 (5): 527–546.

Grünewald, Z. 2022. Will the Tories Ever Resolve Their Internal Battle on Immigration. *New Statesman*, 14 December. https://www.newstatesman.com/politics/conservatives/2022/12/rishi-sunak-immigration-conservatives-internal-battle. Accessed 29 Dec 2022.

Haiven, M. 2020. *Revenge Capitalism: The Ghosts of Empire, the Demons of Capital and the Settling of Unpayable Debts*. London: Pluto Press.

Hanks, S. 2021. The Safeguarding Delusion: Sex Work and Policing in Wales. *Justice, Power and Resistance* 5 (1–2): 91–108.

Home Office. 2019. The Home Office has Awarded New Asylum Accommodation and Support Services Contracts (AASC) Following an Open and Fair Procurement Exercise. *Home Office*, 8 January. https://www.gov.uk/government/news/new-asylum-accommodation-contracts-awarded. Accessed 19 Nov 2022.

Home Office. 2022. Factsheet: Small Boat Crossing since July 2022. *Home Office*, 2 November. https://www.gov.uk/government/statistics/factsheet-small-boat-crossings-since-july-2022/factsheet-small-boat-crossings-since-july-2022. Accessed 19 Nov 2022.

Hymas, C. 2022. Manston Migrant Centre Empty after 6000 Asylum Seekers Sent to Hotels. *Daily Telegraph*, 22 November. https://www.telegraph.co.uk/politics/2022/11/22/manston-migrant-centre-empty-after-asylum-seekers-sent-hotels/. Accessed 29 Nov 2022.

INQUEST. 2013. Jury rules Jimmy Mubenga was Unlawfully Killed. *INQUEST*, 9 July 2013, https://www.inquest.org.uk/jimmy-mubenga-jury-conclusions. Accessed 8 Apr 2023.

INQUEST. 2022. Deaths of Immigration Detainees. *INQUEST*. https://www.inquest.org.uk/deaths-of-immigration-detainees. Accessed 13 Nov 2022.

Institute of Race Relations, the Permanent People's Tribunal and the Groupe d'Information et de Soutien des immigré. 2020. *Deadly Crossing and the militarisation of Britain's border*. London: Institute of Race Relations, the

Permanent People's Tribunal and the Groupe d'Information et de Soutien des immigré.

Kenway, E. 2021. *The Truth About Modern Slavery*. London: Pluto Press.

Kundnani, A. 2007. *The End of Tolerance? Racism in 21st century Britain*. London: Pluto Press.

Kundnani, A. 2021. The Racial Constitution of Neoliberalism. *Race & Class* 63 (1): 51–69.

Laidman, J. 2022. A Tiered Asylum System, Restricting Entry to the UK, and Failing 'Legal' Routes. *Free Movement*, 6 December. https://freemovement.org.uk/a-tiered-asylum-system-restricting-entry-to-the-uk-and-failing-legal-routes/. Accessed 14 Dec 2022

Lawton, K. 2023. Ministers Face Legal Action over £20,000-a-Day Migrant 'Flotel' Barges where Asylum Seekers could be Housed Amid Concerns the Policy Could Hurt Local Tourism. *Daily Mail*, 4 April. https://www.dailymail.co.uk/news/article-11935513/Ministers-face-legal-action-20k-day-migrant-flotel-barges-asylum-seekers-stay.html. Accessed 9 Apr 2023.

Liberty. 2023. Explained: New Immigration Bill. *Liberty*. https://www.libertyhumanrights.org.uk/issue/explained-anti-refugee-bill/. Accessed 24 Mar 2023.

Lloyd, J.M. 2015. Carceral Citizenship in an Age of Global Apartheid. *Occasion* 8: 1–15.

Maggs, J. 2022. Manston: State Violence in a No-Access Border Zone. *IRR News*, 24 November. https://irr.org.uk/article/manston-state-violence-in-a-no-access-border-zone/. Accessed 14 Dec 2022.

McGuirk, S., and A. Pine. 2020. *Asylum for Sale: Profit and Protest in the Migration Industry*. Oakland: PM Press.

Mehrez, H. 2022. Only four Afghan Asylum Seekers Resettled in UK, all in Hastings, after UNHCR Referral. Sussex Live. https://www.sussexlive.co.uk/news/sussex-news/only-four-afghan-asylum-seekers-7909409. Accessed 14 Dec 2022.

Menon, P. 2016. 48,000 Students Wrongly Deported from the UK: Tribunal. *The Hindu*, 28 March. https://www.thehindu.com/news/international/justice-in-sight-for-thousands-of-indian-and-other-students/article8405679.ece. Accessed 13 Nov 2022.

Mills, J. 2019. 'Boris Johnson says Essex Lorry Victims were "Innocent People Hoping for a Better Life"'. *The Metro*, 28 October. https://metro.co.uk/2019/10/28/boris-johnson-says-essex-lorry-victims-innocent-people-hoping-better-life-10997663/ Accessed 28 Dec 2022

Ministry of Justice. 2022. *Offender Management Statistics Bulletin, England and Wales Quarterly: April to June 2022*. London: Ministry of Justice.

Neal, D., and Shaw, S. 2023. Suella Braverman has Just Culled Inspections in Detention Centres—Has She Forgotten Manston? *The Guardian*, 12 January. https://www.theguardian.com/commentisfree/2023/jan/12/suella-braverman-detention-centres-manston-home-office. Accessed 7 Apr 2023.

Norris, S. 2021. Firm linked to Conservatives will Run New Immigration Detention Centre for Women. *Byline Times*, 20 July, https://bylinetimes.com/2021/07/20/firm-linked-to-conservatives-will-run-new-immigration-detention-centre-for-women/ (Accessed 7 Apr 2023)

Parmar, A. 2020. Arresting (non)Citizenship: The Policing Migration Nexus of Nationality, Race and Criminalization. *Theoretical Criminology* 24 (1): 28–49.

Patel, I. 2021. *We're Here Because You were There: Immigration and the End of Empire* London: Verso.

Pearce, F. 1976. *Crimes of the Powerful. Marxism, crime and Deviance*. London: Pluto.

Privacy International. 2021. *The UK's Privatised Migration Surveillance Regime: A Rough Guide for Civil Society*. London: Privacy International.

Rahman, M. 2019. *Safe and Legal Routes of Entry to the UK*. London: Joint Council for the Welfare of Immigrants.

Robinson, V., and Segrott, J. 2022. Understanding the Decision-Making of Asylum Seekers. *Home Office Research Study 243*. London: Home Office.

Shaw, S. 2016. *Review into the Welfare in Detention of Vulnerable Persons: A Report to the Home Office*. Cm 9186. London. Home Office.

Shehadi, S. 2022. Police Report Hundreds of Crime Victims a Month to Immigration Service. *New Statesman*, 27 June. https://www.newstatesman.com/society/2022/06/police-refer-crime-victims-deportation-home-office. Accessed 7 Apr 2023.

Sherwood, H. 2014. UN Special Rapporteur Criticises Britain's "In-Your-Face" Sexist Culture. *The Guardian*, 15 April. https://www.theguardian.com/world/2014/apr/15/un-special-rapporteur-manjoo-yarls-wood-home-office. Accessed 7 Apr 2023.

Sim, J. 2001. The Victimised State. *Criminal Justice Matters* 42: 26–27.

Sim, J. 2004. The Victimised State and the Mystification of Social Harm. In *Beyond Criminology: Taking Harm Seriously*, ed. P. Hillyard, C, Pantazis, S. Tombs, and D. Gordon, 113–182, London: Pluto Press.

Sivanandan, A. 2008. Catching History on the Wing, *IRR News*, 6 November. http://www.irr.org.uk/news/catching-history-on-the-wing/. Accessed 13 Nov 2022.

Spitzer, S. 1975. Towards a Marxian Theory of Deviance. *Social Problems* 22: 638–651.

Stumpf, J. 2006. The Crimmigration Crisis: Immigrants, Crime, and Sovereign Power. *American University Law Review* 56: 67–419.

Tapia, R. 2019. What is the Carceral State. *University of Michigan Carceral State Project*. Michigan: University of Michigan. https://storymaps.arcgis.com/stories/7ab5f5c3fbca46c38f0b2496bcaa5ab0. Accessed 28 Sep 2022.

Taylor, D. 2021. 'UK Asylum Seekers at "Unprecedented" Risk of Suicide Amid Deportation Threat'. *The Guardian*, 21 May. https://www.theguardian.com/uk-news/2021/may/21/uk-asylum-seekers-at-unprecedented-risk-of-suicide-amid-deportation-threat Accessed 22 Dec 2022.

Taylor, D. 2022. Conditions at Manston Asylum Centre Prompt Torture Monitor Visit. *The Guardian*, 30 November. https://www.theguardian.com/uk-news/2022/nov/30/manston-asylum-centre-torture-monitor-visit. Accessed 3 Dec 2022.

Taylor, D. 2023. Home Office Publishes Details of £70m Contract to House Asylum Seekers. *The Guardian*, 29 January. https://www.theguardian.com/uk-news/2023/jan/29/home-office-publishes-details-of-70m-contract-to-house-asylum-seekers. Accessed 21 Mar 2023.

Therrien, A. 2021. Migrant Tragedy is Biggest Loss of Life in Cannel. *BBC News*, 25 November. https://www.bbc.co.uk/news/uk-59406355. Accessed 16 Nov 2022.

Tombs, S. 2015. *Social Protection After the Crisis: Regulation Without Enforcement*. Bristol: Policy Press.

Trilling, D. 2021. The Napier Barracks Fire is an Indictment of Britain's Inhumane Asylum System. *The Guardian*, 2 February. https://www.theguardian.com/commentisfree/2021/feb/02/napier-barracks-fire-britain-asylum-system-priti-patel. Accessed 13 Nov 2022.

UCL-Lancet Commission on Migration and Public Health. 2018. *The Health of a World on the Move*. London: UCL-Lancet Commission on Migration and Public Health.

University of Michigan Carceral State Project. 2019. What is the Carceral State. Michigan: University of Michigan. https://storymaps.arcgis.com/stories/7ab5f5c3fbca46c38f0b2496bcaa5ab0. Accessed 19 Sep 2022.

Walawalker, A., and Bulman, M. 2022. Asylum Seekers 'Effectively Detained' at Home Office Hotels in Potential Legal Breach. *Liberty and the Independent*, 15 October. https://libertyinvestigates.org.uk/articles/asylum-seekers-effectively-detained-at-home-office-hotels-in-potential-legal-breach/. Accessed 13 Nov 2022.

Walker, P. 2023. Asylum Seekers to be Housed on Dorset Barge Despite Local Opposition. *The Guardian*, 5 April. https://www.theguardian.com/uk-news/2023/apr/05/asylum-seekers-to-be-housed-on-dorset-barge-home-office-confirms. Accessed 6 Apr 2023.

Webber, F. 2014. The Fading Red Line: Barnardo's Role in the Detention and Removal of Children. *IRR News*, 15 May. https://irr.org.uk/article/the-fading-red-line-barnardos-role-in-the-detention-and-removal-of-children/. Accessed 13 Nov 2022.

Webber, F. 2022. Impunity Entrenched: Policing the Borders. *IRR News*, 17 January. https://irr.org.uk/article/policing-the-borders-impunity-entrenched/. Accessed 13 Nov 2022.

12

Criminal Law Categories as Ideological Constructs: The Case of Human Trafficking

Shahrzad Fouladvand and Tony Ward

Introduction

In *Power, Crime and Mystification,* Box argues that:

> *criminal law categories are ideological constructs.*...Rather than being a fair reflection of those behaviours objectively causing us collectively the most avoidable suffering, criminal law categories are artful, creative constructs designed to criminalize only some victimizing behaviours, usually those more frequently committed by the relatively powerless, and to exclude others, usually those frequently committed by the powerful against subordinates (Box 1983: 7, original emphasis).

S. Fouladvand (✉)
University of Sussex, Sussex, UK
e-mail: s.fouladvand@sussex.ac.uk

T. Ward
Northumbria University, Newcastle Upon Tyne, UK
e-mail: tony.ward@northumbria.ac.uk

Like other social constructionists, Box aims to show that what is constructed, in this case the legal definition of crime, 'is not determined by the nature of things; it is not inevitable' (Hacking 1999: 6). He contrasts this with something that is defined at least partly in accordance with 'the nature of things', namely 'avoidable suffering' or harm. In Box's view (and ours), there are things like injuries, killings and severe forms of exploitation that no 'fair' categorisation could fail to recognise as avoidable harms (notwithstanding the complexities of the debate about the ontology of harm: see Canning and Tombs 2021: 101–110). The construction of criminal law categories, for Box, is not just social but 'ideological', that is, it has a consistent tendency to reinforce a view of the world consistent with the maintenance of existing structures of power. The gap between the ideological construct of crime and the relatively objective category of avoidable harm is what Box refers to as mystification.

Box's argument makes an important link between legal scholarship and criminology, and also foreshadows the critique of criminal law that underpins zemiological or social harm-based approaches (Canning and Tombs 2021). In this chapter we explore the ideological construction of a pair of criminal law categories that have emerged relatively recently: human trafficking and modern slavery. These categories belong to a form of law that has grown in importance since Box wrote *Power, Crime and Mystification* but has received little attention from critical criminologists: namely transnational criminal law.

The term 'transnational' criminal law (TCL) is used to distinguish this phenomenon from *inter*national criminal law, which has its own rules laid down in international law and its own courts. In TCL, international instruments do not directly criminalise categories of behaviour but instead place an obligation on states to enact laws which have this effect.

In TCL the construction of legal categories takes place at both international and national levels. International legal norms require states to criminalise certain forms of behaviour, but leave it to states to determine precisely how those categories are defined. It therefore raises questions both about the ideological uses of criminal law in domestic politics and social control, and their uses in international relations.

As TCL will be unfamiliar to many readers from a criminological background, we provide an introduction to it in the next section, before returning to Box's work for a closer examination of his view of law and his wider account of mystification. We then discuss the construction of human trafficking and modern slavery as ideological categories linked to immigration control and political struggles over sex work.[1] Next, we focus on one of the most important subcategories of human trafficking, forced criminality, and its role in the policing of the illicit drugs trade in England and Wales. Finally, we discuss governmental collusion in human trafficking as a form of state crime which states, and specifically the United States of America (USA), are actively involved in defining and 'policing'.

Transnational Criminal Law

Transnational forms of criminal law are an increasingly important part of the global legal order. In this form of law, international legal norms identify in broad terms certain categories of behaviour which states undertake to criminalise, but the precise specification of offences is left to national legislation. Therefore, if we wish to understand such offences as ideological constructs, we have to study their construction at both international and national levels. The offences covered by transnational criminal law include corruption, money laundering, terrorism and various forms of trafficking, whether in drugs, arms, endangered species or human beings (Boister 2018). These can be distinguished from offences against international criminal law, i.e., core crimes such as war crimes, crimes against humanity, genocide and the crime of aggression, which are fully defined by international legal instruments and can be tried by the International Criminal Court (ICC). The State parties to the ICC have to criminalise those crimes in their national laws and under the Complementarity regime of the ICC, states have the primacy over national courts while

---

[1] We are aware of the debates about the conflicting layers of understanding sex trafficking from prostitution and migration on the one hand and trafficking as acts involving forced prostitution and forced labour on the other. See for example Kempadoo et al. (2012). Weitzer (2007). In this chapter, we have decided to use sex work.

they have the obligation to cooperate with international investigation and prosecution.[2]

In the case of human trafficking as a transnational criminal category, the key international instruments are the *Palermo Protocol to Prevent, Suppress and Punish Trafficking in Persons, Especially Women and Children* supplemented to the *UN Convention on Transnational Organized Crime*; and the *Council of Europe Convention on Action Against Trafficking in Human Beings*. These 'suppression conventions' (Boister 2018: 20) indirectly facilitate criminalisation of human trafficking in criminal law at the national level. An important (but vague) provision of the *Council of Europe Convention* (Article 26) is the 'non-punishment principle', which requires states to 'provide for the possibility' of exempting victims of trafficking from punishment for crimes they were 'compelled' to commit. The European Court of Human Rights (ECtHR) has also decided that contraventions of the *Palermo Protocol* and *Council of Europe Convention* are *ipso facto* violations of Article 4 of the European Convention on Human Rights, which proscribes slavery, servitude and forced or compulsory labour (*Rantsev v Cyprus and Russia* [2010] 51 EHRR 1).

Despite the fact that the ECtHR provides some limited oversight over legislation and policing, TCL is characterised by an 'adjudication gap' (Fouladvand and Ward 2022: 28). That is, there is no international court with the authority to determine what the words of the *Palermo Protocol* and other international instruments mean. One consequence of this is to create a role for international groups of experts such as GRETA, the *Group of Experts on Action Against Trafficking in Human Beings*, which oversees the implementation of *Council of Europe Convention*. Another consequence is that states have considerable leeway in adopting broad or narrow definitions of trafficking to suit their own international purposes. This has proved particularly important in relation to sex work and forced criminality, which we discuss in the next two sections.

---

[2] Article 17 of the Rome Statute.

Law and Mystification

Box's remarks on law form part of a wider argument about the 'ideological mystification' of deviance. Box does not define the term 'mystification', but it clearly refers to the 'slightly disturbing picture' he paints as follows:

> The process of law enforcement, in its broadest possible interpretation, operates in such a way as to *conceal* crimes of the powerful against the powerless, but to *reveal* and *exaggerate* crimes of the powerless against "everyone" (Box 1983: 5).

Criminal law categories make certain fact-patterns salient by instructing officials to seek out examples of those patterns (usually patterns of individual, intentional wrongdoing) and prove the relevant facts in court. They obscure others by directing officials to ignore them if some legally relevant feature is absent. In particular, they obscure those forms of avoidable harm—harms caused by human acts or omissions—that do not fit criminal law definitions (although they may fit less ideologically salient categories of tort, employment law etc.). In this way, law enforcement produces a picture of crime that 'is not untrue'—in the sense that every published statistic, and most criminal convictions, may be factually correct—but is nevertheless 'inaccurate' (Box 1983: 5). Box's use of 'mystification' bears a loose relation to that of Goffman, who describes mystification as a technique of self-presentation that 'accentuates certain matters and conceals others' (Goffman 1959: 33).

Box (1982: 7) portrays the construction of criminal law categories as 'artful, creative ... designed to criminalize only some victimizing behaviours'. On a literal reading, this seems to attribute a remarkable degree of clear-sighted cynicism to lawmakers. Given that Box was elsewhere at pains to avoid 'the imagery and logic of conspiracy theory' (Box 1983: 213), it is unlikely that he intended to make such an implausible claim. In much the same way that Foucault's theory postulates 'a strategy without a strategist' (Dreyfus and Rabinow 1982: 187), Box appears to have in mind an artful design without a designer. As Foucault put it,

'People know what they do; they frequently know why they do what they do; what they don't know is what they do does' (personal communication quoted by Dreyfus and Rabinow 1982: 187). As we understand Box's analysis, he sees law and ideology as supporting one another in a process that does not require anyone to be fully conscious of it. The categories that ideology makes salient in the minds of lawmakers are endlessly reinforced by officials rooting out acts that fit those categories and dramatically presenting narratives of those acts in the public courts, which act as 'primary definers' of the events narrated and discussed by the mass media (Hall et al. 2013: 60–63). There is no reason to suppose, in many cases, that the lawmakers have any conscious design of mystifying anybody, or that they are anything other than mystified themselves. They do not necessarily know what is done by what they do. Ideology is too 'artful' to have any need for conscious complicity.

Modern Slavery as Mystification?

Read in this way, Box's argument rings true in relation to the construction of the legal categories of human trafficking and modern slavery. As O'Connell Davidson (2015) acknowledges in her important critique of the modern slavery construct, it would be ridiculous to suppose that those who promoted the idea of modern slavery consciously set out to legitimise forms of exploitation which fall outside the categories they proposed to criminalise. 'They call for action against a peculiarly morally repugnant form of suffering, but since this wrong is presented as exceptional to, and incompatible with, the dominant political and economic world order, their project is readily allied to a celebration of the existing status quo' (O'Connell Davidson 2015: 12). How different forms of exploitation should be addressed is an issue remaining to this day (Skrivankova 2014). The anti-trafficking discourse re-emerged in the late twentieth century particularly where the globalised world enhanced the vulnerability of migrants to enslavement and exploitation (Craig et al. 2019: 7). The law and order campaign on what Milivojevic and Pickering (2013: 595) call 'the human trafficking complex' combined three key issues: sex and anti-trafficking as a 'moral crusade'; migration (and paternal control over women's bodies as border crossers); and crime, depicted in terms of folk devils and ideal victims.

Policy makers attempted to inform their policies through quantifying modern slavery and human trafficking which required the police, e.g., in the UK, to have a separate recording category for modern slavery offences and thus effectively to double-count modern slavery offences in terms of both the specific offence and the associated crime, such as drug trafficking or prostitution-related offences (Craig et al. 2019: 17). However, as Faulkner (2017) puts it, the 'moral stance of the contemporary abolitionist movement'[3] (which sees itself as continuing the historic struggle to abolish slavery) hides an implicit racist and imperialist bias in the numbers of those claimed by non-governmental organisations (NGOs) to be living in modern slavery. In her view, these movements are 'being wielded as a hypocritical weapon of morality' (ibid.) which praises the 'best' states fighting modern slavery, which are all Euro-American, and does not acknowledge the West's role in perpetuating inequality, injustice and exploitation overseas.

The law's tendency to deflect attention from major forms of social harm may not be attributable to artful design, but it is entirely plausible to suggest that the upshot of a complex process of negotiation between various powerful and less powerful interest groups is to produce a law that reduces the ability of some groups to resist domination, and is intended to do so. That is what we believe our study of human trafficking will show.

Banal Orthodoxies

An important aspect of Box's approach was to understand how governments perceive the threats which they regard as calling for repressive measures, such as their perceptions of the links between unemployment, crime and disorder at the time he was writing. Policy was driven by a

---

[3] This is the 'contemporary abolitionist movement' championed by the Walk Free Foundation. They produce statistics via the Global Slavery Index and use the numbers in line with naming and shaming policy of the US concerning countries fighting modern/contemporary slavery.

'banal and mundane orthodoxy' (Box 1983: 211), which whether or not it was accurate was real in its consequences. The global orthodoxy which prompted the growth of a transnational legal order to combat human trafficking was one that linked illegal migration to organised crime and entailed an increased focus on the policing and criminalisation of human trafficking. Increasingly, concerns about modern slavery and human trafficking have been framed around organised crime in government policy and addressed from a criminal justice angle (Craig et al. 2019). States considered organised crime as a security problem in the era of globalisation and the debate on organised crime shifted after 1990 from a national to a transnational level (Holmes 2014: ix). The term 'global transnational crime' became prevalent in the mid-1990s (Wright 2006: 22) and a more strategic response at a country level and increasingly global and regional levels started by producing threat-assessments of organised crime groups in reports which were pioneered by the *United Kingdom Threat Assessment for Organised Crime* (UKTA) (Shaw 2011: 2). Within the context of the European Union, human trafficking has been identified as a form of organised crime closely linked with irregular migration and as one of the major challenges for EU internal security (European Commission 2010: 4). Directive 2011/36/EU on 'preventing and combating trafficking in human beings and protecting its victims' is part of a broader policy framework at EU level providing provisions to fight human trafficking as a serious crime that is controlled by transnational organised criminal networks. This has been reflected in a dedicated EU *Strategy on Combating Trafficking in Human Beings* 2021–2025 which has been regarded as a priority under the EU Security Union Strategy (European Commission 2021). The identification of trafficking with transnational organised crime prevailed despite a lack of clear evidence or systematic analysis of data on convicted traffickers (Lee 2011: 62).

The placing of human trafficking in the organised crime framework was aligned with a 'governing through crime' strategy which fuelled a culture of fear (Simon 2006: 6) and presented transnational organised crime as an external 'threat' necessitating a strong response by law enforcement (Lee 2011: 62). The threats posed by non-state actors have been the centre of attention; organised crime groups and the corruption they practise are perceived as 'weakening states' capacity to enforce the rule of law' (Schreier 2009: 218). What has been neglected or underestimated in this process is the complexity of the social organisation of human trafficking, the range of facilitators, abusers and layers of culpability involved in 'doing trafficking' (Lee 2011: 84). The 'war on trafficking' followed the US 'war on drugs' which comprised an important element of American foreign policy, in which 'a transnational police function' assumed increasing importance 'as the coercive mode for the projection of external force' (Andreas and Price 2001: 48). The emphasis has been on the vulnerability of 'modern states' and the importance of intelligence as an important weapon in 'fighting' the 'non-state actors' involved in trafficking (Schreier 2009: 218–219). The role of state actors has not, however, been entirely overlooked, as we discuss below.

This 'Americanization' of international law enforcement (Woodiwiss and Hobbs 2009: 115, 122), influenced the ways in which states and international organisations—including the United Nations—adopted and shaped their organised crime control strategies. The United States Congress enacted the *Trafficking Victims Protection Act* of 2000 (TVPA) just before the UN General Assembly adopted the *Palermo Protocol*. It defined sex and labour trafficking, focusing on 'prevention', 'protection', and 'prosecution' which constitute the main elements of the assessment process of the U.S Department of State's annual reports on *Trafficking in Persons* (TIP) describing and ranking the efforts every country is taking to combat trafficking (see below). Assuming the role of a 'global sheriff' (Chuang 2006: 437) on trafficking, this extraterritorial reach of the TVPA introduced a sanction regime which can hold other countries accountable to U.S. domestic standards if they are noncompliant (ibid.: 439).

In a different field, the Americanisation of the transnational rule of law has gone even further, in a way that calls the legitimacy of the US's role as 'sheriff' sharply into question. In 2020 the former U.S. government imposed sanctions on the ICC prosecutor, Fatou Bensouda, and the head of the Office of the Prosecutor's Jurisdiction, Complementarity, and Cooperation Division, Phakiso Mochochoko (Dworkin 2020). This 'executive order' was a response to the Court's investigation into possible international core crimes committed by the U.S. forces in Afghanistan as part of the U.S. 'war on terror'. The U.S. is still not a member of the ICC and in 1998 during the establishment of the Court along with countries such as China, Iraq, Israel, Libya, Qatar, and Yemen voted against the ICC Rome Statute (Coalition for the ICC, n.d.).

Framing human trafficking in the context of organised crime contributed to the securitisation of border crossings instead of focusing on prevention and protection measures (Lee 2011: 106). Counter-trafficking offensives have promoted a 'war-fighting approach' which highlighted the need to control, deter and immobilise both trafficking offenders and unauthorised migrants (Bigo 2001: 128). Putting in place more rigorous migration controls resulted in increasing 'incentives for the involvement of organised groups, networks and criminal entrepreneurs' to take advantage of people who were prepared to take risks for better life opportunities (Caparini 2014: 21).

In the UK, the Border Agency (UKBA) was abolished in March 2013 and its functions taken back into the Home Office under new divisions, UK Visas and Immigration, Immigration Enforcement and Border Force (UK Parliament). Despite this reform, the immigration system has a three-tiered approach to migration control, combining remote controls, territorial border and in-country controls to create 'a triple line of defence' to 'protect the country from illegal immigration, organised crime and terrorism', constructing 'a new offshore line of defence' (Lee 2011: 12). There can be no doubt that the rhetoric of trafficking has been useful in justifying ever harsher measures against illegal migration. People who arrange for migrants to enter the country illegally are not, in the legal sense, traffickers unless they do it 'with a view' to certain forms of exploitation (*Modern Slavery Act*, 2015, s. 3); but trafficking and smuggling of human beings are regularly conflated in political discourse. For example, Liz Truss, during the Conservative leadership contest, promised a 'strengthened' UK Bill of Rights and to send more asylum applicants to Rwanda because she was 'determined to end the appalling people trafficking we've seen' (Carr 2022). (The use of 'people' rather than 'human' looks like an 'artful' sidestepping of the legal term.) The Government's use of unevidenced claim that survivors of modern slavery and human trafficking are 'misusing the modern slavery identification and protection mechanism' directly has attacked the credibility of victims of human trafficking who need protection and support (UN 2022). For example, the

Sunak Government has recently announced new measures intended to increase removals of Albanian nationals (Gower 2023). The *Illegal Migration Bill*, introduced on 7 March 2023 as a response to the problem of small boats crossing the Channel (see Burnett, this volume), includes provisions which endanger the potential victims of Modern Slavery and Human Trafficking, as the Home Secretary will have a legal duty to remove migrants. In addition, Part 5 of the *Nationality and Borders Act* 2022 made changes to the *Modern Slavery Act* allegedly to help decision-makers to distinguish more effectively between 'genuine' and 'non-genuine' accounts of modern slavery (ibid.). Although the Government has claimed the Illegal Immigration Bill is compatible with the *Council of Europe Convention on Action against Trafficking in Human Beings* (ECAT), they have been unable to confirm whether the Modern Slavery and Human Trafficking provisions of this new Bill are complementing the ECHR requirements. The deliberate *weakening* of human rights protection becomes a way of *strengthening* it in the face of the evil of human trafficking—a near-perfect example not only of 'mystification' but of what O'Connell Davidson (2015: 5) calls the 'new double-think' in which 'cracking down on illegal migration becomes part of a fight to secure fundamental human rights, as opposed to implying a violation of those rights'.

Ironically, this crackdown has prompted fears that it will undermine the legal framework erected to combat trafficking—especially the parts of it that provide some measure of protection for victims. The *Nationality and Borders Act* received Royal Assent on 28th April 2022 and has introduced new changes to immigration, asylum and modern slavery. Provisions in part 5 of the Act will change the identification and protection process of potential victims of modern slavery and human trafficking. NGOs, the Independent Anti-Slavery Commissioner, senior police officers, chief prosecutors and international organisations have raised their concerns that particular provisions in Part 5 will result in fewer victims of modern slavery accessing support and will be damaging to prosecutions (Ariyo et al. 2021). For example, four UN Special Rapporteurs addressed their concerns in a letter (Mullaly et al. 2021). Dame Sara Thornton, the then Independent Anti-Slavery Commissioner, stated that the new provisions were made rather from an immigration approach which can increase the vulnerability of victims of modern slavery and human trafficking (Thornton 2021). ECPAT UK (2022) has also raised their concerns about the impact of the *Nationality and Borders Act* on children which can leave them 'at risk of dangerous journeys, trafficking and criminalisation'.

The depiction of economically driven 'illegal' or irregular migration with organised crime as part of a continuum of threats to the security of destination countries, Caparini (2014) argues, has shaped policy discourse for the past two decades. This prioritisation of criminal justice measures in countering human trafficking as a form of transnational organised crime has ignored the exploitative activities of trafficking facilitators and 'state-induced trafficking harms'. The layers of culpability have not been acknowledged effectively to hold the state and state agents to account (Lee 2011: 83).

While the negotiations leading to the *Palermo Protocol* were dominated by issues of migration and organised crime, they were also influenced by a great deal of lobbying, and sometimes acrimonious debate, between NGOS on both sides of the politics of sex work (Doezema 2005; Kotiswaran 2021). Both the advocates of an 'abolitionist' approach[4] towards prostitution and those advocating greater legal protection for sex workers were working on behalf of subordinate groups, but in contradictory ways and with very different degrees of success. As Ward and Wylie (2017: 79) have argued, in the US 'a curious combination of feminist and faith-based organizations has been a potent force'

---

[4] During the negotiations of drafting process for the 'Protocol to Suppress, Prevent and Punish Trafficking in Persons, Especially Women and Children' (The Trafficking Protocol) in Palermo, there were two main non-governmental organisations (NGOs) concerning prostitution and sex work. One feminist lobby group was the International Human Rights Network represented by the Coalition Against Trafficking in Women (CATW) had an abolitionist approach towards prostitution. They considered all forms of prostitution to be a violation of women's human rights which should be regarded as trafficking. The other group was the Human Rights Caucus led by the International Human Rights Law Group (IHRLG) and the Global Alliance Against Traffic in Women (GAATW). They viewed prostitution as legitimate labour based on consent and they argued for sex workers' rights. The Human Rights Caucus also criticised the abuse of anti-trafficking measures to police female migrant sex workers and restrict their freedom of movement. See for example: Doezema (2002, 2005). Please note also the differences between this approach to 'abolition' with that of penal abolitionism, as advocated by O'Connell Davidson (2020).

in promoting a particular variant of the anti-trafficking agenda, both domestically and internationally (see also Jackson et al. 2017).

In British politics, sex work does not have quite the same importance as it does in the USA as a means of creating alliances between social conservatism and evangelical feminism. Nevertheless, we have seen 'human trafficking' used as a justification for introducing the so-called 'Nordic model'—criminalising the purchase of sexual services, and thereby making sex work an increasingly dangerous underground activity—into Northern Ireland (Gordon 2014). There is little or no evidence of the legislation having the promised effects (Ellison et al. 2019). There is, of course, much more to be said about the issue of sex work and its relation to trafficking than we have space for here (see e.g. Kenway 2021, Ch. 3); the 'Boxian' point we wish to make is simply that it illustrates how the demands of subordinate groups are selectively incorporated into legal categories in ways that further the interests of the powerful (Box 2003: 8).

Race, Drugs and the Politics of Victimhood

In England and Wales, increasing numbers of referrals of possible victims of trafficking to the National Referral Mechanism (NRM) have been related to criminal exploitation and in particular 'county lines', defined by the Government as a form of drug dealing 'using dedicated mobile phone lines or other form of "deal line". They are likely to exploit children and vulnerable adults to move [and store] the drugs and money and they will often use coercion, intimidation, violence (including sexual violence) and weapons' (Home Office 2018: 48). In recent years, there has been a sharp increase of children (predominantly male) referred to the NRM as victims of trafficking, which has largely been driven by 'county lines' cases. 'County lines' accounted for 16% of all referrals to the NRM in 2021, averaging 500 referrals a quarter (Home Office 2022).

This form of exploitation falls in the category of 'abuse of power or of a position of vulnerability' in Article 3 of the UN *Palermo Protocol* in defining human trafficking. In English law this form of exploitation (so far as it relates to children and vulnerable adults) is defined as using a person to provide a service or benefit of any kind, having chosen them on the grounds that they are a child and that an adult would be likely to refuse to be used for that purpose (*Modern Slavery Act*, 2015 s. 3(6)). Anyone who 'arranges travel' for a child 'with a view' to such exploitation commits the offence of human trafficking.

The breadth of this provision is shown in the important case of *R v Karemera, Wabelua, and Alford* (2018). The defendants—'three young black men from inner-London housing estates' (Koch 2020)—were convicted in 2016 of conspiracy to supply heroin and cocaine in what the Court of Appeal described as a 'county drugs lines' operation (Court of Appeal 2018, para. 1). Not content with sentences of 10, 11, and six years imposed on the three defendants, the prosecution, in 'an attempt to deter drug dealers from using the county drugs line system and from exploiting the vulnerable as couriers' (ibid.: para. 3) brought additional charges of human trafficking under a statute in force at the time the couriers were recruited,[5] which was worded similarly to the *Modern Slavery Act*, s. 3(6). The charges were based on the allegations that the three dealers had 'arranged travel' for five couriers aged 14–16, who were used for this purpose on the grounds of their age. The trial judge thought it likely that the young couriers (none of whom gave evidence) were 'willing volunteers' and in these circumstances did not think it was open to the jury to find that they were 'used' on the grounds of their age. Therefore, the Judge ruled 'no case to answer'. However, the prosecution successfully challenged the judge's 'terminating ruling' in the Court of Appeal. The Court held that the Act was 'seeking to protect the young and the vulnerable from their own decision-making' (ibid.: para. 60) and that it was therefore irrelevant whether the couriers had volunteered for their roles, provided that *one* of the reasons for choosing them was their youth, and the likely unwillingness of older people to undertake the task. When the trial resumed two of the defendants pleaded guilty to human trafficking and the third was convicted by the jury. The defendants were sentenced to terms of imprisonment: five years, three years six months and four years respectively.

---

[5] *Asylum and Immigration (Treatment of Claimants*, etc.*) Act* 2004 (as amended) s. 4(1A).

In *Karemera* we see two opposing ideological constructions of the mainly young, black men and women involved in 'county lines' drug dealing. For the trial judge the young couriers were willing recruits to crime; for the Court of Appeal (2018) they were victims of exploitation. As Koch (2020) notes, this willingness to identify young couriers as in need of care and compassion looks at first sight like an exception to the 'punitive turn' (Garland 2002: 142), which Box anticipated more recent writers (e.g. Wacquant 2009) in diagnosing. In marked contrast to the general reluctance of the criminal courts to extend the defence of duress to anyone involved in organised crime (Wake 2017), the *Karemera* decision has contributed to growing prominence of 'county lines' among suspected cases of trafficking. Koch (2020) argues, however, that the 'murky politics of victimhood' associated with modern slavery 'not only conjures images of the internal traitor in disenfranchised working class communities but … activates a host of technical and legal mechanisms of control in the name of saving the vulnerable. Drug dealing is more likely to be seen as a "gang" activity when the dealers are predominantly black' (Clarke and Williams 2016: 5) and applying the most condemnatory label possible to the senior figures in such 'gangs' reinforces this racist stereotype.

It seems unlikely that either the drafting of the legislation or the *Karemera* judgement were 'artfully designed' as a means of dividing drug dealers into two categories of exploiters and exploited. The *Karemera* judgement makes sense in its transnational legal context, since the international conventions on human trafficking do not require any element of coercion or deception for the exploitation of 'children' under 18 to constitute trafficking. Because the court had to consider the law in force at the time of the alleged offences, the case turned on the construction of an obsolete statute, and it is unclear whether the Court of Appeal even considered the effect it would have on the scope of the (then) new defence created by the *Modern Slavery Act*, 2015, s. 45.

Once the legal scope of both the trafficking offence and the s. 45 defence became clear, however, they were able to be put to strategic use, while also creating certain unintended consequences. HM Inspectorate of Constabulary Fire and Rescue Services (2020: 31) has stated that 'modern slavery offences should be pursued whenever possible in county lines cases. Some perpetrators may be deterred by the stigma that can come with a modern slavery conviction, particularly involving children'. No evidence is cited for such a deterrent effect, which would be very hard to demonstrate, but the Inspectorate clearly sees ideological value in the 'modern slavery' label, as well as in the legal power to impose Slavery and Trafficking Prevention Orders which, for example, restrict offenders' use of mobile phones and cars (ibid.: 32). On the other hand, it also fears that 'perversely… the availability of this statutory defence may increase the risk of exploitation' as recruits may be told that they can avoid conviction by claiming to have been trafficked. The evidence for this appears to be what the Inspectors were told by a single 'survivor of county lines exploitation' (ibid.).

This theme has also been taken up, in a somewhat more nuanced way, by the Independent Anti-Slavery Commissioner (2020). She argues both that people who should benefit from the statutory defence are not doing so, and that others may be misusing the defence. She acknowledges that her call for evidence produced only:

> a few cases where defendants were found to be falsely claiming that they were child victims but did not reveal defendants seeking referrals to the NRM [National Referral Mechanism] by concocting false victim narrative[s]. In many cases it was likely that defendants had been groomed and trafficked but had also committed serious crimes. A young person found in possession of crack cocaine, heroin and a large knife has probably been trafficked in the past and/or may be a victim of trafficking at the time of the offence but neither such status [*sic*] automatically means that they should not be prosecuted. I am persuaded that while an opportunistic defendant may attempt to abuse the defence, many cases involve victims of human trafficking who are committing serious offences (ibid.: 9).

In other words, there simply is no neat dichotomy between offenders and victims. Prosecutors are, however, exhorted to draw the line in accordance with the words of the statute, by trying to prove (in the case of a child) that a 'reasonable' child in the same situation would have committed the offence, or (in the case of an adult) that they were not 'compelled' to do the relevant act because they had a 'reasonable alternative' to doing so. The 'reasonable person' is one of the most deeply problematic of all criminal law's ideological constructs. As Norrie (2002) argues, the criminal law addresses itself to an abstract, rational subject, but at the same time it comes under pressure to take account of at least some features of the concrete situations in which individuals find themselves. In the *Modern Slavery Act* this is reflected in the idea that the 'reasonable person' in question shares the 'relevant characteristics' of the actual defendant—that is, their 'age, sex and any physical or mental illness or disability' (s. 45(5))—and is placed 'in the same situation' (s. 45(1)(d)). The trouble is that the more vulnerable a defendant is and the more intimidation and manipulation they have been subjected to, the less likely their behaviour is to resemble that of a 'reasonable person' (Laird 2016; Simpson 2019). This results in seemingly harsh decisions like *R v AAD* (Court of Appeal 2021), where a Vietnamese 'cannabis gardener' who was undoubtedly trafficked succeeded in leaving the premises where he had been tending cannabis plants, but when he failed to find another Vietnamese-speaking person who could help him, he gave up and returned to his traffickers. Though this could easily be interpreted as a sad indication of the helplessness to which he had been reduced, it was held that he had failed to show the element of compulsion necessary for defence.

Mystifying State Crime? The Trafficking in Persons (TIP) Reports

The American public concern and interest about human trafficking emerged in 1990s at the end of Cold War when the policymakers and American civil society actors claimed thousands of women in Eastern Europe and the Middle East sold to sexual slavery (Specter 1998). This took place concurrently with discourses of liberating Third World women from gendered oppression (Risley 2015: 219) which apparently motivated the U.S. anti-trafficking activism. One aspect of the US's role as 'global sheriff' (Chuang 2006: 237) is the work of the State Department in publishing Annual Reports on the anti-trafficking efforts, or lack of efforts, of almost every country in the world. These 'Trafficking in Persons' (TIP) reports assign countries to four tiers (numbered 1–3 with the addition of a 'Tier 2 watch list').[6] Those in tier 3, found to be neither complying nor making significant efforts to comply with the standards set out in the US Trafficking Victims Protection Act (TVPA), face financial sanctions in the form of exclusion from US aid, and US opposition to aid being granted by international bodies such as the IMF. Countries currently on Tier 3 include some whose regimes regularly attract US hostility, such as Venezuela, Cuba and Iran, along with some less obvious countries such as Papua New Guinea and the Gambia (Wooditch 2011: 477). Ward and Wylie (2017: 84) pointed out that:

> Tier 3 countries repeatedly resemble a list of the US's "most wanted"...while many US allies with poor human rights record[s] and/or acknowledged problems with practices such as bonded labour remain forever on the tier 2 watch list without enduring what would be a deserved demotion according to the criteria.

In numerous countries the reports identify not only a lack of effort to investigate and prosecute trafficking, but official complicity or involvement in trafficking. In the 2021 report, 105 countries out of 188 are described in these terms, ranging from China and Russia to the tiny Pacific island nation of Palau. Four are EU member states: Bulgaria, Cyprus, Greece and Romania (U.S. State Department 2022; Fouladvand and Ward 2022).

The evidence for these accusations comes largely from unnamed civil society sources in the countries concerned. This can be frustrating for researchers, since the allegations if true would be of great importance but without some more detail of the data relied upon it is difficult to use the reports as evidence, particularly when (as in the case of China, for

---

[6] TIP Reports provides a guide to the Tiers that Tier 1 will include countries where fully compliant with the minimum standards for elimination of severe forms of trafficking in persons; Tier 2 countries are not fully compliant, but making 'significant efforts' to be compliant with the minimum standards; Tier 2 Watch List was created in 2004) as determined by the Secretary of State to 'require special scrutiny during the following year'.

Tier 3 countries are not fully compliant and not making 'significant efforts' to be compliant with the minimum standards.

example) the allegations go well beyond anything that academic research has been able to discover.[7]

In these reports the US State Department is playing a significant role in the investigation and censure of state crime. This kind of state activity has received relatively little attention in the literature on state crime (e.g. Green and Ward 2004, 2019), which has tended to portray the investigation and censure of state crime as carried out largely by NGOs and international organisations, rather than by states themselves. It is important to consider that state crime, or state complicity in international crime, may itself be an ideological construct which can be used to promote the interests of the powerful, as well as the victims of state crime. As we have argued elsewhere (Fouladvand and Ward 2022) the pressure put upon states to criminalise trafficking has been highly effective in getting states to pass the relevant laws but has been much less effective in making any real impact on the practices designated as 'modern slavery'. As Lee (2013: 2) argues, the tendency to equate control of trafficking with control of migration also has the effect of forcing more migrants to rely upon professional smugglers, some of whom turn out to be traffickers bent on exploiting them in their destination countries. Exactly how this benefits powerful interests, particularly those of the USA, is not a straightforward question. Ward and Wylie (2017: 85–86) argued that:

> there is something about the passion that recent administrations have brought to this issue in comparison to all other 'good causes' or security concerns that makes the bleak calculation of interests or exercise of hegemony seem too parsimonious an explanation of why the US invests so heavily in anti-trafficking activism.

It is, she suggests, more to do with a domestic ideological agenda of 'freedom, feminism and faith' (ibid.) as a combination of feminist and faith-based organisations has been a major force in shaping the US human trafficking response. This was written before the election of Donald Trump but his (and his daughter and aide Ivanka Trump's)

---

[7] Thanks to Anqi Shen for discussion of this point.

anti-trafficking policies and rhetoric did not notably break from earlier approaches, particularly in the legislation against online 'sex trafficking' which passed with bipartisan support (Musto et al. 2021). Trump did, however, intensify the anti-immigration strand of this type of rhetoric:

> Tolerance for illegal immigration is not compassionate – it is cruel. One in three women is sexually assaulted on the long journey north. …Human traffickers and sex traffickers take advantage of the wide open areas between our ports of entry to smuggle thousands of young girls and women into the United States and to sell them into prostitution and modern-day slavery (Trump 2019).

Conclusion

Box's argument that critical criminology should pay attention to criminal law categories as ideological constructs was a potentially fruitful one, which anticipated later critical scholarship in criminal law (e.g. Norrie 2014; Farmer 2016). As we interpret his argument it is neither conspiratorial nor functionalist, but rather pays attention both to the (not necessarily accurate) perceptions of threats to social order on the part of the powerful, and to the efforts of less powerful groups to put their concerns on the legal agenda. Laws made in response to these ideologically salient concerns tend both to perpetuate their salience and to conceal other forms of harm, thus contributing to what Box termed mystification.

The legal constructs which emerge from this process serve a much wider range of ideological purposes than that of diverting attention from socially harmful behaviour that is not criminalised. The law can operate regressively, for example, to forge alliances between evangelicals and evangelical feminists, to legitimise the repressive policing of inner-city communities and in the toughening of immigration controls and promoting US global hegemony. What is perhaps most interesting from both a legal and a criminological point of view is how fine legal points about the precise meaning of statutory provisions can interact with developments in policing strategies: producing, in this case, a bifurcation of drugs traffickers into exploiters and victims and a difficult legal (and tactical) problem about how the line between them is to be drawn. This reinforces our sense that criminal law doctrine is a worthwhile object of study for critical criminologists, as critical criminology is for criminal lawyers.

References

Andreas, P., and R. Price. 2001. From War Fighting to Crime Fighting: Transforming the American National Security State. *International Studies Review* 3 (3): 31–52.

Ariyo, D., and 55 Other Signatories. 2021. *Statement from Anti-Slavery Leaders and Organisations.* https://static1.squarespace.com/static/599abfb4e6f2e19 ff048494f/t/61791619ab13bc63b265ff2a/1635325466766/Antislavery+Sector+Statement+updated.pdf. Accessed 29 Sep 2022.

Bigo, D. 2001. Migration and Security. In *Controlling a New Migration World*, ed. V. Guiraudon and C. Joppke, 121–149. London: Routledge.

Boister, N. 2018. *An Introduction to Transnational Criminal Law.* Oxford: Oxford University Press.

Box, S. 1983. *Power, Crime and Mystification.* London: Tavistock.

Canning, V., and S. Tombs. 2021. *From Social Harm to Zemiology: A Critical Introduction.* London: Routledge.

Caparini, M. 2014. *Trafficking in Human Beings: Learning from Asian and European Experiences.* Singapore: European Union Centre.

Carr, S. 2022. Conservative Leadership Candidate Liz Truss Vows to Extend Rwanda Migrant Scheme July 23. *Daily Mail.* https://www.dailymail.co.uk/news/article-11042267/Tory-leadership-favourite-Liz-Truss-vows-extend-Rwanda-migrant-scheme.html. Accessed 30 Sep 2022.

Chuang, J. 2006. The United States As Global Sheriff: Using Unilateral Sanctions To Combat Human Trafficking. *Michigan Journal of International Law* 27: 437–494.

Clarke, B., and Williams, P. 2016. *Dangerous Associations: Joint Enterprise, Gangs and Racism.* London: Centre for Crime and Justice Studies. https://www.crimeandjustice.org.uk/sites/crimeandjustice.org.uk/files/Dangerous%20assocations%20Joint%20Enterprise%20gangs%20and%20racism.pdf. Accessed 6 Jun 2023.

Coalition for the International Criminal Court (CICC). N.d. United States. https://www.coalitionfortheicc.org/country/united-states. Accessed 31 Jul 2023.

Craig, G., Balch, A., Lewis, H., and Waite, L. 2019. The Modern Slavery Agenda: Politics, Policy and Practice. In *The Modern Slavery Agenda*, eds. G. Craig, A. Balch, H. Lewis, and L. Waite, eds. Bristol: Policy Press.

Doezema, J. 2002. Who Gets to Choose? Coercion, Consent, and the UN Trafficking Protocol. *Gender and Development* 10 (1): 20–27.

Doezema, J. 2005. 'Now You See Her, Now You Don't: Sex Workers at the UN Trafficking Protocol Negotiations. *Social & Legal Studies* 14 (1): 61–89.

Dreyfus, H. L., and Rabinow, P. 1982. *Michel Foucault: Beyond Structuralism and Hermeneutics*. Brighton: Harvester.

Dworkin, A. 2020. Why America is Facing off against the International Criminal Court. http://ecfr.eu/article/commentary_why_america_is_facing_off_against_the_international_criminal_cou/. Accessed 22 May 2023.

Every Child Protected Against Trafficking (ECPAT) UK. 2022. Harmful Nationality and Borders Act Passes. https://www.ecpat.org.uk/news/the-nationality-and-borders-act-received-royal-assent-this-week-after-a-hard-fought-battle-to-increase-rights-and-protections. Accessed 31 Jul 2023.

Ellison, G., C. Ní Dhónnail, and E. Early. 2019. *A Review of the Criminalisation of Paying for Sexual Services in Northern Ireland*. Belfast: Queen's University and Department of Justice.

European Commission. 2010. *The EU Internal Security Strategy in Action: Five Steps Towards a More Secure Europe*. COM 2010 (673). https://eur-lex.europa.eu/LexUriServ/LexUriServ.do?uri=COM:2010:0673:FIN:EN:PDF. Accessed 27 Sep 2022.

European Commission. 2021. *Strategy on Combatting Trafficking in Human Beings* COM (2021) 171. https://eur-lex.europa.eu/legal-content/EN/TXT/PDF/?uri=CELEX:52021DC0171&from=EN. Accessed 15 Mar 2023.

Farmer, L. 2016. *Making the Modern Criminal Law: Criminalization and Civil Order*. Oxford: Oxford University Press.

Faulkner, E. 2017. 40.3 Million Slaves: Challenging the Hypocrisy of Modern Slavery Statistics. https://www.opendemocracy.net/en/beyond-trafficking-and-slavery/403-million-slaves-challenging-hypocrisy-of-modern-slavery-statistics/. Accessed 14 Mar 2023.

Fouladvand, S., and T. Ward. 2022. Comparing Transnational Legal Orders: Criminalisation, Labour Law and Forced Labour. *Journal of International and Comparative Law* 9 (1): 25–50.

Garland, D. 2002. *The Culture of Control*. Oxford: Oxford University Press.

Goffman, E. 1959. *The Presentation of Self in Everyday Life.* New York: Anchor.
Gordon, G. 2014. Trafficking Bill: MLAs Vote to Make Paying for Sex a Crime. October 21. *BBC News.* https://www.bbc.co.uk/news/uk-northern-ireland-29699626. Accessed 30 Sep 2022.
Gower, M. 2023. Modern Slavery Cases in the Immigration System. https://commonslibrary.parliament.uk/research-briefings/cbp-9744/. Accessed 15 Mar 2023.
Green, P., and T. Ward. 2004. *State Crime: Governments, Violence and Corruption.* Pluto Press.
Green, P., and T. Ward. 2019. *State Crime and Civil Activism: On the Dialectics of Repression and Resistance.* London: Routledge.
Hacking, I. 1999. *The Social Construction of What?* Cambridge, MA: Harvard University Press.
Hall, S., C. Critcher, T. Jefferson, J. Clarke, and B. Roberts. 2013. *Policing the Crisis: Mugging, the State and Law and Order,* 2nd ed. London: Bloomsbury.
HM Inspectorate of Constabulary, Fire and Rescue Services. 2020. *Both Sides of the Coin: An Inspection of How the Police and the National Crime Agency Consider Vulnerable Young People who are both Victims and Offenders in 'County Lines' Drug Dealing.* https://www.justiceinspectorates.gov.uk/hmicfrs/publications/both-sides-of-the-coin-county-lines/. Accessed 30 Sep 2022.
Holmes, L. 2014. *Advanced Introduction to Organised Crime.* Cheltenham: Edward Elgar.
Home Office. 2018. *Serious Violence Strategy.* https://assets.publishing.service.gov.uk/government/uploads/system/uploads/attachment_data/file/698009/serious-violence-strategy.pdf. Accessed 31 Jul 2023.
Home Office. 2022. *Modern Slavery: National Referral Mechanism and Duty to Notify Statistics UK, End of Year Summary, 2021.* https://www.gov.uk/government/statistics/modern-slavery-national-referral-mechanism-and-duty-to-notify-statistics-uk-end-of-year-summary-2021/modern-slavery-national-referral-mechanism-and-duty-to-notify-statistics-uk-end-of-year-summary-2021. Accessed 31 Jul 2023.
Jackson, C. A., Reed, G. L., and Brants, B. G. 2017. Strange Confluences: Radical Feminism, Evangelical Christianity as Drivers of US Neo-Abolitionism. In *Feminism, Prostitution and the State: The Politics of Neo-Abolitionism,* eds. E. Ward and G. Wylie. London: Taylor & Francis.
Kempadoo, K., J. Sanghera, and B. Pattanaik. 2012. *Trafficking and Prostitution Reconsidered: New Perspectives on Migration, Sex Work, and Human Rights,* 2nd ed. Boulder: Paradigm Publishers.

Kenway, E. 2021. *The Truth About Modern Slavery*. London: Pluto.
Koch, I. 2020. *The Making of Modern Slavery in Austerity Britain*. June 12. Focaalblog. https://www.focaalblog.com/2020/06/12/insa-koch-the-making-of-modern-slavery-in-austerity-britain. Accessed 27 Sep 2022.
Kotiswaran, P. 2021. The Sexual Politics of Anti-Trafficking Discourse. *Feminist Legal Studies* 29: 43–65.
Laird, K. 2016. Evaluating the Relationship between Section 45 of the Modern Slavery Act 2015 and the Defence of Duress: An Opportunity Missed? *Criminal Law Review* 6: 395–404.
Lee, M. 2011. *Trafficking and Transnational Organised Crime. Trafficking and Global Crime Control*. London: SAGE.
Lee, M. 2013. *Human Trafficking*. Hoboken: Taylor & Francis.
Milivojevic, S., and S. Pickering. 2013. Trafficking in People, 20 Years On: Sex, Migration and Crime in the Global Anti-Trafficking Discourse and the Rise of the 'Global Trafficking Complex.' *Current Issues in Criminal Justice* 25: 585–604.
Mullaly, S., González Morales, F., Obokata, T., and Ní Aolain, F. 2021. Communication OBL GBR 11/2021. November 5. https://spcommreports.ohchr.org/TMResultsBase/DownLoadPublicCommunicationFile?gId=26788. Accessed 30 Sep 2022.
Musto, J., Feherenbacher, A. E., Hoefinger, H., Mai, N., Macioti, P. G., Bennachie, C., Giametta, C., and D'Adamo, K. 2021. Anti-Trafficking in the Time of FOSTA/SESTA: Networked Moral Gentrification and Sexual Humanitarian Creep. *Social Sciences* 10 (2): 58. https://www.mdpi.com/2076-0760/10/2/58. Accessed 16 Feb 2023.
Norrie, A.W. 2002. From Criminal Law to Legal Theory: The Mysterious Case of the Reasonable Glue-Sniffer. *Modern Law Review* 65 (5): 538–555.
Norrie, A.W. 2014. *Crime, Reason and History: A Critical Introduction to Criminal Law*, 3rd ed. Cambridge: Cambridge University Press.
O'Connell Davidson, J. 2015. *Modern Slavery: The Margins of Freedom*. Basingstoke: Palgrave Macmillan.
O'Connell Davidson, J. 2020. *Slavery*. London: Sage.
Risley, A. 2015. "America will not Tolerate Slave Traders": Counter-Trafficking Policies and US Power. *Journal of Women Politics and Policy* 36 (2): 213–238.
Schreier, F. 2009. Human Trafficking, Organsied Crime and Intelligence. In *Strategies Against Human Traficking: The Role of the Security Sector*. ed. C. Friesendorf. Vienna: Study Group Information.

Shaw, M. 2011. *Know Your Enemy: An Overview of Organized Crime Threat Assessments.* International Peace Institute Issue Brief. https://www.files.ethz.ch/isn/133787/ipi_e_pub_know_your_enemy.pdf. Accessed 27 Sep 2022.

Simon, J. 2006. *Governing Through Crime.* New York: Oxford University Press.

Simpson, B. 2019. The Reasonable Victim of Modern Slavery: *R v N* [2019] EWCA Crim 984. *Journal of Criminal Law* 83 (6): 508–512.

Skrivankova, K. 2014. *Forced Labour in the United Kingdom.* York: Joseph Rowntree Foundation.

Specter, M. 1998. Contraband Women—A Special Report. Traffickers New Cargo Naive Slavic Women. January 11. *New York Times.* https://www.nytimes.com/1998/01/11/world/contraband-women-a-special-report-traffickers-new-cargo-naive-slavic-women.html. Accessed 24 May 2023.

Thornton, S. 2021. *Dame Sara responds to the Nationality and Borders Bill.* http://www.antislaverycommissioner.co.uk/news-insights/dame-sara-responds-to-the-nationality-and-borders-bill/. Accessed 31 Jul 2023.

Thornton, S. 2020. *The Modern Slavery Act 2015 Statutory Defence: A Call for Evidence.* Independent Anti-Slavery Commissioner. https://www.antislaverycommissioner.co.uk/media/1478/the-modern-slavery-act-2015-statutory-defence-call-for-evidence.pdf. Accessed 31 Jul 2023.

Trump, D. 2019. *State of the Union Address.* https://edition.cnn.com/2019/02/05/politics/donald-trump-state-of-the-union-2019-transcript/index.html. Accessed 16 Feb 2023.

Trafficking in Persons Report (TIP). 2022. U.S. State Department. https://www.state.gov/reports/2022-trafficking-in-persons-report/. Accessed 31 Jul 2023.

UK Parliament, Public Accounts Committee. 2014. Progress in Reforming the UK Border Agency. https://committees.parliament.uk/work/4306/progress-in-reforming-the-uk-border-agency. Accessed 31 Jul 2023.

UN. 2022. UK: UN Experts Condemn Attacks on Cedibility of Slavery and Tafficking Victims, Office of the High Commissioner on Human Rights. December 22. https://www.ohchr.org/en/press-releases/2022/12/uk-un-experts-condemnattacks-credibility-slavery-and-trafficking-victims. Accessed 15 March 2023.

Wacquant, L.J.D. 2009. *Punishing the Poor: The Neoliberal Government of Social Insecurity.* Durham, NC: Duke Univeristy Press.

Wake, N. 2017. Human Trafficking and Modern Day Slavery: When Victims Kill. *Criminal Law Review* 9: 658–677.

Ward, E., and G. Wylie, eds. 2017. *Feminism, Prostitution and the State: The Politics of Neo-abolitionism.* London: Routledge.

Weitzer, R. 2007. The Social Construction of Sex Trafficking: Ideology and Institutionalization of a Moral Crusade. *Politics & Society* 35 (3): 447–475.

Wooditch, A. 2011. The Efficacy of the Trafficking in Persons Report: A Review of the Evidence. *Criminal Justice Policy Review* 22: 471–493.

Woodiwiss, M., and D. Hobbs. 2009. Organized Evil and The Atlantic Alliance: Moral Panics and the Rhetoric of Organized Crime Policing in America and Britain. *British Journal of Criminology* 106 (49): 115–116.

Wright, A. 2006. *Organised Crime.* Cullompton: Willan.

Wylie, G. 2017. *The International Politics of Human Trafficking.* Basingstoke: Palgrave Macmillan.

Legal Cases Cited

Legal Cases Cited

Court of Appeal (2018) *R v Karemera and Others* [2018] EWCA Crim 1832; [2019] 1 WLR 4761.

Court of Appeal (2021) *R v AAD and others* [2021] EWCA Crim 106.

Rantsev v Cyprus and Russia [2010] 51 EHRR 1.

Part IV

Power, Gender and Sexual Violence

13

Power, Sexual Violence and Mystification

Kym Atkinson and Helen Monk

Introduction

We are effectively facing the decriminalisation of rape in England and Wales. The number of rape convictions in the year ending September 2021 was 1109 (End Violence Against Women Coalition [EVAW], n.d.). This is the lowest number of rape convictions on record. This stands in contrast with the highest number of sexual offences ever recorded during the same time frame, reaching the staggering figure of 170,973 (EVAW, n.d.). Rape also continues to have the lowest charging rate of all crimes (Syal 2022). The complex web of injustice and harms, reliance on myths and stereotypes, the abiding constrictive nature of gendered

K. Atkinson (✉)
Sheffield Hallam University, Sheffield, UK
e-mail: K.Atkinson@shu.ac.uk

H. Monk
Centre for the Study of Crime, Criminalisation and Social Exclusion,
Liverpool John Moores University, Liverpool, UK
e-mail: H.L.Monk@ljmu.ac.uk

subjectivities, and dangerous and narrow definitions of rape, consent, culpability and sexuality, articulated by state institutions and the media, underscore the figures above and are central to the arguments made by Box (1983) in his chapter 'Rape and sexual assaults on females'. Here, we outline the contemporary relevance of Box's work to the current theorisation and experience of, and responses to, sexual violence. To do this, we will concentrate on the developments which have taken place in sexual violence scholarship from a feminist, and predominantly, feminist poststructuralist perspective. We will argue that Box's work has an enduring utility in Critical Criminology. The chapter therefore aims to extend Box's analysis of sexual violence and the process of mystification, by continuing to see this issue through the eyes of the state, whilst also making explicit the discourses which operate in and out of the realm of the state which serve to limit our understanding of sexual violence and their resultant, harmful effects.

The chapter is split into four sections. Firstly, we briefly outline the intersections of Box's approach to the process of mystification and our own perspective in addressing sexual violence at the level of discourse. Secondly, we explore how dominant discourses often obscure the nature, extent and effects of men's violence against women and girls. Thirdly, we address how the process of mystification operates in conjunction with narrow and unworkable definitions of consent. Finally, we explore institutional mystification and the limits of the law in dealing effectively with sexual violence. We consider the resistance to the limitations imposed by the gendered social order which has been generated by feminist scholarship and grassroots organisations.

Discursive Formations of Sexual Violence

In relation to sexual violence, Alcoff (2018: 3) states that rape cultures produce a discursive formation in which:

the intelligibility of claims is not by logical argument or evidence, but by frames that set out who can be victimised, who can be accused, which are plausible narratives, and in what contexts rape may be spoken about, even in private spaces.

It is through this discursive formation that we seek to analyse the enduring legacy of Box's work on the process of mystification with respect to this violence. For us, it is at the level of discourse, and through the construction of knowledge, that we should locate the problematic truths established around sexual violence and examine the disciplinary power that they wield. This understanding of discourse and the socially and culturally constructed nature of experience and meaning is used to extend Box's understanding of a 'cultural repertoire' (Box 1983: 157) of excuses, exonerations and exclusions, at subjective, discursive and structural levels, around sexual violence. It is the discourses through which sexual violence is made intelligible to us that is important. This approach argues that the problem of sexual violence is not separate from the way that it is spoken about as it sets the boundaries around what is sayable and permissible (Alcoff 2018).

It is through a compliance to, and internalisation of, culturally and historically contingent norms that the gendered operation of disciplinary power finds its footing (Foucault 1995). Box contends that a central part of this process is mystification and that '[F]or too long too many people have been socialized to see crime and criminals through the eyes of the state' (1983: 14). We, like Box, seek to contest the dominant lens through which rape and sexual assault are viewed and to dismantle the relationship between power and claims to truth. As Gavey (1989: 463) argues, we should be concerned with 'disrupting and displacing dominant (oppressive) knowledges'. This has been the task for many feminist interventions into sexual violence; to try to lessen the stranglehold that dominant discourses have on the ways in which women live, move, think, act and experience gendered life.

Box's chapter, therefore, represents a challenge not only to the dominant, discursive constructions of rape and sexual assault defined by the state, justice system and the media, but also by liberal and radical criminologies. His central argument, that the realities of sexual violence are mystified through processes of discrediting, minimising and deflection, serve to centralise the gendered nature of this type of serious crime and harm and, as such, his work brought rape under the same ideological gaze as more established critical criminological considerations such as corporate and state crime. To position sexual violence as a crime of power and one which suffers from the same misleading social construction as other crimes gaining attention from critical scholarship at the time was incredibly important. Box moves away from discussions and explanations of rape predicated on biology, pathology, or individualisation and argues that sexual violence is ultimately a cultural expression bolstered by power, inequalities, institutionalised sexism, and fruitful techniques of neutralisation (1983; see also Whyte, this volume). For Box, '[T]he engine of rape is not to be found between a man's loins, but in his mind, and this in turn reflects cultural definitions of gender' (1983: 161). It is to these prevailing cultural constructs of gender, sexuality and violence that the chapter now turns.

Mystification Through Dominant 'Truths'

Box is primarily concerned with analysing the ways in which power relations mystify the violence, masculinity and criminality of rape. Mystification occurs through the intersection and culmination of 'sexist male culture', structural gendered inequalities, a legal system predicated on deep-rooted misogyny and various techniques of neutralisation, all of which form the 'roots of rape' (1983: 163). One contemporary approach is to view these roots of rape and the insidious ways in which they are able to normalise sexual violence as rape culture. Rape culture is understood as:

> a set of general cultural beliefs supporting men's violence against women, including the idea that this violence is a fact of life, that there is an association between violence and sexuality, that men are active while women are passive, and that men have a right to sexual intercourse. (Phipps et al. 2018: 1)

Phipps et al. (2018) urge us to be mindful of the populist energy of this type of concept and the tendency for over-generalisation in its applicability. However, for us here, rape culture is useful in an overarching sense to track and analyse a myriad of ways in which feminist praxis and theory has sought to account for the emission, operation and internalisation of cultural messages and societal norms around what Box (1983: 146) refers to as the 'permissibility of rape'.

Box (1983: 153) states that 'our sexist culture is replete with a library of accounts [...] and techniques of neutralisation [...] which enable the potential rapist to proceed without feeling inhibited by guilt' and, as we will argue, also enables the guilt to be deflected away from the rapist by institutions and deeply ingrained popular and political attitudes more broadly. This mystification occurs, it is suggested, by redescribing the reality of consent, desire, motives and blame of the rapist *and* the victim.

Box is keen to dispel arguments around victim-precipitated rape and his recognition of agency is important following years of feminist praxis. He is clear that our attention should lie with 'the man who *chooses* to rape ... and beyond him, the broader macro-sociological factors which form the context in which that choice is made' (ibid.: 135, emphasis added). One of the ingredients that binds together the subjective and structural elements of rape, as well as the discursive elements, is the construction of masculinity. 'Rape is primarily committed by men…who are relatively more attached and identified with notions of 'manliness' and feel the need to demonstrate this essentializing view of themselves whenever they experience some identity doubts or anxieties' (ibid.: 161). Here, Box is arguing that we examine the maleness of rape itself.

Prevailing cultural messages about what it means to be a real man—virile, aggressive, predatory, tough—identified by Box in 1983, and central to feminist work since, are fundamental to tackling the seemingly intractable problem of sexual violence. But these elements of sexist culture cannot be divorced from the operation of power which sustain and reproduce them. It is important that we understand that these discursive constructions—in a binary sense, the predatory nature of masculinity and by extension the passive nature of femininity—do not tell us what is true but rather what is *accepted* as truth. As such, it is the disciplinary power of these dominant discourses upon which much critical scholarship has tended to focus (Collier 2017; Howe 2008). It is the dominant cultural scripts which fuel the process of mystification and produce plausible and customary narratives on sexual violence. It is precisely because these scripts pass as truth, that they are 'difficult to discern, identify and subvert' (Alcoff 2018: 3).

Box was right, therefore, to argue that we examine the maleness of rape and to do this effectively we must examine power as it relates to men and masculinities and to the 'internal and external forces that complicate the entrenching and constraint of this power' (Collier 2017: 45). Kate Manne (2018) outlines the complexities of misogyny and the ways in which systems of power are able to work together on a 'punishment and reward' arrangement. This is well documented in terms of the policing of women's behaviour and the punishment of 'disorderly' women and, to a lesser extent, the valorisation of women who do conform and the part they often play in sustaining victim-blaming narratives (Manne 2018: 192). The punishment and policing of men who fail to reach or live by the culturally prescribed norms of masculinity are also well-versed. Conceptually often referred to as hegemonic masculinity, this desired form of masculinity separated itself from subordinated masculinities and took on a normative status (Connell and Messerschmidt 2005). Indeed, hegemonic masculinity 'embodied the currently most honoured way of being a man, it required all other men to position themselves in relation to it, and it ideologically legitimated the global subordination of women to men' (ibid.: 832). The operation of hegemonic masculinity is constraining and oppressive for both men and women; and lies at the heart of how we understand sexual violence.

What is less drawn out from this analysis of masculinity, and what is important in relation to the truly epidemic proportions of rape and sexual violence, is the '*positive* and *exonerating* attitudes and practices of which the men who dominate women tend to be the beneficiaries' (Manne 2018: 193; emphasis in the original). Box includes these attitudes in his overall analysis of 'techniques of neutralisation' (Box 1983: 163; see also Whyte, this volume), in terms of the various ways in which we, as a society, remove culpability and responsibility from men's violence against women. 'These techniques of neutralization are not private constructions thought up by rapists. They are part of our cultural repertoire for evading personal responsibility' (ibid.: 157). These techniques of neutralisation include denial of the victim, of harm, of intention or of criminally culpable behaviour, and they continue to underscore how we are encouraged to view rape and sexual violence. For example, one of two former police officers, convicted in 2022 of sharing racist, sexist, misogynistic messages about rape and sexual assault, as well as other deeply offensive material, in a WhatsApp group that also included Wayne Couzens, the convicted rapist and murderer of Sarah Everard, stated that the messages were merely 'jokes' and that any insinuation of harm or upset resulting from them was 'ridiculous' (Cunliffe 2022). This is a well-trodden path for neutralising the impact of sexual violence.

What underlines many of these techniques and enables them to persist with such ferocity is the discursive framing of men's and women's sexuality. The cultural construction of men's sexuality has remained depressingly familiar since Box described it as 'overpowering' and driven by 'biologically determined sexual urges' in 1983 (Box 1983: 153). The framing of men's sexuality in 'natural', uncontrollable terms—urgent, insatiable, potent, and instinctual—is important for the consideration of rape and sexual violation and the social context, which surrounds it. The 'real' man, Box perceptively argued, must dominate his partner or prey by making recourse to 'charm, connivance, or cunning, and if these fail, by coercion' (1983: 145). A culture of (hegemonic) masculinity, an internalised cultural code about appropriate forms of masculinity revolved around the importance of being virile and utilising any means possible to be demonstrably sexually active and aggressive, again, underpins the permissibility of rape. This belief is compounded by another cultural distortion around rape and sexuality, namely that to be dominated, persuaded or even coerced into sexual activity is 'what "real" women really want' too (ibid.: 146). This myth has endless repercussions for women's safety. For example, a survey of public attitudes to rape and sexual violence found that a third of men think that even if a woman has not explicitly consented to sex, it is not rape if she has previously flirted on a date (EVAW 2018). Similarly, almost a quarter (24%) of those asked believed that it is not rape if non-consensual sex occurs in marriage or a long-term relationship (ibid.).

The need to understand women's sexuality, for themselves and for men, is rooted in the apparently 'problematic nature of female sexuality (which contrasts with the virile straightforwardness of male sexuality)' (Smart 1989: 29). Men are taught to portray themselves through sexuality whereas women are taught to submit to the demands of male sexuality. As such, women become the gatekeepers of sexuality; to be passive, submissive, and responsive to sexual advances but also to manage the barometer of these encounters so as not to be too alluring, or encouraging of the insatiable, instinctive, sexual, male drive. These restrictive and punitive discourses about women's sexuality, not only responsibilise women for men's sexuality, but limit their ability to pursue their own desires. A woman's 'desire disqualifies her from protection, and from justice. Once a woman is thought to have said yes to something, she can say no to nothing' (Angel 2021: 4). As Box states, 'the alleged masculine sexual burden become[s] the victim's strict responsibility' (1983: 149). The conflicting expectations placed upon women as the gatekeepers of sexuality identified by Box persist in a nuanced and contemporary way.

The collision of sex, violence and power has been further normalised in the twenty-first century. There is a culture-wide obligation for young women to embrace an ostensibly progressive view which sees a degree of violence as sexy and desired sexuality as violent (Savigny 2020). This dominant construction has further normalised violence against women during sex and has resulted in women being sexually assaulted during otherwise consensual sex (Harte 2019). These acts of assault include being choked, slapped, gagged and spat on. At times, this 'rough' sex results in death. Popularised via the term 'sex games gone wrong', a specific defence to murder which claims that a person consented to the violent acts inflicted upon them and that death was, therefore, a possibility (Yardley 2020). The utilisation of cultural codes to establish a regime of truth around sex in contemporary society further exemplifies a reinscription of Box's techniques of neutralisation; that is, in this example, women get exactly what they have asked for—rough sex and strangulation—erasing guilt, a victim, and, at times, culpability. As Gavey (2005) argues, and as is explored in the next section of this chapter, consent can be given through a lens of reluctance, avoidance, discord or submission. Coercive sexuality, as noted by Box and as central to our and other feminist understandings of sexual violation, *is* normal sexuality.

Mystification Through the Limits of Consent

Opening the chapter on rape and sexual assaults on females, Box (1983: 121) argues that '"normal" sexual encounters merge imperceptibly into sexual assaults of which rape is the most serious, and [...] the former provides the just ingredients out of which the latter can emerge'. Within this argument, there are three key points which have been addressed by feminist scholars, activists and agencies. Firstly, the suggestion that rape is the worst form of sexual violence that can be experienced. Secondly, that the distinction between what is often considered a 'normal' sexual encounter and sexual violence is not quite as clear as the law, criminal justice system and dominant discourse would have us believe. Finally, that many behaviours widely understood as 'normal' sexual encounters, in fact, provide the context, and arguably the justification, for the normalisation of sexual violence. It is these points which this section seeks to address and, following developments in feminist poststructuralist work, where we outline the harm of sexual violence as a violation of subjectivity.

Although this is not a key argument in the chapter, rather a passing comment, the point Box makes, that rape is the most serious form of sexual assault is taken for granted. Decades of feminist work has now highlighted, however, that experiences of sexual violence are interconnected and that a scale on which to place experiences from least to most serious is lacking in its ability to accurately reflect the multiple and often repeated forms of violence women experience and the harms which stem from these. In her seminal text *Surviving Sexual Violence*, Kelly (1988: 76) utilised the concept of a continuum to highlight the 'basic common character that underlies many different events [and] ... a continuous series of elements or events that pass into one another and which cannot be readily distinguished'. Kelly (1988: 76) argues that 'clearly defined and discrete analytic categories', which Box also used, are not useful for explaining sexual violence, nor is a 'hierarchy of abuse' (ibid.) which denotes the seriousness of different forms of violence. She demonstrates that reactions to, and the consequences of, sexual violence, at the point of the incident and over time, depend on a multitude of factors which cannot be inferred from the type of sexual violence experienced, nor can they be separated out from other experiences of violence. Whilst it may be true for many that 'coitus with a stranger holding a gun or a knife to the victim's head is not the same as seduction-turned-into-rape between fairly intimate acquaintances where the "weapon" is persistent verbal pressure and threatened withdrawal of affection' (Box 1983: 126), this misses the point that everyone experiences violence differently, and that coercion is as problematic as physical force. Box falls into the trap of maintaining the elevation of the law's 'truth', that rape involving direct physical violence, weapons and strangers should be taken most seriously, and this is at the expense and relegation of knowledge predicated on women's experience. Although Box clearly argues that rape should be conceptualised more broadly than legal definitions at the time allowed, by drawing distinctions between different types of rape based on perceived 'seriousness', where the presence of direct physical violence, or not, is always key to this distinction, he elevates the law's ability to define in and define out incidents deemed to be harmful cases of sexual violence.

Box discusses the ways in which behaviours deemed 'normal' sexual encounters merge into those considered sexual violence. In addressing this point, he argues that the law excludes some behaviours, and deems them legal, which are similar to those it judges to be illegal. Although Box was writing at a different time, and rape law has changed since the book's publication, much of his critique remains relevant today.

He rightly takes issue with the notion of consent itself and its use as the standard which determines whether rape has taken place, or not. Whilst, as noted above, the law in relation to consent has changed since his chapter was written, the issue of 'reasonableness' remains, that is, whether there is a reasonable belief that someone consents (*Sexual Offences Act*, 2003). As the law concentrates on uncovering whether a victim consented or not, the result is a focus only on rape as a result of direct physical or threatened violence. For Box (1983: 123), 'by making lack of consent the distinguishing feature of rape, the law misses an obvious point. It is not so much the absence of consent, although that has to exist, but the presence of coercion which makes rape fundamentally different from normal acts of sexual intercourse'. The law, he argues, is only able to account for submission under physical coercion, resulting in the omission of 'submission under threats of all types' (ibid.). Returning to Box's original point, the law excludes behaviours which are similar to those it includes and, ultimately, we see the merging of normal sexual encounters and sexual assaults.

These points have again been addressed by feminist scholars since the book's publication, focusing on the limitations of the notion of consent. For Cahill (2001: 171):

> Liberal theories of rape depend on a certain understanding of consent that demands it be freely given, that is, that the alternatives to the encounter in question are not so seriously inconvenient or harmful so as to be virtually unthinkable. Yet this conceptualisation of consent, when taken against political and social structures that seriously limit women's agency and autonomy under many circumstances, proves problematic.

Taking into consideration the gendered, heterosexed discourses discussed in this chapter and in the work of Box, in which men are required to be sexually aggressive and where women secretly yearn to be dominated, the concept of 'reasonableness', a focus in the law and in everyday speech, becomes an issue. As Pateman (1980, cited in Cahill 2001: 173, emphasis in the original) highlights,

> at present it is widely believed that a woman's "no" does *not* constitute a refusal, that it *is* "reasonable" for men to put a lesser or greater degree of pressure on unwilling women in sexual matters, and that it *is* "reasonable" for consent to be inferred from enforced submission.

Such discourses contribute to what Gavey (2005: 3) terms 'the cultural scaffolding of rape'. This cultural scaffolding, it is argued, sets up the preconditions for rape and, taking these discourses into consideration, it becomes clear that an ungendered discourse of consent fails in its ability to conceptualise consent which is freely given.

Gavey (2005: 136) explores the experiences between 'what we might call mutually consenting sex, on the one hand, and rape or sexual coercion on the other'. That is, experiences in which women felt pressured into sex, felt unable to resist, acquiesced, and situations where women ended up having unwanted sex although often without direct force being used. If we conceptualise consent as a scripted, gendered interaction, premised on men's sexual entitlement and women's roles as sexual gatekeepers (Faustino and Gavey 2022), then the ability of women to say no to unwanted sex is constrained within these cultural scripts. For Olufemi (2020: 96) '[t]he happy face of consent' fails because it does not recognise the power relations entangled in sexual encounters. She argues that when consent is understood because of the negotiation of power relations, 'our "yeses" and "no's" do not carry the same weight' (ibid.: 99).

Fundamental to the notion of consent is the requirement to speak out about what you want. Angel (2021: 5) discusses this and questions how women 'can know what we want, when knowing what we want is both something demanded of us and used as a source of punishment?'. For example, footballer Ched Evans had his conviction of guilt overturned following the introduction of sexual history evidence of the alleged victim. Such evidence, in this case, was that during previous consensual sex with other men, 'she liked to have sex "doggie style" and used the phrase "go harder" while having drunken, but consensual, relations with them' (Kale 2016). Furthermore, for women to be able to speak out about what they want, they must also know what it is they want (Angel 2021), which proves difficult in a context where gendered discourses limit the subjective positions available for women to realise their desires. The requirement to speak their sexual desires then, means women must negotiate their way through a tangled web of gendered discourses and cultural expectations which are further restricted by the fact that not everyone's speech is granted the same level of credibility (Code 1995).

Succinctly, Alcoff (2018: 128) argues that consent 'provides a low bar for sexual agency' and we should move away from a singular focus on the concept of consent as a valid way to indicate whether sexual violation has, or has not, occurred. When experiences of sexual violence do not always conform to a simplistic notion of non-consent, but can be understood as violations, intrusions, a result of coercion or something which is unwanted, a clearer understanding of the 'wrong' of sexual violence, is required. From our own perspective, key questions should address what violation we are addressing when we seek to understand the experience of rape and work out ways to challenge its prevalence. How can we understand the violence of subjectivity? How does this violence, and its mystification by state institutions and media outlets, which implicitly and explicitly legitimate it by their actions and non-actions, maintain the gendered social order?

Feminist work in this area, particularly from a poststructuralist perspective, has developed an understanding which recognises the short and long-term harmful and traumatic effects of sexual violence on an individual's sense of self, and subjective functioning, such as the impact on their physical and emotional health, their social, financial, employment and educational lives and, broadly, how an individual negotiates the world following sexual violence.

The discourses and processes of mystification discussed by Box can also be seen to limit the ways in which we understand sexual violence and the legitimate subject positions women can have when it comes to sex, desire and consent. Within this already constrained context, sexual violence can be understood as a violation of subjectivity, a violation which has transformative effects. For Alcoff (2018: 110):

> Sexual violation transforms us. Both victims and perpetrators are transformed, as well as their families, friends and social circles. Just the knowledge that such events are real possibilities in one's life, however remote, has an impact on those who have had no direct experience of them.

Cahill (2001) develops the argument about rape as a gendered, embodied experience, one which has enduring effects, extending beyond the temporal limits of the act of violence itself. She states, 'the social death a rape can impose can qualitatively transform the victim's being' (ibid.: 179) and that an understanding of sexual violence as an embodied experience helps us to see the ways in which women respond to sexual violence and the effects of these experiences on their subjective functioning. Beyond the often traumatic experience of the act itself, there are a range of harms which can potentially follow. One way of conceptualising the multitude of harms which follow an experience of sexual violence is what Bufacchi and Gilson (2016: 32) term 'the ripples of the same act of violence'. These ripples develop and change over time with broader and less clear boundaries than the act itself. Rape and sexual violence more broadly, therefore, should be understood as an *experience*, rather than an act, which is temporally indeterminate, with deeply traumatising and devastating, rippling effects on a person's subjective functioning.

The effects of the prevalence of sexual violence are often that a person will place restrictions on their own behaviour following an experience of, or in anticipation of, violence—such as not walking alone at night, not drinking alcohol, and other well-rehearsed measures women undertake with the hope of avoiding sexual violence (Vera-Gray 2018). This means violence can be seen as productive, in that it alters and reconstitutes a victim's subjectivity. Through a poststructuralist lens, whereby rape is understood as a violation of subjectivity, there is no distinct self that exists separately to the traumatic experience (Cahill 2001). As the survivor of Brock Turner's sexual violence stated, 'my damage was internal, unseen, I carry it with me. You took away my worth, my privacy, my energy, my time, my safety, my intimacy, my confidence [...] I am a human being who has been irreversibly hurt' (Buncombe, n.d.). The notion that there is one event and a defined number of harms which the victim needs to transcend in order to return to herself is insufficient in explaining the ways in which sexual violence alters a person and their position in the world.

Through focusing on the consequences of sexual violation, Alcoff (2018: 110) argues that the distinct harm is a violation of sexual subjectivity, specifically our capacity for sexual agency which encompasses but is not limited to consent, desire, pleasure and will. She points out that sexual violation 'severely constricts the possibilities for [...] self-directed sexual formation' (ibid.: 112). Of course, heterosexed, gendered, raced, classed and disablist discourses also limit the accepted subject positions available for people, whether that relates to sexual violence or not. As

Alcoff (2018) notes, sexual violence should not be viewed as separate from sexuality and the ways in which it has been constructed. The everyday, taken-for-granted forms of heterosexuality (Gavey 2005) regulate our conceptualisation of what counts as sex and sexual violence and restrict our agency.

Through a feminist poststructuralist lens, we can better understand the ways in which sexual violence is a violation of subjectivity, which changes a person's relation to themself. As Alcoff (2018: 120) argues though, 'it is not only the rape that changes her relationship to herself, but the social context that protects rapists'. The following section, therefore, highlights the role of institutions in this violation of subjectivity and the ways in which the law acts as a permitting force, an argument made persuasively by Box.

Institutional Mystification and the Limits of the Law

Box argues that rape and sexual assault are mystified in a plethora of ways. For him (1983: 157) 'men are assisted considerably' in this process 'by the criminal justice system and the media's dramatic representation of rape cases'. This takes many forms, with justice denied because the accused is portrayed as 'sex starved', 'drunk', 'provoked' or 'too enthusiastic' (ibid.: 158). Overlapping with this, the law protects only certain types of women, that is, those who conform to the ways in which women are taught to be, in line with the social construction of femininity and insidious gendered ideals. Those women who deviate from these ideals do not receive the same purported protection from the law (Chadwick and Little 1987; Smart 1995a).

Since the publication of *Power, Crime and Mystification* (1983), understanding of the ways in which appropriate forms of femininity are modified and shaped by other colluding forms of oppression and privilege, such as, but not limited to, race, ethnicity, class, sexuality and ability/disability has developed. It is vital to make these intersectional connections across processes of victimisation and criminalisation, to understand the specific ways in which these complex regimes of inequality impact upon hierarchies of power and gendered experiences, expectations and responses (Walby 2009; Yuval-Davis 2006). For example, rape laws are intended to protect us all, but they do not protect us equally. They are part of a broader apparatus of categorising who has and has not '... communicated through their behaviour and commitments (to men and children) that they recognize their place in the established order of things' (Box 1983: 158). In this highly gendered social order, women do not know or own their own sexuality and they are constrained and punished by the ways in which the law, and the state, more broadly, are able not only to reflect appropriate forms of femininity and sexuality but also to reproduce them (Smart 1995b).

Box (1983) also outlines the role of the media in maintaining and replicating this distinction between 'good' and 'bad' women, worthy, or not, of state 'protection'. In this way, the media, alongside the law and the state, are able to set and reset the discursive parameters of acceptable behaviour and appropriate forms of femininity. These parameters impact significantly on public awareness around sexual violence. Since the book's publication, we have seen the development and impact of social media, and its grip on the discursive climate in which we talk about and understand sexual violence (Gash and Harding 2018), as well as being a medium for the perpetration of sexual violence (Huber 2023). Reporting rates have increased notably since Box published *Power, Crime and Mystification* in 1983, but traumatic and triggering experiences of the criminal justice system, including the dissection of character, appearance, choices and relationships, low conviction rates, pitiful sentencing patterns and a concentration on sensational cases, persist. The message to potential rapists remains clear, 'this is a type of crime for which there is a very low rate of being convicted and imprisoned' (Box 1983: 159).

Feminist scholarship, and grassroots organisations, have built on the evidence and ideas presented since the publication of Box's work on the way in which the legal system, and state more broadly, functions in part to maintain the gendered social order by reinscribing ideal gendered subjectivities. For many, the issues relate to discourse and our wider cultural beliefs about gender, sexuality and, by extension, sexual violence. It is this line of thinking which has led to some significant developments in understanding and challenging the exercise of law's power and this work suggests we should do more than problematise Box's interpretation of the law as an 'unwitting' contributor to the mystification of rape (ibid.: 157). Law plays a central role in how rape is constructed and understood. It plays a significant part, therefore, in the overall 'cultural expression' of rape (ibid.: 161).

Smart (1989: 162) argued that the law, as discourse, can 'refute and disregard alternative discourses and claim a special place in the definition of events'. She maintained that the law has a claim to truth in that it sets itself outside of the social order, 'as if through the application of legal method and rigour, it becomes a thing apart which in turn can reflect on the work from which it is divorced' (ibid.: 11). In this sense, the law is a gendering strategy, (re)producing a series of 'truths' about rape, whilst also disqualifying alternative, supposedly inferior, knowledges (ibid.). Whilst the law has historically established these 'truths', feminists have contested them, instead exposing them as stereotypes and myths which both deny women's experiences and 'refuse women the status as truth-tellers' (Serisier 2018: 71). As a gendering strategy, the ways in which the law operates to produce a 'truth' about sexual violence is clear. Through the deployment of gendered discourses on women's bodies and sexuality, medical discourses on the 'typical' bodily signs of rape (Lees 1997) and a standard of how the 'reasonable woman' would respond if she did not consent to sex (Ussher 1997), the realities of women's actual experiences of sexual violence are mystified. As Smart contends, these are the mechanisms through which the 'law consistently fails to "understand" accounts of rape which do not fit within the narrowly constructed legal definition' (1989: 26).

Of further importance, is the law's discursive framing of 'real' rapists, as monsters or predators, and as someone who would be clearly distinguishable from non-rapists (Manne 2018). This discursive framing has effects, particularly in relation to reporting and speaking out about incidents. As Brison (2014) discussed, the myth that only those who are inhumane, rape, generates a political and popular common sense around rape, which can lead to a disbelief of those who experience sexual violence at the hands of people known to the victim. As these discourses do persist, there are effects on the numbers and types of cases which are deemed truthful and ultimately, 'by scapegoating "the few" as rapists, the law legitimates "the many" as normal' (Jeffreys and Radford 1984: 160). Through claims to truth, the law has the power to disqualify women's experiences of sexual violence (Howe 2008). The law, therefore, needs to be understood as a site of struggle, not simply an unwitting contributor to the mystification of sexual violence, due to its participation in constructing meaning and subjectivities (Smart 1995a). What we must also be mindful of, as Box argues, is that 'the majority of rapists…are not touched directly by the actual operation of the law' (1983: 161). As such, we cannot rely either on the law, or state institutions, despite the contradictions within and between them, as a solution to sexual violence.

Box ends the book with the question, '[A]nd justice for all?' (Box 1983: 219). His vision is one which challenges law and order policy and campaigns as a means to justice as, for him, this often does not reflect the interests of those harmed and instead reinforces and legitimises state punishment. As Box outlined, and as feminist scholarship and activism has shown us in the period since the book's publication, the extension of this power to punish excludes the most marginalised people from access to this limited conceptualisation of justice and reproduces the harms that are supposed to be repaired (Olufemi 2020; Richie 2012). In relation to sexual violence, justice for survivors relates to 'consequences, recognition, dignity, voice, prevention and connectedness' (McGlynn and Westmarland 2019: 179). Justice is not incident based but should instead be understood 'an ever-evolving, nuanced, lived experience' (ibid.). Responses therefore should be built on this knowledge, moving away from a singular focus on punishment through the means of criminal 'justice'.

Following the developments in feminist poststructuralist work in conceptualising the nature and harms of sexual violence, striving for justice would mean expanding the discourse of justice to not only reflect the broader range of harms to subjectivity, but also the harms which stem from engagement with the criminal justice system. Specifically, challenging law's grasp on defining what is, and is not, considered harmful and who, and who is not, understood as a victim or perpetrator is crucial. Ultimately though, to challenge law's exercise in power, it is vital to expand and produce new discourses which challenge the current gendered social order beyond the legal system.

Conclusion

To use rape and sexual assault to highlight the process of mystification was a radical move by Box in 1983. Drawing our attention to the coordinated and surreptitious ways in which sexual violence is concealed, justified and, at times, encouraged, was a powerful statement amongst the scholarship of critical criminology at the time. The inclusion of rape and sexual assault as an example of 'crime' as an ideological construct and as a social control strategy in a collection by a male criminologist, alongside chapters on corporate crime and police crime, with a focus on power and how power is exercised over people, was a progressive step and one which undoubtedly had far reaching implications for centralising the gendered nature of sexual violence in critical criminology and academia.

In this chapter we have argued that many of the central arguments made by Box hold contemporary value and have been both extended and refined by four decades of critical and feminist thought. Ultimately, the mystification of sexual violence continues unabated despite relentless challenge from counter discourses and radical sites of resistance. We continue to problematise the taken-for-granted ideas about sex, sexuality and interpersonal relationships which take hold on subjective, discursive and structural levels but we reach the same broad conclusion that Box did. For agents of the state, broadly conceived, there is 'no way' to 'treat men's violence as a serious crime without undermining the social order it serves so well' (Hanmer et al. 1989: 11). Processes of mystification obscure our view of rape and sexual assault, hindering the fight for women to live a life of freedom and safety in exceptional ways, some of which we have outlined above.

What we believe to be of central importance to the maintenance of the gendered social order via sexual violence is the culturally accepted, 'commonsense' and conventional ideas about gendered identities, heterosexuality and interpersonal relationships. In this chapter, we have outlined the importance of Box's analysis of sexual violence which focuses on the role of the state from a materialist perspective in not responding adequately to the issue. We have also suggested though, that his analysis can be extended through focusing on the operation of harmful and restrictive discourses, from a poststructuralist feminist analysis, which are (re)produced by institutions of the state but are also inherently connected to the broader gendered discourses which shape women's lives outside of the legal arena. By making these connections, and by focusing on discourses outside of the realm of the state, as well as within, we can further understand sexual violence experienced by those who have not necessarily interacted with the criminal justice system, or who have not been harmed in line with restrictive legal definitions. To tackle these discourses and their effects would mean to dismantle normative forms of masculinity and femininity which are ingrained in, and exercised by, all aspects of our society. Whilst this task can seem insurmountable, we have argued that an approach to sexual violence which centralises discourse and works with the complexities of cultural ways of life, can best demand change. As Cahill (2019: 290) argues:

> The anti-rape movement needs to be undergirded with a recognition of the ways in which all discourses that surround and construct the phenomenon of sexual violence – overlapping, intersecting discourses about sex, agency, narrative, race, the self, gender, and so on – shape it into the particular phenomenon that it currently is. Any conceptual or rhetorical approach that assumes a givenness to rape beyond its discursive particularity will by definition miss the mark.

References

Alcoff, L.M. 2018. *Rape and Resistance*. Cambridge: Polity Press.
Angel, K. 2021. *Tomorrow Sex Will Be Good Again*. London: Verso.
Box, S. 1983. *Power, Crime and Mystification*. London: Tavistock.
Brison, S. 2014. Why I Spoke Out About One Rape but Stayed Silent About Another. *Time*, September 19. https://time.com/3612283/why-i-spoke-out-about-one-rape-but-stayed-silent-about-another/. Accessed 19 Sept 2022.
Bufacchi, V., and J. Gilson. 2016. The Ripples of Violence. *Feminist Review* 112 (1): 27–40.
Buncombe, A. n.d. Stanford Rape Case: Read the Impact Statement of Brock Turner's Victim. *Independent*. https://www.independent.co.uk/news/people/stanford-rape-case-read-the-impact-statement-of-brock-turner-s-victim-a7222371.html. Accessed 23 Sept 2022.

Cahill, A. 2001. *Rethinking Rape*. New York: Cornell University Press.
Cahill, A. 2019. Alcoff's *Rape and Resistance*: A Précis. *Philosophical Studies* 177 (2): 289–296.
Chadwick, K., and C. Little. 1987. The Criminalization of Women. In *Law, Order and the Authoritarian State*, ed. P. Scraton, 254–278. Milton Keynes: Open University Press.
Code, L. 1995. *Rhetorical Spaces*. London: Routledge.
Collier, R. 2017. Redressing the Balance? Masculinities, Law and Criminology—Rethinking the 'Man Question'—Forty Years On. In *Women, Crime and Criminology: A Celebration*, ed. H. Monk and J. Sim, 23–56. Centre for the Study of Crime: Criminalisation and Social Exclusion and EG Press Ltd.
Connell, R.W., and J.W. Messerschmidt. 2005. Hegemonic Masculinity: Rethinking the Concept. *Gender and Society* 19 (6): 829–859.
Cunliffe, R. 2022. The Metropolitan Police is a Danger to Women: How Can This Institution Protect Us? *The New Statesman*. https://www.newstatesman.com/quickfire/2022/09/the-metropolitan-police-is-a-danger-to-women. Accessed 22 Sept 2022.
End Violence Against Women (EVAW). 2018. *Attitudes to Sexual Consent: Research for the End Violence Against Women Coalition by YouGov*. End Violence Against Women Coalition. https://www.endviolenceagainstwomen.org.uk/wp-content/uploads/2018/12/1-Attitudes-to-sexual-consent-Research-findings-FINAL-1.pdf. Accessed 7 Aug 2022.
End Violence Against Women (EVAW). n.d. *Rape Justice Now*. London: End Violence Against Women Coalition. https://www.endviolenceagainstwomen.org.uk/campaign/rape-justice-now/. Accessed 14 Aug 2022.
Faustino, M.J., and N. Gavey. 2022. The Failed Promise of Sexual Consent in Women's Experiences of Coercive and Unwanted Anal Sex with Men. *Is Consent Good for Women? A Feminist Symposium on Consent Culture*. Birkbeck College, University of London, June 17.
Foucault, M. 1995. *Discipline and Punish*. New York: Random House Inc.
Gash, A., and R. Harding. 2018. #MeToo? Legal Discourse and Everyday Responses to Sexual Violence. *Laws* 7 (21): 1–24.
Gavey, N. 1989. Feminist Poststructuralism and Discourse Analysis. *Psychology of Women Quarterly* 13: 459–475.
Gavey, N. 2005. *Just Sex? The Cultural Scaffolding of Rape*. East Sussex: Routledge.
Hanmer, J., J. Radford, and E. Stanko, eds. 1989. *Women, Policing and Male Violence: International Perspectives*. London: Routledge.

Harte, A. 2019. A Man Tried to Choke Me During Sex Without Warning. *BBC News*, November 28. https://www.bbc.co.uk/news/uk-50546184. Accessed 22 Sept 2022.

Howe, A. 2008. *Sex, Violence and Crime: Foucault and the 'Man; Question*. Oxon: Routledge Cavendish.

Huber, A. 2023. 'A Shadow of Me Old Self': The Impact of Image-Based Sexual Abuse in a Digital Society. *International Review of Victimology* 29 (2): 199–216.

Jeffreys, S., and J. Radford. 1984. Contributory Negligence or Being a Woman? The Car Rapist Case. In *Causes for Concern*, ed. P. Scraton and P. Gordon, 154–183. Middlesex: Penguin Books.

Kale, S. 2016. How and Athlete Used His Alleged Victim's Sexual History in His Rape Acquittal. *Vice*, October 17. https://www.vice.com/en/article/wje8xy/how-ched-evans-use-alleged-victim-sexual-history-rape-conviction. Accessed 23 Sept 2022.

Kelly, L. 1988. *Surviving Sexual Violence*. Minneapolis: University of Minnesota Press.

Lees, S. 1997. *Ruling Passions: Sexual Violence, Reputation and the Law*. Buckingham: Open University Press.

Manne, K. 2018. *Down Girl: The Logic of Misogyny*. UK: Penguin Random House.

McGlynn, C., and N. Westmarland. 2019. Kaleidoscopic Justice: Sexual Violence and Victim-Survivors' Perceptions of Justice. *Social and Legal Studies* 28 (2): 179–201.

Olufemi, L. 2020. *Feminism Interrupted*. London: Pluto Press.

Phipps, A., J. Ringrose, E. Renold, and C. Jackson. 2018. Rape Culture, Lad Culture, and Everyday Sexism: Researching, Conceptualizing and Politicizing New Mediations of Gender and Sexual Violence. *Journal of Gender Studies* 27 (1): 1–8.

Richie, B. 2012. *Arrested Justice: Black Women, Violence and America's Prison Nation*. New York: New York University Press.

Savigny, H. 2020. *Cultural Sexism: The Politics of Feminist Rage in the #MeToo Era*. Bristol: Bristol University Press.

Serisier, T. 2018. *Speaking Out: Feminism, Rape and Narrative Politics*. London: Springer.

Smart, C. 1989. *Feminism and the Power of Law*. London: Routledge.

Smart, C. 1995a. *Law, Crime and Sexuality*. London: Sage.

Smart, C. 1995b. Law's Power, the Sexed Body and Feminist Discourse. In *Law, Crime and Sexuality*, ed. C. Smart, 70–87. London: Sage.

Syal, R. 2022. Labour Pledges to Place Specialists in 999 Call Centres to Help Rape Victims. *The Guardian*, September 26. https://www.theguardian.com/society/2022/sep/26/labour-pledges-specialists-999-call-centres-help-rape-victims. Accessed 13 Nov 2022.

Ussher, J. 1997. *Fantasies of Femininity: Reframing the Boundaries of Sex*. London: Penguin Books.

Vera-Gray, F. 2018. *The Right Amount of Panic: How Women Trade Freedom for Safety*. Bristol: Policy Press.

Walby, S. 2009. *Globalisation and Inequalities*. London: Sage.

Yardley, E. 2020. The Killing of Women in "Sex Games Gone Wrong": An Analysis of Femicides in Great Britain 2000–2018. *Violence Against Women* 27 (11): 1840–1861.

Yuval-Davis, N. 2006. Intersectionality and Feminist Politics. *European Journal of Women's Studies* 13 (3): 193–209.

14

'Rape Kills the Soul': The Use of Sexual Violence by State and non-State Actors in War and Conflict

Brenda Fitzpatrick

Introduction

It has probably become more dangerous to be a woman than a soldier in an armed conflict. (Cammaert, UNSC/9364, 19 June 2008)

In 1983, Steven Box made the link between rape and power in Chapter 4 of his book, *Power, Crime and Mystification* [*PCM*]. He wrote about how powerbrokers, their agencies, analysts and policymakers mystify and deflect attention away from the real impact of crimes and those who should be held accountable for them. Such mystification applies particularly to rape and sexual violence in war and conflict. These are crimes that have been perpetrated over millennia but never really acknowledged in International Humanitarian Law. Secrecy was

---

Nowrojee (2005: 1)

B. Fitzpatrick (✉)
Care for Africa, Dar Es Salaam, Tanzania
e-mail: brenda.m.fitz@gmail.com

widespread. It went beyond just any one state. It was secrecy at a global level. International power brokers were complicit. Askin listed numerous historical examples (1999: 97–123). In The Hague Convention[1] only one article prohibited sexual violence and it described it as a violation of family honour. In the aftermath of World War Two, 723 pages of reports at the Nuremburg Trials, did not even index rape and the Tokyo War Crimes Trial, which included five supplementary indexes to 22 volumes, barely mentioned rape. The four Geneva Conventions specifically prohibit rape only once and two Additional Protocols include no mention of rape and just one sentence explicitly prohibits sexual violence. The United Nations (UN) *1974 Declaration on the Protection of Women and Children in Emergency and Armed Conflict* included no mention of rape. In 1983, there had been little change.

The failure to acknowledge the traumatising harm of rape in war was everywhere when Box was writing. As late as 1992 when asked about reports of widespread rape in the conflict in the former Yugoslavia, a local churchman in Zagreb agreed that 'of course' women were being raped and added, 'that's war' with accompanying shrugs (Fitzpatrick 1992: 21). The comments indicated the chilling acceptance and normalisation of rape in war and the failure to recognise the difference between a by-product of individual criminal behaviour and the widespread, systemic and state-sanctioned policy of rape occurring in Bosnia and Herzegovina. Some observers even dismissed the notion of rape as a 'weapon of war' as merely semantics designed to bring attention to what was 'just' a women's issue (Fitzpatrick 2016: 1).

Box's Analysis

Forty years after Box highlighted the impact of mystifying the reality of rape and sexual violence and the underlying power relations which protect perpetrators, elements of his analysis can be applied to the widespread rape and sexual violence used as weapons and tactics in

---

[1] The Hague Convention comprises a number of international treaties derived from a several international conferences held in the Netherlands from 1899 to 1907.

conflicts. Box saw the effect of inadequate or non-existent definitions contributing to crimes being buried. Definitions are 'no mere academic questions' (Box 1983: 121). This became obvious when, later, as discussed below, international judiciaries such as the *International Criminal Tribunal for the former Yugoslavia* (ICTY) and the *International Criminal Tribunal for Rwanda* (ICTR) had to confront the absence or inadequacy of definitions of rape in International Humanitarian Law (IHL). Just as Box had recognised that powerful perpetrators were going unpunished, so, too, did the ICTY and ICTR. In these conflicts, powerbrokers were attacking those who were vulnerable. The conflicts epitomised toxic power built into the hegemonic masculinity of patriarchy and the culture of masculine sex socialisation (Box 1983). Civilian populations, women and children, in particular, were made vulnerable by societies' attitudes and assumed values.

Box provided insights into coercion and consent highlighting that consent was often criminally misconstrued and assumed (ibid: 121–127). He urged the expansion of notions of accountability to include powerbrokers, noting that 'the possible clue to our understanding most serious crimes can be located in power, not weakness …' (ibid: 202). He decried that democracies as well as autocracies failed to meet their responsibilities to protect their people, especially women and girls, which reinforced the lack of accountability of corporations, police, judiciaries and powerbrokers (ibid: 201–202).

Understanding Tactical Rape

Towards the end of the twentieth century, global attention was at last drawn to the reality of rape and sexual violence in conflict. The conflicts in the former Yugoslavia and Rwanda in the 1990s and the rulings of The International Criminal Tribunal for the former Yugoslavia (ICTY) and United Nations International Criminal Tribunal for Rwanda (ICTR eventually led to resolution 1325 at the United Nations Security Council (UNSC) in 2000 (UN S/RES/1325, 31 October 2000). This was the beginning of formal recognition that tactical, strategic use of rape and sexual violence violates international law when perpetrated by state or non-state actors. It is a deliberate practice and the result of deliberate policies. It took even longer to accept that there were grounds for holding powerbrokers and perpetrators accountable. Change was a long time coming and it came slowly. But some change did come. It came with recognition of the changing nature of war itself. At the beginning of the twentieth century, 85–90% of conflict-related casualties were military. In the Second World War, approximately half of the casualties were civilians. By the late 1990s, approximately 80% of casualties were civilians. Warfare became gendered, avoiding battle between armed troops and instead controlling territory through strategies with serious impact on non-combatants (Kaldor 2001: 106).

Thirty years or so after Box's writing, this author used the term 'tactical rape' (Fitzpatrick 2016). This term encapsulated the key elements of a widespread policy namely the systemic use of rape by powerbrokers and attempts to confront the mystification of this egregious crime. I defined tactical rape as a strategy to attack those deemed to be enemies in conflicts which may be intra-or inter-state. It targets civilians, mostly but not exclusively women and girls (UN S/RES/2106, 24 June 2013). For this female majority of victims of tactical rape, gendered social, political, economic and physical inequity creates gendered vulnerability. This is a pervasive precondition for the effective use of tactical rape to control, destabilise and destroy the social fabric of civilian communities. It is a widespread, deliberate policy of attack, promoted or condoned by at least one party to a conflict. As will be seen below, the ICTY and ICTR showed that it may constitute a war crime, a crime against humanity, a weapon of genocide, torture or ethnic cleansing. It attacks individuals and communities. The ICTY Trial Chamber quoted testimony from a medical worker:

> The very act of rape, in my opinion – I spoke to these people, I observed their reactions – it had a terrible effect on them. They could, perhaps, explain it to themselves when somebody steals something from them or even beatings or even some killings. Somehow they sort of accepted it in some way, but when the rapes started they lost all hope. Until then they had hope that this war could pass, that everything would quiet down. When the rapes started, everybody lost hope, everybody in the camp,

men and women. There was such fear, horrible. (ICTY Trial Chamber, *Prosecutor v Tadic*: para. 175)

In 2005 Nowrojee quoted Major Brent Beardsley, a professional soldier and member of the UN peacekeeping force in Rwanda:

One, when they killed women it appeared that the blows that had killed them were aimed at sexual organs, either breasts or vagina; they had been deliberately swiped or slashed in those areas. And, secondly, there was a great deal of what we came to believe was rape, where the women's bodies or clothes would be ripped off their bodies, they would be lying back in a back position, their legs spread, especially in the case of very young girls. I'm talking girls as young as six, seven years of age, their vaginas would be split and swollen from obviously gang rape, and then they would be killed in that position. So they were lying in a position they had been raped; that's the position they were in. Rape was one of the hardest things to deal with in Rwanda on our part. It deeply affected every one of us. …amongst all of us the hardest thing that we had to deal with was not so much the bodies of people, the murder of people – I know that can sound bad, but that wasn't as bad to us as the rape and especially the systematic rape and gang rape of children. Massacres kill the body. Rape kills the soul. And there was a lot of rape. (Nowrojee 2005: 1)

Charlesworth and Chinkin (2000: 252) noted:

As well as the immediate degradation, pain and terror, rape survivors frequently experience long-term physical injury and psychological trauma. Fear and shock are also experienced by women who were not themselves subjected to attack.

There has been recognition of associated impacts on women raped in conflict: the risk of sexually transmitted disease and pregnancy; facing childbirth or abortion with reduced health care and intense social and cultural pressures, sometimes against abortion and sometimes against keeping a child conceived by rape. Physical damage may last long after an attack. Vulnerability can be exploited (ibid). Canning and Tombs highlighted socially generated, deliberate harms such as, 'those actions, omissions, policies, conditions, ways of doing things and dominant structures which contribute to the absence of or distortion in self-actualisation' (2021: 10). Expanding on this zemiological analysis, it is argued here that such a harmful outcome can also be generated through tactical rape.

Masculinity and Patriarchy

Hegemonic masculinity can be toxic. Box (1983) talked of the culture of masculinity, meeting a subculture of violence and the male expectations of physical, social and economic advantage. He linked such expectations to the powerful male belief that sex is a right (ibid). He refuted the idea that males have uncontrollable sex desires as one of the library of cultural excuses applied in judicial systems based on a deliberate misunderstanding of the responsibilities of male perpetrators of rape. He questioned simplified concepts which biologise what is essentially a social phenomenon and noted, 'masculine sex role socialisation is a precondition of rape because, first, it reduces women in men's minds to the status of sex-objects, and second, it instructs men to be the initiator of sexual encounters and to be prepared for strong, even if deceitful, resistance' (ibid: 146).

He concluded, 'each type of rape is primarily committed by men…who are relatively attached and identified with notions of "manliness" and feel the need to demonstrate this view of themselves whenever they experience some identity doubts or anxieties' (ibid: 161). Offering an explanation of such manliness and the relation to rape he quoted that 'for a man to have his exclusive sexual property defiled by an intruder is one of the worst things that can happen to him' (Clark and Lewis 1977, cited in ibid: 123). Women suffer when enemies use rape as a form of attack on males who 'own' women. There is an inherent power in gender inequality. Those with power ensure such inequality, promoting and accepting the values of patriarchy. Connell (2009: 141) noted that 'very large numbers of men stand to gain from current arrangements in terms of power, economic advantage, authority, peer respect, sexual access, and so on'. Not surprisingly they will defend that inequality.

As Box intimated, powerbrokers, including military leaders, can exploit notions of masculinity extolling male physical, economic and social supremacy to exploit the engendered vulnerability of women:

> In our culture, the idealization of femininity involves notions of passivity, dependence, submissiveness, and mindlessness; women are taught to need men, to be emotionally and economically dependent upon them, and to look to them for protection in a harsh brutal world of male predators (Box 1983: 148).

Nearly, 10 years after the publication of *PCM*, in 1992, the UN Committee monitoring the *Convention on the Elimination of all Forms of Discrimination Against Women* (CEDAW) formally noted traditional attitudes by which women are regarded as subordinate to men and stereotyped female roles that perpetuate widespread practices involving violence or coercion.

In 2006, the devastating impact of rape was noted by Mililllo:

> …the systematic nature of rape as a tactic of war exists against a backdrop of rigid cultural norms of gender and women's sexuality, social dominance and power within conflicting groups and a soldier's identity as a man and as a member of a particular military group (2006: 196).

In the aftermath of the conflict in the former Yugoslavia, 1992–1995, an eventual judicial response to tactical rape took into account that at least one accused had frequently told his victims that they would give birth to Serb babies. This reflected the patriarchal insistence that babies are always children of fathers (ICTY *Kunarac Indictment* 2001). The pain and suffering of rape victims are exacerbated by the sense of bearing babies of an enemy. This interferes with lines of heritage and cultural identity. For this reason, many pregnant women may be released from captivity. Impregnating a woman considered as belonging to another male is a warrior's act of masculine dominance over the woman and the man (Goldstein 2001: 362).

Box reflected on the relationship between masculinity and the exercise of patriarchal power when describing types of rape including sadistic, dominance and anger rape which can be seen in many conflicts. He concluded that it is essential to emphasise an offender's attachment to being 'manly' and his location within the distributive system of social rewards (1983: 161). While clear distinctions are not realistic it is helpful to consider the differences.

Sadistic rape involves sexuality and aggression becoming fused into violent, mutilating acts (ibid: 127). The Rwandan conflict in 1994 between the Hutu and Tutsi was one of the first conflicts where the use of widespread, tactical rape was recognised. Frequently, these rapes were sadistic. Evidence constantly emphasised attackers' desire to humiliate as well as physically wound. One young witness described being raped along with another sister by two men in the courtyard of their home after it was destroyed by Hutu neighbours and her brother and father had been killed. One of the men told her that the girls were spared so they could be raped; when her mother begged the men, who were armed with bludgeons and machetes, to kill her daughters rather than rape them in front of her, the man replied that the principle was to make them suffer. The girls were raped and on later examination in court the witness said that the man who raped her penetrated her vagina with his penis, saying he did it in an 'atrocious' manner, mocking and taunting them. She said her sister was raped by the other man at the same time, near her, so that they could each see what was happening to the other. Afterwards, she begged for death (ICTR *Prosecutor v Jean-Paul Akayesu* 1998: para. 430). These were rapes intended to inflict serious mental as well as bodily harm.

Box (1983: 150–152) highlighted that rape can express masculinity when a rapist is experiencing a sense of inadequacy, a lack of status. Exerting power over anyone, particularly over a woman perceived as an enemy, can be a means of countering such feelings of inadequacy and provide a strong motivation for rape. Dominating someone otherwise perceived as higher in status could be seen as a personal achievement. In Rwanda, domination rape was evident. Box (ibid: 127) defined this as rape driven by a need to demonstrate power over a victim. Stereotypes portrayed Tutsi women as arrogant, despising Hutu men and as weapons for use by Tutsi men against the Hutu. Comments by rapists were reported by Nowrojee (1996) as including: 'You Tutsi women think you are too good for us'; 'If there were peace you would never accept me'; 'You Tutsi girls are too proud'. Hutu men were warned that anyone who married, befriended or employed a Tutsi woman would be considered a traitor because the Tutsi would not hesitate to transform their sisters, wives and mothers into pistols to conquer Rwanda. 'Tutsi women were always viewed as enemies of the state', said one Tutsi woman: 'It led to a hate that I can't describe' (ibid: 13). Exerting power over Tutsi women helped counter a Hutu male's sense of inadequacy. This was further encouraged because if these were enemies of the state then rape was part of a 'legitimate' defence. Generalising that the Tutsi were responsible for all economic or political problems was a step towards believing that the defence of the State required dominating, even exterminating, all Tutsi. In 1994, the UN Special Rapporteur reported:

> false rumours and tracts designed to inflame ethnic hatred and encourage violence were constantly circulating in Rwanda with the Tutsi portrayed as serious threats to the Hutu. (Degni-Segui 1994: para. 58)

Anger rape was also evident. Box quoted from Groth and Birnbaum (1979, cited in Box 1983: 127), describing rapes are an expression of pent-up anger and characterised by extreme brutality which may have little to do with sexual penetration. 'Exploitation rape', as described by Box (ibid: 128), as taking advantage of vulnerability, was also evident. Each of these types of rape could be identified but they clearly overlap in motivation. Each was an exacerbation of a toxic, hegemonic masculinity. Powerbrokers looking to encourage rape and sexual abuse by attackers found easy routes to manipulation.

Beginning to Demystify

Goldstein (2001) highlighted a number of discourses of rape in war: rape may be an opportunistic crime in war perpetrated by rogue soldiers; a right to rape was at times a reward for triumphant armies or even essential to cater for the male sex drive. These discourses were the pernicious but not necessarily inevitable widespread policy practices of all armed groups (Wood 2009: 34). So, there are grounds for holding tactical rape perpetrators accountable. It took time to recognise that the tactical, strategic use of rape and sexual violence are violations of international law, deliberate practices and the result of deliberate policies by powerbrokers. However, recognition has been limited and in many ways might be viewed as obfuscating a really effective response by international judiciaries and states. Legal definitions and precedents are helpful in providing grounds for holding perpetrators accountable if they actually result in accountability and realistic strategies to ameliorate the social harms generated by sexual violence such as those identified by Box in *Power, Crime and Mystification*. The following analysis highlights the benefits and the shortcomings of attempts to confront the decades of mystification of tactical rape.

The UN Security Council (UNSC) was slow to react to widespread reports of rape in both Bosnia and Herzegovina (former Yugoslavia) and Rwanda in the 1990s. Unusually western media focussed on the use of rape in both conflicts. This may have been because the two conflicts overlapped in time and the two International Tribunals overlapped in areas of legal focus.

I took a team to Zagreb at the informal request of a UN worker who had no mandate to investigate reports of rape camps. The team reported back to UN agencies, NGOs and the media that there was clear evidence of the use of systematic mass rape as a deliberate weapon of war. Dame Anna Warburton was briefed and then led a European Council Investigative Mission, one of the first formal investigations (Fitzpatrick 2016: 41–42). Many NGOs were clamouring for a response.

Eventually, the UN Special Rapporteur reported an alarming number of allegations regarding the use of rape as a weapon of ethnic cleansing in Bosnia and Herzegovina. Human Rights Watch (HRW) reported on crimes at Foca where non-Serb women, and young Muslim women and girls as young as 12 were detained, abused and raped on a daily basis (HRW 1998). The UN Commission of Experts recorded in 1994 approximately 10,000 possible victims noting many others not officially named nor sufficiently identified for formal checks. The reasons for the lack of formal reports were fear of reprisals, fear of social ostracisation and the practical difficulty of finding a place to report (UNSC Commission of Experts 1994, S/1994/674). Lack of reporting in conflict is understandable. Box (1983: 130) noted that fewer than 25% of rape victims in England and Wales report rape even in peacetime, something which has deteriorated even further in recent times (see Atkinson and Monk this volume).

There was a similarly slow response in Rwanda. In refugee camps in Tanzania in 1994, I heard from medical workers that it was likely that all females, including children, had probably been raped (Fitzpatrick 1994). While empirical evidence abounded as early as May 1994, it was notable that the UN investigators who visited Rwanda in June, July and October 1994 and March, April and May 1995 gave no particular attention to rape apart from including it in passing among some problems and a brief reference to women being taken as hostages and the victims of rape. Only in August–September 1995 was special UN attention drawn to systematic rapes (Degni-Segui 1995).

Notably, it was not until 2005 that the policy of Responsibility to Protect (R2P) was endorsed by all member states of the UN. Previously it had been frequently asserted under the Westphalian Treaty that states could not intervene in the internal affairs of other sovereign states. R2P was acceptance that states had a responsibility to protect their citizens and if they failed to do so then other states had a responsibility to intervene. This policy is frequently ignored but it did at least confirm the responsibility of state leaders as power holders to protect their citizens, which, of course, includes women.

Box noted this responsibility in 1983. In Chapter 6, he wrote of the responsibility of democracies to protect and to be accountable to those who elect them (Box 1983). He asserted the real powerlessness of citizens in democracies and their apparent ignorance of what powerbrokers owe them: 'large sections of the public lack the inclination, ability, or power to make accountable those wielding political power, and through them, those wielding economic power' (ibid: 204). When the public is kept ill-informed, it lacks the power to hold leaders accountable for failing to protect and care. Within democracies, despite the rhetoric, the relatively powerless, and the vulnerable, have little power to change internal policies. Citizens are often too distant from powerbrokers. What hope is there then for inhabitants of autocracies or where disinformation and hate propaganda are rife? Accountability of powerbrokers in serious harms and crimes such as the tactical use of rape in war has been limited. Forty years after the publication of *Power, Crime and Mystification*, despite changes in international law and precedents in international judiciaries, it will be seen that powerbrokers are protected by the tangled, complex acceptance of judicial mandates and by priorities set by agencies and other powerbrokers.

The UN and Powerbrokers

The UN has real limitations in its ability or resources to bring to account states which fail to comply with agreed law. Due to the power of veto of certain powers, the UNSC sometimes has difficulties even formalising global condemnation of certain actions. If any one of the five major powers disagrees it is impossible to pass a resolution let alone initiate specific action. But it is at least one way to articulate IHL and formalise expected standards of behaviour by and between states. In 1993, the UN Security Council (UNSC) established the ICTY which irreversibly changed the landscape of International Humanitarian Law regarding rape in conflict.

This court set precedents with judgements on genocide, war crimes and crimes against humanity. It ruled that rape had been used as a weapon of war (ICTY *Prosecutor v Kunarac*, Judgment 2001). It recognised that rape and sexual violence had been a deliberate policy to impose terror (ICTY *Prosecutor v Tadic*, Judgment 1999: para. 649). Significantly, it judged that an individual's senior position, their power, could not protect them from prosecution. Heads of state should have no immunity or impunity from prosecution for crimes committed under their authority (ICTY Celebici, Trial Judgment: para. 354). Those in command of the use of tactical rape and sexual violence could be prosecuted, whether they were in direct or indirect control, encouraging, promulgating, accepting the abuses or deliberately failing to condemn them. Tactical rape and sexual violence were deemed war crimes when committed as part of a strategic or policy-driven plan to gain political or military ascendency over another group or to ethnically cleanse a territory (ICTY *Prosecutor v Kunarac*, Judgment 2001: para. 419).

The power of military and political leaders was challenged. A plan or policy could indicate the systematic nature of the crime and be admissible in court. It was, however, not essential to produce a written plan or policy for an attack to be deemed systematic (Askin 2003: 315). This applied when ruling on tactical rape and sexual violence as crimes against humanity.[2]

In 1995, the ICTR was established to investigate crimes in the Rwandan conflict. Its legal focus often overlapped with the ICTY. In many areas, the ICTR failed to perform well but it produced what is arguably the most significant case in international law regarding rape and genocide (Moreno-Ocampo 2009). This was the first court to recognise tactical rape as a method of committing genocide (ICTR *Prosecutor v Jean-Paul Akeyesu* 1998). Reflecting the terms of the Genocide Convention, there was clear evidence of intent to destroy a particular group (the Hutus) and to inflict great bodily and mental harm from tactical rape as well as other attacks. As noted above, tactical rape was used to impose measures intended to prevent births within the targeted group. Many cases of forced incest and children born of these attacks added to the personal and social shame perceived by victims and communities. Many women suffered such damage to sexual organs that they were unable to bear children. This was the case for many girls who were raped. Prevailing patriarchal attitudes meant children of rapes would not be children of the targeted group but deemed children of the attackers. Given the authority of the Genocide Convention and relevant responsibilities of states to respond, ruling that rape could be a weapon of genocide was a significant step (Moreno-Ocampo 2009).

In line with judgements at the ICTY, those indicted at the ICTR included high-ranking military and government officials, politicians, religious and militia leaders. An important case was eventually brought against a local leader, Jean-Paul Akayesu, who was convicted of rape

---

[2] There is no moral or legal justification for treating perpetrators of atrocities in internal conflicts more leniently than those engaged in international wars. IHL and human rights law apply in conflicts, international or internal. The application and relevance of other international instruments which formulate required protection of human rights, civil and political rights, protection of women and children and which prohibit torture and discrimination are clear. States might ignore and fail to comply but there is a legal basis for justifying intervention by other states.

as genocide. Accounts of tactical rape had been widespread but not mentioned in the original indictments for genocide, crimes against humanity and violations of Article 3 Common to the Geneva Conventions relating to his role as a local authority figure. It was noted that numerous atrocities had been committed with his knowledge and under his supervision. Then statements from particular witnesses linked acts being judged as genocide with the rape of Tutsi women (Neuffer 2000). The indictment was eventually amended with prosecutors suggesting that the reason for the original omission and lack of evidence linking Akayesu to acts of sexual violence 'might' include the shame that accompanies acts of sexual violence as well as insensitivity in the investigation of sexual violence (ibid). The use of 'might' would seem to be an understatement. Akayesu was eventually found guilty, the first conviction for the use of rape as a means of genocide (ICTR *Prosecutor v Jean-Paul Akayesu* 1998: para. 452). The case was a watershed one. Yet, decades later, it remained almost an isolated one—perhaps something akin to what Box (1983) referred to as merely a hollow and symbolic victory for those campaigning against power (see Scott and Sim, this volume). Rape in conflict is both an individualistic and a structural harm, yet it is still usually left to feminist campaigners to push for accountability (Canning 2010). The Akeysu case focussed on an individual powerbroker but failed to confront the institutionalised contributors to rendering women vulnerable, including the violent domination of hegemonic masculinity inherent in society.

Definitions, Consent and Coercion

Taken together, the two Tribunals were responsible for realistic and comprehensive definitions of rape and sexual violence. The ICTY found no definition of rape in international law (ICTY *Prosecutor v Furundzija* 1998: para. 175). The court then referred to the crime of 'forcible sexual penetration by an accused or by a third person under the control of the accused' (ICTY Gagovic & Others 'Foca', Indictment 1996). Sexual violence, which includes rape, was considered to be any act of a sexual nature which is committed on a person under circumstances which are coercive.

In *Power, Crime and Mystification*, Box (1983) highlighted the conflicts between notions of consent and coercion. He discussed the need to clarify the distinction between consent as perceived by a perpetrator and consent as perceived by a rape victim and decried the absence of any real understanding of consent and even less of coercion. Anticipating in part contemporary debates on 'coercive control', he recognised that force could be more than physical:

> …those operating with a concept of rape produced by juridical practice focus only on that type of violence which reflects man's physical superiority over females … and ignore other types of violence which reflect man's economic, organizational, and social superiority. … they exclude an enormous amount of sexual access where the actual or threatened use of violence other than the physical variety is the means of neutralizing the victim's non-consent. (Box 1983: 124)

Women and girls may be forced to submit through other threats. As if in response to these concerns, the ICTY declared that sexual violence covers a broad range of acts and includes rape, molestation, sexual slavery, sexual mutilation, forced marriage, forced abortion, enforced prostitution, forced pregnancy and forced sterilisation (ICTY *Prosecutor v Delalic* 1998: para 496). The ICTR added that sexual violence is not limited to physical invasion of the human body by another human body. It may include acts involving penetration with weapons. Coercive circumstances need not be evidenced by physical force but also by:

> …threats, intimidation, extortion and other forms of duress which prey on fear or desperation may constitute coercion, and coercion may be inherent in certain circumstances, such as armed conflict or the military presence. (ICTR Akeyusu decision 1998: para. 688)

The Akayesu decision recognised the difficulties for rape survivors to provide corroborating evidence. The ICTR was the first to define rape in international law, holding that the key elements of rape could not be captured in mechanical descriptions of objects and body parts (ICTR *Prosecutor v Jean-Paul Akayesu*: paras. 174–186).

The ICTY ruled that any form of captivity vitiates consent (ICTY Furundzija Judgment 1998: para. 271). Emphasis was on violations of sexual autonomy ruled to be violated wherever the person subjected to the act had not freely agreed or was not a voluntary participant. Force, threat or taking advantage of a vulnerable person provided evidence as to whether consent was or was not voluntary. No corroboration of the victim's testimony was necessarily required where circumstances rendered such evidence impossible. Prior sexual conduct of the victim was not admissible in evidence. This was a realistic obviation of legal attempts to undermine the testimony of survivors.

Currently, IHL defines rape as the act of obliging someone to have sexual intercourse against his or her will using force, violence or any other form of coercion. The criminal laws of many countries reflect this definition. This means there is a legal basis for demanding action to prevent, prohibit and prosecute perpetrators. Unfortunately, as will be seen in consideration of the Ukraine conflict 2022, the existence of law does not always benefit the powerless. It can be mystified by rhetoric and be manipulated.

Tactical Rape and International Powerbrokers in the Twenty-First Century

Into the current century, the UNSC took further action responding to tactical rape but this did not happen easily. Many states contested the action by the UNSC before eventually accepting that tactical rape was a security issue for states. The fact that the ICTY and ICTR operated under existing law helped final acceptance because if states were breaching IHL they would be deemed a security risk for them as well as for women and girls. Women, peace and security emerged as an ongoing issue for reporting and consideration at the UNSC. However, problems remained regarding implementation and enforcing accountability.

In 2002, the International Criminal Court (ICC) defined crimes against humanity and referenced widespread or systematic attacks on civilian populations. This was the first independent, permanent, international criminal court recognising not only rape in war but also sexual slavery and other sexualised crimes as crimes against humanity, war crimes and genocide. However, despite this seeming positive progress, in its first 20 years, the ICC procured only one conviction for a crime of sexual violence (Altunjan 2021: Part 1).

Debate continued at the UNSC on resolution 1325 in 2000 which broke new ground recognising that women's situation in peace was closely intertwined with their vulnerability in conflict. In 2008, UNSC resolution 1820 demanded all parties immediately take measures for the protection of women and children. Resources were allocated to UN agencies and personnel to investigate, report and monitor rape and sexual violence in conflicts. Special Rapporteurs in conflict were expected to investigate and report to the UNSC on the issue. States were required to formulate National Action Plans to prevent, monitor and hold perpetrators to account.

In 2009, UNSC resolution 1888 demanded measures including vetting candidates for national armies and security forces to exclude those associated with serious violations of IHL and human rights law including sexual violence. The UN Secretary General (UNSG) was to report to the UNSC regularly on women, peace and security. There was ongoing progress. UNSC resolution 2467 in 2019 required a survivor-centred approach to address conflict-related sexual violence in all UN peace-making, peacekeeping and peace-building initiatives. The resolution called for justice, accountability and reparation for survivors and their families. This was to include children born of sexual violence in conflict who are often stigmatised, stateless and acutely vulnerable to recruitment and radicalisation by armed groups. It recognised the necessity, in prevention and response to support a broad range of civil society actors on the frontlines of conflicts.

Forty Years After *Power, Crime and Mystification*

Despite these resolutions by states to bring other states to account, to prevent, prohibit and prosecute perpetrators, widespread, systemic rape has continued into the twenty-first century. Laws and resolutions have done little to prevent, to bring to account perpetrators or to really demystify the issue. There has been some legal and institutional recognition of the causes, motivations and social harms but forty years after Box's analysis in *Power, Crime and Mystification* rape and sexual violence continued to be a persistent feature of conflicts. Real, effective demystification failed to be achieved. There remained a dearth of direct action to confront or prevent this tactic of attack in war and conflict. Widespread rape and sexual violence were reported in Ukraine, Afghanistan, Democratic Republic of Congo, Central African Republic, Mali, Colombo, Iraq, Libya, Myanmar, Somalia, South Sudan, Sudan, Syrian Arab Republic, Yemen, Ethiopia (especially Tigray), the Chadian Basin including Chad, Niger and Nigeria (Under-Secretary General Report 2022, S/2022/272: para.10).

The widespread practice seemed to be evident in reports from the conflict in Ukraine. With ongoing hostilities and occupied towns and cities, it can be difficult to independently verify some claims. However, within days of the Russian invasion on 24 February 2022, apparently credible reports were emerging which applied 'reasonable grounds to conclude' based on a body of verified information that systemic rape and sexual violence were being perpetrated (OHCHR *Report of the Independent International Commission of Inquiry on Ukraine* A/77/533 2/17 2022). The UN's Office for Coordination of Humanitarian Affairs (OCHA) early on reported multiple cases of sexual violence in Ukrainian cities that had been occupied by Russian forces (OCHA 2022). Reports referred to women, including elderly women, being gang-raped and in some instances killed and Russian soldiers raping Ukrainian women for hours before killing them. There were:

> …multiple reports of Russian soldiers breaking down the doors of cellars and basements where people were sheltering and raping women. Some

women were raped in front of their children and there have been allegations of these violent attacks being filmed and put on porn sites by Russian soldiers. Due to ongoing hostilities and because many occupied towns and cities have been isolated with most telecommunications down, it has been difficult to independently verify these claims and for reports of sexual violence and further atrocities against civilians to come to light. (Office for Coordination of Humanitarian Affairs, OCHA 2022)

There were other apparently credible reports such as those from the UN Special Rapporteur on Sexual Violence in Conflict, Pramila Patten who stated in October 2022 that rapes and sexual assaults by Russian soldiers in Ukraine had become the Kremlin's military strategy and a deliberate tactic to dehumanise the victims of the war. In an interview, Patten stressed her belief that rape was being used as a weapon of war in Ukraine and reports confirming crimes against humanity committed by the Russian forces with testimonies that the age of the victims of sexual violence ranged from four to 82-years-old. She added that victims were mostly women and girls, but also men and boys (Patten 2022a).

The Office of the High Commissioner for Human Rights (OHCHR) reported on the findings of the Human Rights Monitoring Mission to Ukraine which documented 86 cases of conflict-related sexual violence against women, men, and girls, including rape, gang rape, forced nudity and forced public stripping, sexual torture and sexual abuse. In 53 cases, sexual violence was used as part of torture and ill-treatment in the context of detention (Office of the High Commissioner for Human Rights, A/77/533 2/17 2022). Reports suggested that rape in Ukraine by Russian soldiers might be widespread. Those fears were further crystallised following the Russian withdrawal from Bucha, a suburb of the Ukrainian capital Kyiv, where some two dozen women and girls were systematically raped by Russian forces, according to Ukraine's ombudswoman for human rights. (Denisova 2022).

Box's analysis of types of rapists and toxic masculinity seemed to be applicable. His description of sadistic rape had been also echoed. Few lessons had been learned. All indications are that despite progress made in IHL, tactical rape and sexual violence continued to be perpetrated in conflicts. Civilians continued to be targeted and suffered brutal attacks.

In February 2023, Havryshko (2023) wrote about rape as a weapon of war and terror, carried out with 'demonstrable cruelty' in the Ukraine conflict. Patten reported to the UNSC on the gap between aspirations of prevention and the reality on the ground (Patten 2022b). In conflicts, little had changed on the ground. Russian leaders employed agnotological strategies including justifying military action with the media claiming that the Crimea had always been Russian, false claims about neo-Nazi infiltration in Ukraine's government and conspiracy theories about Ukraine/US bioweapons (Organisation for Economic Cooperation and Development, OECD 2022). Ukrainian men and women were deemed enemies, 'the common people' according to a propagandist essay published in the Russian press (Rio Novosti 2022). Mystification by powerbrokers continued.

In December 2022, the EU called for a special tribunal to investigate Russian war crimes in Ukraine. The focus would be the crime of aggression but might cover crimes of sexual violence and rape. Difficulties were evident. If the UNSC tried to establish a special judiciary Russia would have the power to veto it. The International Criminal Court (ICC) announced the issuance of arrest warrants for senior Russian leaders in March 2003 (International Criminal Court [ICC], Press Release). Russia responded that it did not recognise the ICC's jurisdiction (Sauer 2023). The ICC President, Khan, noted, however, that according to Article 27 of the Rome Statute such arrest warrants—for Putin and his Commissioner for Children's Rights—could restrict travel to states which did recognise the ICC (Khan 2023). These warrants represented the first time a head of state of a permanent member of the UNSC had been charged. The charges did not mention sexual violence.

In 2022, the UN General Assembly (GA) called on the permanent members of the UNSC to be accountable for the use of veto (UN General Assembly, GA/12417). Any such action at either the GA or the UNSC is likely to fail. However, the chance of any substantial change to prevent rape and sexual violence in conflict and holding perpetrators to account is unlikely. Keepers of the rule of law might admit the role of hidden powerbrokers but they are either unable or unwilling to prioritise bringing them to account. Democracies make rhetorical statements in the UN but the tangles of rules by which they operate keep powerful criminals protected.

Conclusion

So, much remains to be done to respond to Box's analysis of the mystification around rape. There has been some progress at some levels but this progress remains limited in its real effect in demystifying the route to making more apparent the links between power, crime and social harm. It is progress that the widespread, systemic use of this abuse in war and conflict has been acknowledged. There are now more comprehensive definitions and some very limited case law at international levels. There have been advances in the statements of responsibility of powerbrokers, but very few individuals have been legally held to account.

There is now some recognition, albeit limited to certain international fora, that men and women who are raped and men and women who know that others are being raped are all affected, disempowered. Resistance is attacked. Physical, social and emotional damage are the results. It has been confirmed that a widespread policy of rape contravenes IHL and is a security issue for the international community of states. Judging by the cases brought before the ICC, this seems more important than it being a security issue for women.

It is an advance that powerbrokers can be recognised as responsible and can legally be held to account. Such accountability has been limited to very few instances. There has been some action by UN agencies and NGOs with the appointment of courts and personnel to report, to monitor and to attempt to hold perpetrators accountable. But a handful of indictments and convictions does not represent serious action. Complex, tangled mandates and procedures may be seen as merely further obfuscation and a cynical pretence at demystification.

Certainly, there is public recognition of the deliberate, tactical use of rape and sexual violence in war and conflict. Media and journalists now regularly report on these abuses and violations—with accompanying condemnation.

It has been acknowledged that women and girls made vulnerable in peace—by political, economic, social, cultural and religious powerbrokers—are rendered more vulnerable in conflict. Box's analysis contributed to understanding issues of toxic, hegemonic masculinity to be confronted and there has been some international recognition of the impact on victims and consequently, some policy and humanitarian strategies to confront harms and social structures which engender women's vulnerability. As Canning notes, '[a]ctions which occur during war are not always individualised acts and do not exist within a vacuum, but as part of an overarching social and institutional entity' (Canning 2010: 9). War is gendered. Effective responses to the specifically egregious use of rape and sexual violence in war requires much more work to confront the pervasive hegemonic masculinity in many societies which engage in war and conflict.

The ongoing conflicts where rape and sexual violence are tactics are indications of the inadequacy of such strategies. Legal pronouncements and policy rhetoric are very small first steps but do little to really demystify the reality of the interaction of power, crime and social harm. Definitions are useful and essential to clarify tensions between the reality of coercion vs consent. But definitions are insufficient to demystify crimes when they are either ignored or deemed too complex to apply. Difficulties remain when reaching a balance between the rights of accused and rights of victims and survivors who cannot produce witnesses and who face stigma and emotional stress when testifying. Yet these are not necessarily insurmountable difficulties. As has been seen above, there has been some movement towards confronting the specifics encountered in courts. To bring the atrocious harms of rape and sexual violence in conflict out of the shadows and into the light of social justice is possible. It does, however, need much more work by states and international and national agencies.

The abuses continue. Despite seeming advances, courts are still not holding powerbrokers to account. Prevention is not a reality. For women and girls caught in the power struggles of violent men, there is still no protection. Tactical use of rape remains a mystified social harm. The level of compliance with relevant international norms and resolutions by parties in conflict has remained appallingly low despite the framework put in place by the UNSC. IHL condemns and regulates against tactical rape but IHL continues to be disregarded by many states. There is now clear international law that precludes powerbrokers from escaping prosecution but perpetrators and powerbrokers who either directly or indirectly plan, coordinate, encourage or protect perpetrators are still largely not held accountable. The ICC which issued initial arrest warrants for leaders of the Ukrainian invasion did not mention violations such as the reported tactical use of rape and sexual violence. Even while the complex web of organisational mandates and international agreements render these warrants unlikely to result in accountability this lack of priority or concern is notable.

More must be done. There are agencies and NGOs trying to do more. They must be supported. There are analysts who can bring Box's insights to the notice of the global community. More analysis, data collection and legal prosecution with clear, well-resourced programmes to improve women's status and to prevent abuses must be encouraged and supported. Justice and protection for all women and girls demands the unveiling of this wrongdoing and those responsible for it. Box's calls for demystification of the links between power, sexual violence and social harms must be answered.

References

Altunjan, T. 2021. *The International Criminal Court and Sexual Violence: Between Aspirations and Reality.* Cambridge: Cambridge University Press.

Askin, K, 1999. Sexual violence in decisions and indictments of the Yugoslav and Rwandan Tribunals: Current status. *The American Journal of International Law*, 93:1, January, 97–123.

Askin, K. 2003. Prosecuting Wartime Rape and Other Gender-Related Crimes Under International Law: Extraordinary Advances, Enduring Obstacles. *Berkeley Journal of International Law* 21 (2): 288–349.

Box, S. 1983. *Power, Crime and Mystification.* London: Routledge.

Cammaet Patrick, Retired Major General. quoted in *UN, Security Council Demands Immediate and Complete Halt to Acts of Sexual Violence Against*

Civilians in Conflict Zones, Unanimously Adopting Resolution 1820, (2008) SC/9364, June 19, 2008.

Canning, V. 2010. Who's Human? Developing Sociological Understandings of the Rights of Women Raped in Conflict. *The International Journal of Human Rights* 14 (6): 849–864.

Canning, V., and S. Tombs. 2021. *From Social Harm to Zemiology: A Critical Introduction*. London: Routledge.

Charlesworth, H., and C. Chinkin. 2000. *The Boundaries of International Law: A Feminist Analysis*. Manchester: Manchester University Press.

Clark, L., and D. Lewis. 1977. *Rape: the Price of Coercive Sexuality*. Toronto: Women's Press.

Connell, R. 2009. *Gender In World Perspective*, 2nd ed. Bristol: Polity Press.

Denisova, L. Reported in NPR. Wamsley, L. 2022. *Rape Has Reportedly Become a Weapon in Ukraine, Finding Justice may be difficult*, April 30, 2022.

Fitzpatrick, B. 1992. *Rape of Women in War*. Geneva: World Council of Churches.

Fitzpatrick, B. 1994. *The Rwandan Regional Crisis*. Geneva: World Council of Churches, August.

Fitzpatrick, B. 2016. *Tactical Rape in War and Conflict*. Bristol: Policy Press.

Goldstein, J.S. 2001. *War and Gender*. Cambridge: Cambridge University Press.

Groth, A. N. and Birnbaum. J. 1979. *Men who Rape*. New York: Plenum.

Havryshko, M. S. 2023. *Rape as a Weapon of War*. Eurozine Review., March 14, 2023.

Human Rights Watch (HRW). 1998. *Bosnia and Herzegovina. A Closed Dark Place: Past and Present Human Rights Abuses in Foca*, vol. 10, issue 6, 1, July.

International Criminal Court (ICC). 2023. *Press Release*, March 17, 2023.

Kaldor, M. 2001. *New and Old Wars: Organized Violence in a Global Era*. Cambridge: Polity Press.

Khan, K. 2023. ICC Press Release. *Situation in Ukraine: ICC Judges Issue Arrest Warrants Against Vladimir Vladimirovich Putin and Maria Alekseyevna Lvova-Belova*, March 17, 2023.

Millilo, D. 2006. Rape as a Tactic of War – Social and Psychological Perspectives. *Affilia: Journal of Women and Social Work* 21 (2): 196–205.

Moreno-Ocampo, L. 2009. *Sexual Violence as International Crime: Interdisciplinary Approaches to Evidence*. The Hague: International Criminal Court, June 16.

Neuffer, E. 2000. *The Keys to My Neighbour's House: Seeking Justice in Bosnia and Rwanda*. USA: Picador.

Nowrojee, B. 1996. *Shattered Lives: Sexual Violence during the Rwandan Genocide and Its Aftermath.* Washington: Office of Justice Programs. https://www.ojp.gov/ncjrs/virtual-library/abstracts/shattered-lives-sexual-violence-during-rwandan-genocide-and-its.

Nowrojee, B. 2005. *Your Justice Is Too Slow. Will the ICTR Fail Rwanda's Rape Victims?* United Nations Research Institute for Social Development, November.

Office for Coordination of Humanitarian Affairs, (OCHA). 2022. *Sexual Violence and the Ukraine Conflict*, April 2022.

Organisation for Economic Cooperation and Development. 2022. Disinformation and Russia's war of aggression against Ukraine, November 3, 2022.

Patten, P. 2022a. *Rape used in Ukraine as a Russian 'Military Strategy': UN*, October 14, 2022. https://www.france24.com/en/live-news/20221014-rape-used-in-ukraine-as-a-russian-military-strategy-un.

Patten, P. 2022b. Reports of Sexual Violence in Ukraine Rising Fast. Security Council Hears. *UN News*, June 6, 2022.

Rio Novosti. 2022. https://medium.com/@kravchenko_mm/what-should-russia-do-with-ukraine-translation-of-a-propaganda-article-by-a-russian-journalist-a3e92e3cb64.

Sauer, P. 2023. Russia Says It Does Not Recognise Hague Court Amid Reports of Arrest Warrants. *The Guardian*, March 13.

Sexual Violence and the Ukraine Conflict. 2022. https://reliefweb.int/report/ukraine/sexual-violence-and-ukraine-conflict-april-2022.

Wood, E.J. 2009. Variation in Sexual Violence during War. *Politics and Society* 34 (3): 307–342.

United Nations Documents

Degni-Segui, R. 1994. *Situation of Human Rights in Rwanda* A/49/508 S/1994/1157, October 13, 1994.

Degni-Segui, R. 1995. *Situation of Human Rights in Rwanda* E/CN.4/1996/7, June 28.

Dicarlo, Rosemary A. Under-Secretary General. 2022. *Remarks to the Security Council on Ukraine.* New York. S/2022/272, November 16, 2022

Office of the High Commission for Human Rights (OHCHR). 2022. *Report of the Independent International Commission of Inquiry on Ukraine.* A/77/

533 2/17, October 18, 2022, and update on the human rights situation in Ukraine 1 August–31 October.

UN Security Council. 1994. *Rape and Sexual Assault—Final Report of the United Commission of Experts Established Pursuant to Security Council Resolution 780 (1992). S/1994/674.*

UN Resolutions

UN General Assembly. 2022. *General Assembly Adopts Landmark Resolution Aimed at Holding Five Permanent Security Council Members Accountable for Use of Veto.* GA/12417, April 26, 2022.

UN Security Council. 2000. *Security Council Resolution 1325 (2000) [On Women and Peace and Security].* S/RES/1325, October 31, 2000.

UN Security Council. 2008. *Security Council Resolution 1820 (2008) [On Women and Peace and Security].* S/RES/1820, June 19, 2008.

UN Security Council. 2009. *Security Council Resolution 1888 (2009) [On Women and Peace and Security].* S/RES/1888, September 30, 2009.

UN Security Council. 2013. *Security Council Resolution 2106 (2013) [On Women and Peace and Security].* S/RES/2106, June 24, 2013.

UN Security Council. 2019. *Security Council Resolution 2467 (2019) [On Women and Peace and Security].* S/RES/2467, April 23, 2019.

Tribunal Proceedings and Judgements

ICTR. *Prosecutor v Jean-Paul Akayesu.* ICTR-96-4-T. Decision of September 2, 1998 [The Akayesu decision].

ICTY. *Celebici Case: The Judgment of the Trial Chamber: The Most Significant Legal Aspects.* www.icty.org/sid/7617.

ICTY. Gagovic & Others ('Foca'). Indictment, Confirmed, June 26, 1996. IT-96-23-1322, 332.

ICTY. (International Criminal Tribunal for the former Yugoslavia). Kunarac Indictment, 2001. para. 6.1.

ICTY. *Prosecutor v Delalic.* Judgment. IT-96-21-T, November 16, 1998.

ICTY. *Prosecutor v Furundzija.* Judgment. IT-95-17/1-T, December 10, 1998.

ICTY. *Prosecutor v Kunarac*. Judgment. IT-96-23-T, February 21, 2001.
ICTY. *Prosecutor v Tadic*. Judgment. IT-94-1-A (ICTY App. CH, July 15, 1999).
ICTY. *Prosecutor v Tadic*. Trial Chamber. IT-94-1. para. 175.

15

Gender, Power and Criminalisation

Kathryn Chadwick and Becky Clarke

Introduction

Steven Box's work in the 1980s, particularly his conceptualisation of 'power, crime and mystification', proved to be seminal in the development of criminological research and theorising. His work sat in a moment where the critical debate around theoretical conceptualisation (the causes of crime) and policy discussion (responses to crime) were fragmented. *Power, Crime and Mystification* continued a thread of critical analysis of state institutional responses to 'crime' that featured in previous collaborations and collections, particularly *Policing the Crisis* (Hall et al. 1978) and the later edited volume, *Law, Order and the Authoritarian State* (Scraton 1987).

K. Chadwick (✉) · B. Clarke
Manchester Metropolitan University, Manchester, UK
e-mail: k.chadwick@mmu.ac.uk

B. Clarke
e-mail: r.clarke@mmu.ac.uk

Significantly, these developments were also happening alongside the emergence of realism, in particular left realism (Lea and Young 1984; Kinsey et al. 1986), to which we see Box's work becoming more closely connected later in the decade (Matthews and Young 1986). For us, this juncture in criminological research and theorising of the late 1970s and 1980s is significant and has been instructive in our shared thinking focused on the criminalisation and punishment of women. This opportunity to consider Box's contribution, the relationship of his work to others at that time, and ours in the present moment, has been constructive. A particular feature of his work that we value, and seek to replicate in our own, is the detailed consideration of a wide range of empirical sources.

In the 1980s, Box was writing at a time where feminist critique and the inclusion of women's experiences of crime, harm, criminalisation and punishment into criminological arguments were just emerging. Box was viewed as exceptional as a 'non-feminist writer' and one of the 'few criminologists that have assimilated the approaches and findings of feminists' (Heidensohn 1985: 2–3). That he was one of the few male academics who was engaging seriously with the lives of women is in and of itself significant.

Our focus in this chapter is two-fold. Firstly, we review the significance of Box's book *Power, Crime and Mystification* and examine how this contribution sits among other key studies published in that period looking to evidence and theorise women's crime, criminalisation and punishment. Secondly, we focus on our qualitative empirical work to revisit and develop analyses of women's criminalisation presented in the 1980s (Chadwick and Little 1987). Our particular focus and analysis here are women criminalised under joint enterprise (Clarke and Chadwick 2020) and a longitudinal, collaborative narrative dialogue documenting state intervention for one woman over her life course (Clarke and Leah, 2023).

In conclusion, we assert that, in making sense of justice for women, the harms caused to girls and women as victims and as the criminalised 'offender' need to be connected. In so doing, we affirm that our analysis centres institutional intervention and failures for criminalised women rather than concentrating on causal explanations or pathways to women's crime. Thus, rather than viewing powerlessness as a causal feature of criminality, it is the unequal power of the state to criminalise *some* girls and women that offers the most value for contemporary critical and interventionist social research that seeks to make sense of gender, power and criminalisation. We close the chapter by asking: how do we serve justice to women and what would justice look like for these women?

Placing *Power, Crime and Mystification* in Context

Mainstream criminology up to the late 1960s and into the 1970s was largely based on the experiences of men. The construction, production and dissemination of knowledge was dominated by male discourses, with women being a largely marginal group (Heidensohn 1968, 1985; Smart 1976; Carlen 1983). As Scraton (1990: 17–18) rightly observes:

> An excursion through the twentieth century's developments in criminology is a journey through communities inhabited only by men...... where women and their experiences fail to register even a passing comment from the researchers.

Not surprisingly, criminology failed to address the central questions of why women's relationship to 'crime' and harm was different from men's but also how and why women were treated differently by the police, courts, prisons and systems of punishment. Feminist critiques emerged to deconstruct the existing criminological frames of reference and reconstruct new ways of thinking (Gelsthorpe 2002). The significant early contributions of Frances Heidensohn (1968) and Carol Smart (1976) started redressing the balance, initially focusing on an analysis of women and offending, whilst also moving these debates on considerably by prioritising the significance of centres of power, particularly in relation to patriarchal systems of control in the criminal justice process and endemic across societies.

Box contributed to this growing research base both empirically and conceptually. His work, with colleagues, particularly Chris Hale (Box and Hale 1983, 1984), engaged thoroughly in empirical analysis of women's appearance in official crime statistics, drawing on these and other survey data to develop a comparative analysis of gendered victimisation and criminalisation. The findings of this analyses, whilst relying on official crime data to examine criminalisation, gave a clear space and commitment to bring women's lives 'into' debates about crime, allowing for both a challenge to emerging claims and prompting new threads to the debate.

Two of the six chapters in *Power Crime and Mystification* focused on women, 'crime' and the criminal justice process. Interestingly Box (1983) separated women's experiences, prioritising women as victims in Chapter 4: 'Rape and Sexual Assaults on Females' (see Atkinson and Monk, this volume; Fitzpatrick, this volume) and on women's relationship to offending in Chapter Five: 'Powerlessness and Crime—The Case of Female Crime' (see also Cooper and McCulloch, this volume). In *Women, Crime and Criminology*, Smart (1976) had warned about the dangers of 'ghettoisation' in developing feminist critiques, with fears that the subject would remain marginal to the wider discipline. In developing these chapters, which placed women's experiences as both victims and offenders at the centre of the analysis, whilst connecting the findings to a wider conceptual discussion of crime, Box responded to these concerns, as well as others that Smart outlined in her critique.

At a time when the visibility of women as 'offenders' was growing, there was concern that a moral panic about women's criminality would be whipped up in the media and a public consciousness that rather than being grounded in reality was shaped by political and social anxieties and fears (Smart 1976). Box's analysis became a key source seeking to critique theoretical claims of women's growing criminality, such as those of Pollack (1961) and that of Adler and Simon (1979). Heidensohn (1985) drew on Box's meta-analysis to refute such claims, as do others. Susan Edwards (1984: 168) cited Box and Hale when demonstrating the flaws in the causal assumptions of Alder and Simon's work, naming it 'the critique that out does them all' in relation to these emerging theories arguing that women's emancipation leads to crime. It seems that the ability to draw on the detailed empirical analysis by Box and others offered something which up to this point any debates or theorising had been lacking. Box and Hale (1983) argued for, 'vigorous analysis of relevant data', indicating the criteria that must be fulfilled for various studies (cited in Heidensohn 1985: 157).

Early in the book, Box, utilised his concept of 'mystification' to explore legal definitions and categories, arguing that the legal principle of 'exclusion' (Box 1983: 122) applied to issues of consent in the law particularly related to rape and other forms of violence against women. Box suggested that our knowledge and understanding of violence against women was minimal and less visible than other offence categories. Conversely, he asserted that more was known about women as prostitutes, shoplifters, girls 'beyond parental control' and 'in need of care and protection' (ibid.: 12). These girls and women were often excluded from the protection of the law and often subsequently criminalised:

> The view of women as sexual servant, contracted willingly to serve men, gets extended beyond wives to include a whole category of "sexually worthless" women – prostitutes, whores, drug addicts, alcoholics, sexually experienced, and divorced – who because they lack "respectability" are considered to have no worthwhile reason for not consenting to men and therefore do not deserve legal protection. (ibid.: 122)

This list developed by Box was specific and highlighted those women, particularly as victims, who were not served justice due to the judgments made in relation to their perceived sex lives, femininity and overall character. Yet the list further objectifies women, denies any representation or contextualisation of their real lives and has the potential to reproduce the narratives, explored in detail in the case studies below, that serve to marginalise, exclude, silence and criminalise *some* women.

Chapter Five on female offending perhaps aligns most closely to our work, although we are not without critique of it. Again, this chapter reviewed extensive relevant literature, statistics, self-report studies and data to further our understanding of women's involvement in offending. Having established that women committed far fewer serious 'conventional' crimes than men (ibid.: 168), Box referred to the significance of social processes of labelling in calling out behaviour as 'criminal': '…. It is frequently argued that the outcome may be determined less by the person's actual or presumed behaviour than by their personal attributes, real or imagined'. A person's social characteristics and biography may become central: 'It may be "who" you are rather than "what" you actually did that determines whether your behaviour is seen by others, and you, as criminal' (ibid.: 169).

Developing this, Box presented two views: the 'sentimental or romantic' position whereby gender impacted the outcome in judicial cases enabling women rather than men to escape criminalisation. This is reminiscent of Pollack's (1961) study prioritising the concepts of protection and chivalry in criminal justice proceedings. The second, the 'cynical or sceptical' view purported that those women processed through the criminal justice system were more likely, as everywhere else, to be discriminated against and receive more punitive treatment compared to men. Here, aligning with our case studies which highlight the ways in which vulnerability is criminalised, he used the example of girls and young women deemed to need 'care and protection'.

Returning to his earlier discussion, Box in a lengthy presentation and discussion of empirical evidence questioned why women commit so few serious crimes, exploring whether women's perceived powerlessness leads to liberation or marginalisation in the context of justice. Whilst some useful concepts were explored in this chapter, our critique centres on Box's sole focus on the actions of individual women, their crimes and the causal factors. We recognise here the pull to realist explanations but in our own research and analysis, we look to both state failures to protect women and girls alongside the state's power and capacity to punish *some* women. The gendered processes of criminalisation are our concern.

In his final chapter, Box addressed crime, power, and justice. Alluding to crimes of the powerful, which go unrecognised and uncontrolled, Box noted: 'The possible clue to our understanding most serious crimes can be located in power, not weakness, privilege, not disadvantage, wealth not poverty' (Box 1983: 202). However, he acknowledged that institutional power was 'occasionally used to victimise criminally those who are primarily powerless' (ibid.: 204), that some 'sub populations' (young men and young women increasingly plus those 'ethnically oppressed') did not experience the law fairly or universally. Here he concluded that: 'The criminal justice personnel should be accountable not only for who they criminalise, but why, and in whose interest' (ibid.: 223). Whilst welcoming this analysis, we ask, if institutional power is used 'occasionally', is this random rather than a feature of the system? By demanding that criminal justice 'personnel should be accountable' Box's analysis places the focus on the individual practitioner, rather than power as a feature of systemic structures and institutions of the state. Our analysis, presented in the case studies in this chapter, points to the significance of examining systemic failures and responses in determining gendered processes of criminalisation.

Revisiting Power and Mystification: Challenging State Power and Injustice

We share with Box both the commitment to developing empirical evidence and of examining the significance of power in how the criminal justice process is applied. This leads us to examine the multiple and cumulative institutional decisions and processes that women experience to further conceptualise how gendered criminalisation operates, whilst also supporting an understanding of why *some* women are selected for punishment.

The shared values and principles of critical social research have driven the empirical work we reflect on in this chapter, representing concerted attempts to promote an alternative discourse that questions the connection between relations of power and processes of legitimacy. Central to this aim is a commitment to prioritising several values: 'being there', 'bearing witness' and 'voicing the view from below'; acknowledging injustice; recognising our relationships to marginalised groups and communities; challenging powerful institutions and the significance of our own positionality (Clarke et al. 2017).

We acknowledge how the politics of power to criminalise shapes not only our value base but also our routes to analysis (Clarke and Chadwick 2020). Our research is governed by a deliberately interventionist approach to produce knowledge that resists the harms of criminalisation. Our concern is that research-informed responses to challenge such issues are often met with silence, the suppression of dissenting voices and the continuity of destructive policies and practices which marginalise and socially exclude minoritized groups. Significant here is David Scott's writings on 'rehumanising the other', whereby dehumanisation, demonisation and monstering can be challenged by placing humans at the centre of analyses (Scott 2013). It is necessary then for research to advance knowledge that exposes injustice and to promote understanding that informs policy towards change and social justice.

In summary, our goal is to be interventionist and therefore create space for critical analysis and debate regarding criminal justice policy, of policing and prosecution strategies and of longstanding debate about women's 'offending' and punishment. As Hillyard et al. (2004: 384) point out, critical scholars:

> often share a Milibandian "coincidence of interests" with community-based organizations with respect to documenting the deleterious and often devastating harms generated by the activities of powerful individuals, organizations and institutions and the structural social divisions which both legitimate and, in turn, are legitimated by these activities.

Our work around women, punishment, injustice and specifically the narratives of criminalised women builds on the forementioned work of feminist scholars to not only humanise the stories and lives of women but to also build and develop a critical analysis of the gendered processes of criminalisation. Our analysis is driven by the desire to understand which women become 'defined' in the criminal justice system and subject to criminalisation and punishment.

Our qualitative work includes firstly, a project focussed on joint enterprise prosecutions of women which allows for a unique lens on gendered processes of criminalisation, including 'bad character' inferences outlined earlier by Box. Secondly, a longitudinal, collaborative narrative piece surfacing lifelong institutional intervention in the life of one woman, leading to punitive responses and lifelong harms.[1] Our analysis here builds towards an understanding of our priorities going

---

[1] The narratives we are drawing on in these case studies are taken from extensive pieces of research carried out over several years. Here we illustrate the significance of the narrative methodological approach and the focus of analysis which centres the state's power to criminalise.

forward. We explore similar themes raised by Box concerning questions of justice and what this could/should look like for those women failed by state institutions and subject to ongoing ideological processes of criminalisation.

Case Study 1: Stories of Injustice: Women Criminalised Under Joint Enterprise Laws

Joint enterprise (JE) is a set of legal principles grounded in common law and originating from Victorian times, allowing for the collective punishment of multiple defendants for a single offence (see Cunliffe and Morrison, this volume). There has been a re-emergence in their application in the last two decades with research demonstrating how it is disproportionately used against young people from black and mixed-race communities (Clarke and Williams 2020). In 2018, we undertook a research project to examine the impact of the use of JE with female defendants.

Using a range of strategies, largely dependent on families, campaigners, and prisoners to gather our data, we found that since 2004, there have been at least 109 women (and likely more) convicted in England and Wales under JE. Most of these women have convictions for serious violent offences, with over three-quarters (77%) for murder or manslaughter. As a result, most are serving long or indeterminate prison sentences (the average prison sentence is 15 years). Almost half the women (47%) are serving life sentences with tariffs of 16 years or more, and 20 women have tariffs of between 21 and 30 years.

Yet most of the women (90%), engaged in non-violent crimes with regards to the events related to their JE conviction. In no cases did these women use a deadly weapon, such as a knife or bottle, the type of implements that were the most common causes of death of the victims. In fact, women were often marginal to the violent event, with almost half not present at the scene and almost all never having engaged in any physical

---

A more detailed examination of this research can be accessed in the source material referred to in the case studies.

violence. Regardless, in many cases, the women were criminalised and punished for the most serious offence.

What this research presents is an opportunity to explore the process of criminalisation, how and why have these women been selected for punishment? The findings then present two important points in relation to an early assertion from Box that 'from illegal act to legal punishment there are numerous escape routes. It is as though the offender has to pass through a corridor of connected rooms!' (Box 1971: 167). In gathering women's narratives of JE prosecution, we were able to surface how the power of the state in this process can make aspects of women's lives hyper-visible and facilitated their criminalisation, whilst simultaneously rendering experiences of harm and victimisation silent.

The analysis reveals the multiple and cumulative nature of discretion mobilised by criminal justice agencies, decisions and actions, or omissions, in the process of criminalisation, that lead to these convictions of women under JE laws. In the early stages of investigation and pre-trial, the actions of the police and Crown Prosecution Service (CPS) were significant in their decisions to charge women. Initially, some women were questioned as witnesses whilst others were immediately arrested and charged. The police and CPS conferred prior to the CPS determining the charging decision and the offence for which the woman would stand trial. Plea bargaining was sometimes used by the CPS, where defendants (the women or their co-defendants) via their legal teams were approached by the prosecution to plead guilty as part of a deal. Most of the women maintained their innocence, but the case went to trial, where the prosecution and defence drew on a range of strategies (arguments and narratives) to present their case. In the court, the strategies the prosecution teams selected in building the case narrative, as well as the legal advice from defence teams (including decisions about whether women should speak in the trial and their 'credibility as witnesses'), were critical:

> *I was told [by defence] not to give evidence, or dispute what the surgeon said even though what he was saying was wrong. Said it would make me look like a liar, as who would they believe me or a surgeon. (Ada)*

I was told [by defence] not to give evidence, but the prosecution said things that weren't true and the Judge just allowed it all. (Medina) (cited in Clarke and Chadwick 2020: 22).

At all the stages through this process, inferences about the women, how they were judged and constructed in the court narratives, focussed on their assumed character or lifestyle. Joint enterprise convictions became a sharp window into how such judgements were central to the criminalisation of girls and women:

My abuse was used by the prosecution to paint a bad picture of me. I think also when used by the defence it didn't help. I just don't think they believed me. (Jenna). (cited ibid.: 17)

Prosecution said I knew the victim would be seriously hurt or killed…My lifestyle working for escort agency and that I was on drugs. (Kaylee). (cited ibid.: 19)

My role in the crime was deemed to be as this woman full of hate who somehow managed to convince everyone to end up fighting…the focus was on me and the fact I was a woman. I think I was judged more harshly because I was a woman. Intelligence was equated with ability to deceive and manipulate… and I was judged on my lifestyle and my addiction. (Willow). (cited ibid.: 20).

The prosecution strategies in the JE cases we examined were to develop a case story that constructed women as the facilitators of violence, drawing on a range of arguments and narratives to infer their intent or role. Analysis revealed how the prosecution characterised and presented women in the courtroom, relying on longstanding myths and stereotypes, with these gendered narratives further layered with class stigma and racism:

They said I associated with gang members. It was all phone calls between me and one Co-Defendant (CoD). I didn't know the rest of them before the night. (Aliyah). (cited ibid.: 21)

Our primary research shows how the media selected phrases from the prosecution narrative and used them for their headlines. In local newspapers, cases involving Black or Black mixed-race girls and women were reported as 'Honey trap girl', 'Good riddance honey trap killer', 'girls in gang culture' or 'gang violence' (Clarke and Chadwick 2020).

These court narratives, echoed and amplified in the media reporting of cases, not only decontextualised women's lives but also presented opportunities for these objectifying and misogynistic accounts to facilitate processes of criminalisation (see: Jewkes 2015; Kennedy 2018). In our narratives, we heard the context of one young woman's life:

> *I was mentally weak and unstable so I accepted all of his abuse. I was unaware of their criminal activity that he had a knife. I apparently lured my boyfriend to be murdered. (Lisa).* (cited in Clarke and Chadwick 2020: 16)

In these Joint Enterprise cases, as with many others, we were directed to understand the innocence or guilt of women, whether they were 'worthy of leniency' through these racialised and classed gendered narratives (Hudson 2002; Brennan and Vandenberg 2009). The women's accounts, as with this final quote from Lisa, also captured the repeated failure of the police and other agencies to protect women from violence or respond to their health needs. As we have argued elsewhere, there is an urgent need to critically examine the 'hidden role of institutions, legislation, policies and practices', in the lives of girls and women (Clarke and Chadwick 2018: 64).

Case Study 2: Institutional Intervention—Power and Resistance in Women's Lives

An evaluation for the national charity *Women in Prison* in 2015 (Clarke et al. 2015) provided the opportunity to advocate for an alternative approach to research, one which would evolve into an in-depth understanding of institutional intervention for one criminalised young woman.

Using a narrative approach in two initial planned qualitative sessions, one young woman, who had been recently released from prison, struck up what was to become an un-ending collaboration with one of the authors. Facilitating both understanding and more concerted campaigning and intervention work, this collaborative and slow approach to research (Sinha and Back 2014; Mason 2021), enabled us to 'take seriously' the need to contextualise and historicise the criminalisation of girls and women through a life story, tracing the structural relations of gender and class through the power of the state to both define her and intervene over her life course.

As Segrave and Carlton (2010: 291) observe, the lives of criminalised women are often lived under scrutiny by and contact with the state:

> Institutional intervention featured in women's lives from a young age, along with the constant presence and intervention of welfare and criminal justice agencies.... Yet while state intervention was a constant in the women's lives from an early age, this was never experienced or intended as a positive or supportive attempt to assist young women to address traumatic experiences.

It is valuable to consider how these approaches we have utilised, both in this narrative work and the wider project on Joint Enterprise convictions of women drawn on above, are distinct from those employed by Steven Box and colleagues. Whilst both are empirical in nature, and arguably whilst both approaches attempt to frame the findings in sociopolitical contexts, Box's preference for quantitative analysis as a method could mean that controlling for variables and locating statistical significance was prioritised over explanatory nuance and depth. Although Box's work provides a useful critique and challenge to theoretical arguments such as the emancipation leads to crime thesis (Edwards 1984), what the approach is less able to facilitate is the generating of new ideas that enable us to make sense of state punishment and harm in the lives of those women subject to criminalisation.

In contrast to the potential of the narrative life story work, we present both above and here to de-mystify power in the lives of criminalised girls and women, who have often also been failed as children in the care of the state and/or as victims of interpersonal and institutional forms of violence and harm. As Plummer reminds us, life stories 'have work to perform: they are never just stories. And we need to always look to the contrasting political roles they can play' (Plummer 2001: 221). For us to understand how the exercise of patriarchal power operates in the lives of women, and importantly write against the othering of criminalised women, we must employ approaches that resist objectification, but instead prioritise space for women to contextualise and historicise their experiences of policing and punishment (Krumer-Nevo and Benjamin 2010; Krumer-Nevo and Sidi 2012; Clarke et al. 2017).

Analysis from this single case narrative revealed how welfare and criminal justice practitioners share the power to define. The following quote is not only revealing of the multiple forms of institutional power in operation but it also surfaces a resistance to these gendered narratives about girls and women as 'vulnerable' or 'powerless':

I was a little bugger, yeah [laughs], but no, I wasn't bad. Obviously it weren't my fault I was put in care. I don't know, I hold my hands up. I've, well, I've been in the wrong place and hmm, I can't get the words out, I put myself in you know, like, what they call risky situations, where I was maybe at risk. I was messing with the wrong crowd and not caring about myself so much at the time. And there are times where, you know when I look back at younger days and think, oh, I don't know.

There's that one, "vulnerable". I hate that word, vulnerable [laughs], *yes I really do hate that word. Yeah because when I'm back all the way down here* [points on a paper timeline we have created to her childhood] *obviously with what has happened to me in my life, I was vulnerable.* [long pause]

Then, later, between being in care and having my own child, I don't know. I don't see myself as vulnerable…no, I try and say no. Other people might say yeah but I don't want it. I don't like that word. When I was in care they said I was putting myself in danger going places and with people, maybe I was, but they were trying to control me. That's another word "controlling"!! (cited in Clarke and Leah, 2023)

A rebuttal to assumptions of powerlessness is evident in other work around social policy. In Ellis's work, girls in residential care also reject the label of vulnerability, as a denial of their agency and survival in the face of many interpersonal and institutional harms:

> People say I'm vulnerable because I do let people take advantage of me but I'm not vulnerable because if I were vulnerable I wouldn't even be alive now, never mind alive and looking well. (cited in Ellis 2018: 161)

In centring women as powerless, albeit in a book seeking to focus on power and mystification, Box risked contributing to pathologizing narratives of girls and women. Rather than focus on the women's power (lessness), we advocate for empirical work, such as the collaborative and detailed narrative approach, which surfaces the continuities and patterns in institutional power in the lives of girls and women, including an ongoing power to silence:

> There's more stuff I would have wanted to say there I felt like I was holding back you know. There's this barrier, it's like I can't go over it. I stop myself from saying it and speaking.
> I just feel like I can't escape from them. (cited in Clarke and Leah, 2023)

Our collaborative work presented in this chapter, represents an approach to critical social research, whilst markedly different to that of Box's, shares his broader intention to surface policies and practices that are often mystified or concealed.

Centring the Power to Criminalise Girls and Women

In this final section, we revisit arguments on women's criminalisation from the 1980s to the contemporary moment reflecting on the significance of Box's work in theorising women's criminality to these ongoing debates. His work, alongside others at the time (Edwards 1984; Heidensohn 1985), was influential in rejecting earlier claims that women's criminality was increasing due to liberation and emancipation, with a further focus on discussions of either lenient or harsh punishments for women (Pollack 1961; Adler and Simon 1979). For Box, powerlessness, marginalisation and persistent social control (see also Heidensohn 1985), contributed to low crime rates for women and girls. Box also alluded to some girls and women, deemed to be 'out of control', disproportionately entering the criminal justice system. This was instructive and undoubtedly influenced later theorisation. However, the emphasis in Box's work was on understanding the actions and motivations of individual women lawbreakers, rather than examining the systemic, institutional and structured responses to the few women who are criminalised.

Four decades later, criminology, including feminist theorising, remains fragmented along these lines. There is still a pull to centre causes and pathways to crime and the significance of coercive control rather than examining the processes that lead to women's criminalisation. Much of this research and policy work, whilst recognising that 'women offenders' are often disadvantaged and victimised women, experiencing gendered harms, violence, mental ill health, poverty and often come from fractured family backgrounds (see Corston 2007; Batchelor 2009; Barlow 2016), focus their attention on individual women, the choices they make, the circumstances of their offences and ultimately responsibilise women for their actions rather than examining structural inequalities and injustice in producing criminalisation. As we have argued elsewhere: 'the shift within neoliberalism to a responsibilising agenda dissipates the state's role in addressing discrimination, inequalities and marginalisation by making individuals accountable for their own choices, lives and personal and even societal failures' (Clarke and Chadwick 2018: 63).

Our analysis does not seek to examine 'criminal women' or to explain why women offend. Rather, a deeper scrutiny of state power is required. However, our analysis does not dismiss the significance of the experiential or indeed of women's agency. The powerful testimonies in our case studies through the voices of the women surface their agency and knowledge, something missing from Box's work and earlier studies. In the JE cases, there are examples of women wanting to exert their agency and take responsibility for lesser crimes (Hulley et al. 2019; Clarke and Chadwick 2020). The single longitudinal case study highlights the ways that girls and women resist the narratives of themselves as vulnerable and powerless (Ellis 2018; Clarke and Leah, 2023). Further studies looking to explore women's agency and accountability in relation to serious violence incidents, highlight women's willingness to reflect on their own actions and context. This is absent from state narratives of women's actions (Ballinger 2000, 2019; Morrisey 2003; Barlow 2016; Hulley et al. 2019).

Our analysis, rather than viewing powerlessness as a causal feature of criminality, asserts that it is the unequal power to criminalise and punish girls and women that must be prioritised. We focus on the processes that create and reinforce criminalised status alongside an examination of lived experiences of social and state control. To do this, we revisit earlier work that conceptualised gendered processes of criminalisation (Carlen 1983; Edwards 1984; Chadwick and Little 1987), alongside contemporary contributions (Segrave and Carlton 2010; Clarke and Chadwick 2018).

Prioritising Determining Contexts

Previously (Clarke and Chadwick 2018), we argued that by using the term 'criminalised women' the state's decision, through its institutions used to regulate, control and punish, are recognised and revealed. Central to our work and analysis are three determining contexts, to be examined in the remainder of this section: class and economic relations, patriarchal power and processes of racialisation. Firstly, the political and economic context of women's lives, impacts how power and poverty shape their lives. Significantly in his later work, Box (1987) points to the disproportionate negative impact on women during times of economic recession and welfare cuts.

Later research on the feminisation and criminalisation of poverty showed that *some* women's experiences of poverty are qualitatively different from that of men. For example, Pat Carlen (1988) pointed to groups of women disproportionately affected: those looking after children and other dependants, unpaid; lone women with children, whether or not in employment; elderly women; women with low earnings. Box and Hale's (1982, 1985) work was instrumental in showing how in a particular historical moment the impact of structural relations was intensified. Focussed on the period of the 1980s in the UK under the Thatcher government, the significance of economic recession was prioritised.

Arguably the last fifteen years, whilst more protracted and extended, from the global financial crisis of 2008, through the UK Government's 'austerity' project, to the now repackaged 'cost of living' crisis, we see gendered forms of economic marginalisation and poverty grow again. Sylvia Walby (2016) referring to a 'crisis in the gender regime' showed how women's everyday realities were marked by poverty and marginalisation. She reviewed a House of Commons Report showing that 72% of 2010 budget reductions were borne by women, with women's unemployment the highest for 25 years. The 2020 analysis from the Women's Resource Centre echoed much of this earlier research. Examining women and poverty during the Covid Pandemic, they revealed women were more likely to be living in poverty. This was particularly the case for black and minoritized women with one quarter reporting difficulties faced in feeding their families and children. The work of Amina Mama (1984) and more recent empirical research by Awugo Emejulu and Leah Bassel (2016), demonstrated the significance of the relationship between the British state and Black and Minority Ethnic women at times of economic crisis.

This economic context is crucial to understanding the processes of criminalisation that *some* women experience. We are not however arguing that economic marginalisation, poverty and powerlessness is a causal factor to explain women's involvement in and a reason why they may turn to crime. Our empirical work, illustrated in this chapter, shows how ideological narratives, arguably intensified in moments of economic crisis (Hall et al. 1978), that centre class stigma and racialisation lead to some women being perceived as problematic, in need of intervention and ultimately for *some* selected for criminalisation and punishment.

Carlen (2002) showed how expectations around femininity and gender, particularly motherhood, sexuality and relationships became central to women's criminalisation. In one case we examined, two female co-defendants were on trial with three men. Two of the three male co-defendants were fathers, but this was not a feature of the trial, they were not judged on the parenting of their children or as fathers. This was not the case for the women defendants in the trial. The Judge chose to foreground the young women as mothers in her remarks:

> ... a feckless mother of X unfortunate children... mercifully will not be burdened with you for their upbringing... your child who will be protected from you... the state picks up the pieces of your fecklessness. (cited in Clarke and Chadwick 2020: 24)

These judgements and statements were not confined to judges. Prosecution and in some cases even defence teams, undermined their own clients through such judgements, using gendered narratives as a strategy to construct meaning and imply blameworthiness. These narratives were also echoed in media reporting, where a woman's status as a mother became central, with every opportunity taken to refer to women as single parents or having children by multiple partners:

> 'A sadistic single mum, tortured ex-boyfriend'
> 'Her defence said she had 3 children under 5 by different fathers'
> 'Drug dealer mother'. (cited in Clarke and Chadwick 2020: 28)

Economic relations and class stigma are closely connected to patriarchal power relations and processes of racialisation. Carlen's (1983) empirical study of women's imprisonment in Scotland some forty years ago showed how patriarchal power was exercised through state intervention and economic relations. A double standard of morality operated whereby women were judged and punished accordingly. 'A high proportion of the women who eventually are selected to appease the public's punitive obsession are those who in the eyes of the Sheriff have failed as mothers' (Carlen 1983: 66). She continued: 'A woman who is still running a household and looking after her children is more likely to be a candidate for a non-custodial penalty than is her sister who, in rebelling against marital tyranny, has also stepped out with domesticity and motherhood. The latter goes to Cornton Vale – again and again and again' (ibid.: 70). Further research supported these claims that experiences of criminal justice were impacted by the perceived adherence of women to dominant discourses of femininity, resulting in the application of various labels—'mad', 'bad wives and mothers', 'victim', to justify their punishment (Allen 1987; Carlen and Worrall 1987; Morrisey 2003; Ballinger 2009). Similar labels and judgements are applied to girls deemed to be 'risky', 'out of control', 'drunken', 'ladettes', 'over sexualised', requiring intervention and punishment (Hudson and Cain 2002; Chesney-Lind and Eliason 2006; Worrall 2019; Hodgson 2023).

The 2020 *Stories of Injustice* report concurs with these findings. Our examination of the language used by judges to describe women in JE cases and their perceptions of the women are central to the construction of them as blameworthy. The Judge's summing up and sentencing remarks often focus on judgements of their character and behaviour rather than their actions related to the alleged offence. Additionally, the prosecution and media narratives for those women identifying their ethnicity as Black, 'Black British', 'Black Caribbean', 'Black African' or else as mixed-race 'White and Black Caribbean', focus on girls and women as the 'honey trap' 'girl in the gang' or as the woman 'luring' men to violent situations (Clarke and Chadwick 2020). Similar representations can be found in US-based research, of Black and Latina women in contact with the criminal justice system constructed as sexually dangerous or 'jezabelled' (Slakoff and Brennan 2019).

Processes of racialisation and racism are key factors in the criminalisation and punishment of minoritized women. Feminist scholars have examined women's experiences as both offender and victim, pointing to the difficulties and discrimination experienced by women when seeking both protection and justice (Patel 2003; Chigwada-Bailey 2003). Significantly, prior to this work, Ruth Hall's, *Ask Any Woman* (1985: 48) survey examining the extent of women's fear of and experiences of rape and sexual violence, made a significant contribution in naming 'racist sexual assault', to signify that for minoritized women racism and sexism may be interconnected and inseparable.

The development and importance of this theorisation have been considerable. Mapping and analysing women's experiences as determined by the intersections of gender, age, class and racialisation have gathered momentum. Significantly, early academic activists including bell hooks (1981, 1984, 2000) and Kimberle Crenshaw (1991) demanded an analysis which prioritises interlocking systems and centres of oppression. For bell hooks, the focus was 'imperialist, white supremacist, capitalist patriarchy' (hooks 2000: 9), to make sense of inequalities and power, moving beyond individual, social, familial and cultural explanations to the institutional and structural relations which determine lives. Drawing on this work, more recently an edited collection examining feminist responses to injustices of the state and its institutions (Atkinson et al. 2023), called for an 'intersectional feminist lens' (Atkinson et al. 2023: 13) in theorising gendered state injustice, with the need to 'explore the ways in which "race", ethnicity, social class, age, sexuality and disability impact upon experience and state and institutional discrimination and power' (ibid.: 7).

Processes of criminalisation can be understood as not just a response to those women selected for punishment but as a cautionary tale for *all* women, functioning to maintain gendered expectations and stereotypes in a patriarchal society. Anette Ballinger (2007: 476) reminded us that the different responses to women through their criminal justice journey are reflective of the 'state's role in the production and reproduction of the gendered social order'. The processes of criminalisation then, must be located in the wider context of those structural relations that shape women's lives. As we are arguing here, these relations are not only reflective of gender but also class and economic relations and racism within society. Significantly, in focussing on the response to girls and women and the power to punish, their criminalisation not the 'causes' of their 'crime' surfaced. Additionally, in exposing harm and injustice, action is demanded.

Conclusion

We share with Box the desire to examine ideological functions of 'crime' and criminalisation, as well as a deep commitment to engaging in a detailed empirical analysis of the gendered nature of policing and punishment. The undoubted status of Box as one of the first (male) researchers engaging in such issues with this gendered lens is reflective of his genuine positive legacy.

Yet from the standpoint of today, with that obvious benefit of hindsight, we also see in his work some of the assumptions we are seeking to critique. First, we argue that we can only make sense of justice for women when analysis that disconnects experiences of girls and women's harm as a 'victim' and harm as the criminalised 'offender' are allied, in order that the failures and impact of *both* are recognised. Second, we challenge the longstanding continuities in a prioritising of explanatory causes or crime, or women's pathways into offending, instead of analysis which centres institutional intervention and failures for criminalised women. Third, we reject explanations that centre women as powerless, when we see women in the system and outside of it actively resisting and surviving failed intervention and the criminalising definitions and strategies to silence them that further cause harm. It is not women's powerlessness that should be the subject of our analysis, but the power of the state to select *some* girls and women for policing and punishment.

Our collaborative work presented in this chapter, represents an approach to critical social research (Clarke et al. 2017), that whilst remarkably different to that of Box perhaps extols a shared intention—to surface policies and practices that are often mystified or concealed (Mathiesen 2004). We contend that the current criminal justice system is inadequate in ensuring justice, accountability, addressing harm and preventing further violence.

Our final reflections return to the issue of Justice. Indeed, Box finished his book by calling for justice for all. That so many of the women who are subject to punishments are marginalised and have been failed by state institutions at an earlier point, whether in relation to protection, care or support, requires us to reimagine what justice might look like for girls and women in the twenty-first century. Again, we are drawn to the edited collection on feminist responses to injustice which prioritised a commitment to politics, intervention and resistance (Atkinson et al. 2023). Concurring with our work the authors argue that a feminist conceptualisation of justice—a feminist jurisprudence—should not just focus on 'crime' and the criminal justice system but recognise wider intersecting harms 'that result from injustices perpetrated at structural, subjective and discursive levels' (ibid.: 17) and 'consider a variety of theoretical, methodological and activist implications for achieving justice', which centre the experiences of those facing injustice (ibid.: 21). Indeed, in rethinking and in pursuit of justice, given the extent of state power and its role in creating harms, it is not enough to call for reforms of state institutions, 'it is key that these are undertaken alongside a broader commitment to radical, transformative change in society and its institutions' (ibid.: 17).

In solidarity with these goals, the priorities and commitment in our work to date and moving forward are threefold and interconnected. First, to produce knowledge with and alongside those subject to these processes of criminalisation. Second, to centre interventionist principles that move the debate beyond and outside of academia. Finally, to work with grassroots campaigning groups to build collective power that can challenge and resist state failures and harms in the pursuit of intervention and radical change.

References

Adler, F., and R. Simon, eds. 1979. *The Criminology of Deviant Women*. Boston: Houghton Mifflin.

Allen, H. 1987. *Justice Unbalanced: Gender, Psychiatry, and Judicial Decisions*. Milton Keynes: Open University Press.

Atkinson, K., U. Barr, H. Monk, and K. Tucker. 2023. *Feminist Responses to Injustices of the State and Its Institutions. Politics, Intervention, Resistance*. Bristol: Bristol University Press.

Ballinger, A. 2000. *Dead Woman Walking*. Aldershot: Ashgate.

Ballinger, A. 2007. Masculinity in the Dock: Legal Responses to Male Violence and Female Retaliation in England and Wales, 1900–1965. *Socio Legal Studies* 16 (4): 459–481.

Ballinger, A. 2009. Gender, Power and the State: Same as It Ever Was? In *State, Power, Crime: Readings in Critical Criminology*, eds. R. Coleman, J. Sim, S. Tombs, and D. Whyte. London: Sage.

Ballinger, A. 2019. 'A Crime of Almost Unspeakable Cruelty and Wickedness': Gender, Agency and Murder in Scotland—The Case of Jeannie Donald. *Social & Legal Studies* 28 (4): 429–449.

Barlow, C. 2016. *Coercion and Women Co-offenders: A Gendered Pathway into Crime*. Bristol: Policy Press.

Batchelor, S. 2009. Girls, Gangs and Violence: Assessing the Evidence. *Probation Journal* 56 (4): 399–414.

Box, S. 1971. *Deviance, Reality and Society*. London: Holt, Rinehart and Winston.

Box, S. 1983. *Power, Crime and Mystification*. London: Tavistock Publications.

Box, S. 1987. *Recession, Crime and Punishment*. London: Macmillan.

Box, S., and C. Hale. 1982. Economic Crisis and the Rising Prisoner Population in England and Wales. *Crime and Social Justice* 17: 20–35.

Box, S., and C. Hale. 1983. Liberation and Female Criminality in England and Wales. *The British Journal of Criminology* 23 (1): 35–49.

Box, S., and C. Hale. 1984. Liberation/Emancipation, Economic Marginalization, or Less Chivalry. *Criminology* 22 (4): 473–497.

Box, S., and C. Hale. 1985. Unemployment Imprisonment and Prison Overcrowding. *Contemporary Crises* 9 (3): 209–228.

Brennan, P.K., and A.L. Vandenberg. 2009. Depictions of Female Offenders in Front-Page Newspaper Stories: The Importance of Race/Ethnicity. *International Journal of Social Inquiry* 2 (2): 141–175.

Carlen, P. 1983. *Women's Imprisonment*. London: Routledge and Kegan Paul.

Carlen, P. 1988. *Women, Crime and Poverty*. Milton Keynes: Open University Press.

Carlen, P., ed. 2002. *Women and Punishment: The Struggle for Justice*. Cullompton, Devon: Willan Publishing.

Carlen, P., and A. Worrall, eds. 1987. *Gender, Crime and Justice*. Milton Keynes: Open University.

Chadwick, K., and C. Little. 1987. The Criminalisation of Women. In *Law, Order and the Authoritarian State*, ed. P. Scraton. Milton Keynes: Open University Press.

Chesney-Lind, M., and M. Eliason. 2006. From Invisible to Incorrigible: The Demonization of Marginalized Women and Girls. *Crime, Media, Culture* 2 (1): 29–47.

Chigwada-Bailey, R. 2003. *Black Women's Experiences of Criminal Justice: Race, Gender and Class: A Discourse on Disadvantage*. Hook: Waterside Press.

Clarke, B., and Leah. 2023. The Panopticon Looms: A Gendered Narrative of the Interlocking Powers of Welfare Intervention and Criminalisation. *Child and Family Social Work*.

Clarke, B., and K. Chadwick. 2018. From 'Troubled' Women to Failing Institutions: The Necessary Narrative Shift for the Decarceration of Women

Post-Corston. In *Women's Imprisonment and the Case for Abolition: Critical Reflections on Corston Ten Years On*, ed. L. Moore, P. Scraton, and A. Wahidin. London: Routledge.
Clarke, B., and K. Chadwick. 2020. *Stories of Injustice: The Criminalisation of Women Convicted Under Joint Enterprise Laws*. Manchester: Manchester Metropolitan University. https://barrowcadbury.org.uk/wp-content/uploads/2020/11/Stories-of-Injustice-women-and-JE.pdf.
Clarke, B., K. Chadwick, and P. Williams. 2017. Critical Social Research as a 'Site of Resistance': Reflections on Relationships, Power and Positionality. *Justice, Power and Resistance* 1 (2): 261–282.
Clarke, B., K. Chadwick, T. O'Hara, and A. Wood. 2015. *An Evaluation of the 'Triangle Project': A National Service for Women in Prison in England and Wales*. London: Women in Prison.
Clarke, B., and P. Williams. 2020. (Re)producing Guilt in Suspect Communities: The Centrality of Racialisation in Joint Enterprise Prosecutions. *International Journal for Crime, Justice and Social Democracy* 9 (3): 116–129.
Corston, B. 2007. *The Corston Report: The Need for a Distinct, Radically Different, Visibly-led, Strategic, Proportionate, Holistic, Woman-Centred, Integrated Approach*. London. Home Office.
Crenshaw, K. 1991. Mapping the Margins: Intersectionality, Identity Politics, and Violence Against Women of Color. *Stanford Law Review* 43 (6): 1241–1299.
Edwards, S. 1984. *Women on Trial*. Manchester: Manchester University Press.
Ellis, K. 2018. Contested Vulnerability: A Case Study of Girls in Secure Care. *Children and Youth Services Review* 88: 156–163.
Emejulu, A., and L. Bassel. 2016. Minority Women, Austerity and Activism. *Race and Class* 57 (2): 86–95.
Gelsthorpe, L. 2002. Feminism and Criminology. In *The Oxford Handbook of Criminology*, ed. M. Maguire, R. Morgan, and R. Reiner, 3rd ed. Oxford: Oxford University Press.
Hall, R.E. 1985. *Ask Any Woman: A London Inquiry into Rape and Sexual Assault: Report of the Women's Safety Survey Conducted by Women Against Rape*. London: Falling Wall Press.
Hall, S., C. Critcher, T. Jefferson, J. Clarke, and B. Roberts. 1978. *Policing the Crisis*. London: Macmillan.
Heidensohn, F. 1968. The Deviance of Women: A Critique and an Enquiry. *British Journal of Sociology* XIX: 2.
Heidensohn, F. 1985. *Women and Crime*. London: Macmillan.

Hillyard, P., J. Sim, S. Tombs, and D. Whyte. 2004. Leaving a 'Stain upon the Silence': Contemporary Criminology and the Politics of Dissent. *The British Journal of Criminology* 44 (3): 369–390.
Hodgson, J. 2023. An Anti-Carceral Feminist Response to Youth Justice Involved Girls. In *Feminist Responses to Injustices of the State and Its Institutions. Politics, Intervention, Resistance*, ed. K. Atkinson, U. Barr, H. Monk, and K. Tucker. Bristol: Bristol University Press.
hooks, b. 1981. *Ain't I A Woman: Black Women and Feminism*. London: Pluto
hooks, b. 1984. *Black Women Shaping Feminist Theory*. ProQuest Information and Learning.
hooks, b. 2000. *Feminist Theory: From Margin to Center*, 2nd ed. London: Pluto Press.
Hudson, A., and M. Cain. 2002. *'Troublesome Girls:' Towards Alternative Definitions and Policies*. London: Sage.
Hudson, B. 2002. Restorative Justice and Gendered Violence: Diversion or Effective Justice? *The British Journal of Criminology* 42 (3): 616–634.
Hulley, S., B. Crewe, and S. Wright. 2019. Making Sense of 'Joint Enterprise' for Murder: Legal Legitimacy or Instrumental Acquiescence? *The British Journal of Criminology* 59 (6): 1328–1346.
Jewkes, Y. 2015. *Media and Crime*, 3rd ed. London: Sage.
Kennedy, H. 2018. *Eve Was Shamed: How British Justice Is Failing Women*. London: Penguin Books.
Kinsey, R., J. Lea, and J. Young. 1986. *Losing the Fight Against Crime*. Oxford: Blackwell.
Krumer-Nevo, M., and O. Benjamin. 2010. Critical Poverty Knowledge: Contesting Othering and Social Distancing. *Current Sociology* 58 (5): 693–714.
Krumer-Nevo, M., and M. Sidi. 2012. Writing Against Othering. *Qualitative Inquiry* 18 (4): 299–309.
Lea, J., and J. Young. 1984. *What Is to Be Done About Law and Order?* London: Penguin.
Mama, A. 1984. Black Women, the Economic Crisis and the British State. *Feminist Review* Special Issue 17: 22–34.
Mason, W. 2021. Radically Slow? Reflections on Time, Temporality, and Pace in Engaged Scholarship. In *Temporality in Qualitative Inquiry*, ed. B.C. Clift, J. Gore, and S. Gustaffson et al. London: Routledge.
Mathiesen, T. 2004. *Silently Silenced: Essays on the Construction of Acquiescence in Modern Society*. Hook: Waterside.
Matthews, R., and J. Young, eds. 1986. *Confronting Crime*. London: Sage.

Morrisey, B. 2003. *When Women Kill: Questions of Agency and Subjectivity.* London: Routledge.

Patel, P. 2003. The Tricky Blue Line: Black Women and Policing. In *From Homebreakers to Jailbreakers: Southall Black Sisters*, ed. R. Gupta. New York: Zed Books.

Plummer, K. 2001. *Documents of Life 2: An Invitation to a Critical Humanism.* London: Sage.

Pollack, O. 1961. *The Criminality of Women.* New York: A.S. Barnes.

Scott, D. 2013. Rehumanising the Other and the Meaning of Justice: An Essay on the Contribution of Barbara Hudson. *European Group for the Study of Deviance and Social Control:* Newsletter. November 2013.

Scraton, P., ed. 1987. *Law, Order and the Authoritarian State.* Milton Keynes: Open University Press.

Scraton, P. 1990. Scientific Knowledge or Masculine Discourses? Challenging Patriarchy. In *Feminist Perspectives in Criminology*, ed. L. Gelsthorpe and A. Morris. Milton Keynes: The Open University Press.

Segrave, M., and B. Carlton. 2010. Women, Trauma, Criminalisation and Imprisonment. *Current Issues in Criminal Justice* 22 (2): 287–305.

Sinha, S., and L. Back. 2014. Making Methods Sociable: Dialogue, Ethics and Authorship in Qualitative Research. *Qualitative Research* 14 (4): 473–487.

Slakoff, D.C., and P.K. Brennan. 2019. The Differential Representation of Latina and Black Female Victims in Front-Page News Stories: A Qualitative Document Analysis. *Feminist Criminology* 14 (4): 488–516.

Smart, C. 1976. *Women, Crime and Criminology.* London: Routledge and Kegan Paul.

Walby, S. 2016. *Cascading Crises and the World of Work: Implications for Women's Economic Empowerment and Decent Work.* Geneva. New York: UN Women Expert Group Meeting, Preparation for UN Commission on the Status of Women.

Women's Resource Centre. 2020. *Women and Poverty During the Pandemic.* https://www.wrc.org.uk/women-and-poverty-during-the-pandemic. Accessed 3 July 2023.

Worrall, A. 2019. Troubled or Troublesome? Justice for Girls and Young Women. Youth Justice. *Contemporary Policy and Practice*, 28–50. London: Routledge.

16

Mystification, Violence and Women's Homelessness

Vickie Cooper and Daniel McCulloch

Introduction

Between 2011 and 2021, the number of women in England who were homeless increased by 88%, making women the fastest-growing group of the homeless population (Schofield 2021). Next to housing inequality, one of the main causal factors contributing to women's homelessness is domestic violence. Violence, homelessness, and gender are intimately linked. Studies of homelessness repeatedly show that 'rates of violence against homeless women are high, measured against any standard' (Jasinski et al. 2010: 1), and that homeless women are at greater risk of violence and victimisation than compared to housed women (Dej 2020). What is more, homeless women are more at risk of sexual violence compared to homeless men (Jasinski et al. 2010). The prevalence of

---

V. Cooper (✉) · D. McCulloch
Criminology and Social Policy, The Open University, Milton Keynes, UK
e-mail: victoria.cooper1@open.ac.uk

D. McCulloch
e-mail: daniel.mcculloch@open.ac.uk

© The Author(s), under exclusive license to Springer Nature Switzerland AG 2023
D. G. Scott and J. Sim (eds.), *Demystifying Power, Crime and Social Harm*, Critical Criminological Perspectives, https://doi.org/10.1007/978-3-031-46213-9_16

violence and victimisation in the lives of homeless women is systemic and is rarely a one-off event, but instead occurs multiple times over, as women move in and out of homelessness over a protracted period.

Homelessness is a highly gendered phenomenon. The causal factors contributing to women's homelessness and strategies they adopt to navigate space and place are distinct from the experience of homeless men (Cloke et al. 2010). To mitigate the risk of violence, it is widely understood that as a 'survival strategy', homeless women make themselves less visible and form relationships to conceal their visibility (Mayock et al. 2015; Klodawsky 2006). While the range of survival strategies adopted by homeless women may vary according to cultural and geographical context, they nevertheless help to frame the understandings of homelessness as a highly gendered phenomenon.

Using Steven Box's concept of mystification, this chapter will first set out the ways in which the state conceals harm and violence caused to marginal populations, while at the same time framing these groups as 'problem populations' by emphasising their supposedly pathological tendencies. Second, this chapter considers the ways in which policy constructions and definitions of homelessness can furthermore be understood as part of the process of mystification, where local states produce contradictory political responses 'that neither admits nor denies homelessness, that neither provides homes nor leaves the homeless on the streets' (Marcuse 1988: 85). We argue that dominant political narratives that seek to mystify social problems like homelessness, make claims that allow governments to maintain power over how social problems are defined, about which groups are affected by it and assert control over institutional responses. Here we draw on the analytical framework of 'maximalist' and 'minimalist' understandings of definitions of homelessness and related policy frameworks and in doing so demonstrate the material and institutional impacts of mystification. Third, this chapter will argue that the historical construction of homelessness has largely drawn upon the male experience and that policy provision for homeless women, or lack of, has been linked to these historical constructions. Here, we draw upon the ways in which homeless women are subject to a complex ideology, understood through constructions of gender and the home, and what this means for homeless women who are ideologically, out of place. Finally, this chapter explores the gendered experience of women's homelessness and ongoing risks of violence which fundamentally shape the survival strategies they adopt, such as remaining hidden from public and formal homeless spaces. Here we emphasise the failure of institutional and official provision of support to homeless women, where an absence of gender-specific resources effectively forces homeless women to pursue informal and hidden routes that are not necessarily safe but may be safer than the official institutional route.

'Nothing but Mystification'[1]

Those familiar with the work of Steven Box (1983) will recognise his call for 'radical reflexiveness' when thinking about marginalisation and social control, and the utility of criminal law designed to criminalise, stigmatise and demoralise so-called 'problem populations'. In his seminal book, *Power Crime and Mystification*, Box frames the notion of ideological mystification to describe the ways in which marginalised and disadvantaged groups in society are subjugated and subordinated through processes of criminalisation and punishment. He argues that:

> crimes of the powerless are revealed and exaggerated, and this serves interests of the powerful because it legitimizes their control agencies, such as the police and prison service, being strengthened materially, technologically, and legally, so that their ability to survey, harass, deter, both specifically and generally, actual and potential resistors to political authority is enhanced. (Box 1983: 6)

The key point Box raises is that through processes of ideological mystification, politicians and governments can frame certain activities and behaviours in ways that lead to the stigmatisation and demonisation of marginalised groups and individuals, and legislate against their behaviours in ways that maximise social control policy and intervention and ensure their criminalisation. Mystification helps to produce

---

[1] Box (1983: 12).

common-sense understandings of crime, who are the perpetrators or victims of crime, and where are the geographical criminal 'hotspots'. These common-sense tropes serve to produce a crucial blind spot that concerns the systemic nature of corporate and political criminality. As Box presciently points out, the state constructs everyday views and assumptions about marginalised groups, 'by concealing and hence mystifying its own propensity for violence and serious crime on a much larger scale' (ibid.: 14). For Box, law enforcement 'operates in such a way as to conceal crimes of the powerful against the powerless, but to reveal and exaggerate crimes of the powerless against everyone' (1983: 5). Box sees the instrumental value of criminal law as ideologically mirroring 'the interests of particular powerful groups' (ibid.: 7). But the capacity of the state to conceal corporate criminality, while weaving a dominant narrative about the causal relationship between so-called problem populations and deviance is not achieved through state coercion alone, though Box does address that. To fully comprehend the intricacies of mystification and how it plays out through state institutions, Box pays equal attention to deviant perceptions of marginalised groups through the process of stigmatisation and demonisation. Here, he draws on the example of unemployment and the fatigued trope that unemployment leads to crime. Ideological responses to such tropes all hinge upon *perceptions* surrounding, for example, the fear of crime, social unrest, and disorder, which are amplified through various state apparatuses.

Borrowing from Hall et al. (1978), Box argues that fear, criminality, and unemployment are mediated and reproduced by the media, an ideological apparatus of the state. Through the technical and bureaucratic organisation of what is considered to be 'newsworthy', verified and validated by 'primary definers' of certain topics, the media reproduces 'the existing structure of power in society's institutional order' (Hall et al. 1978: 58). What we are left with, argues Box, is the 'official view' of social problems and disadvantaged groups that are mediated by public and private agencies to produce everyday common-sense understandings about their alleged problems and failings. '[i]n this illusion', argues Box, poverty and criminality are seen 'as effects of moral inferiority, thus rendering the "dangerous" class deserving of both poverty and punishment' (Box 1983: 13–14).

Mystification and Constructions of Homelessness

No strangers to processes of mystification and political ideology that shape dominant understandings of their plight, homeless people are familiar with the deluge of negative public perceptions that stigmatise them as 'flawed' and 'undeserving' populations. As the visibility of social problems like homelessness amplifies, so too does public perceptions that fixate on the 'deviant' meanderings and activities associated with the status of being homeless. Over the last four decades, local governments have invested significant time and energy into the ideological construction of homeless populations, portraying them as inherently deceptive and undeserving of any meaningful support, while gradually transferring the most vital and urgent support for affordable and adequate housing supply to the private market. With the manufacturing of stigma, governments can shape public perception in order to maintain popular support for the uneven distribution of resources in ways that adhere to the 'anti-welfare' political agenda pursued by many states in the Global North, while gradually transferring the most vital and urgent support for affordable and adequate housing supply to the private market. Anti-welfare ideology, argue Jensen and Tyler (2015), rides on the trope that welfare expenditure has stagnating effects on economic growth and that the private market can provide better, higher-quality goods and services to meet the public's needs, and at lower costs. Ideological tropes such as these obfuscate a more serious political shift occurring amongst the powerful class which involves the extraction of value from public assets and consolidation of private wealth (Cooper and Whyte 2017). Despite the social injurious effects of uneven distribution of wealth, the myth prevails in dominant public narratives that so-called 'welfare dependents' are a problem population, particularly populations like the homeless who are so far removed from participating 'in the roles supportive of capitalist society' (Spitzer 1975: 645). Thus, politicians and governments attempt to shine a light down on disenfranchised groups, such as the homeless populations, framing them as 'deceptive', 'deviant' and/or 'work shy' individuals, in need of the state intervention through workfare-style programmes. For Box, marginalised groups who fall outside of the capitalist mode of production become eligible for state intervention and are managed in ways that reinforce everyday perceptions about individual and pathological failings of the poor. Here he draws on the notion of 'social junk' coined by Spitzer (1975: 645), which represents 'a costly yet relatively harmless burden to society'. Discrete populations managed as 'social Junk' do not represent any great threat to society, and the corresponding approach to managing these populations, Spitzer (1975: 645) argues, is usually 'to regulate and contain rather than eliminate and suppress the problem'.

This critical perspective chimes with Marcuse's (1988) analysis of homelessness, as he argues that 'the dominant response to homelessness will both require recognition of the problem and the prohibition of effective action to solve it' (1988: 85). However, slightly different from Box and Spitzer above, Marcuse is mostly concerned with the legitimation crisis that is at the centre of state responses to social problems. Homelessness, he argues, produces an intellectual realisation and moral outrage about the pervasiveness and limitations of market capitalism, evidenced by and through a lack of basic shelter, unaffordable housing and spike in abject poverty:

> Homelessness in the midst of plenty outrages our sense of well-being and social justice, and our sense of order and discipline. It touches a critical pillar upon which the whole organisations of our lives depend: the sense of home. (ibid.: 83)

Marcuse's take on managing homeless populations reveals something contradictory and nuanced about the regulation of so-called problem populations. If the heightened visibility of homelessness has the capacity to delegitimate 'the machinery of the system' (ibid.: 83), then governments must find ways to neutralise the moral outrage; they must be seen to be doing something about homelessness, while at the same time not jeopardising or slowing down the pace of private market capitalism. On this point, Marcuse (1988: 85) argues that governments and politicians must design policy interventions that 'neither admits nor denies homelessness'; they must show that they are addressing the inequalities

16 Mystification, Violence and Women's Homelessness

confronting homeless people through the funding of homeless service provision, while at the same time advancing market capitalism which, directly or indirectly, results in the eviction and homelessness of low-income households. Understood in this way, processes of mystification do not necessarily involve complete denial or exclusion of social problems like homelessness from public discourse, but rather relies upon a contradictory political logic that shapes definitional understandings and frames causal factors in ways that highlight some recognition of the problem, but ultimately achieves very little to resolve it.

Whether the goal is for dominant groups to completely distance themselves from the harms they perpetrated, as Box (1983) would argue, or whether it is to show some recognition of the social problem, but only in limited ways, dominant groups have the power to shape and influence how social problems like homelessness are understood and defined. In *Power, Crime and Mystification*, Box (1983) argues that dominant groups ideologically construct definitions of crime, and 'create the illusion that the "dangerous" class is primarily located at the bottom of various hierarchies' (ibid.: 13). Here we expand on the Boxian analysis by highlighting the dominant political narratives that seek to stereotype the characteristics and behavioural traits that lead to homelessness, which, in so doing, helps to depoliticise and neutralise political decision-making that can create or exacerbate the problem of homelessness.

Dominant political narratives that seek to neutralise social problems such as homelessness, allow governments to maintain power over how social problems are defined. Jacobs et al. (1999) argue, constructions of homelessness matter for understanding policy approaches to homelessness and housing, whereby 'the struggle by different vested interests to impose a particular definition of homelessness on the policy agenda is critical to the way in which homelessness is treated as a social problem' (1999: 11). For Jacobs et al., definitions of homelessness broadly vary between 'maximalist' and 'minimalist' policy frameworks. Under the minimalist framework, homelessness is narrowly defined, where governments and policy programmes frame the causes of homelessness as a behavioural outcome related to, for example, substance misuse, addiction, mental health, or lack of engagement with the labour market.

Under this framework, as is the case in England, routine administrative practices are designed to distinguish between 'deserving' and 'undeserving' homeless individuals, with the view to exclude so-called undeserving applicants from receiving meaningful housing provision.

By contrast, maximalist policy frameworks identify the causes of homelessness as lying within wider structural issues, such as labour market and housing market conditions. Policy responses and practices that adhere to the maximalist definitions of homelessness may involve interventions that maintain the necessary structural conditions and welfare infrastructure that prevents homelessness from occurring and provides targeted intervention to minimise the deleterious socio-economic effects of recession. Interventions under the maximalist policy response may include, by way of example, building genuinely affordable housing or legislative intervention that protects vulnerable households from eviction. Given the emphasis here on structural causes and factors, there is barely any distinction between supposed deserving and undeserving homeless groups within maximalist policy frameworks.

What is the purpose of pursuing a minimalist policy framework that manifestly classifies homeless groups as deserving and undeserving, and disqualifies the latter undeserving group from receiving any meaningful support? The way that governments respond to homelessness, we argue, can be linked to definitional constructions of homelessness. In the context of crime, Box argues that definitions of social problems matter for understanding policy frameworks because policy responses will often mirror the ideological construction and dominant narrative about the problem in question. When considering definitions of homelessness, it is crucial to take into consideration the 'different vested interests' because dominant groups have the power to shape understandings of homelessness in ways that support much wider political aims (Jacobs et al. 1999: 11). In England, the minimalist policy framework adopted in homelessness, advances anti-welfare political objectives as it seeks to administer housing reform and change at the level of the individual, while concealing the unfettered dominance of the private housing market that can cause and exacerbate conditions of homelessness. Definitions of homelessness that broadly focus on individual causes and individual needs have not only shaped administrative support structures and implemented eligibility tests but also serve to conceal the structural causes and conditions of homelessness. Systematic tools of homelessness assessment, for example, help to distinguish between those who are 'statutorily homeless'[2] and those who are not. With these tools of assessment, homeless applicants are routinely administered through complex gate-keeping processes (Robertson 2012), which lead to the exclusion and disqualification of thousands of adults and children from official definitions of statutory homelessness (Watson and Austerberry 1986). Administering groups within restrictive parameters of 'eligibility' allow governments to maintain a sense of legitimacy over their responses to homelessness. By determining which applicants are eligible for, or deserving of some mode of housing provision, governments effectively reinforce the idea that another 'undeserving' group of homeless people really does exist, that there is a 'social junk', who sit on the bottom rungs of disenfranchisement and are therefore in need of therapeutic, welfare or law enforcement intervention (Spitzer 1975).

It is for these reasons, amongst others that homelessness is profoundly bedevilled with definitional problems, mainly due to the contradictory institutional and political logic, as raised by Marcuse (1988), where policy frameworks include some homeless groups while excluding others. In collecting data about the incidence and responses to statutory homelessness, states render a small population who qualify for statutory support as the official and visible form of homelessness, at least in policy terms. Outside of official statutory homelessness, states often also collect data about the incidence of rough sleeping, however rough sleeping occupies a contradictory position in terms of its visibility: it is both the most visible form of homelessness to the public, but with barely any meaningful policy action, rough sleeping is also made invisible in policy terms. Relating to the multiplicity of homeless definitions, many people experiencing homelessness will experience 'hidden homelessness', which

---

[2] Statutory homelessness refers to those people who are owed a legal duty of care and assistance by their local authority.

describes a form of homelessness that is not captured by official statistics and is often ignored in policy; but is widely recognised by most non-government agencies.

As this chapter will show, the Boxian concept of mystification plays a vital role in the ways in which states define and develop policy responses to homelessness. Definitions of homelessness and politics interact in critical ways, whereby definitions, and the resulting inclusion of particular social groups can help to shed some light and knowledge about a social problem and its causes, and in some cases lead to meaningful political intervention, whereas the omission of key populations from official streams of knowledge can distort the scale of the problem and skew understandings about the main causal factors. In the following section, we examine the relative invisibility of homeless women in official knowledge and policy responses to homelessness, which has resulted in a lack of recognition and meaningful policy intervention.

Mystification and Women's Hidden Homelessness

The intellectual significance of *Power, Crime, and Mystification* can be found in its attention to what is concealed from the 'official view' and how common-sense understandings of particular social problems in society are constructed by the exclusion and invisibility of other social groups. Just as it is important to challenge the level at which marginalised groups are criminalised, punished, and stigmatised, Box also gives attention to what is omitted and concealed from the construction of everyday problems. In the context of crime and criminality, Box argues that female criminality has historically been rendered invisible from conventional understandings of crime and criminality and that criminological studies have either reproduced sexist attitudes or demonstrated a cursory, tokenistic interest in analyses of women and crime. Following Smart's (1976) seminal text, *Women, Crime and Criminology*, Box (1983) seeks to demystify the orthodox view that perpetrators of crime are mainly men. Here he highlights how systemic patriarchal oppression and women's economic marginalisation can lead to female criminality in areas of theft, property, and social security-related offences. Although these debates concerning the invisibility of women were made in relation to crime and criminality, they chime with the epistemic issues relating to women and homelessness.

Homelessness has been historically constructed as a problem that is mainly experienced by men, which has been used to frame dominant understandings of homelessness—both politically and within research (O'Sullivan 2016; Neale 1997; Watson and Austerberry 1986). While historiographies of homelessness are vast and rich in detail, homeless women feature far less than homeless men. As Mayock et al. (2015: 878) argue, 'gender tends not to be at the forefront of analytic attention and gains only cursory consideration in most studies of homelessness amongst "single" people'. This lack of analytical attention is especially the case when considering understandings of long-term homelessness, where men's experience tends to prevail over women's. Indeed, several academic and policy studies tend to present women's homelessness as a relatively new phenomenon, where the increasing visibility of homeless women and children from the 1970s onwards was treated as a new problem (see for example DePastino 2003).

Homeless women's invisibility is partly due to men being the main visible group, whose disadvantage and deprivation is more readily 'seen' and understood at critical moments of socio-economic decline. This is certainly reinforced by the complex historical framings of homeless women, who were depicted as either visible, defiant 'vagrants' and managed by law, or as respectable homeless women whose desire to remain hidden was supported through philanthropic charity groups (O'Brien 2018). Throughout history, homeless women have been isolated in ways that are different from men. To elaborate on this point further, O'Sullivan (2016) notes that it was more commonplace for homeless women to be found in refuges and asylums, as opposed to 'privately delivered lodging houses that provided communal shelter-type accommodation' (ibid.:16). Given the differential historical responses, the visibility of men's experience has garnered wider recognition, resulting in policy and institutional responses that seek to respond to homelessness as a homogenous experience, despite homelessness being a highly gendered phenomenon (O'Sullivan 2008).

Revisiting the notion of ideological mystification, we are concerned with causal factors leading to women's homelessness that are excluded from common-sense understandings of socio-economic and cultural conditions pertinent to women. According to Box (1983), mystification is achieved by echoing the official statistics in front of us and concealing the wider political and economic reality of circumstances surrounding poverty or powerlessness and ignoring the differential treatment of men and women when considering social problems. These ideas are particularly pertinent to women's homelessness because what is concealed from everyday understanding of women's homelessness is the ideological construction of gender in relation to the home. According to Jasinski et al. (2010: 57), homeless women are 'subject to an even more complex ideology' because of the normative assumptions surrounding the home and gender. Definitional constructions of gender are co-constructed through meanings of space and place, where there is a profound 'connection of space and place with gender and the construction of gender relations' (Massey 1994: 2). The elusive place called 'home' and the nostalgic beat of belonging are crucially linked and personified by the idealised norms and expectations of women in society. Although the meaning of 'home' is not fixed, it has been historically linked to normative assumptions of gender and family relations, such as 'ideas of companionate marriage, children and shared activities' (Neale 1997: 39). And even though gender roles for women in society have significantly changed and shifted from home life to public life, the ideological construction of women as belonging within the home environment, as primary homemaker, wife, and mother, still very much exist today (Watson 2000; McCarthy 2018; Dej 2020).

The interdependent meanings of gender and home cannot be overstated enough when thinking about the broader invisibility of homeless women and societal responses, or lack thereof. Feminist studies focusing on the causal relationship between violence and homelessness argue that domestic abuse is a significant contributing factor to women's homelessness and view the home as a primary site wherein violence and psychological abuse are reoccurring events (Dej 2020). Studies overwhelmingly show that homeless women are exposed to extreme and persistent violence within the home setting, where they encounter multiple experiences of victimisation over a long period of time (Wardhaugh 2017; Jasinski et al. 2010; Mayock et al. 2015). Relatedly, it is furthermore important to underline the correlation between experiences of childhood violence and homelessness, with evidence showing that experiences of violence in childhood can also increase the risk of homelessness for women. McCarthy (2018: 973) notes in her study of homeless women that abuse and violence 'featured as part of women's childhood relationships, as they navigated a world in which relationship violence was part of the everyday'.

Until now, we have focused on women's experiences of homelessness as being without a home. However, given the systemic nature of domestic abuse in the lives of homeless women, understandings of homelessness cannot be reduced to the physical and material reality of being outside of the home. The notion of being 'homeless at home' is a useful concept for capturing the psychological unravelling of living in fear, feeling insecure and having no control within the home environment. In those circumstances, it is intimated that people who do not feel at home are 'homeless at home' (Wardhaugh 1999: 94). Furthermore, and conceptually, being homeless at home introduces an important paradigmatic shift as it prompts a reassessment of the home as being a comfortable and harmonious space to exist within, or lament for. In the context of domestic abuse, the home is re-framed as possibly the most significant site of crime, harm, and violence, whereby women with acute trauma may connect the idea of being housed or having a home, with feelings of isolation, fear, and violation. Therefore, by taking into account the complex traumatic experiences that occur from within the home, it is possible to foreground the unsettling relationship that many homeless women may have with the idea of the 'home', as opposed to presenting the home as a common pursuit of happiness and belonging (McCarthy 2018; Wardhaugh 2017).

While homeless women shine a light on the sinister reality of the home as a site of harm, violence and insecurity, they are othered for disrupting the idea of the home 'as a source of identity and as a foundation of social order' (Wardhaugh 1999: 106), and for transgressing gendered meanings of the home. As a result, homeless women and women who are 'homeless at home' are often viewed as being responsible for their own situation and to some degree, are made to bear responsibility for the consequential outcomes. Their culpability is based on the false premise that they can escape abuse within the home at any time and move into alternative accommodation where there is none (Wardhaugh 1999). To avoid the stigma of being in an abusive relationship and/or blamed for making themselves homeless, it is argued that many homeless women conceal their experiences of violence and victimisation from statutory homeless services (Posada-Abadía et al. 2021: 216–217).

Homeless Women and Permutations of Violence

In the context of crime and victimisation, Box (1983) highlights the contradictory cultural norms surrounding sexual violence against women, where representations of women as being 'vulnerable' and in need of 'protection' collide with techniques of neutralisation that mobilise feelings of shame and stigma, resulting in women being held responsible for their own victimisation. It is not difficult to see the same cultural and gendered contradictions play out in the field of women's homelessness. Here we are concerned with the structural failings that, on the one hand, seek to responsibilise women for their own safety, and on the other hand, fail to prevent victimisation through wholly inadequate housing and policy provision that is available for homeless women. These points combined, it is not difficult to see how those cultural norms of women being shamed or stigmatised for the violence perpetrated against them are reinforced by the structural, fiscal norms that chisel away at housing programmes and support for homeless women. As the discussion below will highlight, homeless women would no doubt prefer to address their homelessness problem using the formal route of state support, however, given the structural inadequacies in supporting them, the informal and potentially more dangerous route tends to be the one that is most traversed. Although Box (1983) does not refer to the social problem of homelessness per se, it is clear to see how the state's propensity to cause structural harm and violence in the context of homeless women is concealed by the cultural norms that seek to blame women for their own victimisation and responsibilise them for their own safety.

It should by now be apparent that violence and victimisation in the lives of homeless women is rarely a one-off; it is a recurring experience. Where the causal relationship between domestic violence and homelessness is well understood, experiences of violence and victimisation continue in everyday experiences of homelessness. Homeless women experience much greater levels of victimisation compared to the general population and everyday experiences of homelessness are underpinned by multiple episodes of physical assault, theft, harassment, and sexual violence. So prevalent is the risk of violence that women must constantly adopt survival strategies to avoid it. To manage the ongoing fear of sexual violence, for example, homeless women are forced to adopt a range of survival strategies which may include: removing themselves from the public gaze by choosing private institutional spaces, such as hostels or day centres; or acquiring masculine appearances, such as 'dressing as men' (Wardhaugh 1999: 104; Jasinski et al. 2010). Relatedly, it is argued that women are more inclined to pursue informal forms of accommodation, to 'avoid sleeping on the streets or being accommodated in emergency shelter' and more generally, to mitigate the ongoing risk of violence and sexual violence (Klodawsky 2006: 368). Homeless women are understood to move more frequently in and out of official and unofficial routes of housing support as they seek alternative forms of accommodation as and when it becomes available, such as staying with friends and family and forming relationships with men (Huey 2012). Even where these strategies are imperfect or themselves entail other risks (Reeve et al. 2006), such alternative routes help women to remain hidden from official institutional homeless spaces (Mayock et al. 2015; Klodawsky 2006).

Following this gendered logic and everyday experience, women's homelessness is understood to be mainly hidden (Mayock et al. 2015). While the above discussion underlines some of the gendered harms that help to explain the general invisibility of homeless women, it is crucial to connect their invisibility to formal policy frameworks, particularly when thinking about the lack of service provision for homeless women and gate-keeping measures used by statutory authorities that so often results in their exclusion. Not only are homeless women invisible in terms of dominant understandings of homelessness and knowledge about who is affected, but they are more so hidden and underrepresented in terms of policy provision and intervention. Despite the gendered disparities leading to women's homelessness, such as domestic violence, sexual violence, or being the sole carer for children, there are barely any gender-specific policy understandings of women's experiences of homelessness (Mayock et al. 2015). The barriers to accessing statutory homelessness provision of support are well understood and chime with the minimalist legislative frameworks as discussed earlier in this chapter. These barriers may well divert homeless women away from applying for statutory provision of support and force them into informal and unofficial routes for seeking accommodation. For example, stringent eligibility tests in homelessness law in England, such as assessment around intentionality and priority need, mean that homeless people seeking formal support must first satisfy the local authority that they have done everything in their power to prevent themselves from becoming homeless, or as Bevan (2021: 961) succinctly puts it, the intentionality test is a way of examining 'how the homeless applicant itself assessed, balanced and responded to their own housing risk.' Second, applicants must furthermore satisfy the local authority that they are *more* vulnerable than the 'ordinary person if made homeless' (ibid.), which, given the legal comparator, is not easy to prove or qualify. Many argue that eligibility tests such as intentionality and vulnerability act as barriers and play a gate-keeping function that prevents women from accessing official provision of support to be rehoused.

In cases where homeless women do make formal applications and qualify as 'statutorily homeless', they can expect to wait months or years to be rehoused. In England alone, we are looking at approximately 75,000 women and 120,000 children living in temporary accommodation (Wilson and Barton 2020; Schofield 2021). In fact, local authorities use temporary accommodation so frequently, and not always as a short-term resort, that one homeless charity, *Shelter*, reported that temporary accommodation is 'effectively becoming the new social housing with some families having to watch their children grow up in it, with no idea when they might be able to access a stable and suitable home' (Rich and Garvie 2020: 27). In the event that statutorily homeless women with children are eventually offered permanent housing, Malos and Hague (1997: 399) argue that the 'eventual offer of property may not provide anything worthy of the name of "home"'. For homeless women with children who are assessed as ineligible and thus disqualified from receiving statutory housing support, it is not uncommon for social services to be drawn upon for the arrangement of temporary accommodation for children.[3] In light of these gate-keeping barriers and general poor quality support provided by official housing authorities, we should not be at all surprised that homeless women will seek informal routes for rehousing and will try to remain hidden.

Recent legislative shifts may suggest that homeless women are receiving greater support than in the past, but this is far from the case. In England and Wales, the *Homelessness Reduction Bill* 2017 claims that homeless service providers should meet the support needs of key issues, including 'victims of domestic abuse', but service provision for women has significantly diminished in the last decade (Towers and Walby 2012) and where support is provided, domestic violence services and responses to homelessness 'have remained largely or wholly distinct.' (Mayock et al. 2015: 140). Cuts to public expenditure rolled out since 2010 have resulted in a sharp decline in domestic abuse services and related support available for marginalised women. To make matters far worse, cuts to domestic service provision have occurred alongside the drastic reduction in homelessness service provision (McCulloch 2017). In particular,

---

[3] In the case of *Nzolameso v Westminster City Council [2015] UKSC 22*, the Supreme Court judges ruled that Westminster City Council's offer of property was not sufficient to discharge their legal obligations towards Ms Nzolameso. Due to cuts in housing benefit subsidies and subsequent rent arrears, Ms Nzolameso and her five children were made homeless. They were assessed by Westminster local authority as homeless: in priority need and unintentionally homeless, which qualifies her family for maximum local authority housing support ('main duty'). However, Westminster authority wanted to house the family 'out of the area', in a 5-bedroom property, in Bletchley Milton Keynes, claiming that they didn't have a close enough connection to Westminster. Westminster authority provided temporary accommodation during the appeal process and until she applied to the Court of Appeal. When she was refused a judicial review of that decision, Westminster authority ceased to provide any temporary accommodation. Subsequently, the children's services department provided accommodation for her five children, who were separated between three different foster families, while Ms Nzolameso had to source her own accommodation (see McGuire and Hutchings 2015).

provision of support for women experiencing domestic violence, such as Women's Aid, which provides refuge for women and children fleeing from domestic abuse, and Women's Centres that provide key community support for women on the margins of the criminal justice system now struggle to provide the same quality of support and have a far less reach due to the significant reduction of funds (Cooper and Mansfield 2020). Despite the disproportionate impact austerity is having upon the lives of disenfranchised women and the institutional neglect they continue to experience, governments are claiming they have improved support for homeless women. It is this contradictory political logic, we argue, that underpins processes of mystification: not excluding homeless women entirely, but neither providing meaningful support or critical intervention that resolve their homelessness.

Institutional responses to women who are victims of crime and violence during episodes of homelessness do not look much better. Although it is well understood that homeless women encounter far greater levels of violence compared to the general population, research shows that crimes against them are grossly underreported, and as a result, their experiences of victimisation remain under the radar (Scurfield et al. 2009). There are several reasons why women do not report their crime, but perhaps the most significant reason, one that contributes more generally to key debates around the politics of victimisation (Christie 1986), is that homeless individuals do not assume 'the ideal victim' status (ibid.). Relegated to the bottom of 'ideal victim' type, homeless women are seen to transgress conventional ideologies of the home, as discussed above. Othered for transgressing the conventional norms of the home and blamed for engaging in so-called 'risky behaviour', such as drug and alcohol consumption, studies show that homeless people rarely approach criminal justice authorities as a route for protection and safety because victimisation is expected in homeless settings and police 'might take criminal reports from homeless people less seriously' (Nilsson et al. 2020: 340). Such issues with reporting leads to a general invisibility concerning the victimisation of homeless women which, in turn, produces a skewed official knowledge about experiences of crime and victimisation confronting them.

16 Mystification, Violence and Women's Homelessness   425

Conclusion

A vital text for our time, *Power, Crime, and Mystification* shines a crucial light on what is omitted and concealed from definitional understandings of social problems and seeks to lift the veil on the state's propensity for causing structural harm by advancing the power of the dominant class. By elaborating on the concept of ideological mystification, Box demystifies the ideological framing of social problems like crime and marginalisation, and although Box (1983) did not refer to the social problem of homelessness, his ideas are crucial for unravelling, or rather demystifying the ideological constructs that produce common-sense understandings of homelessness.

This chapter has explored how dominant understandings of homelessness have been historically constructed as a socio-economic problem largely experienced by men, whereas women's homelessness tends to be presented as a relatively new phenomenon. Women's relative absence from understanding of homelessness is largely due to the historical construction of their homelessness as a personal affliction, treated and concealed by philanthropic organisations or asylums. Crucially linked to the invisibility of homeless women, is the gendered ideological construction of the home, whereby meanings of home are linked to gendered norms surrounding marriage, motherhood and care-giving. Othered for transgressing the gendered social order of the home and for disrupting normative meanings of the home as a place of sanctuary, homeless women are materially and ideologically out of place. The causal factors contributing to women's homelessness and the survival strategies they must adopt are distinct from men's experiences. Due to the ongoing risk of violence and sexual violence, homeless women are more likely to pursue informal routes for support, conceal their visibility, and remain hidden. While this is certainly true, it is equally important to also consider the failure of statutory provision and institutional neglect that can lead to women becoming hidden homeless. Rather than protect and support women on the verge of becoming homeless, official routes of housing support and legal duty of care may well compromise women's safety and push them further onto the margins of the state as women pursue informal routes for housing, to remain hidden from the 'official view'.

Using a Boxian analysis for thinking about homelessness helps to shine a light on what is concealed from the official view. Beginning with the concept of mystification, this chapter drew on the ways in which the ideological construction of social problems can 'render invisible the vast amount of avoidable harm, injury and deprivation imposed on the ordinary population by the state' (Box 1983: 14). However, and in the context of homelessness, mystification does not necessarily result in the complete subjugation and exclusion of homeless groups. Instead, we argued that social problems like homelessness are neither denied nor solved through any meaningful intervention, or to frame this conundrum slightly differently, the dominant political approach has been to show 'recognition of the problem and the prohibition of effective action to solve it' (Marcuse 1988: 85). This contradictory political logic, or mystification, allows governments to define the homeless problem and construct minimalist policy frameworks that seek to ascertain 'eligibility' and segregate 'unintentionally' and 'vulnerable' homeless applicants from applicants who are defined as 'intentionally' homeless and not vulnerable enough. All we are left with is the 'official view', as Box argues, and in the context of women's homelessness, the official view is desperately limited.

References

Bevan, C. 2021. Reconceptualising Homelessness Legislation in England. *The Modern Law Review* 84 (5): 953–973.

Box, S. 1983. *Power Crime and Mystification*. Tavistock Publications.

Christie, N. 1986. The Ideal Victim. In *From Crime Policy to Victim Policy*, ed. E. Fattah, 17–30. London: Macmillan.

Cloke, P., P. May, and S. Johnsen. 2010. *Swept Up Lives: Re-envisioning the Homeless City*. Oxford: Wiley-Blackwell.

Cooper, V., and M. Mansfield. 2020. Marketisation of Women's Organisations in the Criminal Justice Sector. In *Marketisation and Privatisation in Criminal Justice*, ed. K. Alberston, M. Corcoran, and J. Philips, 203–220. Bristol: Policy Press.

Cooper, V., and D. Whyte. 2017. Introduction. In *The Violence of Austerity*, ed. V. Cooper and D. Whyte, 1–34. London: Pluto.

Dej, E. 2020. *A Complex Exile: Homelessness and Social Exclusion in Canada*. Columbia: University of British Columbia Press.

DePastino, T. 2003. *Citizen Hobo: How a Century of Homelessness Shaped America*. Chicago: University of Chicago Press.

Hall, S., C. Critcher, T. Jefferson, J. Clarke, and B. Roberts. 1978. *Policing the Crisis: Mugging, the State and Law and Order*. Basingstoke: Macmillan Press.

Huey, L. 2012. *Invisible Victims: Homelessness and the Growing Security Gap*. Toronto: Toronto University Press.

Jacobs, K., J. Kemeny, and T. Manzi. 1999. The Struggle to Define Homelessness: A Constructivist Approach. In *Homelessness: Public Policies and Private Troubles*, ed. S. Hutson and D. Clapham, 11–28. Cassell.

Jasinski, L.J., D.J. Wesley, K.J. Wright, and E.E. Mustaine. 2010. *Hard Lives, Mean Streets: Violence in the Lives of Homeless Women*. Northeastern University Press.

Jensen, T., and I. Tyler. 2015. 'Benefits Broods': The Cultural and Political Crafting of Anti-welfare Commonsense. *Critical Social Policy* 35 (4): 470–491.

Klodawsky, F. 2006. Landscapes on the Margins: Gender and Homelessness in Canada. *Gender, Place and Culture* 13 (4): 365–381.

Malos, E., and G. Hague. 1997. Women, Housing, Homelessness and Domestic Violence. *Women's Studies International Forum* 20 (3): 397–409.

Marcuse, P. 1988. Neutralizing Homelessness. *Socialist Review* 88 (1): 69–97.

Massey, D.B. 1994. *Space, Place, and Gender*. Minnesota: University of Minnesota Press.

Mayock, P., S. Sheridan, and S. Parker. 2015. 'It's Just Like We're Going Around in Circles and Going Back to the Same Thing …': The Dynamics of Women's Unresolved Homelessness. *Housing Studies* 30 (6): 877–900.

McCarthy, L. 2018. (Re)conceptualising the Boundaries Between Home and Homelessness: The Unheimlich. *Housing Studies* 33 (6): 960–985.

McCulloch, D. 2017. Austerity's Impact on Rough Sleeping and Violence. In *The Violence of Austerity*, ed. V. Cooper and D. Whyte, 171–177. London: Pluto Press.

McGuire QC, B., and M. Hutchings. 2015. Judicial Review as Sliding Scales: Some Pointers from Recent Homelessness Case Law. *Judicial Review* 20 (3): 152–156.

Neale, J. 1997. Theorising Homelessness: Contemporary Sociological and Feminist Perspectives. In *Homelessness and Social Policy*, ed. R., Burrows, N. Pleace, and D. Quilgars, 35–49. Routledge.

Nilsson, S.F., M. Nordentoft, S. Fazel, and T.M. Laursen. 2020. Homelessness and Police-Recorded Crime Victimisation: A Nationwide, Register-Based Cohort Study. *The Lancet Public Health* 5 (6): e333–e341.

O'Brien, A. 2018. 'Homeless' Women and the Problem of Visibility: Australia 1900–1940. *Women's History Review* 27 (2): 135–153.

O'Sullivan, E. 2008. Pathways Through Homelessness: Theoretical Constructions and Policy Implications. In *'In My Caravan, I Feel Like Superman': Essays in Honour of Henk Meert*, ed. J. Doherty and B. Edgar, 1963–2006, 79–108. FEANTSA/Centre for Housing Research, University of St. Andrews.

O'Sullivan, E. 2016. Women's Homelessness: A Historical Perspective. In *Women's Homelessness in Europe*, ed. P. Mayock and J. Bretherton, 15–40. Basingstoke: Palgrave Macmillan UK.

Posada-Abadía, C.I., C. Marín-Martín, C. Oter-Quintana, and M.T. González-Gil. 2021. Women in a Situation of Homelessness and Violence: A Single-Case Study Using the Photo-Elicitation Technique. *BMC Women's Health* 21 (1): 1–15.

Reeve, K., R. Casey, and R. Goudie. 2006. *Homeless Women: Still Being Failed Yet Striving to Survive*. London: Crisis.

Rich, H., and D. Garvie. 2020. *Caught in the Act: A Review of the New Homelessness Legislation*. London: Shelter. https://england.shelter.org.uk/professional_resources/policy_and_research/policy_library/report_caught_in_the_act. Accessed 16 Aug 2022.

Robertson, G. 2012, October 5. *No Way Through*. Inside Housing. https://www.insidehousing.co.uk/insight/no-way-through-33188. Accessed 16 Aug 2022.

Schofield, M. 2021. *Fobbed Off: The Barriers Preventing Women Accessing Housing and Homelessness Support, and the Women-Centred Approach Needed to Overcome Them*. London: Shelter. https://england.shelter.org.uk/professional_resources/policy_and_research/policy_library/fobbed_off_the_barriers_preventing_women_accessing_housing_and_homelessness_support. Accessed 16 Aug 2022.

Scurfield, J., P. Rees, and P. Norman. 2009. Criminal Victimisation of the Homeless: An Investigation of Big Issue Vendors in Leeds. *Radical Statistics* 99: 3–11.

Smart, C. 1976. *Women, Crime and Criminology: A Feminist Critique*. London: Routledge and Kegan Paul.

Spitzer, S. 1975. Toward a Marxian Theory of Deviance. *Social Problems* 22 (5): 638–651.

Towers, J., and S. Walby. 2012. Measuring the Impact of Cuts in Public Expenditure on the Provision of Services to Prevent Violence Against Women and Girls. *Safe-the Domestic Abuse Quarterly* 41: 1–58.

Wardhaugh, J. 1999. The Unaccommodated Woman: Home, Homelessness and Identity. *The Sociological Review* 47 (1): 91–109.

Wardhaugh, J. 2017. *Sub City: Young People, Homelessness and Crime*. London: Routledge.

Watson, S. 2000. Homelessness Revisited: New Reflections on Old Paradigms. *Urban Policy and Research* 18 (2): 159–170.

Watson, S., and H. Austerberry. 1986. *Housing and Homelessness: A Feminist Perspective*. London: Routledge.

Wilson, W., and C. Barton. 2020. Households in Temporary Accommodation (England). *House of Commons Library, Briefing Paper*, 2110. London: HMSO.

Part V

Demystifying Social Harm

17

Standing on the Shoulders of a Criminological Giant: Steven Box and the Question of Counter-Colonial Criminology

Biko Agozino

Introduction

...nothing gets more up the nose of some contemporary criminologists than the assertion that ideas, no matter how orthodox in their pedigree or dizzying in their complexity, have to be abandoned if the results of 'hypothesis testing' research fail(s) to support them. (Box, cited in Young 1988: 95–96)

Power, Crime and Mystification [PCM] remains the classic that it was when it was first published. The book builds on previous insights by Box which were critical of the commonsensical notion in criminology that poverty was the main cause of crime. This chapter celebrates the work by Box (1983), with a focus on the first chapter of *PCM*, to show his conclusion that the exercise of power is more of a cause of crime than

B. Agozino (✉)
Sociology and Africana Studies, Virginia Tech, Blacksburg, VA, USA
e-mail: agozino@vt.edu

© The Author(s), under exclusive license to Springer Nature Switzerland AG 2023
D. G. Scott and J. Sim (eds.), *Demystifying Power, Crime and Social Harm*, Critical Criminological Perspectives, https://doi.org/10.1007/978-3-031-46213-9_17

poverty and that the powerful routinely get away with crimes and social harms, remains relevant to criminology and decolonization struggles.

Given that the theorem by Box rejecting the supposed association between crime and poverty appears counterintuitive to most people, this chapter will start with an appreciation of an earlier iteration of the argument in Box and Ford (1971). In that journal article, it was specified that 'the facts don't fit' (ibid.: 31) with reference to the expected relationship between poverty and crime. This observation can be used as a background to understanding Box's more elaborate statement of the theory in 1983. Following this re-examination of the poverty–crime thesis via Box and Ford, this chapter proceeds to an appreciation of the contribution of *PCM*. The influence of Box in criminology is outlined and this is followed by a discussion on the applicability of Box to the decolonization paradigm in criminology.

The Poverty and Crime Thesis

In 1971, Steven Box and Julienne Ford offered a groundbreaking critique of empiricist positivism in criminology in their co-authored journal article, 'The Facts Don't Fit' (Box and Ford 1971). That paper demonstrated an eye-opening claim that poor people are not more crime-prone than rich people and that claims to the contrary are just 'logical legerdemain' or magic tricks (ibid.: 31). The article posited that criminologists were in the business of creative writing when they try to explain known facts about crime, just like Sherlock Holmes. It used to be fashionable to attribute the causes of crime to biological determinism or physical characteristics such as the fiction of atavistic stigmata invented by Lombroso. Anyone who disagreed with such 'facts' would have been thought to be biased, foolish or crazy at the time that the fad was a central discourse in the conquering and colonizing army that Lombroso served as a surgeon (Melossi 2020).

If poverty was the main cause of crime, women should be more criminal than men given that they are more likely to be poorer than men in patriarchal societies (see Cooper and McCulloch, this volume). Carol Smart (1990) has pointed out that the atavistic stigmata alleged by

Lombroso is more applicable to men than to women who tend to be more likely to be crime victims than criminals themselves. Box (1983) made a similar observation by devoting a chapter to crimes of sexual violence against women (see Atkinson and Monk this volume; Fitzpatrick, this volume). Women tend to make up about 7% of prison populations in most countries around the world despite being poorer than men on average (see Chadwick and Clarke, this volume).[1]

Box and Ford's (1971) view that 'the facts don't fit' appears valid, particularly in relation to the question of bias in the collection and collation of official criminal statistics. As they noted:

> From our knowledge of the kinds of persons who commit one type of crime rather than another, it is clear that "ordinary" crimes tend to be committed more by persons from the less powerful and under-privileged sections of society, whereas "respectable" crimes are, as the label suggests, more likely to be committed by persons from the more privileged and powerful sections of the community. Thus, even if the police cleared up as many respectable crimes as ordinary crimes, there would still be proportionately more middle class offenders excluded than were reported to the police initially. (ibid.: 35)

It is still the case that within criminology and other disciplines, it is assumed as factual that poverty causes crime. The most popular versions of such claims are found in theories that assume a negative correlation between criminality and social class—as one rises, the other declines and vice versa. This assumption is embraced by those on the right and on the left of the ideological, sociological and political divides with few exceptions.

The poverty–crime assumption is also held by people on the streets, by law enforcement agents, by the media and by policy makers and is

---

[1] Although the population of women in prisons globally has increased by 60% from the year 2000 to 2022, it has been reported by the World Prison Brief that: 'Women and girls make up 6.9% of the global prison population. In African countries, the proportion of female prisoners is 3.3%, compared to 5.9% in Europe, 6.7% in Oceania, 7.2% in Asia, and 8.0% in the Americas'. https://www.prisonstudies.org/news/world-female-prison-population-60-2000#:~:text=Women%20and%20girls%20make%20up,and%208.0%25%20in%20the%20Americas. (Accessed 04/24/2003).

found in popular culture. Elvis Presley represented this in the lyrics of 'In the Ghetto' in which he asserted that without help, the little baby born in the ghetto will grow up to be an angry young man someday. Cocoa Tea also repeats this assertion in 'Poverty', a song that says that hunger and poverty are the causes of crime. Bob Marley also sang on the album 'Natty Dread' that 'them belly full (but we hungry)'. The good intention here is to call for poverty to be eliminated from society. Malcolm X said that African Americans were being manipulated into a life of poverty and crime but he added that the real criminals were in corporate and government offices. Fela Kuti concurs in almost all of his songs, especially in 'ITT: International Tief Tief' and 'Beasts of No Nation'. Both Martin Luther King Jr. and Nelson Mandela suggested in several speeches that poverty should be made history, not because it is the cause of crime but, because it is evidence of oppression and exploitation that should be treated as harms if not as crimes. Du Bois (1896) had long ago established that African Americans were overrepresented in official crime statistics because law enforcement ignored crimes of the powerful and railroaded even innocent African Americans into the convict lease system (Gabbidon 2020).

Box and Ford (1971) analysed the leading theorists at the time who propagated similar poverty–crime views including Robert K. Merton, Albert Cohen, Donald Cressey, Richard Cloward and Lloyd Ohlin, who held similar flawed assumptions about the reasonableness of the expectations that different social classes have different criminal behaviour propensities. Within criminology, the focus on the criminality of black people and racial crimes was challenged by Paul Gilroy (1982) by dismissing the myth of black criminality as asserted by Left Realists[2] who joined the tabloid press in asking the leaders of the black community to rein in their youth or the police will do it for them, without calling on the leaders of the white community to control their own youth. There is no such thing as black or white crime. Box and Ford (1971) concluded that:

---

[2] Left realism was a perspective in critical criminology that emerged in the late 1970s/early 1980s. It was intended to engage more directly with Labour Party politics. Its influence in criminology substantially declined after the late 1990s.

> Distinctions have to be made between primary law-violating behaviour, the official records of criminal behaviour, and secondary law-violating behaviour which results from official criminalization or reward-learning processes. Each of these requires a different explanation, and the facts of one should not be taken as the empirical basis on which an explanation of the others is constructed. (ibid.: 48)

Thus, they demystified the myth around poverty and crime and looked to the question of labelling just as Hall et al. (1978) did in *Policing the Crisis* seven years later.

However, Box and Ford (1971) wrote their powerful article without explicitly mentioning that the Labour Party government of Harold Wilson had just orchestrated a genocidal war in Biafra that killed 3.1 million people, mostly of Igbo descent, in 30 months from 1967 to 1970 for the protection of the interests of British oil companies (Curtis 2020; Achebe 2012; Ekwe-Ekwe 2019; Jacobs 1987).[3] According to Roger Morris (1977: 122):

> London … armed Nigeria and supported the starvation blockade with equal cynicism to protect its own post-colonial economic and political interests in West Africa. The Wilson government was beset by the widespread British public concern with the disaster, to which Whitehall's policy was, as one senior Foreign Office official put it to his American counterpart, "To show conspicuous zeal in relief while in fact letting the little buggers starve out." On one occasion late in the war, Wilson would tell Ferguson that casualties of the famine were no object. He would

---

[3] "On Mr. Wilson: His role as their true enemy was as clear as Lyndon Johnson's role in Vietnam. He had placed his Government fully at the service of the lust of British Shell and British Petroleum for the great Biafran oilfields, which produced crude oil so pure it can be used directly in diesel engines. The Ibos, who made up nine million of Biafra's pre war population of 14 million—five times the population of Ireland then, but perhaps only three times Ireland's now—were the people whom the English could never control in Colonial days. Mr. Wilson's goal was neocolonialism for Nigeria, a condition, I may add, that one sees in other presumably independent African countries. There, at the first sign of an administrative complication, from immigration procedures to hotel bills, a white man materializes to straighten things out. As long as their lanterns burned, this never happened in Biafra. But it was estimated that as many as 20 official missions—trade, sanitation and so on—had been sent to Nigeria from London in 1969." https://www.nytimes.com/1970/01/25/archives/an-epitaph-for-biafra-an-epitaph-for-biafra.html. (Accessed on 04/24/2023).

accept a half million dead Biafrans, said Wilson earnestly, if that was what it took to secure the old Nigeria.

Chinua Achebe analysed the genocide against the Igbo in Biafra to show that it was not a case of individual offenders as conventional criminologists would have it but institutionalized, nationalized and internationalized victimization of the innocent men, women and children of Igbo descent:

> What terrified me about the massacres in Nigeria was this: If it was only a question of rioting in the streets and so on, that would be bad enough, but it could be explained. It happens everywhere in the world. But in this particular case a detailed plan for mass killing was implemented by the government—the army, the police—the very people who were there to protect life and property. Not a single person has been punished for these crimes. It was not just human nature, a case of somebody hating his neighbour and chopping off his head. It was something far more devastating, because it was a premeditated plan that involved careful coordination, awaiting only the right spark. (Achebe 2012: 83)

Achebe admitted that he was neither a social scientist nor a lawyer, professions that should be addressing genocidal crimes or what Wayne Morrison (2004: 68) dubbed 'the companion that criminology neglected'. The methodology of self-reported criminality and statistical significance measures are not suitable for the subject matter of decolonization struggles. This is because those engaged in the struggle and the organized criminals they are up against have never concealed their stories but rather published profusely in books and articles, posts, music, fine arts, drama, cinema, dance, textiles, architecture, struggles, celebrations and commemorations. The state's definition of reality still dominates official discourse and the mass media, but without being able to totally conceal the huge crimes and harms that are done to the people by states, criminal justice systems and corporations.

Crime, Power and Ideological Mystifications

This chapter now returns to *PCM*. The discussion focuses on the first chapter of the book where Box reflected on the debate about facts that do not fit theories; arguing that there is no negative correlation between socio-economic class and deviance. Reiman and Leighton (2012) support this conclusion with an explanation of why *The Rich Get Richer and the Poor Get Prison*—not because the poor are more crime-prone, but because law enforcement turns a blind eye to what Frank Pearce (1976) called *Crimes of the Powerful*.

The chapter starts with the kind of alarmist tabloid newspaper types of headlines that echo the law and order priorities of official statistics: 'Murder! Rape! Robbery! Assault! Wounding! Theft! Burglary! Arson! Vandalism! These form the substance of the annual official criminal statistics on indictable offences…' (Box 1983: 1). There is no mention of genocide, slavery, colonialism, apartheid, racism, sexism and imperialism in the laundry list of indictable offences (Nkrumah 1965). Box noted that the index offences were on the increase in the decade from 1970 to 1980 and such increases were used to justify the increase in police powers and repressive fetishes of the prison industrial complex. The mythologization of crime and power relations can be exposed by examining the null hypothesis that there is no relationship between increasing crimes and increasing budgets for law enforcement. It is not as if crime went down to zero, there would be more support for the defunding of repressive state apparatuses. Instead, any declines would be used to justify the original hypothesis that there is a relationship between law enforcement effectiveness and any declines in crime rates; to justify increased funding rather than defunding at the expense of 'education, health, unemployment welfare, and social services, nothing much justifies the optimism' (ibid.: 1). As noted above, he opened with these haunting words: 'Murder! Rape! Robbery! Assault! Wounding! Theft! Burglary! Arson! Vandalism!' Then he observed that: 'The number of recorded serious crimes marches forever upward' (ibid.).

Maybe not 'forever', but it may have been the case for the decade that Box focused on, 1970–1980. Recorded crime was on the rise then but 'forever upward' was negated from a peak in 1995 with estimates of a sustained downward trend in serious crimes since then, according to the UK government.[4] These estimates of declining crime rates highlighted by the Conservative government at the time represented the priorities of the government whereas corporate crime, domestic violence, police corruption and racial attacks were not and are still not prioritized by the state and successive governments. People may not be willing to report all crimes especially when crimes are common. Whether crime goes up or down, the budget for law enforcement keeps rising forever upward. The Netherlands closed dozens of prisons after running out of convicts to house due to increasing civility in the wider society and even when serious crimes are involved, they chose to rely on alternatives to long prison sentences.[5] Yet, their criminal justice budget is not likely to be positively related to the falling recorded crime rates in support of the defunding hypothesis. Since their budget is beefed up with personnel costs, the abolition of prisons may still not result in zero spending on security, law and order.

Box (1983) demystifies the power relations implicit in claims to authority to regulate, discipline and punish others by indicting the state and the international community for their direct and proxy involvement in genocidal wars in poorer countries. As he put it:

> The criminal law includes and reflects our proper stance against "murderous" acts of terrorism conducted by people who are usually exploited or oppressed by forces of occupation. But it had no relevance, and its guardians remained mute ten years ago, when bombs, with the United States' and allied governments' blessing, fell like rain on women and children in Cambodia …, or when the same governments aid and support other political/military regimes exercising mass terror and partial genocide against a subjugated people …. The criminal law, in other words, condemns the importation of murderous terrorist acts usually against powerful individuals or strategic institutions, but goes all quiet when governments export or support avoidable acts of killing usually against the underdeveloped countries' poor. Of course there are exceptions—the

---

[4] See https://www.ons.gov.uk/peoplepopulationandcommunity/crimeandjustice/bulletins/crimeinenglandandwales/yearendingmarch2022.

[5] See https://www.theguardian.com/world/2019/dec/12/why-are-there-so-few-prisoners-in-the-netherlands.

Russian "invasion" of Afghanistan was a violation of international law and a crime against humanity. It may well have been, but what about Western governments' involvement in Vietnam, Laos, Cambodia, Chile, El Salvador, Nicaragua, Suez, and Northern Ireland? Shouldn't they at least be discussed within the same context of international law and crimes against humanity? And if not, why not? (Box 1983: 11)

This view that violence by states against people (including people of other states) should be treated as harm even when there is no political will to treat them as human rights crimes, is in line with zemiological (Canning and Tombs 2021) and decolonization perspectives (Agozino 2003, 2018) that have directly and indirectly followed Steven Box, Stuart Hall, Angela Davis, Jeffrey Reiman, Frank Pearce, among others. The major cause of crime is the abuse of power and not poverty/powerlessness given the absolute abuse of absolute power by states and corporations, to paraphrase Lord Acton who indicted the religious clergy.

The surprising thing for criminology is that few of the major authorities on decolonization were trained as criminologists, raising the question that Stan Cohen (1993) posed in his reflections on apartheid in South Africa and the first edition of the *Oxford Handbook of Criminology*: What was so unique about British criminology that made it ignore the biggest cases of crime around the world, especially in a *Handbook* that was bigger than the Bible—the human rights crimes that kill millions? Even when critical criminologists like Schwendinger and Schwendinger attempted to break the silence on genocide, Cohen (1993: 98) noted that: 'Firstly, they cite as examples of other socially injurious action (their only examples) genocide and economic exploitation'. Now, besides the fact that these are hardly morally equivalent categories, genocide is crucially different from economic exploitation. It is recognized in current political discourse as a crime by the state; it is clearly illegal by internal state laws; and since the Nuremberg Judgements and the 1948 UN Convention Against Genocide, it is a 'crime' according to international law. Genocide belongs to the same conceptual universe as 'war crimes' and 'crimes against humanity'. 'By any known criteria, genocide is more self-evidently criminal than economic exploitation' (ibid.).

Steven Box had to cite a historian, a linguist and a political scientist to support the reference to genocidal crimes committed by powerful countries in poorer countries that criminologists tend to ignore in their bulky textbooks. As Stephen Pfohl observed in his 'Foreword' to *Counter-Colonial Criminology* (Agozino 2003), there is something 'hauntingly unreal' (Pfohl 2003: xii) about criminology obsessing about crimes of the sort encoded in the French Penal Code of 1791 but choosing to ignore the biggest types of real crime against humanity such as slavery against which the enslaved Africans successfully rose to win their freedom and abolish slavery in Haiti by defeating the French, Spanish and British troops who attempted to restore slavery.

Box (1983: 11) also notes the obsession with crimes of the poor by criminologists but he insists that the facts do not fit the theory that correlates poverty with criminality. The poor are afraid of crimes and incivilities like public drunkenness, loud parties, mugging, drug addiction, domestic violence, racial attacks and graffiti in their communities but many of the rich get away with murder because the state focuses almost exclusively on crimes of the poor (Box 1983: 2). Even among the poor, it is often the more socially, economically, politically or physically stronger that bully the relatively weak (Agozino 2003). Therefore, what is needed is not just disempowerment but to make those who exercise power democratically accountable at all levels. What is needed is the decolonization of power relations in the interest of all (Ibid).

At the international level, some states and corporations openly take sides in criminally harmful ways for which they should be held accountable according to those pursuing a zemiological analysis (Canning and Tombs 2021). For example, Canning (2019: 46) observed that women and asylum seekers are infantilized and subjected to 'degradation by design' to force them to give up their claims for indefinite leave to remain in northern Europe. The fear of crime is real in poor communities but Box et al. (1988: 353) insist that the priorities of the government contribute to this fear whereas investing in those communities would help to reduce incivilities, some of which may not amount to serious crimes.

Pre-Box, conventional criminology followed the commonsense example of accepting the official statistics and priorities of the state without realizing how those statistics were intended to be used as tools for holding successive governments accountable over the enormous resources at their disposal, to ensure that such powers are not abused by the government of the day, and to distil 'facts' from 'myths' about official statistics (McClintock 1974). Conventional criminology now recognizes that there are dark figures in official statistics consisting of crimes unknown to the police but the solution to this recognition is usually to try and find true crime figures by relying on crime and victimization surveys rather than seek to support the defunding of known repressive forces in the pursuit of penal abolitionism in line with #BlackLivesMatter, #EndSARS and critical criminology (Onyeozili et al. 2021). But the point is not so much about the statistics or number crunching, it is about the fact that conventional criminology still ignores genocide, slavery, state sanctioned assassinations, the harms of colonialism, patriarchy and imperialism (Nkrumah 1965). It is to this issue of applicability that the chapter now turns.

The Applicability of *Power, Crime and Mystification* to Decolonization Theory

The book, *Black Women and the Criminal Justice System: Towards the Decolonisation of Victimisation* (Agozino 1997, 2018) highlighted enslavement, colonialism, apartheid and internal colonialism as systems of organized crimes that did serious harm to millions of people for hundreds of years. This fact is recognized in what is known as the colonial model in criminology (Gabbidon 2020) based on the decolonization work of Frantz Fanon (1963). The colonial model sees the conditions of the African Diaspora under racist-sexist-imperialism as being comparable to internal colonialism and settler colonialism in Latin America and elsewhere (Hall 1980). What is usually not specified in the theory of internal colonialism is the question of what is to be done about the harms of colonialism contrary to the focus of Fanon who prioritized the explanation of the various approaches to decolonization, including reparations. Box (1983) also raised the question of what is to be done about the huge crimes carried out by imperialist countries in poor countries around the world and he called for justice to be done in the interest of all.

Apart from the relative silence on decolonization by theories of internal colonialism, Edward Said (1993) challenged the theory of communicative action by Habermas for mentioning the colonization of the lifeworld by monetary power but without addressing the struggles for decolonization in different parts of the world, unlike Fanon. Agozino (1997, 2018) extended this concern about institutional colonization and decolonization struggles by calling for the victimization of the innocent to be decolonized from the expanding empire of punishment. This call is consistent with the observation of Box (1983) that the allegation of crimes against humanity by Western countries indicting Russia should be applied to the Western countries themselves for their support of the invasion and bombing of innocent millions in poorer countries and not flung exclusively at the Soviet Union for invading Afghanistan. He wrote this in 1983 long before the Russian war in Ukraine that started in 2022. But even Box did not extend his critique of Russia and the West for possible crimes against humanity to the genocide in Biafra that was facilitated with the supply of warplanes by the Soviet Union and with small arms and patrol boats supplied by the UK to kill millions and blockade them (Achebe 2012; Ekwe-Ekwe 2019).

A further insight from Box (1983) that is applicable to the decolonization of criminology is the critique of the punitive turn in the exercise of state power which has always been punitive anyway. Once criminologists recognize that decolonization is not a punitive practice but a reparative movement, then the coupling of crime and punishment in theories of modernity (Garland 1990) would be decentered in favour of reparative praxis (Agozino 2021). Citing Box (1983) among other authorities, I have linked reparative justice with decolonization as a more feasible model than punitive justice models. Without reparative justice, decolonization would remain incomplete. The recognition that genocide has been inflicted by imperialist countries against poorer countries does not presuppose that there will be punishment calibrated to fit the crimes or harms since no punishment would ever fit such crimes. Steven Box concentrated on what is to be done to tackle the structural conditions that make such crimes possible. However, Box did not clearly express the fact that such crimes against humanity tend to take racist forms and do not have only class-specific impacts (Hall 1980). Jock Young (1988) noted, in an obituary, that Box benefited from criticism about his relative lack of gender awareness and took on the task of addressing gender and class issues but Young did not raise a similar concern about the awareness of anti-racism contrary to the incisive contributions of Hall et al. (1978), Gilroy (1982) and Davis (1981), to mention but a few.

The survey of contributions from critical criminology in my *Counter-Colonial Criminology* led to the conclusion that each paradigm is in need of further decolonization by adopting lessons from counter-colonial struggles around the world. This is consistent with the conclusion of Box that the exercise of state power is more a cause of crime than poverty (Agozino 2003). This conclusion does not imply that the response to crime must always be the punitive disempowerment of the culprits in line with the punitive turn in state power. The problem is that, in general, criminology continues to describe the punitive turn in state policies without offering a decolonization and abolitionist perspective, as some, albeit a minority of criminologists, are now doing. The point is more about the fact that the punitive turn taken by different states around the world has not impacted the powerful in terms of the punishment of the powerful as represented by those who have engaged in state atrocities legitimated by racism, imperialism, patriarchy, homophobia and neo-colonialism (Nkrumah 1965). The application of Box to decolonization suggests that the deepening of democratization and the institution of reparative justice would be a more effective response to crimes of powerful states, corporations and individuals.[6] But what does a decolonized criminology compatible with a Boxian analysis look like?

An influential text on the decolonization of criminology was written by Blagg and Anthony (2019) with lots of support for counter-colonial

---

[6] "In 2002, the Khulumani Support Group for victims of Apartheid brought a suit against five corporations for providing infrastructure to South Africa's Apartheid regime. The case also used the Alien Tort Claims Act that allows non-US citizens to charge offenders of human rights. Again, the ATCA has been criticized by corporations, and the Act's relevance is now under review in the United States Supreme Court. The South African President Zuma approved of the lawsuit, 'hoping that reparations would help South Africa come to terms with the apartheid's legacy'" (Rothe and Kauzlarich 2016: 187).

criminology through its emphasis on the need to turn conventional criminology upside down from the point of view of Indigenous peoples; the need to move beyond the postcolonial perspective because the past is not over; the need to decolonize criminological methodologies in the interest of intellectual activism; the similarities of militarized state borders and the militarized prison industrial complex; the importance of emphasizing Indigenous justice and not just restorative justice; the irony of carceral feminism on Indigenous women who were supposedly being saved from Indigenous men; and the need to decolonize Indigenous self-policing and patrols.

Cunneen and Tauri (2016) in the innovative text, *Indigenous Criminology*, offer the first comprehensive theory of the impact of colonial criminal justice systems on Indigenous peoples; the importance of a comparative perspective on settler colonialism and criminology; the value of Indigenous knowledge systems in criminology; the importance of committed objectivity and scholar activism in criminological methodology; the need to prioritize Indigenous voices in opposition to deaths in custody; the prison industrial complex; the struggle for reparative justice; and the importance of the decolonization perspective in criminology. Further, the work of Box has directly and indirectly influenced my own work on counter-colonial criminology, something that has attracted much support from international colleagues (Kitossa 2012; Tauri and Deckert 2014; Cunneen and Tauri 2016; Onwudiwe 2000; Oriola 2006).

Had Steven Box lived longer, he would most likely have embraced innovations from what de Sousa Santos (2014) called 'epistemologies of the south' that Box may have contributed to. It is worth repeating that a key demand of Box (1983) was for *justice to be extended to all.* This also demands the exposing and challenging of injustice. The work of the historian, Elkins (2005, 2022), thus contributes to what can be considered a Boxian critique of the legacies of white supremacist-sexist-imperialist violent policies inflicted in gulags around the world. Such violence was disguised as 'punitive expeditions' (Onyeozili et al. 2021: 12) or what Onyeozili (2004/2017: 205) called 'gunboat criminology'. Elkins (2021: 106–110) obviously borrows from Fanon (1963) the activist principle that scholars can bear witness to such state violence that deserves to be addressed through reparative justice (Agozino 2002, 2021; Feagin et al. 2015). Reparative justice would be more effective than the unlikely calibration of punishment to fit the crimes of the powerful under the commodity fetishism of paying the price for imperialist harms.

Let us return though to the work of Elkins (2022). She was clear about the systemic nature of the British Empire's violence:

> ......the....iron fist...the permanent scars it left on subjects' bodies and minds. The violence it inflicted was not abstract. It took the form of electric shock, faecal and water torture; castration; forced hard labour; sodomy with broken bottles; and vermin; forced marches through landmines; shin screwing; fingernail extraction; and public execution. Failure to confront these practices diminishes the raw lived experiences in the empire and the legacy they left behind. (Elkins 2022: 28)

These horrific atrocities were differentiated by gender. In India:

> ....defaulters were publicly flogged, and their virginal daughters were dragged into public view, where they were cruelly "violated by the basest and wickedest of mankind". It did not end there.... "The wives of the people of the country only differed in this; that they lost their honour in the bottom of the most cruel dungeons...... But they were dragged out, naked and exposed to the public view, and scourged before all the people.... They put the nipples of the women into the sharp edges of split bamboos and tore them from their bodies". (ibid.: 42)

Elkins (2021) was also clear about bearing witness to these atrocities. In a major legal case in England concerning the systemic violence perpetrated by the British in Kenya, she was engaged by the claimants and cross examined by the respondents. The judge found her evidence helpful to the court. Elkins wrote two witness statements, one of which summarized her book in 200 pages, partly because her book that the litigants relied upon was being put on trial for allegedly relying on oral history. Yet she also relied heavily on hundreds of archival sources, despite the destruction of documents by the colonial UK government. The court asked the historian for evidence regarding which colonial state, colonized

Kenya or colonial UK, was responsible for destroying evidence, whether such destruction was the work of a few bad apples or whether it was part of systematic state policy? It turned out that the demand for discovery led to hidden boxes with relevant evidence, though some were reclassified as top secret (Elkins 2021: 106–110).

Criminologists were apparently not called as expert witnesses by either the respondents or the litigants. This is an indication that the discipline of criminology will also benefit from the development of interest in decolonization and reparative justice given that a literary theorist, Gopal (2020), has shown how decolonization struggles ended up helping to improve conditions for citizens in Europe through tolerance for dissent at home and through welfare reforms. The decolonization of criminology will undoubtedly help contribute to Box's demand for justice for all.

Conclusion: Standing on the Shoulders of a Criminological Giant

Without being exposed to the inspirational work of Box and the work of others like him, I would not have been able to make original contributions of my own in the ways that I did and at the times and places that I did. But, of course, the influence of Box was only part of the body of work that influenced my own writings. I am pleased to say that I engaged in much of this work while based at Liverpool John Moores University where I also had the pleasure of co-teaching the work of Box and others to Criminal Justice and Sociology students while learning from this body of work myself.

I have been able to stand on the proverbial shoulder of a criminological giant to see farther by introducing the decolonization perspective in criminology but such a view was implicit in the work of Box and many others. I simply made decolonization more visible as an on-going struggle to which the thoughts of Box and others created an enabling environment for my own thoughts to develop. Of course, there were other influences in other political and organizational activities that were not part of my criminology work, a field in which the work of Box is highly regarded. I hope more of such regards rub off on my own work which contributes to the decolonization paradigm and the abolitionist perspective in preference for reparative justice, especially in cases of huge state or corporate crimes. Punishment is not always the best way to respond to crimes and harms whereas reparations for the victimized would be more substantial than punitiveness. I am proud to say that I stand on the giant shoulders of Box all the time to support my own work.

The policy implication of the demystification of crime, harm and power is that the crimes and harms of the powerful are rarely punished as crimes in the way the crimes of the powerless are severely punished. Instead of hoping against hope that the powerful will be punished as severely as the poor who break the law, we should follow the *Abolition Democracy* of Angela Davis (2005) and push for the withering away of the prison industrial complex and the defunding of the police and we should support the abolition of prisons to free up more resources for community interventions.[7]

References

Achebe, C. 2012. *There Was a Country: A Personal History of Biafra*. London: Penguin.
Agozino, B. 2002. *Reparative Justice*. African Independent Television, Lagos.
Agozino, B. 2003. *Counter Colonial Criminology: A Critique of Imperialist Reason*. London: Pluto Press.
Agozino, B. 2018/1997. *Black Women and the Criminal Justice System: Towards the Decolonisation of Victimization*. Aldershot, Ashgate, reissued, London, Routledge Revivals Series.
Agozino, B. 2018. The Withering Away of the Law: An Indigenous Perspective on the Decolonisation of the Criminal Justice System and Criminology. *Journal of Global Indigeneity* 3 (1). http://ro.uow.edu.au/jgi/vol3/iss1/2.
Agozino, B. 2020. Africana Liberation Criminology. In *Routledge Handbook on Africana Criminologies*, ed. B. Agozino, V. Saleh-Hanna, E.C. Onyeozili, and N.P. Dastile, 18–31. London: Routledge.

---

[7] See for example, Fanon (1963), Davis (1981, 2003, 2005), Derrida (2001), Gilmore (2007), Tutu and Tutu (2014), Agozino (2018b), Jackson (2016), Dastile and Agozino (2019), Elechi (2020), Agozino and Ducey (2020), Feagin, et al. (2015) and Agozino (2020).

Agozino, B. 2021. Reparative Justice: The Final Stage of Decolonization. *Punishment & Society* 23: 613–630.
Agozino, B. 2022. Genocidist Discourse and Intellectuals in Africa. *Journal of Central and Eastern European African Studies* 2 (1): 13–30. https://jceeas.bdi.uni-obuda.hu/index.php/jceeas/article/view/86. Accessed 24 June 2023.
Agozino, B., and K. Ducey. 2020. Articulation of Liberation Criminologies and Public Criminologies: Advancing a Countersystem Approach and Decolonization Paradigm. In *Routledge Handbook of Public Criminologies*, ed. K. Henne and R. Shah, 59–72. London: Routledge.
Agozino, B., V. Saleh-Hanna, E.C. Onyeozili, and N.P. Dastile, eds. 2020. *Routledge Handbook on Africana Criminologies*. Routledge: London.
Blagg, H., and T. Anthony. 2019. *Decolonising Criminology: Imagining Justice in a Postcolonial World*. London: Palgrave Macmillan.
Box, S. 1983. *Power, Crime and Mystification*. London: Tavistock.
Box, S., and J. Ford. 1971. The Facts Don't Fit: On the Relationship Between Social Class and Criminal Behaviour. *Sociological Review* 19: 31–52.
Box, S., C. Hale, and G. Andrews. 1988. Explaining the Fear of Crime. *British Journal of Criminology* 28 (Summer) 3: 340–356.
Canning V. 2019. Degradation by Design: Women and Asylum in Northern Europe. *Race and Class* 61 (1): 46–63. Accessed 24 June 2023.
Canning, V., and S. Tombs. 2021. *From Social Harm to Zemiology: A Critical Introduction*. Bristol: Policy Press.
Cohen, S. 1993. Human Rights and Crimes of the State: The Culture of Denial. *Australian and New Zealand Journal of Criminology* 26 (2): 97–115. John Barry Memorial Lecture, University of Melbourne, 30 September 1992.
Cunneen, C., and J. Tauri. 2016. *Indigenous Criminology*. Bristol: Policy Press.
Curtis, M. 2020. How Britain's Labour Government Facilitated the Massacre of Biafrans in Nigeria to Protect Its Oil Interests. https://www.dailymaverick.co.za/article/2020-04-29-how-britains-labour-government-facilitated-the-massacre-of-biafrans-in-nigeria-to-protect-its-oil-interests/.
Dastile, N.P., and B. Agozino. 2019. Decolonizing Incarcerated Women's Identities Through the Lens of Prison Abolitionism. *South African Crime Quarterly* 68: 21–32.
Davis, A.Y. 1981. *Women, Race and Class*. London: The Women's Press.
Davis, A.Y. 2003. *Are Prisons Obsolete?* New York: Seven Stories Press.
Davis, A.Y. 2005. *Abolition Democracy: Beyond Empire, Prisons and Torture*. New York: Seven Stories Press.

de Sousa Santos, B. 2014. *Epistemologies of the South: Justice Against Epistemicide*. London: Routledge.
Derrida, J. 2001. *On Cosmopolitanism and Forgiveness*. London: Routledge.
Du Bois, W.E.B. 1896. *The Philadelphia Negro: A Social Study*. Philadelphia: University of Pennsylvania Press.
Ekwe-Ekwe, H. 2019. *The Longest Genocide from 1966*. Darkar: African Renaissance Press.
Elechi, O.O. 2020. Mbari and Ubuntu in Indigenous Africana Criminologies. In *The Routledge Handbook on Africana Criminologies*, ed. B. Agozino, E.C. Onyeozili, N.P. Dastile, and V. Saleh-Hanna, 32–40. London: Routledge.
Elkins, C. 2005. *Imperial Reckoning: The Untold Story of Britain's Gulag in Kenya*. New York: Henry Holt and Co.
Elkins, C. 2021. History on Trial: Mau Mau Reparations and the High Court of Justice. In *Reparations: A Global Perspective*, ed. J. Bhabha, M. Matache, and C. Elkins, 101–118. Philadelphia: University of Pennsylvania Press.
Elkins, C. 2022. *Legacy of Violence: A History of the British Empire*. London: The Bodley Head.
Fanon, F. 1963. *The Wretched of the Earth*. New York: Grove Press.
Feagin, J., H. Vera, and K. Ducey. 2015. *Liberation Sociology*, 3rd ed. New York: Paradigm Books.
Gabbidon, S.L. 2020. *Criminological Perspectives on Race and Crime*, 4th ed. London: Routledge.
Garland, D. 1990. *Punishment and Modern Society*. Oxford: Clarendon.
Gilmore, R.W. 2007. *Golden Gulag: Prisons, Surplus, Crisis and Opposition in a Globalizing California*. Berkeley: University of California Press.
Gilroy, P. 1982. The Myth of Black Criminality. In *The Socialist Register 1982*, ed. M. Eve and D. Musson, 47–56. London: The Merlin Press.
Gopal, P. 2020. *Insurgent Empire: Anticolonial Resistance and British Dissent*. London: Verso.
Hall, S. 1980. Race, Articulation and Societies Structured in Dominance. In *Sociological Theories: Race and Colonialism*, ed. UNESCO, 305–344. Paris: UNESCO.
Hall, S., C. Critcher, T. Jefferson, J. Clarke, and B. Roberts. 1978. *Policing the Crisis: Mugging, the State and Law and Order*. London: Palgrave Macmillan.
Jacobs, D. 1987. *The Brutality of Nations*. New York: Knopf.
Jackson, M. 2016. The Abolition of Prisons and Indigenous Self-Determination. Keynote Address at the Forum for Indigenous Research Excellence, University of New South Wales, Wollongong, Australia. https://www.youtube.com/watch?v=mPnf0cbFIuo/. Accessed 24 June 2023.

Kitossa, T. 2012. Criminology and Colonialism: The Canadian Context. *The Journal of Pan African Studies* 4 (10): 204–226.
Melossi, D. 2020. Changing Representations of the Criminal. *British Journal of Criminology* 40: 296–320.
McClintock, F.H. 1974. Facts and Myths About the State of Crime. In *Crime, Criminology and Public Policy*, ed. R. Hood. Oxford: Heinemann.
Morris, R. 1977. *Uncertain Greatness: Henry Kissinger and American Foreign Policy*. New York: Harper and Row.
Morrison, W. 2004. Criminology, Genocide and Modernity: Remarks on the Companion That Criminology Ignored. In *The Blackwell Companion to Criminology*, ed. C. Sumner, 66–88. Oxford, Blackwell Publishers.
Nkrumah, K. 1965. *Neo-colonialism: The Last Stage of Imperialism*. London, Thomas Nelson & Sons, Ltd.
Onwudiwe, I.D. 2000. Review of Black Women and the Criminal Justice System by Biko Agozino, Ashgate Publishing Company. *Journal of Social Pathology* 1998: 245–247.
Onyeozili, E.C. 2004/2017. Gunboat Criminology. In *Pan African Issues in Crime and Justice*, ed. B. Agozino and A. Kalunta-Crumpton, 205–227. Farnham: Ashgate, reissued by Routledge, 2017.
Onyeozili, E.C., B. Agozino, A. Agu, and P. Ibe. 2021. *Community Policing in Nigeria*. Fourth Dimension Publishers; and Virginia Tech Publishing.
Oriola, T. 2006. Biko Agozino and the Rise of Post-Colonial Criminology. *African Journal of Criminology and Justice Studies* 2 (1): 104–131.
Pearce, F. 1976. *Crimes of the Powerful: Marxism, Crime and Deviance*. London: Pluto Press.
Pfohl, S. 2003. Foreword. In *Counter-Colonial Criminology: A Critique of Imperialist Reason*, ed. B. Agozino, xi–xiv. London: Pluto Press.
Reiman, J., and P. Leighton. 2012. *The Rich Get Richer and the Poor Get Prison*. New York: Pearson.
Rothe, D.L., and D. Kauzlarich. 2016. *Crimes of the Powerful: An Introduction*. Oxford: Routledge.
Said, E. 1993. *Culture and Imperialism*. London: Penguin.
Smart, C. 1990. Feminist Approaches to Criminology or Postmodern Woman Meets Atavistic Man. In *Feminist Perspectives in Criminology*, ed. L. Gelsthorpe and A. Morris, 70–84. Milton Keynes: Open University Press.
Tauri, J.M., and A. Deckert. 2014. Editorial Comments on Indigenous Criminology and Counter-Colonial Criminology. *African Journal of Criminology and Justice Studies* 8 (1): i–iv.

Tutu, D., and M. Tutu. 2014. *The Book of Forgiving*. New York: Harper Collins.

Young, J. 1988. Steven Box (1937–1987). *The British Journal of Criminology* 28 (1, Winter): 95–96.

18

The Policing of Youthful 'Social Dynamite' and Neo-liberal Capitalism: Continuities, Discontinuities and Alternatives

Jodie Hodgson

Introduction

In *Power, Crime and Mystification*, Box (1983) identifies two significant problems with penal policy and sentencing practices under Conservative rule during the early 1980s. Firstly, he argued that the 'short, sharp shock' (ibid: 3) law and order crusade was not a reaction to 'democratic pressures from below' (ibid: 219). Instead, it represented an effort to reduce the anxieties of the powerful, which were generated by the economic recession, rising unemployment, 'youthful rebellion' (ibid: 220), and the crisis of capitalism this represented. Secondly, he argued that the crusade of criminalisation and imprisonment of young offenders which followed, directed the focus away from crimes of the powerful and served to rupture opposition to capitalist domination by creating an understanding, supported by police-recorded crime statistics, that the 'crime problem' (ibid: 1) is one caused by uneducated, young, Black males,

J. Hodgson (✉)
Manchester Metropolitan University, Manchester, England, UK
e-mail: J.Hodgson@mmu.ac.uk

living in inner city areas. It is through the creation of this common sense understanding as to who the 'real' criminals are that mystification and distraction occur, causing the powerless to gaze upwards to the state for protection.

Focussing predominantly on the field of youth justice and responses to young peoples' offending and deviant behaviour since Box's pioneering work, this chapter charts the continuities and changes in relation to what he described as the policing of youthful 'social dynamite' (Box 1983: 209). To begin, the chapter will revisit the key points raised in Box's initial arguments concerning the ways in which the state used its power to 'victimise criminally' (ibid: 204) the behaviour of young people. The focus of the chapter then moves on to critically analyse the continuities and discontinuities in the state's response to managing young people through shifting youth justice and crime control landscapes.

To this end, the chapter explores how penal politics, policies and policing, within an intensified era of neo-liberalism, have contributed to new strategies through which youthful 'social dynamite' (Box 1983: 209) is regulated and controlled. The chapter will draw critical attention to the persistent failures of the youth justice system's response to vulnerable young people who encounter its services and the non-intervention by the state to address such vulnerability. Finally, the chapter concludes that whilst the state's approach to the control and regulation of young people in conflict with the law has changed, since the publication of *Power, Crime and Mystification,* the approach remains one which is punitive and harmful to young people. The harms committed by the state and the most powerful continue to be subject to mystification through processes of misdirection and distraction.

Welfarism, Regulation and the Policing of Youthful 'Social Dynamite'

Prior to the late 1970s, welfarism was the dominant policy framework for responding to youth crime in England (Garland 2001: 34). It was recognised as modernist in value and shaped by a focus on the treatment and rehabilitation of young people who offend, as opposed to their criminalisation (Garland 2001; Muncie and Hughes 2002). This view culminated in the introduction of *The Children and Young Persons Act* (1969). This legislation supported a rise in the age of criminal responsibility and the decriminalisation of children through welfare policies, as opposed to criminal justice intervention (Muncie and Hughes 2002).

This welfare endeavour was brought to an abrupt halt following the election of the Conservative Government in 1979. Conservative politics at this time was characterised by a deep-seated hostility to the discourse of welfarism and rehabilitation and favoured, as Sim (2009: 2) noted, 'an apparatus of punishment, underpinned and legitimated by a political and populist hostility to offenders'. As such, the party pledged its commitment to begin reversing many of the progressive elements of the social welfare state, established in the post-war years, by 'rolling back the state … [and] building a state apparatus that … [was] stronger and more authoritarian than before' (Garland 2001: 98), comprising of what has come to be known as 'neo-liberalism' and 'neo-conservatism' (ibid: 98).

As Box (1983: 204) states, the Conservative Party was 'not idling' in its response to crime and criminal justice and the 1980s was a time in which the state's power to 'victimise criminally' the powerless expanded. Characterised by both authoritarianism and interventionism, changes to penal policy and sentencing practices were introduced. The Criminal Justice Act 1982, for example, not only enabled the judiciary to sentence young offenders to prison, something which the 1969 Act had obstructed but it also reduced the age limit for imprisonment from 17 to 15 (Box 1983: 220). Box described such legislative changes as reflecting a 'strong desire to move wayward adolescents from the "caring" hands of social workers … to the calloused hands of prison officers' (Box 1983: 220).

He (ibid: 206) detailed the 'strengthened armoury' of the state, as new prisons were built and the number of police officers increased. Young people bore the brunt of these changes. Incarceration in detention centres and prisons rose sharply. As Box (ibid) detailed, those criminalised were disproportionately young Black and Minority Ethnic men and boys.

Whilst girls and young women remained predominantly absent from Box's analysis, the changes in responses to the state's approach to crime control, which reflected a shift away from welfarism towards a justice model of intervention, *also* had a pernicious impact on girls. This was because the informal policing and social control of girls' behaviour, which formed the basis of intervention for 'troublesome' girls under welfarism, was now replaced by criminalisation (Worrall 2001). As such, 'increasing numbers of young women were being incarcerated, not on spuriously benevolent welfare grounds but on spuriously equitable "justice" grounds' (ibid: 86). The chapter returns to this issue below.

The changes in penal policy and sentencing can be understood in the context of the economic crisis of the 1970s, which threw up massive numbers of unemployed young people—the 'social dynamite' (Box 1983: 209) discussed earlier in this chapter. The state responded to this youthful 'social dynamite' (ibid: 209) through increased authoritarianism and stringent, marginalising and harmful economic policies. Young people and Black and Minority Ethnic people, residing in deprived inner-city areas were those most affected by these stringent and oppressive economic policies. Such reality, Box (ibid) argued, gave the state reason to be anxious in terms of the impact unemployment, inadequate living standards and stringent welfare provision might have on the ability of its institutions to govern those most disproportionately affected and maintain social order.

The increased use of imprisonment and severity of sentencing which accompanied this growth in unemployment and the deepening economic crisis, he asserted, was not a response to increased crime but was rather an 'ideologically motivated response to the perceived threat of crime posed by the swelling population of economically marginalised persons' (ibid: 212). As he noted:

> During times of economic crisis, state coercion increases in response to the perceived threat, real or imagined, of public disorder including crime waves. The judiciary, being an integral part of the state control apparatus, makes its contribution to this increased level of coercion by imprisoning more, particularly those typifying the actually, or potentially, disruptive problem populations. (ibid: 217)

Relevant to this analysis is the distinction he made between 'social junk', those that must be 'managed' such as the sick, elderly or mentally ill, and 'social dynamite' that must be controlled such as the under and unemployed. Those considered 'social junk' were perceived as a 'fiscal problem', whilst those considered 'social dynamite' were those who were able to work, and thus were perceived to be more problematic as their existence questioned the operation of the capitalist mode of production which, in turn, threatened a 'crisis of legitimacy' (ibid: 207–209). In relation to this troublesome population of youthful 'dynamite', he argued that:

> Because they can distance themselves from the consent to be governed, are likely to be perceived by those in positions of power and authority as potential disruptives, thus constituting a threat, real or imagined, to social discipline, law and order. Consequently, this problem population has to be suppressed or eliminated in order to preserve ideological and social hegemony. (ibid: 209)

The criminal justice system and 'its capacity to extend the use and length of prison sentences' was 'one of the first line defences available to the powerful' (ibid: 209).

New Labour: New (in)Justice

Whilst the 1970s and 1980s had a pernicious impact on many groups of young people, the Conservative government's focus on reducing state welfare and intervention created a bifurcated dual system approach to youth justice (Carrabine 2010). This consisted of less serious offending being met with minimal intervention and diversion, and maximum intervention and youth custody being reserved for those deemed to require increased levels of state surveillance and monitoring (Jamieson and Yates 2009). Despite a substantial decrease in the use of custody for young people during this time, this approach was not advantageous for all young people as the bifurcated system 'provided a strategy whereby those groups regarded as the volatile fraction of the surplus population could be managed' (ibid: 80). As such, historical processes of criminalisation continued and Black and Minority Ethnic young people continued to be disproportionately represented across all stages of the youth justice system.

During the 1990s, the state's approach to the control and regulation of young people began to shift and intensify. In the context of far-reaching economic depression, high rates of unemployment, social unrest and a rise in recorded crime, public confidence in the Conservative Party's law and order policies had declined. A public focus on youth crime, magnified by the murder of James Bulger,[1] was politically exploited by both the Labour and Conservative parties and both battled to demonstrate who could provide the most hardened response to youth crime (Goldson 2002). Combined with emergent managerial and actuarial discourses, described by Garland (2001) as a new strategy for exercising state power and governing individuals, New Labour 'sought to redefine itself in the law-and-order landscape' (Crawford and Newburn 2002: 477), whilst supporting the ideology of a 'third way' in politics which was successful in the 1997 general election. The ideology of this third-way politics emphasised that 'in an age when globalisation had placed control of the economy beyond the competence of national governments, social policy becomes the pre-eminent issue' (Pitts 2001: 35). For New Labour, the central focus of such social policy was youth crime. Following Box's arguments, this focus on youth crime can be understood in the context of strengthening the control and regulation of specific groups of young people. Drawing upon Box's analysis, this focus on youth crime served as the pathway in which the state could reinforce its authority and instil discipline amongst relatively powerless groups of young people, whilst powerful state actors remained unaccountable for the most serious crimes located in power, privilege and wealth.

Following their success in the 1997 general election, New Labour promptly initiated a radical restructuring of the existing youth justice system. Acting on the recommendations of the *Misspent Youth Report* (Audit Commission 1996), which promoted a restructuring of the youth justice system in line with 'the "actuarial" techniques of classification, risk

---

[1] James Bulger was a two-year-old boy who was abducted and murdered by two ten-year-old boys in Merseyside, England. See Scraton and Haydon (2002) for a discussion of the impact the crime had on the policing and regulation of young people in England and Wales.

assessment and resource management' (Muncie 1999: 150), risk management and crime prevention became the central features of their new youth justice strategy. The most potent manifestation of these reforms, in terms of strengthening the state's capacity to govern young people, was *The Crime and Disorder Act* 1998. The act introduced a series of legislative changes targeting those deemed to be at risk of offending (Jamieson and Yates 2009).

These changes included the abolition of *doli incapax*, the introduction of child safety orders, local child curfews, detention and training orders, parenting orders, anti-social behaviour orders, sex offender orders, reparation orders, final warnings and action plan orders, all of which mobilised new layers of social control directed towards young people. These additional layers of social control were underpinned by new and distinct strategies of risk management, responsibilisation and pre-emptive early intervention (Crawford 2003; Gelsthorpe and Morris 1999; Muncie 1999; Williams and Squires 2021), which not only accounted for an intensification in the criminalisation of young people but also individualised young people's offending behaviour and neglected the significance of macro-structural relations of power in shaping the experiences of criminalised young people (Gelsthorpe and Morris 1999; Phoenix 2016).

The focus on the policing and regulation of young people during the late twentieth and early twenty-first century, served to widen the net of state control to a much broader group of young people and the number entering the youth justice system and being subject to intervention significantly increased. Between 2002–2003 and 2006–2007, the number of children and young people subject to youth justice intervention increased by 28% (Solomon et al. 2007). Rather than reflecting an actual increase in youth crime, these increases can be understood in the context of a rise in the targets concerning offences brought to justice between 2002 and 2007/08 introduced by New Labour, which created an incentive to criminalise minor offending (Sharpe 2012; Bateman 2008, 2015). As such, 'young people figured prominently among the criminalised' (Morgan 2009: 60).

The changes to legislation and policy which added new layers to existing forms of social control, through new strategies of risk management and assessment continued to produce gendered, class, racial and ethnic disparities, which served to intensify the regulation and control that young people were already subject to. Boys and young men from Black and Minority Ethnic communities continued to be disproportionately subject to criminal justice intervention and police surveillance. This is demonstrated by the significant increase in the use of stop and search for Black young people and disproportionality in youth custody sentences (Webster 2015).

The additional focus on risk management also had specific consequences for girls. The focus on predicting the risk of future offending led to the 'concept of need [being] fused with risk to create 'dynamic risk/criminogenic need' (Hannah-Moffat 2005: 31). For girls, this meant their gender-specific needs, for example, 'past abuse, and trauma', were reconstructed as criminogenic need and thus reframed as individualised problems, which in turn isolated their offending and criminalisation from the broader structural inequalities, which are pivotal to the forms of oppression and victimisation girls experience (ibid: 43). This had a significant net-widening impact for girls. Between 2002/3 and 2005/06, there was a 78% increase in the number of girls apprehended for violent crime (Youth Justice Board 2004, 2007, cited in Sharpe 2012: 33) and a 25% increase in girls receiving a custodial sentence between 2002/3 and 2006/7 (Sharpe 2012).

System Shrinkage and Diversion: The Same but Different

Since 2009, there has been a significant reduction in youth justice intervention for young people and a substantial increase in the diversion of young people away from the formal system. This deduction occurred simultaneously with the introduction of targets, in 2008, focussed on reducing system contact for young people (Bateman 2015). Between 2011 and 2021 there was an 81% reduction in the number of children receiving a sentence or a caution and an 82% reduction in first time entrants to the youth justice system (Youth Justice Board 2022). This system shrinkage continued following the election of the Conservative Government in 2015. Whilst such changes may be interpreted as a positive development, the reality is that this depletion of criminalised young people is driven by neo-liberal political ideology, 'the unsustainability to soaring sanction detections' (Bateman 2015: 78) and austerity as opposed to any top-down transformative intentions concerning the rights and well-being of children and young people. It has also done nothing to address the disciplinary practices of over-policing of Black, minority and ethnic young people via old, new and distinct strategies of regulation and control. The chapter returns to this issue below.

Recent research by Smith and Gray (2019) suggests that youth justice now operates on more diverse models and approaches, implemented by practitioners at a local level, however, youth justice assessments, which determine intervention continue to be framed through the lens of risk management and crime prevention. In other words, New Labour's legacy of iatrogenic consequences of the risk-led, responsibilising, early interventionist responses to young people's deviant behaviour have continued. Further, this system shrinkage does not automatically mean a relaxation in the state's regulation of young people, as a diversion from formal youth justice intervention continues to operate through 'actuarial risk assessment' and 'welfare-oriented' interventionism (Kelly and Armitage 2015: 118). Research, exploring contemporary models of youth justice practice, undertaken by Smith and Gray (2019) supports this argument. They suggest that 'offender management' and 'targeted intervention' models continue to conflate young people's welfare needs with offending risk factors (ibid: 554).

As Phoenix (2016: 135) has argued, responsibilising and risk management approaches are 'fundamentally unjust because they target the lawbreaking behaviour of young people already marginalised by class, gender and cultural inequalities while simultaneously practising a form of radical non-interventionism regarding the crimes … committed against them'. This argument illuminates how such approaches in responding to young people's deviant and offending behaviour individualise the reasons for offending and situate young people as the problem to be managed (Johns 2018).

Thus far, the chapter has explored the recent history of youth justice in England since the publication of *Power, Crime and Mystification*. The chapter has drawn attention to the role of political ideologies and opportunism in shaping the youth justice agenda throughout recent decades. It has explored how the changes in the regulation and control of young people have had deleterious consequences for all young people but those from the most marginalised, in particular Black and Minority Ethnic young people, have often experienced the harsher end of these consequences. Whilst the impact of these political strategies and ideologies can still be felt, the remainder of the chapter will now move on to focus on current examples of the state's attempt to control and regulate young people and how they represent not only a continuation of historical processes of injustice examined by Box in 1983, but also new developments overlaying the strategies in operation at the time Box was writing.

Continued Injustice

It is important to note that the social control and regulation of young people in the third decade of the twenty-first century is effectuated in a variety of policy contexts, punitive penal settings and practices and disciplinary and non-interventionist risk management techniques. Whilst Box's intervention did not come at a time in which some of these exact issues were present, his work provided a pivotal starting point for framing the lens through which the contemporary approaches to the control and regulation of young people can be critically understood. Drawing upon the key themes of power, mystification and criminalisation, the chapter will now consider two current injustices relating to the policing and regulation of young people, first the incarceration of young people in the youth custodial estate and second, responses to girls in conflict with the law.

The two examples discussed in this chapter are not exhaustive and there are many more examples, which represent prominent cause for concern. These include, although not limited to, the legal apparatus of joint enterprise (Williams and Clarke 2016, 2018), the increasing use of disciplinary alternative schools (Selman 2017), the criminalisation of looked-after children (Fitzpatrick et al. 2022) and the management of, and responses to, gangs and serious youth violence (Smithson et al. 2013).

Young People and The Youth Custodial Estate

As demonstrated, in England and Wales, trends in youth justice policy and practice have been subject to shifting political and social landscapes. Significant changes in the numbers of children encountering the youth justice system and changing models of practice have in the last decade become most reflective of the changing nature of youth justice. However, significant problems still exist. Such problems consist of; (i) the criminalisation and incarceration of highly vulnerable young people in general, (ii) the over-representation of Black and Minority Ethnic young people in the custodial estate and (iii) the inadequacy of the youth secure estate.

Whilst there have been several examples of continuities and discontinuities of the state's response to the regulation of young people since the publication of *Power, Crime and Mystification*, the current state of youth custody clearly reflects the continuities in the state's approach to managing youthful 'social dynamite' (ibid: 209), through the racialised criminalisation of young Black people and their imprisonment. Box (1983: 5) noted how those typically convicted of crime and imprisoned were disproportionately young males between the ages of 15–20, often 'uneducated' or unemployed, coming from working class backgrounds in inner-city areas and frequently, Black. Of central importance to this chapter and the arguments put forward by Box is the continuation of such historical processes of criminalisation and imprisonment of young Black, Minority and Ethnic young people, at a time when the youth justice system has and continues to reduce its contact with young people overall.

In 2022, statistics published by the Youth Justice Board revealed that children from a Black and Minority Ethnic background accounted for 29% of those sentenced to youth custody in 2021. This is an 11% increase for young Black people in the last decade compared to a 21%

decrease in the number of White children sentenced to custody in the same period. Further, Black children were more likely to be sentenced to custody and serve longer sentences compared to their White counterparts (Her Majesty's Inspectorate of Probation 2021; Youth Justice Board 2022). In addition to being incarcerated at a higher rate than their White counterparts, once in youth custody Black children and young adults experienced the highest incidences of physical restraint (Youth Justice Board 2022). The fact that these groups of young people remain in the youth justice system and subject to state control and regulation, is evidence of the eagerness of the state to continue to perpetuate the criminal labelling of those most disadvantaged within society. This disproportionality also extends to youth unemployment. For example, in 2022, a research briefing on unemployment and ethnicity revealed that young people from a Black ethnic background aged 16–24 years old experienced the highest rates of unemployment between July 2021 and June 2022 compared to all other ethnicities in the same age group (House of Commons Library 2022).

This disproportionality, as stated, represents the continuation of historical processes of criminalisation of Black, Minority and Ethnic young people, identified by Box. Further, this disproportionality is not surprising when understood in the context of intensifying, draconian state powers, which have served to target, control and regulate young people, perpetuate the 'myth of black criminality' (Gilroy 1982) and expand the carceral estate.

There is a plethora of research, which demonstrates how such young people become the targets of draconian police powers, ultimately resulting in their incarceration. The police target, disproportionately, young males from lower class backgrounds, not in education or employment, who live in socially deprived, inner-city areas (May et al. 2010; Mcara and Mcvie 2005). Consequently, Black, ethnic and White working class young people become 'permanent suspects' (Webster 2015: 40) constantly being regulated and surveilled by state agents, in contrast with the non-regulation and non-surveillance of corporate criminals discussed by Box in *Power, Crime and Mystification*.

Williams and Squires (2021: 15) have argued that the criminalisation of young Black males represents a 'strong and continuing characteristic of urban crime control' reflective of the racialised policing of the 'mugging crisis' explored by Hall et al. (1978). Supporting this analysis, existing research on the use of stop and search, serious youth violence and gang policy and interventions and joint enterprise convictions and prosecutions has revealed that racialised criminalisation continues to be a key feature of the policing of youthful 'social dynamite' (Williams and Squires 2021; Williams and Clarke 2016, 2018), which can ultimately result in the increased imprisonment of Black and Minority Ethnic young people.

Such a response is not new as Gilroy (1982: 47) has previously argued, 'the rule of law and maintenance of public order have appeared in forms which involve a racist appeal to the "British Nation" and have become integral to maintaining popular support for the government in crisis conditions'. This not only resonates with the arguments made by Box in 1983 but is also pertinent for providing an understanding of the criminalisation and disproportionate representation of young Black people in custody as those apprehended are receiving more punitive sentences, many of which are custodial (Fatis et al. 2021).

Not only are the most disadvantaged and marginalised and predominantly Black or ethnic young people being incarcerated within the existing criminal justice system and youth justice secure estate, but also this estate continues to expand and new techniques of control and regulation, continue to emerge. The 'PRU[2] to prison pipeline' (Perera 2020: 20) and the increasing use of pupil referral units as 'warehouses' for disadvantaged young people are examples of this (Selman 2017: 217). Young Black people are disproportionately represented in pupil referral units and the term 'PRU to prison pipeline' provides 'a concise description of the nexus between schools and prison' (Perera 2020). Such 'schools' can be understood as an expansion of the carceral state, specifically targeted towards young people in an intensified neo-liberal era (Selman 2017).

---

[2] PRU refers to a Pupil Referral Unit, which is alternative education provision for children and young people who are removed from mainstream education.

Not only does the current state of youth custody demonstrate the continuity of the disproportionate criminalisation and incarceration of Black children and young people since the time of Box's intervention and the institutional racism they are subject to, but it also provides an insight into many other significant problems child prisoners experience. Trauma and adverse childhood experiences are prevalent amongst young people in youth custody and thus make them highly vulnerable (Liddle et al. 2016). Although at present, the state criminalises fewer young people compared to the populist punitiveness of the New Labour era, those who are still within its reach are some of the most marginalised and excluded young people, whose complex needs and adverse formative experiences remain neglected or unaddressed by state institutions (Phoenix 2016).

Not only does the United Kingdom imprison its most vulnerable and disadvantaged children and young people, but it also has the highest rate of child imprisonment in Western Europe (Children's Rights Alliance for England 2018) and is the only state in Europe, which still allows children under 18 years of age to be given a life sentence. Between 1995 and 2013, there were 361 life sentence convictions for offences committed whilst under the age of 18 (Children's Rights Alliance for England 2016).

These children, as Scott (2017) notes, are subject to regimes of 'deliberate harm which leads to thousands of children being physically, psychologically and emotionally damaged every year'. Youth custody, regardless of the sentence length, continues to be an unsafe place for children and young people, particularly in relation to abuse, solitary confinement, the use of force and high levels of self-harm. In 2017, the Chief Inspector of Prisons stated there was 'not a single establishment that we inspected in England and Wales in which it was safe to hold children and young people' (HM Inspectorate of Prisons 2017: 9). Subsequent reports have continued to emphasise these concerns and in 2021, the same annual report revealed that conditions had continued to deteriorate, particularly within Secure Training Centres where it was found that 'violence between children and towards staff … was unacceptably high' (HM Inspectorate of Prisons 2022: 83).

The imprisonment of children in the youth secure estate continues to be condemned on the basis that it infringes Article 37 of the United Nations Convention on The Rights of a Child. However, as Scott

(2017) notes, there is a general acceptance, both public and political, of the incarceration of children in our society, despite an ever-increasing plethora of evidence detailing its harmful effects on those who are imprisoned.

Girls, Young Women and (in)Justice

As noted above, *Power, Crime and Mystification* focussed on young, predominantly Black, men as 'social dynamite' (Box 1983: 209). The high rates of unemployment and low educational attainment of this group represented a 'crisis of legitimacy' (ibid) due to the threat they posed to the capitalist social order. However, in comparison, the position of young women as 'social dynamite' (ibid) remained unexplored within Box's analysis.

Girls in contact with the criminal justice system have been 'socially constructed within a range of legal, welfare, and political discourses' (Worrall 2004: 44). Attempts to socially control and regulate girls' behaviour in line with dominant discourses of 'acceptable' femininity have remained a constant theme within criminal justice and welfare responses focussed upon girls' deviance (Cox 2003; Gelsthorpe and Worrall 2009). However, in comparison to their young, male and adult, female counterparts, the state's approach to the treatment of, and responses to, girls in the justice system has been neglected in criminological inquiry and policy and practice discourse (Agenda Alliance 2022).

This remains a contemporary issue. For example, high-profile reports aimed at reforming how the criminal justice system responds to women in conflict with the law, such as The Corston Report (2007) and The Female Offender Strategy (Ministry of Justice [MoJ] 2018), have neglected to address issues specific to girls. Further to this, girls account for less than 20% of young people involved in the justice system and thus represent a minority in both custody and community sentences (Agenda Alliance, 2021). One consequence arising from this neglect is that girls' voices are effectively 'muted' (Worrall 1990: 162) and the various and discursive mechanisms of social control and regulation they are subject to by the criminal and youth justice systems are not interrogated substantially. For Worrall (1990: 164), this muting of their voices forms part of a broader process of 'multiple discursive oppression which is subtle and sophisticated'.

Whilst contributions to feminist scholarship have demonstrated how processes of muting and marginalisation persist in contemporary criminal justice responses to criminalised women (Barr 2019; Monk et al. 2019; Atkinson et al. 2022) more recent contributions relating to girls in the youth justice system are less available. Those examples which do exist highlight the harmful ways in which the state, through criminal justice and welfare agencies, continues to shape the subjectivities of girls, attempts to regulate and control their behaviour and fails to effect transformative change for them.

For example, the development of gender-specific provision and programming, focussed upon the delivery of relationships, health and strength-based programming[3] (Morgan and Patton 2002) for girls in the justice system, fails to effect 'institutional or structural change' for them and thus serves to reinforce their unequal position within the heteropatriarchal order of society (Goodkind 2005: 61). Drawing upon empirical research findings which emerged from qualitative research with girls and practitioners involved in two girls' programmes in North America, Goodkind (2009) has further argued that the focus on promoting self-change and individual development, central to these programmes, reinforced the idea that girls have an individual responsibility to effect change in their lives. For Goodkind (2009: 397), this focus on responsibilisation for self-change reflects the ways in which the 'intersection of neoliberalism with feminist values' has translated into the disempowerment of girls.[4]

---

[3] Strength-based programming in the context of gender-specific provision is focussed on providing girls with opportunities to learn new skills, as well as teaching them skills that build upon their existing strengths (Morgan and Patton 2002).

[4] It is important to note here that not all feminist perspectives and positionalities promote and support gender-specific provision and approaches to girls embroiled in the youth justice system. Critics, for example, have argued that gender-specific provision and responsivity underpinned by feminist values have been used to underpin carceral expansion, thus emphasising a conflict between carceral and anti-carceral feminist ideologies. See Musto (2019) for further discussion.

My research (Hodgson 2022) on offending girls' experiences of Restorative Justice (RJ) demonstrates further the diversification of social control strategies and the themes of power and criminalisation affecting girls and young women involved in the criminal justice system. My research draws attention to the centrality of the gendered politics of shame and stigma in RJ conferencing used with girls. The gendered politics of shame and stigma power, which function as part of a political economy of subjugation and dehumanisation, cannot be separated but in fact are exacerbated for girls participating in an RJ conference, and the wider structural relationship between stigma power, shame and gender situate RJ as part of a continuum of patriarchal power and an apparatus and informal sanction employed to socially control and regulate gender subjectivities (Hodgson 2022). Further, the absence of critical considerations of gender and the social construction of masculinity and femininity within official policy and discourse on RJ, has meant that the potential for RJ conferencing to (re)produce unequal power relations and inequality for girls who are already marginalised is exaggerated but remains unexplored (ibid).

Further, examples include Tosouni (2019), who in her research on girls detained in custodial institutions, has drawn critical attention to the ways in which the incorporation of gender-responsive programmes has served to contribute towards the continuum of harm, neglect and injustice detained girls are subject to. Clarke and Chadwick (2020) have also drawn attention to the ways in which racist and gendered narratives played a role in the criminalisation and punishment of girls and women convicted under Joint Enterprise laws[5] (see Clarke and Chadwick, this volume; Cunliffe and Morrison, this volume). They found that a common prosecution strategy in Joint Enterprise cases with female defendants was to rely 'on myths and stereotypes and gendered narratives, further layered with class stigma and racism' to pursue their criminalisation (ibid: 4).

The examples discussed above support the argument that criminal justice intervention not only fails to effect transformative change for

---

[5] Joint Enterprise is a common law doctrine, which allows the prosecution of more than one individual for the same offence. See JENGbA, (n.d) for further discussion and the next chapter, Cunliffe and Morrison (this volume).

girls embroiled in the justice system, but it also enables the expansion and reinforcement of the formal and informal punishment of girls through carceral expansion (Goodkind 2005; Musto 2019). In addition to this, there is also the issue of the state's non-intervention in the private sphere and how this represents continuities in reinforcing the existing social order built upon gendered, racial and class oppression. As Edwards (1989) has noted, there is a 'clear existence of a public/private divide in law, which organises and ratifies a different level of response to similar conduct in two terrains, including a different level of police response and priorities' (Edwards 1989: 4). Edwards described a 'deepening chasm between the … laws designed to regulate public conduct (and especially potential group and public violence) … and those designed to regulate private situations (ibid: 1)'. This distinction, she argued, demonstrated 'the discrimination and partiality of particular laws, clearly imbued with value judgments about who and what forms of violence should be regulated' (ibid). She argued that the criminal justice system like other institutions is built on 'patriarchal attitudes and patriarchal structures of power' (ibid: 26), which reinforce women's subordination. Such attitudes and ideologies influence the criminal justice system's response to crime and victimisation and therefore 'incidents within the private domain, for example violence against women and sexual misconduct, have been considered less serious than incidents involving violence and sexual abuse occurring in public' (ibid: 26).

This argument is still relevant when considering the media sensationalism and disproportionate criminalisation and incarceration of Black and mixed heritage boys and young men for crimes relating to serious youth violence and knife crime (Perera 2020; Williams and Squires 2021), compared to the prevalent experiences of rape and domestic violence criminalised girls have experienced (Agenda Alliance 2022; Covington and Bloom 2007). This is demonstrated by existing scholarship which has emphasised that the dominant discourse on knife crime has focussed on incidents, which have occurred in the public sphere as opposed to the private sphere, despite knife crime regularly featuring in domestic violence offences and femicide (Cook and Walklate 2020; Long et al 2020). The use of weapons and the perpetration of violence by men in the public sphere continues to dominate public and political discourse on crime control. Therefore, the focus is on the risk management, prevention and punishment of structurally marginalised young people of colour (Fatsis et al. 2021; Williams and Clarke 2018) at the expense of focussing on knife crime or other acts of violence against women and girls.

As highlighted by Atkinson et al. (2022: 13), this process means that violence perpetrated within the private sphere is 'edged out of the debate'. Ultimately, this removes girls' offending from the broader structural inequalities which are pivotal to the forms of oppression and victimisation they experience, whilst simultaneously ideologically mystifying and distracting attention away from the crimes and social harms committed against them.

Conclusion

Box's intervention was integral to stimulate and promote an understanding of how the exercise of state power plays a fundamental role in shaping the ideological conditions and the material and lived realities of those who form part of, and experience, intersecting social divisions and disadvantages. Box's arguments, emphasising how the control and regulation of young people positioned as 'social dynamite' (Box 1983: 209) were pursued through criminalisation and incarceration has provided a basis and a point of comparison through which this chapter has been able to explore the continuities and discontinuities of the state's response to managing and regulating young people in the decades, which have followed the publication of *Power, Crime and Mystification*. Central to the analysis provided by Box (ibid: 57) was the issue of power, how it is exercised and by whom and how it is maintained, structurally, within capitalist society through processes of 'mystification and misdirection'. As demonstrated within this chapter, this analysis continues to be significant and applicable today when considering the extent and impact of the criminalisation and imprisonment of young people, the effects of which are felt across the different axes of social divisions and structural disadvantages emerging from race and ethnicity, social class and gender, all of which can be understood as a product of an intensified neo-liberal agenda in which risk management has become a primary approach deployed to control 'troublesome' populations of young people (ibid: 209).

Since the publication of *Power, Crime and Mystification*, youth justice responses to young people in general have wavered between various philosophies and approaches, ranging from welfarism, justice-based approaches, risk management and early interventionism and diversion. Each of these approaches represent different responses to the management, regulation and control of young people and have different consequences. In the four decades since Box's intervention, different groups of young people have been criminalised by the state following these different approaches. Whilst approaches to the management, regulation and control of young people have remained far from consistent, as the shifting landscape of youth justice has demonstrated, the disproportionate criminalisation of Black and Minority Ethnic young people who have remained 'perpetual suspects' (Long 2021: 344), and the systemic neglect of girls and young women and their relationship with the criminal justice system, have continued.

Overall, the approach has remained one which is and has continuously been punitive towards young people in conflict with the law and the law in conflict with young people. This is demonstrated by the issues discussed in this chapter. As Box (1983: 7) notes, following Sumner, the law is an ideological construct, which does not reflect '… those behaviours objectively causing us collectively the most avoidable suffering'. Rather, it is constructed in a way, which serves to criminalise only some harmful behaviour—those 'committed by the relatively powerless and to exclude others, usually those frequently committed by the powerful against subordinates' (ibid). Thus, the 'mystification and misdirection' of crimes committed by the powerful also remains a continuity (ibid: 57). To this end, the state's power to victimise, criminally or otherwise, serves a purpose. Despite the contradictions and contingencies within and between state institutions, it reinforces existing capitalist, hetero-patriarchal, sexist, ageist, ableist and racist structures, which serve the interests of the powerful while reinforcing the punishment and social control of young people in general, and young, Black and Minority Ethnic people, in particular.

References

Agenda Alliance for Women and Girls at Risk. 2021. *Young Women's Justice Project Literature Review*. London: Alliance for Youth Justice.
Agenda Alliance for Women and Girls at Risk. 2022. *'We've Not Given Up' Young Women Surviving the Criminal Justice System*. London: Alliance for Youth Justice.
Atkinson, K., Ú. Barr, and H. Monk. 2022. Introduction: Denying Oppression a Future—Gender, the State and Feminist Praxis. In *Feminist Responses to Injustices of the State and its Institution*, ed. K. Atkinson, Ú. Barr, H. Monk, and K. Tucker, 3–39. Bristol: Bristol University Press.
Commission, Audit. 1996. *Misspent Youth Report*. London: Audit Commission.
Barr, Ú. 2019. *Desisting Sisters: Gender, Power and Desistance in The Criminal (in)Justice System*. Basingstoke: Palgrave Macmillan.
Bateman, T. 2008. Target Practice: Sanction Detection and the Criminalisation of Children. *Criminal Justice Matters* 73 (1): 2–4.
Bateman, T. 2015. Trends in Detected Youth Crime and Contemporary State Responses. In *Youth Crime and Justice*, ed. B. Goldson and J. Muncie, 67–82. London: Sage Publications.
Box, S. 1983. *Power, Crime and Mystification*. London: Routledge.
Carrabine, E. 2010. Youth Justice in the United Kingdom. *Essex Human Rights Review* 7 (1): 12–24.
Children's Rights Alliance for England. 2016. *Inhuman Sentencing of Children in the United Kingdom Briefing for the 27th Session of the Human Rights Council Universal Periodic Review in April 2017 Submitted by the Child Rights International Network*. https://home.crin.org/. Accessed 3 July 2023.
Children's Rights Alliance for England. 2018. *State of Children's Rights in England 2018 Policing and Criminal Justice*. London: Children's Rights Alliance for England.
Clarke, B., and K. Chadwick. 2020. *Stories of Injustice: The Criminalisation of Women Convicted Under Joint Enterprise Laws*. London: Barrow Cadbury Trust.

Cook, E. A., and S. Walklate. 2020. Gendered Objects and Gendered Spaces: The Invisibilities of 'Knife' Crime. *Current Sociology* [Online], June 27, 1–16.

Corston, J. 2007. *The Corston Report: A Review of Women with Particular Vulnerabilities in the Criminal Justice System*. Home Office. https://www.clinks.org/resources-reports/who-careswhere-next-women-offender-services. Accessed 19 Aug 2016.

Covington, S., and B.E. Bloom. 2007. Gender Responsive Treatment and Services in Correctional Settings. *Women and Therapy* 29 (3–4): 9–33.

Cox, P. 2003. *Gender, Justice and Welfare: Bad Girls in Britain, 1900–1950*. Basingstoke: Palgrave Macmillan.

Crawford, A. 2003. Contractual Governance of Deviant Behaviour. *Law and Society* 30 (4): 479–505.

Crawford, A., and T. Newburn. 2002. Recent Developments in Restorative Justice for Young People in England and Wales. *British Journal of Criminology* 42 (3): 476–495.

Edwards, S.M. 1989. *Policing 'Domestic' Violence: Women, the Law and the State*. London: SAGE.

Fatis, L., J. Ilan, H. Kadiri, A. Owusu-Bempah, E. Quinn, M. Shiner, and P. Squires. 2021. *Missing the Point: How Policy Exchange Misunderstands Knife Crime in the Capital*. Identities, Global Studies in Culture and Power. https://www.identitiesjournal.com/blog-collection/missing-the-point-how-policy-exchange-misunderstands-knife-crime-in-the-capital. Accessed 3 July 2023.

Fitzpatrick, C., K. Hunter, J. Shaw, and J. Staines. 2022. *Final Report Disrupting the Routes Between Care and Custody for Girls and Women*. Centre for Children and Family Justice Research. https://www.cfj-lancaster.org.uk/files/pdfs/care-custody-report.pdf. Accessed 3 July 2023.

Garland, D. 2001. *The Culture of Control: Crime and Social Order in Contemporary Society*. Oxford: Oxford University Press.

Gelsthorpe, L., and A. Morris. 1999. 'Much Ado About Nothing': A Critical Comment on Key Provisions Relating to Children in the Crime and Disorder Act. *Child and Family Law Quarterly* 11 (3): 209–221.

Gelsthorpe, L., and A. Worrall. 2009. Looking for Trouble: A Recent History of Girls, Young Women and Youth Justice. *Youth Justice* 9 (3): 209–223.

Gilroy, P. 1982. *The Myth of Black Criminality. In Socialist Register*. London: Merlin.

Goodkind, S. 2005. Gender-Specific Services in the Juvenile Justice System: A Critical Examination. *Affilia* 20 (1): 52–70.

Goodkind, S. 2009. You Can Be Anything You Want, But You Have to Believe It. Commercialized Feminism in Gender-Specific Programs for Girls. *Signs Journal of Women in Culture and Society* 34 (2): 397–422.

Goldson, B. 2002. New Punitiveness: The Politics of Child Incarceration. In *Youth Justice: Critical Readings*, ed. J. Muncie, G. Hughes, and E. McLaughlin, 386–400. London: Sage Publications.

Hall, S., C. Critcher, T. Jefferson, J. Clarke, and B. Roberts. 1978. *Policing the Crisis: Mugging, the State, and Law and Order*. London: Macmillan.

Hannah-Moffat, K. 2005. Criminogenic Needs and the Transformative Risk Subject. *Punishment and Society* 71 (1): 29–51.

Her Majesty's Inspectorate of Probation. 2021. *The Experiences of Black and Mixed Heritage Boys in the Youth Justice System*. Manchester: Her Majesty's Inspectorate of Probation.

HM Chief Inspectorate of Prisons for England and Wales. 2017. *HM Chief Inspector of Prisons for England and Wales Annual Report 2016–17*. https://www.justiceinspectorates.gov.uk/hmiprisons. Accessed 3 July 2023.

HM Chief Inspectorate of Prisons for England and Wales. 2022. *HM Chief Inspector of Prisons for England and Wales Annual Report 2021–2022*. https://assets.publishing.service.gov.uk/government/uploads/system/uploads/attachment_data/file/1089500/hmip-annual-report-2021-22.pdf. Accessed 3 July 2023.

Hodgson, J. 2022. *Gender, Power and Restorative Justice: A Feminist Critique*. Cham, Switzerland: Palgrave Macmillan.

House of Commons Library. 2022. *Research Briefing: Unemployment and Ethnic Background*. https://commonslibrary.parliament.uk/research-briefings/sn06385/. Accessed 3 July 2023.

Jamieson, J., and J. Yates. 2009. Young People, Youth Justice and the State. In *State, Power, Crime*, eds. R. Coleman, J. Sim, S. Tombs, and D. Whyte, 76–89. London: Sage Publications.

JENGbA (Joint Enterprise Not Guilty by Association). nd. http://jointenterprise.co/default.html. Accessed 3 July 2023.

Johns, D. 2018. *A Social Ecological Approach to 'Child-Friendly' Youth Justice*. London: National Association of Youth Justice.

Kelly, L., and V. Armitage. 2015. Diverse Diversions: Youth Justice Reform, Localized Practices and a 'New Interventionist Diversion'? *Youth Justice*. 15 (2): 117–133.

Liddle, M., G. Boswell, S. Wright, V. Francis, and R. Perry. 2016. *Trauma and Young Offenders: A Review of the Research and Literature*. London: Beyond Youth Justice.

Long, J., E. Wertens, E., Harper, K., Brennan, D., Harvey, H., Allen, R., and Elliot, K, 2020. *Femicide Census: UK Femicides 2009– 2018.*

Long, L. 2021. The Ideal Victim: A Critical Race Theory (CRT) approach. *International Review of Victimology* 27 (3): 344–362.

May, T., T. Gytang, and M. Hough. 2010. *Differential Treatment in the Youth Justice System.* EHRC Research Report 50. London: Equality and Human Rights Commission.

McAra, L., and S. Mcvie. 2005. The Usual Suspects? Street-life, Young People and the Police. *Criminal Justice* 5 (1): 5–36.

Ministry of Justice (MoJ). 2018. *Female Offender Strategy.* London: Home Office.

Monk, H., J. Gilmore, and W. Jackson. 2019. Gendering Pacification: Policing Women at Anti-fracking Protests. *Feminist Review* 122 (1): 64–79.

Morgan, M., and P. Patton. 2002. Gender-Responsive Programming in the Justice System—Oregon's Guidelines for Effective Programming for Girls. *Federal Probation* 66 (2): 57–65.

Morgan, R. 2009. Children and Young People: Criminalisation and Punishment. In *Youth Offending and Youth Justice*, ed. M. Barry and F. McNeill, 56–77. London: Jessica Kingsley Publishers.

Muncie, J. 1999. Institutionalized Intolerance: Youth Justice and the 1998 Crime and Disorder Act. *Critical Social Policy* 19 (2): 147–175.

Muncie, J., and G. Hughes. 2002. Modes of Governance: Political Realities, Criminalization and Resistance. In *Youth Justice: Critical Readings*, ed. J. Muncie, G. Hughes, and E. McLaughlin, 1–18. London: Sage Publications.

Musto, J. 2019. Transing Critical Criminology: A Critical Unsettling and Transformative Anti-Carceral Feminist Reframing. *Critical Criminology* 27: 37–54.

Perera, J. 2020. *How Black Working-Class Youth are Criminalised and Excluded in the English School System.* London: Institute for Race Relations.

Phoenix, J. 2016. Against Youth Justice and Youth Governance, For Youth Penality. *The British Journal of Criminology* 56 (11): 123–140.

Pitts, J. 2001. *The New Politics of Youth Crime: Discipline or Solidary?* Basingstoke: Palgrave.

Scott, D. 2017. *When Prison Means Life: Child Lifers and the Pains of Imprisonment.* Harm and Evidence Research Collaborative. The Open University. https://www.open.ac.uk/researchcentres/herc/blog/when-prison-means-life-child-lifers-and-pains-imprisonment. Accessed 3 July 2023.

Scraton, P., and D. Haydon. 2002. Challenging the Criminalization of Children and Young People: Securing a Rights Based Agenda. In *Youth Justice:*

Critical Readings, ed. J. Muncie, G. Hughes, and E. McLaughlin, 311–328. London: Sage Publications.

Selman, K.J. 2017. Imprisoning 'Those' Kids: Neoliberal Logics and the Disciplinary Alternative School. *Youth Justice* 17 (3): 213–231. https://doi.org/10.1177/1473225417712607.

Sharpe, G. 2012. *Offending Girls: Young Women and Youth Justice*. London: Routledge.

Sim, J. 2009. *Punishment and Prisons: Power and the Carceral estate*. London: Sage Publications.

Smith, R., and P. Gray. 2019. The Changing Shape of Youth Justice: Models of practice. *Criminology and Criminal Justice* 19 (5): 554–571.

Smithson, H., R. Ralphs, and P. Williams. 2013. Used and Abused: The Problematic Usage of Gang Terminology in the United Kingdom and Its Implications for Ethnic Minority Youth. *British Journal of Criminology*. 53 (1): 113–128.

Solomon, E., C. Eades, R. Garside, and M. Rutherford. 2007. *Ten Years of Criminal Justice Under Labour: An Independent Audit*. London: Centre for Crime and Justice Studies.

Tosouni, A. 2019. *Gendered Injustice: Uncovering the Lived Experience of Detained Girls*. London: Routledge.

Webster, C. 2015. Race, Youth Crime and Youth Justice. In *Youth Crime and Justice*, eds. B. Goldson, B. and J. Muncie, 31–48. London: Sage Publications.

Williams, E., and D. Squires. 2021. *Rethinking Knife Crime Policing, Violence and Moral Panic?* Cham, Switzerland: Palgrave Macmillan.

Williams, P., and B. Clarke. 2016. *Dangerous Associations: Joint Enterprise, Gangs and Racism. An Analysis of the Processes of Criminalisation of Black, Asian and Minority Ethnic Individuals*. London: Centre for Crime and Justice Studies.

Williams, P., and B. Clarke. 2018. The Black Criminal Other as an Object of Social Control. *Social Sciences* 7 (11): 234. https://doi.org/10.3390/socsci7110234.

Worrall, A. 1990. *Offending Women: Female Lawbreakers and The Criminal Justice System*. London: Routledge.

Worrall, A. 2001. Girls at Risk? Reflections on Changing Attitudes to Young Women's Offending. *Probation Journal* 48 (2): 86–92.

Worrall, A. 2004. Twisted Sisters, Ladettes and the New Penology: The Social Construction of Violent Girls. In *Girls Violence: Myths and Realities*, ed. C. Alder and A. Worrall, 41–60. New York: New York Press.

Youth Justice Board. 2022. *Youth Justice Statistics 2020/21*. London: Youth Justice Board.

19

Demystifying Injustice: Joint Enterprise Law and Miscarriages of Justice

Janet Cunliffe and Gloria Morrison

Introduction

This chapter explores a controversial issue, which has come to the fore since the publication of *Power, Crime and Mystification* (Box, 1983)—that of the interpretation and application of Joint Enterprise (JE) laws, a doctrine enshrined in English common law. It is written from the perspective of two leading activists who, over the last decade and more, have been campaigning for the abolition of this law and of life sentences for children and the broader promotion of social justice. Our campaigning has been done through *Joint Enterprise Not Guilty by Association* [JENGbA], a grassroots group, founded in 2010 by ourselves. It aims to combat the widely condemned doctrine of JE and particularly, Parasitic Accessorial Liability (PAL). JE describes the situation where two or more people are convicted for participating in the same crime.

J. Cunliffe · G. Morrison (✉)
JENGA (Joint Enterprise Not Guilty by Association), England, UK
e-mail: gloriamorrison420@outlook.com

It is a policy driven by the tough-on-crime rhetoric pursued by successive governments for several decades. Yet, until recently, very few people, including senior MPs and the wider public, had heard of it. JENGbA aims to raise awareness of this profoundly unjust law and work towards its abolition. It is coordinated and run by the family members of those convicted under the doctrine.

JE has been a cause of concern for several years. In 2006, the Law Commission, which advises the Government on legal reform, made wide-ranging recommendations for changes to legislation and a year later, claimed the current homicide law was a 'rickety structure set upon shaky foundations' (Law Commission 2006, cited in Justice, nd), with some of the rules established in the seventeenth century. In 2006, the commission suggested a three-tier system for homicide cases based on their seriousness. However, the Labour Government at the time decided against overhauling the system (Justice, nd).[1] If it had been implemented, most of our JE prisoners could not have been charged with first-degree murder.

This chapter addresses five issues. First, it outlines some key themes from *Power, Crime and Mystification*, which contextualise JENGbA's work. Second, it discusses the formation and ethos of JENGbA. Third, it provides an overview of the scope and application of JE laws, noting the 'usual suspects' who are prosecuted and punished through the elastic interpretation of this law. Fourth, it highlights the group's legal activism and how JENGbA directly intervened in the case of R v Jogee [2016] UKSC. Even though, in this case, the Supreme Court fundamentally changed the law of accessorial liability, many wrongfully convicted people still remain in prison, blocked by the Court of Appeal's refusal to overturn unsafe JE convictions unless 'substantial injustice' is demonstrated (Krebs 2019). Fifth, it focusses on other important aspects of JENGbA's campaigning work over the last decade. Here, the chapter outlines some of our strategies including challenging the dominant narrative that the JE doctrine is about gangs, 'broken Britain' and controlling

---

[1] In its 2006 report, the Law Commission proposed a three-tier system of general homicide offences: first-degree murder (which would attract the mandatory life sentence); second-degree murder (with a discretionary life sentence); and manslaughter (with a discretionary life sentence). See Justice, (nd).

'feral' youth. Taking inspiration from Box (1983) and breaking through the power and mystifications of the law, we argue that JE is a tool used by the police and the Crown Prosecution Service (CPS) to unjustly imprison people for life for crimes committed by others. We note that a large proportion of those convicted of JE are young and Black, thus shining a critical spotlight on wider issues of racial injustice. This part of the chapter also discusses some of the latest campaigns and strategies pursued by JENGbA. We conclude by outlining our aspirations for a future where the harmful and unjust consequences of JE laws have been successfully de-mystified and abolished in line with Box's call for 'justice for all' (Box 1983: 219). JENGbA's campaigning also illustrates the new sites of resistance that have emerged since *PCM* was published. So, while the power of the authoritarian state has intensified since 1983, and imposed further, draconian measures on particular, targeted groups, in the case of this chapter racialised, young people, as ever, these measures have not been uncritically accepted. Through our work, and that of other organisations, state power has been contested both ideologically and through our demands for a radical change in policy. Both struggles remain ongoing.

Joint Enterprise and the Relevance of Steven Box

The first thing that struck us when reading *Power, Crime and Mystification* (Box 1983) was that, while it was published some forty years ago, it continues to powerfully speak to the present. Below, we highlight three key themes in the book, which resonate with the campaign priorities of JENGbA, and then reflect further upon them as we move through the chapter.

Box (1983: 2) states that, 'For every hundred persons convicted of…serious crimes, 85 are male. Amongst this convicted male population those aged less than 30 years, and particularly those aged between 15 and 21 years are over-represented'. This is exactly what is happening today with JE convictions. There is an over-criminalisation and disproportionate use of JE against young people, and Black youths, in particular. Box (1983) drew upon the ideas of Steven Spitzer to talk about 'social dynamite' (cited in ibid: 209) who 'have to be *controlled*' (ibid, original emphasis). Groups labelled as 'social dynamite' are often from impoverished backgrounds and collectively are considered a threat to social order. JE is a means of collectively controlling and displacing young people, disproportionately Black. By taking out whole groups of networked people (in the language of the state—gangs), JE can be understood as operating via the logic of 'social dynamite', where those convicted are presented as a threat who need to be controlled through the criminal law:

> Thus, the typical people criminally victimising and forcing us to fear each other and fracture our sense of "community" are young uneducated males who are often unemployed, live in a working class impoverished neighbourhood, and frequently belong to an ethnic minority. These villains deserve…"law and order".... .(Box 1983: 2)

This 'law and order' ideology has shaped the rhetoric of successive governments, with each competing to be tougher on crime than the previous one (Hall et al. 2013). This insidious rhetoric has led to a ratcheting up and intensification in punitiveness in the UK. Even though the death penalty was abolished in 1969, we still allow prisoners to endure a living death through JE. When we first began the campaign in 2010, the average sentence handed down was 15 years and 12 for those under 17. Now, we are seeing 17-year olds serve sentences of 24 years while the average sentence is 25 years.[2]

JE is used almost exclusively on working class and marginalised communities. But the doctrine could just as easily be implemented for other criminal activities such as the Downing Street lockdown parties, the Grenfell Tower fire, deaths in police custody, and aiding and abetting police officers who know their colleagues are dangerous and probably criminals (see Drake and Scott, this volume; White and Williams, this volume; Jackson, this volume).

---

[2] An increasing level of punitiveness is reflected in all life sentences. During our campaign work, we have found sentences are higher if it is a JE conviction, but this knowledge is based on our own data which we have not currently published. In 2020, the average length of time served for life sentences for murder was 16.5 years. 10% of prisoners sentenced to life imprisonment for murder in the period from 2010 to 2018 served 24 years or more (Leary 2020).

This discussion leads us to reflect upon one of the key concepts that Box explored, namely mystification, the ideological 'fog' that rendered invisible the true nature and extent of social harm (Box 1983: 12). This is a helpful concept when thinking about the interpretation and application of JE laws, particularly in the context noted above where JE is inappropriately applied to the powerless when it seems like a legal framework that is much more applicable to the harms perpetrated by those with power. He notes that the state provides:

> a particular and partial ideological version of serious crime and who commits it, but it does so by concealing and hence mystifying its propensity for violence and serious crimes on a much larger scale. (Box 1983: 14)

The definition of serious crime then both distort the harms of the powerless and misdirects attention away from the social harms of the powerful. As campaigners, it seems that JE law is mystified, and this ideological 'fog' hides the great injustice and misinterpretation of this law.

One further aspect derived from reading the book is the elasticity of law (see Burnett, this volume). The way that evidence is marshalled through JE illustrates how it is stretched to cover more than just one person and is applied to groups of people using the same evidence. Indeed, this over-stretched evidence is often very flimsy. Just as significantly, the very interpretation of JE can be brought into question and the way it is disproportionately deployed to control those from impoverished backgrounds who are considered a threat by state agents. We particularly note this with reference to the number of children who receive life sentences under JE laws.

Finally, Box highlights the problem of collective and public ignorance, thereby exposing the lack of knowledge and understanding about the most serious harms such as those perpetrated by corporations and the state (ibid: 16–17). It is a point which is implicit within much of the book while the construction of ignorance is closely tied to the way knowledge is distorted. JENGbA's campaigning work can be seen as following a pathway charted by Box in that our interventions are also about exposing and challenging collective public ignorance. Like him, we would like to transform common sense understandings of JE, which are grounded in partial and incorrect assumptions, into a much better understanding that is informed by the families and the people who have had to live with the cruel injustice of JE sentences. For us, reading Box today highlights a key element in our activism; we also want to expose how the current perceptions and applications of JE law are shaped by collective ignorance.

Responding to Injustice—the Formation of JENGbA

JENGbA was co-founded by the authors in 2010 to highlight wrongful JE convictions after their sons were convicted of murder. Neither of them committed, assisted, encouraged or knew about what was going to happen. People have been convicted of murder on the 'possibility of foresight', which might seem an odd turn of phrase but in the UK's legal system, a prosecutor can claim a defendant could possibly foresee what someone else might do. Whether by association (a friend or relative), by a phone call (we once witnessed a Judge say that teenagers 'phone each other more than they do their fathers') or simply because they like the same music can, and has resulted in, a conviction for murder. We have cases where the prosecution will argue that if a defendant's phone is switched off, or has no signal to connect them to the scene of a crime, it is because they have gone 'radio silent'. The prosecution will infer, rather than prove with real evidence, that they knew the crime was going to happen.

The authors met after the BBC Panorama programme, *Lethal Enterprise* (2009), filmed one of us (Jan) discussing her son Jordan Cunliffe's case. The filmmaker had witnessed some of the trial and knew something was dreadfully wrong with his conviction. However, the Judge had imposed a gagging order on the press reporting his severe disability. Jordan had Keratoconus, an eye condition which left him with less than 10% vision in both eyes. The prosecution at the outset of the trial said that they would not challenge his serious visual impairment so would not need an expert witness to give evidence. But when Jordan took the stand the same prosecutor stated that while Jordan would tell the jury he was blind, he had been playing football that day and if he could kick a ball then he could kick a man to death, even though he was barefoot at the time. This was all the while knowing that Jordan had not even touched the victim let alone kicked him. The expert witness who could have explained his blindness was not called. Thus, the jury never understood his disability. After being found guilty of murder, Jordan had one cornea transplant as he had turned sixteen. When he returned to court to be sentenced with a bandage over his transplant, the Judge told him he did not need to stand as he was clearly unable to see!

Gloria's son's best friend[3] had also been found guilty of murder even though he was the first person attacked by a group of men and was semi-conscious during a stabbing that he had no intention or foresight. He had been training to be a youth offending officer at the time and took part in a prison film about JE questioning the legitimacy of his conviction when he had not committed the crime. The producer contacted us and suggested that we should meet, which we did in 2009. It was at that initial meeting that we recognised that a campaign was needed. We had no legal knowledge or idea that it would become a national campaign of huge significance.

After the Panorama documentary was aired, Gloria was contacted by the CEO of a multinational company because he was perplexed about how people in prison did not understand why they were there. Under the company's corporate responsibility arm, he gave us the resources to kick-start JENGbA, which was officially launched in 2010. Before the launch, we inserted an advert in the prison newspaper *Inside Time* asking if anybody who had been convicted under JE could come to a meeting in the House of Commons (Woffinden 2010). We had to keep booking a bigger room as more and more prisoners and their families contacted us and that is how we started recording the number of JE prisoners.

---

[3] Ken is Gloria's son's best friend, but he calls her mum, and she considers him her son.

At that point, another key founder of JENGbA[4] who was fighting her nephew's wrongful JE conviction had contacted the playwright Jimmy McGovern, who met with our families and recognised a terrible injustice was happening. Jimmy agreed to become JENGbA's patron and helped launch the campaign in Liverpool as well as writing the widely acclaimed film *Common* (BBC 2014).

As a grassroots campaign, we wanted to support prisoners and their families and decided that a newsletter to the prisoners would offer a direct lifeline to the campaign's struggles and achievements. We organised monthly meetings around the country. We visited universities, reached out to community groups and gave talks using cases we supported to show how egregious JE was. We held marches and contacted MPs and met with Jeremey Corbyn MP who was a member of the *House of Commons Justice Select Committee* (JSC). He suggested a brief inquiry into JE, which was held in 2012. Our evidence was based on submissions from prisoners indicating what had happened to them to secure a wrongful conviction much to the annoyance of certain MPs on the Committee who thought the prisoners' (approximately 60 submissions) evidence was partisan. The inquiry's recommendations supported our case with the chair Lord Beith confirming they believed it was leading to wrongful convictions (Justice Select Committee 2012).

In a BBC Radio 4 programme, (BBC 2010), almost a year after the *Panorama* episode was aired (BBC 2009), the former commissioner of the Metropolitan Police, Lord Blair, said a change in the law was 'extremely sensible':

> While murder must remain a very specific crime, with a very serious penalty attached to it, there are, and I think everybody can see it, different kinds of murder and different levels of culpability in those murders and I think the Americans have a very sensible idea that there are degrees of murder. (BBC 2010)

Embracing the Law Commission's recommendations in 2006 for a three-tier system (see earlier), the then-Director of Public Prosecutions,

---

[4] We have worked closely with Cath O Hanlon and Yvonne Belardini in our work with JENGbA.

Keir Starmer also voiced his support. However, the former Labour Lord Chancellor, Lord Falconer, said he was not convinced about the need for change:

> The message that the law is sending out is that we are very willing to see people convicted if they are a part of gang violence - and that violence ends in somebody's death.
> Is it unfair? Well, what you've got to decide is not "does the system lead to people being wrongly convicted?" I think the real question is "do you want a law as draconian as our law is, which says juries can convict even if you are quite a peripheral member of the gang which killed?"
> And I think broadly the view of reasonable people is that you probably do need a quite draconian law in that respect. (BBC 2010)

Our numbers of prisoners and families steadily grew as the CPS realised that the use of JE was an easy tool for obtaining convictions without having to *actually prove* what defendants had done. They had found a sledgehammer to crack a walnut regardless of the fact it created victims of miscarriages of justice. The evidential bar in JE is shockingly low and often those convicted and serving life sentences have told us they did not recognise who the prosecutors were describing until it dawned on them it was they themselves. This is often because those with the least evidence against them are identified as the 'ringleader', even when they can be the youngest of the group. One of the cases we support concerns two brothers, one of whom was in prison when he phoned his brother on an illegal mobile phone to ask him to top up his credit. He was two weeks away from release for a crime he did commit and accepted his guilt. After a shooting in Sheffield, both brothers were charged with murder and convicted including the young man in prison who received thirty-five years for that phone call.

We visit prisoners and that became an integral part of understanding how defendants became caught up in a JE conviction. Our numbers were also pointing to something else, namely that JE was targeting young, black men and boys and those from working-class communities. We contacted different Trade Unions and were invited to talk to their members, who early on were unaware that such a law existed and that it could so easily lead to murder convictions. An early campaign talk with the *National Association of Probation Officers*, led to a delegate taking the floor. She indicated that she had recently been looking at the file of a young man who had served 17 years and could not understand what it was he was supposed to have done (JENGbA 2013).

A follow-up inquiry by the JSC had been scheduled for 2015. Serving prisoners gave us a heads-up that academics from Cambridge University were conducting a study on mandatory sentencing (Crewe, Hulley and Wright 2016). The 2003 *Criminal Justice Ac*t Schedule 21 took the discretionary powers in sentencing away from Judges so in cases of murder the starting point for using a knife was 15 years, and 30 years if a gun was used. Serving prisoners made JENGbA aware of the research so we contacted the authors. When they revealed their findings, at that point unpublished, we asked if they intended to submit evidence to the Committee, which they confirmed they would. They gave oral evidence and it was a pin-drop moment. Out of the 298 young prisoners they interviewed, 50% had been convicted using JE and 40% of those were Black. Once again, the Committee's recommendations called for data to be collected on JE convictions, once again it was promised by the CPS (Justice Select Committee 2015) and once again those recommendations were ignored.

JENGbA has built strong alliances with MPs across the political parties throughout our years of campaigning. Jeremy Corbyn MP was appointed JE's special rapporteur by the JSC. Andrew Mitchell MP has been incredibly supportive to the extent that he and others have visited some of our prisoners. We have encouraged prisoners and their families to lobby their MPs who will invariably say they cannot support individual cases and; as we noted earlier, academic research has played a crucial role in widening our support network.

We have attended various conferences and fundraisers and had the honour to meet Paddy Hill of the Birmingham Six and the late Gerry Conlon of the Guildford Four. As campaigners for justice, we were struck by their resolute passion, their unwavering anger at the criminal injustice system and how they maintained the corruption was as bad as it had always been. When Keir Starmer, the then Director of Public Prosecutions (DPP), agreed to meet us so we could express our genuine concerns about wrongful convictions, and how we felt about the yet-to-be published prosecutors' guidance on JE charging, we thought this could be a great opportunity to dissuade over-zealous prosecutors from overcharging young people. This guidance had been recommended by the JSC and as the inquiry and its follow-up inquiry were both born from the voices of the campaign, there was a sense of confidence that the right thing would be done. Starmer had already spoken publicly about a three tier system regarding cases of homicide. We sat around a table with unknown policymakers, who told us they were not allowed to talk about specific cases. After a long wait and being told Starmer would not be attending the meeting, he did eventually join us. His initial comment was that we would not like the guidance and that anything we did not agree with would not be changed. He told us that as DPP his hands were tied and that JE was a matter for Parliament. Had we not just been to Parliament with a cross-party group of MPs? When he became an MP we had another meeting with him to ask what he could do to help us. He was as vague as he had been as DPP which was a little hard to square with him being a 'leading human rights lawyer'.

The 'Usual Suspects'

According to the CPS, JE is:

> an aspect or form of secondary liability, and not an independent liability. Joint Enterprise can apply where two or more persons are involved in an offence or offences. A principal is one who carries out the substantive offence and performs the conduct element of the offence and the secondary party is one who assists or encourages the principal to commit the substantive offence. (Crown Prosecution Service 2019)

However, a secondary party can be prosecuted and punished as if he/she were a principal offender. Secondary liability principles can be applied to most offences, but the majority of the people JENGbA supports are serving life sentences for a murder they did not commit.

Supported by the media, there is a shared incorrect narrative that JE is about gangs, 'broken Britain' and 'feral' youth (Morrison and Cunliffe 2022). This doctrine is a tool used by the state to imprison people for life for crimes committed by others. Individuals can be wrongly charged and convicted when they have been close to a crime, have a random connection with the actual perpetrator via texting or engage in a phone call which is most often used as 'critical evidence'. Many defendants may not even have been at the crime scene but can be convicted of murder by association. More recently, young men, and increasingly young women, have been targeted, where often the sole evidence against them is their choice of music, especially rap or drill music (*The Guardian* 2019). Trials often open with defendants being shown taking part in a video, rapping or making 'gang' signs. This is a signal to the juries that they are criminals before a shred of evidence is produced.

If it is a complex legal doctrine surely ordinary people sitting on a JE trial jury will have little or no understanding of archaic legal phrases, nor will they fully understand what a guilty verdict will mean. Many people do not realise children can be sentenced to mandatory life with a minimum tariff. For example, if a child is found guilty in a JE case where a weapon is used and he/she is not the main defendant—that is they are not the person who used the weapon that caused the fatal injury but are a secondary party—the Judge will have to follow sentencing guidelines, and give him/her a life sentence, even though the trial process proved they did not commit murder and, in many cases, committed no violence. The Judge will have a starting point of, for example, 20 years so this means those convicted may well be released early for good behaviour and that once a sentence ends, they return to normal life. However, JE prisoners are released on life licence for 99 years with the possibility of recall, a Damocles sword hanging over them for the rest of their lives.[5]

JENGbA currently supports approximately 1400 prisoners and their families but we believe that number to be conservative. In 2022, a study

---

[5] At the time of writing (July, 2023), a new Victims and Prisoners Bill was passing through the UK Parliament, which will give a politician, the Secretary of State for Justice, the power to intervene in decisions made by the independent Parole Board to release prisoners. There have also been attempts during the passage of this bill to change the law with regard to resentencing Indeterminate Public Protection (IPP) prisoners.

by the *Centre for Crime and Justice Studies* confirmed that since the 2016 Supreme Court decision (R v Jogee) the law on parasitic accessorial liability had '*taken a wrong turn in 1984*' (Mills, Ford and Grimshaw 2021, original emphasis). The number of people convicted using JE has in fact risen, with young, black men still being targeted. We have families frequently contacting us but post-trial because they had never heard of JE and did not believe an individual could be convicted of murder when they had not murdered anyone. Mills et al., (ibid) drew upon national data to assess the use of JE in prosecutions for serious violence in England and Wales over the previous fifteen years (i.e. 2006–2021). Theirs was the first publication to track multi-defendant cases and secondary suspects over this significant period. When a family or prisoner contacts us we send them a support pack which includes a questionnaire and a stamped addressed envelope. As a grassroots-led campaign, we did not realise that the data we were collecting was so important. At the beginning of the campaign, we only asked for minimal information whereas, now, the questionnaire asks about, ethnicity, dependents, the names of the Judge, prosecutor, and police force and whether the gang narrative was used. One of the main questions journalists and students ask is how many people are serving life sentences under JE. Numerous Freedom of Information [FOI] requests to the Ministry of Justice have all come back unanswered. They simply do not record the data. This is reinforced by the difficulties in obtaining data from them. The studies by academics and investigative journalists over the last decade—the Bureau of Investigative Journalism (2014), Clarke and Williams (2016), the Lammy Review (2017), Clarke and Chadwick (2021), and the report by the United Nations (2023)—all shine a critical light onto the serious injustices taking place. Williams and Clarke (2016) highlighted the disproportionate and racist application of JE, while Clarke and Chadwick (2021) pointed out that of the 103 women they interviewed, only 2 had inflicted any violence and that was minor while over one hundred women were serving life sentences for a murder they had not committed (see also Chadwick and Clarke, this volume).

These reports vindicated JENGbA's claims that JE is racist and discriminatory. Our concerns led us to contact *Liberty* and ask whether a legal challenge was possible against the Ministry of Justice due to the lack of transparency on data. They advised us to pursue a Judicial Review (JR) against the CPS as they refused to record ethnicity, age, gender and disabilities in their decisions to charge. JENGbA's JR challenged the CPS's failure to gather and monitor data regarding the protected characteristics of those prosecuted under JE, contending that this breached the Public Sector Equality Duty in section149 of the *Equality Act* 2010. The JR was successful although the CPS, while not conceding a breach of duty, has agreed to implement a pilot scheme and thereafter, a full national scheme for gathering and reviewing equalities data on JE prosecutions. It has also committed to consult relevant stakeholders, including JENGbA, on the form of the final national scheme.[6]

In 2020, JENGbA decided to rewrite our manifesto (JENGbA 2020). We wanted to address the fact that we imprison children in the UK for crimes they have not committed. It called for the abolition of detention settings for children. This is the cornerstone of everything JENGbA stands for. We do not forget the men (many of whom went into prison as children), and the women (many of whom have had to abandon their own children to a 'state' upbringing) whose challenges to their wrongful convictions we support. We want to address the fact that in England and Wales presently, children are being caged in often appalling violent and neglectful settings in the name of being 'tough on crime'.

In March 2022, in England and Wales, there were 8610 people serving a life sentence of any kind (Jarman and Vince 2022: 15). This is the highest number of Lifers in Western Europe, and more than France, Germany and Italy combined. The data below provides a snapshot:

- In 2018, the UK had 855 Lifers in prison. This was the highest number of Lifers in Western Europe, 10% of the prison population and higher than the USA's 9.5%;
- Between 2006 and 2016, 197 children were given life sentences in the UK. The average age was 16 but the youngest was just 13;
- In 2018, the BIPOC (Black, indigenous, people of colour) population of children in prison had risen from 24% in 2007 to 46%;

---

[6] The CPS have also asked JENGbA about this process and we are currently (July, 2023) in discussions about what our response should be.

- Three out of 10 children are sent to prison for non-violent offences. (2016–2017) (Scott 2019).

Reading these statistics begs the question: what is going on in our criminal justice system where it is acceptable to still put vulnerable children and adolescents into places of harm under the pretext of protecting the public? Besides the fact that prisons do more harm than good, (Scott 2018, 2020), especially regarding young people (Scott 2016), we must examine why imprisoning children can be considered a route to safer communities. When a child goes to prison, especially but not exclusively, a child convicted using the now discredited and racist doctrine of JE, it devastates communities. It is not only the families mourning the loss of their child, but their friends will no longer have any trust in the criminal justice system. It is a system they recognise as an extension of the apparatus to harass and condemn young people for their friendship groups and musical choices.

Legal Activism

We started the campaign to challenge a law, which we instinctively knew was wrong. Although we are non-practitioners, we have learnt the law and now can hold our own with lawyers and King's Counsels (KCs). The criminal justice system needs root and branch reform, beginning with the abolition of JE, life imprisonment for children and mandatory life sentences. There is a real need for the Police and the CPS to distribute their charging decisions to each individual charged. This is crucial so they understand why they have been charged and allows them to build a defence case that fits those charging decisions. Young people, in particular, will defend themselves against the murder charge alone, and will adequately prove during the trial process that they did not commit murder. However, they will still be convicted of murder because they did not defend themselves against the prosecutor's assertions that they had possible foresight, or there was a tacit agreement in the form of a wink or a nod or even a knowing look. They will have no understanding that their mere presence at the scene will lead to a conviction, as it is interpreted as encouraging and assisting, even if they did nothing.[7]

On 18th February 2016, and following years of tireless campaigning by our families and prisoners, we were ultimately successful in R v Jogee [2016] UKSC 8, when the Supreme Court abolished PAL (Parasitic Accessorial Liability) and reinstated the principles of traditional accessorial liability. The Supreme Court ruled that for over three decades, the courts had been relying on foresight and not intention. They agreed that possible foresight that the principal offender might commit a crime was not sufficient. The Supreme Court acknowledged that the law had taken a 'wrong turn' as far back as 1984. There was an audible gasp from the packed courtroom. And when the news was relayed to the prisoners via the media, we had been told that prisoners up and down the country were ecstatic, believing they would finally get justice. As did we. However, it was a bittersweet victory and actually quite cruel. In spite of the judgement which arguably was supposed to set the law back on course, and render many JE convictions unsafe, to date only two appeals against conviction have been successful. In short, the same law is still being abused.

The acknowledgment in R v Jogee [2016], that it was the Judges who had misinterpreted the law and therefore they were to blame for thirty years of injustice was vindication for all that we had been saying about JE. And if it gave campaigners nothing else it gave us hope and the knowledge that we had been right all along.

Let us look closer at Ameen Jogee's case. He was originally convicted of murder in June 2011, despite the fact it was his friend who stabbed the victim and did so inside a house. This happened while Ameen was outside. The case had originally been rejected by the Court of Appeal and it was only because of a lengthy legal process and the full support of his outstanding legal team and JENGbA that managed to get the case before

---

[7] It should be noted that we recommend that all transcripts from court should be given electronically to each convicted individual immediately and free of charge so if they want to appeal they have the resources and access to their papers which are currently destroyed after six years. Defence lawyers should be able to interview jurors after they make their decision to ascertain how they came to that verdict. These things happen in the US legal system, which many look down on as worse than our own. Appeal also has the same vision as JENGbA and are campaigning for a similar approach here.

the Supreme Court. The Court's decision quite rightly acquitted Ameen of murder, yet the CPS were offered the chance of a retrial. Again, an area of law that is baffling for lay people; If the most senior Judges in the land decide a conviction is unsafe, why do they offer the CPS another opportunity to gain a conviction again using the same evidence as before? Why would they want to put the bereaved families of the victim through the trauma of a trial process again?

At his retrial, Ameen was found not guilty of murder but guilty of manslaughter. Another bizarre decision because a number of campaigners attended the trial and the only evidence against him was a witness to the murder who declared he was innocent. She claimed the police took three witness statements and made changes to the third. She insisted that they use her first witness statement, which confirmed Ameen had been outside and took no part in the murder. This fitted squarely with his lawyer's defence that he was not a murderer, he was just in the wrong place at the wrong time.

The decision in Jogee was not automatically retrospective either, instead to obtain an appeal, all those convicted under the wrong interpretation of the law, Parasitic Accessorial Liability or PAL, had to prove they had suffered a 'substantial injustice'. This was the clause (paragraph 100) that was deliberately inserted into the Jogee judgement of 2016. It was only after digesting the judgement that it became clear this was done to stop what the Judges foresaw might be a floodgate of appeals by the wrongly convicted. Applicants to the Court of Appeal must now demonstrate that they have suffered a substantial injustice before even being given the right to appeal. This test is an added burden on top of an already difficult appeals process and one that is proving impossible to meet.

The first cases to go back to the Court of Appeal to challenge the substantial injustice test were known as R v Johnson [2016] EWCA Crim 1613. Several JE appeals were heard in one sitting and the court was packed with families. Although no appellants were allowed to attend in person, some were able to watch via a video link that we have been reliably informed had appalling sound quality. A number of the cases were at the appeal stage, but waited to see the outcome of Jogee so expectations were high. Michael Hall had paid privately for his QC so he had direct access to him. Michael and his girlfriend had had an altercation over a taxi outside a pub when one of Michael's friends chased a man and kicked him twice in the head, sadly the second blow being fatal, unbeknownst to Michael and Laura. They had woken up to the news that someone had died, went to the police station to assist the police and were later charged with, and then convicted of, murder.

Months after R v Johnson, the Appeal Court's judgement had still not been handed down. Families were anxiously asking if JENGbA knew when this would happen. We called Michael's sister who had direct access to his barrister who was surprised we did not know it was listed for five days later. We shared that information on our social media platform, only to have families call their lawyers who knew nothing about the judgement being handed down. They called the Court of Appeal who confirmed it was at 10 am on Monday 31st October 2016.

It then transpired that the Lord Chief Justice had put a gagging order on the decision. So, instead of an empty court, he encountered a packed courtroom and press gallery. As he denied the appeals for every case, mothers and girlfriends cried and screamed. When the clerk said all rise, the brother of someone serving 24 years stomped his feet and shouted, 'No Justice, No Peace' which the other families echoed. This is the first time we had protested openly in court and it came from anger and the knowledge that we had been shafted yet again. We were warned by our lawyers that we could still be held in contempt of court, so when we met the press we had to say we were seeking legal advice. It was transmitted by the media but at 12 pm, the Home Secretary reneged on her promise to hold an inquiry into Orgreave and that became the lead story burying our stories of further injustices (Stone 2016).[8]

R v Johnson has rendered appeals virtually impossible. There is now an incredibly onerous legal burden to prove a person's innocence. Permission to appeal will only be granted to those who can prove that they

---

[8] In 1984, during the miners strike, striking miners were picketing Orgreave colliery. The police attacked the peacefully picketing miners and arrested 94 for unlawful assembly and violent disorder, all of whom were acquitted when it transpired that the police had attacked the miners and not the other way around. This was at a time when riot was punishable by life imprisonment. The Orgreave campaign had been demanding a full inquiry into the incident where many miners were seriously injured (Stone 2016).

would not have been convicted if the law had been properly applied, as Judges argue that the decisions by juries are final and irreversible, even though they were being directed to apply the wrong law. The guidance for the substantial injustice test is unreachable and has hindered criminal appeals partly because there is no way of knowing what evidence the jury believed.

Of the two appeals which have been successful following Jogee, the first was John Crilly[9] whose conviction for murder was reduced to manslaughter (R v Crilly [2018] EWCA Crim 168). After the appeal, John was taken back to prison and released that evening after being issued with his licence agreement, one that would be in place for a further five years, (February 2023). He said, 'If you take the foresight burden of proof away, and go on intent, which you are supposed to do, it's impossible to convict me of murder. It's that simple really' (BBC 2018). He had planned a burglary with his co-defendant. Unbeknown to both, the homeowner was still in the property. John claimed he wanted to leave but his co-defendant, David Flynn struck the victim and the blow was fatal.

The second successful acquittal was in 2021. Phillipe Sonsongo, a 14-year old, was convicted of JE murder in 2017. He was convicted as a secondary party to a stabbing and his post-conviction diagnosis for autism spectrum disorder (ASD) and Attention Deficit Hyperactivity Disorder (ADHD) was seen to amount to fresh evidence that could have impacted the jury's original decision (R v Sonsongo [2021] EWCA Crim 1777).

---

[9] John Crilly went on to fight a terrorist on London Bridge after an attack that took place at Fishmongers' Hall, claiming the lives of Jack Merritt and Saskia Jones. His courage led to him receiving the Highest Commendation Award from the Metropolitan Police and the Queen's Gallantry Award for Bravery.

Changing the Narrative Through Grassroots Campaigning

It is important to challenge the dominant narrative that the JE doctrine is about gangs, 'broken Britain' and the control of 'feral' youth. As with all grassroots campaigns, the work behind opposing the legal establishment has been, and is, an uphill battle. It was a role taken on mainly by women. JENGbA was created by the legal establishment, it was not a campaign that came out of nowhere; it was precisely because the use of JE was unjust, unfair and discriminatory towards working class and minority ethnic communities that we were forced to form JENGbA.

As discussed earlier, one of the key issues raised by Box is social ignorance. As he noted:

> The conditions of life for the powerless, created by the powerful are simply ignored by those who explain crime as a manifestation of individual pathology or local neighbourhood friendships and cultural patterns – yet in many respects the unrecognised victimisation of the powerless by the powerful constitutes a part of those conditions under which the powerless choose to commit crimes. (Box 1983: 14)

The public's ignorance regarding JE and sentencing is such that what they believe to be the case is very far removed from reality. If JE is policy-driven, we can confidently say it is driven by ignorance. The law says ignorance is no defence yet a legal doctrine like JE is driven by, and thrives on, ignorance and powerlessness.

This brings us back to JE being a deterrent to gang-related crime. How can it be? How can a legal doctrine which people know nothing about be a deterrent? And if we were to believe it was a deterrent, and all the young people that have been convicted pre-Jogee 2016 when foresight was enough to convict a person of murder, why was this not the police message at the time? When asked about JE, why did successive Justice Ministers dismiss just how low the burden of proof to conviction lay? There is no consistency in verdicts. Prosecutors remain hell-bent on winning at all costs rather than delivering justice. Some Judges will dismiss defendants on lack of evidence part way through a trial while others will argue that it should be a matter for the jury. The number of children serving life sentences in the UK tells us we have a huge problem. It is not that we have a generation of homicidal children and teenagers but we have a corrupt and draconian legal system that refuses to rectify injustices because politicians believe being tough on crime appeals to the voting public.

To start to draw this chapter to a close let us reflect on some of the work that lies directly in front of us. JENGbA has aimed to shine a critical spotlight on wider issues of racial injustice and has long campaigned against the mystification of the fact that the largest proportion of those convicted of JE are young, minority ethnic people. This picks up on a key theme discussed at the end of *Power, Crime and Mystification* namely that the prison population in the early 1980s was becoming younger and more racialised.

The statistics are huge and rightly worrying to the untrained eye. When they stand alone, with no background they represent gainful convictions for very violent offences. They reassure the public that the most dangerous in society are behind bars and will be for decades. What the statistics do not reveal, and it is telling that FOI requests to the Ministry of Justice and the CPS hit a brick wall, is that many of these convictions were gained using the discredited JE doctrine. JENGbA believes that there are more people serving life for a murder they did not commit than actual murderers.

Charlotte, the sister of Alex Henry, has, since her brother's conviction, trained as a lawyer. She is responsible for a Private Members Bill in Parliament aiming to abolish the substantial injustice test. We have several MPs sponsoring it and it has passed its first reading in the House of Commons. JENGbA now has the support of *Liberty*,[10] to challenge the lack of data from the CPS on murder charges and convictions. Felicity Gerry KC has called for an audit of all those serving life sentences who were secondary parties after Jogee, and this will be one of our next challenges.

The Howard League for Penal Reform is now supporting JENGbA by helping collate our data into a digital format, which will be one of the

---

[10] See Liberty (2023).

most exhaustive data sets on JE in England and Wales. Jimmy McGovern wrote *Common* (BBC 2011) based on our cases and the lead actor Andy Teirnan has also agreed to be a patron as has Maxine Peake, another actor. Support from other campaigns and individuals is key as JENGbAs comprises people from all walks of life who would have never met if it had not been for the most diabolical of injustices, which are *convictions by design*.

We are also intending to hold a family inquiry via family listening days around the country to empower our families, often the most disenfranchised and powerless, to become activists in their own right. This was Box's main message and why he questioned how a society defines crime and what is the difference between justice and social control? Those with power fear campaigns like ours that educate and inform. The powerful are more concerned with regulating, controlling and demoralising relatively powerless groups like JENGbA rather than tackling crime, the causes of crime and those criminals they ignore because they are in positions of power.

Conclusion

It is time to tell the truth and deliver a justice system the public can trust, not only to protect themselves from the violence of others and from State violence. What we mean here by State violence is the wrongful arrest, the wrongful conviction and the wrongful imprisonment of ourselves or our children using a law that is complex and obscure. It is hard to maintain innocence regarding a little-known law. Everything reverts back to ignorance. Everything is based on lies or false information. The answer to violence surely cannot be more violence. We must examine why imprisonment can be considered a route to safer communities. As US writer and activist Angela Davis (2003) states about the US prison system; 'Prisons do not disappear problems, they disappear human beings […] in order to convey the illusion of solving social problems'. We will continue organising, encouraging activism, media work and lobbying until the authors' hopes and aspirations for a future where the harmful and unjust consequences of JE laws have been successfully de-mystified and abolished in line with Box's call for 'justice for all' (Box 1983: 219).

References

BBC. 2009. *Panorama: Lethal Enterprise*. London: BBC.
BBC. 2010. *BBC Radio 4 Today Programme*. www.bbc.co.uk, September.
BBC. 2014. *Common*. London: BBC.
BBC. 2018. *BBC 5 Live Breakfast*. www.bbc.co.uk, April.
Box, S. 1983. *Power, Crime and Mystification*. London: Routledge.
Bureau of Investigative Journalists. 2014. *Revealed: Thousands Prosecuted Under Controversial Law*. BIJ Online https://www.thebureauinvestigates.com/stories/2014-03-31/revealed-thousands-prosecuted-under-controversial-law-o. Accessed 6 June 2023.
Clarke. B., and K. Chadwick. 2021. *Stories of Injustice*. Manchester: Manchester Metropolitan University. https://www.crimeandjustice.org.uk/sites/crimeandjustice.org.uk/files/Stories%20of%20injustice.pdf.
Clarke, B., and P. Williams. 2016. *Dangerous Associations*. London: CCJS.
Crewe, B., S. Hulley, and S. Wright. 2016. *Life Imprisonment from Young Adulthood: Adaption, Identity and Time*. Basingstoke: Palgrave.
Crown Prosecution Service (CPS). 2019. *Secondary Liability: Charging Decisions on Principals and Accessories*. https://www.cps.gov.uk/legal-guidance/secondary-liability-charging-decisions-principals-and-accessories Accessed 6 June 2023.
Davis, A.Y. 2003. Masked Racism: Reflections on the Prison Industrial Complex. In *History is a Weapon*. historyisaweapon.com. Accessed 6 June 2023.
Hall, S., C. Critcher, T. Jefferson, J. Clark, and R. Roberts. 2013. *Policing the Crisis*, 2nd ed. London: Macmillan Palgrave.
Jarman, B., and C. Vince. 2022. *Making Progress? What Progression Means for People Serving the Longest Sentences*. London: Prison Reform Trust.
JENGbA. 2013. Joint Enterprise Laws. Paper Delivered to the *National Association of Probation Officers Annual Conference* [NAPO].
JENGbA. 2020. *Manifesto*. https://jointenterprise.co.
Justice Select Committee. 2012. *Brief Inquiry on Joint Enterprise*. London: HMSO.

Justice Select Committee. 2015. *Follow up Inquiry on Joint Enterprise*. London: HMSO.
Justice., nd. *Homicide Law Reform*. https://justice.org.uk/homicide-law-reform/#:~:text=In%20its%202006%20report%20the,with%20a%20discretionary%20life%20sentence). Accessed 6 July 2023.
Krebs, B., ed. 2019. *Accessorial Liability after Jogee*. London: Hart Publishing.
Lammy, D. 2017. *Lammy Review*. London: HMSO.
Leary, J. 2020. How Long do Murderers Serve in Prison? *Full Fact*. https://fullfact.org/crime/how-long-do-murderers-serve-prison/. Accessed 6 July 2023.
Liberty. 2023. *Holding Our Own*. London: Liberty. https://www.libertyhumanrights.org.uk/wp-content/uploads/2023/04/HoldingOurOwn_Digital-DoubleSpreads.pdf. Accessed 6 June 2023.
Morrison, G., and J. Cunliffe. 2022. *Submission of Evidence on Behalf of JENGbA to Liberty: Serious Youth Violence Report*. London: Liberty.
Mills, H., M. Ford, and R. Grimshaw. 2021. *The Usual Suspects*. London: CCJS.
Scott, D. 2016. When Prison Means Life. *The Justice Gap*. https://www.thejusticegap.com/prison-means-life-child-lifers-pains-imprisonment/. Accessed 6 June 2023.
Scott, D. 2018. *Against Imprisonment*. Hook: Waterside Press.
Scott, D. 2019. *Why We Should Abolish Imprisonment for Children and Young People*. Open Learn: The Open University. https://openlearn.medium.com/why-we-should-abolish-imprisonment-for-children-and-young-people-3bec0b0dd9e8. Accessed 6 June 2023.
Scott, D. 2020. *For Abolition*. Hook: Waterside Press.
Stone, S. 2016. Battle of Orgreave Home Secretary Amber Rudd Rules out Inquiry. *The Independent*, October. https://www.independent.co.uk/news/uk/politics/home-secretary-rules-out-inquiry-into-1984-battle-of-orgreave-between-miners-and-police-a7389151.html. Accessed 6 June 2023.
The Guardian. 2019. Stop Criminalising Our Musicians. *The Guardian. Letters*, February 3. https://www.theguardian.com/law/2019/feb/03/stop-criminalising-our-musicians. Accessed 6 July 2023.
United Nations. 2023. *A Working Group of Experts of People from African Decent*. New York: United Nations [see contribution by Felicity Gerry KC and JENGbA].
Woffinden, B. 2010. Guilty by Association. In *Inside Time,* May 2010. https://insidetime.org/guilty-by-association/. Accessed 6 July 2023.

Legal Cases Cited

R v Jogee [2016] UKSC.
R v Johnson [2016] EWCA Crim 1613.
R v Crilly 2018] EWCA Crim 168.
R v Sonsongo [2021] EWCA Crim.

20

Punishment in 'This Hard Land': Conceptualising the Prison in Power, Crime and Mystification

Joe Sim

Introduction

Although Steven Box did not devote a specific chapter to prisons in *Power, Crime and Mystification (PCM)*, nonetheless, the institution's brooding, malevolent presence looms large in the book (Box 1983). This chapter explores three issues arising from his analysis. First, it focusses on his conceptualisation of the political economy of the prison operating as a *capitalist, state* institution in legitimating, defending and reproducing a decaying, corrosively unequal and violent, neoliberal, social order. Forty years later, this analysis retains its analytical potency in illustrating the institution's pivotal role, despite the endless prison crises generated by contingencies, contradictions and points of contestation, in maintaining this order.

This is taken from Bruce Springsteen's song of the same name.

J. Sim (✉)
School of Justice Studies, Liverpool John Moores University, Liverpool, UK
e-mail: J.Sim@ljmu.ac.uk

Second, the chapter critically analyses the cynical process of distortion and denial mobilised by the state to mystify the nature and extent of avoidable deaths in prison. From the perspective of prisoners, prison regimes eviscerate human beings, mortifying them and reducing them to cusps of their full humanity. It is this coercive and degrading environment, which provides the psychologically withering context for prison deaths, especially self-inflicted deaths. Following Box, the key question is not *how* but *why* these deaths occurred then and still occur now. This context is mystified and hidden behind a positivist discourse of individual abnormality and bureaucratic inefficiency.

Finally, it considers Box's demand for state institutions to be made democratically accountable within a broader theoretical and political framework of 'justice for all' (Box 1983: 219). Democratic accountability underpins contemporary struggles to replace the insidious culture of immunity and impunity, which shields and protects staff *at all levels* of the prison system from being held accountable for their actions, *and* their non-actions which have had, and continue to have, a devastating impact on prisoners and their families.

Box and the Prison: The Radical Context

Box's analysis of the prison was built on the work of critical criminologists, which had developed in the 1970s (Mathiesen 1974; Fitzgerald 1977; Fitzgerald and Sim 1979). Taking an abolitionist position, these, and other writers, challenged the supplicant relationship between liberal academics, traditional reform groups and the state. Together, this penal lobby had become 'acceptable' to the state and had been incorporated by it (Ryan 1978; Mathiesen 1980). The lobby had a misguided, indeed delusional, hope that more prisons, and the policy 'strategy' of crisis/reform/crisis/reform, which had failed so miserably over two centuries, would suddenly and magically bring stability and make them work 'better' in controlling and punishing the poor, powerless, destitute and vulnerable (Foucault 1979).

The praxis of liberal reformers was constructed around a reductive theoretical, political, research and policy discourse which reinforced the 'stultifying idea that nothing lies beyond the prison' (Davis, cited in Ryan and Sim 2016: 716) as a response to those few lawbreakers who were caught and processed through the system. In short, the very existence of the institution was never challenged. At the same time, liberals ignored the deeply embedded social divisions around social class, gender, 'race', sexuality, ability/disability and age, which, not only devastated psyches and decimated lives, but which were also central to the operationalisation of criminal justice power, particularly in terms of the state's laser focus downwards on the morals and behaviour of the powerless while leaving the callous amorality and systemic criminality of the powerful, and their acolytes, free from policing, regulation and control. This systemic process of non-intervention provided clear evidence (if any was needed) of:

> ....the unadulterated hypocrisy of the powerful and their remorseless focus on crimes committed by the powerless and the dispossessed while their corrosive crimes and misdemeanors, often euphemistically labeled as honest mistakes, [were] effectively ignored. (Sim 2020a: 21)

The critical academic work Box identified challenged the cosy and cloying relationship between liberal academics and the state. It rejected the theoretical and methodological naiveté of conventional criminology and its political supplication—aided by the promise of grant-funded research—at the altar of state power. Additionally, this work both supported, and was supported by, a number of radical, grassroots, activist organisations, which had emerged at the same time—the *National Prisoners Movement (PROP)* and *Radical Alternatives to Prison (RAP)*. These organisations unapologetically placed prisoners' voices and experiences at the heart of their campaigning while fiercely rejecting the idea that the crisis-ridden system could ever be reformed. Rather, it needed to be radically transformed and ultimately abolished.

It is in this context that Box made a number of critical observations about the coercive, dehumanising role of the prison, which transcended the liberal pieties that had come to pass as the 'truth' about the institution. The chapter now turns to five dimensions in his analysis which feed into the continuities in punishment forty years on.

Prisons and the Continuities in Punishment

First, Box contrasted the punishment of 'people too poor to pay fines' with those engaged in corporate criminality, a concept which was, and is, almost entirely absent in the uncritical, atheoretical, ahistorical, empiricist work of liberal academics and the compromised interventions of reform organisations. As he noted, '[i]f there is no way of implementing justice for the largest and worst offending corporations then it is surely unjust to pursue with such *ruthless and cruel tenacity* the majority of those eventually condemned to prison' (Box 1983: 78–79, emphasis added). This socially unjust process has intensified since the early 1980s (Sim 2009). The vast majority of human beings mortifyingly and often violently 'churned' through the blistering regimes in prisons, and other sites of state confinement, are destitute, dispossessed and vulnerable (Sawyer and Wagner 2020). Therefore:

> ……..contrary to the state's "truth", prisons are not teeming with stereotypically, dangerous people. Rather, they are decaying dustbins filled with those pejoratively labelled as social trash scraping out an often-desperate existence on the margins of a grossly unequal and unjust society: the unemployed and never employed; the sexually abused; the psychologically traumatised; the homeless; those with drug, alcohol and mental health issues; pupils disproportionately excluded from school; and those with physically traumatic brain injuries. They also contain a disproportionate number of people who have tried to kill themselves; who have been through the social care system; or who have observed domestic violence. Women prisoners are overrepresented in the majority of these categories……. (Sim 2023: 885)

In contrast, as in Box's time, the rampant criminality of the powerful, remains unpoliced, unregulated and unpunished. For them, for the last four decades, it has been 'business as usual' (Tombs 2016: 51).

Second, he pointed to the racialisation of the prison population, particularly in institutions for younger people such as Borstals and Detention Centres. It was, he wrote, 'no mere coincidence' that prisoners were 'getting younger…and blacker' (Box 1983: 218) given that the rate of unemployment among this group was increasing. It was 'on the unemployed and unemployable that the long arm of the law falls like a dead weight' (ibid.: 219). By 2022, 27% of the prison population came from a Black, Asian or minority ethnic group:

> If our prison population reflected the ethnic make-up of England and Wales, we would have over 9,000 fewer people in prison—the equivalent of 12 average-sized prisons......There is a clear direct association between ethnic minority group and the odds of receiving a custodial sentence. (Prison Reform Trust 2022: 30).[1]

Third, building on Stephen Spitzer's brilliant analysis of the pejorative categorisation and searing social control of those groups labelled as 'social dynamite' and the systemic neglect of those labelled as 'social junk' (Spitzer 1975), Box argued that for the 'social dynamite' such as the unemployed and under-employed, prisons were integral to their control and to the ferocious law and order policies pursued by the government of the sanctified (at least in the eyes of a besotted minority of the population) Margaret Thatcher. Their role was not about controlling serious crime. Instead, they were designed:

> .....to instil discipline, directly and indirectly on those people no longer controlled by the soft-discipline-machine of work and who might become growingly resentful that they are being made to pay the price for economic recession. Whilst the powerful are getting away with crimes whose enormity appears to sanctify them, the powerless are getting prison. (Box 1983: 219)

Forty years on, both nationally and internationally, the repressive, pain-inducing role of the prison continues. The process of punishing those seeking to eke out their existence in the wastelands of a compassionless, brutal social order, if anything, has intensified since the early 1980s. The expansion, refashioning and rebranding of the state to target,

---

[1] For children, the percentage was even higher. In January 2022, while '[b]lack children account[ed] for 4% of the 10-17 year old population', they accounted for '18% of stop and searches (where ethnicity was known); 15% of arrests; 12% of children cautioned or sentenced; 34% of children in custody on remand; 29% of the youth custody population (increased from 18% ten years ago)' (Fraser 2022).

regulate and punish the surplus detritus generated by the brutality of neoliberalism's political economy has seen:

> ....policing, punitive, military and security apparatuses, mobilized to monitor, discipline and punish those troublesome populations at risk of turning into Hegel's "rabble"...States are increasingly called on to *select, eject and immobilize*. (Shammas 2018: 415, original emphasis)

According to Valeria Vegh Weis, a longer historical perspective is needed which recognises that crime control has changed little since the fifteenth century. There has been a '....continuity in the functioning and features in this control' (Vegh Weis 2017: 289). She has developed Spitzer's initial thesis, which, as noted above, Box utilised to analyse the mechanisms through which the state controlled the 'social dynamite' and 'social junk', the 'wasted lives' thrown up by contemporary capitalism (Bauman 2007). For Vegh Weis, the category of 'social junk' needed to be expanded to acknowledge the systematic over-criminalisation of contemporary paupers living destitute and insecure lives in the ruthless shadows of neoliberalism. This expansion would include those who:

> ....facing a highly competitive labour market.... can only survive on charity, the scarce remnants of social assistance, sporadic jobs and subsistence self-employment.....social junk has been the target of bulimic over-criminalisation as a result of the perpetration of minimum-harmful behaviours: mostly, criminalized survival strategies and the absorption of social assistance into a criminal logic that turns it into what may be called *punitive welfare*. (Vegh Weis 2017: 226, original emphasis)

For the poor and destitute, the pain-inducing implications are profound:

> Crime control has expanded until swallowing social assistance itself (which can be called *punitive welfare*), leading the assisted into the criminal orbit if they fail to accomplish administrative requirements. Also those behaviours that during the disciplining social order were approached through social administration or therapeutic agencies become absorbed by crime control. (ibid.: 281, original emphasis)

The state's brutal interventions into the lives of contemporary paupers has been reinforced by expanding the complex network of public *and* private agencies involved in the technological surveillance of them, their families and their communities and the punishment, which follows if they deviate from established, 'respectable' norms and values (Wacquant 2009). In an age of 'surveillance capitalism' (Zuboff 2019) a 'surveillance continuum' (Coleman and Sim 2005: 637) from CCTV to the creation of mass databases, often based on racist profiling, (Williams and Clarke 2016) has underpinned the growth of a 'biometric state'[2] (Statewatch 2022: front cover). It is worth repeating that the brutal focus of these anti-democratic developments is relentlessly downwards, there is little or no upward gaze from the state towards the powerful and their criminality. For the state, forgiveness cuts one way. Like Box's materialist analysis from the early 1980s, understanding these links forty years on:

> ….helps preserve a materialist reading of the structural origins of these sectors [modern paupers] under the capitalist production system, enabling a more enlightening reading of the systematic over-criminalisation mechanisms deployed against paupers throughout capitalist history. (Vegh Weis 2017: 256)

Fourth, in the context of the catastrophic, economic crisis that gripped the UK in the late 1970s and early 1980s, at least for the poor, and the devastating rise in unemployment that followed, Box pointed to the intensification in the state's authoritarianism and the judiciary's role in this repressive process. Judges and magistrates were 'sending more and more people to prison' (Box 1983: 206). And contrary to the liberal discourse that the judiciary, as a body, was value free and apolitical, in

---

[2] This is the use of 'biometric identification systems' by states such as fingerprints and facial images at border crossings, and elsewhere to combat, among other things, '"illegal" immigration'. For Statewatch, '[i]n a context of systemic racism and discrimination and a continued drive by both national governments and EU institutions to identify increasing numbers of foreign nationals in order to deport and/or exclude them from their territory, the attempt to extend and entrench the deployment and use of biometric technologies must be interrogated and challenged, as part of the broader fight against state racism and ethnic profiling, and for racial equality and social justice' (Statewatch 2022: 3).

practice, judges and magistrates were central to the coercive response to the crisis:

> ....during times of economic crisis, state coercion increases in response to the perceived threat, real or imagined, of public disorder including crime waves. The judiciary, being an integral part of the state control apparatus, makes its contribution to this increased level of coercion by imprisoning more, particularly those typifying the actual, or potentially, disruptive problem populations. (ibid.: 217)

Finally, in highlighting the increasingly authoritarian exercise of state power for the powerless, while ignoring the crimes of the powerful from violent men to corporate criminality within the political economy and hyper-masculinity of Thatcherite neoliberalism, Box added another dimension to the critical analysis of 'the great moving right show', which formed the beating heart of Thatcherism (Hall 1988). And while the state institutions which nurtured and succoured, legitimated and defended this authoritarian drive were themselves contradictory, contingent and contested by those at the sharp end of their everyday coercive and violent practices, nonetheless, throughout the 1980s and beyond, these institutions, including prisons, uninhibitedly 'work[ed] for the clampdown', that was unfolding (Sim 1987: 190).

Building more prisons was one coercive strand in the 'state's strengthened armoury' (Box 1983: 205). This was more than ironic. As the Introduction to this volume indicates, in October 1983, the month before the publication of *PCM*, Leon Brittan, Margaret Thatcher's new, hard-line Home Secretary announced the biggest prison-building programme of the twentieth century, as well as increasing the sentencing powers of the courts (Ryan and Sim 1984). These regressive policies were reflected in the changes to the wider criminal justice system directed at the usual suspects: the destitute, dispossessed and socially vulnerable. This repressive, authoritarian, 'statist' strategy was dialectically linked to an 'anti-statist' strategy as the state withdrew from policing and regulating other key areas of social life, including the policing of the powerful (Hall, cited in Sim 2009: 27).

PCM captured this repressive conjunctural moment articulated through the consolidation of the Thatcher government's corrosive grip on power after the Conservative Party's General Election victory in June 1983. The book's prescience lay in dissecting a prison machine being built to control, desecrate and punish the powerless, a regressive development, which continued over the following decades under successive Labour, Coalition and Conservative governments (Sim 2000; Ryan and Sim 2016). The further tightening of the authoritarian screw by a sybaritic Boris Johnson, and his government of 'chums' (Kuper 2022) that occurred following the Conservative's election victory in 2019, can be traced back to their Thatcher-inspired time at Oxford in the 1980s: '[p]olitically [he] shared with most Oxford Tories of his generation a generalised faith in Thatcherism…She stood for unabashed material advancement for the winners, and a world in which Britain could still make the rules through willpower alone' (ibid.: 70). The Eton-educated, Oxford generation of the 1980s, also perfectly crystallised Box's point about the non-criminalisation of the powerful. The all-male Bullingdon Club, which included Johnson and David Cameron, embodied a sense of entitlement, underpinned, as ever, by a culture of immunity and impunity. Its members:

> …went around in a pack sacking restaurants or the rooms of new members, smashing bottles on the street, humiliating hired sex workers and "debagging" (removing the trousers of) lower-caste outsiders. They would then add insult to injury by compensating "pleb" victims with money. The message: *The rules don't apply to our class.* (ibid.: 52, original emphasis)

Four decades on, the ruthless drive to enforce law and impose order has followed the same, grim trajectory (See Scott and Sim, this volume). The further intensification in the coercive capabilities of the state's power has been underpinned by yet another prison-building programme, which would add to the 120 prisons already operating. In August 2019, the government indicated that:

………..it would spend up to £2.5 billion to create 10,000 prison places in addition to the approximately 3,500 places already under way. In the 2020 Spending Review, the Government stated it would spend more than £4 billion towards delivering 18,000 prison places across England and Wales by the mid-2020s. The 18,000 places would include the 10,000 places at four new prisons (announced in August 2019), the expansion of a further four prisons, the refurbishment of the existing prison estate and the completion of ongoing prison builds…… The 2021 Spending Review said the Government would spend £3.8 million to provide 20,000 prison places. (Beard 2023: 6)

It was 'the biggest prison building programme in a generation' (Hansard, 27 October 2021: column 277). By March 2027, the prison population was expected to be in the range of 93,100 to 106,300 (Beard 2023).

This expansion points to a key issue concerning the nature and direction of the state's law and order spending. Between 2015/2016 and 2019/2020, over £18 billion was spent on prisons while nearly £122 billion was spent on Public Order and Safety (HM Treasury 2021: Tables 10.1 and 10.5). Such a regressive pattern of expenditure was moving in one authoritarian direction. This point is graphically illustrated by the state's abject response to domestic violence. Between 2010 and 2019, funding for services was cut by 25%, despite the fact that in 2018 domestic homicides, with their overwhelmingly female victims, had reached 3 a week and had climbed to a five-year high (Sisters Uncut 2019).

In a Boxian sense, this process has not only been mystified through being 'sold' as a signal that the government was prepared to provide huge sums to maintain law and order, despite the clear failure of this policy in the past which is never discussed, but also it raises a broader question about whose order is being maintained and whose safety is being protected.

Demystifying Deaths in Prison

Contentious deaths in state custody became increasingly visible in the late 1970s and early 1980s. One reason for this increasing visibility was due to the emergence of a number of radical grassroots organisations such as *INQUEST* founded in 1981 and *Women in Prison*, founded in 1983. These organisations, built on the shared membership, interventions and political campaigning of the earlier radical groups discussed above—*Radical Alternatives to Prison (RAP)* and the *National Prisoners Movement (PROP)*—while carving out their own, radical spaces to campaign around the neglected issues of women in prison and preventable deaths in custody. *INQUEST* campaigned around the slogan 'truth, justice and accountability' for those who were either dying violently at the heads, hands and feet of state agents or who took their own lives as a result of the systemic indifference, and contempt, displayed towards them by prison staff who at least in theory, owed a duty of care to them (Ryan 1996).

Box discussed a number of notorious deaths in state custody during this period pointing out that:

> In each of these "sudden" deaths in police (and prison) custody, a number of people have suspected murder or at least manslaughter – suspicions which have not diminished....official passivity is even more surprising considering that in many instances coroner's courts returned verdicts of "misadventure", "accidental death", "suicide", or "unlawful killing". (Box 1983: 82–3)

Barry Prosser, whose violent death in August 1980 in Birmingham prison provoked outrage, was one such case identified in *PCM*. Barry was on remand for causing *criminal damage to a door handle*. Giving evidence at his inquest, a doctor noted that he had 'died of Shock (sic), due to rupture of the stomach and oesophagus caused by a crushing injury' (Coroner's Court, Birmingham, cited in Sim 2009: 31). He described how Barry's body was covered in bruises 'from head to toe'. This included injuries to his feet, anus and private parts:

> I think the probability is that the injuries to the private parts and the anus came before the [fatal] blow. It is not impossible to visualise the situation where he got a kick or a stamp in the groin and in the back passage after having received his severe injury to the abdomen. That would have been a perfectly ghastly and wholly unnecessary thing to have done. It would have been a sadistic act……. During my examination, I found no injuries that could be described as defensive injuries. That indicates to me that as well as his feet being stamped on, that it raises the possibility that others were holding him. If one is retaliating, one is not necessarily going to show signs of retaliation with one[']s fists…….There were two bursts one to the gullett (sic) or the oesophagus and one to the stomach. These two ruptures are very close to each other and in my view there were two ruptures of the stomach and the oesophagus as well as ruptures to the back of the lungs and they were all caused by one and the same blow. (ibid.)[3]

In the year *PCM* was published, there were 64 deaths in prison, 37 were classified as 'natural' and 27 as self-inflicted. Between 1980 and 1990, there were 770 deaths including 10 homicides, 380 'natural' deaths, 362 self-inflicted deaths and 18, which were attributed to other causes (Ministry of Justice n.d.). Altogether, between 1978 and early March 2022, 6891 prisoners died, 2785 or (40.4%) of these deaths were self-inflicted (INQUEST and Ministry of Justice, cited in Sim 2023: 898).

As noted above, INQUEST was formed in 1981, two years before the publication of *PCM*. From the beginning, the charity was concerned with deconstructing and demystifying the state's 'truth' around deaths in prison, and in other sites of state detention. Like Box, it developed a critical analysis of prison deaths and the state's neutralising strategies, which individualised the issue and distracted attention away from the debasing toxicity of prison regimes which underpinned these deaths. Their casework highlighted a number of issues.

---

[3] The inquest jury returned a verdict of 'unlawful killing'. In March, 1982, three prison officers were subsequently tried for Barry's murder. They were found not guilty. In the same month, the Home Office announced that they would not face disciplinary action because there were 'no grounds to justify the officers' dismissal or proceedings under the code of discipline for prison officers'. (*The Times*, 25 March 1982, cited in Sim 2009: 34).

First, INQUEST critiqued the state's discourse around 'natural' deaths inside. This discourse medicalised and normalised these deaths thereby mystifying their premature nature, the searing context in which they occurred and distracted attention from the fact that they could have been avoided and prevented. On the contrary, 'INQUEST ['s] casework and monitoring shows many of these deaths are premature and far from "natural"' (INQUEST 2022).

Second, in terms of self-inflicted deaths, the state's 'truth' mystified the systemic culture of indifference which underpinned, and gave meaning to, *why* individuals decided to kill themselves in prison. State agents, and the few media commentators who were interested in these deaths, focussed on the pathological abnormality of the individual prisoner's psychology and character. They voyeuristically fixated 'on the deficiencies of the deceased' (Sim 2020b: 238) and applied 'negative reputations' to the dead. This strategy operated 'to protect the operational policies and practices which obtain in custodial situations' resulting in 'the authorities effectively marginalis[ing] those people who self-mutilate, attempt suicide, or die though suicide, neglect or acts of brutality' (Scraton and Chadwick, cited in ibid.: 238).

Being 'abnormal' also worked with respect to those few state servants linked to specific deaths. They were characterised as deviating from a benevolent occupational norm making them different:

> from the vast majority of their peers who, it is argued, benevolently apply the prison rules without prejudice. The corrosive, authoritarian culture of prison officers, based on institutionalised retaliation towards prisoners who complain.....is thereby transformed within this discourse into a problem with the personality, behaviour, attitude and training of individual staff, or their inability to cope with stressful situations causing them to inexplicably and uncharacteristically "snap". (ibid.)

Finally, there was the discourse of 'bureaucratic mismanagement' (ibid.). This discourse was built around failing to: identify vulnerable prisoners; share information between staff; carry out in-depth risk assessments; learn lessons from previous deaths; and implement recommendations from the Prison Inspectorate and from coroners' inquests concerning prisoner safety. In the latter case, as INQUEST noted, 'the current system for learning lessons and implementing changes is not fit for purpose' (INQUEST 2020: 7). These failures meant that, even on its own terms, the state was failing to fulfil its duty of care to prisoners while ignoring the brittle structures erected to, theoretically, instil a modicum of democratic accountability into a system pitifully devoid of it.

The language underpinning these failures was also problematic. In practice, the searing nature of prison regimes made *all* prisoners vulnerable to self-harm and self-inflicted death, not just the vulnerable few. The alleged 'science' behind risk assessment was, in practice, an exercise in classificatory power. For Kate Brown:

> ….notions of vulnerability sometimes operate to strip power away from populations that are already marginalised….Although they help some individuals to avoid blame for their difficulties, vulnerability discourses emphasise personal reasons for difficulties experienced by individuals, diverting attention from structural issues. (Brown 2016: 45 and 51, emphasis added)

The risk to prisoners from a harm-inducing environment was, therefore, mystified and hidden behind the individualised discourse of the prisoner at risk caused by bureaucratic mismanagement and inefficiency. In short, the process of mystification ensured that the vulnerable prisoner became the issue *not* the pathologically dangerous prison.

Since the publication of *PCM* in the early 1980s, deaths in prison, and other sites of state punishment, have remained highly contentious. This is not surprising given that prison regimes remain 'bleak, retributive [and] unforgiving'. They are 'built on systemic indifference' and imposing 'pain and punishment' into lives, which are already fractured (Sim 2023: 889). In Box's time they were, and forty years on continue to be, 'debasing places of terror and trauma, degradation and humiliation, dread and foreboding' which differentially impact on: women and girls, Black, Asian and minority ethnic prisoners, as well as younger, older and LGBTQ+ prisoners (ibid.).

Additionally, the state's 'punitive obsession' (Playfair 1971) has spilled over into other social arenas. The penal and welfare systems have become increasingly calibrated, to 'form a single organisational mesh flung at the same clientele mired in the fissures and ditches of the dualizing metropolis' (Wacquant, cited in Ryan and Sim 2016: 724)

The impact of this punitive mentality has been devastating. A 59-year-old diabetic was sanctioned for missing two appointments, despite carrying out two periods of unpaid work. While caring for his mother who had dementia, he had applied for a job. However, he was:

> …..later found dead at home. He had £3.44 in his bank account, and with his electricity cut off, the fridge where he kept his insulin was no longer working. He died from diabetic ketoacidosis, caused by a lack of insulin. (Lansley 2022: 219)

Between December 2011 and April 2018, over 34,000 people, many of whom were disabled, died under the Department of Work and Pension's (DWP) watch:

> They died either waiting for the DWP to sort their claims or after it said they were well enough to work or start moving towards work. Moreover, in 2018 alone there could have been 750 (if not more) people who took their own lives while claiming from the DWP. But across five years, the department only reviewed 69 cases of people taking their own lives. (Topple 2021)

Finally, the punitive, welfare discourse had also led to 'social murder by destitution'. In other words, as with deaths in custody, these deaths were preventable. They included: homeless people dying on the streets and in temporary accommodation; deaths from malnutrition; and deaths generated because the poor were unable to heat their homes due to benefit cuts. The state's callousness and lack of compassion brutally illustrated 'the long-standing association between poor material conditions and social murder' (Grover 2019: 347).

What is to be done? Box pointed to a number of strategies designed to contest and contain the untrammeled power of the state which remain directly relevant to contemporary struggles around its institutions and its agents. It is to a consideration of these strategies to which the chapter now turns.

Box, Democratic Accountability and Utopian Thinking

PCM was unusual in that unlike the majority of criminology texts at the time, critical or otherwise, Box raised the issue of democratic accountability, transparency and responsibility in relation to the criminal justice system. This issue was also beginning to materialise in other arenas. The Greater London Council's Police Committee Support Unit, and the local monitoring groups the Council funded, demanded police accountability in London, particularly regarding the Met's racist use of stop and search powers. The research and activism of feminist academics, and grassroots organisations, regarding violence towards women and girls also raised significant issues about the responsibility of men for this violence and the criminal justice system's systemic failure to respond to this violence (Greater London Council Police Committee 1982; Hall 1985).

Box was one of the first critical criminologists to make the link between prisons and the need to make those who worked in them, and in the criminal justice system more generally, democratically accountable for their actions *and* inactions. He pointed out that prisons operated 'behind a shield of undemocratic secrecy' (Box 1983: 203). Furthermore, 'successive Home Secretaries have used the lack of public knowledge and scrutiny of prisons to support their particular needs' (Fitzgerald and Sim, cited in ibid.: 203). In a prescient passage, he noted that:

> The governing political party seems increasingly unable to check the cabinet. The cabinet no longer seems to have control over the prime minister, a position that has moved from being "first amongst equals" to simply being "first" full stop. The executive has lost its grip over its social control agencies such as the prison service which appears increasingly to be run by the Prison Officers Association, and the police, which seems to be driven mainly by the Chief Police Officers Association and the Police Federation. (ibid.: 203)

The question of holding to account those who exercise penal power—from state agents on the landings through to those who run and manage prisons at the highest levels of the state—remains central to the work of grassroots, prisoners' rights organisations four decades on.

Once again, the work of INQUEST is relevant here. The charity's praxis regarding democratic accountability chimes with Box's concerns. From its inception in 1981, the charity raised a series of questions around self-inflicted deaths in custody, in particular. First, it challenged the language the state used to describe deaths in custody; INQUEST popularised the term self-inflicted death as opposed to suicide. Second, it focussed on the structures of democratic accountability which were theoretically supposed to govern the work of prison staff and hold them accountable but which, in practice were failing miserably to protect prisoners and guarantee their safety. As an example in Liverpool prison, the complaints system was completely failing prisoners: 'only 20% of prisoners feeling that their complaints were dealt with seriously' (HM Chief Inspector of Prisons cited in Sim 2019: 45). Additionally, there was 'no legal advice service…no "access to justice" laptops were available…Information about the Section 2, Respect 32 HMP Liverpool Criminal Casework Review Commission and the Legal Ombudsman was not displayed. Legal visits continued to start late' (HM Chief Inspector of Prisons 2018: 31–2).

Furthermore, the prison effectively ignored the recommendations made in previous inspections, which were supposed to improve the regime. In 2015, 89 recommendations had been made, '…..only 23 had been achieved, 14 had been partially achieved and 53 had not been achieved' while in the area of safety, a key area of concern according to the state 'only three out of 15 recommendations had been achieved, two had been partially achieved and 10 had not been achieved' (ibid.).

The state's failure to ensure that its agents, *at whatever level of the state*, were democratically accountable generated further questions:

> ………where does responsibility lie when the state fails in its duty of care? What if state servants willfully ignore official recommendations about learning lessons and preventing future deaths?.....[W]hat should be done about prison staff if their actions are directly linked to self-inflicted deaths through systemic indifference towards prisoners? In short, what does justice and accountability look like…..? (Sim 2020b: 241)

Third, INQUEST argued that a 'crucial part' of its work was 'to bring about accountability, both as an absolute requirement for bereaved families seeking answers about how their relative died and to prevent another death from happening' (INQUEST, cited in ibid.: 245). The charity identified:

> ....the abject failure of the state to live up to its own rhetoric in terms of protecting prisoners and ensuring their safety. The state's duty of care towards them is fractured and broken. This lack of care is not accidental, but arises from values, attitudes and cynical negativity deeply embedded in the occupational culture of prison staff on the ground and the incompetence, inefficiency and mismanagement of those above them. (ibid.)

Crucially, grappling with the issue of democratic accountability is *not* a deviation into a liberal theoretical and political position as some on the left would argue. Marx, himself, had recognised that the 'democratization of society' was based on 'democratization in the state' (Draper, cited in Panitch and Albo 2017, cited in Sim 2020b: 246). Therefore:

> .....linking the often-brutal, discretionary exercise of penal power to structures of democratic accountability, designed to control state agents, would be a significant step in removing the nefarious culture of impunity and immunity institutionalised across all levels of the prison system. (ibid.: 246–7)

For Paul Raekstad: 'we need a definition of democracy that makes determinate demands on institutions; that we can use to criticise institutions like capitalism and the state and use to guide their process of replacement' (cited in ibid.: 247).

The last page of *PCM* returned to the issue of democratic accountability. For Box: 'criminal justice personnel should be accountable not only for *who* they criminalise, but *why*, and in *whose* interests' (Box 1983: 223, original emphasis). Such demands were:

> Not utopian.....Rather they reside essentially within the democratic ideal. They are, therefore, only demands that principles espoused in public

by our political leaders are translated into practice. We have for too long ignored crimes of the powerful, allowed the poor to be imprisoned scapegoats, and encouraged criminal justice personnel to act subversively. Justice has suffered, and so have well all. (ibid.)

In defending utopianism, demanding radical policy changes and linking them to democratic accountability, Box was making a crucial point, namely that utopianism and democracy were not mutually exclusive terms representing a binary divide, which was unbridgeable. In fact, it was the reverse, a point captured by Russell Jacoby two decades later. For him, dichotomising the discourse of reform and the discourse of utopianism missed a fundamental point:

> The choice we have is not between reasonable proposals and an unreasonable utopianism. Utopian thinking does not undermine or discount real reforms. Indeed, it is almost the opposite; practical reforms depend on utopian dreaming - or at least utopian thinking drives incremental improvements. (Jacoby 2005: 1)

The 'anti utopian age' (ibid: ix) of the last 40 years has reduced democratic politics to puerile, infantile political maneuvering and focus group populism. Demands for the fundamental transformation of the criminal justice system *and* broader changes in the structures of power and powerlessness which are wrecking the bodies and minds of the majority of the population nationally and internationally but which stray beyond this narrow political and populist terrain, leave their protagonists open to the charge of being motivated by starry-eyed utopianism. For Jacoby, the problem lies *not* with utopianism but the fixation on the present: 'in an age of permanent emergencies, more than ever we have become narrow utilitarians dedicated to fixing, not reinventing the here and now' (ibid.: ix).

Conclusion

PCM brilliantly exposed the link between the political economy of punishment and the prison's parasitic role in facilitating the humiliation and punishment of the powerless while the rich and powerful, with the odd exception, could continue to operate within a culture of immunity and impunity which ignored and condoned their rampant criminality. Box highlighted the hypocrisy of a prison system whose claims about rehabilitation, care and compassion mystified the grim imposition of pain and punishment onto a scapegoated minority while leaving the vast majority of lawbreakers, including corporate, white collar and state criminals, free to pursue their socially harmful, destructive behaviour with little or no reprisals, or fear of reprisals. For him, '….prisons function not only to demoralise and fracture potential resistance to domination, but they also supply ideological fodder by way of providing a massive legitimation to the portrait of crime and criminals so artfully and cynically constructed by legislators and those who influence them' (Box 1983: 222). Forty years on from the Thatcher governments of the 1980s, this point is still as profound, political and poignant as it was when it was written in 1983.

Box's analysis can be captured in two simple, inter-related questions which have profound moral and political implications. As noted above, by March 2027, the prison population is expected to be in the range of 93,100 to 106,300 (Beard 2023).[4] What will be the demographics of this group? And who will be targeted and criminalised by the wider criminal justice system between now and then? Given the punitive history of the last two centuries, then the answers are indisputable. Both the prison population, and those being ignominiously and often violently processed through the wider system, will not be drawn from the self-entitled, hypocritical, criminogenic ranks of the rich and powerful but from the economic and political descendants of those for whom the

---

[4] In June 2023, the Prison Governors' Association warned that prisons would be full by July and threated to take legal action if the Government tried to 'squeeze any more prisoners in'. (Inside Time 2023). Thanks to David Scott for pointing out this reference to me.

prison was designed to inflict pain and punishment two hundred years ago. The direction of the punitive wind is entirely predictable.

Those involved in disciplines like Criminology, Psychology and Policing 'Studies' might also ask themselves these same questions and consider the answers. Such self-reflection would allow them to move from consciously and unconsciously legitimating the amoral criminal injustice system, which currently prevails, and the deeply unequal social order it supports, and shift their thinking towards a system based on social justice, democratic accountability and, ultimately, the removal of the excoriating social divisions which scar and decimate lives, as Box demanded. They might also decide to remove themselves from the research grant gold rush, *whatever the source*, which, while pouring funds into the coffers of the corporate university system, has, with a few honourable exceptions, done little, if anything, to deliver a fair, equitable and democratically accountable criminal justice system. Snake oil does not come close to describing much of what passes for research in these, and other disciplines, at this historical moment.

In an age of 'philistine barbarism' (Hall, cited in Sim and Tombs 2019), radical transformation through an insurgent praxis is desperately needed. Confronting and replacing the pistons of retribution and revenge which are driving the machinery of contemporary state punishment for the powerless while leaving the powerful as free as ever to engage in their illegalities and perpetuate their catastrophic social harms is a moral as well as a political question. Box recognised this forty years ago. Forty years later, his theoretical insights and policy prescriptions remain as relevant and urgent as ever if a fundamental change to the criminal injustice system, and to the wider society, is to happen.

Acknowledgements Thanks to David Scott for his comments on an earlier draft of this chapter.

References

Bauman, Z. 2007. *Wasted Lives: Modernity and Its Outcasts*. Cambridge: Polity.

Beard, J. 2023. *The Prison Estate in England and Wales*. London: House of Commons Library.

Box, S. 1983. *Power, Crime and Mystification*. London: Tavistock.

Brown, K. 2016. Beyond Protection: 'The Vulnerable' in the Age of Austerity. In *Social Policies and Social Control: New Perspectives on the 'Not-So-Big Society,'* ed. M. Harrison and T. Sanders, 39–52. Bristol: Policy Press.

Coleman, R., and J. Sim. 2005. Contemporary Statecraft and the 'Punitive Obsession': A Critique of the New Penology thesis. In *The New Punitiveness: Current Trends, Theories, Perspectives*, ed. J. Pratt, D. Brown, M. Brown, S. Hallsworth, and W. Morrison, 101–118. Cullompton: Willan.

Fitzgerald, M. 1977. *Prisoners in Revolt*. Harmondsworth: Penguin.

Fitzgerald, M., and J. Sim. 1979. *British Prisons*, 1st ed. Oxford: Basil Blackwell.

Foucault, M. 1979. *Discipline and Punish: The Birth of the Prison*. Harmondsworth: Peregrine.

Fraser, K. 2022. Annual Statistics: A Youth Justice System Failing Black Children. https://www.gov.uk/government/news/annual-statistics-a-system-failing-black-children. Accessed 29 Aug 2022.

Greater London Council Committee. 1982. *A New Police Authority for London: A Consultation Paper on Democratic Control of the Police in London*. London: Greater London Council.

Grover, C. 2019. Violent Proletarianisation: Social Murder, the Reserve Army of Labour and Social Security "Austerity" in Britain. *Critical Social Policy* 39 (3): 335–355.

Hall, R. 1985. *Ask Any Woman*. Bristol: Falling Wall Press.

Hall, S. 1988. *The Hard Road to Renewal*. London: Verso.

Hansard. 2021. *Ways and Means Financial Statement*, 27 October. London: House of Commons.

HM Chief Inspector of Prisons. 2018. *Report on an Unannounced Inspection of HMP Liverpool by HM Chief Inspector of Prisons 4–15 September 2017*. London: Her Majesty's Inspectorate of Prisons.

HM Treasury. 2021. *Public Expenditure Statistical Analyses 2021*. London: HMSO CP507

INQUEST. 2020. *INQUEST Submission to the Justice Select Inquiry into the Coroner Service*. London: INQUEST.

INQUEST. 2022. INQUEST Responds as new data shows 2021 had highest number of deaths in prison ever recorded. https://www.inquest.org.uk/moj-data-jan2022. Accessed 31 Jan 2022.

Inside Time. 2023. Prisons Will Be Full by July, Governors Warn. *Inside Time*, 5 June. https://insidetime.org/prisons-will-be-full-by-july-governors-warn/. Accessed 12 Jun 2023
Jacoby, R. 2005. *Past Imperfect*. New York: Columbia University Press.
Kuper, S. 2022. *Chums: How a Tiny Caste of Oxford Tories Took Over the UK*. London: Profile Books.
Lansley, S. 2022. *The Richer the Poorer: How Britain Enriched the Few and Failed the Poor, A 200-Year History*. Bristol: Policy Press.
Mathiesen, T. 1974. *The Politics of Abolition*. London: Martin Robertson.
Mathiesen, T. 1980. *Law, Society and Political Action*. London: Academic Press.
Ministry of Justice. n.d. *Deaths in Prison Custody 1978–2019*. London: Ministry of Justice deaths-prison-custody-1978–2020.ods (live.com). Accessed 21 Jul 2022.
Playfair, G. 1971. *The Punitive Obsession*. London: Gollancz.
Prison Reform Trust. 2022. *Bromley Briefings Prison Factfile. Winter 2022*. London: Prison Reform Trust.
Ryan, M. 1978. *The Acceptable Pressure Group*. Farnborough: Teakfield.
Ryan, M. 1996. *Lobbying from Below: INQUEST in Defence of Civil Liberties*. London: UCL Press.
Ryan, M., and J. Sim. 1984. Decoding Leon Brittan. *The Abolitionist* 16: 3–7.
Ryan, M., and J. Sim. 2016. Campaigning for and Campaigning Against Prisons: Excavating and Re-affirming the Case for Prison Abolition. In *Handbook on Prisons*. ed. Y. Jewkes, J. Bennett, and B. Crewe, 2nd ed. 712–733. London: Routledge.
Sawyer, W., and P. Wagner. 2020. *Mass Incarceration: The Whole Pie 2020*. www.prisonpolicy.org/reports/pie2020.htmlative. Accessed 17 Jul 2022.
Shammas, V. 2018. Superfluity and Insecurity: Disciplining Surplus Populations in the Global North. *Capital and Class* 42 (3): 411–418.
Sim, J. 1987. Working for the Clampdown: Prisons and Politics in England and Wales. In *Law, Order and the Authoritarian State*, ed. P. Scraton, 190–211. Stony Stratford: Open University Press.
Sim, J. 2000. One Thousand Days of Degradation": New Labour and Old Compromises at the Turn of the Century. *Social Justice* 27 (2): 168–192.
Sim, J. 2009. *Punishment and Prisons: Power and the Carceral State*. London: Sage.
Sim, J. 2019. Aching Desolation: Liverpool Prison and the Limits of Penal Reform in England and Wales. *Critical and Radical Social Work* 7 (1), March: 41–58.

Sim, J. 2020a. Foreword. In *For Abolition: Essays on Prisons and Socialist Ethics*, D. Scott, 21–24. Hook: Waterside Press.

Sim, J. 2020b. Challenging the Desecration of the Human Spirit: An Alternative Criminological Perspective on Safety and Self-Inflicted Deaths in Prison. In *Justice Alternatives*, ed. P. Carlen and L.A. Franca, 237–250. Oxon: Routledge.

Sim, J. 2023. Confronting State Power: Dissenting Voices and the Demand for Penal Abolition. In *The Oxford Handbook of Criminology*, ed. A. Liebling, S. Maruna, and L. McAra, 7th ed., 884–908. Oxford: Oxford University Press.

Sim, J., and S. Tombs. 2019. The Johnson Government: Working for the Brexit Clampdown. https://ccseljmu.wordpress.com/2019/08/19/the-johnson-government-working-for-the-brexit-clampdown/.

Sisters Uncut. 2019. A Decade of Austerity. https://www.sistersuncut.org/2019/12/02/a-decade-of-austerity/. Accessed 31 Jul 2023.

Spitzer, S. 1975. Toward a Marxian Theory of Deviance. *Social Problems* 22 (5): 638–651.

Statewatch. 2022. *Building the Biometric State: Police Powers and Discrimination*. London: Statewatch.

Tombs, S. 2016. *Social Protection After the Crisis: Regulation Without Enforcement*. Bristol: Policy Press.

Topple, S. 2021. 35,000 Deaths Later, the DWP Still Denies Its Problems Are "Systemic" *The Canary* 27 June. https://www.thecanary.co/uk/analysis/2021/06/27/35000-deaths-later-the-dwp-still-denies-its-problems-are-systemic/. Accessed 25 Mar 2022.

Vegh Weis, V. 2017. *Marxism and Criminology*. Chicago: Haymarket Books.

Wacquant, L. 2009. *Punishing the Poor: The Neoliberal Government of Social Insecurity*. Durham: Duke University Press.

Williams, P., and B. Clarke. 2016. *Dangerous Associations: Joint Enterprise, Gangs and Racism*. London: Centre for Crime and Justice Studies.

Zuboff, S. 2019. *The Age of Surveillance Capitalism*. London: Profile Books.

21

Demystifying Murder: Open University Pedagogy, Social Murder and the Legacy of Steven Box

Deborah H. Drake and David Gordon Scott

Introduction

Power, Crime and Mystification [PCM] considered the key question of why some harmful acts and behaviours are defined as illegal whilst others are not. In the 40 years since its publication, the themes, ideas, and concepts introduced in Box's book have provided invaluable insights for critical criminological praxis and critical pedagogy. The analysis Box provides sensitises our critical consciousness to the role of the powerful in generating serious and deadly harms and other forms of social suffering whilst at the same time designating such harmful behaviours, actions, and consequences as non-criminal. Crucially, Box reveals that many serious harms undertaken by powerful actors or institutions are 'mystified' or left unacknowledged as harm. Box's sophisticated attempts at demystification not only show how state power and its ideological apparatus can and does invisibilise certain social harms but also emphasises the role of state power in the definition and punitive response to criminalised harms. It is the furthering of this goal of demystifying serious and deadly harms and rethinking our collective responses to such harms that is our main focus here. This chapter is therefore concerned with critically exploring a less discussed aspect of Box's work, namely understanding *PCM* as a form of critical pedagogy.

Whilst no quantitative assessment (to our knowledge) has been undertaken on the legacy of *PCM* to the critical criminological curriculum in universities in the United Kingdom (UK), United States of America (USA) or elsewhere, in this chapter we provide an in-depth qualitative discussion of how this book inspired a 60-credit, level one Open University (UK) criminology module, *DD105: Introduction to Criminology*, one of the largest standalone criminology modules in Europe. Although our module is also informed by the ideas of C. Wright Mills and the application of the 'criminological imagination' (Barton et al. 2007; Drake and Scott 2019a), it consistently applies key insights from Box (1983) in its 32 weeks of study. Indeed, Mills (1959/2000) and Box (1983) are the two intellectual pillars upon which the module stands. Across the module's teaching materials, a number of case studies are informed by Box's arguments on the mystification of serious and deadly harms. The module covers such case study topics as: deaths in police custody (Drake and Scott 2019b); intentional state killings through war and the death penalty (Drake and Scott 2019c, d); unintentional state and corporate harms, injuries, and deaths (Drake and Scott 2019e; Drake et al. 2019a, b); and the potentially deadly harms of social and economic inequalities (Drake and Scott 2019f). Box's influence on our thinking and, as a result, on our curriculum and our students has been substantial. Since its launch in October 2019, *DD105: Introduction to Criminology* has been presenting ideas informed by Box (1983) to thousands of Open University (OU) students in the UK every year.[1]

In the first part of this chapter, we reflect on the rationale of the critical 'Open University pedagogy' that underscored our thinking as we wrote our module. In the second part, we move on to applying Box's ideas about the way different harms are constructed. Box (1983) points out that some criminalised harms—such as intentional homicide (i.e. murder)—are constructed in such a way that excludes other forms of avoidable death, notably those which are likely to be committed more often by those in power. In the words of Box (1983: 8–9):

> … in the criminal law, definitions of murder, rape, robbery, assault, theft, and other serious crimes are so constructed as to exclude many similar, and in important respects, identical acts, and these are just the acts likely to be committed more frequently by powerful individuals …

We extend this insight from Box by exploring the concept of 'social murder', an idea first introduced by the Chartists in England in the early 1840s to refer to the deadly harms of the 1834 *New Poor Law* and later formalised and popularised in the writings of Friedrich Engels (1845/2009), notably to illustrate the increase in child deaths following the introduction of industrialisation.[2] We describe how we reframe 'murder' to include other avoidable and premature deaths and, in so doing, shed light on the mystification of its legal definition and the power of the state to both generate and prevent such deaths. This goal of 'demystifying murder' was the main intention in the making of the OU film *Grenfell Tower and Social Murder* (OU 2019a), and we discuss this film in some detail in the chapter's third part. It is worth noting here that the commissioning of the film *Grenfell Tower and Social Murder* (and indeed the other films made for this module, which include ones focussed on

---

[1] For reasons of OU marketing confidentiality, we are not permitted to give full or recent numbers of student registrations on DD105, but as an illustration we can note that there were more than 4000 students registered on the module in 2019–2020.

[2] It should be noted that the book was first written by Engels in German between 1842 and 1844 but that the English translation was not published until 1887.

'brandalism', 'subvertising',[3] anti-fracking activism in West Lancashire and the case for abolishing child imprisonment) illustrate the contradictions that exist in contemporary Higher Education in the UK today. In a time when undoubtedly there is a strong emphasis on the developments around *Police Studies* and the shift in the role of universities to training state agents, the 'criminological imagination' underscoring the bespoke films on *DD105: Introduction to Criminology* illustrates the contradictions and contingencies that still exist for producing critical, pedagogical work, which stands in opposition to the 'disimagination machine' that Henry Giroux (2013: 257) so eloquently describes as defining the neo-liberal university in the twenty-first century (Scott and Sim, this volume; Jackson, this volume).

Overall, this chapter draws attention to the way the ideas of Box (1983) can be utilised and applied to a selection of carefully chosen examples of events in everyday life, to help inform undergraduate studies about the role of power, mystification and the state and how 'crime' and harm are currently understood. *PCM* is also about how conventional crime is responded to and how corporate crime is often neglected; points crucial to the examples we selected, including the Grenfell Tower fire, discussed below. We reflect further upon alternative, non-penal, approaches to preventing/reducing harm and the broader legacy of Steven Box at the close of the chapter as a way of ending this volume focused on *PCM*.

DD105: Introduction to Criminology and OU Critical Pedagogy

Critical pedagogy is an educational philosophy privileging independent, reflective, and critical thinking (Freire 1970/2005). Teaching is conceived as a political intervention aiming to facilitate the emergence of an emancipatory 'critical consciousness' empowering individuals and

---

[3] Brandalism and Subvertising are terms, which refer to interventions by artists and activists that aim to subvert the ideological message of corporate brands and advertising (Drake and Scott 2019g).

challenging social and economic inequalities. An institution, which is, in essence, founded on the notion of critical pedagogy is The Open University (OU). The OU is a distance-learning public University in the UK, founded in 1969 (Weinbren 2014). The concept and idea of the OU, which is an open-access university, threatened an elitist view of who University-level education was for. The OU dared to compete in an educational and political environment that was hostile to its existence. It was viewed as a pet project of labour MP Jennie Lee who encountered resistance from both inside and outside the labour party to its teaching model and widening participation mission. The need to 'prove itself' amongst other more traditionally established higher education providers led the university to develop a powerfully inclusive and supportive approach to teaching and learning. No entry requirements and a principled commitment to openness combined with a drive for academic rigour and quality assurance that resulted in a teaching model that has an inherently disruptive and critical pedagogical approach.

In practice, this led to the development of what can be called 'OU pedagogy'. This involves the creation of accessible, inspirational, and user-friendly learning materials. In academic terms, it means distilling a corpus of knowledge of complex ideas, data, and evidence and bringing it to life in ways that make it meaningful, interesting, easy to follow, and comprehend for learners. It also means making it useful and applicable to students and their lives—wherever they are, whatever their circumstances—so that they can make it their own and use it in whatever way they see fit. For over fifty years, OU pedagogy has entailed 'teaching through text' and correspondence tuition, 'teaching through film and audio', and other forms of technology using a multi-media and blended approach to learning.

Teaching criminology at the OU has a lengthy history, beginning in 1981 with the third-year 60-credit module *D335: Issues in Crime and Society*, which produced a well-received, externally published reader (Fitzgerald et al. 1981). This module self-consciously built on the developments of critical criminology up to that point in time. Criminologist Stanley Cohen was the external examiner during the development of the module and supported its interdisciplinary approach and the way it sought to challenge how criminology was generally being taught elsewhere. Moreover, in 1996, the replacement module *D315: Crime Order and Social Control* was launched, and its textbooks came to shape the way criminology was taught in many universities in the UK and abroad (Muncie and McLaughlin 1996; McLaughlin and Muncie 1996a, 1996b). In keeping with this tradition at the OU, we began to think about how to conceive what would become the first-ever entry-level criminology module taught at the university, *DD105: Introduction to Criminology* (Drake et al. 2019a, b).

Building on more recent developments in critical criminology, including the broadening of the definition of crime, punishment and the state by taking a zemiological or social harm approach, we began from a starting point that questioned the way harms in society are defined, acknowledged and responded to. By doing so, we opened up the notion that the subject matter of criminology should be rethought and rearticulated in a way that can transcend existing legal boundaries, and the exclusionary logic that underpins them (Giroux 2010, 2020). We also started from the premise that such a destabilisation of existing meanings and definitions around 'crime' could be a useful tool for facilitating new ways of thinking about criminological subject matter leveraging a shift away from punitive 'law and order' approaches, something which was also important for Box (1983). In addition, we wanted to avoid the repetition of administrative criminological tropes and circumvent simple and procedural explanations of how the police, courts, and prisons operate. Instead, we wanted students to leave the module thinking differently and with the beginning of a more expansive 'criminological imagination' and an ability to challenge dominant views on who the 'criminals' and 'victims' are (Mills 1959/2000; Barton et al. 2007; Drake and Scott 2019a).

The teaching materials internally produced by the OU included two in-house published edited books (Drake et al. 2019a, b; Downes et al. 2019), which comprised of 19 chapters in total and several bespoke films (including three bespoke animations on 'State', 'Power', and 'Crime', respectively [OU 2019b, c, d]). One of the films, which ended up being multi-award-winning, considered the Grenfell Tower fire in London that happened on 14th June 2017. We discuss this film in some detail later in this chapter as part of our reflection on the influence that Box has had on our thinking, learning, and teaching. But for the time being it is worth noting that we were particularly interested in the point Box illuminates when he argues that a more nuanced and detailed consideration of the role of the criminal law is needed because: '[w]e are encouraged to see murder as a particular act involving [only] a very limited range of stereotypical factors, instruments, situations and motives' (Box 1983: 8).

When we began writing our module, we were conscious that students are often drawn to criminology with a sense of fascination with murder, serial killers, and other criminal activity that is sensationalised in popular culture, news media, and 'true' crime television programmes. The latter, in particular, seem to be intrinsic to the viewing habits of students and the wider population. The fact that a number of criminologists give their name to these programmes only reinforces the idea that they are a legitimate source of knowledge about crime and criminality. We wanted to build on this interest by covering similar topics to those touched on in popular culture and in the mass media and social media, such as the problem of murder, but in a critical and imaginative way. Box's work steered us towards situating murder within the broader category of avoidable death. Influences in critical criminology, penal abolitionism, and zemiology invited us to consider what other types of avoidable acts or practices tend to result in death or severe injury.

We wanted to open up a space for ourselves and our students to systematically question 'which harms are criminal', 'why are some avoidable deaths criminalized and others ignored', 'who is responsible for such harms', 'how are such harms brought to public attention', and 'how are they responded to by the state?' These questions, along with a drive to promote emotional engagement that could engender feelings of empathy rather than moral indifference, were central to our critical pedagogy. In his classic text, Paulo Freire (1970/2005) highlights the importance of connecting politics, culture, and education and raising the critical consciousness of individuals so they can understand their own oppression and subsequently undertake emancipatory transformative action. Additionally, following Gramsci (1971), the educator, whose role is almost interchangeable with that of the learner, should engage in reciprocal learning—learning the unique language and culture of a given community or group of people—so as to be able to convert 'common sense' into 'good sense' (see also Mayo 1999).

For Giroux (1992), the human subject is in itself a 'transient border crosser' constantly becoming sensitized to the pain and suffering of others. This stands in direct opposition to apathy and moral indifference. The topics and problems covered in undergraduate criminology modules provide ample subject matter for opportunities for a critical pedagogy inspired by Box (1983) to challenge 'common sense' moralities, sensitize 'border crossings', and generate empathy, compassion, and understanding amongst the student cohort. Indeed, Box (1983) confronts the opposite of empathy—the problem of moral indifference—head-on in *Power, Crime and Mystification*, most notably through his consideration of the indifference to corporate harm:

> [A]ny discussion of crime must be cognizant of the fact that serious adverse consequences can and often do follow from being indifferent to the outcome of one's actions (or inactions). To avoid considering these consequences on the grounds that they were not intended is not only to be blind to much human suffering, but also to accept the relative positions of intentions compared with indifference on a common-sense hierarchy of immorality (Box 1983: 21).

Taking inspiration from the ideas of Jeffrey Reiman (1979, cited in Box 1983; see also Reiman and Leighton 2010), Box (1983: 21) argues that the harms of power often demonstrate a great 'disdain for humanity in general' and this indifference, he maintains, is a higher form of immorality than that of conventional 'street level' crime, albeit one which often goes unrecognised (Mills 1956/2001; Drake et al. 2019a, b). Further, the harms of corporations 'should be conceptualised so as to include acts of omission as well as the more obvious acts of commission' (Box 1983: 21). The acknowledgement of the potentially deadly harm and suffering generated by the polices and actions of both 'commission and omission' by those in positions of power and authority wound up being central to the pedagogy of our module. The key point we aimed to work through with our students was, following Box (1983), to explore more deeply the ways that intentional homicides and other avoidable deaths are defined (or not) as *crimes* by the state and, also, to critically consider other serious and deadly harms that are not so defined. As Box (1983: 9) poetically noted:

> Other types of avoidable killing are either defined as a less serious crime than murder, or as a matter more appropriate for administrative or civil proceedings, or as events beyond the justifiable boundaries of state interference. In all these instances, the perpetrators of these avoidable killings deserve, so we are told, less harsh community response to those committing legally defined murder. The majority of people accept this because the state, by excluding these killings from the murder category, has signified its intention that we should not treat them as capital offenders. As the state can muster a galaxy of skilled Machiavellian orators to defend its definitions, and has, beyond these velvet tongues, the iron fist of police and military physical violence, it is able to persuade most people easily and convincingly.

Avoidable Deaths and Social Murder

The strict legal definition of intentional homicide (or murder) means that there are only certain circumstances when the killing of a human being at the hands of another is viewed as a 'crime'. A key question that we asked in our module was: 'when should an avoidable death be defined as intentional homicide?' An avoidable death occurs when a human life ends, but when it could (and should) have been saved. Avoidable deaths include those that arise through the deliberately harmful actions of others (such as those defined as intentional homicide). But it also includes many other forms of premature death, including, for example, those related to deaths in the workplace; self-inflicted deaths in custody; state killings; and people who die because of inadequate provision of shelter, warmth, or food. This considerably expands the categories of death outside of those that are normally focussed on in criminal law (Box 1983; Dorling 2003; Hillyard and Tombs 2003; Freudenberg 2014; Drake and Scott 2019f; Scott 2020—see also Grover, this volume).

Throughout the materials designed for our module, we asked students to reflect on how they thought about murder and whether classifying it as an avoidable death comparable to other causes of premature death that are avoidable changed the way they thought about it. We demonstrated the ways in which doing so could allow a sobering picture to emerge. We made the point that there are a variety of other causes of premature death that are far more likely than murder, such as suicide, road traffic accidents, or lung disease (Drake and Scott 2019f). Comparing statistics on types of preventable death is not to say that any of the causes of death are more or less serious than any other. The end result—the loss of a human life—is equally tragic regardless of the circumstances. What is worth thinking about, however, is the relative importance and attention that is given by society to the different causes of death, and which avoidable deaths come under the remit of the criminal law, and which do not. Therefore, whilst there is not a neat binary between neglect and intention (for example, there may be situations when avoidable harms result from what can only be considered as 'intentional neglect') the pedagogical aim of *DD105: Introduction to Criminology* was to question the exclusive focus on legal definitions of *intentional* homicide.

We presented our students with an alternative way of defining the premature ending of a life, drawing on a concept that has been adopted by critical criminologists, that of 'social murder'. Friedrich Engels (1845/2009) gives a clear indication of how avoidable deaths can be caused systematically from the way a given society is set up and organised. Engels suggests that too often those amongst the working class:

> …inevitably meet a too early and an unnatural death, one which is quite as much a death by violence as that by the sword or bullet; when it deprives thousands of the necessaries of life, places them under conditions in which they cannot live – forces them, through the strong arm of the law, to remain in such conditions until that death ensues which is the inevitable consequence – knows that these thousands of victims must perish, and yet permits these conditions to remain, its deed is murder just as surely as the deed of the single individual (Engels 1845/2009: 126).

Whilst such avoidable deaths can be seen more as neglect rather than intention, the social conditions that people find themselves forced to live in nevertheless undermine 'the vital [life] force gradually, little by little, and so hurries them to the grave before their time' (ibid.: 126–7). This problematisation of deaths occurring sooner than they should because of social, living, or working conditions is what is meant by 'social murder' and whilst this concept is not directly drawn upon by Box (1983), it is clearly consistent with his overall analysis of avoidable harms. For example, in *PCM* he discusses the systemic failings at 'Swan Hunters' Shipyard to provide a 'proper safe environment' (Box 1983: 23) for its workers in September 1976, which resulted in a number of avoidable deaths in a fire aboard HMS Glasgow whilst under repairs in their dry docks. As he (ibid.) presciently put it, in harmful situations like large fires, resulting avoidable deaths are determined merely by 'anyone who just happens to be there', something also true at Grenfell Tower on the evening of the 14th June 2017.

Demystifying Murder: The Grenfell Tower Fire Film

Grenfell Tower was a 24-storey high-rise block of flats in North Kensington, West London. On 14th June 2017, a fire broke out and burned for over 60 hours. The 2018 official number of recorded deaths of the tower-block residents was 72 (INQUEST 2019), and at least 70 other residents were injured, some seriously. There were also other serious harms—psychological, emotional, and financial—which were created through the fire which would negatively impact upon the well-being of members of the local community as well as the direct survivors of Grenfell Tower fire for many years to come (OU 2019a). The Grenfell Tower fire started after a Hotpoint fridge-freezer caught fire in one of the 127 flats in the building (BBC 2017a). It was reported in the media as one of the deadliest structural fires in recorded history in the United Kingdom and the worst UK residential fire since World War II (Aljazeera 2022). The building's cladding and poor internal maintenance were key factors in both why the fire spread so rapidly and why residents were unable to escape.

Grenfell Tower underwent a £10 million refurbishment in 2014–2016, including renovations of the first four floors of the building, a new heating system, and total refurbishment work on its exterior. The exterior modernisation included the fitting of rain-screen cladding and insulation. It is believed that around eight tonnes of cladding panels and 18 tonnes of insulation foam were attached to the tower during refurbishments (Reed and Clare 2017). Before its refurbishment, Grenfell Tower was constructed of 'virtually incombustible concrete' (Bowcott 2018). However, the cladding selected for the outer layer of the building during the refurbishment was highly combustible.

When the building caught fire, it is estimated that the tower would have released '14 times more heat than a key government test allows' (Reed and Clare 2017). The cladding's plastic core would have burned 'as quickly as petrol' (ibid.), and the fire 'rose 19 storeys through the cladding in just 12 minutes' (Booth 2018). For just an extra £5000 (safer cladding was just £2 per square metre more expensive than the sheets used), much more fire-resistant materials could have been fitted (Knapton and Dixon 2017). Grenfell Tower residents had raised concerns around the risk of fire at the tower for years, but their concerns had not been addressed (BBC 2017b). The first inquiry report, released in October 2019, found:

> compelling evidence that the external walls of the building failed to comply with Requirement B4(1) of Schedule 1 to the Building Regulations 2010, in that they did not adequately resist the spread of fire having regard to the height, use and position of the building. On the contrary, they actively promoted it (Moore-Bick 2019: 5).[4]

---

[4] According to the *April 2023 Grenfell Inquiry Newsletter*, it is hoped that the drafting of the report of the second phase of the Grenfell Tower inquiry will be completed 'before the end of 2023' (Grenfell Tower Inquiry 2023). It goes on to note that publication will not be until some point in 2024 as '[v]arious practical steps will then need to follow, such as proof-reading, typesetting and printing, all of which take time. We shall send the report to the Prime Minister, as required by our terms of reference, as soon as we can but that will probably not be possible before the beginning of next year [2024]. The Prime Minister will decide when the report will be published and by whom, but we are ready to act quickly if he asks us to publish it, as

Prior to the fire, the victims of Grenfell Tower were let down on at least eight occasions by a series of legislative and health and safety shortcomings, including around the relaxation of building regulations and failure to undertake appropriate risk assessments; the fitting of unsafe cladding as part of the refurbishment; missing sprinklers and inadequate fire exits (i.e. second staircase) and firebreaks; and failure of the government to learn from previous tower block fires (Knapton and Dixon 2017; Drake et al. 2019a, b). As survivor testimonies attest, in the aftermath of the fire, Grenfell residents felt that they had been treated with disdain (OU 2019a; INQUEST 2019).

As educators, we immediately recognised that the Grenfell Tower fire raised many key issues that students (and society in general) could learn from about the nature of 'social murder'. To create sensitive and yet poignant learning materials for our students, we commissioned a film and worked with a film production company to carefully and compassionately research residents' experiences of the fire (Scott and Hamlett 2019). We worked closely with *Justice4Grenfell*[5] who advised us on who they felt were ready to talk and were at a point where they could 'tell their story'. A careful and trusting collaboration led to extremely powerful testimonies from many survivors, relatives of the deceased, and the residents who appreciated being able to tell their stories on film. The people who shared their stories with us included Antonio Roncolato, who was trapped in the tower for many hours, and Joe Delaney, from the *Grenfell Tower Action Group*, who was a resident in the adjoining 'finger of flats' connected to the tower at ground level (Scott and Hamlett 2019; OU 2019a). The *Grenfell Tower and Social Murder* film gave a platform for the powerful testimonies and first-hand accounts of the survivors. In so doing the film evidenced the ongoing neglect and moral indifference that led to the fire and how the warnings of the tenants were continuously ignored. This disavowal of the voices and shared humanity

---

we think likely'. We are conscious that as we write this chapter (July 2023), we have recently marked the sixth anniversary of the Grenfell fire, and yet, so little progress has been made in terms of truth and accountability.

[5] Justice4Grenfell (J4G) is a community-led organisation, seeking justice, in the aftermath of the Grenfell fire, for the bereaved families, survivors, evacuated residents, and the wider local community.

of the survivors is understood in the film as an illustration of systemic indifference and institutionalised contempt.

The more we understood about the circumstances of the fire the more we saw the benefit of focusing on tenants' perspectives—the people closest to the situation—for our future students to gain a personalised understanding of what happened at Grenfell. Clarrie Mendy, who lost her first and second cousins, Khadija Saye and Mary Mendy, in the fire, provided a powerful interview and talked about the loss and how, in her opinion, the cause of the fire was down to neglect by the local authority and how this neglect and contempt continued in the way the survivors were being housed in substandard conditions, months after the fire took place. She also poignantly noted:

> … what are we going to do afterwards with the tower? Is this tower in the sky going to be a constant reminder of man's inhumanity against man?

The *Grenfell Tower and Social Murder* film, which was produced over a seven-month period from mid-2017 to early-2018, created a space for the testimonies from survivors and families of the bereaved that was not then available.[6]

From a critical pedagogical perspective, the film was intended to convey the importance of listening to the voices of those who are least likely to be heard. It had the capacity to open a portal for students to gain a deeper understanding of human and social tragedy. This seemed especially important for people who felt that their voices had not been heard, and that lives had been lost because of the national and local state's systemic moral and political indifference. From the perspective of Giroux (1992), The *Grenfell Tower and Social Murder* film could provide students with a chance to explore a transient border crossing—allowing them to cross the border into the worlds of Grenfell residents

---

[6] David Scott and Sian Hamlett interviewed the survivors and bereaved families for the film in October 2017, only four months after the fire. The filming team was honoured that people who were suffering, feeling lost, and traumatised, opened themselves up to camera, agreed to be interviewed and share their pain. They trusted that their stories would be told truthfully and that what they shared could reach and help influence the ideas and thinking of Open University students over a 10-year period (which could result in 50,000 or more students watching the film).

and become sensitised to their direct experiences and to bear witness empathically and compassionately to their suffering (Quinney 2000). The challenge in creating the film was to generate an informed and well-researched 'good sense' understanding of the tragedy, that was accessible and understandable to all who would watch it, but which also 'held' the audience to allow them to process what they were watching. OU critical pedagogy aims to help others to think through difficult and controversial issues in ways that facilitate shared understanding. It is a way of preparing people for wider engagement in political and democratic processes, democratic accountability, and the importance of learning to see multiple perspectives. Our consideration of the Grenfell fire was also an attempt to deconstruct the mystification around the fire itself as the local state immediately mobilised to socially construct the fire in very particular ways that included victim blaming.

Ethics and the Making of the Grenfell Tower and Social Murder Film

The story of making a film like *Grenfell Tower and Social Murder* (OU 2019a) also, necessarily, raises numerous ethical concerns. The loss of 72 lives and the life-changing harms and damage to many others (Tombs 2020) were both the forefront and the background of the ethical and political dimensions that needed to be very carefully and compassionately navigated. There had to be limitations on what the film could and could not do. It could not heal the trauma experienced by so many of the survivors and loved ones of those who died. It could not redress the hurt and abandonment that the residents of the tower had experienced in the years leading up to the fire. Also, no film could ever fully represent what had happened in all its nuances nor fully reflect the feelings of the local community. What the film *could* do, however, was highlight the concerns of local people; provide a record of their recollections; allow them to give their accounts and see these reflected in a film that affirmed their own understandings of the causes of the fire; and give some of those who suffered as a result of the fire a voice they may not have otherwise had.

But of key significance here, what the film could also do was present a competing account of the fire from the perspective of the tower residents and bereaved families through the interpretive lens of 'social murder'. *Grenfell Tower and Social Murder* attempted to highlight the harms of the powerful and allow survivors to express their righteous anger, outrage, and frustration over how little their lives had seemed to matter to those who had made the decisions that made the Grenfell Tower fire possible. The residents themselves were best placed to highlight the broader failings around democratic accountability that had led to the devastation of this local community. The making of the film included a heavy burden of responsibility for us as critical, activist academics—to the local people to provide a fair representation of what had happened—to raise questions and support those who watched the film reflect on the nature and gravity of the Grenfell fire and why it happened in the first place.

As noted above, *Grenfell Tower and Social Murder* (OU 2019a) was initially made for *DD105: Introduction to Criminology*, but once it was finished, it became clear that the evidence it presented, and the interpretation it gave of events 'from below' was a useful resource that could support some of the former residents begin to process what had happened and perhaps, also act as a conduit through which they could talk about their experiences. At the time that the film was finalised, several former residents had yet to find new, long-term, or suitable accommodation. There remained much debris and toxic material from the fire around the local area. Many of the bereaved and survivors were only just starting to process the trauma and loss generated by the fire. The residents were also just dealing with the news that the public inquiry into the fire was going to be paused until 2020. It seemed a timely moment for our film to be shared more widely in an effort to highlight its social, emotional, physical, and psychological harms. We also felt there was a strong ethico-political case for highlighting the idea that the fire could be understood as a form of 'social murder'. Such an interpretation could help raise questions and stimulate democratic debate on what happened and what should be done to ensure that this kind of human devastation is never repeated.

A special screening of the film was arranged at the Electric Cinema in the Borough of Kensington and Chelsea[7] in February 2019. Sixty-five local residents attended and following the screening there was a 72-second silence in memory of the 72 people who died. The special screening was significant because it provided an opportunity for the OU to show their appreciation to the local community for their support in making the film. It also provided an opportunity for the local community to come together, offer mutual support, express their grief, and at times, their anger at the way the government and local authorities responded to and subsequently investigated the disaster. *Justice4Grenfell* has expressed gratitude and appreciation that the film led to a wider recognition both nationally and internationally about what had happened (Scott and Hamlett 2019).

The *Grenfell Tower and Social Murder* film was a powerful ethico-political intervention and received international recognition. In late 2018, it won the Life Changing Award at the *British Documentary Film Festival*. At the *Event and Visual Communication Association* (EVCOM) *Clarion Awards*, which celebrate excellence across cause-driven corporate film, live events, and experiences, the film took Gold in two categories: Education and Training, and Social Welfare. The judges noted that the film received a unanimously high score and was described as 'compelling', 'raw', and 'powerful'. The film was awarded gold in the educational category at the *New York Festival's TV & Film Awards* in May 2020. It also received a further five national nominations at film Awards in the UK and Ireland, including a nomination for best educational film at the Learning on Screen Awards in 2018 as well as being shortlisted for the *Arts and Humanities Research Council* (AHRC) Research Film of the Year 2018.

The film provided important teaching material for our undergraduate module, but it went beyond that. It also provided an important interpretation of the fire which 'demystified murder' in terms of both the context leading up to it and what needed to change in terms of policy in its aftermath. For the film's creators, David Scott and Sian Hamlett (Hamlett

---

[7] This is the borough in West London where Grenfell Tower was situated. Kensington and Chelsea is the richest borough in England and Wales (Drake et al. 2019a, b).

Films) and some of the contributors, such as criminologist Steve Tombs, the avoidable and premature deaths in the fire were a terrible example of social murder that reflected the key concerns of Steven Box (1983). The fire happened because of negligence and moral indifference; the placing of profit over human beings; the abject long-term national policy decisions on the deregulation of building standards and social housing; and acts of both commission and omission on the part of the local authorities charged with the care of those living within Grenfell Tower (OU 2019a; Tombs 2020).

Scrutinising the State

What the state defines as a 'serious crime' does not necessarily reflect the most serious or harmful events, behaviours, and actions in society but instead often reflects the interests of power, privilege, and social status (Box 1983). Demystification involves seeing and interpreting social harm and suffering from the perspective of the powerless—what some have referred to as 'criminology from below' (Sim et al. 1987: 7). This view from below does not only question existing definitions of serious crime but also looks up at the workings of the state, scrutinising both its acts of commission and acts of omission (Box 1983). The concerns here resonate strongly with the point Box (1983) raises about the deficit in structures of democratic accountability. Of the 23 criminal convictions related to the fire in the period from 2017–2020, virtually all (22 convictions) were for minor frauds perpetrated by people from impoverished social backgrounds; indeed, many of those imprisoned for defrauding the council in the aftermath of the fire had no fixed abode (Tombs 2020). There have (at the time of writing in June 2023) been no legal charges laid against any of the corporations involved. This class-biased legal response to the fire and the virtual absence of any developments towards legal accountability for state-corporate harm, shines a spotlight on the sustained failure to hold the state and the powerful to account, something highlighted by Box in *PCM* 40 years ago. This critique is not therefore from a position that assumes the state is a protector delivering 'justice for all', but rather that power and social harm are often conjoined, and those with the greatest power in society in the past have perpetrated many of the most serious harms in human history (Drake and Scott 2019b, c).

Our module, *DD105: Introduction to Criminology* constantly reiterates (either implicitly or explicitly) the importance of clarifying the rights to which all human beings are entitled. The idea of universal rights can move us beyond definitions of crime that are predicated only on criminal law (Stanley 2006). The focus on universal rights (and especially the 'right to life') in critical criminology continues to gain momentum and may, over time, provide a means by which to better highlight the instances when they are breached and violated. As an alternative to following a state-set agenda that largely reflects the interests of the powerful, it is important for criminologists to ask difficult questions that highlight when dangerous states or other powerful bodies are acting against the interests of citizens and are not being held to account for those actions. Criminology, as a discipline, is not asking such questions often enough.

Our teaching of social murder at The Open University attempts to 'demystify murder'. This has involved two things: first, 'looking up' at the harms of the state, and secondly, questioning the suitability of the criminal law as our default mechanism for responding to social harms. When asking our students to 'look up', our teaching materials point directly to the deadly harms perpetrated by those in power, through either their intentional actions or through state and corporate inaction and moral indifference—'social murder'. Box (1983: 202) is undoubtedly correct to argue how essential it is that we collectively understand that the root of much serious harm is 'located in power, not weakness, privilege not disadvantage, wealth not poverty'. It should come as no surprise that he (ibid) argues that to effectively reduce serious harms the accumulation of (political, economic, and social) power must be restricted, for it is only:

> by spreading power thinly, just as a good farmer would spread manure over a field instead of concentrating it in one place, [that] the stink of rotten absolute power can be avoided.

Such a redistribution of power requires political change and a dramatic shift in our collective understanding of social relationships. Yet, as Box (1983: 223) maintains, to create such a collective understanding what is required is not just academic rigour and insight. What is also needed are interventions that can educate public audiences, challenge hegemonic assumptions and beliefs, and generate widespread 'solidaristic action' (ibid.) that can force progressive social and political transformation. In our pedagogic approach to *DD105: Introduction to Criminology*, we share these aims and aspirations.

But our concern and pedagogy go beyond the limits of definitions of serious 'crime', to also critically considers how we respond to it. The criminal law has, historically, been ineffective as a response to acts or events that could be called social murder, including acts of gross negligence by corporations (Drake et al. 2019a, b; Scott 2020). In a context where the criminal law (through legal loopholes, under enforcement, or just simply non-criminalisation) systematically fails to hold to legal account states and corporations and other powerful actors and institutions that perpetrate serious and deadly harms, Box (1983: 79) makes the crucial point that:

> … if there's no way of implementing justice for the largest and worst offending corporations then it is surely unjust to pursue with such ruthless and cruel tenacity the majority of those eventually condemned to prison … when we [have] fail[ed] to punish those practising minor acts of genocide, let us be merciful on those committing comparatively minor acts of violence.

Building on Box's clear and astute point above, it makes little sense that the criminal processes should exercise their weighty power over individual perpetrators of harm and yet consistently fail to use it in the face of corporate harms. There is no hesitation to apportion blame to individuals committing minor acts of violence with little or no regard for the complex, interwoven contexts or social and personal circumstances that inevitably preceded their actions. And yet the criminal law's powerlessness in the face of corporate cases is, in part, blamed on the complexity of prosecuting such activities. There is a perversity in the fact that the criminal law is able to ignore the complexity of an individual person's life course and hold them entirely responsible for everything that led up to their harmful deed and yet it will not proceed with prosecuting large corporations because it bows under the weight of complexity and diffuse levels of corporate responsibility (see also Tombs, this volume; Whyte, this volume). In one case, the law blatantly ignores complexity and context and proceeds anyway, in the other it folds under the weight of it. The real differences between the two sets of circumstances are power and the dominant construction of morality, and Box's work helps to highlight both for us (see also Scott and Sim, this volume). As emphasised earlier, whereas moral condemnation and blame abounds for those involved in 'street level' harmful conduct, the disdain and contempt shown for humanity from those in positions of power when people die in cases like Grenfell Tower is arguably a much 'higher form of immorality' (Mills 1956/2001: 343) and yet it fails to be widely conceived as such.

Conclusion

It is essential that ALL avoidable and premature deaths are examined and understood in the different and multifaceted social contexts in which they occur. Talking about social murder is not just about looking at individual blame and intention, although this can also be one of the factors considered. If the problem of avoidable deaths is, instead, framed through the language of social murder, then it potentially becomes more possible for the multiplicity of factors that led to it to be brought into full view. It signals the opportunity to take a different approach to the way harms in society are examined, thought about, and understood. This requires an alternative conception of responsibility for harm that goes beyond individual responsibility and the search for an individual murderer. It means questioning current notions of criminal blameworthiness and the systemic lack of holding to account those responsible for the most egregious harms committed against the wider population. Further, it also, potentially, means thinking about the urgent need for a collective 'social responsibility' for reducing social harm as a whole (Scott 2018). For Box (1983: 223), what was ultimately required was:

> ... establishing institutional democratic procedures through which people's demands can be communicated to elective, responsive responsible or removable leaders ... [who are working for] the interest of all of us equally and not covertly making or masking differential benefits accruing to the powerful, privileged and the wealthy.

A focus on decontextualised and narrowly focused individual, criminalised blame takes us further away, not closer to, such a worthy objective of democratic accountability, a deeper appreciation for the importance of context and the drive for greater social equality. This is one of the key messages Box articulated in *Power, Crime and Mystification*. And this is one of the key messages of *DD105: Introduction to Criminology*, in general, and the Grenfell Tower and Social Murder film, in particular. This reflects the influence of his legacy forty years from the publication of the book. It may be concluded then (as this and the previous essays in this volume demonstrate), that *Power, Crime and Mystification* and the work of Steven Box remains seminal for a whole new generation of critical scholars today.

Acknowledgements Many thanks to Joe Sim for his careful reading and helpful comments on earlier drafts of this chapter.

References

Aljazeera. 2022. Memorials Held Five Years on from London's Worst Residential Fire: London Marks the Fifth Anniversary of the Grenfell Tower Fire That Killed 72 People. 14 June 2022 [Online]. https://www.aljazeera.com/news/2022/6/14/memorials-held-five-years-on-from-londons-worst-residential-fire. Accessed 3 Aug 2022.

Barton, A., K. Corteen, D. Scott, and D. Whyte. 2007. Conclusion: Expanding the Criminological Imagination. In *Expanding the Criminological Imagination*, ed. A. Barton, K. Corteen, D. Scott, and D. Whyte, 198–214. London: Routledge.

Booth, R. 2018. Grenfell Firefighters Deny Response Was Affected by Racism. *Guardian,* 7 June [Online]. https://www.theguardian.com/uk-news/2018/jun/07/grenfell-firefighters-deny-response-was-affected-by-racism. Accessed 9 Jun 2022.

Bowcott, O. 2018. Refurbishment Made Grenfell Tower a Death Trap, Inquiry Hears. *Guardian,* 5 June [Online]. https://www.theguardian.com/uk-news/2018/jun/05/dangerous-building-works-turned-grenfell-tower-death-trap-inquiry. Accessed 9 Jun 2022.

Box, S. 1983. *Power, Crime, and Mystification.* London: Routledge.

BBC, 2017a. Grenfell Tower: Fire Started in Hotpoint Refrigerator, Say Police. 23 June 2017 [Online]. https://www.bbc.co.uk/news/uk-40380584. Accessed 9 Jun 2022.

BBC. 2017b. Concerns Raised About Grenfell Tower "For Years". 14 June 2017. [Online]. https://www.bbc.co.uk/news/uk-england-london-40271723. Accessed 9 Jun 2022.

Drake, D.H., J. Muncie, and D. Scott. 2019a. What Is Crime? In *Introduction to Criminology 1,* ed. D.H. Drake, D. Scott, and A. Nightingale, 33–54. Milton Keynes: The Open University.

Drake, D.H., and D. Scott. 2019a. The Criminological Imagination. In *Introduction to Criminology 2,* ed. J. Downes, G. Mooney, A. Nightingale, and D. Scott, 237–257. Milton Keynes: The Open University.

Drake, D.H., and D. Scott. 2019b. Victims and Perpetrators. In *Introduction to Criminology 1,* ed. D.H. Drake, D. Scott, and A. Nightingale, 131–156. Milton Keynes: The Open University.

Drake, D.H., and D. Scott. 2019c. Dangerous States. In *Introduction to Criminology 1,* ed. D.H. Drake, D. Scott, and A. Nightingale, 157–182. Milton Keynes: The Open University.

Drake, D.H., and D. Scott. 2019d. Death Penalty: State-Sanctioned Murder? In *Introduction to Criminology 1,* ed. D.H. Drake, D. Scott, and A. Nightingale, 183–208. Milton Keynes: The Open University.

Drake, D.H., and D. Scott. 2019e. Law and Order or Harm and Disorder: Contesting Crime. In *Introduction to Criminology 1,* ed. D.H. Drake, D. Scott, and A. Nightingale, 55–78. Milton Keynes: The Open University.

Drake, D.H., and D. Scott. 2019f. The Murder Puzzle: Intentional Homicide, Avoidable Deaths and Social Murder. In *Introduction to Criminology 1,* ed. D.H. Drake, D. Scott, and A. Nightingale, 105–130. Milton Keynes: The Open University.

Drake, D.H., and D. Scott. 2019g. Graffiti: Art, Crime or Political Resistance? In *Introduction to Criminology 1*, ed. D.H. Drake, D. Scott, and A. Nightingale, 7–32. Milton Keynes: The Open University.

Drake, D.H., D. Scott, and A. Nightingale, eds. 2019b. *Introduction to Criminology 1*. Milton Keynes: The Open University.

Dorling, D. 2003. Prime Suspect: Murder in Britain. In *Beyond Criminology*, ed. P. Hillyard, C. Pantazis, S. Tombs, and D. Gordon, 178–191. London: Pluto.

Downes, J., G. Mooney, A. Nightingale, and D. Scott, eds. 2019. *Introduction to Criminology 2*. Milton Keynes: The Open University.

Engels, F. 1845/2009. *The Condition of the Working Class in England*. Oxford, Oxford University Press.

Fitzgerald, M., G. McLennan, and J. Pawson, eds. 1981. *Crime and Society: Readings in History and Theory*. London: Routledge and Kegan Paul; and The Open University Press.

Freire, P. 1970/2005. *Pedagogy of the Oppressed* (30th Anniversary Edition). New York: Continuum.

Freudenberg, N. 2014. *Lethal But Legal: Corporations, Consumption, and Protecting Public Health*. Oxford: Oxford University Press.

Giroux, H.A. 1992. *Border Pedagogy*. New York: Routledge.

Giroux, H.A. 2010. Rethinking Education as the Practice of Freedom: Paulo Freire and the Promise of Critical Pedagogy. *Policy Futures in Education* 8 (6): 715–721.

Giroux, H.A. 2013. The Disimagination Machine and the Pathologies of Power. *Symploke* 21 (1): 257–269.

Giroux, H.A. 2020. *On Critical Pedagogy*, 2nd ed. London: Bloomsbury.

Gramsci, A. 1971. *Selections from the Prison Notebooks*. London: Lawrence and Wishart.

Grenfell Tower Inquiry. 2023. *April 2023 Newsletter*. https://www.grenfelltowerinquiry.org.uk/news/april-2023-newsletter. Accessed 18 May 2023.

Hillyard, P., and S. Tombs. 2003. Beyond Criminology. In *Beyond Criminology* ed. P. Hillyard, C. Pantazis, S. Tombs, S., and D. Gordon, 10–29. London: Pluto.

INQUEST. 2019. Family Reflections on Grenfell: No Voice Left Unheard. London: INQUEST. https://inquest.eu.rit.org.uk/Handlers/Download.ashx?IDMF=47e60cf4-cc23-477b-9ca0-c960eb826d24. Accessed 9 Jun 2022.

Knapton, S., and H. Dixon. 2017. Eight Failures That Left People in Grenfell Tower at the Mercy of an Inferno. *The Telegraph*. 15 June 2017

[Online]. https://www.telegraph.co.uk/news/2017/06/15/eight-failures-left-people-grenfell-tower-mercy-inferno/. Accessed 9 Jun 2022.

Mayo, P. 1999. *Gramsci, Freire and Adult Education*. London: Zed Books.

McLaughlin, E., and J. Muncie, eds. 1996a. *Controlling Crime*. London: Sage.

McLaughlin, E., and J. Muncie, eds. 1996b. *Criminological Perspectives*. London: Sage.

Mills, C. W. 1956/2001. *The Power Elite*. Oxford: Oxford University Press.

Mills, C. W. 1959/2000. *The Sociological Imagination*. Oxford: Oxford University Press.

Moore-Bick, M. 2019. *Grenfell Tower Inquiry: Phase 1 Report Overview*. London: Crown Copyright. https://assets.grenfelltowerinquiry.org.uk/GTI%20%20Phase%201%20report%20Executive%20Summary.pdf. Accessed 14 May 2022.

Muncie, J., and E. McLaughlin, eds. 1996. *The Problem of Crime*. London: Sage.

Quinney, R. 2000. *Bearing Witness to Crime and Social Justice*. New York: SUNY Press.

Reed, J., and S. Clare. 2017. Grenfell Cladding "14 Times Combustibility Limit". BBC News. 19 July 2017 [Online]. https://www.bbc.co.uk/news/uk-40645205. Accessed 9 Jun 2022.

Reiman, J., and P. Leighton. 2010. *The Rich Get Richer and the Poor Get Prison: Ideology, Class and Criminal Justice*, 9th ed. London: Allyn & Bacon.

Scott, D. 2018. *Against Imprisonment*. Hook: Waterside Press.

Scott, D. 2020. *For Abolition*. Hook: Waterside Press.

Scott, D., and S. Hamlett. 2019. *Grenfell Tower and Social Murder*. https://oucriminology.wordpress.com/2019/05/. Accessed 9 Jun 2022.

Sim, J., P. Gordon, and P. Scraton. 1987. Introduction. In *Law, Order and the Authoritarian State*, ed. P. Scraton, 1–71. Milton Keynes: Open University Press.

Stanley, L. 2006. Towards a Criminology for Human Rights. In *Expanding the Criminological Imagination*, ed. A. Barton, K. Corteen, D. Scott, and D. Whyte, 168–197. London: Routledge.

The Open University (OU). 2019a. Grenfell Tower and Social Murder. *DD105: Introduction to Criminology*. https://learn2.open.ac.uk/mod/oucontent/view.php?id=1673415&section=6.2 [closed site]. Accessed 9 Jun 2022.

The Open University (OU). 2019b. The State. *DD105: Introduction to Criminology*. https://learn2.open.ac.uk/mod/oucontent/view.php?id=1895339&section=7.1 [closed site]. Accessed 9 Jun 2022.

The Open University (OU). 2019c. Power. *DD105: Introduction to Criminology*. https://learn2.open.ac.uk/mod/oucontent/view.php?id=1895339&section=7.2 [closed site]. Accessed 9 Jun 2022.

The Open University (OU). 2019d. Crime. *DD105: Introduction to Criminology*. https://learn2.open.ac.uk/mod/oucontent/view.php?id=1895339&section=7.3 [closed site]. Accessed 9 Jun 2022.

Tombs, S. 2020. Home as a Site of State-Corporate Violence: Grenfell Tower, Aetiologies and Aftermaths. *Howard Journal of Crime and Justice* 59 (2): 120–142. https://onlinelibrary.wiley.com/doi/full/https://doi.org/10.1111/hojo.12360.

Weinbren, D. 2014. *The Open University. A History*. Manchester: Manchester University Press.

Index

A

Abolition 508
Accountability 353, 360, 361, 364, 366, 367, 371, 373
Anti-corruptionism 90, 91, 93, 94, 96
Anti-statism 31
Austerity 203, 204, 206–218
Avoidable harm 540, 541

B

Bourdieu, P. 83, 85–88, 94
Boxian 445, 446
Boxian morality 42
Box, Steven 183, 200, 273, 274, 277, 278, 281, 282, 284, 285, 288, 291, 292, 481, 483–486, 500, 502, 503

C

Campaigns 483, 484, 487–489, 491, 493, 495, 498, 500
Capitalism 82, 83, 94–96, 98, 204, 206, 208, 211, 212, 217
Carceral 274, 276–282, 288, 292
Challenges 363
Child Lifers 494
Climate crimes 149, 154, 156–159
Climate criminality 131, 133, 134, 137
Climate crisis 149, 157, 160, 161
Colonialism 439, 443–446
Commodification 206–209, 212, 213, 217, 218
Conceal 408, 410, 414–416, 418, 420, 421, 425, 426
Conflicts 351–354
Consent 328, 331, 333–340, 343
Contemporary criminology 38

Continuities and discontinuities 24
Control 58, 61, 65–67, 69–72, 74–76
Corporate corruption 83
Corporate crime 57–61, 63–72, 74–76, 85, 103, 106, 107, 109, 115, 118–120
Corporate deviance 123
Corruption 223–226, 228, 229, 231, 234, 235, 238, 240
County lines 311, 313, 314
Crime 182–184, 186–188, 190–196, 198–200, 433–437, 439–445, 449
Crimes of the powerful 82–84, 86, 92, 94, 149–152, 154, 156, 164, 166
Criminalisation 192, 204, 273, 277, 278, 281, 289, 380–382, 384–391, 393–396, 398, 399, 401, 455, 457–459, 461, 462, 464–468, 471–474
Criminal law 299–303, 315, 318, 319
Criminology 224, 225, 228, 235–237, 239, 240, 242
Critical criminology 103, 104
Critical pedagogy 531, 532, 534, 535, 537, 538, 545
Custody 459, 462, 465–469

DD105: Introduction to Criminology 532, 534, 536, 540, 546, 549, 550, 552
Deaths in custody 517, 521, 523
Decolonization 434, 438, 441–446, 448, 449
Democratic accountability 4, 33, 39, 42, 508, 520, 522–525, 527
Demystification 532, 548
Demystifying 481
Denial 107, 109–111, 114, 117
Deviance 103, 106, 107
Discourse 328, 329, 331, 334, 335, 337–340, 342–346
Discretion 230
Diversion 459, 462, 463, 474

Ecocide 130, 131, 133–135
Environmental crime 125, 128, 131, 132, 137
Environmental uncertainties 61, 66
Ethnicity 466, 473
Exclusion 413, 415, 416, 422, 426
Extinction Rebellion (XR) 160–162

Failed institutions 387
Foucault, Michel 274, 276
Fridays for Future (FFF) 160, 161

Gender 327–330, 337–346, 407–409, 417–422, 425, 462, 463, 470–473
Gendered narratives 389, 390, 392, 397
Green criminology 131, 132, 149, 154
Grenfell Tower fire 534, 536, 541, 543, 546

H

Hall, Stuart 5, 6, 8, 13, 15, 16, 22, 25–28, 34, 35, 42, 44
Harm 183, 188–191, 194, 195, 197, 199, 200
Hegemony 274
Homeless women 407–409, 416–425
Human trafficking 300–302, 304–315, 317

I

Ideology 83, 84, 87, 88, 151, 167, 168, 274, 276, 277, 282, 284
Immigration control 274, 277, 280–282, 284, 285, 288–292
Imperialism 439, 443, 445
Indigenous justice 446
Injustice 380–388, 391, 392, 394, 397–401, 483, 485, 486, 488, 490, 496, 497, 499, 501
INQUEST 517–520, 523, 524
Institutional harms 393
Institutional racism 251
Interventionist research 381
Invisibility 416–418, 421, 424, 425

J

Joint enterprise (JE) 380, 386–391, 394, 398, 481–497, 500–503
Justice 481–483, 489, 490, 492, 493, 495, 496, 498, 500–503

L

Law 328, 335–337, 341–344, 481–486, 488, 489, 492, 493, 495–497, 499, 500, 502, 503

Law-and-order 223, 240

M

Manufactured crisis 212, 217
Masculinity 353, 356–359, 364, 369, 372
Modern slavery 300, 301, 304–306, 308–310, 313, 314, 317
Murder 482, 484, 486–493, 495–501
Mystification 5, 10–12, 18–20, 26, 31, 83–86, 88–90, 94, 182–184, 186, 187, 190, 193–199, 224, 225, 230, 238, 240, 248–250, 252, 254–256, 258–260, 262, 264, 265, 274, 281, 282, 284, 290–292, 300, 301, 303, 304, 309, 318, 328–332, 335, 339, 341, 343–345, 408–411, 413, 416, 418, 424–426, 520, 532–534, 545

N

Neoliberalism 95, 96, 182–186, 189, 190, 192–194, 196, 198, 199
Neo-Marxism 274
Neo-Marxist 71

O

Official view 410, 416, 426
Order 224, 227, 229, 230, 236, 242
Organisational crime production 64
Organisational goals 63

P

Parasitic Accessorial Liability (PAL) 481, 493, 496, 497
Patriarchy 443, 445
Planetary collapse 123
Police 223–242
Police violence 249, 254–257, 259–261
Poststructuralism 328, 335, 339–341, 344, 345
Poulantzas, Nicos 185, 187–189, 193
Poverty 433–437, 441, 442, 445
Power 223–233, 235–238, 240, 241, 329–332, 334, 338, 342, 344, 345, 433, 439–442, 444, 445, 449, 532–534, 536, 538, 548–551
Powerbrokers 351, 353, 354, 357, 359–362, 364, 366, 370–373
Prisons and social order 511
Punishment 380, 381, 385–388, 391–393, 396, 398–400, 509, 510, 513, 520, 526, 527

R

Race 311, 473
Racialisation 510
Racism 439, 445
Rape 327–333, 335–343, 345, 346, 351–372
Reform 119
Regulation 58, 63–72, 74–76, 111, 115–117
Rentiership 95, 96
Reparative 444–449
Research 224, 225, 235–237, 239–241
Resistance 4, 21, 33, 34, 44, 390, 392, 400, 526
Responsibilisation 461, 470
Restorative Justice (RJ) 471
Risk management 461–464, 473, 474

S

Sexuality 328, 330, 333–335, 341–343, 345
Sexual violence 328–333, 335, 336, 338–346, 351–353, 360, 362–365, 367–373
Sex work 301, 302, 310, 311
Social junk 204, 206, 209, 212, 213, 217, 218
Social justice 13, 17, 33, 39, 513, 527
Social murder 211, 212, 533, 539–541, 543, 546, 548–552
Social order maintenance 75
Social security 203, 206–209, 211–213, 215–218
Social theory 226
Sousveillance 260
State 408, 410–412, 415, 416, 420, 425, 426
State and corporate power 123, 133
State authoritarianism 31
State-corporate crime 149, 153, 154, 157, 158, 165
State-corporate relationships 67, 70, 74
State crime 301, 317
State power 117, 133, 186, 189, 200, 385, 394, 401
State violence 284, 285
Structural power 107, 108

Index   561

Tactical rape 353, 354, 356–360, 362–364, 366, 369, 373
Techniques of neutralisation (ToN) 103, 104, 106–109, 111, 112, 114, 115
The Open University (OU) 533–536, 541, 543, 545–549
The state 58–61, 66–75, 182–186, 189, 190, 192, 193, 195, 196, 199, 200, 533, 534, 536, 537, 539, 548, 549
Transgress 419, 424, 425
Transnational criminal law (TCL) 300–302

United Nations Security Council (UNSC) 353, 360, 362, 366, 367, 370, 373

Utopianism 525

Victimhood 111, 112, 311, 313
Violence 204, 210–213, 215–217, 223–225, 228–231, 233, 235, 238, 240, 241, 407–410, 418–425

Wage labour 206–208, 211–213, 215, 217
War 351, 352, 354, 357, 359–362, 367–372

Young people 456–469, 473–475
Youth Activism 158

GPSR Compliance
The European Union's (EU) General Product Safety Regulation (GPSR) is a set of rules that requires consumer products to be safe and our obligations to ensure this.

If you have any concerns about our products, you can contact us on

ProductSafety@springernature.com

In case Publisher is established outside the EU, the EU authorized representative is:

Springer Nature Customer Service Center GmbH
Europaplatz 3
69115 Heidelberg, Germany